The Development of Social Engagement

Series in Affective Science

The Development of Social Engagement

Neurobiological Perspectives

Edited by

Peter J. Marshall

Nathan A. Fox

UNIVERSITY PRESS

2006

OXFORD
UNIVERSITY PRESS

Oxford University Press, Inc., publishes works that further
Oxford University's objective of excellence
in research, scholarship, and education.

Oxford   New York
Auckland   Cape Town   Dar es Salaam   Hong Kong   Karachi
Kuala Lumpur   Madrid   Melbourne   Mexico City   Nairobi
New Delhi   Shanghai   Taipei   Toronto

With offices in
Argentina   Austria   Brazil   Chile   Czech Republic   France   Greece
Guatemala   Hungary   Italy   Japan   Poland   Portugal   Singapore
South Korea   Switzerland   Thailand   Turkey   Ukraine   Vietnam

Published by Oxford University Press, Inc.
198 Madison Avenue, New York, New York 10016

www.oup.com

Oxford is a registered trademark of Oxford University Press

Library of Congress Cataloging-in-Publication Data
The development of social engagement: neurobiological perspectives /
edited by Peter J. Marshall, Nathan A. Fox.
    p. cm. — (Series in affective science)
Includes bibliographical references and index.
ISBN-13: 978-0-19-516871-6
ISBN: 0-19-516871-2
1. Neurobiology.   2. Sociobiology.   3. Emotions.   4. Social psychology.   5. Social
psychiatry.   6. Autism.   I. Marshall, Peter J.   II. Fox, Nathan A.   III. Series.
QP360.D486 2005
612.8—dc22   2005008736

9 8 7 6 5 4 3 2 1

Printed in the United States of America
on acid-free paper

Preface

We have assembled a diversity of leading researchers to present findings related to social engagement across a range of contexts, domains, and species. In this sense, we feel that the volume gives a taste of contemporary work on social engagement across a variety of levels of analysis.

In the opening chapter, we introduce some of the themes that run throughout the volume, including an attempt to define early social engagement in terms of its subcomponents, and an overview of some current biological approaches to the study of social engagement in infants and young children. Some of the remaining chapters pursue similar themes, while others take different directions. In chapter 2, Polak-Toste and Gunnar provide a thorough introduction to approach-related behavior as an important but understudied component of temperament that reflects developing processes of social engagement. The following series of chapters is then devoted to cognitive capacities associated with the development of social engagement, including face processing (de Haan & Groen), joint attention (Mundy & Acra), language development (Pruden, Hirsh-Pasek, & Golinkoff), and social cognition (Sabbagh). The third section of the volume takes a different perspective, aiming to provide a description of selected current work on social engagement processes across a variety of mammalian species. The chapters in this section concern the neurobiology of social bonds (Lim & Young), the neurobiology of maternal behavior (Lévy & Fleming), and specific aspects of play (Pellis & Pellis). While the emphasis on development may be more muted in parts of these chapters, they provide a fascinating window on current comparative work on social engagement processes in both juveniles and adults, with a particular focus on neurochemical mechanisms. Following this series of chapters, Keller and Chasiotis provide a consideration of evolutionary perspectives in social engagement. The final three chapters of the volume cover deviations in the development of social engagement. Two developmental disorders that are in many ways signified by deficits or deviations in social engagement are covered in detail. First, Bernier, Webb, and Dawson describe work on impairments in social engagement in autism, with a focus on recent studies aimed at elucidating some of the specific biological mechanisms underlying these impairments in individuals with autistic spectrum disorders. Second, Tager-Flusberg and Plesa-Skwerer describe the unique profile of social engagement shown by individuals with Williams syndrome. The final chapter in the volume is a thorough treatment of the social and emotional effects of early institutionalization. It has long been observed that children raised in institutional environments have a range of difficulties associated with social and emotional functioning. In this closing chapter, Rutter provides a summary of recent work that has described some of the mechanisms involved in the development of these difficulties.

This volume provides the reader with a overview of current work on selected aspects of social engagement processes, and it is our hope that it can be read by researchers across a range of disciplines. Relatedly, we had two goals when formulating the volume: First, it is intended to introduce the behavioral scientist to state-of-the-art thinking and research in the neurobiology of social engagement. Second, it is meant to introduce the neuroscientist to cutting-edge behavioral research in social development.

In closing, we would like to extend our thanks to Catharine Carlin for her helpful guidance throughout the editorial process and to Anne Enenbach for shepherding the volume through the final stages of production.

Peter J. Marshall & Nathan A. Fox

Contents

Contributors

C. Françoise Acra
Department of Psychology
University of Miami
FHF Building
5665 Ponce De Leon Boulevard
Coral Gables, FL 33146
E-mail: cacra@umiami.ir.miami.edu

Raphael Bernier
UW Autism Center
University of Washington
Box 357920
University of Washington
Seattle, WA 98195
E-mail: rab2@u.washington.edu

Athanasios Chasiotis
Universität Osnabrück
Fachbereich Humanwissenschaften
Seminarstr.20
D-49069 Osnabrück
Germany
E-mail: Athanasios.Chasiotis@uos.de

Geraldine Dawson
UW Autism Center
University of Washington
Box 357920
University of Washington
Seattle, WA 98195
E-mail: dawson@u.washington.edu

Michelle de Haan
Institute of Child Health
University College London
London WC1N 3JH
United Kingdom
E-mail: m.de-haan@ich.ucl.ac.uk

Alison S. Fleming
Department of Psychology
University of Toronto at Mississauga
Mississauga, Ontario
L5L 1C6
E-mail: afleming@credit.erin.utoronto.ca

Nathan A. Fox
Department of Human Development
3304 Benjamin Building
University of Maryland
College Park, MD 20742
E-mail: nf4@umail.umd.edu

Roberta Michnick Golinkoff
School of Education
University of Delaware
Newark, DE 19716
E-mail: Roberta@udel.edu

Margriet Groen
Department of Experimental Psychology
South Parks Road
Oxford OX1 3UD
United Kingdom
E-mail: margriet.groen@psy.ox.ac.uk

Megan R. Gunnar
Institute of Child Development
University of Minnesota
51 East River Road
Minneapolis, MN 55455–0345
E-mail: gunnar@tc.umn.edu

Kathy Hirsh-Pasek
Department of Psychology
Temple University
Weiss Hall
1701 North 13th Street
Philadelphia, PA 19122–6085
E-mail: khirshp@temple.edu

Heidi Keller
Universität Osnabrück
Fachbereich Humanwissenschaften
Seminarstr.20
D-49069 Osnabrück
Germany
E-mail: Heidi.Keller@uos.de

Frédéric Lévy
INRA-CNRS Research Unit for
   Reproductive and Behavioural
   Physiology
INRA Research Center
University of Tours
Nouzilly, France 37380
E-mail: Frederic.Levy@tours.inra.fr

Miranda M. Lim
954 Gatewood Road
Yerkes Research Center
Emory University
Atlanta, GA 30322
E-mail: mmlim@emory.edu

Peter J. Marshall
Department of Psychology
Temple University
1701 North 13th Street
Philadelphia, PA 19122
E-mail: pjmarsh@temple.edu

Peter C. Mundy
Department of Psychology
University of Miami
P.O. Box 248185
Coral Gables, FL 33124
E-mail: pmundy@umiami.ir.miami.edu

Sergio M. Pellis
Department of Psychology and
   Neuroscience
University of Lethbridge
4401 University Drive
Lethbridge, Alberta
Canada T1K 3M4
E-mail: pellis@uleth.ca

Vivien C. Pellis
Department of Psychology and
   Neuroscience
University of Lethbridge
4401 University Drive
Lethbridge, Alberta
Canada T1K 3M4
E-mail: pellvc@uleth.ca

Daniela Plesa-Skwerer
Department of Anatomy and
   Neurobiology
Boston University School of Medicine
715 Albany Street L-814,
Boston, MA 02118–2526
E-mail: dplesas@bu.edu

Cindy P. Polak-Toste
Department of Human Development
University of Maryland
3304 Benjamin Building
College Park, MD 20742
E-mail: cpolak@umd.edu

Shannon M. Pruden
Department of Psychology
Temple University
1701 North 13th Street
Philadelphia, PA 19122
E-mail: spruden@temple.edu

Sir Michael Rutter
Box P080
Social, Genetic and Developmental
   Psychiatry Research Centre
Institute of Psychiatry
De Crespigny Park
Denmark Hill
London SE5 8AF
United Kingdom
E-mail: j.wickham@iop.kcl.ac.u

Mark A. Sabbagh
Psychology Department
Queen's University
Kingston, Ontario, Canada
K7L 3N6
E-mail: sabbagh@psyc.queensu.ca

Helen Tager-Flusberg
Department of Psychology
Boston University
64 Cummington Street
Boston, MA 02215
E-mail: htagerf@bu.edu

Sara Jane Webb
UW Autism Center
University of Washington
Box 357920
Seattle, WA 98195
E-mail: sjwebb@u.washington.edu

Larry J. Young
Center for Behavioral Neuroscience
Yerkes Research Center
Emory University
954 Gatewood Drive
Atlanta, GA 30322
E-mail: lyoun03@emory.edu

The Development of Social Engagement

1

Biological Approaches to the Study of Social Engagement

Peter J. Marshall
Nathan A. Fox

O ver the last two decades, there has been a burgeoning interest in the biological mechanisms subserving social behavior in both human and nonhuman animals (Carter, Lederhendler, & Kirkpatrick, 1997). There are multiple reasons for this increase in interest. In part, it has been fueled by the increasing sophistication and availability of techniques and assays to monitor or record nervous system activity. For instance, in terms of the measurement of brain activity, newer techniques such as functional magnetic resonance imaging (fMRI), magnetoencephalography (MEG), and near infrared spectroscopy (NIRS) have joined more established methodologies such as electroencephalography (EEG) and event-related potentials (ERP). The application of these new technologies, as well as technological improvements in older technologies, has resulted in a sharp increase in the number of research studies examining the relations between various aspects of social behavior and the activity of a multitude of physiological systems (Cacioppo et al., 2002). As part of this endeavor, developmental scientists have begun to use some of these new neurobiological techniques to address fundamental questions about human development (Casey & de Haan, 2002; Dawson & Fischer, 1994; Johnson, 1997). One promising aspect of this work is the potential use of converging methods, combining findings from the realms of functional neuroimaging and electrophysiology with data from comparative, neuropsychological, and computational approaches (Casey & Munakata, 2002).

Another reason for the surge in interest is an increasing acceptance of studying biological mechanisms (Kagan, 1994), including evolutionary and genetic influences on behavior. Whereas initial evolutionary applications to human social behavior generated much controversy (Segerstrale, 2001)—and indeed such applications continue to evoke debate—evolutionary social psychology has found a niche in the contemporary landscape of psychology. Theorists have also focused an evolutionary lens on child development (Bjorklund & Pellegrini, 2000). These developments have been accompanied by an increased awareness of comparative approaches and the development of highly specified animal models relating neurophysiology to behavior across multiple levels of explanation (Cacioppo, 2002). Although evolutionary, comparative, and developmental approaches may be asking quite different questions, it appears that cross-disciplinary fertilization among these approaches hold much promise. For instance, the eclectic model of Porges (2003) provides much insight into why such cross-domain considerations are so important in understanding social engagement processes in humans.

A third reason for this renewed interest in the biology of social behavior relates to the emergence of cognitive neuroscience. With its roots in cognitive science, cognitive neuroscience has emerged as a substantive discipline. Researchers have realized the interconnections between social behavior and cognition, as well as the influence of affect on cognitive processes. As part of this integration, a new discipline has emerged at the intersection of cognitive neuroscience and social behavior: social cognitive neuroscience (Adolphs, 2003a; Blakemore, Winston, & Frith, 2004). In turn, social cognitive neuroscience can be seen as representing a subdiscipline within the field of social neuroscience, which encompasses a wide array of topics, including social cognition, motivation, emotion, the biology of social relationships and affiliative behavior, individual differences, and relations to health (Cacioppo et al., 2002). Work within this wider field has also generated perspectives on how to integrate social and biological perspectives, emphasizing the value of multilevel approaches. Such an integrative approach is also key to the success of social cognitive neuroscience (Adolphs, 2003b).

One specific subdiscipline of cognitive neuroscience, developmental cognitive neuroscience, developed rapidly in the 1990s and continues to address key developmental questions (de Haan & Johnson, 2003; Johnson, 1997). Many of the research themes being addressed in developmental cognitive neuroscience have implications for social and emotional aspects of development. Although these links have often not been made explicit, more recently there has been an intersection between aspects of social cognitive neuroscience and developmental findings from cognitive neuroscience. In adults, much work in the domain of social cognitive neuroscience has focused on determining patterns of neural activity associated with understanding the actions, minds, and emotions of others, as well as with aspects of higher emotional processes such as moral reasoning, deception, and fairness (C. D. Frith & Wolpert, 2004). Functional neuroimaging technologies such as fMRI have become prime tools for such research in adults. While the use of such techniques requires careful experimental design and interpretation (Cacioppo et al., 2003), they have enriched the study of social cognition in adults by allowing researchers to image neural activity during processes related to mentalizing. U. Frith and Frith (2003) provide a summary of such mentalizing tasks in adults, in which the brain activity of participants is assessed while they read examples of "false belief" stories in which the behavior of a character in the story is driven by a false belief about the mental states of others. Regional brain activation during the comprehension of false belief stories is compared with that during control stories, which involve physical, nonhuman causes of events rather than events that are the direct result of human behavior. The mentalizing stories typically elicit activity in the medial prefrontal cortex (MPFC), the temporal poles, and the superior temporal sulcus (STS). Particular attention has been focused on the role of the MPFC, particularly paracingulate cortex (Brodmann's area 32), which has sometimes been considered to be part of the anterior cingulate. U. Frith and Frith (2003) cite evidence suggesting that the paracingulate cortex is in fact structurally and functionally distinct from the rest of the cingulate cortex.

In studying the neurobiological correlates of social cognitive processes in infants and young children, the developmental neuroscientist is faced with a number of important issues. First, fMRI and positron emission tomography (PET) applications to infants and very young children remain restricted by ethical constraints (Hinton, 2002). Studies using these technologies have typically examined infant or child populations with neurological disorders, although some recent studies have presented fMRI findings from typically developing infants (e.g., Dehaene-Lambertz, Dehaene, & Hertz-Pannier, 2002). Second, the behavioral processes reflecting mentalizing (or the beginnings of this capacity) are not as amenable to neurophysiological investigation in infants and young children as are the mature capacities in typical adults. In terms of the development of behaviors related to social cognition, there has been a substantial amount of behavioral research which has focused on areas such as imitation, joint attention, and face processing. However, in part because of methodological constraints and our relative lack of knowledge about the development of the brain areas involved, only a relatively small amount of work has focused on the developmental neurophysiology of social cognition. As detailed in a number of other chapters in this volume, developmental research from a neurobiological perspective has tended to focus on the development of specific aspects or precursors of social cognition (e.g., Mundy & Acra, this volume; Sabbagh, this volume).

One primary area of interest in research on the development of social cognition concerns the interactions between cognition and emotion. An example comes from research examining prefrontal cortex (PFC) development in young children. Dorsolateral regions of the PFC have been found to subserve more cognitive aspects of executive function (abstract reasoning, problem solving), whereas other more ventral and medial areas (medial PFC and orbitofrontal cortex) are responsible for the integration of affect with cognitive information. The role of ventromedial PFC in emotional development is of much interest (Happeney, Zelazo, & Stuss, 2004), in part because the development of orbitofrontal cortex has also been related to the increasing capacity for mentalizing (U. Frith & Frith,

2003). The explicit links between cognition and emotion have also been explored in adults by Adolphs (2001), who outlines the sequence of stimulus processing in the nervous system, beginning with the perception, recognition, and evaluation of social stimuli. The latter involves processing of stimulus features by sensory and association cortices, which allow the representation of the social environment. In addition, brain networks involving the fusiform gyrus and superior temporal sulcus work with other structures such as the amygdala, orbitofrontal cortex, cingulate, and somatosensory cortices to build up this representation. This central representation then modulates the effector systems involved in motor behavior and emotional output. In addition, the produced social behavior itself becomes an important source of perceptual input.

While neurobiological theories of mentalizing aspects of social cognition have been advanced in adults, developmental models are still constrained by our limited knowledge of nervous system development in relation to the development of social behavior. However, recent biological perspectives on early social development have often focused on young infants' "preparedness" for social engagement. In part, this focus developed through an increasing level of interest in social capacities in early infancy: For an eloquent summary of findings in this area, see Bugental and Goodnow (1998). Indeed, much of this research explicitly discusses the "innate" social abilities or preferences of newborns or young infants. Despite problems with defining innateness (Samuels, 2004), it is clear that even very young infants are particularly tuned to social stimuli (U. Frith & Frith, 2003). In addition, a variety of work has suggested that even in the first year of life, infants are developing notions about the goal-directed nature of actions, an ability which may provide the basis for the development of more complex inferences about others' intentions (Woodward, Sommerville, & Guajardo, 2001).

Components of Social Engagement

It is widely recognized that most social behaviors are composite or complex behavioral processes that are themselves the product of a number of behavioral subcomponents. This implies the need to break down social behavior into subcomponents that are amenable to direct behavioral and neurobiological investigation. Implicit in this approach is the recognition that understanding the complexity of social engagement will not occur until we understand the behavior and neurobiology of each of the subcomponent processes.

Added to this discussion are the dimensions of developmental change in the organism, the nature of capacities for perceiving and identifying social stimuli, and the mechanisms for learning the rules of the social world. Indeed, a developmental approach provides an appropriate start for examining the subcomponent processes involved in social engagement. One might begin by identifying the perceptual abilities that are available to the infant and the kinds of discrimi-nations that are made by newborns. One can then list the goals or attainments that are necessary for normative social engagement and then study how the young infant learns or attains these goals. For example, human infants may be born with specialized perceptual abilities to process faces (Morton & Johnson, 1991). They learn that certain faces and people provide reinforcement, reward, or se-curity more than others, and that people often share affective information via facial expression, gesture, and voice (Walker-Andrews, 1997). Indeed, one of the processes by which social information is shared and learned is through imi-tation of facial expressions (Field, Woodson, Greenberg, & Cohen, 1982; Meltzoff & Moore, 1983). A developmental approach allows one to examine just how these subcomponent processes merge to form the complex behavioral pro-cesses we call social engagement.

What are the key components of social engagement? In answering this ques-tion, it is helpful to divide up the list of components into those that are inherent in the individual versus those that are dyadic. For example, the ability to per-ceive faces and perhaps to discriminate between facial expressions of emotion is inherent in the individual, as is the ability to express a range of emotions. In contrast, learning the rules of turn taking, social referencing, and joint attention involves dyadic interaction.

A second approach to carving up the subprocesses involved in social engage-ment is to examine those processes involved in the experience of emotion. In-fants are born with the capacity to experience both positive and negative affect, and these emotions are associated with their learning about the social world (Abe & Izard, 1999). Human infants find both human faces and positive social en-gagement to be rewarding. Moreover, human social contact, in the form of face, voice, touch, and kinesthetic input, serves to reduce states of distress in the in-fant. This distress, at first, may be the result of physical discomfort (e.g., hun-ger, temperature) but very soon includes distress that is the result of the infant's response to novelty or uncertainty. As infants mature in their perceptual and cognitive abilities, novel aspects of the social context may be more or less threat-ening and elicit distress and negative affect. The ability of a caregiver to reduce that distress and create or provide an environment in which the infant can ex-plore with freedom and safety is a major impetus for the formation of social preference and what has been termed a social bond or attachment to a specific caregiver or caregivers (Ainsworth, Blehar, Waters, & Wall, 1978). Thus the experience of positive affect in social interaction, and the reduction of distress and negative affect via social interaction both work to facilitate the rewarding aspects of social engagement.

A third element to social engagement is the notion of shared affective expe-rience. There is a great deal of discussion regarding this aspect of social interac-tion. Some researchers believe it is a uniquely human characteristic to understand that someone else has an affective experience similar to one's own and that both individuals may share in that experience (Tomasello & Haberl, 2003; Tomasello & Rakoczy, 2003). The construct of joint attention has received a great deal of interest as an initial indicator of shared affective experience. Here, too, there are subcomponent behaviors that precede this complex behavioral process that might inform the emergence of this skill. For example, young infants engage in a behavior known as social referencing, a dyadic process in which one perceives an emotion signal (e.g., facial or vocal expression) targeted at the infant, who then modifies his behavior as a function of that signal (Klinnert, Emde, ButterWeld, & Campos, 1986). A young infant might approach a dangerous object, a caregiver might send a signal via face or voice that would convey the danger of the object, and the infant would halt his approach. Or an unfamiliar person might approach the infant, and the infant would look to the caregiver (thus, the social referencing goes both ways—the caregiver or adult first signaling the infant, as well as the infant looking to the caregiver for information). If the caregiver smiles, that may signal that the unfamiliar person is friendly. Social referencing, then, in its elementary form, provides the infant with information from the facial or vocal emotional signs of another. This process may be an important step in later using facial or vocal signs of affect to share emotional experiences.

Little work has been done on the underlying components of complex social engagement behaviors like social referencing. Instead, the neuroscientific investigation of early social engagement has drawn heavily on the literature on the cognitive neuroscience of development (Nelson & Luciana, 2001). In particular, researchers examining early social cognition and brain development have drawn from work in specific areas such as face processing, as well as related constructs such as imitation and joint attention. Various aspects of this work are described in the current volume, but we also present our perspective on two of these developments here (face processing and imitation). We then go on to briefly outline another fruitful research area which highlights the intersection of neurobiological and developmental approaches, the study of early temperament.

Psychophysiological Aspects of Face Processing

Face processing in infancy and early childhood has been an area of intense research interest for developmental scientists (Pascalis & Slater, 2003). Of particular relevance to the current volume is the relation between face processing and brain development (see de Haan & Groen, this volume). One particularly interesting aspect of this work concerns infants' attention to facial expressions of emotion. Various researchers have utilized ERP techniques to examine the early processing of facial expressions, an approach that has provided valuable information about perceptual and discrimination processes (de Haan, Johnson, & Halit, 2003). In contrast, very few studies have examined other psychophysiological measures related to the attentional and affective processing of facial expressions. Two studies by D. H. Marshall, Marshall, and Fox (2005) investigated whether the startle reflex of infants can be modulated by viewing various facial expressions or by behavioral episodes designed to elicit different emotions. In adults, a large research literature has examined the modulation of eyeblink startle responses to acoustic probes presented during visual processing using electromyographic (EMG) techniques. This literature has clearly shown that the magnitude of the eyeblink startle response is modulated by the valence of the visual stimulus. Negatively valenced stimuli tend to potentiate the startle response, while positively valenced stimuli tend to inhibit the startle response. However, very few studies have examined the modulation of the startle response by emotionally valenced stimuli in infants. Marshall et al. (2005) monitored infants' startle responses to short acoustic probes (100 dB SPL) during the presentation of happy, angry, or neutral facial expressions. The magnitude of the startle responses was then compared across the three facial affect conditions. The results indicated a pattern of startle modulation opposite to that documented in adults: The startle reflex of the infants was potentiated during the viewing of happy faces and was inhibited during the viewing of angry faces. Differences in heart period and looking time between the affective conditions suggested that these findings were driven, at least in part, by greater allocation of attentional resources to angry expressions. Specifically, heart period deceleration was greatest and viewing time was longest for angry faces compared with the other two stimulus types. A follow-up study involved the use of a modified paradigm with an independent sample of 9-month-olds to examine whether behavioral episodes designed to induce positive or negative affect in the infant would modulate the eyeblink startle response. Acoustic startle probes were presented while infants were engaged in a pleasant game of peekaboo, an affectively neutral presentation of a spinning bingo wheel, and a mildly frustrating arm restraint episode. The results revealed startle potentiation during the unpleasant condition of arm restraint and startle inhibition during the pleasant condition of peekaboo, indicating that the startle reflex can be modulated by affective experience in 9-month-old infants when they are engaged in affectively charged activities. In this second study, the pattern of startle modulation was similar to the effect seen with visual stimuli in adults, but opposite to the effect seen in the previous study, which had employed photographs of facial expressions. These two studies point to the complex interactions between attention and emotion in understanding face processing in infants. This complexity becomes particularly apparent when these studies are examined in relation to the study of Balaban (1995), who found the adult pattern of eyeblink startle modulation to be present in 5-month-old infants. Balaban's study has sometimes been used to signify the maturation of emotion-processing systems in the infant brain (e.g., systems involving the amygdala; see de Haan & Groen, this volume). However, as noted previously, Marshall and colleagues found an opposite effect at 9 months of age, with concurrent autonomic and looking time data for the 9-month-olds suggesting that differential allocation of attention was an important factor in determining the direction of startle modulation. In addition, the development of novelty preferences over infancy may also explain the changes in the patterning of startle modulation to affective facial expression seen between 5 and 9 months of age in the studies of Balaban (1995) and Marshall et al. (2005). For instance, 4-month-old infants look longer at joyful expressions than at angry or neutral ones, but at 7 months of age infants look longer at fearful than at happy faces (see de Haan & Nelson, 1998). Changes in infants' preferences for different facial expressions may therefore be an important factor in determining the direction of startle modulation. In this sense, the two studies of D. H. Marshall and colleagues neatly illustrate some of the complexity involved in parsing out attentional from affective processes in early processing of emotionally valenced stimuli, including facial expressions.

Imitation, Social Cognition, and Mirror Neurons

Part of the social repertoire of newborns and young infants is imitation, which is viewed as infants' capacity to map adult biological motion onto their own body movements (Meltzoff & Moore, 1983). In terms of the underlying neurobiological processes, a number of researchers have related the recent neuroscience findings on "mirror neurons" to infant imitation (Meltzoff, 2002). Mirror neurons, a class of neurons originally found in the premotor cortex (area F5) of macaque monkeys, exhibit specific firing patterns when the monkey carries out an action or observes another individual carrying out a similar action (Gallese, Fadiga, Fogassi, & Rizzolatti, 1996). While there are important differences between the monkey work and research on mirror neurons in humans, there is a variety of evidence for a mirror neuron system in humans with similar functionality (for review see Rizzolatti & Craighero, 2004). However, there is very little work specifically examining the development of such a system in infants and children. Clues for this research direction come from neurophysiological research with human adults, examining the mirror neuron system as a potentially important substrate underlying action understanding and imitative learning. Recent work has shown that a mirror neuron system exists in humans and may be monitored using noninvasive electroencephalographic (EEG) techniques that are appropriate for use with developmental populations. One proposed candidate index of the mirror neuron system in humans is suppression of the mu rhythm in the electroencephalogram (EEG). The mu rhythm occurs over central electrode sites in the frequency range of 8 to 13 Hz in adults and is suppressed (reduced in amplitude) by movement, intended movement, or observed movement (Gastaut, Dongier, & Courtois, 1954). The emergence of the mu rhythm in infancy and early childhood has been documented in a longitudinal sample of typically developing infants and young children. P. J. Marshall, Bar-Haim, and Fox (2002) showed that the mu rhythm is particularly strong in early development, appearing in the first year of life at a peak frequency of 6 to 9 Hz in the EEG signal over central electrode sites. This finding is consistent with other findings of a central rhythm in infancy that is particularly prominent during quiet attention, and unlike posterior alpha rhythms, is minimally reactive to changes in illumination or eye opening/closing (Hagne, Persson, Magnusson, & Petersen, 1973; Smith, 1941). More recently, Galkina and Boravova (1996) and Stroganova, Orekhova, and Posikera (1999) have implied a functional relation between the central oscillation in the EEG of infants and young children and the classical adult mu rhythm.

Due to the similarities between mu suppression in the EEG and the properties of the mirror neurons documented in monkeys, there has been recent interest in mu rhythm suppression as an index of the mirror neuron system in humans. Other methods have also been used to examine human mirror neuron system function in adults (e.g., fMRI, TMS, PET, MEG), but electroencephalographic techniques hold the most promise for work with infants and young children because of their noninvasive nature and the relative ease of data collection. Indeed, studying the mirror neuron system in infants and children holds great potential. Recent findings about the properties of the mu rhythm in adults, as well as other studies of the human mirror system using other techniques, suggest that developmental studies of the mirror neuron system may be very profitable not only for studies of imitation but also for examining related aspects of social cognition and the understanding of intentionality. These findings include the following: (a) Mu rhythm suppression in adults is typically stronger when observing actions directed toward objects (e.g., a hand grasping an object) compared with observing an empty hand grip (Muthukumaraswamy & Johnson, 2004); (b) activation of the human mirror system is more evident for the observation of a human model performing an action compared with the same action performed by a robot model (Tai, Scherfler, Brooks, Sawamoto, & Castiello, 2004); (c) activation of the human mirror neuron system to observation of tool use is stronger with goal-directed rather than non-goal-directed tool use and is dependent on an individual's experience with a specific action. In a fascinating recent study, Jarvelainen, Schurmann, and Hari (2004) monitored mirror system activation during observation of goal-directed use of chopsticks (e.g., picking small objects from a plate and moving them to another plate) compared with non-goal-directed chopstick use (using the same movements without touching or moving the objects). Indeed, mirror system activation was stronger during the goal-directed action condition and was related to experience: The magnitude of mirror system activation was significantly correlated with participants' chopstick use over the last year. In summary, these recent findings suggest that in humans, mirror system activation is found more strongly for goal-directed actions on objects carried out by people. In addition, the strength of mirror system activation may depend on the degree of experience that an individual has with the observed action.

The fundamental principle of mirror neuron system function relates to the "common coding" theory, which proposes that perception of others' actions maps directly onto internal motor representations of these actions (Prinz, 1997). However, imitative learning in humans must clearly go beyond perception-action equivalence: Rhesus monkeys possess mirror neurons in premotor cortex, but they do not imitate the actions of conspecifics. It is likely that in humans, the common coding aspect of the mirror system in premotor cortex is one part of a complex network involving other brain regions such as the superior temporal sulcus, orbitofrontal cortex, dorsal medial frontal cortex, and inferior parietal cortex. Each part of this network may play a particular role in the sense of agency and the inference of beliefs, goals and intentions to explain human actions and ultimately make inferences about others' mental states (U. Frith & Frith, 2003). Although the importance of motor cognition in social understanding has been debated (Jacob & Jeannerod, 2005), there has been a great deal of interest in the specific role of the motor component of the mirror neuron system in social cognition (Jackson & Decety, 2004). It is has also been suggested that without the common coding component of perception and action in motor cortex, the functioning of the wider network would be severely compromised, which would have implications for many aspects of social cognition (Meltzoff & Decety, 2003).

In this sense, studies of the mirror neuron system in children may have implications for studying developmental disorders such as autism. Indeed, a recent EEG study has suggested that the mirror neuron system is dysfunctional in children and adults with autism (Oberman et al., 2005). This study showed that typically developing subjects showed the expected mu suppression (relative to baseline) to both the movement of their own hand and the movement of a hand shown on videotape. An autistic group showed mu suppression to their own hand movement but not to the videotaped hand movement. Neither group showed mu suppression during a condition showing two bouncing balls. This work raises some very interesting questions, and the replication and extension of these findings are extremely important. In addition, the relations of these findings to imitative deficits in autism need to be clarified. Williams, Whiten, Suddendorf, and Perrett (2001) made a strong case for mirror system dysfunction being a key deficit in autistic spectrum disorders, based on the deficits in elicited imitation in autistics that have been noted across many studies. Such dysfunction does not result in a deficit in simple imitation: Autistic children may show excessive levels of simple out-of-context imitation and may not be impaired on object-oriented imitation where the imitation can be carried out through affordance learning (e.g., does not involve novel actions). In contrast, autistic participants appear to be impaired on action-oriented imitation involving novel gestures and tasks. In a recent review, Williams, Whiten, and Singh (2004) further propose that the imitational deficit in autism reflects a deficit in self-other mapping that may have a basis in a dysfunctional mirror neuron system.

In addition to the putative role of motor and premotor cortices in mirror neuron system function, a complex network of neural systems are also responsible for attending to, orienting to, and processing social stimuli. It has already been suggested that certain aspects of this network are dysfunctional in autism. A variety of evidence has accumulated to suggest that the functioning of the amygdala, the superior temporal sulcus region, and the fusiform gyrus may be impaired in autistic individuals (Pelphrey, Adolphs, & Morris, 2004). Mundy (2003) also provides an elegant account of current developmental knowledge about the role of the dorsal medial frontal cortex (DMFC) and anterior cingulate cortex (AC) regions in autistic spectrum disorders. These regions are closely connected to motor and premotor cortex, but we know little about the relations between these structures, the mirror neuron system, and imitation. In addition, developmental research on these relations is needed to clarify the mechanisms involved in the development of social cognition. In terms of neurophysiological measures, it is possible that the mu rhythm in the EEG may be a candidate index for use in potential studies of imitative development. While such studies need to be carefully designed and finely controlled, they may advance our knowledge in the field.

Social Engagement and Temperament

One example of a biological approach to individual differences in social and emotional development is the study of temperament. The study of individual differences in behavioral style in infancy and early childhood has been of much interest to psychophysiologists, neuroscientists, and developmental psychologists, and provides an excellent example of research at the intersection of these disciplines (see also Polak-Toste & Gunnar, this volume). Temperament has been conceptualized as "characteristic individual differences in the way basic emotions are experienced and expressed" (Goldsmith, 1994, p. 69). Emotions are generally seen as interpersonal phenomena, and "characteristic" implies cross-situational stability and temporal stability. Temperament research has tended to focus on individual differences in behavior with a view to uncovering differences in underlying physiological systems. In this sense there has been a large amount of theorizing and research on the biological aspects of temperament, particularly in regard to temperamental traits involving reactions to unfamiliarity. Perhaps the best example of this interface is the behavioral inhibition paradigm developed by Kagan and colleagues. Kagan's classic longitudinal studies in the 1980s focused on behavioral inhibition in toddlers and young children (Kagan, Reznick, Clarke, Snidman, & Garcia-Coll, 1984; Kagan, Reznick, Snidman, Gibbons, & Johnson, 1988). These studies and others began to elucidate physiological correlates of the behaviorally inhibited profile (for review see P. J. Marshall & Stevenson-Hinde, 2001), with much of this work being originally based on animal models of fear conditioning. This has proved to be an extremely fertile interdisciplinary area that has provided a model for other such cross-domain endeavors in developmental psychology (Fox, Henderson, Marshall, Nichols, & Ghera, 2005).

Although neurobiological models of withdrawal tendencies and fear in infancy and childhood are relatively advanced, such models are less well established for the development of positive affect and approach-related behaviors. This mirrors the fact that compared with withdrawal behaviors, much less is known about the neurobiology of the development of positively valenced approach behaviors in infancy and early childhood. Rather than simply being at the low end of a continuum of fear, infants showing high levels of approach behaviors toward unfamiliar stimuli may be utilizing a different set of psychological processes and distinct underlying neurobiological systems, compared with infants who are wary and withdrawn in response to novelty. Infants who exhibit high motor reactivity and positive affect to novel auditory and visual stimuli appear to form a unique and independent temperamental group, displaying greater consistency in their social behavior over time than temperamentally fearful infants (Fox, Henderson, Rubin, Calkins, & Schmidt, 2001). Such infants, who are consistently low in fear to novelty and high in sociability from infancy into early childhood, have been called "temperamentally exuberant" to describe the combination of their high arousal and positive approach behaviors. However, it should be noted that high levels of positive affect and approach are not always optimal. Infants displaying high approach behaviors often find themselves at odds with caregivers because they often are frustrated by restrictions or boundaries. We have argued that the development of response inhibition skills is critical for temperamentally exuberant children in the development of regulated social behavior (Fox, Henderson, & Marshall, 2001). In the absence of such skills, temperamentally exuberant children may exhibit impulsivity, anger, and high activity levels during emotional challenge (see Polak-Toste & Gunnar, this volume).

One current challenge for temperament researchers is to elucidate the specific relations between individual differences in the activity of target physiological systems and variations in behavioral tendencies. A relevant example of a prominent physiological measure used in temperament research is that of frontal EEG asymmetry. Asymmetries in EEG activation over frontal electrode sites have been associated with approach and withdrawal tendencies across a variety of studies in infants and children (Fox, 1991). Reduced levels of alpha band power over the left frontal region relative to the right frontal region, indicating greater left-sided EEG activation of neural tissue, have been associated with positive emotion and approach tendencies. The opposite pattern of increased relative EEG activation over the right frontal region (as indicated by reduced alpha band power) has in turn been associated with negative affect and withdrawal processes. In a recent special issue of *Biological Psychology* dedicated to coverage of current work on frontal EEG asymmetry, a number of prominent researchers in the area provide some theoretical guidance for interpreting the role of frontal EEG asymmetry in behavioral processes. The theoretical and empirical approaches expressed in this collection of articles provide some very useful guidelines not only for interpreting frontal EEG asymmetry but also at a broader level of applying physiological analyses to the understanding of behavior. For example, a key theme throughout the special issue is that it is important to discern whether the observed asymmetry is a mediator, moderator, or correlate of the behavior (Cacioppo, 2004; Coan & Allen, 2004; Davidson, 2004). Specifically, frontal EEG asymmetry may be a mediator when the asymmetrical neural activation produces tonic approach or withdrawal tendencies, or it may be a moderator when it dampens or augments the processes that produce the state changes in approach or withdrawal. These kinds of considerations are important to apply to temperament research as well as to wider themes within the context of social neuroscience and may take us beyond the level of reporting associations to a more thorough interpretation and discussion of mechanisms (see also Adolphs, 2003).

References

Abe, J. A., & Izard, C. E. (1999). The developmental functions of emotions: An analysis in terms of differential emotions theory. *Cognition & Emotion, 13,* 523–549.

Adolphs, R. (2001). The neurobiology of social cognition. *Current Opinion in Neurobiology, 11,* 231–239.

Adolphs, R. (2003a). Cognitive neuroscience of human social behaviour. *Nature Reviews Neuroscience, 4,* 165–178.

Adolphs, R. (2003b). Investigating the cognitive neuroscience of social behavior. *Neuropsychologia, 41,* 119–126.

Ainsworth, M. S., Blehar, M. C., Waters, E., & Wall, S. (1978). *Patterns of attachment: A psychological study of the strange situation.* Hillsdale, NJ: Lawrence Erlbaum.

Balaban, M. T. (1995). Affective influences on startle in five-month-old infants: Reactions to facial expressions of emotion. *Child Development, 66,* 28–36.

Bjorklund, D. F., & Pellegrini, A. D. (2000). Child development and evolutionary psychology. *Child Development, 71,* 1687–1708.

Blakemore, S. J., Winston, J., & Frith, U. (2004). Social cognitive neuroscience: Where are we heading? *Trends in Cognitive Sciences, 8,* 216–222.

Bugental, D. B., & Goodnow, J. G. (1998). Socialization processes. In N. Eisenberg (Ed.), *Handbook of child psychology: Vol. 3. Social, emotional, and personality development* (pp. 389–462). New York: Wiley.

Cacioppo, J. T. (2002). Social neuroscience: Understanding the pieces fosters understanding the whole and vice versa. *American Psychologist, 57,* 831–834.

Cacioppo, J. T. (2004). Feelings and emotions: Roles for electrophysiological markers. *Biological Psychology, 67,* 235–243.

Cacioppo, J. T., Berntson, G. G., Adolphs, R., Carter, C. S., Davidson, R. J., McClintock, M. K., et al. (Eds.). (2002). *Foundations in social neuroscience.* Cambridge, MA: MIT Press.

Cacioppo, J. T., Berntson, G. G., Lorig, T. S., Norris, C. J., Rickett, E., & Nusbaum, H. (2003). Just because you're imaging the brain doesn't mean you can stop using your head: A primer and set of first principles. *Journal of Personality and Social Psychology, 85*, 650–661.

Carter, C. S., Lederhendler, I. I., & Kirkpatrick, B. (1997). *The integrative neurobiology of affiliation.* New York: New York Academy of Sciences.

Casey, B. J., & de Haan, M. (2002). Introduction: New methods in developmental science. *Developmental Science, 5*, 265–267.

Casey, B. J., & Munakata, Y. (2002). Converging methods in developmental science: An introduction. *Developmental Psychobiology, 40*, 197–199.

Coan, J. A., & Allen, J. J. (2004). Frontal EEG asymmetry as a moderator and mediator of emotion. *Biological Psychology, 67*, 7–49.

Davidson, R. J. (2004). What does the prefrontal cortex "do" in affect: Perspectives on frontal EEG asymmetry research. *Biological Psychology, 67*, 219–233.

Dawson, G., & Fischer, K. W. (1994). *Human behavior and the developing brain.* New York: Guilford.

de Haan, M., & Johnson, M. H. (Eds.). (2003). *The cognitive neuroscience of development.* Hove, UK: Psychology Press.

de Haan, M., Johnson, M. H., & Halit, II. (2003). Development of face-sensitive event-related potentials during infancy: a review. *International Journal of Psychophysiology, 51*, 45–58.

de Haan, M., & Nelson, C. A. (1998). Discrimination and categorization of facial expressions of emotion during infancy. In A. Slater (Ed.), *Perceptual development: Visual, auditory, and speech perception in infancy* (pp. 187–310). Hove, UK: Psychology Press.

Dehaene-Lambertz, G., Dehaene, S., & Hertz-Pannier, L. (2002). Functional neuroimaging of speech perception in infants. *Science, 298*, 2013–2015.

Field, T. M., Woodson, R., Greenberg, R., & Cohen, D. (1982). Discrimination and imitation of facial expressions by neonates. *Science, 218*, 179–181.

Fox, N. A. (1991). If it's not left, it's right: Electroencephalograph asymmetry and the development of emotion. *American Psychologist, 46*, 863–872.

Fox, N. A., Henderson, H. A., & Marshall, P. J. (2001). The biology of temperament: An integrative approach. In C. A. Nelson & M. Luciana (Eds.), *Handbook of developmental cognitive neuroscience* (pp. 631–646). Cambridge, MA: MIT Press.

Fox, N. A., Henderson, H. A., Marshall, P. J., Nichols, K. E., & Ghera, M. M. (2005). Behavioral inhibition: Linking biology and behavior within a developmental framework. *Annual Review of Psychology, 56*, 235–262.

Fox, N. A., Henderson, H. A., Rubin, K. H., Calkins, S. D., & Schmidt, L. A. (2001). Continuity and discontinuity of behavioral inhibition and exuberance: Psychophysiological and behavioral influences across the first four years of life. *Child Development, 72*, 1–21.

Frith, C. D., & Wolpert, D. M. (Eds.). (2004). *The neuroscience of social interaction: Decoding, imitating, and influencing the actions of others.* Oxford, UK: Oxford University Press.

Frith, U., & Frith, C. D. (2003). Development and neurophysiology of mentalizing. *Philosophical Transactions of the Royal Society of London. Series B: Biological Sciences, 358*, 459–473.

Galkina, N. S., & Boravova, A. I. (1996). Formation of electroencephalographic mu- and alpha-rhythms in children during the second to third years of life. *Human Physiology, 5*, 540–545.

Gallese, V., Fadiga, L., Fogassi, L., & Rizzolatti, G. (1996). Action recognition in the premotor cortex. *Brain, 119*, 593–609.

Gastaut, H., Dongier, M., & Courtois, G. (1954). On the significance of "wicket rhythms" in psychosomatic medicine. *Electroencephalography and Clinical Neurophysiology, 6*, 687.

Goldsmith, H. H. (1994). Parsing the emotional domain from a developmental perspective. In P. Ekman & R. J. Davidson (Eds.), *The nature of emotion: Fundamental questions* (pp. 68–73). New York: Oxford University Press.

Hagne, I., Persson, J., Magnusson, R., & Petersen, I. (1973). Spectral analysis via fast fourier transform of waking EEG in normal infants. In P. Kellaway & I. Petersen (Eds.), *Automation of clinical EEG* (pp. 3–48). New York: Raven.

Happeney, K., Zelazo, P. D., & Stuss, D. T. (2004). Development of orbitofrontal function: Current themes and future directions. *Brain and Cognition, 55*, 1–10.

Hinton, V. J. (2002). Ethics of neuroimaging in pediatric development. *Brain and Cognition, 50*, 455–468.

Jackson, P. L., & Decety, J. (2004). Motor cognition: A new paradigm to study self-other interactions. *Current Opinion in Neurobiology, 14*, 259–263.

Jacob, P., & Jeannerod, M. (2005). The motor theory of social cognition: A critique. *Trends in Cognitive Science, 9*, 21–25.

Jarvelainen, J., Schurmann, M., & Hari, R. (2004). Activation of the human primary motor cortex during observation of tool use. *Neuroimage, 23*, 187–192.

Johnson, M. H. (1997). *Developmental cognitive neuroscience*. Oxford, UK: Blackwell.

Kagan, J. (1994). *Galen's prophecy: Temperament in human nature*. New York: Basic Books.

Kagan, J., Reznick, J. S., Clarke, C., Snidman, N., & Garcia-Coll, C. (1984). Behavioral inhibition to the unfamiliar. *Child Development, 55*, 2212–2225.

Kagan, J., Reznick, J. S., Snidman, N., Gibbons, J., & Johnson, M. O. (1988). Childhood derivatives of inhibition and lack of inhibition to the unfamiliar. *Child Development, 59*, 1580–1589.

Klinnert, M. D., Emde, R. N., Butterfield, P., & Campos, J. J. (1986). Social referencing: The infant's use of emotional signals from a friendly adult with mother present. *Developmental Psychology, 22*, 427–432.

Marshall, D. H., Marshall, P. J., & Fox, N. A. (2005). The emotional modulation of the startle response in 9–month-old infants. Manuscript in preparation.

Marshall, P. J., Bar-Haim, Y., & Fox, N. A. (2002). Development of the EEG from 5 months to 4 years of age. *Clinical Neurophysiology, 113*, 1199–1208.

Marshall, P. J., & Stevenson-Hinde, J. (2001). Behavioral Inhibition: Physiological correlates. In W. R. Crozier & L. E. Alden (Eds.), *International handbook of social anxiety* (pp. 53–76). Chicester, UK: John Wiley.

Meltzoff, A. N. (2002). Imitation as a mechanism of social cognition: Origins of empathy, theory of mind, and the representation of action. In U. Goswami (Ed.), *Blackwell handbook of childhood cognitive development* (pp. 6–25). Oxford, UK: Blackwell.

Meltzoff, A. N., & Decety, J. (2003). What imitation tells us about social cognition: A rapprochement between developmental psychology and cognitive neuroscience. *Philosophical Transactions of the Royal Society of London. Series B: Biological Sciences, 358*, 491–500.

Meltzoff, A. N., & Moore, M. K. (1983). Newborn infants imitate adult facial gestures. *Child Development, 54*, 702–709.

Morton, J., & Johnson, M. H. (1991). CONSPEC and CONLERN: A two-process theory of infant face recognition. *Psychological Review, 98*, 164–181.

Mundy, P. (2003). Annotation. The neural basis of social impairments in autism: The role of the dorsal medial-frontal cortex and anterior cingulate system. *Journal of Child Psychology and Psychiatry, 44*, 793–809.

Muthukumaraswamy, S. D., & Johnson, B. W. (2004). Changes in rolandic mu rhythm during observation of a precision grip. *Psychophysiology, 41*, 152–156.

Nelson, C. A., & Luciana, M. (2001). *Handbook of developmental cognitive neuroscience.* Cambridge, MA: MIT Press.

Oberman, L. M., Hubbard, E. M., McCleery, J. P., Altschuler, E. L., Ramachandran, V. S., & Pineda, J. A. (2005). EEG evidence for mirror neuron dysfunction in autism. *Cognitive Brain Research, 24*, 190–198.

Pascalis, O., & Slater, A. (Eds.). (2003). *The development of face processing in infancy and early childhood: Current perspectives.* Hauppage, NY: Nova Science Publishers.

Pelphrey, K., Adolphs, R., & Morris, J. P. (2004). Neuroanatomical substrates of social cognition dysfunction in autism. *Mental Retardation and Developmental Disabilities Research Reviews, 10*, 259–271.

Porges, S. W. (2003). Social engagement and attachment: A phylogenetic perspective. *Annals of the New York Academy of Sciences, 1008*, 31–47.

Prinz, W. (1997). Perception and action planning. *European Journal of Cognitive Psychology, 9*, 129–154.

Rizzolatti, G., & Craighero, L. (2004). The mirror-neuron system. *Annual Review of Neuroscience, 27*, 169–192.

Samuels, R. (2004). Innateness in cognitive science. *Trends in Cognitive Sciences, 8*, 136–141.

Segerstrale, U. (2001). *Defenders of the truth: The sociobiology debate.* Oxford, UK: Oxford University Press.

Smith, J. R. (1941). The frequency growth of the human alpha rhythms during normal infancy and childhood. *The Journal of Psychology, 11*, 177–198.

Stroganova, T., Orekhova, E., & Posikera, I. (1999). EEG alpha rhythm in infants. *Clinical Neurophysiology, 110*, 997–1012.

Tai, Y. F., Scherfler, C., Brooks, D. J., Sawamoto, N., & Castiello, U. (2004). The human premotor cortex is "mirror" only for biological actions. *Current Biology, 14*, 117–120.

Tomasello, M., & Haberl, K. (2003). Understanding attention: 12- and 18-month-olds know what is new for other persons. *Developmental Psychology, 39*, 906–912.

Tomasello, M., & Rakoczy, H. (2003). What makes human cognition unique? From individual to shared to collective intentionality. *Mind & Language, 18*, 121–147.

Walker-Andrews, A. S. (1997). Infants' perception of expressive behaviors: Differentiation of multimodal information. *Psychological Bulletin, 121*, 437–456.

Williams, J. H., Whiten, A., & Singh, T. (2004). A systematic review of action imitation in autistic spectrum disorder. *Journal of Autism and Developmental Disorders, 34*, 285–299.

Williams, J. H., Whiten, A., Suddendorf, T., & Perrett, D. I. (2001). Imitation, mirror neurons and autism. *Neuroscience and Biobehavioral Reviews, 25*, 287–295.

Woodward, A. L., Sommerville, J. A., & Guajardo, J. J. (2001). How infants make sense of intentional action. In B. F. Malle & L. J. Moses (Eds.), *Intentions and intentionality: Foundations of social cognition* (pp. 149–169). Cambridge, MA: MIT Press.

2

Temperamental Exuberance: Correlates and Consequences

Cindy P. Polak-Toste
Megan R. Gunnar

Temperamental exuberance is a complex construct that has been operationalized in a variety of ways, including positive affectivity, surgency/extroversion, and impulsivity. It is thought to emerge from motivational states associated with a positive valence (e.g., sensitivity to reward, strong reward expectancies). Although at one time temperamental exuberance was studied as merely the low end of the temperamental dimension of fearfulness or behavioral inhibition, more recently developmental researchers have begun to identify some of its unique behavioral and neurobiological aspects, including how early individual differences in this phenotype contribute to later social and emotional development (Denham, McKinley, Couchoud, & Holt, 1990; Derryberry & Reed, 1994; Eisenberg, Wentzel, & Harris, 1998; Hirshfeld et al., 1992; Raine, Reynolds, Venables, Mednick, & Farrington, 1998; Rothbart, Ahadi, & Hershey, 1994). Several lines of inquiry at various levels of analysis have been applied toward understanding temperamental exuberance, but much of the developmental work examining this construct remains largely descriptive and constrained by the history of its relation to the construct of behavioral inhibition.

Given that no single framework has emerged from which to examine exuberance, the primary objective of this chapter is to introduce several areas of research in which progress is being made and to examine how this progress can help to elaborate and clarify current conceptualizations of this phenotype. To achieve these objectives, we will focus on four broad issues. First, we will review the few existing attempts to conceptualize temperamental exuberance in the developmental literature. Second, we will discuss neurobiological models that may hold explanatory value and place them in the context of the behavioral descriptions of exuberance in the child development literature. Because several of these models have been used as explanatory models for behavior disorders, we will then examine the evidence for relations between temperamental exuberance and behavior problems in children. This discussion will highlight the need to consider exuberance in relation to the child's developing self-regulation or self-control competencies, in order to predict whether temperamental exuberance may be associated with problematic behavior and poor developmental outcomes. Finally, we will review the literature relating stress and exuberance as a means of understanding whether exuberance is more than just low behavioral inhibition, and whether this behavioral phenotype may in fact be associated with elevated stress system activity in specific contexts. Throughout this review we will ask whether there is evidence that temperamental exuberance is more than simply low temperamental behavioral inhibition. Although the evidence is not yet extensive, we will argue that it is sufficient to encourage continued attention to this temperamental phenotype as a separate construct with a potentially unique underlying neurobiological profile and with particular implications for children's behavioral and emotional development.

Temperamental Approach: The Behavioral Phenotype

Although developmental researchers have been examining children's temperament for a number of decades (e.g., Thomas, Chess, & Birch, 1968), they have only recently begun to include assessments of positive emotionality (see Rothbart, 1981). Much of the attention in research on temperament has been to aspects of children's behavior that are of concern to parents and caregivers, as evinced by the focus on dispositions associated with behavioral resistance (e.g., difficult temperament; Lee & Bates, 1985) and fear/anxiety (e.g., Kagan, Reznick, & Snidman, 1987). However, just as positive affect cannot be understood as simply low negative affect, the range of temperamental variation in children is not captured merely by noting that some children are not temperamentally difficult and/or temperamentally fearful or inhibited. In part, interest in temperamentally exuberant children grew out of recognition that among the children who were low in behavioral inhibition or fearful reactions to novel, arousing stimuli were some who seemed to revel in such stimulation. At least three research orientations have been taken to the study of such children. Because these orientations tend to operationalize exuberance somewhat differently, it is useful to review each in turn.

High Positive Affectivity and Exuberant Temperament

The work by Fox and colleagues (Fox, Henderson, Rubin, Calkins, & Schmidt, 2001; Fox, Henderson, & Marshall, 2001) on exuberant temperament grew out of observations of 4-month-olds responding to a battery of stimuli originally developed by Kagan (1991, 1994) to identify infants predisposed to show behavioral inhibition later in infancy. This battery exposed babies to repetitive, intense, and/or novel stimuli. Some infants were observed to react to the stimuli with high levels of motor activity and distress. Fox, however, noted that some infants exhibited another clear pattern of response: Another subset of babies were very motorically reactive, but this reactivity was combined with high positive affectivity and apparent delight in arousing, intrusive, and novel stimulation. When these infants were followed longitudinally in the paradigms that Kagan had used to assess the emergence and continuity of extreme behavioral inhibition, they not only were likely to be extremely uninhibited but also exhibited greater stability in their uninhibited classification than did those infants selected to be extremely fearful and inhibited (Fox, Henderson, Rubin, et al., 2001).

Fox and colleagues conceptualized these high motor/high positive affect infants as developing not simply into low inhibited or "disinhibited" children, but rather into children whose core characteristics were high positive affectivity, impulsivity, and high physical activity (Fox, Henderson, Rubin, et al., 2001). Exuberant children were noted by Fox and colleagues to be sociable with unfamiliar peers and adults, to approach novelty fearlessly and quickly, and to take more risks in ambiguous and "scary" situations. Indeed, it was their rapid approach to situations that in most children provoke some tentativeness (e.g., rapidly approaching a noisy and unpredictable toy robot) that suggested that impulsivity was either an outgrowth or a core component of these children's exuberant temperament. However, because the paradigms used to assess these children later in development were originally developed to assess inhibited and uninhibited children, the results of this work do not provide unambiguous behavioral evidence that exuberance differs from the low end of the behavioral inhibition continuum.

Goldsmith and his colleagues have also conceptualized exuberance as involving the display of intense positive affectivity combined with approach to highly stimulating activities (Pfeifer, Goldsmith, Davidson, & Rickman, 2002). In a longitudinal study of children between the ages of 4 and 7 years, these researchers employed a composite of exuberance that was derived from a series of games contained in the Preschool Laboratory Assessment Battery (PS-LabTAB; Goldsmith, Reilly, Lemery, Longley, & Prescott, 1993). Those used to assess exuberance were labeled "Making a Car Go," "Surprise! It's a Pop-Up Snake," and "Bubbles," which were vignettes designed to elicit high-intensity joy (for formal characteristics theoretically specified as relevant to joy, see Campos, Barrett, Lamb, Goldsmith, & Stenberg, 1983). Importantly, these episodes of the PS-LabTAB tend to elicit positive emotionality from most children. For example, "Surprise! It's a Pop-Up Snake" involves a jar disguised as containing peanuts that actually contains a spring covered in cloth that shoots out when the jar is opened. While the first trial with this "gag" toy is startling, the fact that it is a joke is quite transparent to preschool-aged children. Thus, the sudden change in stimulation when the snake pops out quickly becomes a predictable, child-controllable, safe event, making this a test of exuberance or high positive affectivity rather than one of behavioral inhibition. Preschool children easily become involved in the joke and are delighted when they are told they can go and play it on their parent. Indeed, extremely exuberant children are so thrilled and stimulated by the reward value of playing a joke on mom or dad that they have trouble containing themselves long enough to play the trick. During this episode and the other two, children's behavioral responses were scored in terms of their latency to approach, the amount of smiling and laughter expressed, and the latency to smile during the games. The scores for each of the three episodes were then added together to form a composite score of exuberance.

In the same study, different episodes ("Scary Mask," "Risk Room," and "Stranger Approach") from the PS-LabTAB were used to derive measures of behavioral inhibition at 7 years of age. These situations were derived from work by Kagan (1991, 1994) and were designed to elicit inhibition of approach to novel, unfamiliar, and often ambiguous or scary stimuli. In this sense, these episodes were similar to the ones used by Fox, Henderson, Rubin, et al. (2001) as they followed the high motor/high positive infants into the toddler and preschool years. For example, in the Risk Room a child and mother are escorted into a room containing a balance beam, a tunnel to crawl through where the exit cannot be seen from the entrance, steps to climb to a platform from where the child can jump onto a mattress, a large black box with a hole shaped as a mouth with teeth that the child can put her hands in, a gorilla mask on a pole, and so on. After the child is allowed a period of free play, an experimenter enters the room and encourages the child to play with the items. In the study by Pfeifer et al. (2002), behavioral inhibition in the Risk Room was the sum of the number of objects touched, latency to the first touch, latency to vocalize to the experimenter, approach to mother, and tentativeness of play.

At 7 years, scores for exuberance were not correlated with scores for inhibition (the correlation coefficient was near zero), indicating that exuberance is not the same construct as low behavioral inhibition. The sample under study had been selected at 32 months of age based on a laboratory assessment of behavioral inhibition. Children were selected for high or low levels of behavioral inhibition based on time spent near mother, failure to approach an unfamiliar child, and long latencies to play with toys in a play session. Disinhibited or uninhibited children quickly approached the toys, were talkative and sociable, and spent extremely little time near their mothers. These researchers also selected children intermediate on the dimension of behavioral inhibition, with all three groups returning for testing at 7 years. Scores on exuberance at 7 years were related to the inhibition groupings at 32 months of age. However, it was not the extremely inhibited toddlers who differed from the extremely uninhibited toddlers on 7-year exuberance ($Ms = -.04$ and $.26$, respectively, $SEs = .14$ and $.11$). Rather, it was the group who were intermediate in inhibition as toddlers who were the least exuberant at 7 years ($M = -.33$, $SE = .15$). These researchers also derived a composite measure of inhibitory control and impulsivity from parental report of child temperament in order to index effortful and reactive aspects of inhibition at 7 years of age. Interestingly, this measure was negatively correlated with the 7-year laboratory assessment of inhibition ($r = -.43$) and positively correlated with the exuberance composite ($r = .36$), suggesting that impulsivity/inhibition in situations that are not highly emotionally charged (i.e., situations assessed via parental report of temperament) may be involved in both fearful inhibition and exuberant approach.

Surgency and Exuberance

Rothbart and her colleagues (e.g. Rothbart, 1981; Rothbart, Ahadi, Hershey, & Fisher, 2001) have developed an elaborate model of temperament that includes assessment of what may be similar to exuberance. Their model is based on analyses of caregiver report items designed to assess theoretically derived temperament dimensions reflecting two central constructs of temperament: reactivity and self-regulation. In this model, *reactivity* refers to the arousability of motor, emotional, and sensory response systems; *self-regulation* refers to processes that modulate reactivity, including attention focusing and inhibitory control (i.e., the effortful inhibition of prepotent response tendencies). Their emphasis on the affective nature of temperament led Rothbart and colleagues to include numerous items related to smiling and laughter, positive anticipation, pleasure in quiet activities, and joy to highly arousing stimuli that were only minimally assessed by other researchers studying children's temperament.

Rothbart's (1981) Infant Behavior Questionnaire (IBQ) is one of the most widely used caregiver report measures of infant temperament. Two of the scales on the IBQ, Smiling and Laughter, and Activity Level, clearly fit the exuberance construct as it has been discussed by Fox (see earlier discussion). The IBQ has recently been revised to include additional items related to positive emotionality (IBQ-R; Garstein & Rothbart, 2003). Principal axis factor analysis on the IBQ-R scale scores collected from 360 infants aged 3 to 12 months identified a factor that was labeled Surgency/Extroversion. Scales loading highly on this factor were Activity Level (e.g., "When put in the bath water, how often did the baby splash and kick?"); Smiling and Laughter (e.g., "How often during the week did the baby smile or laugh when given a new toy?"); High Intensity Pleasure (e.g., "During a peek-a-boo game, how often did the baby smile?"); Positive Anticipation (e.g., When given a new toy, how often did the baby get very excited about getting it?"); and Vocal Reactivity (e.g., "When being dressed/undressed during the last week, how often did the baby coo or vocalize?"). Perceptual Sensitivity or the detection of slight or low-intensity stimulation from the environment also loaded on this factor in infancy, although this scale generally loads on a dimension of self-regulation during early and middle childhood.

Rothbart and her colleagues have also developed a caregiver report instrument, the Children's Behavior Questionnaire (CBQ; Rothbart, Ahadi, Hersey, & Fisher, 2001), to assess various dimensions of temperament in early and middle childhood. This instrument includes 15 scales and has been administered to mothers of children aged 4 to 8 years in the United States, the People's Republic of China, and Japan (see Ahadi, Rothbart, & Ye, 1993; Rothbart et al., 2001). Using principle component analyses and both exploratory and confirmatory factor analyses, Rothbart and her colleagues have consistently obtained three major factors from the CBQ, one of which they label Surgency/Extroversion. Across both early and middle childhood, the following scales load highly on Surgency/Extroversion: Activity Level, Impulsivity, High Intensity Pleasure, and Shyness (loads negatively). Scales that are inconsistently associated with Surgency/Extroversion are Positive Anticipation/Approach and Smiling and Laughter.

Since Positive Anticipation/Approach is conceptually the scale that should most clearly reflect motivational approach systems (see later discussion of neurobiological models), it is surprising to find it inconsistently associated with Surgency/Extroversion. However, the reason suggested for this finding is instructive. This temperamental dimension sometimes loads highly on both Surgency and another factor that Rothbart has labeled Negative Affectivity, which includes a scale reflecting Anger and Low Frustration Tolerance. Rothbart (Rothbart, Derryberry, & Posner, 1994) and others (e.g., Stifter & Fox, 1990) have noted that beginning in infancy, children who are high in approach motivation or positive anticipation are more likely to exhibit angry reactions when blocked from achieving their goals and/or when they are physically confined or restrained. This analysis suggests that low frustration tolerance and angry reactions may be observed for highly exuberant children because their exuberant temperament leads them to experience more intense reactions to goal blocking. However, it seems unlikely that anger and low frustration tolerance are at the core of this temperamental phenotype given that the expression of anger is not a global characteristic but most often emerges in response to a frustrating event. Also, there is evidence that the development of attentional and behavioral control systems dampens anger expressions, suggesting that whether or not highly exuberant children are also observed to be angry or frustrated may depend on the development of self-regulatory competencies (Fox, Henderson, & Marshall, 2001; Rothbart, Ahadi, & Evans, 2000).

The fact that the Smiling and Laughter scale does not consistently load on the Surgency/Extroversion factor at first would appear to call into question the interpretation of this factor as reflecting exuberance. However, while the general relations have been inconsistent, Smiling and Laughter sometimes loads both on Surgency/Extroversion and on the Effortful Control factor related to self-regulation. Items that make up the Smiling and Laughter scale include both ones reflecting intense positive affectivity and ones reflecting less intense positive emotionality. As noted by Pfeifer and colleagues (2002), exuberance should reflect intense positive affectivity rather than calm contentment. Similarly, in research on adult personality, Depue (Depue & Collins, 1999; Morrone-Strupinsky & Depue, 2004) has demonstrated that the higher-order personality factor of Positive Affectivity or Extroversion is actually composed of two unique dimensions: Affiliation, which reflects warmth, affection, and the enjoyment of close interpersonal relationships, and Agency, which reflects the experience of a sense of potency in accomplishing goals and attaining social dominance or leadership. Thus, the temperamental dimension of Smiling and Laughter may not be uniquely associated with Surgency/Extroversion because it reflects both smiling and laughter motivated by contentment, warmth, and affiliation, as well as smiling and laughter stimulated by goal attainment and the anticipation of reward.

Given our question of whether exuberance can be differentiated from low levels of behavioral inhibition, one important question is whether consistent the Shyness scale consistently loads on the Surgency/Extroversion factor. While Shyness also often cross-loads on Negative Affectivity, its presence on the Surgency/ Extroversion factor reflects the difficulty of clearly differentiating exuberance from behavioral inhibition. It may also point to another difficulty in differentiating these constructs. Specifically, with both constructs it may be important to differentiate responses to social and nonsocial stimuli, a distinction that may be of increasing importance as children develop. Thus, for example, it is difficult to differentiate between social and nonsocial fear in infancy (e.g., Garstein & Rothbart, 2003), but by the toddler period (Goldsmith, 1996) and certainly by early childhood (Rothbart et al., 2001), questionnaire items assessing social and nonsocial fear cohere separately. Behavioral measures of social and nonsocial fear also decrease in their association from infancy through the preschool years (e.g., Fox, Henderson, Rubin, et al., 2001; Sanson, Pedlow, Cann, Prior, & Oberklaid, 1996; Scarpa, & Raine, 1995). Whether exuberance in play with objects and exuberance in response to social stimulation become differentiated during early childhood is not yet known but may be important to determine.

Neurobiological Models Relevant to Exuberance

Another approach to conceptualizing the exuberant phenotype is to examine neural systems purported to support strong approach tendencies and pleasure in highly stimulating activities. Several theorists have attempted to identify neural systems relevant to these behavioral dimensions. Their models roughly fall into ones describing neural pathways involved in reward and models of the nervous system that postulate patterns of stimulation seeking (or avoidance) in the service of regulating arousal. As support for the argument that exuberance and behavioral inhibition reflect different underlying neural circuitry, these models can be contrasted with models describing the neural bases of inhibited behavior. We will first consider models of responses to reward-ing stimulation, followed by models of stimulation seeking in the service of regulating arousal.

Gray's Motivational Systems

Elaborating principles of classical conditioning derived from animal research, Gray (1970, 1971, 1982a, 1982b, 1987a, 1987b) proposed a motivationally based view of temperament. Gray's model centered on the notion that individual differ-ences in temperamental approach and withdrawal were due to variations in the sensitivity of certain neural circuits to particular classes of stimuli. Gray identified three systems that have specific input-output relations and have been associated with specific brain regions: the flight-fight (F-F) system, the behavioral activa-tion system (BAS; Gray, 1987a), and the behavioral inhibition system (BIS; Gray, 1982b).

Gray envisioned the BAS and the BIS as mutually competitive systems. In his model, the BAS facilitates responses to conditioned and unconditioned ap-petitive stimuli such that the presentation of stimuli associated with reward and/or the termination of punishment results in approach behavior and positive affect. The key neural elements related to the BAS include two interrelated subsystems: (a) a *caudate motor system* that includes regions of the nonlimbic cortex (e.g., motor, sensorimotor, and association cortices), the caudate putamen, dorsal glo-bus pallidus, ventral lateral thalamus, and substantia nigra; and (b) an *accumbens motor system* that contains prefrontal and cingulated cortex, nucleus accumbens, ventral globus pallidus, and dorsomedial thalamic nucleus. When activated, the BAS recruits reward-related ascending dopamine projections from the substan-tia nigra, amygdala, and nucleus accumbens to facilitate approach behavior. In contrast to the BAS, the BIS is thought to respond to signals of nonreward, un-conditioned fear stimuli, and novelty, thus resulting in behavioral inhibition, an increase in physiological arousal, heightened attention and information process-ing, and the emotion of anxiety. More recently, Gray (Gray & McNaughton, 2000) has revised his initial concept of BIS (Gray, 1982b) to stress that the BIS is activated only when an organism is required to move toward a source of dan-ger to achieve a desired outcome. Therefore, according to this new theory, the BIS is now activated only when there is simultaneous activation of the BAS. The core of the BIS system, the subcortical septal-hippocampal formation, is linked to a number of brain regions, such as the thalamus, midbrain, and orbital prefrontal cortex, which are thought to provide a "bottom-up" mechanism for the inhibition of ongoing behavior.

Gray's model of the behavioral inhibition system is similar in its behavioral predictions to Kagan's (1991) model of extreme behavioral inhibition. These models differ, however, in their emphasis on the amygdala as a critical source of inhibition in response to novelty. Kagan has argued that extremely inhibited children have lower thresholds for activation of the amygdalar fear circuit. The amygdala is a gray mass located in the dorsomedial portion of the temporal lobe, positioned in front of and partly above the tip of the inferior horn of the lateral nucleus (Parent, 1996). Three nuclei within the amygdala (the medial, central, and basolateral nuclei) are particularly sensitive to novelty. Because these nuclei receive, either directly or indirectly, an enormous array of convergent sensory information and because efferents from these synapse on the hypothalamus, basal forebrain, ventral striatum, and various autonomic centers in the brain stem, the amygdala is viewed as an important relay through which external stimuli can influence or modulate cortical, motor, autonomic, and neuroendocrine targets. Kagan's emphasis on the amygdala is partly based on elegant work by LeDoux (e.g., LeDoux & Phelps, 2000), who has analyzed the neural pathways underlying conditioned fear responses. One related issue is that behavioral inhibition is also thought to involve unconditioned fear, which is not mediated by the three main nuclei of the amygdala. Recent work by Davis and colleagues (e.g., Davis, 1998) suggests that unconditioned fear involves pathways through the bed nucleus of the stria terminalis, which has been termed part of the "extended amygdala."

Returning to the BAS/BIS model, Gray has specifically linked the BAS circuit to individual differences in impulsivity, which has implications for the conceptualization of exuberance. Gray argues that individuals with a more reactive BAS are more likely to show conditioned approach than are individuals with a less reactive BAS. However, while the active opposition between the BAS and BIS systems in Gray's motivational system suggests that the neural systems for approach and inhibition may be differentiated, in reality both systems are likely to be activated as organisms navigate their environments. Obtaining relatively "pure" indices of the behavioral expression of BAS and BIS may therefore be difficult. Furthermore, when researchers have applied Gray's model to questions of behavior disorders, they have tended to focus on variations in strength of the BIS as the locus of problems in impulsivity and undercontrol (see, e.g., Fowles, 1980; Gray, 1970, 1971, 1982a, 1982b, 1987a, 1987b; Gorenstein & Newman, 1980; Newman, Patterson, & Kosson, 1987). Thus both in Gray's model and in Kagan's neurobiological model of inhibition, variations in exuberant approach may tend to be explained by variations in the strength of systems supporting behavioral inhibition.

Panksepp's Seeking System

Research on reward pathways in the central nervous system have often used measures of an animal's willingness to self-stimulate brain areas (see review by Panksepp, 1998). Panksepp has argued that this work, rather than identifying the neural basis of reward, points to neural systems that support the anticipation of rewarding stimuli and strong approach motivation. He has termed these neural systems the "Seeking System." The pathways he discusses bear strong resemblance to those described by Gray as components of the BAS. They include areas within the orbital frontal cortex, the basolateral amygdala, and the lateral hypothalamus (Panksepp, 1998). These specialized circuits are thought to facilitate approach to rewarding stimuli by regulating locomotor movement via (a) dopaminergic projections to the nucleus accumbens and the pedunculopontine nucleus and (b) interactions with the midbrain dopamine systems that project from the substantia nigra and the ventral tegmental area. In mammals, stimulation of the medial forebrain bundle of the lateral hypothalamus in which the major sets of dopaminergic pathways arise has been found to promote approach behaviors such as exploration, foraging, and reward seeking (Panksepp, 1998). In human adults, stimulation of these systems produces feelings of energy and invigoration similar to those elicited by drugs such as cocaine and amphetamines that act on the dopaminergic system (Panksepp, 1998).

Depue's Behavioral Facilitation System

The Behavior Facilitation System (BFS; Depue & Collins, 1999) is another model that is based on the supposition that dopamine facilitates motor functions associated with approach to rewarding stimuli. Two major circuits have been theorized as constituting the BFS. The first includes the nucleus accumbens, ventral pallidum, and dopaminergic neurons, which are thought to function collectively to code the intensity of rewarding stimuli. The second, composed of the medial orbital cortex, amygdala, and hippocampus, has been theorized as the circuit responsible for integrating the salience of the reward. In the BFS model, individual differences in approach arise as a result of variations in dopaminergic projections to limbic and frontal sites encoding the salience intensity of reward and those acting to promote contextual processing.

In contrast to the BAS, the BFS posits that when a reward-goal is blocked, aggressive behavior toward the obstacle may be expressed so that the reward can be attained. Individuals with a more reactive BFS are therefore described as being quick to initiate approach and as having a tendency to experience strong positive affect given the potential of receiving a reward. They also may show high levels of frustration when their goals are blocked. Interestingly, dopamine agonists such as amphetamines have been found to enhance aggressive behaviors, in addition to increasing the motor systems related to approach behaviors. In this sense, activation of the dopamine system may in fact also facilitate irritable aggression aimed at removing a frustrating obstacle (Depue & Collins, 1999).

Stimulus Seeking and Arousal

The major models developed in the 1960s describing sensation seeking (Zuckerman, 1969) and extroversion (Eysenck, 1967) were based largely on arousal theories of motivation and emotion (e.g., Duffy, 1962; Hebb, 1955; Lindsley,

1951). The central tenet of these theories is that individuals differ in the extent to which they can be physiologically "aroused" and therefore also vary in the amount of stimulation they need to function at an "optimal" level. Eysenck (1967) hypothesized that individual differences in the degree of introversion or extroversion result from an imbalance between excitatory and inhibitory neural mechanisms. He suggested that the properties of the ascending reticular activating system (ARAS, a brain stem structure regulating the amount of information entering the cortex) differed in introverts and extroverts such that it allowed large amounts of stimulation to reach the cortex of introverts and allowed only low levels of stimulation to reach the cortex of extroverts. Eysenck therefore posited that the dampening or inhibiting of sensory input by the ARAS in extroverts would eventually cause chronic underarousal and thus result in sensation-seeking behavior by these individuals. Zuckerman (1969, 1991) also employed the notion of optimal level of arousal, but he used it to describe individual differences in sensation seeking. In this model, sensation-seeking behavior is thought to reflect a compensatory mechanism arising from reduced activity in the dopaminergic system. High sensation seekers were therefore thought to have lower levels of tonic activity in the dopaminergic system and thus engage in "risky behaviors" to increase the activity of this system.

Laterality and Models of Approach

Clinical and empirical data employing a number of methodologies have suggested that the right and left frontal regions of the cortex are differentially involved in the experience and expression of motivation and emotion (e.g., Gainotti, 1972; Robinson & Price, 1982; Robinson, Kubos, Starr, Reo, & Price, 1984; Rossi & Rosadini, 1967; Sackeim et al., 1982; Sackeim & Gur, 1978). The extant literature concerning asymmetrical involvement of the left and right cortical regions indicates that left frontal cortical activity is associated with approach motivation and positive affect, whereas right frontal cortical activity is associated with withdrawal motivation and negative affect (e.g., Coan & Allen, 2003; Davidson & Fox, 1989; Tomarken, Davidson, Wheeler, & Kinney, 1992). Indices of frontal cortical activity have most often employed electroencephalography (EEG) to examine asymmetries in alpha power (Davidson, Jackson, & Larson, 2000), which are in turn related to asymmetries in cortical activation (Lindsley & Wicke, 1974).

Evidence suggests that lateralization of frontal cortical activity reflects a trait, since the pattern of activity in this region demonstrates reasonable test-retest reliability (e.g., Tomarken et al., 1992). In adults, patterns of baseline frontal EEG asymmetry have been found to predict individual differences in emotional responses such that individuals with relatively greater resting right frontal cortical activity show more negative affect in response to films aimed at inducing fear and disgust, and less positive affect in response to positive emotion–inducing films (Jones & Fox, 1992; Tomarken, Davidson, & Henriques, 1990; Wheeler, Davidson, & Tomarken, 1993). Similar relations between patterns of right frontal EEG asymmetry and the tendency to express negative affect have also been identified in infancy. For instance, baseline right frontal EEG asymmetry was found to predict crying in response to maternal separation in 10-month-old infants (Davidson & Fox, 1989). Davidson and Fox (1982) also found that infants showed greater left frontal cortical activation in response to a film clip of an actress generating a happy facial expression as compared with a sad facial expression. Given that infants and children identified as exuberant display high levels of both approach behavior and positive affect, it is reasonable to expect that they would display greater patterns of left frontal EEG asymmetry as compared with other types of children. To date, no work has examined patterns of frontal EEG asymmetry and exuberance, although the work of Fox and colleagues has examined the relations between patterns of frontal EEG asymmetry and disinhibition or low behavioral inhibition to novelty. In a longitudinal study of children displaying continuous patterns of either inhibited or uninhibited behavior, children who continuously displayed uninhibited behavior over the first 4 years of life showed greater relative left frontal EEG activation than did children who continuously displayed inhibited behavior over the same time period (Fox, Henderson, Rubin, et al., 2001). Given that the continuous display of disinhibited behavior was associated with patterns of left frontal EEG asymmetry, these data lend support to the prediction that exuberance, also conceptualized as an approach-related motivation, would also be associated with patterns of left frontal EEG asymmetry.

Summary of Approach Systems

The various neurobiological models presented here have implicated dopamine reward systems in behavioral approach and reward. The models differ only slightly in their emphasis on the other neural systems that are implicated in individual differences in approach tendencies. Thus, Gray emphasizes the balance between the BAS and BIS systems in regulating approach to rewarding stimulation, whereas Depue and colleagues emphasize interactions between the BFS and systems supporting aggression and attack under conditions of goal blocking. As we have seen in the child developmental literature, both impulsivity and anger/frustration have been associated with temperamental exuberance. These neurobiological models argue that rapid approach to rewarding stimuli, which might be viewed as "impulsive approach," may be a component of exuberant temperament. Additionally, impulsivity in the form of failure to inhibit approach in the presence of stimuli that should arouse the inhibition system may in fact reflect the balance of approach and inhibition systems. In this sense, impulsivity may be less of a "core" construct underlying exuberance than approach-related tendencies, but parsing approach and impulsivity remains a challenge empirically.

The models presented here also suggest that anger and low frustration tolerance reflect an interaction of the systems supporting approach and those supporting aggressive responses to goal blocking. This interaction may be qualified by neurobiological studies examining laterality and motivated approach and withdrawal. As with Gray's model, this work suggests that approach-withdrawal or positive-negative affect systems tend to be interactive and competitive. Thus, exuberance, which should be associated with high left relative frontal EEG activation, should be difficult to qualitatively differentiate from behavioral inhibition, which should be associated with high relative right frontal EEG activation. Indeed, Davidson and colleagues (Sutton & Davidson, 1997) have integrated Gray's BAS/BIS model into their work on frontal EEG laterality. However, it has also been noted that some forms of anger, particularly anger associated with approach responses to remove obstacles to goals, is associated with left-biased frontal EEG asymmetry (Harmon-Jones, 2003). Thus, although anger/frustration may not be a core component of the exuberance phenotype, it may be challenging to operationally differentiate it from exuberance.

The models focusing on stimulation seeking as a means of regulating arousal suggest that exuberant children should be disturbed by conditions of low stimulation. Importantly, none of the laboratory episodes that have been used to examine exuberance have confronted children with prolonged periods of low stimulation. However, using Rothbart's factor analyses of parental report questionnaires, it is noteworthy that the scale labeled "low pleasure" (which assesses whether the child enjoys quiet, low-level stimulation) negatively loaded onto the surgency/extroversion factor. Thus, exuberance might involve aversion to quiet, low-stimulation activities, as well as pleasure in highly stimulating play. Designing situations to assess this hypothesis might help to firm up behavioral descriptions and conceptual understanding of the exuberant phenotype.

Exuberance and Behavior Problems

All the neurobiological models of approach suggest that high levels of approach behavior will be sustained if there is an inability to activate appropriate inhibitory mechanisms. This raises questions of whether children who appear to be extremely exuberant also tend to exhibit problematic behavior related to a lack of inhibition. The challenge of disentangling problems resulting from failure to engage inhibitory neural systems from ones based on overengagement of exuberant approach systems presents a difficulty in terms of assessing the pure contribution of exuberant temperament to behavioral outcomes. However, relations between exuberance and behavior problems are likely to depend on whether the exuberant child is able to flexibly regulate his or her behavior to match the demands and opportunities of different settings. Thus, as noted by Rubin and colleagues (Rubin, Coplan, Fox, & Calkins, 1995), exuberance is likely to be a double-edged sword, one that when well regulated supports positive outcomes, but when poorly regulated tends to result in behavior problems in the externalizing realm.

The interpretation of studies of the relation between exuberance and behavioral outcomes for children may vary depending on whether the researchers emphasize the positive emotionality components of exuberance or instead emphasize the rapid approach and delight in highly stimulating activities. Those who have emphasized positive emotionality tend to observe fairly uniform positive outcomes. These researchers have tended to focus on happy or cheerful moods and have generally found that the display of positive affect is associated with more positive social and emotional development (e.g., Denham et al., 1990; Eisenberg et al., 1998; Scaffer, 1966). For example, Denham and colleagues found that teacher reports of children's dispositional positive emotionality were positively related to children's dispositional sympathy (Denham et al., 1990). A number of researchers have also suggested that positive affect may act as a buffer or increase resilience, since children displaying this characteristic are more likely to receive greater attention from adult caregivers. For example, highly active and outgoing children in institutions were less likely to show behavioral maladjustment than children who did not display this pattern of behavior (Scaffer, 1966). Although some work has attempted to examine the nature of positive affect and its role in social development in infancy (e.g., Spitz, 1983; Stern, 1977), research examining these relations remains largely descriptive.

More recently, researchers have begun to examine relations between the strong approach component of exuberance and behavioral adaptation. This work suggests that these tendencies may contribute to the development of externalizing behavior problems (Derryberry & Reed, 1994; Hirshfeld et al., 1992; Raine et al., 1998; Rothbart, Ahadi, & Hershey, 1994). For example, children who displayed strong approach tendencies in the laboratory assessments of responding to novel, ambiguous, or strange events at 21 months, 4 years, 5 years, and 7.5 years of age were significantly more likely to be diagnosed with oppositional disorder at 8 years of age as compared with all other children in the sample (Hirshfeld et al., 1992). However, as noted earlier, when approach tendencies are examined under conditions that also elicit strong inhibition of approach in some children, it is difficult to differentiate whether such behavior problems are due to weak inhibitory or strong approach dispositions.

All the neurobiological models discussed here that posit a balance between inhibitory and approach systems in the regulation of approach have focused on what has been termed "reactive" inhibition (Nigg, 2003; Rothbart & Bates, 1998). Reactive inhibition is organized around systems that respond with inhibition of activity in the face of novelty or cues of punishment. Recently, developmental researchers have increasingly focused their attention on the development of a self-regulatory system that emerges and develops rapidly over the early childhood years. Presumably this system supports the child's flexible regulation of behavior, allowing him or her to override prepotent tendencies to approach and also to inhibit approach. According to Rothbart (Rothbart, Derryberry, & Posner, 1994), the development of a system of effortful control allows the child to act in the service of future goals, overriding both reactive approach and avoidance responses when appropriate.

In searching for neurobiologically based models of effortful regulation, Rothbart has argued that the development of attention regulatory systems and systems that support the inhibition of prepotent responses provides a useful heuristic. Posner and colleagues (e.g., Posner & Peterson, 1990; Posner & Driver, 1992; Posner & Raichle, 1994) have provided a framework from which to explore the attentional self-regulatory processes, identifying three networks involved in selective attention: the posterior orienting network, the vigilance system, and the anterior attentional network. Each of these networks is uniquely involved in the activity of particular components of selective attention. The posterior attention system is involved in orienting toward sensory stimuli (e.g., Posner & Rothbart, 1991) and is responsible for shifting attention from one location to another by allowing attention to disengage and reengage. At a neural level, the posterior network is thought to involve parts of the superior colliculus, pulvinar, and parietal lobe. Strong connections between the anterior cingulate and the posterior parietal lobe are hypothesized to exist and to facilitate voluntary control over orienting by high-level cognitive strategies (Rothbart, Posner, & Hersey, 1995). The vigilance system is associated with the ability to maintain an alert state or to maintain focus on a selected location and is thought to involve norepinephrine input to the right lateral frontal lobe from the locus coeruleus (Posner & Raichle, 1994; Posner & Rothbart, 1991; Rothbart, Posner, & Boylan, 1990). The lateralization of the vigilance system has been attributed to the close association of the right hemisphere to autonomic systems associated with selective attention, such as the cardiovascular system (Rothbart et al., 1990). Tucker and his colleagues (Tucker & Derryberry, 1992; Tucker & Williamson, 1984) have put forward a similar model of "alertness" that involves the tonic activation system, which is posited to facilitate self-protective behavior by directing attention toward important stimuli and thwarting distraction. Unlike Posner's vigilance system, however, the tonic activation system involves dopaminergic input to the object-processing area of the left hemisphere from the ventral tegmental area.

Although no work has directly examined the relation between temperamental approach and the vigilance system, current notions about the behavioral manifestations of dysregulation in this system may provide an initial direction from which to begin to conceptualize this link. Deficits in the vigilance system have been hypothesized to underlie attention-deficit/hyperactivity disorder (ADHD) in children, since one of the most commonly observed behavioral characteristics of children diagnosed with this disorder is distractibility (Rothbart et al., 1995). While it is unlikely that disturbances in the vigilance system are directly implicated in overly exuberant behavior, an examination of temperamental exuberance in children with attention deficit disorders may be useful in understanding the different behavioral manifestations of ADHD. Specifically, it may be that the hyperactivity component that is observed in some but not all children with attention deficits may reflect interactions between disturbances in the vigilance system and exuberant temperament. In addition, given Depue and colleagues' (Depue & Collins, 1999) discussion of the relations between the BFS and aggression systems, it may also be that the aggressive behavior noted for some but not all children with attention deficits reflects interactions between deficits in the vigilance system and exuberant temperament.

The anterior or executive attention system is the network responsible for voluntary attentional and inhibitory processes (Posner & Raichle, 1994; Posner & Rothbart, 1991). The most common method used to examine the executive control of attention involves the use of conflict tasks, such as the various versions of the Stroop (1935) or flanker tasks (Eriksen & Eriksen, 1974). Considerable evidence now suggests that these types of tasks activate midline frontal areas, such as the anterior cingulate and the lateral prefrontal cortex (Bush, Luu, & Posner, 2000; MacDonald, Cohen, Stenger, & Carter, 2000). Studies employing functional magnetic resonance imaging (fMRI) have consistently shown that activity in both the anterior cingulate and the orbitofrontal cortex in children and adults correlates with better performance on tasks involving inhibitory control (Casey, Giedd, & Thomas, 2000). For example, in a study examining selective attention via the go/no-go paradigm, children (7–12 years) and adults (21–24 years) were found to show reliable activation in the anterior cingulate, middle frontal gyri, and orbitofrontal gyri in both children and adults. Children showed greater overall prefrontal activation, particularly in the dorsolateral prefrontal regions. Adults in turn showed the most robust activity in more ventral regions of the prefrontal cortex (Casey et al., 1997). Therefore, since better inhibitory control is associated with the activation of the anterior cingulate and the prefrontal cortex, one source of individual differences in children's display of inhibitory control may stem from the functioning of these neural components.

Much of the work guiding the current efforts to understand the anterior attentional system in children with strong appetitive motivations draws from the study of adult personality (Derryberry, 1987; Newman, 1987; Newman, Patterson, Howland, & Nichols, 1990). For example, laboratory investigations employing conditioned reward and punishment such as Newman's modified go/no-go task have provided evidence that individuals identified as extremely extroverted and adults with disinhibitory psychopathologies have trouble inhibiting their responses (Newman, 1987; Newman, Patterson, Howland, & Nichols, 1990). In addition, when reward or punishment cues were predetermined and were noncontingent on the subjects' response during the same task, both extreme extroverts and adults with disinhibitory psychopathologies overresponded to approach-reward-related cues and responded more quickly to trials after punishment compared with individuals identified as anxious or introverted (e.g., Nichols & Newman, 1986; Newman et al., 1990).

Effortful regulatory systems that presumably reflect the development of the anterior attention system show marked development over the early and middle childhood years. Indeed, a number or investigators have been developing tasks to assess the early periods of emergence and organization of the anterior attention network (e.g., Gerardi-Caulton, 2000; Rothbart, Ellis, Rudea, & Posner, 2003). Children who are able to inhibit dominant responses during toddlerhood are described on parental report measures of temperament as more capable of attentional shifting and focusing, as displaying lower levels of impulsive behavior, and as being less prone to frustration (Gerardi, Rothbart, Posner, & Kepler, 1996). A lack of inhibitory control has been attributed to a variety of childhood problems (Ruff & Rothbart, 1996). For example, boys between the ages of 4 to 6 years with good attentional control tended to deal with anger by using nonhostile verbal methods rather than more overt aggressive methods (Eisenberg, Fabes, Nuyman, Bernzwieg, & Pinuelas, 1994). Also, effortful control was negatively related to anger in children between the ages of 6 and 7 years of age (Rothbart, Ahadi, et al., 1994). As noted previously, the interaction between a strong approach system and the aggression system proposed by Depue and colleagues suggests that the development of attention and effortful control systems that would allow the child to contain and redirect angry, aggressive reactions to goal blocking might be particularly important for reducing the likelihood that extremely exuberant children will exhibit behavior problems. Consistent with this view, a number of investigators have suggested that the development of response inhibition skills is especially critical for the regulation of behavioral and physiological arousal in children with strong approach motivations because it can help them modulate their behavior (Rothbart et al., 2000; Fox, Henderson, & Marshall, 2001). For example, preschoolers rated high in exuberance and *low* in regulatory abilities were observed to have difficulties in their peer interactions and were reported to display more externalizing problems than children rated high in exuberance and *high* in regulatory abilities (Rubin et al., 1995).

Although most of the work on effortful regulation and behavior has focused on the regulation of negative behaviors and emotional states, difficulties in regulating high levels of positive affect and reward-seeking tendencies may also create problems for children. Certainly, many researchers have argued that problems in such areas as the delay of gratification, impulse control, and other regulatory competencies may increase the likelihood that exuberant children will have difficulty regulating their exuberance to achieve social goals (e.g., Calkins, 1994; Campbell, 2000; Cole, Michel, & Teti, 1994; Eisenberg et al., 1996; Kochanska, Murray, & Coy, 1997; Underwood, 1997).

In sum, the development of effortful regulatory competencies may moderate relations between exuberant temperament and behavior problems. In practice, because systems of exuberant approach, reactive inhibition, anger/frustration, and effortful control likely operate dynamically in most situations, it may be difficult to disentangle assessments of these dimensions in naturalistic contexts, and thus specific behavioral tasks may be needed to examine their interactions in relation to behavioral outcomes for children. Furthermore, while positive emotionality and approach are often conceptualized as supporting social and emotional adjustment, an inability to restrain excitement may in fact represent a liability to the developing child. Understanding both the "protective" and the "detrimental" factors associated with temperamental approach in specific developmental environments therefore seems to be an important step in helping put children on a pathway toward positive social and emotional development.

Exuberance, Stress Reactivity, and Cortisol

The neurobiological systems purported to underlie the exuberant phenotype are not ones associated with heightened reactivity or poor regulation of stress-sensitive physiological systems. Indeed, to the extent that the exuberant child is capable of approaching the world with joy and excitement, we might expect that this disposition would be stress protective. Consistent associations with low stress reactivity, however, would constitute a problem for the construct. Specifically, because the neurobiological systems purported to underlie behavioral inhibition have their outputs through stress-sensitive autonomic and neuroendocrine systems (Rosen & Schulkin, 1998), consistent evidence for low sympathetic and adrenocortical activity among exuberant children would lend support to the contention that exuberance is nothing more than extremely low behavioral inhibition.

Unfortunately, most of the work on stress and temperament involves studies of children who vary in behavioral inhibition. Even when those studies find that individuals low on behavioral inhibition are also low in autonomic and neuroendocrine reactivity (e.g., Kagan et al., 1987; Kalin, Larson, Shelton, & Davidson, 1998), we cannot conclude that low inhibition is equivalent to high exuberance. To date, the most informative work comes from studies using the CBQ completed by teachers or parents (for review see Gunnar, 2001). In these studies, the higher-order dimension of Surgency/Extroversion has been examined in relation to measures of salivary cortisol. As noted earlier, shyness loads negatively on this temperament dimension and thus is not a pure measure of exuberance. However, in most of these studies, because the target temperament dimension was shyness, additional analyses were performed that allow differentiation of the core exuberant dimensions (e.g., high-intensity pleasure) from scales that might actually reflect low inhibition (e.g., impulsivity and shyness). The results of this work are notable, since not only is Surgency/Extroversion not always negatively correlated with activity of the stress-sensitive adrenocortical system, but at times positive associations have been noted.

Positive associations between Surgency/Extroversion and measures of salivary cortisol have most often been reported under conditions in which children are entering new social groups. This has been examined for preschool-age children starting a new year of preschool (Gunnar, Tout, de Haan, Pierce, & Stansbury, 1997) or entering a new playgroup (Granger, Stansbury, & Henker, 1994). It has also been examined for school-age children at the beginning of a new school year (Bruce, Davis, & Gunnar, 2002; Davis, Donzella, Krueger, & Gunnar, 1999). In all these studies, salivary cortisol levels were noted to be higher and/or more labile among more exuberant than shy/inhibited children during the morning hours in the first days or weeks of classroom entry. Similar evidence for dominant, assertive men has been noted in studies of adults during basic training for the military (Hellhammer, Buchtal, Gutberlet, & Kirschbaum, 1997).

In several of these studies, significant correlations were found between measures of salivary cortisol and scales measuring high-intensity pleasure, whereas no significant relation has been found between cortisol and scales assessing impulsivity and shyness. Results such as these certainly call into question glib assumptions that activation of this hormonal stress system are always associated with poor outcomes (de Kloet, Oitzl, & Joels, 1999) and support arguments that positive outcomes tend to be obtained when this system is activated transiently under conditions of challenge. Beyond this, however, these data suggest that exuberant children, rather than having high thresholds for responding to novelty and challenge, may well be exquisitely sensitive to such stimuli, allowing the pathways sensitive to novelty to regulate increased activity of the adrenocortical system (e.g., Davis et al., 1999; de Haan, Gunnar, Tout, Hart, & Stansbury, 1998; Gunnar, Tout, de Haan, Pierce, & Stansbury, 1997). Because the hormone produced by this system (i.e., cortisol in humans) helps to raise glucose levels to support cognitive and behavioral responses to challenge (de Kloet et al., 1999), the increased activity noted in these studies might well support exuberant behavioral and emotional responses to new social situations.

However, it is also possible that the heightened cortisol levels obtained in at least some of these studies reflect emotional and behavioral challenges experienced by underregulated, exuberant children. Indeed, there are now several studies suggesting that Surgency/Extroversion is not, by itself, related to heightened activity of the adrenocortical system. Rather, it is the combination of high surgency and low effortful control that predicts elevated cortisol responses. This was noted in a study of preschoolers in which the children played a game of memory against an adult experimenter (Donzella, Gunnar, Krueger, & Alwin, 2000). The children were shown that if they won a series of these games, they would win the grand prize, which consisted of the opportunity to launch a Nerf rocket. The game was rigged so that the child initially won several games and was one game away from the grand prize. The child then lost several games, at which point the adult was one game away from being the one to launch the rocket. In the end, naturally, the child won the final games and the grand prize. Only a minority of children exhibited significant elevations in cortisol in this competitive challenge; however, those who did were overwhelmingly described by teachers as being high on surgency and low on effortful control. In another recent study with preschoolers, the combination of high surgency and low effortful control was shown to predict aggressive behavior. This, in turn, predicted peer rejection and elevated cortisol levels assessed in the classroom (Gunnar, Sebanc, Tout, Donzella, & van Dulman, 2003).

Thus, there is little evidence in these studies that exuberance, at least as measured using parent and teacher reports, is simply the low end of behavioral inhibition and thus associated with low stress reactivity. Furthermore, there is fairly good evidence that children who are exuberant, again as measured as Surgency/Extroversion, may sometimes exhibit heightened activity in stress-sensitive systems such as the adrenocortical system. At least in some cases, however, their stress vulnerability would appear to be due to failures in the ability to effortfully and perhaps flexibly regulate their exuberance and to control angry and aggressive reactions when there are threats to goal attainment.

Conclusions and Future Directions

One of the primary objectives of this chapter has been to introduce several areas of research in which progress is being made toward our understanding of the complex temperamental construct of exuberance. Because the extant literature does not contain standard assessments of exuberance, the temperamental dimensions included in different assessments and the relations among the scale content of the various instruments must be examined in comparing results across studies and ages.

Standard assessments of exuberance have been difficult to create given that current conceptualizations of the phenotype are meager. Some advances have been made toward understanding the biological and psychological concomitants of temperamental exuberance, but the large number and wide variety of traits still associated with this phenotype suggest more work is needed to differentiate core components of the construct from aspects of behavior that may reflect interactions of exuberance with situational and/or other temperamental or dispositional factors. Considerably more work is needed to conceptually and empirically differentiate exuberance from low behavioral inhibition. Similarly, work is needed to identify facets of positive affectivity that may be close to the core of exuberance from those that may be more closely associated with affiliation and easygoing or amenable dispositions. Finally, work is needed to determine the factors that relate exuberance to anger or frustration. This latter point intersects with the need to carefully examine relations between exuberance and behavior problems. We have argued that these associations are most likely to emerge when exuberant children do not develop the ability to effortfully regulate their exuberance or manage anger or frustration. However, the possibility that extreme exuberance and the neurobiology that gives rise to it might be associated more directly with behavior disorders should also be considered. Finally, the fact that exuberance, perhaps particularly if undercontrolled, has been associated with poor peer relations, externalizing problems, and elevations in stress hormone activity should encourage attention to this temperamental phenotype.

Most models of temperament have at their foundation the notion that temperament develops over time (Rothbart & Derryberry, 1981). Given the strong likelihood that both exogenous and endogenous factors influence the expression and stability of temperamental exuberance, models of this phenotype should be placed into a developmental framework. Particular emphasis should be placed on the ways in which different attentional systems may influence the expression of motivational systems at different points in development. Although the pathways between the expression of temperamental exuberance in early infancy and later social and emotional development will involve the influence of early temperamental dispositions, social experiences, and relationships, a more precise understanding of the biological and psychological processes of temperamental approach will facilitate our understanding of the way in which this phenotype influences the development of psychopathology or promotes social and emotional well-being.

Acknowledgments This work was supported by a National Institute of Mental Health Research Scientist Award (MH00946) to the second author.

References

Ahadi, S. A., Rothbart, M. K., & Ye, R. M. (1993). Child temperament in the U.S. and China: Similarities and differences. *European Journal of Personality, 7*, 359–378.

Bruce, J., Davis, E. P., & Gunnar, M. R. (2002). Individual differences in children's cortisol response to the beginning of a new school year. *Psychoneuroendocrinology, 27*, 635–650.

Bush, G., Luu, P., & Posner, M. I. (2000). Cognitive and emotional influences in the anterior cingulate cortex. *Trends in Cognitive Science, 4*, 215–222.

Calkins, S. D. (1994). Origins and outcomes of individual differences in emotion regulation. *Monographs of the Society for Research in Child Development, 59*(2–3 Serial No. 240), 53–72.

Campbell, S. B. (2000). Early externalizing behavior problems: Toddlers and preschoolers at risk for later maladjustment. *Development and Psychopathology, 12*, 467–488.

Campos, J. J., Barrett, K. C., Lamb, M. E., Goldsmith, H. H., & Stenberg, C. (1983). Socioemotional development. In M. M. Haith and J. J. Campos (Eds.), *Handbook of child psychology: Vol. 2. Infancy and developmental psychobiology* (pp. 783–915). New York: Wiley.

Casey, B. J., Castellanos, F. X., Giedd, J. N., Marsh, W. L., Hamburger, S. D., Schubert, A. B., et al (1997). Implication of right frontostriatal circuitry in response inhibition and attention-deficit/hyperactivity disorder. *Journal of the American Academy of Child and Adolescent Psychiatry, 36*, 374–382.

Casey, B. J., Giedd, J. N., & Thomas, K. M. (2000). Structural and functional brain development and its relation to cognitive development. *Biological Psychology, 54*, 241–257.

Coan, J. A., & Allen, J. B. (2003). Frontal EEG asymmetry and the behavioral activation and inhibition systems. *Psychophysiology, 40*, 106–114.

Cole, P. M., Michel, M. K., & Teti, L. O. (1994). The development of emotion regulation and dysregulation: A clinical perspective. *Monographs of the Society for Research in Child Development, 9*(2–3, Serial No. 240), 73–100.

Davidson, R. J., & Fox, N. A. (1982). Asymmetrical brain activity discriminates between positive and negative affective stimuli in human infants. *Science, 218*, 1235–1236.

Davidson, R. J., & Fox, N. A. (1989). Frontal brain asymmetry predicts infants' response to maternal separation. *Journal of Abnormal Psychology, 98*, 127–131.

Davidson, R. J., Jackson, D. C., & Larson, C. I.. (2000). Human electroencephalography. In J. T. Cacioppo & L. G. Tassinary (Eds.), *Handbook of psychophysiology* (2nd ed., pp. 27–52). New York: Cambridge University Press.

Davis, M. (1998). Are different parts of the extended amygdala involved in fear versus anxiety? *Biological Psychiatry, 44*, 1239–1247.

Davis, E. P., Donzella, B., Krueger, W. K., & Gunnar, M. R. (1999). The start of a new school year: Individual differences in salivary cortisol response in relation to child temperament. *Developmental Psychobiology, 31*, 93–101.

de Haan, M., Gunnar, M. R., Tout, K., Hart, J., & Stansbury, K. (1998). Familiar and novel contexts yield different associations between cortisol and behavior among 2-year-old children. *Developmental Psychobiology, 3*, 93–101.

de Kloet, E. R., Oitzl, M. S., & Joels, M. (1999). Stress and cognition: Are corticosteroids good or bad guys? *Trends in Neurosciences, 22*, 422–426.

Denham, S. A., McKinley, M., Couchoud, E. A., & Holt, R. (1990). Emotional and behavioral predictors of preschool peer ratings. *Child Development, 61*, 1145–1152.

Depue, R. A., & Collins, P. F. (1999). Neurobiology of the structure of personality: Dopamine, facilitation of incentive motivation, and extroversion. *Behavioral and Brain Sciences, 22*, 491–569.

Derryberry, D. (1987). Incentive feedback effects on target detection: A chronometric analysis of Grays' model of temperament. *Personality and Individual Differences, 8*, 855–865.

Derryberry, D., & Reed, M. A. (1994). Temperament and the self-organization of personality. *Development and Psychopathology, 6*, 653–676.

Donzella, B., Gunnar, M. R., Krueger, W. K., & Alwin, J. (2000). Cortisol and vagal tone responses to competitive challenge in preschoolers: Associations with temperament. *Developmental Psychobiology, 37*, 209–220.

Duffy, G. (1962). *Activation and behavior*. London: Wiley.

Eisenberg, N. A., Fabes, R. A., Guthrie, I. K., Murphy, B. C., Massk, P., Holmgren, R., et al. (1996). The relations of regulation and emotionality to problem behavior in elementary school. *Development and Psychopathology, 8*, 141–162.

Eisenberg, N. A., Fabes, R. A., Nuyman, M., Bernzwieg, J., & Pinuelas, A. (1994). The relations of emotionality and regulation to children's anger-related reactions. *Child Development, 65*, 109–128.

Eisenberg, N. A., Wentzel, M. N., & Harris, J. D. (1998). The role of emotionality and regulation in empathy-related responding. *School Psychology Review, 27,* 506–522.

Eriksen, B. A., & Eriksen, C. W. (1974). Effects of noise letters upon the identification of a target letter in a nonsearch task. *Perception and Psychophysics, 16,* 143–149.

Eysenck, H. J. (1967). *The biological basis of personality.* Springfield, IL: Thomas.

Fowles, D. C. (1980). The three-arousal model: Implications of Grays' two-factor learning theory for heart rate, electrodermal activity and psychopathy. *Psychophysiology, 17,* 87–104.

Fox, N. A., Henderson, H. A., & Marshall, P. J. (2001). The biology of temperament: An integrative approach. In C. A. Nelson & M. Luciana (Eds.), *Handbook of developmental cognitive neuroscience* (pp. 631–646). Cambridge, MA: MIT Press.

Fox, N. A., Henderson, H. A., Rubin, K. H., Calkins, S. D., & Schmidt, L. A. (2001). Continuity and discontinuity of behavioral inhibition and exuberance: Psychophysiological and behavioral influences across the first four years of life. *Child Development, 72,* 1–21.

Gainotti, G. (1972). Emotional behavior and hemispheric side of the lesion. *Cortex, 8,* 41–55.

Garstein, M. A., & Rothbart, M. K. (2003). Studying infant temperament via a revision of the infant behavior questionnaire. *Infant Behavior and Development, 26,* 64–86.

Gerardi, G., Rothbart, M. K., Posner, M. I., & Kepler, S. (1996, April). *The development of attentional control: Performance on a spatial Stroop-like task at 24, 30, and 36 and 38 months of age.* Poster session presented at the annual meeting of the International Society for Infant Studies, Providence, RI.

Gerardi-Caulton, G. (2000). Sensitivity to spatial conflict and the development of self-regulation in children 24–36 months of age. *Developmental Science, 3,* 397–404.

Goldsmith, H. H. (1996). Studying temperament via construction of the Toddler Behavior Assessment Questionnaire. *Child Development, 61,* 218–235.

Goldsmith, H. H., Reilly, J., Lemery, K. S., Longley, S., & Prescott, A. (1993). *Preliminary manual for the Preschool Temperament Assessment Battery* (Tech. Rep. version 1.0). University of Wisconsin, Madison, Department of Psychology.

Gorenstein, E. E., & Newman, J. P. (1980). Disinhibitory psychopathology: A new perspective and a model for research. *Psychological Review, 87,* 301–315.

Granger, D. A., Stansbury, K., & Henker, B. (1994). Preschoolers' behavioral and neuroendocrine responses to social challenge. *Merrill-Palmer Quarterly, 40,* 20–41.

Gray, J. A. (1970). The psychophysiological basis of introversion-extroversion. *Behavioral Research Therapy, 8,* 249–266.

Gray, J. A. (1971). *The psychology of fear and stress.* New York: McGraw-Hill.

Gray, J. A. (1982a). *The neuropsychology of anxiety: An enquiry into the function of the septo-hippocampal system.* New York: Oxford University Press.

Gray, J. A. (1982b). Precis of the neuropsychology of anxiety: An enquiry into the functions of the septohippocampal system. *Behavioral and Brain Sciences, 5,* 469–534.

Gray, J. A. (1987a). Perspectives on anxiety and impulsivity: A commentary. *Journal of Research in Personality, 21,* 493–509.

Gray, J. A. (1987b). *The psychology of fear and stress.* New York: Cambridge University Press.

Gray, J. A., and McNaughton, N. (2000). *The neuropsychology of anxiety: An inquiry into the function of the septo-hippocampal system.* 2nd ed. Oxford: Oxford University Press.

Gunnar, M. R. (2001). The role of glucocorticoids in anxiety disorders: A critical analysis. In M. W. Vasey & M. Dadds (Eds.), *The developmental psychopathology of anxiety* (pp. 143–159). New York: Oxford University Press.

Gunnar, M. R., Sebanc, A. M., Tout, K., Donzella, B., & van Dulman, M. M. H. (2003). Peer rejection, temperament, and cortisol activity in preschoolers. *Developmental Psychobiology, 43,* 346–358.

Gunnar, M. R., Tout, K., de Haan, M., Pierce, S., & Stansbury, K. (1997). Temperament, social competence, and adrenocortical activity in preschoolers. *Developmental Psychobiology, 31,* 65–85.

Harmon-Jones, E. (2003). Clarifying the emotive functions of asymmetrical frontal cortical activity. *Psychophysiology, 40,* 838–848.

Hebb, D. O. (1955). Drives and the C.N.S. (conceptual nervous system). *Psychological Review, 62,* 243–254.

Hellhammer, D. H., Buchtal, J., Gutberlet, I., & Kirschbaum, C. (1997). Social hierarchy and adrencortical stress reactivity in men. *Psychoneuroendocrinology, 22,* 643–650.

Hirshfeld, D. R., Rosenbaum, J. F., Biederman, J., Bolduc, E. A., Faraone, S. V., Snidman, N., et al. (1992). Stable behavioral inhibition and its association with anxiety disorder. *Journal of the American Academy of Child and Adolescent Psychiatry, 31,* 103–111.

Jones, N. A., & Fox, N. A. (1992). Electroencephalogram asymmetry during emotionally evocative films and its relation to positive and negative affectivity. *Brain and Cognition, 20,* 280–299.

Kagan, J. (1991). Temperamental factors in human development. *American Psychologist, 46,* 856–862.

Kagan, J. (1994). *Galen's prophecy.* New York: Basic Books.

Kagan, J., Reznick, J. S., & Snidman, N. (1987). The physiology and psychology of behavioral inhibition in children. *Child Development, 58,* 1459–1473.

Kalin, N. H., Larson, C., Shelthon, S. E., & Davidson, R. J. (1998). Asymmetric frontal brain activity, cortisol and behavior associated with fearful temperament in rhesus monkeys. *Behavioral Neuroscience, 112,* 286–292.

Kochanska, G., Murray, K., & Coy, K. (1997). Inhibitory control as a contributor to conscience in childhood: From toddler to early school age. *Child Development, 68,* 263–277.

LeDoux, J. E., & Phelps, E. A. (2000). Emotional networks in the brain. In M. Lewis & J. M. Haviland-Jones (Eds.), *Handbook of emotions* (2nd ed., pp. 157–172). New York: Guilford.

Lee, C. L., & Bates, J. E. (1985). Mother-child interaction at age two and perceived difficult temperament. *Child Development, 56,* 1314–1325.

Lindsley, D. B. (1951). Emotion. In S. S. Stevens (Ed.), *Handbook of experimental psychology* (pp. 473–516). New York: Wiley.

Lindsley, D. B., & Wicke, J. D. (1974). The electroencephalogram: Autonomous electrical activity in man and animals. In R. Thompson & M. N. Patterson (Eds.), *Bioelectrical recording techniques* (pp. 3–79). New York: Academic Press.

MacDonald, A. W., III, Cohen, J. D., Stenger, A.V., & Carter, C. S. (2000). Dissociating the role of the dorsolateral prefrontal and anterior cingulated cortex in cognitive control. *Science, 288*, 1835–1839.

Morrone-Strupinsky, J. V., & Depue, R. A. (2004). Differential relation of two distinct, film-induced positive emotional states to affiliative and agentic extroversion. *Personality and Individual Differences, 36*, 1109–1126.

Newman, J. P. (1987). Reaction to punishment in extraverts and psychopaths: Implications for the impulsive behavior of disinhibited individuals. *Journal of Research in Personality, 21*, 464–480.

Newman, J. P., Patterson, C. M., Howland, E. W., & Nichols, S. L. (1990). Passive avoidance in psychopaths: The effects of reward. *Personality and Individual Differences, 11*, 1101–1114.

Newman, J. P., Patterson, C. M., & Kosson, D. S. (1987). Response preservation in psychopaths. *Journal of Abnormal Psychology, 96*, 145–148.

Nichols, S. L., & Newman, J. P. (1986). Effects of punishment on response latency in extraverts. *Journal of Personality and Social Psychology, 50*, 624–630.

Nigg, J. T. (2003). Response inhibition and disruptive behaviors: Toward a multiprocess conception of etiological heterogeneity for ADHD combined type and conduct disorder early-onset type. *Annals of the New York Academy of Sciences, 1008*, 170–182.

Panksepp, J. (1998). *Affective neuroscience: The foundations of human and animal emotions*. New York: Oxford University Press.

Parent, A. (1996). *Carpenter's human neuroanatomy*. Media, PA: Williams and Wilkins.

Pfeifer, M., Goldsmith, H. H., Davidson, R. J., & Rickman, M. (2002). Continuity and change in inhibited and uninhibited children. *Child Development, 73*, 1474–1488.

Posner, M. I., & Driver, J. (1992). The neurobiology of selective attention. *Current Opinion in Neurobiology, 2*, 165–169.

Posner, M. I., & Peterson, S. E. (1990). The attention system of the human brain. *Annual Review of Neuroscience, 13*, 25–42.

Posner, M. I., & Raichle, M. E. (1994). *Images of mind*. New York: Scientific American Library.

Posner, M. I., & Rothbart, M. K. (1991). Attentional mechanisms and conscious experiences. In M. Rugg & A. D. Miner (Eds.), *The neuropsychology of consciousness* (pp. 91–112). London: Academic Press.

Raine, A., Reynolds, C., Venables, P. H., Mednick, S. A., & Farrington, D. P. (1998). Fearlessness, stimulation-seeking, and large body size at age 3 years as early predispositions to childhood aggression at age 11 years. *Archives of general psychiatry, 55*, 745–751.

Robinson, R. G., Kubos, K. L., Starr, L. B., Reo, K., & Price, T. R. (1984). Mood disorders in stroke patients: Importance of location of lesion. *Brain, 107*, 81–93.

Robinson, R. G., & Price, T. R. (1982). Post-stroke depressive disorders: A follow-up study of 103 patients. *Stroke, 13*, 635–641.

Rosen, J. B., & Schulkin, J. (1998). From normal fear to pathological anxiety. *Psychological Review, 105*, 325–350.

Rossi, G. F., & Rosadini, G. R. (1967). Experimental analyses of cerebral dominance in man. In D. H. Millikan & F. L. Darley (Eds.), *Brain mechanisms underlying speech and language* (pp. 167–189). New York: Grune and Stratton.

Rothbart, M. K. (1981). Measurement of temperament in infancy. *Child Development, 52*, 569–578.

Rothbart, M. K., Ahadi, S. A., & Evans, D. E. (2000). Temperament and personality: Origins and outcomes. *Journal of Personality and Social Psychology, 78*, 122–135.

Rothbart, M. K., Ahadi, S. A., & Hershey, K. L. (1994). Temperament and social behavior in childhood. *Merrill-Palmer Quarterly, 40*, 21–39.

Rothbart, M. K., Ahadi, S. A., Hershey, K. L., & Fisher, P. (2001). Investigation of temperament at three to seven years: The Children's Behavior Questionnaire. *Child Development, 72*, 1394–1408.

Rothbart, M. K., & Bates, J. E. (1998). Temperament. In N. Eisenberg (Ed.), *Handbook of child psychology Vol. 3. Social, emotional, and personality development* (pp. 105–176). New York: Wiley.

Rothbart, M. K., & Derryberry, D. (1981). Development of individual differences in temperament. In M. E. Lamb & A. L. Brown (Eds.), *Advances in developmental psychology* (Vol. 1, pp. 37–86). Hillsdale, NJ: Erlbaum.

Rothbart, M. K., Derryberry, D., & Posner, M. I. (1994). A psychobiological approach to the development of temperament. In J. E. Bates & T. D. Wachs (Eds.), *Temperament: Individual differences at the interface of biology and behavior* (pp. 83–116). Washington, DC: American Psychological Association.

Rothbart, M. K., Ellis, L. K., Rudea, M. R., & Posner, M. I. (2003). Developing mechanisms of temperamental effortful control. *Journal of Personality, 71*, 1113–1143.

Rothbart, M. K., Posner, M. I., & Boylan, A. (1990). Regulatory mechanisms in infant development. In J. T. Enns (Ed.), *The development of attention: Research and theory* (pp. 3–79). Oxford, England: North-Holland.

Rothbart, M. K., Posner, M. I., & Hersey, K. L. (1995). Temperament, attention, and developmental psychopathology. In D. Cicchetti & D. J. Cohen (Eds.), *Manual of developmental psychopathology* (Vol. 1, pp. 315–340). New York: Wiley.

Rubin, K. H., Coplan, R. J., Fox, N. A., & Calkins, S. D. (1995). Emotionality, emotion regulation, and preschoolers' social adaptation. *Development and Psychopathology, 7*, 49–62.

Ruff, H. A., & Rothbart, M. K. (1996). *Attention in early development: Themes and variations.* New York: Oxford University Press.

Sackeim, H., Greenberg, M. S., Weimen, A. L., Gur, R. C., Hungerbuhler, J. P., & Geschwind, N. (1982). Hemispheric asymmetry in the expression of positive and negative emotions: Neurological evidence. *Achieves of Neurology, 39*, 210–218.

Sackeim, H., & Gur, R. C. (1978). Lateral asymmetry in intensity of emotional expression. *Neuropsychologia, 16*, 473–481.

Sanson, A., Pedlow, R., Cann, W., Prior, M., & Oberklaid, F. (1996). Shyness ratings: Stability and correlates in early childhood. *International Journal of Behavioral Development, 19*, 705–725.

Scaffer, H. R. (1966). The onset of fear of strangers and the incongruency hypothesis. *Journal of Child Psychology and Psychiatry, 6*, 95–106.

Scarpa, A., & Raine, A. (1995). The stability of inhibited/uninhibited temperament from ages 3 to 11 years in Mauritian children. *Journal of Abnormal Psychology, 23*, 607–619.

Spitz, R. A. (1983). The smiling response: A contribution to the ontogenesis of social relations. In R. N. Emde (Ed.), *Rene A. Spitz: Dialogues from infancy* (pp. 98–124). New York: International University Press.

Stern, D. N. (1977). *The first relationship: Infant and mother*. Cambridge, MA: Harvard University Press.

Stifter, C. A., & Fox, N. A. (1990). Infant reactivity: Physiological correlates of newborn and 5-month temperament. *Developmental Psychology, 26*, 582–588.

Stroop, J. R. (1935). Studies of interference in serial verbal reactions. *Journal of Experimental Psychology, 18*, 643–662.

Sutton, S. K., & Davidson, R. J. (1997). Prefrontal brain asymmetry: A biological approach and inhibition systems. *Psychological Science, 8*, 204–210.

Thomas, A., Chess, S., & Birch, H. (1968). *Temperament and behavior disorders in children*. New York: New York University Press.

Tomarken, A. J., Davidson, R. J., & Henriques, J. B. (1990). Resting frontal brain asymmetry predicts affective responses to films. *Journal of Personality and Social Psychology, 59*, 791–801.

Tomarken, A. J., Davidson, R. J., Wheeler, R. E., & Kinney, L. (1992). Psychometric properties of resting anterior EEG asymmetry: Temporal stability and internal consistency. *Psychophysiology, 29*, 576–592.

Tucker, D. M., & Derryberry, D. (1992). Motivated attention: Anxiety and the frontal executive functions. *Neuropsychiatry and Behavioral Neurology, 5*, 233–252.

Tucker, D. M., & Williamson, P. A. (1984). Asymmetric neural control systems in human self-regulation. *Psychological Review, 91*, 185–215.

Underwood, M. K. (1997). Top ten pressing questions about the development of emotion regulation. *Motivation and Emotion, 21*, 127–147.

Wheeler, R. E., Davidson, R. J., & Tomarken, A. J. (1993). Frontal brain asymmetry and emotional reactivity: A biological substrate of affective style. *Psychophysiology, 30*, 82–90.

Zuckerman, M. (1969). Theoretical formulations. In J. P. Zubek (Ed.), *Sensory deprivation: Fifteen years of research* (pp. 407–432). New York: Appleton-Century-Crofts.

Zuckerman, M. (1991). *Psychobiology of personality*. Cambridge, England: Cambridge University Press.

3

Neural Bases of Infants' Processing of Social Information in Faces

Michelle de Haan
Margriet Groen

The human face is a special visual stimulus that conveys a variety of important nonverbal information (e.g., age, gender, identity, and emotional state) that adults can quickly and accurately perceive. Faces may be particularly salient to infants because, unlike adults, they cannot take advantage of verbal information conveyed through language as a means of communication. Indeed, from the first moments after birth, infants show a preference for orienting toward faces (Goren, Sarty, & Wu, 1975; Johnson, Dziurawiec, Ellis & Morton, 1991; Maurer & Young, 1983; Valenza, Simion, Cassia, & Umilta, 1996); look longer at the mother's face than a stranger's face (Bushnell, Sai, & Mullin, 1989; Pascalis, de Schonen, Morton, Deruelle, & Fabre-Grenet, 1995); and appear to be able to notice the difference between at least some facial expressions of emotion (Field, Woodson, Greenberg, & Cohen, 1982; Field, Cohen, Garcia, & Collins, 1983). Although several studies document these and other impressive face-processing abilities in young infants, investigators have only relatively recently begun to investigate the mechanisms that underlie these early skills and their development. The aim of this chapter is to review infants' abilities to perceive and respond to faces and the emotional signals they convey as social stimuli distinct from other objects, and to consider the neural and experiential contributions to the development of these skills.

Perception of Faces

Perceiving the Category "Face"

Over the past decades there has been continuing interest in determining when infants first perceive a face as distinct from other types of object. Initially it was thought that infants were not able to do so until at least several months after birth. However, the results of several studies demonstrating that newborn babies will move their eyes, and sometimes their heads, longer to keep a moving facelike pattern in view than several other comparison patterns suggest that this ability is present around the time of birth (Goren et al., 1975; Johnson et al., 1991; Maurer & Young, 1983; Valenza et al., 1996). It seems that all that is needed to elicit a response is a very schematic version of the face: Just a triangular arrangement of three blobs for eyes and a mouth is sufficient (Johnson & Morton, 1991).

Currently, there remains a debate as to the best interpretation of these results (for further discussion see de Haan, Humphreys, & Johnson, 2002). Some authors have argued that they are best explained by a social hypothesis. In this view, infants have an innate preference for facelike stimuli that is based on a specific knowledge of the configuration of the face. For example, in the Conspec/Conlern hypothesis, an innate, subcortical mechanism (Conspec) causes newborns to orient specifically to patterns with elements arranged in a facelike pattern in preference to other patterns (Morton & Johnson, 1991). Computational modeling suggests that this type of orienting mechanism could be the result of prenatal learning of internally generated input patterns (Bednar & Miikkulainen, 2003). In contrast, other authors account for the same data with a sensory hypothesis. A common theme in the various formulations of this hypothesis is that no aspect of the system is responding specifically to faces. Instead, the preferential orienting of the newborn to faces is just a consequence of more general mechanisms guiding visual attention. For example, newborns show a preference for looking at patterns with a greater number of elements in the top half compared with patterns with a greater number of elements in the lower half (Turati, Simion, Milani, & Umilta, 2002). Thus, infants' apparent preference for facelike patterns, which naturally tend to have more elements in the upper half, may simply be a result of this more general orienting tendency (Turati et al., 2002). Whichever explanation for newborns' preferential orienting to faces is correct, there is a consensus that the infant is born with perceptual biases that could serve to guide subsequent experience with faces.

At approximately 8 weeks of age, there is a marked change in infants' responses to faces: Their preferential following of peripheral moving faces declines (Johnson et al., 1991) and a preference for fixating faces longer than other patterns presented in the central visual field emerges (Maurer & Barrera, 1981). This behavioral change is thought to be due to functional development of visual cortical pathways that inhibit the following response and mediate the new fixation response (Johnson & Morton, 1991).

Although 2-month-old infants do look longer at centrally presented faces than at least some other patterns, factors such as stimulus complexity can be equally or more salient in attracting their attention. For example, in one series of studies (Haaf, 1974, 1977), 1- to 5-month-olds' looking times were measured to a set of four stimuli that varied independently in complexity (number of elements) and facedness (number of facial features in the proper place). One- to 2-month-old infants' looking was determined solely by the complexity of the pattern, look-ing longer at more complex patterns, whereas older infants' looking was affected by both the complexity and the facedness of the pattern.

At this age, infants' representation of the face also appears quite different from adults in that it seems to be based primarily on the eyes rather than the entire constellation of facial features. For example, 2-month-olds look equally long at the full face and a face with only eyes present (nose and mouth missing), and look at both of these longer than at a face with only nose and mouth present (eyes missing; Maurer, 1985). Moreover, the position of the eyes in the face does not appear to make a difference to the infants in their preference, even though they are able to discriminate among faces with eyes in varying positions following habituation (Maurer, 1985). Thus, at 2 months of age the eyes are a more salient feature of the face than the nose or mouth, but where the eyes are located is immaterial to the babies' preference for facelike drawings.

By approximately 3 months of age, infants do appear to be able to form a mental representation of the category "face" based on particular faces they ex-perience in the visual environment. This was demonstrated in a study in which 1- and 3-month-old infants were familiarized to four individual faces, after which their abilities to recognize both the previously unseen morphed average of the four familiar faces and one of the four unaltered familiar faces were tested (de Haan, Johnson, Maurer, & Perrett, 2001). Babies at both ages were able to rec-ognize the individual faces seen during familiarization, but only the 3-month-olds showed evidence of recognizing, and thus having mentally computed, the average of the four familiar faces. These results suggest that the ability of ba-bies to form a mental category of the face based on the actual faces they expe-rience emerges sometime between 1 and 3 months of age.

It may not be until 4 to 6 months of age, however, that infants begin to have a more adultlike representation of the face that is based less exclusively on the eyes (see Maurer, 1985). Even at this age, the importance of the eyes appears to persist, as is demonstrated in studies of infants' social interactions with adults. For example, in 9- and 12-week-olds the combination of eye contact and a sweet taste is sufficient to induce a preference for the viewed individual's face (Blass & Camp, 2001), and in 3- to 5-month-olds smiling decreases during a social interaction when the adult partner's eyes are averted and recovers when mutual gaze is reestablished (Hains, Muir, & Franke, 1994).

Perception of Facial Expressions

Definitions: What Are Facial Expressions?

The ability to pick out a face from other objects and patterns in the visual envi-ronment is an important skill, but equally important is the ability to read the various types of information the face itself contains, such as facial expressions of emotion. Facial expressions of emotion can be defined as characteristic movements of the face that adults readily identify as representing discrete emotions (Ekman, 1972). Although there remains a debate regarding the degree to which recognition of facial expressions is universal across cultures and the degree to which recognition is influenced by socialization within a culture (for a history and discussion of this debate, see Ekman, 1998), a number of emotional expressions are recognized relatively consistently across different cultures and are described as the "basic" emotions. For the purposes of this chapter, we will focus on these basic emotions (happiness, surprise, fear, anger, disgust, and sadness) rather than on "secondary" emotions (e.g., pride, jealousy) because the perception of the latter is typically considered to develop later and thus has not been studied during the first year of life.

The process of recognizing facial expressions of emotion is typically described as involving at least two steps: perception and recognition of meaning. Perception of a facial expression involves the basic ability to perceive the features that define one expression and allow it to be discriminated from another expression. Infants' perception of facial expressions is typically tested by examining their discrimination abilities (e.g., whether they notice the difference between a happy and sad expression) or their categorization abilities (e.g., whether they notice that happy expressions posed by different individuals all belong to the same category that excludes other expressions). Recognition of the meaning of an expression refers to the ability to link this percept to some other source of information regarding its meaning. In adults, a variety of sources of information are potentially available to contribute to recognition of the meaning of an expression (Adolphs, 2002): (a) knowledge of the verbal label for the expression, (b) conceptual knowledge about the emotion the expression conveys, (c) perception of an emotional response in the self that viewing the expression triggers, and (d) knowledge about the motor representations required to produce the expression. Infants clearly have fewer sources of information about the meaning of expressions, since, for example, they cannot verbally label them. However, young infants can demonstrate their understanding of meaning of expressions in other ways. In the following sections we will review evidence concerning infants' abilities to perceive and recognize the meaning of facial expressions of emotion.

Discrimination

There are some compelling reasons to believe that infants may be insensitive to differences among facial expressions in their first weeks of life. First, the newborn's visual system is far from mature at birth. For example, at birth visual acuity is between 10 and 30 times poorer than adults', and the ability to change the shape of the eye's lens to focus on stimuli at different distances is poor (reviewed in Slater, 2001). Second, there is evidence that newborns may not even process the internal features of the face. For example, newborns look longer at the mother's face than a stranger's face when her full face is presented but not when only her internal features are presented (Pascalis et al., 1995). These results suggest that newborns are not attending to the internal features of the face but instead are basing their recognition on the external contour (e.g., face shape, hair). This interpretation is consistent with studies showing that, both for faces and for other patterns, young infants tend not to notice a shape or pattern if it appears within a larger frame (Maurer, 1983; Milewski, 1976; but see Farroni, Valenza, Simion, & Umilta, 2000). Together, these results lead to the expectation that very young infants cannot discriminate among different facial expressions.

In spite of these reasons to suspect a lack of ability, two studies have reported that infants just 36 hours old are able to discriminate among facial expressions (Field, Cohen et al., 1983; Field et al., 1982). In both studies infants were presented with a happy, sad, or surprised expression posed by a live female model until they looked for less than 2 seconds, and then saw the other two expressions presented the same way. Infants increased their looking when the expression changed, suggesting that they noticed the difference between them (see Nelson & de Haan, 1997, for a discussion of possible methodological problems that might influence the interpretation of this result). These results suggest that newborns are able to process some aspects of the internal features of the face, at least enough to tell apart happy, sad, and surprised expressions. This conclusion is supported by another study showing that newborns are also able to detect the direction of eye gaze in a face (Farroni, Csibra, Simion, & Johnson, 2002).

The main focus of most studies of older infants' abilities to perceive facial expressions has been to document the age at which different expressions are discriminated. Overall, these studies suggest that by 3 to 7 months of age infants can discriminate among some, but not all, expressions. Three-month-olds can discriminate happy from surprised faces (Young-Browne, Rosenfeld, & Horowitz, 1977), and smiling faces from frowning faces (Barrera & Maurer, 1981), but they do not consistently discriminate sad faces from surprised faces and show no evidence of discriminating sad faces from happy faces (Young-Browne et al., 1977). In addition, 3- to 6-month-olds can discriminate among happy, surprised, and angry expressions (McGrath, 1983), although one study found that 7-month-olds could not discriminate happy from angry expressions (Caron, Caron, & MacLean, 1988). By 4 months of age, infants in a visual preference test look longer at joyful expressions than at angry or neutral ones (LaBarbera, Izard, Vietze, & Parisi, 1976) and look longer at happy faces with toothy smiles than at sad faces (Oster & Ewy, 1980, cited in Oster, 1981), but they look equally long at angry and neutral faces (LaBarbera et al., 1976) or at happy faces with closed mouths when paired with sad faces (LaBarbera et al., 1976). Five-month-olds can discriminate between sad and fearful faces and can discriminate both of these expressions and an interest expression from angry, but only if they are first habituated to angry and then tested with the other expressions, not if they are tested in the reverse order. At the same age, infants show no evidence of discriminating joy from anger or interest (Schwartz, Izard, & Ansul, 1985) and at 6 months show no evidence of discriminating surprise from fearful expressions (Nelson & Horowitz, 1980). At 7 months of age, infants look longer at fearful than at happy faces in a visual preference test (de Haan & Nelson, 1998; Kotsoni, de Haan, & Johnson, 2001; Nelson & Dolgin, 1985) and can discriminate between happy and fearful faces in a habituation-dishabituation test, but only if they first habituate to happy and are then tested with fear, not if they are tested in the reverse order.

By 7 months of age, infants can also correctly match vocal expressions of emotion to the correct dynamic facial display of an emotion. Seven-month-olds look longer at the facial expression concordant with a vocal expression when tested with happy-angry (Soken & Pick, 1999; Walker, 1982), happy-neutral (Walker, 1982), angry-sad (Soken & Pick, 1999), interested-angry (Soken & Pick, 1999), and interested-happy pairs (Soken & Pick, 1999), but they do not consistently do so for happy-sad pairs (see Soken & Pick, 1999, for a negative result and Walker, 1982, for a positive result). Infants' matching appears to be based on information relevant to the emotion and not merely temporal synchrony between the audio and visual portions of the stimuli, because these results hold even when the audio stimulus is played out of synchrony with the face (Soken & Pick, 1999; Walker, 1982).

Overall, the results of these studies suggest that within the first half year of life infants are able to discriminate at least some of the features of the face that denote different expressions to adults. The results are most extensive and most consistent with respect to the ability to discriminate happy from other expressions: With only one exception (Schwartz et al., 1985), the results of several studies are in agreement that during the first few months of life infants are able to discriminate happy from surprised, angry, and fearful expressions (Barrera & Maurer, 1981; Field et al., 1982; Field et al., 1983; Kotsoni et al., 2001; LaBarbera et al., 1976; McGrath, 1983; Nelson, Morse, & Leavitt, 1979; Nelson & Dolgin, 1985; Soken & Pick, 1999; Walker, 1982). However, in several studies infants had difficulty discriminating happy from sad expressions (Young-Browne et al., 1977; Oster & Ewy, 1980) even by 7 months of age (Soken & Pick, 1999; but see Caron et al., 1988; Walker, 1982). Interestingly, one study has demonstrated that infants as young as 3.5 months of age can discriminate between happy and sad expressions, but only when posed by the mother and not when posed by a stranger (Kahana-Kalman & Walker-Andrews, 2001), suggesting that a familiar facial context might facilitate infants' abilities to tell apart expressions. Discrimination between other expressions has been less extensively studied: In particular, discrimination of disgust from other expressions has not been investigated.

Categorization

Studying infants' abilities to discriminate among facial expressions provides important information about whether they can perceive the differences among them. However, this approach is limited in that it does not provide information as to whether infants can perceive the same categories of expressions as adults do. That is, do infants treat various types of happy expressions (e.g., posed with different intensities, by different models) as belonging to the same category, in spite of the fact that they can notice the difference among them? If infants are able to recognize that an expression is the same even when posed in differing ways, it suggests that they have formed a perceptual category for the expression and that their responses are not limited to a particular individual model's face, and are unlikely to be based only on local differences in pattern information.

Infants' abilities to categorize expressions have been tested most frequently for happy and fearful expressions (Kotsoni et al., 2001; Ludemann & Nelson, 1988; Nelson et al., 1979; Nelson & Dolgin, 1985). In one such study (Nelson et al., 1979), 7-month-olds were familiarized to two different models posing happy expressions and were then shown a new model showing a happy expression and a fearful one. Infants looked longer at the fearful expression than the happy one, suggesting that they recognized the happy expression as familiar despite the change in model and were able to discriminate this expression from the fearful one. These results were not due to the infants' inability to discriminate between the different examples within an expression category; that is, they treated the different happy faces as belonging to the same category in spite of being able to tell them apart.

In contrast to these results, infants of this age do not show evidence of categorization if they are first familiarized to different models posing fearful expressions (Nelson et al., 1979). Subsequent studies have replicated and extended this pattern. For example, 7-month-olds showed categorization of happy following habituation to happy faces posed by (a) multiple male or female models (Nelson & Dolgin, 1985), and (b) by female models that varied in how intensely the expressions were depicted (Kotsoni et al., 2001; Ludemann & Nelson, 1988). However, across numerous studies, 6- to 7-month-old infants showed no evidence of categorizing fear or surprise when habituated to multiple models posing these expressions and then tested with happy expressions (Caron, Caron, & Myers, 1982; Nelson & Dolgin, 1985; Ludemann & Nelson, 1988).

In addition to the work documented above, infants' abilities to categorize other expressions have also been tested. Four- to 6-month-old infants are able to categorize fear and anger, but they show evidence of categorizing surprise only if they are tested with anger and not when tested with fear (Serrano, Iglesias, & Loeches, 1992). In another study, 4- to 9-month-olds showed evidence of categorizing happy, angry, and neutral expressions (Serrano, Iglesias, & Loeches, 1995), although these results contradict those of a previous study using the same types of expressions (Phillips et al., 1990). In the studies showing evidence of categorization (Serrano et al., 1992, 1995), the investigators did not test whether infants could discriminate among exemplars within a category; thus the results could have occurred because infants failed to discriminate between the different examples of the same expression, rather than because they formed a true category in spite of being able to notice the difference among the exemplars.

The studies described above demonstrate that, at least for some expression categories, infants are able to perceive the similarity among different examples of the same expression. However, since these studies provided category structure within the experiment (i.e., during the familiarization phase only examples from one category were presented), they do not provide information as to whether the nature of infants' perceptual categories for expressions is similar to adults'. For example, adults show categorical perception of facial expressions. Categorical perception refers to a discontinuity of discrimination at the category boundary of a physical continuum, with greater difficulties in discriminating member pairs of the same category than members of different categories even though the amount of physical difference between both pairs is the same (Harnad, 1987). In the visual domain, this has been studied perhaps most extensively for perception of color, where it has been shown that adults are superior at discriminating pairs of colors that cross a color boundary compared with pairs that are equally physically different but are both within the same color category. To study categorical perception of emotional expressions, realistic drawings (Etcoff & Magee, 1992) or photographs (De Gelder, Teunisse, & Benson, 1997; Young et al., 1997) are changed in equal steps so that a face showing one expression is gradually transformed into another expression. With these types of stimuli, adults show the classic pattern of categorical perception, with enhanced discrimination of faces that cross an emotion category compared with pairs that are equally different but are both within the same emotion category. A recent study shows that, at 7 months of age, infants also appear to respond to expressions as categories rather than as a continuum: (a) When their visual preference for fear is tested by pairing a fearful face with different degrees of happy-fear blend, the preference emerges suddenly rather than gradually over the happy-fear continuum, and (b) following familiarization to happy, they show recovery of looking to cross-category fearful faces but not within-category happy faces (Kotsoni et al., 2001).

What Information Do Infants Use to Perceive Expressions?

Few studies have investigated what perceptual information infants use to discriminate and categorize facial expressions. There is some evidence to suggest that certain features of the face that are relevant to expression are more salient than others. Nelson and Horowitz (1980) familiarized 6-month-olds to a surprised face and then tested them with that face and either (a) the same surprised face but with eyes changed to show fear, or (b) the same surprised face with the mouth changed to show fear, or (c) a fearful face. Infants showed evidence of discrimination only between the surprised face and the surprised face with the fearful eyes, suggesting that the eye region may be more important than the mouth for discriminating surprised from fearful faces.

A few studies have investigated the influence of inversion on infants' perception of facial expression. In adults, inversion of the face is known to disproportionately decrease speed and increase errors in recognition of facial identity compared with recognition of other objects. This effect is typically interpreted as the disruptive effect that inversion has on encoding configural information (e.g., spacing of features) that is important for fast and accurate recognition of facial identity. Investigations of adults' perception of facial expression have suggested that, at least for some expressions, recognition is impaired by inversion, suggesting that perception of facial expressions of emotion may also rely on configural encoding (e.g., Fallshore & Bartholow, 2003; McKelvie, 1995).

Infants, like adults, appear to be affected by inversion when processing facial expression. For example, one study found that 7-month-old infants are able to tell apart two different facial expressions whether upright or inverted, but they have difficulty categorizing facial expressions in inverted faces (Kestenbaum & Nelson, 1990). Several other studies have reported that visual preferences between expressions observed when they are presented upright disappear when the same expressions are presented upside down. For example, 7-month-olds' visual preference for fearful compared with happy faces (de Haan & Nelson, 1998), and for happy compared with angry face/voice films (Walker, 1982), disappears when the faces are inverted, and 4-month-olds' preference for a toothy smile over a sad face disappears when the faces are inverted (Oster & Ewy, 1980, cited in Oster, 1981). These results might suggest that infants' differential looking to the upright pairs is based on configural information that is no longer easily perceived when the faces are inverted.

Within the first days of life, newborns appear to be able to orient to faces and to detect differences in emotional expression within the face. Moreover, within the first few months they are also able to group together the faces they see to form categories. This allows them by 3 months of age to form a mental representation of the category of "face" that is based on faces they have seen in their visual environment and allows them by 6 to 7 months of age to group facial expressions into categories that resemble those of adults.

Although these abilities are impressive, it is important to keep in mind that they do not necessarily provide evidence that infants have any understanding of the communicatory function that the emotional information in the face conveys. For example, studies using computational modeling indicate that the physical properties of facial expressions provide sufficient information to divide them into the typical emotion categories, even without any conceptual knowledge. Given that there is evidence that infants are sensitive to statistical regularities in perceptual inputs from an early age (e.g., Fiser & Aslin, 2002), it is possible that their perceptual abilities reflect primarily "bottom-up" processing. In the following section, we will review evidence that addresses the question of whether infants are able to recognize the social meaning of faces.

Recognizing the Face as a Social Stimulus

As discussed in the previous section, recognition of a face as a social stimulus involves linking the specific perceptual representation of that expression with one of several types of knowledge, only some of which may be potentially available to young infants. For example, infants may express their understanding of the meaning of facial expressions of emotion in at least two ways (Soken & Pick, 1999): (a) The expression may trigger a specific response in the infant, such as facial expressions of his or her own and/or vocalizations and body movements that are consistently related to particular expressions, and (b) the infant may use the facial expressions to regulate his or her behavior. In the following, we discuss evidence from imitation, patterns of visual attention, response to still faces, and social referencing, suggesting that infants within the first year of life have some understanding of the meaning of faces.

Imitation

Although infants do preferentially orient to facelike patterns, this does not necessarily mean that they have any "understanding" of the face as a special social stimulus. However, two studies have reported that newborns, including those born prematurely, are able to imitate facial expressions of emotion (Field et al. 1982; Field et al., 1983): Adults viewing videotapes of infants seeing happiness, sadness, or surprised expressions were able to guess at a level above chance which expression the infant was viewing on the basis of the infant's face alone. This could represent an early form of a mechanism that also contributes to adults' recognition of emotion. In adults, the *simulation theory* of expression recognition argues that viewing facial expressions of emotion triggers an emotional response in the perceiver that mirrors the emotion being viewed. In one formulation of this view, seeing an expression triggers an imitation of the expression in the viewer's face, which then would trigger the related emotional state in the viewer and thereby contribute to understanding of the other person's emotional state. Evidence to support this view comes from a variety of sources in adults (reviewed in Adolphs, 2002), including studies showing that (a) viewing facial expressions results in expressions in one's own face that mimic the expression shown (these may not be readily visible but are detectable in recordings of facial muscle activity; Dimberg, 1982; Jaencke, 1994; Hess & Blairy, 2001), and (b) production of emotional expressions can lead to changes in emotional experience (e.g., Adelman & Zajonc, 1989). Seen in the light of simulation theory, the ability of newborns to imitate facial expressions might reflect the beginnings of one pathway for understanding emotional meaning.

This finding is in accordance with reports that infants couple their own expressive behaviors to the mother's expression (Trevarthen, 1979, 1998), and that during face-to-face interactions mothers complement what the infant is expressing (Legerstee & Varghese, 2001; Stern, 1983). In contrast, it has been argued that, at least in very young infants, imitation of facial gestures may not represent imitation of emotion per se because they are also known to "imitate" very nonspecific actions, such as imitating the looming of a pencil with a tongue protrusion. Some facial gestures that newborns "imitate" may be a more general reaction to an interesting stimulus rather than an imitation of a specific action or emotional state (Jones, 1996).

Visual Attention

Another way in which infants might express a level of understanding of emotional expressions is by relatively automatic, adaptive responses that they produce when viewing specific facial expressions. For example, infants appear to respond to fearful expressions with increased attention (e.g., Nelson & Dolgin, 1985), and to angry expressions by averting their gaze (e.g., Schwartz et al., 1985). These reactions may represent an early form of recognition of the meaning of the expressions in that they can be viewed as adaptive: Increased vigilance in response to another's fearful face may elicit help or quicker perception of the threat, while looking away from anger is a submissive gesture that may prevent an aggressive encounter.

These spontaneous reactions may influence how babies respond in the typical looking-time-based tests of discrimination and categorization, and can also provide an account for the observed effects of order of testing (described in the previous section). Babies' tendency to respond to fearful faces with increased vigilance might explain why they prefer to look at fearful expressions rather than happy ones (e.g., Nelson & Dolgin, 1985) and why they continue to show an interest in looking at fear even following habituation (and thus fail to show categorization when habituated to fear; e.g., Nelson et al., 1979). Similarly, infants' tendencies to look away from anger expressions might explain why babies prefer to look at happy rather than angry expressions (e.g., Soken & Pick, 1999), and might also explain why they can categorize anger from some other expressions only when they are habituated to anger, since in the test trials they will show short looks to anger even if it is the novel expression (Schwartz et al., 1985).

Still Face

By 3 months of age, infants appear to have some expectations regarding the nature of social interactions involving faces. One framework that has been used quite extensively to study the young infant's social understanding and expectancies for the human face has been the still-face paradigm (Tronick, Als, Adamson, Wise, & Brazelton, 1978). In the classic version of this paradigm, a mother poses a stationary, silent, neutral facial expression after a period of face-to-face interaction. Infants show gaze aversion and lack of positive affect during the still-face experience compared with normal interactions, a reaction called the *still-face response*. It has been suggested that infants read the emotional expressions in the maternal face and voice during the contingent, face-to-face interactions and that the still-face response is a reaction to a violation of their expectations for continued maternal responsiveness. This classic procedure has been modified in various ways to examine the sensitivity of the infant to various aspects of facial and vocal stimulation during the interactions. In one study designed to compare responses to human faces and objects (Ellsworth, Muir, & Hains, 1993), 3- and 6-month-olds were presented with either an interactive human face or a hand puppet with a schematic face that first responded with contingent movement and sound, then had a still-face or still-object period, and then resumed contingent interaction. In all cases, infants' visual attention decreased during the still period and thus differentiated only active versus dynamic stimulation. However, they smiled almost exclusively at the interacting human face. These results suggest that by 3 months of age infants show responsiveness to the social significance of the face. This is consistent with other claims that by this age infants direct their affiliative responses toward people but not objects (Brazelton, Koslowski, & Main, 1974; Legerstee, Pomerleau, Malcuit, & Feider, 1987; Spitz & Wolf, 1946; but see Frye, Rawling, Moore, & Myers, 1983).

There is evidence that the still-face effect is influenced to a large extent by changes in the adult's facial expression. For example, if maternal facial expression becomes static but the mother continues to interact vocally with the infant, a large still-face effect is produced. However, if maternal facial expressions remain positive and dynamic but the mother's voice is turned off, the still-face effect is not obtained, suggesting that the still-face effect is generated largely by absence of maternal contingent facial, rather than vocal, expression (Gusella, Muir, & Tronick, 1988). Moreover, further studies have shown that infants also produce less positive affect to an upside-down interactive smiling face than an upright interactive smiling face (Muir & Rach-Longman, 1989), and also show a decrease in smiling if the face changes from happy to sad (D'Entremont, 1994).

Social Referencing

Another way that infants' understanding of emotional expressions has been assessed is by the examination of social referencing. In this paradigm, infants are placed in an ambiguous situation (e.g., a stranger approaching, a novel unusual toy), and the mother poses a positive, negative (usually fearful) or neutral expression. The experimenter then observes whether the infant attends to the mother, and whether the mother's posed expression modulates the infant's behavioral or emotional response to the novel situation. These types of studies have shown that infants as young as 9 to 12 months are guided by the parent's reactions. However, at this age the infant's response may be based more on the voice than the face, since infants of the same age show behavioral regulation in response to a voice alone (Mumme, Fernald, & Herrera, 1996), and when they attend to the parent, they do not look more at the face than at other parts of the body (Walden & Ogan, 1988). However, during the second year of life infants begin to show a preference to look directly at the parent's face during the situation (Walden & Ogan, 1988) and guide their behavioral reactions based on these expressions (Walden & Baxter, 1989; Walden & Ogan, 1988).

There is evidence to support the possibility that infants have at least some ability to recognize the social importance of faces and the emotional information they convey even in the first months of life. However, this understanding is based primarily on particular attentional and emotional reactions triggered by the faces, and in this way infants' understanding is still immature. By the second year of life, infants appear to have a more advanced understanding, whereby they seek out the face as a source of emotional cues and guide their behavior based on the cues perceived. The extent to which infants' understanding of facial expressions involves mainly a positive-negative differentiation or involves more specific understanding of different types of positive or negative expressions is not entirely clear.

Mechanisms of Development of Face and Emotion Processing

The studies reviewed in the previous section indicate that during the first year of life, infants are able to detect faces and derive something about the emotional meaning they convey. In the following two sections, we consider the basis for these abilities and how they develop, Wrst by examining the neural correlates of face and emotion processing and then by examining the influence of experience.

Neural Bases

Occipitotemporal Cortex

Studies of brain-damaged patients (Damasio, Tranel, & Damasio, 1990, reviewed in Farah, 1996), single-cell recordings in monkeys (Perrett, Rolls, & Caan, 1982; Desimone 1991), and electroencephalographic (EEG), magnetoencephalographic, and functional magnetic resonance imaging (fMRI) studies (Watanabe, Kakigi, Koyama, & Kirino, 1999; Kanwisher, McDermott, & Chun, 1997; McCarthy, Puce, Gore, & Allison, 1997; for a description of these techniques, see Casey & de Haan, 2002) in healthy people all support the view that particular regions in the lateral and ventral occipitotemporal cortex are central to face processing in adults. Some authors have argued that the fusiform gyrus functions as a discrete "face module" that operates to detect faces in the visual environment; others have emphasized that faces and objects are represented in a more distributed and overlapping way in the ventral temporal cortex (Haxby et al., 2001). However, even those who argue for a more distributed system note that faces may be a unique category in that the pattern of activation they elicit is more focal and less influenced by attention than the pattern elicited by other objects (Ishai, Ungerleider, Martin, Schouten, & Haxby, 1999).

According to one view, a network including the inferior occipital gyrus, the fusiform gyrus, and the superior temporal sulcus is important for the early stages of face processing (Haxby, Hoffman, & Gobbini, 2002). In this view, the inferior occipital gyrus is primarily responsible for early perception of facial features (Haxby et al., 2002). For example, activation in the inferior occipital gyrus, but not in the fusiform gyrus or superior temporal sulcus, changes in response to faces shown at different angles (frontal vs. diverted; George, Driver, & Dolan, 2001). In contrast, the fusiform gyrus and the superior temporal sulcus are involved in more specialized processing (Haxby et al., 2002). In particular, the fusiform gyrus is thought to be involved in the processing of invariant aspects of faces (such as the perception of unique identity), whereas the superior temporal sulcus is involved in the processing of changeable aspects (such as perception of eye gaze, expression, and lip movement; Haxby et al., 2002; Hoffmann & Haxby 2000; Hasselmo, Rolls, & Baylis, 1989; see Elgar & Campbell, 2001, for discussion of a two-route model in the context of developmental disorders).

The question of whether similar pathways mediate face processing in young infants is a matter of debate. While newborns' preferential orienting toward facelike stimuli in the visual environment might appear to be evidence in favor of the functioning of these cortical areas, there is evidence that in fact this response is mediated by a subcortical retinotectal pathway (Johnson & Morton, 1991). For example, newborns show the preference only under conditions to which the subcortical systems are sensitive (i.e., when stimuli are moving and are in the peripheral visual field but not when they are in the central visual field). Further experimental evidence in support of this view is that infants orient more toward facelike patterns than inverted face patterns in the temporal, but not the nasal, visual field (Simion, Valenza, Umilta, & Barba, 1998). Since the retinotectal (subcortical) pathway is thought to have greater input from the temporal hemifield and less input from the nasal hemifield than the geniculostriate (cortical) pathway, this asymmetry in the preferential orienting to faces is consistent with subcortical, but not cortical, involvement. The lack of preferential orienting to faces in the nasal field is not simply due to a general lack of sensitivity, since in this same visual field there is increased responding to an optimal spatial frequency nonface stimulus over another nonface stimulus (Simion et al., 1998). This evidence is consistent with the hypothesis that the preferential orienting to faces is mediated by a subcortical mechanism; however, because the visual cortex of the newborn is at least partially functional (Maurer & Lewis, 1979), it might also contribute to the response. One possible role of the earlier-developing subcortical system is to provide a "face-biased" input to the slower-developing occipitotemporal cortical system and to provide a mechanism whereby an initially more broadly tuned processing system becomes increasingly specialized to respond to faces during development.

A small number of studies using fMRI or event-related potentials (ERPs) suggest that occipitotemporal cortical pathways are involved in infant face processing by 2 to 3 months of age. In the single fMRI study in infants, 2-month-olds' activation in the inferior occipital gyrus and the fusiform gyrus, but not the superior temporal sulcus, was greater in response to a human face than to a set of three diodes (Tzourio-Mazoyer et al., 2002). This study demonstrates that areas involved in face processing in adults can also be activated by faces by 2 months of age, although it does not address the question of whether these areas are specifically activated by faces rather than other visual stimuli. The superior temporal sulcus, suggested to be involved in the processing of information relevant to social communication, was not activated in this study, possibly because the stimuli (static, neutral) were not optimal for activating processing in the superior temporal sulcus. However, the observation that activation in the superior temporal sulcus has been found in adults even in response to static, neutral faces (e.g., Kesler-West et al., 2001) argues against this interpretation. It is possible that the superior temporal sulcus plays a different role in the face-processing network in infants than in adults, since in primates its connectivity with other visual areas is known to differ in infant compared with adult monkeys (Kennedy, Bullier, & Dehay, 1989).

ERP studies support the idea that cortical mechanisms are involved in face processing from at least 3 months of age. However, these studies also suggest that, when cortical mechanisms do become involved in infants' processing of faces, they are less "tuned in" to faces than is the mature system. For example, two studies have shown that face-responsive ERP components are more specific to human faces in adults than in infants (de Haan, Pascalis, & Johnson, 2002; Halit, de Haan, & Johnson, 2003). In adults, the N170, a negative deflection over occipitotemporal electrodes that peaks approximately 170 ms after stimulus onset, is thought to reflect the initial stage of the structural encoding of the face (Bentin, Allison, Puce, Perez, & McCarthy, 1996). Although the location in the brain of the generator(s) of the N170 remains a matter of debate, it is generally believed that regions of the fusiform gyrus (Shibata et al., 2002), the posterior inferior temporal gyrus (Bentin et al., 1996; Shibata et al., 2002), the lateral occipitotemporal cortex (Bentin et al., 1996; Schweinberger et al., 2002), and the superior temporal sulcus (Henson et al., 2003) are involved. The N170 is typically of larger amplitude and/or has a longer latency for inverted than upright faces (Bentin et al., 1996; de Haan, Pascalis, & Johnson, 2002; Eimer, 2000; Itier & Taylor, 2002; Rossion et al., 2000), a pattern that parallels behavioral studies showing that adults are slower at recognizing inverted than upright faces (Carey & Diamond, 1994). In adults, the effect of inversion on the N170 is specific for human faces and does not occur for inverted compared with upright exemplars of nonface object categories (Bentin et al., 1996; Rebai, Poiroux, Bernard, & Lalonde, 2001; Rossion et al., 2000), even animal (monkey) faces that share the basic eyes-nose-mouth arrangement with the human face (de Haan et al., 2002).

In young infants, two components believed to be precursors to the adult N170 are elicited during viewing of faces: the N290 and the P400. Infants' ERP responses also differ from adults in that (a) they do not show an inversion effect specific to human faces until 12 months of age (even though they are able to tell the difference between upright and inverted faces by at least 3 months of age); (b) their responses occur at a latency approximately 100 to 200 ms slower than adults; (c) even at 12 months of age, their responses are spread over a longer time range compared with adults; and (d) the spatial distribution of both the N290 and the P400 shifts laterally (thereby becoming more adultlike) between 3 and 12 months of age. Together, these results suggest that infants' processing of the face becomes more specific to human faces over the first year of life, that processing of the face occurs more quickly and becomes more discrete with age, and possibly that the configuration of neural generators that contribute to this component change with age (for discussion see de Haan, Johnson, & Halit, 2003).

The basic information about the face as processed by the occipitotemporal areas is fed forward to brain areas involved in recognition of familiarity, facial expression, and other facial information. With respect to facial expressions, neuroimaging and neuropsychological studies with human adults suggest that regions involved in perception and recognition of facial expressions of emotion include (in addition to the occipitotemporal cortex) the amygdala, the orbitofrontal cortex, the basal ganglia, and the somatosensory cortex (for a review of the evidence in adults, see Adolphs, 2002). The involvement of these regions in face processing will be discussed in turn.

The Amygdala

The amygdala is a heterogeneous collection of nuclei located in the anterior temporal lobe (Amaral, Price, Pitkanen, & Carmichael, 1992). Substantial input to the amygdala comes from the more advanced areas along the ventral visual stream in the temporal cortex, but not from earlier levels in the hierarchy of visual processing. Conversely, projections from the amygdala back to the visual cortex terminate not only in the higher-order visual areas but also in primary visual cortex (Amaral, 2002). In addition to this cortical route, the amygdala also receives projections from a subcortical visual route via the superior colliculus and pulvinar. The subcortical pathway is believed to be involved in rapid, coarse processing of facial expression information, which in turn can modulate the cortical pathway that is involved in slower, more detailed analysis (Adolphs, 2002).

The amygdala has been associated with processing of emotion and social behavior in a variety of tasks in both animals (Daenen, Wolterink, Gerrits, & Van Ree, 2002; Bachevalier, 1994; Amaral, 2002) and human adults (Adolphs, 2002). With respect to humans, several studies have shown that lesions to the amygdala impair emotion recognition, even when they leave other aspects of face processing intact (e.g., identity recognition; Adolphs, Tranel, Damasio, Damasio, 1994). Lesion studies also indicate that recognition of fear is particularly vulnerable to such damage (Adolphs et al., 1994; Adolphs et al., 1999; Calder et al., 1996; Broks et al., 1998). Functional imaging studies in healthy adults and school-age children complement these findings, with some studies showing that the amygdala responds to a variety of positive, negative, or neutral expressions (Thomas et al., 2001; Yang et al., 2002), and other studies suggesting that the amygdala is particularly responsive to fearful expressions (Morris et al., 1996; Whalen et al., 2001). Whether the amygdala is disproportionately activated by fear compared with other expressions may depend in part on the nature of the task. The results of some studies have suggested that the greater activation to fearful faces may occur only during tasks involving passive or implicit processing of fear (Hariri, Bookheimer, & Mazziotta, 2000), and that when adults are instead required to explicitly label emotions, there is actually a deactivation of the amygdala to fearful faces (Critchley, Daly, Phillips, et al., 2000). Other studies have suggested that the amygdala may respond more generally to emotional signals that serve as primary reinforcers, including signals related to sadness and happiness as well as fear (Blair, 2003).

A variety of roles for the amygdala in the processing of facial expressions by adults have been proposed, including providing top-down feedback to early stages of face processing via connections to visual cortex, retrieving conceptual knowledge about the viewed expression via projections to other regions of cortex and medial temporal lobe, and/or triggering emotional responses via connections to motor structures, the hypothalamus, and brain stem nuclei (reviewed in Adolphs, 2002). Certainly, the amygdala's very rapid response to emotional stimuli suggests that it might be part of a route for top-down influence on early perceptual processing in the occipitotemporal cortex. For example, in an fMRI study by George et al. (2001), the correlation between activity in the amygdala and the fusiform gyrus increased when faces with direct gaze were shown. Since direct gaze is thought to be a particularly important signal for social interaction, this shows a link between brain regions processing faces as visual objects and those extracting affective significance. ERP studies in adults have also found that affective judgments of faces (Pizzagalli et al., 2002) and facial expressions of emotion (Sato, Kochiyama, Yoshikawa, & Matsumura, 2001) modulate early activity in the occipitotemporal cortex. Thus, one role of the amygdala could be to modulate perceptual representations via feedback. This might contribute to fine-tuning the categorization of facial expression and the allocation of attention to certain features of the expression.

There is also evidence that the amygdala plays a role in processing facial expressions in infants and children. The eyeblink startle response is a reflex blink initiated involuntarily by sudden bursts of loud noise. In adults, these reflex blinks are augmented by viewing slides of unpleasant pictures and scenes, and they are inhibited by viewing slides of pleasant or arousing pictures and scenes (Lang, Bradley, & Cuthbert, 1990, 1992). Based on work in animals, it has been argued that fear potentiation of the startle response is mediated by the central nucleus of the amygdala, which in turn directly projects to brain stem centers that mediate the startle and efferent blink reflex activity (Davis, 1989; Holstege, Van Ham, & Tan, 1986). Balaban (1995) used a procedure very similar to that used with adults to examine the psychophysiology of infants' responses to facial expressions. Five-month-old infants watched slides depicting eight different adults posing happy, neutral, and angry expressions. Each slide was presented for 6 seconds, followed 3 seconds later by an acoustic startle probe. Consistent with the adult literature, infants' blinks were augmented when they viewed angry expressions and were reduced when they viewed happy expressions, relative to when they viewed neutral expressions. These results suggest that by 5 months of age, portions of the amygdala circuitry underlying the response to facial expressions may be functional.

Studies of children with developmental disorders involving deficits in face processing provide converging evidence for the amygdala's role in young children's abilities to recognize facial expressions. For example, autism, a disorder characterized by social impairments, deficits in language, and the presence of stereotypical or repetitive behaviors (American Psychiatric Association, 1994), is associated with impairments in face recognition and anatomical abnormalities in the amygdala (reviewed in Bachevalier, 1994, and Sweeten, Posey, Shekhar, & McDougle, 2002). Autistic individuals are able to discriminate between faces differing in identity (Hauck, Fein, Maltby, Waterhouse, & Feinstein, 1998), but their performance is impaired on more demanding tasks, or when elements of emotion are included (Davies, Bishop, Manstead, & Tantam, 1994; Tantam, Monaghan, Nicholson, & Stirling, 1989). Autistic individuals seem to use a different, more "feature-based," strategy to process faces and facial expressions, suggesting that at least part of their difficulty is in perceptual processing of faces (but see Blair, 2003, for a different view). Their processing of faces is also associated with atypical neural correlates: The brain regions typically activated in response to faces and facial expressions (e.g., the amygdala, as well as the occipitotemporal cortical regions described previously) are not activated in individuals with autism when they are viewing these stimuli (Critchley, Daly, Bullmore, et al., 2000; Schultz et al., 2000; Pierce et al., 2001). Instead, faces maximally activate aberrant and individual-specific neural sites that are typically involved in nonface object recognition (e.g., frontal cortex, primary visual cortex, or even inferior temporal gyri; Pierce et al., 2001; Critchley, Daly, Bullmore, et al., 2000). Moreover, autistic individuals pay particular attention to the mouth instead of the eye region (Klin, Jones, Schultz, Volkmar, & Cohen, 2002).

Furthermore, in a test in which one has to infer the mental state by the expression of the eyes, performance of individuals with autism was impaired and the typical activation of the amygdala was not observed (Baron-Cohen et al., 1999).

Converging evidence for the role of the amygdala in processing of facial information also comes from Turner syndrome. Individuals with this syndrome have been found to be impaired at face recognition, identification of facial expressions of emotion (especially fear), and processing of displays of the eye region affording social and affective information (Lawrence et al., 2003a; Lawrence et al., 2003b). As in autism, preliminary structural imaging evidence suggests anatomical abnormalities in the amygdala in this syndrome (Good et al., 2001).

Interestingly, there is evidence that early damage to the amygdala may have a more pronounced effect on recognition of facial expression than damage sustained later in life. For example, in one study of emotion recognition in patients who had undergone temporal lobectomy as treatment for intractable epilepsy, emotion recognition in patients with early, right mesial temporal sclerosis, but not those with left-sided damage or extratemporal damage, showed impairments on tests of recognition of facial expressions of emotion but not on comparison tasks of face processing (Meletti et al., 2003). This deficit was most pronounced for fearful expressions, and the degree of deficit was related to the age of first seizure and epilepsy onset.

Whether the amygdala functions as a top-down influence in early perceptual processing in young infants is not clear. Two ERP studies have examined 7-month-old infants' responses to fearful compared with happy or angry expressions (de Haan & Nelson, 1998; Nelson & de Haan, 1996). These studies demonstrated that ERPs differed for happy compared with fearful faces beginning at approximately 140 to 260 milliseconds after stimulus onset, but ERPs did not differ from angry compared with fearful faces at any latency up to 1,700 milliseconds after stimulus onset. These results demonstrate that 7-month-olds can rapidly distinguish positive from negative expressions. However, due to the small number of electrodes used, these studies unfortunately were not able to examine the infant N290 or P400 responses (see earlier discussion) to determine whether there was any evidence of modulation of these occipitotemporal components by emotional expression, or synchronization of these responses with more anterior frontotemporal activity (e.g., as in adults; Sato et al., 2001). It is interesting to note that, even in adult ERP studies, there has been no evidence to date of early-latency amygdala activity that might reflect activation of the subcortical processing route (Blair, 2003).

In summary, converging evidence from a variety of sources suggests an important role for the amygdala in processing facial expressions of emotion, particularly fearful expressions, in adults. Although there is little information regarding the neuroanatomical development of the amygdala in human infants, there is some evidence from studies using the eyeblink startle response and studies examining children with early lesions or developmental disorders to suggest that the amygdala may also play a role in processing facial expression early in life. One possible role the amygdala may play is to provide top-down input into the occipitotemporal areas involved in processing perceptual information in the face. In this way, the amygdala may provide a signal to these regions that mark faces and facial expressions as emotionally salient, and may play a role in shaping perceptual representations of these categories (Grelotti, Gauthier, & Schultz, 2002). Whether and when the amygdala also begins to play a role in other aspects of emotion processing, such as providing inputs to brain areas storing conceptual knowledge or involved in motor responses, remains unclear.

Frontal Cortex

Specific regions of the frontal cortex appear to play a role in adults' recognition of facial expressions of emotion. For example, damage to the orbitofrontal cortex (OFC), especially the right OFC, can impair recognition of emotion from the face and voice (Hornak, Rolls, & Wade, 1996), and electrophysiological recordings in patients have shown selectivity for faces over objects (Marinkovic, Trebon, Chauvel, & Halgren, 2000) and discrimination between happy and fearful facial expressions (Kawasaki et al., 2001) in the right prefrontal cortex. Furthermore, several imaging studies in healthy adults have implicated the prefrontal cortex in emotion recognition, especially when the task requires explicit identification of emotions (Nakamura et al., 1999; Narumoto et al., 2000). It has been proposed that the OFC is particularly involved in the processing of angry expressions, and that it plays a role in modulation of behavioral responding that is necessary for appropriate reaction to angry faces (Blair, 2003). The OFC, like the amygdala, may provide top-down influences on early perceptual processing, and links to conceptual knowledge and motor responses (Adolphs, 2002).

With respect to infants, there are no studies that directly relate orbitofrontal or prefrontal cortex activity to expression recognition, but there is some indirect evidence from EEG studies that could indicate involvement of frontal cortex in emotion recognition early in life. Hemispheric asymmetry in the EEG recorded over the frontal lobes has been associated with a broad set of emotion-processing situations in adults, children, and infants. In general, differential activation (as reflected by a decrease in alpha activity) of the left and right frontal regions has been associated with positive and negative emotion, respectively. These frontal asymmetries have been interpreted as reflecting a fundamental dichotomy between the two hemispheres in the control of two basic circuits, each mediating different forms of motivation and emotion. In one view, the left frontal region is associated with an approach system that facilitates appetitive behavior and generates certain types of positive affect, while the right frontal region is associated with a withdrawal system that facilitates the withdrawal of an individual from sources of aversive stimulation and generates certain forms of negative affect (e.g., fear, disgust; Kinsbourne, 1978, in Fox, 1994; Davidson,

1994, 2000; Gray, 1994; see Dawson, 1994, for a somewhat different formulation of the lateral differences in terms of emotion regulation). Studies with infants suggest that they may show a similar pattern of laterality of frontal activation under a variety of emotion-eliciting circumstances. With regard to the processing of facial expressions, one study (Davidson & Fox, 1982) found that 10-month-old infants show greater relative left frontal activation in response to happy facial expressions in comparison to sad facial expressions. This result provides some preliminary evidence that by 10 months of age, the frontal circuits involved in emotion processing are at least partially active. However, these results are not conclusive, as it cannot be firmly concluded that activity recorded over frontal scalp actually originates in frontal cortex.

Other Brain Areas

Two other brain areas that have been implicated in emotion recognition in adults are the basal ganglia and the somatosensory cortex. With respect to the basal ganglia, neuropsychological and neuroimaging studies provide evidence that they are involved in recognition of expressions, possibly particularly for the expression disgust (Phillips et al., 1997; Adolphs, 2002). There is no evidence regarding whether the basal ganglia are also involved in emotion recognition in infants, or indeed whether infants can discriminate or categorize disgust expressions.

With regard to the somatosensory cortex, emotion recognition has been found to be impaired in patients with lesions in the right ventral primary and secondary somatosensory areas, and to a lesser extent in the insula and anterior supramarginal gyrus (Adolphs, Damasio, Tranel, Cooper, & Damasio, 2000). These findings provide some support for the simulation theory discussed earlier. The fact that infants imitate facial expressions of emotion could indicate that this component of the neural system is, at least partly, online at an early age. However, the neural bases of infants' imitative behavior have yet to be determined.

In adults, the occipitotemporal cortex, amygdala, orbitofrontal cortex, basal ganglia, and somatosensory cortex are all thought to contribute to recognition of the face and the emotions it conveys. Knowledge of whether the same structures are involved in infants' abilities is limited, but evidence suggests that the occipitotemporal cortex, the amygdala, and possibly the frontal regions are involved during the first year of life. Perhaps surprisingly, the one functional imaging study of infants did not indicate activation of the superior temporal sulcus, a region associated with processing of facial emotion in adults. Whether this reflects a limitation of the stimuli used or a delayed functional development of this region compared with regions such as the fusiform gyrus remains to be determined. The role of other regions believed to be involved in adults' processing of expressions, such as the basal ganglia and the somatosensory cortex, also requires further investigation.

Studies with adults have suggested that visual experience plays an important role in establishment of category-specific activations of the occipitotemporal cortex such as those observed for faces (Gauthier, Tarr, Anderson, Skudlarski, & Gore, 1999; Gauthier, Skudlarski, Gore, & Anderson, 2000). In the next section, we will consider the role of experience in development of processing of faces and facial expressions.

Visual Experience

Based on newborns' preferences for facelike stimuli and on the face-processing deficits that can result from brain damage early in life, it has been claimed that an experience-independent mechanism exists that directs attention to facelike patterns (Morton & Johnson, 1991) and that the anatomical localization of the ability to identify and recognize faces is specified in the genome (Farah, Rabionitz, Quinn, & Liu, 2000). Whether or not face-processing abilities have a genetic component, several studies suggest that visual experience is necessary for at least some aspects of face processing to develop normally. For instance, patients with congenital cataracts who were deprived of patterned visual input from birth until 2 to 6 months of age show deficits in particular aspects of face processing even after at least 9 years of "normal" visual input. These patients show normal processing of featural information in the face (e.g., subtle differences in the shape of the eyes and mouth), but show impairments in processing configural information (i.e., the spacing of features within the face; Le Grand, Mondloch, Maurer, & Brent, 2001; Geldart, Mondloch, Maurer, de Schonen, & Brent, 2002). These studies suggest that visual input during early infancy is necessary for the normal development of at least some aspects of face processing.

Experience with particular facial expressions in the visual environment may also play a role in development of infants' abilities to recognize them. In this view, infants will be able to discriminate best among familiar expressions and perform more poorly with less familiar expressions. Studies have shown that by 7 months of age, infants have typically seen certain expressions more than others; for example, they have seen happy expressions more than angry ones, and both happy and angry expressions more than sad ones (Malatesta, Grigoryev, Lamb, Albin, & Culver, 1986; Malatesta & Haviland, 1982). Thus, infants may be particularly good at discriminating happy expressions from other expressions because they are most familiar with happy ones.

The familiarity hypothesis has also been used to provide an explanation for the order effects observed in some studies. For example, as described earlier, infants show evidence of categorization of happy and fearful expressions only if they are habituated to happy and tested with fear, not if they are habituated to fear and tested with happy. One interpretation is that when infants view a more familiar expression during familiarization/habituation, they are able to categorize it and discriminate it from a more novel expression. However, if infants view a less familiar expression during habitation, they may have difficulty categorizing it and discriminating it from another expression.

One study attempted to directly test this idea by examining 7-month-olds' abilities to discriminate happy, surprised, and fearful expressions (Ludemann & Nelson, 1988). The prediction was that less familiar expressions would be more difficult to habituate to, and thus discrimination would not be present when a less familiar expression was the habituating stimulus. In this instance, since surprise expressions are less familiar than happy expressions at this age, discrimination for happy/surprise should be present only when happy was the habituating stimulus and not when surprise was the habituating stimulus. In contrast, since surprise is a more familiar expression than fear at this age, discrimination of surprise/fear should be present when surprise was the habituating stimulus but not when fear was. The results supported these predictions and suggest that less familiar expressions are more difficult to habituate to, at least in static photographs.

If experience plays an important role in normative development of expression recognition, infants who experience atypical early emotional environments should show an atypical pattern of abilities. For example, Pollak and colleagues have found that perception of the facial expression of anger, but not other expressions, is altered in children who are abused by their parents. Specifically, they report that, compared with nonabused children, abused children show a response bias for anger (Pollak, Cicchetti, Hornung, & Reed, 2000), identify anger based on less perceptual input (Pollak & Sinha, 2002), and show altered category boundaries for anger (Pollak & Kistler, 2002). These results suggest that atypical frequency and content of their emotional interactions with their caregivers results in a change in the basic perception of emotional expressions in abused children. On this basis, one might predict that exposure to this type of environment during infancy would lead to a different (possibly enhanced) pattern of response to anger in habituation studies.

Consistent with these results is the argument that the basis for the face-processing deficits observed in autism is their reduced amount of visual experience due to lack of interest in social stimuli. This suggests that valuable insights can be gained from studying the role of social interest and its emotional circuitry (e.g., the amygdala) in the development of face processing (Grelotti et al., 2002).

The complicated interplay between infant and parent emotionality in infants' development of the processing of facial expressions is illustrated by a study involving infants of depressed mothers. Field, Pickens, Fox, Gonzalez, & Nawrocki (1998) found that 3-month-old infants of depressed mothers did not display the "normal" pattern of longer looking and decreased left frontal EEG activation in response to sad faces/voices compared with happy ones. In another study, the amount of "social referencing" (defined as the amount of contact sought by the infant with the primary caregiver) displayed by 7-month-old infants viewing fearful facial expressions was related to the pattern of frontal EEG activity

(Groen, 2002). Infants who made fewer attempts to seek contact with the primary caregiver while viewing fearful faces showed greater left frontal activation, scored higher on a temperamental measure of negative emotionality, and had mothers who scored lower on positive emotionality. Conversely, infants who made more attempts at social referencing showed greater right frontal activation, scored lower on negative emotionality, and had mothers who scored higher on positive emotionality. The pattern of increased left frontal activation could be interpreted as suggesting that the infants are treating fearful expressions as relatively familiar, while the relative right frontal activation in infants who show more instances of social referencing could be interpreted as reflecting a more novel response that disrupts the ongoing interaction with the environment (Groen, 2002).

Summary and Conclusions

Our review of the behavioral literature on infants' perception of faces and facial expressions indicates that from the first days of life, infants orient to faces and can tell different facial expressions apart. However, infants do not appear to begin to form perceptual categories of faces until some months later. In addition to these perceptual abilities, infants appear to have some appreciation of the social importance of faces and the emotional information they convey, even in the first months of life. However, this understanding is immature in that it is based primarily on particular attentional and emotional reactions triggered by the faces. By the second year of life, infants appear to have a more advanced understanding and are able to seek out the face and use its emotional content to guide their own behavior. However, even then, infants' conceptual understanding of emotion is not adultlike (e.g., they have not learned to attach verbal labels to the range of emotions).

Our review of the neuropsychology and neuroimaging of recognizing facial expressions suggests that some of the same regions that are believed to mediate adults' expression recognition are also utilized by infants. The evidence is strongest for the ventral occipitotemporal cortex and amygdala, while for other areas, such as the frontal cortex, superior temporal sulcus, basal ganglia, and somatosensory cortex, the evidence is weaker or absent. There is also some evidence that a subcortical mechanism exists that is active from birth and operates to orient infants' visual attention to faces. The influence of this mechanism appears to decline at about 2 months of age, but whether its activity is still detectable at some level later in life remains to be determined. It is possible that the subcortical mechanism, which orients the infant to faces, and the amygdala, which processes information about the social salience of the face, together provide routes through which experience with faces can influence the occipitotemporal cortical areas involved in face processing (de Haan, Humphreys, & Johnson, 2002).

It is also possible that the different neural substrates involved in expression recognition mature at different rates. For example, it is possible that the amygdala and ventral occipitotemporal areas may contribute more to the recognition of faces early in life than the superior temporal sulcus or frontal cortical areas, whose influence may emerge later or more slowly. If this is true, then early lesions of the occipitotemporal areas or the amygdala might impair expression recognition early in life, whereas lesions to any of the areas might impair recognition later in life.

Accumulating evidence points to the importance of experience in shaping the brain systems involved in processing faces and facial expressions. An intriguing question is whether such effects reflect perceptual learning (as in adults) or reflect a mechanism unique to the developing nervous system. Parallels between perceptual learning and the development of face recognition have been used to argue in favor of the former (e.g., Gauthier & Nelson, 2001). However, the finding that atypical experience for a limited period early in life can have a lasting impact on face-processing abilities argues in favor of the latter (Le Grand et al., 2001). Future studies in which the neurocognitive mechanisms involved in perceptual learning and the typical development of perceptual expertise are compared may help to shed some light on this issue.

In summary, the ability to recognize facial expressions of emotion is reasonably sophisticated within the first year of life, although this ability continues to develop through childhood. At the neurobiological level, this observation can be accounted for by the relatively early maturation of structures such as the occipitotemporal cortex and amygdala, and the relatively late maturation of other cortical structures and their connections. Increasing evidence points to the important role that experience plays in shaping responses to faces in general and to facial expressions of emotion in particular. Future investigations will help to determine how the various neural components of the face-processing system are assembled into the widespread network involved in this ability in adults, and how experience shapes the construction of this system and its ultimate sensitivity to the social-emotional content of the human face.

References

Adelman, P. K., & Zajonc, R. (1989). Facial efference and the experience of emotion. *Annual Review of Psychology, 40,* 249–280.

Adolphs, R. (2002). Recognizing emotion from facial expressions: Psychological and neurological mechanisms. *Behavioural and Cognitive Neuroscience Reviews, 1,* 21–61.

Adolphs, R., Damasio, H., Tranel, D., Cooper, G., & Damasio, A. R. (2000). A role for somatosensory cortices in the visual recognition of emotion as revealed by three-dimensional lesion mapping. *Journal of Neuroscience, 20,* 2683–2690.

Adolphs, R., Tranel, D., Damasio, H., & Damasio, A. (1994). Impaired recognition of emotion in facial expressions following bilateral damage to the human amygdala. *Nature, 372,* 669–672.

Adolphs, R., Tranel, D., Hamann, S., Young, A. W., Calder, A. J., Phelps, E. A., et al. (1999). Recognition of facial emotion in nine individuals with bilateral amygdala damage. *Neuropsychologia, 37*, 1111–1117.

Amaral, D. G. (2002). The primate amygdala and the neurobiology of social behavior: Implications for understanding social anxiety. *Biological Psychiatry, 51*, 11–17.

Amaral, D. G., Price, J. L., Pitkanen, A., & Carmichael, T. (1992). Anatomical organization of the primate amygdaloid complex. In J. Aggleton (Ed.), *The amygdala: Neurobiological aspects of emotion, memory, and mental dysfunction* (pp. 1–66). New York: Wiley-Liss.

American Psychiatric Association. (1994). *Diagnostic and statistical manual of mental disorders* (4th ed). Washington, DC: American Psychiatric Association.

Bachevalier, J. (1994). Medial temporal lobe structures and autism: A review of clinical and experimental findings. *Neuropsychologia, 32*, 627–648.

Balaban, M. T. (1995). Affective influences on startle in five-month-old infants: Reactions to facial expressions of emotion. *Child Development, 66*, 28–36.

Baron-Cohen, S., Ring, H. A., Wheelwright, S., Bullmore, E. T., Brammer, M. J., Simmons, A., et al. (1999). Social intelligence in the normal and autistic brain: An fMRI study. *European Journal of Neuroscience, 11*, 1891–1898.

Barrera, M. E., and Maurer, D. (1981). The perception of facial expressions by the three-month-old infant. *Child Development, 52*, 203–206.

Bednar, J. A., & Miikkulainen, K. (2003). Learning innate face preferences. *Neural Computation, 15*, 1525–1557.

Bentin, S., Allison, T., Puce, A., Perez, E., & McCarthy, G. (1996). Electrophysiological studies of face perception in humans. *Journal of Cognitive Neuroscience, 8*, 551–565.

Blair, R. J. R. (2003). Facial expressions, their communicatory functions and neurocognitive substrates. *Philosophical Transactions of the Royal Society of London. Series B: Biological Sciences, 358*, 561–572.

Blass, E. M., & Camp, C. A. (2001). The ontogeny of face recognition: Eye contact and sweet taste induce face preference in 9- and 12-week-old human infants. *Developmental Psychology, 37*, 762–774.

Brazelton, T. B., Koslowski, B., & Main, M. (1974). The origins of reciprocity: The early mother-infant interaction. In M. Lewis & L. A. Rosenblum (Eds.), *The effect of the infant on its caregiver* (pp. 46–76). Oxford, England: Wiley-Interscience.

Broks, P., Young, A. W., Maratos, E. J., Coffey, P. J., Calder, A. J., Isaac, C. L., et al. (1998). Face processing impairments after encephalitis: Amygdala damage and recognition of fear. *Neuropsychologia, 36*, 59–70.

Bushnell, I. W., Sai, F., & Mullin, J. T. (1989). Neonatal recognition of the mother's face. *British Journal of Developmental Psychology, 7*, 3–15.

Calder, A. J., Young, A. W., Rowland, D., Perett, D. I., Hodges, J. R., & Etcoff, N. L. (1996). Facial emotion recognition after bilateral amygdala damage: Differentially severe impairment of fear. *Cognitive Neuropsychology, 13*, 699–745.

Carey, S., & Diamond, R. (1994). Are faces perceived as configurations more by adults than by children? *Visual Cognition, 1*, 253–274.

Caron, A. J., Caron, R. F., & MacLean, D. J. (1988). Infant discrimination of naturalistic emotional expressions: The role of face and voice. *Child Development, 59*, 604–616.

Caron, R. F., Caron, A. J., & Myers, R. S. (1982). Abstraction of invariant face expressions in infancy. *Child Development, 53*, 1008–1015.

Casey, B. J., & de Haan, M. (2002). Introduction: New methods in developmental science. *Developmental Science, 5*, 265–267.

Critchley, H. D., Daly, E. M., Bullmore, E. T., Williams, S. C. R., Van Amelsvoort, T., Robertson, D. M., et al. (2000). The functional anatomy of social behaviour. Changes in cerebral blood flow when people with autistic disorder process facial expressions. *Brain, 123*, 2203–2212.

Critchley, H. D., Daly, E., Phillips, M., Brammer, M., Bullmore, E., Williams, S., et al. (2000). Explicit and implicit neural mechanisms for processing of social information from facial expressions: A functional magnetic imaging study. *Human Brain Mapping, 9*, 93–105.

Daenen, E. W. P. M., Wolterink, G., Gerrits, M. A. F. M., & Van Ree, J. M. (2002). The effects of neonatal lesions in the amygdala or ventral hippocampus on social behaviour later in life. *Behavioural Brain Research, 136*, 571–582.

Damasio, A., Tranel, D., & Damasio, H. (1990). Face agnosia and the neural substrates of memory. *Annual Review of Neuroscience, 13*, 89–109.

Davidson, R. J. (1994). Asymmetric brain function, affective style, and psychopathology: The role of early experience and plasticity. *Development and Psychopathology, 6*, 741–758.

Davidson, R. J. (2000). The neuroscience of affective style. In M. Gazzaniga (Ed.), *The new cognitive neurosciences* (2nd ed., pp. 1149–1159). Cambridge, MA: MIT Press.

Davidson, R. J., & Fox, N. (1982). Asymmetrical brain activity discriminates between positive versus negative affective stimuli in human infants. *Science, 218*, 1235–1237.

Davies, S., Bishop, D., Manstead, A. S. R., & Tantam, D. (1994). Face perception in children with autism and Asperger's syndrome. *Journal of Child Psychology and Psychiatry and Allied Disciplines, 35*, 1033–1057.

Davis, M. (1989). The role of the amygdala and its efferent projections in fear and anxiety. In P. Tyrer (Ed.), *Psychopharmacology of anxiety* (pp. 52–79). Oxford, England: Oxford University Press.

Dawson, G. (1994). Development of emotional expression and emotion regulation in infancy: Contributions of the frontal lobe. In G. Dawson & K. Fisher (Eds.), *Human behavior and the developing brain* (pp. 346–379). New York: Guilford.

De Gelder, B. L. M. F., Teunisse, J. P., & Benson, P. J. (1997). Categorical perception of facial expressions: Categories and their internal structure. *Cognition and Emotion, 11*, 1–23.

de Haan, M., Humphreys, K., & Johnson, M. H. (2002). Developing a brain specialized for face perception: A converging methods approach. *Developmental Psychology, 40*, 200–212.

de Haan, M., Johnson, M. H., and Halit, H. (2003). Development of face-sensitive event-related potentials during infancy: A review. *International Journal of Psychophysiology, 51*, 45–58.

de Haan, M., Johnson, M. H., Maurer, D., & Perrett, D. I. (2001). Recognition of individual faces and average face prototypes by 1- and 3-month-old infants. *Cognitive Development, 16*, 659–678.

de Haan, M., & Nelson, C. A. (1998). Discrimination and categorization of facial expressions of emotion during infancy. In A. Slater (Ed.), *Perceptual development: Visual, auditory, and language development in infancy.* London: University College London Press.

de Haan, M., Pascalis, O., & Johnson, M. H. (2002). Specialization of neural mechanisms underlying face recognition in human infants. *Journal of Cognitive Neuroscience, 14,* 199–209.

D'Entremont, B. (1994). Young infants' responding to static and dynamic happy and sad expressions during a social interaction. *Infant Behavior and Development, 17,* 600.

Desimone, R. (1991). Face-selective cells in the temporal cortex of monkeys. *Journal of Cognitive Neuroscience, 3,* 1–8.

Dimberg, U. (1982). Facial reactions to facial expressions. *Psychophysiology, 19,* 643–647.

Eimer, M. (2000). Effects of face inversion on the structural encoding and recognition of faces: Evidence from event-related brain potentials. *Brain Research. Cognitive Brain Research, 10,* 145–148.

Ekman, P. (1972). Universal and cultural differences in facial expressions of emotion. In J. K. Cole (Ed.), *Nebraska Symposium on Motivation* (Vol. 19, pp. 207–283). Lincoln: University of Nebraska Press.

Ekman, P. (1998). Charles Darwin's *The expression of the emotions in man and animals* (3rd ed.). London: HarperCollins.

Elgar, K., & Campbell, R. (2001). Annotation: The cognitive neuroscience of face recognition: Implications for developmental disorders. *Journal of Child Psychology and Psychiatry, 42,* 705–717.

Ellsworth, C. P., Muir, D. W., & Hains, S. M. (1993). Social competence and person object differentiation: An analysis of the still-face effect. *Developmental Psychology, 29,* 63–73.

Etcoff, N. L., & Magee, J. J. (1992). Categorical perception of facial expressions. *Cognition, 44,* 227–240.

Fallshore, M., & Bartholow, J. (2003). Recognition of emotion from inverted schematic drawings of faces. *Perceptual and Motor Skills, 96,* 236–244.

Farah, M. J. (1996). Is face recognition "special"? Evidence from neuropsychology. *Behavioural Brain Research, 76,* 181–189.

Farah, M. J., Rabionitz, C., Quinn, G. E., & Liu, G. T. (2000). Early commitment of neural substrates for face recognition. *Cognitive Neuropsychology, 17,* 117–123.

Farroni, T., Csibra, G., Simion, F., & Johnson, M. H. (2002). Eye contact detection in humans from birth. *Proceedings of the National Academy of Sciences of the United States of America, 99,* 9602–9605.

Farroni, T., Valenza, E., Simion, F., & Umilta, C. (2000). Configural processing at birth: Evidence for perceptual organisation. *Perception, 29,* 355–372.

Field, T., Pickens, J., Fox, N. A., Gonzalez, J., & Nawrocki, T. (1998). Facial expression and EEG responses to happy and sad faces/voices by 3-month-old infants of depressed mothers. *British Journal of Developmental Psychology, 16,* 485–494.

Field, T. M., Cohen, D., Garcia, R., & Collins, R. (1983) Discrimination and imitation of facial expressions by term and preterm neonates. *Infant Behaviour and Development, 6,* 485–489.

Field, T. M., Woodson, R. W., Greenberg, R., & Cohen, C. (1982). Discrimination and imitation of facial expressions by neonates. *Science, 218,* 179–181.

Fiser, J., & Aslin, R. N. (2002). Statistical learning of new visual feature combinations by infants. *Proceedings of the National Academy of Sciences of the United States of America, 99,* 15822–15826.

Fox, N. A. (1994). Dynamic cerebral processes underlying emotion regulation. *Monographs of the Society for Research in Child Development, 59*, 152–166.

Frye, D., Rawling, P., Moore, C., & Myers, I. (1983). Object-person discrimination and communication at 3 and 10 months. *Developmental Psychology, 19*, 303–309.

Gauthier, I., & Nelson, C. A. (2001). The development of face expertise. *Current Opinion in Neurobiology, 11*, 219–224.

Gauthier, I., Skudlarski, P., Gore, J. C., & Anderson, A. W. (2000). Expertise for cars and birds recruits brain areas involved in face recognition. *Nature Neuroscience, 3*, 191–197.

Gauthier, I., Tarr, M. J., Anderson, A. W., Skudlarski, P., & Gore, J. C. (1999). Activation of the middle fusiform "face area" increases with expertise in recognising novel objects. *Nature Neuroscience, 2*, 568–573.

Geldart, S., Mondloch, C. J., Maurer, D., de Schonen, S., & Brent, H. P. (2002). The effect of early visual deprivation on the development of face processing. *Developmental Science, 5*, 490–501.

George, N., Driver, J., & Dolan, R. J. (2001). Seen gaze-direction modulates fusiform activity and its coupling with other brain areas during face processing. *NeuroImage, 13*, 1102–1112.

Good, C., Elgar, K., Kuntsi, J., Akers, R., Price, C., Ashburner, J., et al. (2001). Gene deletion mapping of the X-chromosome: Human brain mapping. *NeuroImage, 13*, S793.

Goren, C., Sarty, M., & Wu, P. (1975). Visual following and pattern discrimination of face-like stimuli by newborn infants. *Pediatrics, 56*, 544–549.

Gray, J. A. (1994). Three fundamental emotion systems. In P. Ekman & R. J. Davidson (Eds.), *The nature of emotion: Fundamental questions* (pp. 243–247). New York: Oxford University Press.

Grelotti, D. J., Gauthier, I., & Schultz, R. T. (2002). Social interest and the development of cortical face specialisation: What autism teaches us about face processing. *Developmental Psychobiology, 40*, 213–225.

Groen, M. A. (2002, March). *Effects of emotional reactivity in response to facial expressions in 7-month-old infants*. Poster session presented at the 44th meeting of Experimental Psychologists, Chemnitz, Germany.

Gusella, J. L., Muir, D., & Tronick, E. Z. (1988). The effect of manipulating maternal behavior during an interaction on three- and six-month-olds' affect and attention. *Child Development, 59*, 1111–1124.

Haaf, R. A. (1974). Complexity and facial resemblance as determinants of response to facelike stimuli by 5- and 10-week-old infants. *Journal of Experimental Child Psychology, 18*, 480–487.

Haaf, R. A. (1977). Visual response to complex facelike patterns by 15- and 20-week-old infants. *Developmental Psychology, 13*, 77–78.

Hains, S. M., Muir, D. W., & Franke, D. (1994). Eye contact modulates infant affect during infant-adult interactions. *Infant Behavior and Development, 17*, 679.

Halit, H., de Haan, M., & Johnson, M. H. (2003). Cortical specialisation for face processing: Face sensitive-event related potential components in 3- and 12-month-old infants. *NeuroImage, 19*, 1180–1193.

Hariri, A. R., Bookheimer, S. Y., & Mazziotta, J. C. (2000). Modulating emotional responses: Effects of a neocortical network on the limbic system. *Neuroreport, 11*, 43–48.

Harnad, S. (1987). *Categorical perception: The groundwork of cognition*. New York: Cambridge University Press.

Hasselmo, M., Rolls, E. T., & Baylis, G. C. (1989). The role of expression and identity in the face-selective responses of neurons in the temporal cortex of the monkey. *Behavioural Brain Research, 32*, 203–218.

Hauck, M., Fein, D., Maltby, N., Waterhouse, L., & Feinstein, C. (1998). Memory for faces in children with autism. *Child Neuropsychology, 4*, 187–198.

Haxby, J. V., Gobbini, M. I., Furey, M. L., Ishai, A., Schouten, J. L., & Pietrini, P. (2001). Distributed and overlapping representations of faces and objects in ventral temporal cortex. *Science, 293*, 2425–2430.

Haxby, J. V., Hoffman, E. A., & Gobbini, M. I. (2002). Human neural systems for face recognition and social communication. *Biological Psychiatry, 51*, 59–67.

Henson, R. N., Goshen-Gottstein, Y., Ganel, T., Otten, L. J., Quayle, A., & Rugg, M. D. (2003). Electrophysiological and haemodynamic correlates of face perception, recognition and priming. *Cerebral Cortex, 13*, 795–805.

Hess, U., & Blairy, S. (2001). Facial mimicry and emotional contagion to dynamic emotional facial expressions and their influence on decoding accuracy. *International Journal of Psychophysiology, 40*, 129–141.

Hoffman, E., & Haxby, J. V. (2000). Distinct representations of eye gaze and identity in the distributed human neural system for face perception. *Nature Neuroscience, 3*, 80–84.

Holstege, G., Van Ham, J. J., & Tan, J. (1986). Afferent projections to the orbicularis oculi motoneural cell group: An autoradiographical tracing study in the cat. *Brain Research, 374*, 306–320.

Hornak, J., Rolls, E. T., & Wade, D. (1996). Face and voice expression identification in patients with emotional and behavioural changes following ventral frontal lobe damage. *Neuropsychologia, 34*, 247–261.

Ishai, A., Ungerleider, L. G., Martin, A., Schouten, J. L., & Haxby, J. V. (1999). Distributed representation of objects in the human ventral visual pathway. *Proceedings of the National Academy of Sciences of the United States of America, 96*, 9379–9384.

Itier, R. J., & Taylor, M. J. (2002). Inversion and contrast polarity reversal affect both encoding and recognition processes of unfamiliar faces: A repetition study using ERPs. *NeuroImage, 15*, 353–372.

Jaencke, L. (1994). An EMG investigation of the coactivation of facial muscles during the presentation of affect-laden stimuli. *Journal of Psychophysiology, 8*, 1–10.

Johnson, M. H., Dziurawiec, S., Ellis, H. D., & Morton, J. (1991). Newborns' preferential tracking of face-like stimuli and its subsequent decline. *Cognition, 40*, 1–19.

Johnson, M. H., & Morton, J. (1991). *Biology and cognitive development: The case of face recognition.* Oxford, England: Blackwell.

Jones, S. S. (1996). Imitation or exploration? Young infants' matching of adults' oral gestures. *Child Development, 67*, 1952–1969.

Kahana-Kalman, R., & Walker-Andrews, A. S. (2001). The role of person familiarity in young infants' perception of emotional expressions. *Child Development, 72*, 352–369.

Kanwisher, N., McDermott, J., & Chun, M. M.(1997). The fusiform face area: A module in human extrastriate cortex specialized for face perception. *Journal of Neuroscience, 17*, 4302–4311.

Kawasaki, H., Adophs, R., Kaufman, O., Damasio, H., Damasio, A. R., Granner, M., et al. (2001). Single-unit responses to emotional visual stimuli recorded in human ventral prefrontal cortex. *Nature Neuroscience, 4*, 15–16.

Kennedy, H., Bullier, J., & Dehay, C. (1989). Transient projection from the superior temporal sulcus to area 17 in the newborn macaque monkey. *Proceedings of the National Academy of Sciences of the United States of America, 86*, 8093–8097.

Kesler-West, M. L., Andersen, A. H., Smith, C. D., Avison, M. J., Davis, C. E., Kryscio, R. J., et al. (2001). Neural substrates of facial emotion processing using fMRI. *Brain Research. Cognitive Brain Research, 11*, 213–226.

Kestenbaum, R., & Nelson, C. A. (1990). The recognition and categorization of upright and inverted emotional expressions by 7-month-old infants. *Infant Behavior and Development, 13*, 497–511.

Klin, A., Jones, W., Schultz, R., Volkmar, F., & Cohen, D. (2002). Visual fixation patterns during viewing of naturalistic social situations as predictors of social competence in individuals with autism. *Archives of General Psychiatry, 59*, 809–816.

Kotsoni, E., de Haan, M., & Johnson, M. H. (2001). Categorical perception of facial expressions by 7-month-old infants. *Perception, 30*, 1115–1125.

LaBarbera, J. D., Izard, C. E., Vietze, P., & Parisi, S. A. (1976). Four- and six-month old infants' visual responses to joy, anger, and neutral expressions. *Child Development, 47*, 535–538.

Lang, P. J., Bradley, M. M., & Cuthbert, B. N. (1990). Emotion, attention, and the startle reflex. *Psychological Review, 97*, 377–395.

Lang, P. J., Bradley, M. M., & Cuthbert, B. N. (1992). A motivational analysis of emotion: Reflex-cortex connections. *Psychological Science, 3*, 44–49.

Lawrence, K., Campbell, R., Swettenham, J., Terstegge, J., Akers, R., Coleman, M., et al. (2003a). Interpreting gaze in Turner syndrome: Impaired sensitivity to intention and emotion, but preservation of social cueing. *Neuropsychologia, 41*, 894–905.

Lawrence, K., Kuntsi, J., Campbell, R., Coleman, M., & Skuse, D. (2003b). Face and emotion recognition deficits in Turner syndrome: A possible role for X-linked genes in amygdala development. *Neuropsychology, 17*, 39–49.

Legerstee, M., Pomerleau, A., Malcuit, G., & Feider, H. (1987). The development of infants' responses to people and a doll: Implications for research in communication. *Infant Behavior and Development, 10*, 81–95.

Legerstee, M., & Varghese, J. (2001). The role of maternal affect mirroring on social expectancies of three-month-old infants. *Child Development, 72*, 1301–1313.

Le Grand, R., Mondloch, C. J., Maurer, D., & Brent, H. P. (2001). Early visual experience and face processing. *Nature, 410*, 890.

Ludemann, P. A., & Nelson, C. A. (1988). Categorical representation of facial expressions by 7-month-old infants. *Developmental Psychology, 24*, 492–501.

Malatesta, C. Z., Grigoryev, P., Lamb, C., Albin, M., & Culver, C. (1986). Emotion socialization and expressive development in preterm and full-term infants. *Child Development, 57*, 316–330.

Malatesta, C. Z., & Haviland, J. M. (1982). Learning display rules: The socialization of emotion expression in infancy. *Child Development, 53*, 991–1003.

Marinkovic, K., Trebon, P., Chauvel, P., & Halgren, E. (2000). Localised face processing by the human prefrontal cortex: Face-selective intracerebral potential and post-lesion deficits. *Cognitive Neuropsychology, 17*, 187–199.

Maurer, D. (1983). The scanning of compound figures by young infants. *Journal of Experimental Child Psychology, 35*, 437–448.

Maurer, D. (1985). Infants' perception of facedness. In T. M. Field & N. Fox (Eds.), *Social perception in infants* (pp. 73–100). Norwood, NJ: Ablex.

Maurer, D., & Barrera, M. (1981). Infants' perception of natural and distorted arrangements of a schematic face. *Child Development, 52*, 196–202.

Maurer, D., & Lewis, T. L. (1979). A physiological explanation of infants' early visual development. *Canadian Journal of Psychology, 33*, 232–252.

Maurer, D., & Young, R. (1983). Newborns' following of natural and distorted arrangements of facial features. *Infant Behavior and Development, 6*, 127–131.

McCarthy, G., Puce, A., Gore, J. C., & Allison, T. (1997). Face-specific processing in the human fusiform gyrus. *Journal of Cognitive Neuroscience, 9*, 605–610.

McGrath, S. K. (1983). Discrimination of facial expressions by three- to six-month-old infants. *Dissertation Abstracts International, 43*, 3721.

McKelvie, S. J. (1995). Emotional expression in upside-down faces: Evidence for configurational and componential processing. *British Journal of Social Psychology, 34*, 325–334.

Meletti, S., Benuzzi, F., Rubboli, G., Cantalupo, G., Stanzani Maserati, M., Nichelli, P., et al. (2003). Impaired facial emotion recognition in early-onset right mesial temporal epilepsy. *Neurology, 60*, 426–431.

Milewski, A. E. (1976). Infants' discrimination of internal and external pattern elements. *Journal of Experimental Child Psychology, 22*, 229–246.

Morris, J. S., Frith, C. D., Perrett, K. I., Rowland, D., Young, A. W., Calder, A. J., et al. (1996). A differential neural response in the human amygdala to fearful and happy facial expressions. *Nature, 383*, 812–815.

Morton, J., & Johnson, M. H. (1991). CONSPEC and CONLERN: A two-process theory of infant face recognition. *Psychological Review, 98*, 164–181.

Muir, D. W., & Rach-Longman, K. (1989). One more with expression: On de Schonen and Mathivet's (1989) model for the development of face perception in human infants. *Current Psychology of Cognition, 9*, 103–109.

Mumme, D. L., Fernald, A., & Herrera, C. (1996). Infants' responses to facial and vocal emotional signals in a social referencing paradigm. *Child Development, 67*, 3219–3237.

Nakamura, K., Kawashima, R., Ito, K., Sugiura, M., Kato, T., Nakamura, A., et al. (1999). Activation of the right inferior frontal cortex during assessment of facial emotion. *Journal of Neurophysiology, 82*, 1610–1614.

Narumoto, J., Yamada, H., Iidaka, T., Sadato, N., Fukui, K., Itoh, H., et al. (2000). Brain regions involved in verbal or non-verbal aspects of facial emotion recognition. *Neuroreport, 11*, 2571–2576.

Nelson, C. A., & de Haan, M. (1996). Neural correlates of visual responsiveness to facial expressions of emotion. *Developmental Psychobiology, 29*, 1–18.

Nelson, C. A., & de Haan, M. (1997). A neurobehavioral approach to the recognition of facial expressions in infancy. In J. A. Russell & J. M. Fernandez-Dols (Eds.), *The psychology of facial expression* (pp. 176–203). Cambridge, England: Cambridge University Press.

Nelson, C. A., & Dolgin, K. (1985). The generalized discrimination of facial expressions by 7-month-old infants. *Child Development, 56*, 58–61.

Nelson, C. A., & Horowitz, F. D. (1980). Asymmetry in facial expression. *Science, 209*, 834.

Nelson, C. A., Morse, P. A., & Leavitt, L. A. (1979). Recognition of facial expressions by seven-month-old infants. *Child Development, 50*, 1239–1242.

Oster, H. (1981). "Recognition" of emotional expression in infancy? In M. E. Lamb & L. R. Sherrod (Eds.), *Infant social cognition: Empirical and theoretical considerations* (pp. 85–125). Hillsdale, NJ: Erlbaum.

Pascalis, O., de Schonen, S., Morton, J., Deruelle, C., & Fabre-Grenet, M. (1995). Mother's face recognition by neonates: A replication and an extension. *Infant Behavior and Development, 18*, 79–85.

Perrett, D., Rolls, E. T., & Caan, W. (1982). Visual neurons responsive to faces in monkey temporal cortex. *Experimental Brain Research, 47*, 329–342.

Phillips, M. L., Young, A. W., Senior, C., Brammer, M., Andrew, C., Calder, A. J., et al. (1997). A specific neural substrate for perceiving facial expressions of disgust. *Nature, 389*, 495–498.

Phillips, R. D., Wagner, S. H., Fells, C. A., & Lynch M. (1990). Do infants recognize emotion in facial expressions? Categorical and "metaphorical" evidence. *Infant Behavior and Development, 13*, 71–84.

Pierce, K., Mueller, R.-A., Ambrose, J., Allen, G., & Courchesne, E. (2001). Face processing occurs outside the fusiform "face area" in autism: Evidence from functional MRI. *Brain, 124*, 2059–2073.

Pizzagalli, D. A., Lehmann, D., Hendrick, A. M., Regard, M., Pascual-Marqui, R. D., & Davidson, R. J. (2002). Affective judgements of faces modulate early activity (~160 ms) within the fusiform gyri. *NeuroImage, 16*, 663–677.

Pollak, S. D., Cicchetti, D., Hornung, K., & Reed, A. (2000). Recognizing emotion in faces: Developmental effects of child abuse and neglect. *Developmental Psychology, 36*, 679–688.

Pollak, S. D., & Kistler, D. J. (2002). Early experience is associated with the development of categorical representations for facial expressions of emotion. *Proceedings of the National Academy of Sciences of the United States of America, 99*, 9072–9076.

Pollak, S. D., & Sinha, P. (2002). Effects of early experience on children's recognition and facial displays of emotion. *Developmental Psychology, 38*, 784–791.

Rebai, M., Poiroux, S., Bernard, C., & Lalonde, R. (2001). Event-related potentials for category-specific information during passive viewing of faces and objects. *Internal Journal of Neuroscience, 106*, 209–226.

Rossion, B., Gauthier, I., Tarr, M. J., Despland, P., Bruyer, R., Linotte, S., et al. (2000). The N170 occipito-temporal component is delayed and enhanced to inverted faces but not inverted objects: An electrophysiological account of face-specific processes in the human brain. *Neuroreport, 11*, 69–74.

Sato, W., Kochiyama, T., Yoshikawa, S., & Matsumura, M. (2001). Emotional expression boosts early visual processing of the face: ERP recording and its decomposition by independent component analysis. *Neuroreport, 12*, 709–714.

Schultz, R. T., Gauthier, I., Fulbright, R. K., Anderson, A. W., Volkmar, F., Skudlarski, P., et al. (2000). Abnormal ventral temporal cortical activity during face discrimination among individuals with autism and Asperger syndrome. *Archives of General Psychiatry, 57*, 331–340.

Schwartz, G., Izard, C., & Ansul, S. (1985). The 5-month-old's ability to discriminate facial expressions of emotions. *Infant Behavior and Development, 8*, 65–77.

Schweinberger, S. R., Pickering, E. C., Jentzsch, I., Burton, A. M., & Kaufmann, J. M. (2002). Event-related brain potential evidence for a response of inferior temporal cortex to familiar face repetitions. *Brain Research. Cognitive Brain Research, 14*, 398–409.

Serrano, J. M., Iglesias, J., & Loeches, A. (1992). Visual discrimination and recognition of facial expressions of anger, fear, and surprise in 4- to 6-month-old infants. *Developmental Psychobiology, 25*, 411–425.

Serrano, J. M., Iglesias, J., & Loeches, A. (1995). Infants' responses to adult static facial expressions. *Infant Behavior and Development, 18*, 477–482.

Shibata, T., Nishijo, H., Tamura, R., Miyamoto, K., Eifuku, S., Endo, S., et al. (2002). Generators of visual evoked potentials for faces and eyes in the human brain as determined by dipole localization. *Brain Topography, 15*, 51–63.

Simion, F., Valenza, E., Umilta, C., & Barba, B. D. (1998). Preferential orienting to faces in newborns: A temporal-nasal asymmetry. *Journal of Experimental Psychology: Human Perception and Performance, 24*, 1399–1405.

Slater, A. (2001). Visual perception. In G. Bremner & A. Fogel (Eds.), *Blackwell handbook of infant development* (pp. 5–34). Malden, MA: Blackwell.

Soken, N. H., & Pick, A. (1999). Infants' perception of dynamic affective expressions: Do infants distinguish specific expressions? *Child Development, 70*, 1275–1282.

Spitz, R., & Wolf, K. M. (1946). The smiling response: A contribution to the ontogenesis of social relations. *Genetic Psychology Monographs, 34*, 57–125.

Stern, D. N. (1983). The goal and structure of mother-infant play. *Psychiatrie-de-l'Enfant, 26*, 193–216.

Sweeten, T. L., Posey, D. J., Shekhar, A., & McDougle, C. J. (2002). The amygdala and related structures in the pathophysiology of autism. *Pharmacology, Biochemistry and Behavior, 71*, 449–455.

Tantam, D., Monaghan, L., Nicholson, H., & Stirling, J. (1989). Autistic children's ability to interpret faces: A research note. *Journal of Child Psychology and Psychiatry, 30*, 623–630.

Thomas, K. M., Drevets, W. C., Whalen, P. J., Eccard, C. H., Dahl, R. E., Ryan, N. D., et al. (2001). Amygdala response to facial expressions in children and adults. *Biological Psychiatry, 49*, 309–316.

Trevarthen, C. (1979). Communication and cooperation in early infancy: A description of primary intersubjectivity. In M. M. Bullowa (Ed.), *Before speech: The beginning of interpersonal communication* (pp. 321–347). New York: Cambridge University Press.

Trevarthen, C. (1998). The concept and foundations of infant intersubjectivity. In S. Braten (Ed.), *Intersubjective communication and emotion in early ontogeny* (pp. 15–46). New York: Cambridge University Press.

Tronick, E., Als, H., Adamson, L., Wise, S., & Brazelton, T. B. (1978). The infant's response to entrapment between contradictory messages in face-to-face interaction. *Journal of the American Academy of Child Psychiatry, 17*, 1–13.

Turati, C., & Simion, F. (2002). Newborns' recognition of changing and unchanging aspects of schematic faces. *Journal of Experimental Child Psychology, 83* 239–261.

Turati, C., Simion, F., Milani, I., & Umilta, C. (2002). Newborns' preference for faces: What is crucial? *Developmental Psychology, 38*, 875–882.

Tzourio-Mazoyer, N., de Schonen, S., Crivello, F., Reutter, B., Aujard, Y., & Mazoyer, B. (2002). Neural correlates of woman face processing by 2-month-old infants. *NeuroImage, 15*, 454–461.

Valenza, E., Simion, F., Cassia, V. M., & Umilta, C. (1996). Face preference at birth. *Journal of Experimental Psychology: Human Perception and Performance, 22*, 892–903.

Walden, T. A., & Baxter, A. (1989). The effect of context and age on social referencing. *Child Development, 60*, 1511–1518.

Walden, T. A., & Ogan, T. A. (1988). The development of social referencing. *Child Development, 59*, 1230–1240.

Walker, A. S. (1982). Intermodal perception of expressive behaviors by human infants. *Journal of Experimental Child Psychology, 33*, 514–535.

Watanabe, S., Kakigi, R., Koyama, S., & Kirino, E. (1999). Human face perception traced by magneto- and electro-encephalography. *Brain Research/Cognitive Brain Research, 8*, 125–142.

Whalen, P. J., Shin, L. M., McInerney, S. C., Fisher, H., Wright, C. I., & Rauch, S. L. (2001). A functional MRI study of human amygdala responses to facial expressions of fear versus anger. *Emotion, 1*, 70–83.

Yang, T. T., Menon, V., Eliez, S., Blasey, C., White, C. D., Reid, A. J., et al. (2002). Amygdalar activation associated with positive and negative facial expressions. *Neuroreport, 13*, 1737–1741.

Young, A. W., Rowland, D., Calder, A. J., Etcoff, N. L., Seth, A., & Perrett, D. I. (1997). Facial expression megamix: Tests of dimensional and category accounts of emotion recognition. *Cognition, 63*, 271–313.

Young-Browne, G., Rosenfeld, H. M., & Horowitz, F. D. (1977). Infant discrimination of facial expressions. *Child Development, 48*, 555–562.

4

Joint Attention, Social Engagement, and the Development of Social Competence

Peter C. Mundy
C. Françoise Acra

U nderstanding the ontogeny of the human capacity for social engagement is an especially important goal for developmental research because competence in social interactions contributes to a wide array of adaptive outcomes in children and adults, from school readiness and academic success (Blair, 2002; Raver, 2002) to risk and resilience in the face of vulnerability for developmental psychopathology (Masten & Coatsworth, 1998). Definitions of social engagement and social competence vary, but they typically emphasize a capacity for a prosocial behavioral style that is based on (a) the capacity to monitor, relate, and integrate the behavior of self and others, (b) the ability to regulate attention and emotional reactivity in the dynamic flow of social interaction, and (c) the tendency to express positive emotions and to be sociable and agreeable with peers as well as adults (Eisenberg et al., 1997; Masten & Coatsworth, 1998; Rothbart & Bates, 1998). Given this broad definition, it is not surprising that the study of infant precursors of social engagement and social competence often focuses on paradigms for the study of attachment and related patterns behaviors or the study of temperament and processes associated with effortful control, emotional regulation, and executive functions (e.g., Calkins & Fox, 2002; Fox, Henderson, Rubin, Calkins, & Schmidt, 2001; Kochanska, Murray, & Coy, 2000; Masten & Coatsworth, 1998; Rothbart, Posner, & Rosicky, 1994). It is perhaps less well recognized, though, that joint attention constitutes an essential form of social engagement in infancy, and indeed throughout the life span. Therefore, the study of joint attention offers an important paradigm for research on the psychological processes that contribute to the early development of social competence.

Joint attention skills refer to the capacity of individuals to coordinate attention with a social partner in relation to a third object or event. In the first years of life, this capacity may only involve the social coordination of overt aspects of visual attention, such as when a toddler shows a toy to a parent. This capacity eventually becomes more elaborate and integral to the social coordination of covert aspects of attention, as when social partners share or coordinate attention to psychological phenomena, such as ideas, intentions, or emotions (Tomasello, 1995).

Components of this capacity begin to emerge between 3 and 6 months of age (D'Entremont, Hains, & Muir, 1997; Morales, Mundy, & Rojas, 1998; Scaife & Bruner, 1975) and are elaborated into several different forms at least through 18 months of age (Carpenter, Nagell, & Tomasello, 1998; Block et al., 2003). One component involves the infant's ability to follow the direction of gaze, head turning, and/or a pointing gesture of another person (Scaife & Bruner, 1975). This behavior has been referred to as Responding to Joint Attention skill (RJA; Seibert, Hogan, & Mundy, 1982; Mundy et al., 2003). Another type of skill involves the infant's use of eye contact and/or deictic gestures (e.g., pointing or showing) to spontaneously initiate coordinated attention with a social partner. This type of protodeclarative act (Bates, 1976) may be referred to as Initiating Joint Attention skill (IJA; Seibert et al., 1982; Mundy et al., 2003). These behaviors, especially IJA, appear to serve social functions. That is, the goal and reinforcement of these behaviors have been interpreted to revolve around the sharing of experience with others and the positive valence that such early social sharing has for young children (Mundy, 1995; Rheingold, Hay, & West, 1976). Alternatively, social attention coordination may also be used for less social, but more instrumental, purposes (Bates, 1976). For example, infants and young children may use eye contact and gestures to initiate attention coordination with another person to elicit aid in obtaining an object or event. This may be referred to as a protoimperative act (Bates, 1976) or Initiating Behavior Regulation/Requests (IBR; Mundy et al., 2003). Although other aspects of behavior may be assessed in early social communication paradigms, such as the tendency to take turns in interactions with others (Seibert et al. 1982; Mundy et al. 2003), the content of this chapter will focus on these three types of behaviors, which are illustrated in figure 4–1.

Each of these behaviors may be measured in the context of an interaction with a social partner, and to a greater (see figure 4–1c) or lesser extent (see figure 4–1d), each involves intersubjectivity or sharing of experience with another person. The tendency to enter into intersubjective episodes with others is regarded as a fundamental aspect of human social engagement (Trevarthen & Aitken, 2001). On this basis, some measures of joint attention may be considered to display significant *content validity* for the study of social engagement in infancy.

It is also important to note that infants display significant variability in joint attention, especially IJA, and this variability reflects stable individual differences

Figure 4–1. Illustrations of (top left) Responding to Joint Attention (RJA); (top right) Initiating Joint Attention (IJA), "pointing"; (middle row and bottom left) IJA, "alternating gaze"; and (bottom right) Initiating Behavior Regulation/Requests (IBR), "pointing" from the Early Social Communication Scales (Seibert, Hogan, & Mundy, 1982; Mundy et al., 2003).

in social engagement tendencies among infants aged 6 to 18 months (Block et al., 2003; Morales et al., 2000; Morales et al., 1998; Henderson, Yoder, Yale, & McDuffie, 2002; Mundy & Gomes, 1998; Mundy, Card, & Fox, 2000; Wetherby, Allen, Cleary, Kublin, & Goldstein, 2002). Using the Early Social Communication Scales (ESCS; Seibert et al., 1982; Mundy et al., 2003), Block et al. (2003) observed significant test-retest reliability for IJA from 9 to 12, 12 to 15, and 15 to 18 months in a longitudinal study of 87 typically developing infants. In this study, significant reliability was also observed for RJA from 12 to 15 and 15 to 18 months and for IBR from 9 to 12 and 12 to 18 months. Furthermore, individual differences in infant joint attention behaviors also appear to be consistent across paradigms such that IJA behavior on the ESCS is correlated with infants' active participation in opportunities for joint attention with their caregivers (Vaughan et al., 2003a). What contributes to the stability of differences in these infant skills, especially IJA? Does this stability extend beyond infancy and contribute to difference in the social proclivities of children and adults? These are important but not necessarily well-recognized issues for research on joint attention and social development. However, as recent longitudinal data to be reviewed later in this chapter suggest, it seems very likely that answers to these questions will provide important information on the processes that underlie individual differences in social engagement across the life span.

A third observation of note is that relatively few significant cross-domain correlations (e.g., IJA with RJA at 12 months) have been observed in studies using the ESCS (Block et al., 2003; Mundy et al., 2000; Mundy & Gomes, 1998). This suggests that the ESCS measures of different types of infant joint attention skills reflect overlapping but distinct dimensions of behavior employed by infants to engage in social interactions. That is, different types of joint attention skills may reflect different constellations of processes that are involved in the development of social engagement and social competence in infancy (Mundy et al., 2000; Mundy & Willoughby, 1996).

In addition to their content validity and reliability, measures of joint attention have considerable *construct validity* for research on the early development of social engagement and social competence. Current theory in this regard can be summarized in terms of four interrelated hypotheses about the nature of joint attention development: (a) The self-organizing hypothesis suggests that joint attention skills reflect the ability to engage with others in a manner that facilitates social learning (e.g. Baldwin, 1995; Mundy & Neal, 2001); (b) the social-cognition hypothesis suggests that joint attention constitutes a form of early engagement that is integral to the development of the ability to understand others' thoughts, intentions, and feelings (e.g., Bretherton, 1991; Tomasello, 1995); (c) the social-motivation hypothesis suggests that joint attention skills reflect sensitivity to the reward value of sharing with others (Dawson et al., 2002; Trevarthen & Aitken, 2001; Mundy, 1995); (d) the neurodevelopmental executive hypothesis suggests that joint attention development reflects specific cortical and subcortical social executive functions that play critical roles in typical and atypical social development (Mundy, 2003; Vaughan & Mundy, in press). One of these social executive functions involves the capacity for the integrative and comparative monitoring of one's own behavior in conjunction with monitoring the behavior of a social partner (Mundy, 2003).

In the remainder of this chapter, each of these hypotheses will be considered in turn, along with related research. Then the construct validity of measures of joint attention for the study of social engagement will be considered by reviewing research on children with autism and children with disturbances of attachment, as well as research on the biobehavioral continuity between infant joint attention and childhood social outcomes. The latter indicates that infant joint attention is predictive not only of childhood cognitive and language outcomes (e.g., Ulvund & Smith, 1996) but also of individual differences in childhood social interactive competence in typically developing children (Vaughan et al., 2003a), "at-risk" children (Acra, Mundy, Claussen, Scott, & Bono, 2003; Sheinkopf, Mundy, Claussen, & Willoughby, 2004), and children with autism (Lord, Floody, Anderson, & Pickles, 2003; Sigman & Ruskin, 1999). These data provide perhaps the strongest support for the validity of infant joint attention measures in the study of processes associated with social engagement and social competence.

The Self-Organizing Hypothesis

The development of joint attention skills has long been considered a major milestone of infancy (Bakeman & Adamson, 1984; Bruner, 1975; Bates, Benigni, Bretherton, Camaioni, & Volterra, 1979). The ability to attend to what other people attend to is fundamental to participation in most, if not all, human social interactions and social learning situations. For example, much of early language learning in the second year occurs by way of incidental learning in unstructured social interactions. In such interactions several things may occur: (a) A parent provides an incidental learning opportunity by referring to a new object or event in the environment, but (b) an infant may need to discriminate among a number of stimuli in the environment to focus on the correct object/event to acquire the appropriate new word association. Thus, the infant is confronted with the possibility of referential mapping errors (Baldwin, 1995). To deal with this problem, infants may utilize the direction of gaze of the parent (i.e., use a form of RJA skill; figure 4–1b) to limit the number of potential referents to attend to, and increase the likelihood of a correct word-learning experience (Baldwin, 1995). Similarly, when an infant initiates bids for joint attention, the responsive caregiver may follow the child's line of regard and take advantage of the child's focus of attention to provide a new word in a context that maximizes the opportunity to learn (cf. Tomasello, 1995). Hence, joint attention may be regarded as an early developing *self-organizing facility* that is critical to much of subsequent social and cognitive development (e.g., Baldwin, 1995; Mundy & Neal, 2001).

If true, the self-organizing hypothesis has a number of important implications for the study of joint attention and social engagement. For example, the early emergence of deficits in joint attention appears to be a characteristic of the syndrome of autism (Curcio, 1978; Mundy, Sigman, Ungerer, & Sherman, 1986; Mundy, 1995). If the self-organizing hypothesis is true, these deficits not only may reflect pathological processes in these children but also would contribute to subsequent pathology by reducing their opportunities of social learning

(Mundy & Neal, 2001). This type of negative feedback may also contribute to suboptimal development for other groups of children who appear to display joint attention deficits, such as those with disorganized attachment (Claussen, Mundy, Mallik, & Willoughby, 2002).

The self-organizing hypothesis may have implications for the measurement of joint attention in infancy. If joint attention skills assist in the self-organization of social information processing and social learning early in development, then individual differences in infants' frequency or consistency of use of joint attention skills may be associated with differences in the social learning opportunities available to children early in development. Therefore, in addition to assessments of whether or not infants are capable of a particular joint attention skill at a given age (Carpenter et al., 1998), it may also be useful to assess how often infants use a particular skill in social interactions. Instruments for measuring joint attention skills in infant-examiner paradigms provide this level of continuous frequency measurement (e.g., Seibert et al., 1982; Wetherby et al., 2002). Indeed, much of the research reviewed in this chapter has employed one of these instruments, the ESCS, which is a 20-minute structured social interaction platform for rating the frequency and consistency of joint attention and other social communication behaviors in infants from 6 to 24 months of age (Mundy et al., 2003; Seibert et al. 1982). The ESCS paradigm is illustrated in figure 4–1.

The self-organizing hypothesis is relatively new to the literature on joint attention. Nevertheless, two studies provide some data of relevance. Bono, Daley, and Sigman (2004) examined the treatment responsiveness of 23 children with autism to varying intensities of intervention over a 1-year period (6–43 hours of intervention per week). ESCS data were collected at baseline, and the Reynell Language Development Scales were used to assess outcome. The results revealed that scores from the IJA and RJA scales of the ESCS predicted individual differences in language outcome. Surprisingly, differences in intervention intensity were not associated with language outcomes. However, Bono et al. (2004) did observe a significant interaction of intervention intensity by RJA score. Children with autism who more consistently responded correctly on RJA trials displayed more evidence of benefiting from higher intensities of intervention (i.e., more social learning opportunities) than did children with less consistent RJA skills.

Another study examined the relation between joint attention at 15 months of age and 24-month outcome in infant-caregiver dyads who showed secure ($N = 22$) or insecure ($N = 21$) attachment patterns (Crowson, 2001). Twenty-four-month outcome in this study was measured in terms of performance on standardized measures of cognitive and language development, as well as with a measure of the tendency of toddlers and caregivers to engage in joint attention in a 12-minute social interaction paradigm (Bakeman & Adamson, 1984; Tomasello & Farrar, 1986). Crowson (2001) found that RJA was related to cognitive and language outcomes in both groups. However, the relations of IJA to these outcomes appeared to be conditional on attachment security: In the Secure Attachment group, 15-month IJA was not related to outcome. However, the tendency of caregivers to follow the line of regard of their infants to establish joint attention at 24 months was related to individual differences in language development, replicating earlier observations by Tomasello and Farrar (1986). This aspect of maternal behavior was not related to language development in the insecure group, and the group differences on this correlation were significant even though there was no difference in caregiver "following in" behavior across the groups. Alternatively, in the Insecure group, the tendency of infants to display IJA behaviors at 15 months (e.g., showing) with a tester was related to infants' tendencies to initiate joint attention in interaction with caregivers at 24 months, and both of these behavior tendencies were associated with language development in this group. These observations were interpreted to suggest that higher IJA skills enabled infants to engage their caregivers and self-organize social interactions to a degree that may decrease their developmental risk incurred by the less sensitive caregiving that is associated with insecure attachment status.

Joint Attention and Social Cognition

Bruner (1975) proposed that before language acquisition, infants develop the ability to intentionally share information with social partners (i.e., communicate) through nonverbal means, such as pointing or showing gestures and eye contact. Bruner and Sherwood (1983) used the term *joint attention* to refer to a subset of these skills and suggested that they reflected a general preverbal cognitive platform that was essential to language development. The notion that preverbal infants *intentionally* share information with others was subsequently elaborated to suggest that joint attention specifically reflects social-cognitive development in infancy (Bretherton, 1991). In brief, the logic of this hypothesis is as follows: If infants use gestures and eye contact to intentionally communicate with others, they must have some awareness not only of the social signal value of their behaviors but also that others have powers of perception and intentions that may be affected by the infant's behavior. Thus, theory has come to suggest that joint attention development reflects the emergence of social cognition or infants' "understanding" that others have intentions (Baron-Cohen, 1995; Tomasello, 1995; Leslie, 1987).

Indeed, if one observes a 15-month-old alternate gaze to share his or her pleasure in an object, or point to show, or point to obtain an object (see figure 4–1c, 4–1b, and 4–1d, respectively), it is difficult to escape the interpretation that the infant possesses some degree of understanding that others have emotions and intentions that may be shared or directed (Bretherton, 1991). Although this is an intuitive and plausible perspective on joint attention, relatively little empirical work has been conducted on this hypothesis. One study followed a sample of 13 typically developing infants from 20 to 44 months of age as part of a study on the early identification of autism (Charman et al., 2000). At 20 months of age, an alternating gaze measure was employed (see figure 4–1c), which involved children spontaneously initiating eye contact with a tester or parent when presented with an interesting toy. After controlling for differences in IQ and language development, the 20-month IJA alternating gaze measure was a significant predictor of 44-month social-cognitive ability on a "theory-of-mind" (ToM) measure, which taps the ability to understand another person's beliefs.

One aspect of the social-cognitive hypothesis that remains unclear is the age of onset of the social-cognitive component of joint attention. Some have argued that true joint attention does not occur until the infant or toddler is capable of the simultaneous awareness of self and other contemplating a common object, thought to occur sometime in the second year (Tomasello, 1995). However, more recent research and theory has adopted a perspective which suggests that social cognition may only gradually become part of joint attention after several months of practice with social attention (Brooks & Meltzoff, 2002; Moore, 1996; Werner & Kaplan, 1963). Indeed, the rudiments of joint attention, especially RJA, may emerge between 3 and 6 months of life (Scaife & Bruner, 1975; D'Entremont et al., 1997; Hood, Willen, & Driver, 1998; Morales et al., 1998), and this occurs well before theory suggests that social-cognitive processes affect or organize behavior (Mundy & Sigman, 1989; Tomasello, 1995). Moreover, recent empirical efforts indicate that infants display RJA skills in the first year of life, but that these skills become associated with social cognition only in the second year of life (Brooks & Meltzoff, 2002; Woodward, 2003).

One way to conceptualize this aspect of joint attention development is to think in terms of two phases: a "learning to" phase and a "learning from" phase (Vaughan & Mundy, in press). In the first year of development, several basic processes such as early operant learning (Corkum & Moore, 1998) and intersensory integration (Flom & Pick, 2003) may play a critical role in joint attention development. Theoretically, other basic processes are also critical to the "learning to" phase of development, including processes associated with motivation for social engagement, attention regulation, imitation, and the related capacity for the integrated monitoring of self and others (Meltzoff & Moore, 1997; Mundy, 1995; Mundy et al., 2000; Pomares, Mundy, Vaughan, Block, & Delgado, 2003; Sheinkopf et al., 2004; Trevarthen & Aitken, 2001). With practice, the numerous processes involved in social attention coordination become integrated and routinized so that infants gradually move into the "learning from" phase of joint attention development, hypothetically at about 8 months. Around this time, practice effects and neurodevelopmental maturation begin to free up enough cognitive resources (e.g., "M-Space"; see Case, 1987) to make it increasingly likely that infants have the capacity not only to engage in joint attention but also to process and compare proprioceptive information about their own experience of an object or event with exteroceptive information about their social partners' experience of the same object or event (Mundy, Sigman, & Kasari, 1993). This comparative process in the context of social interactions about a common referent provides the infant with information about self and other that contributes to the development of an awareness that others have thoughts or feelings that are similar to (or different from) the infant's (Bruner, 1975; Werner & Kaplan, 1963). Based on their own experience, this comparative information allows infants to simulate the experience of others, which gives rise to social cognition (Frith & Frith, 2001; Stich & Nichols, 1992). This theoretical perspective therefore suggests that joint attention may be viewed as a contributing *cause* of social-cognitive development, as much as or more than it is a *consequence* of social-cognitive development. From this perspective, joint attention may be reasonably viewed as a special form of infant social engagement that promotes aspects of cognitive development that are especially important for subsequent social competence (Mundy & Neal, 2001). Theoretically, this is another example of the self-organizing functions of infant joint attention skill development. However, if this line of thinking is correct, the social-cognitive hypothesis may be insufficient to fully explain the nature of individual differences in joint attention, especially in the early "learning to" phase of development. In this regard, it may be useful to consider the motivation of infants to engage in joint attention episodes.

Social Motivation, Affect, and Joint Attention

In examining the behaviors displayed by infants in figure 4–1, researchers may ask at least two questions: How are infants able to share attention and experience with others? Why do infants share attention and experiences with others? The second question leads to reflection on the motivational factors and processes that contribute to the human tendency to share experience with others. For example, consider the following vignette. You are going to be part of the audience at an event that you are sure you will thoroughly enjoy (a play, a concert, a sporting event, etc.). You have a choice: You can go alone or take a friend along. Many, if not most, people will choose the company of a friend. Moreover, during the event, there is a strong likelihood that you and your friend will exchange eye contact and experience a sense of relatedness at some point in response to your shared experience of an especially interesting or emotionally stimulating incident that occurs during the event. In that moment the two of you are socially engaged in joint attention, much like the infant in figure 4–1c. Why do we, as infants, children, and adults, engage in this behavior even when viewing the event by ourselves would be pleasurable? Does the sharing of experience with others hold some positive reward value that motivates people to engage in acts of joint attention throughout the life span? Does this motivation system assist in bootstrapping the development of joint attention and its critical early self-organizing functions in human social development? Some would respond with an unequivocal yes to these questions and go on to suggest that human beings have an intrinsic motivation for sharing of experience or intersubjectivity that is important for the early organization of social and cognitive development (e.g., Trevarthen & Aitken, 2001; Hobson, 2002).

One of the factors that may organize early development is an intrinsic preference to orient to social stimuli and faces (Bard, Platzman, Lester, & Suomi, 1992; Valenza, Simion, Cassia, & Umilta, 1996) and related motivation processes that promote face-to-face mother-infant interaction involving the facial and vocal expression of positive affect (Trevarthen, 1979; Stern, 1985). In particular, Trevarthen and Aitken (2001) suggest that there is an intrinsic motivation function to share affective experience with others. In its first phase of development, this involves face-to-face sharing of nonverbal emotional information, or what has been referred to as *primary intersubjectivity* (Trevarthen, 1979). In terms of neural development, this motivation system is theoretically mediated by orbitofrontal and temporal brain systems involved in the perception of social stimuli (e.g., facial affect) and the association of these stimuli with positive reward value (Trevarthen & Aitken, 2001). According to this model, sensitivity to the reward value of these stimuli is inherent to human beings and possibly mediated by a neuropeptide-based endogenous social reward system (Panksepp, 1979). However, research suggests that this social reward system may also be affected by external operant reinforcement and learning (Corkum & Moore, 1998). In either event, this motivation system serves to organize early behavior and to prioritize social orienting, social interactions, and social information processing (Dawson, Meltzoff, Osterling, Rinaldi, & Brown, 1998; Mundy & Neal, 2001; Trevarthen & Aitken, 2001). This prioritization assures a sufficient input of social information to the infant to allow the next step, which is the development of a more elaborate capacity for sharing of experience with others, vis-à-vis a third object or event. This capacity has been termed *secondary intersubjectivity* (Trevarthen & Aitken, 2001) or *joint attention* (Bruner & Sherwood, 1983; Tomasello, 1995).

The social reward system involved in joint attention likely goes beyond the ventral brain systems described by Trevarthen and Aitken (2001) to include more dorsal cortical regions, including the anterior cingulate (Eisenberger, Lieberman, & Williams, 2003; Mundy, 2003). More important, the strength of this motivational system is likely to vary from individual to individual, either because of inherent biological differences in sensitivity to social reward or through differences in the learned reward value of social stimuli (Dawson et al., 2002; Mundy, 1995; Mundy & Willoughby, 1998). The resulting variability in social motivation significantly contributes to differences among infants in the tendency to engage in different types of joint attention skills. Moreover, when the motivation to share experience with others or to engage in episodes of joint attention and intersubjectivity chronically slips below some critical threshold, the risk for psychopathology increases (Mundy, 1995; Mundy & Willoughby, 1996; Trevarthen & Aitken, 2001).

If joint attention and sharing of experience with others have positive reward value for infants, it may then be reasonable to expect that affect, especially positive affect, may play a role in joint attention development. In this regard, Adamson and Bakeman (1985) provided the seminal observation that, from late in the first year through the second year, the exchange of positive affect becomes increasingly characteristic of infant-caregiver interactions involving joint attention. However, it was not clear whether different types of joint attention skills had different affective characteristics until Kasari and her colleagues published a paper on the nature of joint attention deficits in autism (Kasari, Sigman, Mundy, & Yirmiya, 1990).

The early development of autism is characterized by a specific pattern of impairment in the development of joint attention skills. In particular, IJA development appears to be chronically and robustly disturbed in autism, although an early impairment in RJA development eventually remits, and IBR and other forms of early social communication skills (e.g., social turn-taking) appear to be less impaired relative to delayed and typically developing controls (Curcio, 1978; Loveland & Landry, 1986; Mundy, Sigman, & Kasari, 1994; Mundy et al., 1986; Sigman & Ruskin, 1999; Wetherby & Prutting 1984). In his initial observations, Kanner (1943) had suggested that the social impairments of autism involved a biologically based impairment of affective relatedness to others. Therefore, to examine the role of affect in disturbances of joint attention in autism, Kasari and her colleagues (1990) integrated ESCS ratings of joint attention with systematic ratings of facial affect. Several important observations were noted in this study. First, in the typical control sample, infants conveyed positive affect significantly more often to social partners in the context of IJA bids compared with IBR or RJA behaviors. Children with Down syndrome and autism did not display differences in affect across IJA and IBR measures, but for different reasons. The Down syndrome children displayed equally high rates of positive affect across both IJA and IBR bids, but the children with autism displayed equally low rates of positive affect in IJA and IBR. Positive affect was not a major component of RJA for any group.

These results suggested that the sharing of positive affective experiences with others is a major component of IJA behavior in typical development, and that an attenuation of positive affect sharing may be an important component of IJA deficits in children with autism (Kasari et al., 1990). To examine this issue further, we reexamined the association of affect and joint attention in an independent and larger sample of typically developing infants. This study again revealed approximately 60% of all IJA bids displayed by toddlers in the second year involved the conveyance of positive affect, whereas less than 30% of IBR and RJA bids involved the sharing of positive affect (Mundy, Kasari, & Sigman, 1992). These data were interpreted to suggest that IJA in the second year might provide an operational definition of the development of secondary intersubjectivity, or the tendency of infants to initiate episodes of positive affective sharing with a social partner (see figure 4–1c). Of course, one possibility is that the positive affect in IJA is a reactive, rather than an intentional, sharing of positive affective experience with others. That is, when engaged in triadic attention deployment, infants may smile in response to looking at the face of a social partner rather than as a conveyance of their own preexisting affective state. However, our recent data indicate that, between 8 and 10 months, there is a developmental shift in the association of affect with IJA (Venezia, Messinger, Thorp, & Mundy, 2004). Prior to 10 months, when typically developing infants engage in an alternating gaze IJA bid (see figure 4–1c), they tend to display affect reactively, that is, after they look at the face of their social partner. After 10 months of age, infants tend to smile first and then convey their ongoing affective reaction to an object or event with an IJA bid. One interpretation of these results is that after 10 months, infants begin to display a pattern of behavior that is consistent with the possibility that they are intentionally sharing affect with others as part of an IJA bid (Venezia et al., 2004).

Data on the facial emotion component of IJA are consistent with the hypothesis that at least this type of joint attention may reflect a prosocial motivation to share affective experiences with others. If this is true, environmental factors that may affect infants' social motivational status, such as their caregiving milieu, may also be expected to have specific effects on IJA. Indeed, Wachs and Chan (1986) observed that a more positive social home environment was related to the development of IJA skills (protodeclaratives), but not to IBR skill development (protoimperatives). Subsequently, two other studies have indicated that attachment may be related to joint attention development and especially to IJA development (Schölmerich, Lamb, Leyendecker, & Fracasso, 1997; Claussen et al., 2002). However, like the data from Crowson (2001), these studies did not reveal an effect for secure versus insecure attachment groups, but rather an effect for disorganized attachment versus other classifications. In the Claussen et al. (2002) study, for example, at-risk infants (with in utero cocaine exposure) with either secure, insecure, and disorganized attachment status were compared on the ESCS at 12 and 18 months of age. The results revealed no effect of attachment on RJA, but an attenuation of IBR and IJA development in the disorganized group. IBR development was lower for the disorganized group, but it increased from 12 to 18 months of age. However, IJA bids actually decreased from 12 to 18 months in the toddlers from disorganized attachment dyads. One interpretation of these results is that less than optimal caregiving associated with disorganized attachment may lead to a general attenuation of the tendency of the toddler to initiate communicative bids, and to a *reduction* over the 12-to-18-

month period in the social motivation for secondary intersubjectivity, as measured by the development of IJA bids.

A similar set of observations has been provided in a study of children adopted from institutional orphanages in Asia at an adoption clinic at the University of Minnesota (Kroupina, Kuefner, Iverson, & Johnson, 2003). Infants entered these institutions shortly after birth, but many of these orphanages had few attendants. Therefore, while they provided for the physical needs of the children, they often provided minimal social-emotional nurturance. As children were adopted, they were brought to the United States at different ages and after different lengths of stay in these institutions. The ESCS was administered as part of a broader developmental assessment of these children at the university clinic. The results revealed that age of adoption or length of stay in the orphanage did not have an effect on RJA or IBR development, both of which exhibited monotonic age-related increases. However, the age-related development of IJA was U-shaped such that, after about 14 months of living in the orphanages, the IJA development of the infants displayed a significant and systematic age-related decline. This profile of declining IJA skill is very similar to the pattern observed by Claussen et al. (2002) in their study of infants with substantial biosocial risk and disorganized attachment status. These data raise the hypothesis of a critical period for appropriate social stimulation, reinforcement, and motivation that may be needed for the adequate IJA development in the second year of life.

If joint attention, or at least IJA, development is indeed related to affective and social motivation processes, it may be expected that aspects of temperament, especially emotional reactivity, may also be associated with IJA development. Data from two recent studies are consistent with this possibility. Neither IBR or RJA displays significant relations with indexes of emotional reactivity (Vaughan et al., 2003b), although RJA may be related to parents' reports of visual attention control (Morales et al., 2000). Alternatively, Vaughan et al. (2003) observed that 9-month infant-tester IJA on the ESCS was significantly related to parent reports of "low pleasure" or a heightened tendency to express positive affect on the Infant Behavior Questionnaire (Rothbart, 1981). Parents' ratings of fearful responsiveness to novelty were later associated with IJA at 12 months. Finally, in a follow-up study, Vaughan et al. (2003b) observed that 12-month IJA was related to 24-month parent reports of the tendency of toddlers to display positive emotional reactivity.

These data suggest there may be developmental shifts in temperamental contributions to IJA in an infant-examiner paradigm, from positive emotional reactivity, to negative emotional reactivity at the end of the first year, and then back to positive emotional approach tendency by the middle of the second year. Indeed, we have observed that 12-month IJA may be an especially meaningful marker of vigilance in infants from poor caregiving environments that may be negatively related to cognitive and behavioral outcome (Sheinkopf et al., 2004;

Neal et al., 2003). Moreover, we have also observed a nonlinear pattern of IJA on the ESCS in two typical samples, with an increase in bids observed between 9 and 12 months (Block et al., 2003) but a *decrease* observed between 12 and 15 months, and then an increase (rebound) observed between 15 and 18 months (Block et al., 2003; Mundy et al., 2000). This shifting pattern may reflect changes in the temperamental contributions to IJA over this period, as well as at least two phases of development integration and maturation between 9, 12, 15, and 18 months. It is interesting to note that the decline between 12 and 15 months observed in typical development coincides with the point of decline in IJA that has been observed among infants in less than optimal caregiving (Kroupina et al., 2003; Claussen et al., 2002). Unlike these "at-risk" infants, typical infants display a rebound in IJA development from 15 to 18 months. Nevertheless, examining the nature of the nonlinear pattern of IJA development in the 9-to-18-month period may provide useful information on typical and atypical social engagement and social competence in infants.

As summarized here, the research literature is beginning to suggest that some forms of joint attention such as IJA (as opposed to RJA or IBR) may reflect the tendency of infants to engage others in the spontaneous sharing of affective experience of objects or events. This tendency for affective sharing may reflect a broader motivational tendency to engage in intersubjectivity with others that may in turn be affected by environmental caregiving factors. Moreover, an attenuation of IJA may be a marker of developmental risk. However, it is not just environmental social-motivation factors that contribute to individual differences in joint attention development. Theoretically, observations of associations with temperament measures suggest that joint attention development may also be associated with constitutional factors. Furthermore, observations of syndrome-specific deficits in autism also suggest that constitutional aspects of neurodevelopment contribute to individual differences in the tendency to engage in joint attention with others. Indeed, there is a growing literature on the neurodevelopment of joint attention that raises several hypotheses about the processes that may contribute to this form of social engagement.

The Neurodevelopment of Joint Attention

Autism is a biologically based disorder (Dawson, Osterling, Rinaldi, Carver, & McPartland, 2001) that may be more prevalent than once thought, with the spectrum of autism-related disorders occurring at a rate of 2 to 6 per thousand (Fombonne, 2003). As noted earlier, a pathognomic feature of this syndrome is impaired social and communicative development, one important characteristic of which is a robust early disturbance of joint attention development (Mundy et al., 1986; Mundy & Sigman, 1989). Observations of joint attention deficits in autism are well replicated and appear to be universal among young children with autism (Filipek et al., 1999). As previously noted, young children with autism display deficits in both IJA and RJA skills. However, there is evidence of a dissociation in the course of these joint attention impairments with age. In the first years of life, children with autism display a clear deficit in RJA skills. However, they begin to display basic RJA-related gaze following by 2 years of age (Charwarska, Klin, & Volkmar, 2003), and problems in RJA appear to remit to a significant degree among older children with autism or those with higher mental ages (Mundy, Sigman, & Kasari, 1994; Leekam & Moore, 2001; Sigman & Ruskin, 1999). Conversely, deficits related to IJA appear to remain robust throughout childhood (Baron-Cohen, 1989; Lord et al., 2003; Mundy et al., 1994; Sigman & Ruskin, 1999). As suggested earlier, IJA reflects spontaneously generated social attention coordination behaviors, whereas gaze following, or RJA, involves the perception of, and response to, the social cues of another person. Compared with RJA, IJA may therefore be more affected by executive and social-motivation processes involved in the generation and self-initiation of behavioral goals (Mundy, 1995; Mundy et al., 2000). In particular, IJA deficits in autism appear to reflect impairment in the tendency to spontaneously initiate episodes of shared affective experience of an object or event with a social partner. In contrast, this process does not appear to be involved to a great extent in RJA (Kasari et al., 1990). Indeed, an impaired capacity to "spontaneously share experience with others" is now considered to be a cardinal symptom of autism (American Psychiatric Association, 2000).

The literature on joint attention disturbances in autism has numerous implications. First, examining the neural substrates of an early emerging cardinal symptom such as joint attention impairment may be essential to understanding the neurodevelopmental etiology of this disorder. Second, if IJA and RJA are each associated with a different course of impairment in autism, it is possible that these two forms of joint attention reflect different constellations of neurological processes.

Caplan and colleagues (1993) provided what may have been the first data on this issue. They studied the behavioral outcome of 13 infants who underwent hemispherectomies in an attempt to treat their intractable seizure disorders. The ESCS was used to assess the postsurgical development of joint attention and related behaviors among these children. Positron emission tomography (PET) data were gathered prior to surgical intervention. These data indicated that metabolic activity in the dorsal frontal cortex, especially the left frontal cortex, predicted the development of IJA skill in this sample. However, the capacity of these children to respond to the joint attention bids or to initiate requesting bids was not observed to relate to any of the PET indexes of cortical activity. Moreover, metabolic activity recorded from other brain regions (e.g., ventral-orbitofrontal, temporal, parietal, or occipital cortices) was not significantly associated with joint attention or other social communication skills in this study. Thus, dorsal frontal activity appeared to be specifically related to the development of the tendency to spontaneously initiate social attention coordination with others to share experience.

A post hoc explanation of this frontal connection to IJA was offered in a later paper (Mundy, 1995). By about 10 months of age, a frontal and left lateralized system emerges that plays a role in the executive and emotional processes associated with approach tendencies involved in positive social affiliative behaviors (Fox, 1991). Mundy (1995) suggested that IJA impairment in autism may reflect a disturbance in the emergence of this left-frontal "social approach" system. Based on earlier work (Panksepp, 1979), the specific hypothesis was that pathology in autism involved the early onset of a disturbance in frontally mediated sensitivity to the reward value of social stimuli. This insensitivity hypothetically creates an affective social-motivation imbalance that results in a robust decrease in the tendency to direct attention to social stimuli. This, in turn, leads to a dramatic reduction in the tendency of infants with autism to initiate joint attention bids and a related reduction in social information input to the child that results in a marginalization of subsequent social-cognitive and social behavior development (Dawson et al., 1998; Mundy, 1995; Mundy & Neal, 2001).

To begin to test aspects of this model, a study conducted at the laboratory of Nathan Fox at the University of Maryland (Mundy et al., 2000) examined the hypothesis that electroencephalographic (EEG) activity in a left-lateralized, frontal-cortical system would be a significant correlate of IJA development in typical infants. Baseline EEG and ESCS joint attention data were collected on 32 infants at 14 to 18 months of age. The results indicated that individual differences in 18-month IJA were predicted by a complex pattern of 14-month EEG activity in the 4-to-6-Hz frequency band that included indices of left medial-frontal EEG activation, as well as indices of right central deactivation, left occipital activation, and right occipital deactivation. Although the location of the generators of the EEG data could not be definitively determined in this study, the frontal correlates of IJA reflected activity from the left frontal electrode (F3) of the 10/20 placement system (Jasper, 1958). This electrode was positioned above a point of confluence of Brodmann's areas (BA) 8 and 9 of the medial-frontal cortex of left hemisphere (Martin, 1996), which includes aspects of the frontal eye fields and supplementary motor cortex that are commonly observed to be involved in attention control (Posner & Petersen, 1990). Moreover, theory on the development of attention (Posner & Petersen, 1990) suggested that, in addition to medial-frontal cortical activity, the signal from frontal electrodes may also reflect activity in the anterior cingulate (Brodmann's area 24), a subcortical structure contiguous with the ventral surface of Brodmann's cortical areas 8/9 (Martin, 1996). In contrast, neither RJA nor IBR measures were associated with a similar pattern of EEG activity (Mundy et al., 2000). RJA at 18 months, however, was predicted by EEG indices of left parietal activation and right parietal deactivation at 14 months.

These data suggested that at least two neural systems, a temporal and parietal system for RJA and a dorsal-medial cortical system for IJA, may be involved in joint attention development. Other research provides support for this dual-process model and has provided details about the nature of the processes involved in these two systems (see Mundy, 2003; Vaughan & Mundy, in press, for recent reviews). Here we will briefly consider the relevant research, beginning with information on the connections between RJA-related behaviors and parietal and temporal brain systems.

RJA and Parietal-Temporal Processes

Wicker, Michel, Henaff, and Decety (1998) observed that neural centers in the posterior superior temporal sulcus (STS) were activated in response to faces with direct or horizontally averted eye gaze but not to faces with downward eye gaze. However, Wicker et al. (1998) did not observe differences between direct and averted eye gaze conditions. Alternatively, Puce, Allison, Bentin, Gore, and McCarthy (1998) reported that videos of face stimuli with gaze moving horizontally from forward to averted gaze elicited greater posterior STS activation than did faces with static forward gaze. Face matching on the basis of direction of gaze also elicited activation of neurons in the left posterior STS, while identity-based face matching elicited bilateral activation from the fusiform and inferior occipital gyri (Hoffman & Haxby, 2000). Similarly, George, Driver, and Dolan (2001) reported that direct gaze stimuli elicited more activation in the fusiform gyrus than averted gaze stimuli. Kingstone, Friesen, and Gazzaniga (2000) have also reported data on gaze following in two split-brain patients that were consistent with the notion that parietal as well as temporal subsystems specialized for face processing and processing of information relevant to spatial orientation, combine to support the development of gaze following. Finally, Hooker (2002) used whole-brain fMRI to compare neural activity in response to (a) horizontal eye movement stimuli that provided directional information about where a visual stimulus would appear, or (b) arrow stimuli that provided equivalent directional information, or (c) eye movements that did not provide directional information. Hooker (2002) observed more activity in the STS in the first condition than in either of the other conditions. Hooker (2002) also reported more activity in the fusiform gyrus and prefrontal cortex in the eye-motion control condition (condition c) than in the other conditions. These data were consistent with the notion that the STS may develop a specialization for processing gaze-related, social-spatial orientation information.

The results of these human imaging studies are consistent with earlier reports from comparative research that provide experimental evidence of temporal (i.e., STS) and parietal involvement in gaze following (Emery, 2000). In two studies, presurgical monkeys demonstrated a clear ability to discriminate face stimuli on the basis of direction of gaze (Campbell, Heywood, Cowey, Regard, & Landis, 1990; Heywood & Cowey, 1992). After resection of the STS, however, the gaze discrimination abilities of the monkeys fell to chance levels. Eacott, Heywood, Gross, and Cowey (1993) compared two groups of monkeys (with and without STS lesions) on a task requiring discriminating between pairs of eyes directed straight ahead or averted 5 or more degrees. The results indicated that the nonlesioned monkeys were capable of discriminating targets involving horizontal eye gaze shifts of greater than 5 degrees, but the STS lesion animals were not.

Few studies have reported a significant connection between RJA or gaze following and activity in the frontal cortices. In this regard, Calder et al. (2002) suggested that task difficulty needs to be considered: Most studies have examined passive gaze following on tasks that did not require the perception or inference of intentions on the basis of eye gaze. These authors suggested that more complex presentations of sequences of gaze stimuli may elicit inferential social-cognitive processing, and evidence of more dorsal contributions to the neural substrate of gaze following. To this end, Calder et al. (2002) used PET to examine the neural responses of 9 female volunteers to a relatively complex sequence of faces with gaze averted left or right, direct gaze, and gaze-down orientations. Hypothetically, this procedure elicited interpretation of the nature of meaning of the gaze direction (i.e., the intentionality of gaze direction). In this paradigm, evidence of activation in the dorsal-medial frontal cortex (DMFC; BA 8/9), the anterior cingulate (AC; BA 32), and the STS was observed in response to horizontal gaze aversion. Unlike most other studies, this study employed a sample of women rather than men. Therefore, it is unclear whether an as yet unrecognized gender effect may have also played a role in these observations.

Another line of connection to the STS-parietal systems has been provided by Meltzoff and Decety (2003). These authors reviewed research indicating that imitation is associated with neural activity in the STS and parietal lobes, as well as the dorsal cortical supplementary motor areas (BA 8/9). In particular, they note that the abundance of mirror neurons in STS and parietal lobes may potentiate the role of these cortical regions in the mediation of imitation. Mirror neurons are a specific class of motor neurons that are active both when a particular action is performed by an individual and when an individual observes the same action performed by another person (Gallese & Goldman, 1998). Thus, the proposed location of the neural substrates of imitation overlaps with the systems that are thought to mediate the development of gaze following and RJA. From a task-analytic point of view, this makes a great deal of sense. Gaze following and RJA basically involve copying the eye movements and/or head turns of a social partner. Alternatively, IJA behaviors do not appear to involve a discernible social copying component. Indeed, RJA development has been observed to display a significant path of association with imitation development in a longitudinal study of typically developing infants (Pomares et al., 2003). However, there were no observations of significant associations between the development of IJA and imitation. Thus, it may be useful in future research to better under-stand the degree to which gaze following/RJA and imitation reflect common and unique biobehavioral processes in early development. Indeed, the importance of this issue has long been recognized in research on autism because this syn-drome involves deficits in imitation as well as joint attention skill development (e.g., Rogers & Pennington, 1991).

IJA and Frontal Processes

The study of the initiation of behaviors, although critical for understanding the development of typical and atypical social engagement, is more difficult than the study of responsive, perceptual behaviors such as RJA. Consequently, fewer imaging studies have been conducted on IJA or its analogues. Nevertheless, a recent EEG study conducted by Henderson et al. (2002) has extended, as well as replicated, the observations of Mundy et al. (2000).

Henderson et al. (2002) employed the ESCS in a study of the degree to which baseline EEG at 14 months of age predicted 18-month joint attention develop-ment in a sample of 27 typically developing infants. To improve the spatial reso-lution of their data, they used a high-density array of 64 electrodes. Moreover, since the total ESCS scores for measures of IJA and other domains used in Mundy et al. (2000) were composites of several behaviors, they reasoned that the exact nature of the associations with EEG activity were unclear. Therefore, Henderson et al. (2002) compared the EEG correlates of only two types of behaviors: self-initiated pointing to share attention with respect to an active mechanical toy (IJA pointing), and self-initiated pointing to elicit aid in obtaining an out-of-reach object (IBR pointing). In the ESCS, the former involves pointing to a toy that is within easy reach, and the latter involves pointing to a toy that is out of reach.

Henderson et al. (2002) found no significant correlations between any of the 14-month EEG data and IBR pointing at 18 months. However, in the 3- to 6-Hz band, a 14-month EEG signal indicative of greater brain activity over the medial-frontal cortex was strongly associated with more IJA pointing at 18 months. These correlations involved electrodes that were placed above cortical regions corresponding to Brodmann's areas 8, 9, and 6. Henderson et al. (2002) also analyzed data from the 6- to 9-Hz band, which revealed 15 significant cor-relations between EEG power in this band at 14 months and IJA pointing at 18 months of age. Again, higher bilateral activities corresponding to the previously identified medial-frontal sites were strong predictors of IJA pointing at 18 months. In addition, IJA pointing at 18 months was also predicted by activity from the orbitofrontal, temporal, and dorsolateral frontal cortical regions. Thus, this study suggested that IJA development may reflect an integration of dorsal cortical func-tions (Mundy et al., 2000) with ventral "social brain" and dorsolateral functions identified in other studies (Dawson et al., 2002; Griffith, Pennington, Wehner,

& Rogers, 1999). However, there was little evidence for parietal involvement in IJA.

The study of Henderson et al. (2002) also provided information about the social specificity of the link between IJA and dorsal cortical brain activity. As noted previously, the specific medial-frontal cortical areas involved in IJA as suggested by data from Mundy et al. (2000) and Henderson et al. (2002) correspond to aspects of both the frontal eye fields and supplementary motor cortex associated with the control of saccadic eye movement and motor planning (Martin, 1996). Therefore, these associations could simply reflect the motor control of the eye movements and/or gestural behaviors that are intrinsic to joint attention behaviors. However, the simple elegance of the Henderson et al. (2002) study controls for this possible interpretation. The gross motor topography of IJA pointing and IBR pointing are virtually identical on the ESCS. Therefore, a neuromotor explanation of the different cortical correlates of IJA and IBR appears unlikely. Instead, since IJA pointing and IBR pointing appear to serve different social communicative functions, it is reasonable to assume that the difference in EEG correlates of these infant behaviors also reflects differences in the neurodevelopmental substrates of these social communicative functions.

The data from Henderson et al. (2002) suggest that IJA behaviors reflect a complex system of brain activity that includes not only the dorsal-medial cortex but also activity associated with dorsolateral cortex and ventral orbitofrontal cortex. Several neuropsychological studies have provided data consistent with this more complex systems view of IJA. Two studies have observed that IJA and RJA in young children are associated with performance on a spatial reversal task that involves dorsolateral mediation of response inhibition, planning, and memory (Griffith et al., 1999; McEvoy, Rogers, & Pennington, 1993). Thus, a contribution from dorsolateral frontal cortex may not be specific to IJA, but a general frontal component of both RJA and IJA.

Another important neuropsychological insight was provided by Dawson et al. (2002), who found that joint attention ability in autistic children appears to be significantly correlated with neuropsychological measures associated with an orbitofrontal brain system, rather than a dorsolateral frontal system. This study was based on the hypothesis that IJA disturbances in autism involve an impairment of the reward sensitivity that is mediated by an orbitofrontal and temporal circuit (Dawson et al., 2002; Mundy, 1995). To assess this dimension, the authors presented children with a delayed non-match-to-sample (DNMS) task. This task measures children's sensitivity to reinforcement and has previously been associated with orbitofrontal cortex activity in comparative research. Dawson et al. (2002) also used an A-not-B reversal task previously associated with dorsolateral activation. The results indicated that joint attention in both children with autism and typical controls was associated with performance on the DNMS task but not with performance on the A-not-B task.

Thus, consistent with findings from Henderson et al. (2002), this study provided evidence of a more ventral frontal contribution to joint attention. However, Dawson et al. (2002) used a composite measure of IJA and RJA in their study, and therefore it was difficult to determine if this more ventral component was associated specifically with IJA.

This issue has been addressed in a recent study (Nichols, Fox, & Mundy, 2005). The authors examined the relations of DNMS task performance with measures of IJA and RJA in the 14-to-18-month period in 39 typically developing infants. Because previous research had implicated the dorsal-medial cortex with IJA, the authors also included a behavioral task that hypothetically may be related to activity in this brain system. The dorsal-medial cortex appears to play a fundamental role in self-monitoring and self-awareness (Bush, Luu, & Posner, 2000; Craik et al., 1999; Frith & Frith, 1999, 2001; Johnson et al., 2002; Stuphorn, Taylor, & Schall, 2000). For example, recent research indicates that the DMFC plays a role in encoding and recalling words and actions that involve self-referential awareness, but not necessarily those that do not involve self-reference (Craik et al., 1999; Johnson et al., 2002). Therefore, Nichols et al. (2005) used a measure of infant self-recognition as a means for accessing this domain of behavior. They hypothesized that if the data from Henderson et al. (2002) were correct, then it was likely that variance in both an orbitofrontal-related behavior (DNMS) and a putative dorsal-medial related behavior (self-recognition) would make unique contributions to the explanation of variance in IJA development.

Consistent with these hypotheses, both a composite of the DNMS and the self-recognition tasks (combined from the 14-, 16-, and 18-month data) made significant contributions to a multiple regression for 18-month IJA. However, these measures did not contribute to the explanation of 18-month RJA data. Hence, similar to the findings of Henderson et al. (2002), these data suggest that both orbitofrontal and dorsal-medial frontal systems make a contribution to IJA development. The integrated functioning of these two brain systems may be critical not only for IJA development but also for later-developing aspects of social engagement and social competence.

On the Nature of Dorsal-Medial Cortical Functions

The anterior attention system involves the DMFC (BA 8/9) and the anterior cingulate (BA 24). This anterior network may become functional after the posterior parietal system and is thought to make numerous contributions to the planning, self-initiation, and self-monitoring of goal-directed behaviors, including visual orienting (Rothbart et al., 1994). Of particular importance here is the contribution of the anterior attention system to the capacity to share attention across dual tasks or foci of attention (Birrell & Brown, 2000; Rushworth, Hadland, Paus, & Siplia,

2002; Stuss, Shallice, Alexander, & Picton, 1995). This capacity may play a role in infants' ability to maintain representations of self, a social partner, and an interesting object, while flexibly switching attention between these foci in IJA behaviors (Mundy et al., 2000). This attention-switching facility of the anterior system plays a critical role through its contribution to the supervisory attention system (SAS; Norman & Shallice, 1986), which functions to guide behavior, especially attention deployment, depending on the motivational context of the task (e.g., Amador, Schlag-Rey, & Schlag, 2000; Bush et al., 2000).

Ultimately, the anterior attention system comes to participate in monitoring and representing the self, and directs attention to internal and external events (Faw, 2003). Relatedly, two research groups have reported that self-referenced memory processes preferentially activate the dorsal-medial frontal cortical component of this anterior system (Craik et al., 1999; Johnson et al., 2002). Another important set of observations about self-monitoring indicates that when people make an erroneous response in an attention deployment task, there is a negative deflection in the response-locked ERP, called the error-related negativity (ERN; Luu, Flaisch, & Tucker, 2000; Bush et al., 2000). Source location suggests that the ERN emanates from an area of the DMFC proximal to the anterior cingulate (AC) cortex (Luu et al., 2000). Observations of the ERN suggest that there are specific cell groups within the DMFC/AC that not only are active in initiating a behavioral act, such as orienting to a stimulus, but also are involved in processing the positive or negative outcome of the response behavior (i.e., accuracy and reward or reinforcement information; see, e.g., Amador et al., 2000; Holroyd & Coles, 2002). Thus, like the orbitofrontal cortex, the DMFC appears to play a role in the appraisal of the valence of stimuli, in the generation or modulation of emotional responses to stimuli, and in mediating the subjective experience of emotion and reward in social behavior (e.g., Hornak et al., 2003; Lane, Fink, Chua, & Dolan, 1997; Ochsner, Bunge, Gross, & Gabireli, 2002; Teasdale et al., 1999). Indeed, specific lesions of the orbitofrontal cortex or DMFC (BA 9 and AC) appear to be associated with deficits in voice and face expression recognition, social behavior, and appraisal of subjective emotional states (Hornak et al., 2003).

Finally, with respect to directing attention to external and internal events, Frith and Frith (1999, 2001) have argued that the DMFC/AC integrates proprioceptive information of the self (e.g., emotions or intentions) with exteroceptive perceptions processed by the STS about the goal-directed behaviors and emotions of others. This integrative activity may be facilitated by the abundance of connections between the DMFC/AC and the STS (Morecraft, Guela, & Mesulam, 1993). Indeed, cell groups in and around BA 8/9 may be especially well connected to the STS (Ban, Shiwa, & Kawamura, 1991). We have described this putative facility for the integration of proprioceptive self-information with exteroceptive social perceptions as a social executive function (SEF) of the DMFC and AC system (Mundy, 2003). Hypothetically, this SEF utilizes the DMFC/AC facility to split attention among multiple representations in working memory to compare and integrate the actions of self and others. This integration gives rise to the capacity to infer the intentions of others by matching them with representations of self-initiated actions or intentions (Stich & Nichols, 1992), and recent research by Lau and colleagues (2004) indicates that the representation of self-intentions occurs within areas of the DMFC that include the supplementary motor cortex. Once this integration begins to occur in the DMFC/AC, a fully functional, adaptive human social-cognitive system emerges with experience (Frith & Frith, 1999, 2001).

This last line of theory suggests that functions of the dorsal-medial cortex may be expected to be related to social-cognitive abilities. Indeed, functional imaging studies indicate that dorsal-medial frontal cortical activity is the most consistent correlate of performance on ToM tasks in adults. Fletcher et al. (1995) used PET to examine the cortical metabolic activity associated with performance either on ToM problem-solving stories or "physical" nonsocial problem-solving stories. Performance of six typical adult men on the ToM stories was associated with increased blood flow in an area of the left medial-frontal gyrus corresponding to Brodmann's area 8. However, this was not the case for the physical stories. Goel, Grafman, Sadato, and Hallett (1995) reported a study that also used PET to examine the neural correlates of social-cognitive task performance in typical adults. They observed that only tasks involving inferences about other people's minds activated a neural network in the left dorsal-medial frontal lobe, including part of the left medial-frontal gyrus. These authors concluded that when inferential reasoning depends on constructing a mental model about the beliefs and intentions of others, the participation of the DMFC is required. Of course, even with the control conditions used in these studies, the possibility remains that the observed associations of the DMFC with ToM task performance were affected in some fashion by non-social-cognitive processes. This issue of specificity is far from resolved. Nevertheless, at least one study suggests that while general inferential reasoning processes also seem to involve frontal activation, this activation appeared to be centered on more dorsolateral areas of the frontal cortex (Brodmann's area 46), rather than the more dorsal-medial areas 8/9 associated with social cognition (Goel, Gold, Kapur, & Houle, 1997).

Another important issue is that since imaging studies of ToM often use stories or verbal stimuli, language-related processes may affect the functional localization of ToM skills. Several studies have addressed this possibility. Gallagher et al. (2000) used functional magnetic resonance imaging (fMRI) to examine brain metabolic activity in response to both verbal ToM stories and nonverbal ToM tasks that involved the processing of visually presented cartoons. They observed considerable overlap in the bilateral brain activation associated with both tasks, specifically in the paracingulate area of the DMFC. The paracingulate area refers to a subcortical frontal structure that forms the ventral border between the DMFC and the AC cortex of the limbic system. Brunet, Sarfati, Hardy-Bayle, and Decety (2000) used PET to examine processing of comic strips depicting stories involving either the attribution of intention to characters or understanding physical causal sequences with characters. The comparison of these conditions suggests that the former involved increases in regional cerebral blood flow in the right DMFC (BA 9) and bilateral anterior-cingulate, as well as the areas of the right inferior-frontal cortex, right cerebellum, and right and left temporal cortices. Several researchers have also utilized another nonverbal ToM paradigm that capitalizes on the tendency of people to anthropomorphize and to perceive animate and intentional behavior in cleverly organized movement sequences of geometric forms (Castelli, Happe, Frith, & Frith, 2000; Klin, 2000; Schultz, Romanski, & Tsatsanis, 2000). Klin (2000) has coined the term *social attribution task* (SAT) for this type of paradigm. Castelli et al. (2000) observed that task performance of six healthy adults on an SAT task was associated with PET indices of activation in the medial-frontal cortex (BA 9), the superior and ventral temporal regions, and the occipital cortex. Similarly, Schultz et al. (2000) have reported that processing on an SAT task recruited bilateral activation of the DMFC (BA 9) in their typical sample.

An important control condition was also included in a study by Sabbagh and Taylor (2000). Recording event-related potentials (ERP) using a dense EEG electrode array (128 sites), they presented university students with a paradigm that compared false-belief theory of mind task performance with an analogous nonsocial task. Just as a false-belief task involves thinking about the belief held within someone's mind, this analogous nonsocial task involved thinking about the pictures held within a camera (see Leslie & Thaiss, 1992). Sabbagh and Taylor (2000) observed significantly larger ERPs from the left dorsolateral and dorso-medial cortex in the ToM false-belief task (e.g., electrode sites approximately above BA 9/10/46) compared with the false-image task.

Longitudinal Studies

The previous section provided an overview of the theoretical rationale for the links between research on infant joint attention development and the study of social engagement and social competence. This theory raises a critical hypothesis: If joint attention reflects important aspects of the development of social engagement, there should be evidence of continuity between joint attention and the subsequent development of social competence in childhood. Data relevant to this hypothesis have recently been provided in studies of children with autism, children at risk for poor developmental outcomes, and children with typical development. For example, Sigman and Ruskin (1999) followed a sample of 51 children with autism for 6 to 8 years. At the beginning of this study, the children were 3 to 6 years old. They were assessed with the ESCS, as well as other social-emotional measures such as an index of empathy. Standardized cognitive and language data were also collected at the inception of the study. A variety of outcome data were collected, including measures of the frequency of initiations of play by the children with autism with peers as an index of individual differences in social engagement. An important observation in this study was that IJA behavior in the children with autism (as well as in a control sample) was a significant predictor of individual differences in social engagement 6 to 8 years later, even after considering covariance with language and cognitive development. RJA behavior, on the other hand, was related to language but not to social outcomes in these children. In a related study, Travis, Sigman, and Ruskin (2001) have also observed that measures of both IJA and empathy make significant concurrent contributions to the explanation of variance in the level of peer engagement and prosocial behavior in a structured task among higher-functioning 8- to 15-year-old children with autism.

Similar longitudinal observations have recently been reported by Cathy Lord and her colleagues (2003). These authors followed 95 children with autism from 2 to 9 years of age. At the outset of this study, the intellectual and language level of the children was assessed. Their social status was assessed with parent report on the Autism Diagnostic Interview (ADI) and with direct observations on the Autism Diagnostic Observation Schedule (ADOS). In addition to composite social, communication, and repetitive behavior symptom domain scores, the ADI and the ADOS provide measures of IJA and RJA. The IJA and RJA measures obtained from the ADOS are very similar to those derived from the ESCS. At outcome, social engagement was assessed with observations on the Penn Interactive Peer Play Scale (PIPPS; Fantuzzo et al., 1995). The PIPPS yields three factors: a prosocial Interaction measure, an avoidant Disconnection measure, and an externalizing Disruption measure that are combined into a total social engagement score. ADI and ADOS domain scores did not predict social interaction outcome. However, ADOS IJA scores predicted PIPPS total social engagement scores above and beyond variance associated with verbal IQ. Thus, at least two studies have indicated that IJA is a significant predictor of individual differences in the long-term social outcomes of children with autism (Lord et al., 2003; Sigman & Ruskin, 1999). Furthermore, other studies suggest that the basic phenomenon observed is a general developmental finding rather than one that is limited to children with this syndrome.

Sheinkopf et al. (2004) report data from a longitudinal study of 30 infants with in utero cocaine exposure. In this study, joint attention skills (i.e., IJA, RJA, and IBR) were assessed with the ESCS at 12, 15, and 18 months of age, and composite (average) measures of these domains were computed. Since these children were participants in a preschool intervention program at the Linda Ray Intervention Center (LRIC), it was possible to gather data on social outcomes from preschool teacher reports of peer-related classroom behavior at 36 months of age. These reports were gathered using the Adaptive Social Behavior Inventory (ASBI; Hogan, Scott, & Bauer, 1992), the PIPPS (Fantuzzo et al., 1995), and selected subscales from the Child Behavior Checklist (CBCL; Achenbach,

1992). Three aggregate scores were derived from teacher reports on these measures to provide measures of adaptive and problem behaviors: (a) A Disruptive Behavior score was derived by standardizing and calculating the mean of CBCL Aggression, ASBI Disrupt, and PIPPS Disruption scales; (b) a Withdrawn Behavior score was derived by standardizing and calculating the mean of CBCL Anxiety, CBCL Withdrawn, and PIPPS Disconnection; and (c) a Positive Social Behavior score was derived by standardizing and calculating the mean of ASBI Comply, ASBI Express, and PIPPS Interaction.

The results indicated that IJA, RJA, and IBR all made significant contributions to the prediction of Disruptive Behavior, with IJA and RJA negatively associated with teacher reports of more disruptive behavior, and IBR positively related to this dimension (Sheinkopf et al., 2004). The results also indicated that RJA was negatively associated with teacher reports of Withdrawn Behavior but positively associated with Positive Social Behavior. Thus, processes associated with IJA (e.g., self-monitoring, social motivation) appeared to be associated with decreased risk for externalizing disturbance in this sample. Processes associated with RJA (e.g., social information processing, attention regulation) were also associated with decreased risk for externalizing and internalizing disturbances and an increased likelihood of displaying what preschool teachers regarded as prosocial behaviors. Alternatively, it may have been that higher rates of IBR reflect an impulsive and object reward-driven style of behavior in this sample of young children at risk for externalizing disturbance. Finally, it is also important to note that variance associated with cognition and language did not appear to mediate the associations between joint attention measures and social behavior outcomes in this study (Sheinkopf et al., 2004).

The study reported by Sheinkopf et al. (2004) is especially important because it is among the first to document continuity between the development of joint attention and childhood social development in groups of children other than those affected by autism. However, it was not clear if follow-up to 36 months was adequate to capture stable differences in the social development of "at-risk" children. Therefore, researchers have continued to follow this sample of children, and preliminary results from this longer-term longitudinal data set have been reported (Acra et al., 2003). This research team followed 42 children who graduated from the LRIC at age 36 months. Follow-up was conducted when the children were 6 to 7 years old. At that time, cognitive and language outcomes were measured with the Differential Abilities Scales (DAS; Elliott, 1990) and the Woodcock Language Proficiency Battery-Revised (WLPB-R; Woodcock, 1991). Social outcomes were examined with both teacher and parent report on the Social Skills Rating Scales (SSRS; Gresham & Elliott, 1990) and the Behavior Assessment System for Children (BASC; Reynolds & Kamphaus, 1992). The results indicated that joint attention measures were correlated with social outcomes on both parent and teacher report data. Therefore, parent and teacher report data were reduced to composite measures. In particular, theory relating to joint attention development suggested a focus on two dimensions of behavior: prosocial behavior or social competence, and a measure of attention dysregulation/externalizing behavior. Hence, parent and teacher reports were reduced to composites for Social Competence (parent and teacher SSRS Social Skills summary scores, BASC Adaptability summary scores, and BASC Social Skills summary scores) and Hyperactivity and Attention Problems (parent and teacher SSRS Hyperactivity scores, BASC Hyperactivity scores, and BASC Attention Problems scores).

Consistent with data reported by Sheinkopf et al. (2004), 18-month IJA measures were positively related to first-grade Social Competence but negatively associated with Hyperactivity and Attention Problems. However, unlike the data from Sheinkopf et al. (2004), RJA was significantly associated with language development but not with social development. Moreover, IBR displayed the same pattern of correlations as IJA, that is, a significant positive association with Social Competence and a significant negative association with Hyperactivity and Attention Problems. Not surprisingly, cognition, language, and especially reading ability were also significantly correlated with Social Competence and with Hyperactivity and Attention Problems. Multiple regression analyses revealed that 18-month IJA, but not IBR, made a significant contribution to both first-grade Social Competence and Hyperactivity and Attention problems, when variance associated with this aspect of development (e.g., reading ability) was accounted for. Thus, across these two studies (Acra et al., 2003; Sheinkopf et al., 2004), the most consistent finding was that IJA displayed a significant and long-term association with social behavior outcomes in a high-risk sample, just as it has in samples of children with autism (Lord et al., 2003; Sigman & Ruskin, 1999).

Many important questions remain to be examined with regard to these findings. One of these concerns whether the associations between infant joint attention and social outcomes in atypical or at-risk samples is a robust developmental phenomenon that may be observed in typically developing children. Data relevant to this issue have been presented in a report by Vaughan et al. (2003a), who followed 41 typically developing infants from 12 to 30 months of age. ESCS data were collected at 12 months of age, and parent report data on dimensions of temperament that are expected to be related to joint attention were collected at 24 months of age (i.e., Inhibitory Control, Pleasure Reactivity, Social Approach, Attention Shifting, and Attention Focusing), along with standardized cognitive and language assessments. Finally, at 30 months, social outcomes were assessed with parent report data on the Infant-Toddler Social Emotional Assessment (ITSEA; Carter & Briggs-Gowan, 2000), which provides scaled scores for Externalizing Behavior, Social Competence, Internalizing Behavior, and Dysregulation.

The results of this study indicated that 12-month IJA was negatively related to Externalizing behavior at 30 months of age. Twelve-month RJA was also negatively related to parental reports of Externalizing Behavior at 30 months, as was parent report of Inhibitory Control at 15 months. Other variables reflecting cognition, language, or gender did not mediate these results. Moreover, when combined in a multiple regression, 12-month IJA and RJA as well as 15-month reports of Inhibitory Control all made significant contributions to parental reports of Externalizing Behaviors at 30 months.

Summary

How do we measure social engagement and social competence in infancy? Data from recent longitudinal studies suggest that infant joint attention reflects an important component of this critical dimension of development. Five studies involving four independent samples have indicated that infants' tendencies to initiate joint attention bids predict aspects of social engagement and social competence in childhood. This observed continuity between infancy and childhood extends across intervals from 18 months to 3 to 10 years. Moreover, observations suggest that more frequent IJA bids in infancy may be a useful marker of relative vulnerability to poor social outcomes in at-risk children. With regard to the latter, observations suggest that IJA measures may help to identify children at risk for hyperactivity and attention problems (Acra et al., 2003) or children who may be more resistant to the negative effects of moderate attachment disturbances (Crowson, 2001). Of course, these findings require replication before the clinical implications of infant joint attention assessment can be fully evaluated. Nevertheless, it currently appears to be the case that measures of joint attention may present unique data about processes related to developmental continuity, risk, and resilience in social outcomes for a wide range of children.

Although recent, these findings are not unexpected given our understanding of the nature of joint attention development. An enhanced capacity to attend to what others attend to, and to share experiences and information with others, is a defining functional characteristic of human social development. This capacity serves a major organizational function around which social-cognitive, self-regulatory, and social-emotional systems are organized in early biobehavioral development (Mundy, 1995). It is clear that this capacity may be augmented or attenuated across development, depending, for example, on the caregiving environment to which children are exposed (Claussen et al., 2002; Kroupina et al., 2003). It is also clear that if biological systems go awry, this can severely impact the development of joint attention, as has been illustrated by the repeated observation that early disturbance of joint attention development is a hallmark of autism (Mundy & Neal, 2001). This observation has contributed to the impetus for research on the neural substrates of typical and atypical joint attention development, which raises new and important hypotheses. One of these hypotheses is that different neural systems play a greater or lesser role in the development of different types of joint attention skills (Mundy et al., 2000). In particular, RJA may be mediated by STS and parietal systems that serve to prioritize processing of the spatial orientation of gaze and related postural spatial information (see Vaughan & Mundy, in press). Alternatively, IJA may be mediated by a combination of orbitofrontal and dorsal frontal systems that prioritize a complex system of processes, including the capacities to associate reward with goal-directed social behavior, to shift attention across multiple foci, and to relate proprioceptive self-monitored information with exteroceptive monitoring of the behaviors of others (Dawson et al., 2002; Mundy, 1995, 2003). A third hypothesis is that engagement in joint attention contributes to processes involved in learning about the common psychological processes of self and others (Mundy & Neal, 2001). Hence, joint attention development both reflects and contributes to the early developmental processes that are critical for social engagement and social competence.

Acknowledgments   The preparation of this chapter was supported by NIH grant HD38052 (P. Mundy, P.I.).

References

Achenbach, T. M. (1992). *Child Behavior Checklist, 2-3 Manual*. Burlington, VT: University Medical Education Associates.

Acra, C. F., Mundy, P., Claussen, A., Scott, K., & Bono, K. (2003, April). *Infant joint attention and social outcomes in 6 to 7 year-old at risk children*. Paper presented at the biennial meeting of the Society for Research in Child Development, Tampa, FL.

Adamson, L. B., & Bakeman, R. (1985). Affect and attention: Infants observed with mothers and peers. *Child Development, 56*, 582–593.

Amador, N., Schlag-Rey, M., & Schlag, J. (2000). Reward predicting and reward detecting neuronal activity in the primate supplementary eye field. *Journal of Neurophysiology, 84*, 2166–2170.

American Psychiatric Association. (2000). *Diagnostic and statistical manual of mental disorders* (4th ed., text revision). Washington, DC: author.

Bakeman, R., & Adamson, L. (1984). Coordinating attention to people and objects in mother-infant and peer-infant interaction. *Child Development, 55*, 1278–1289.

Baldwin, D. A. (1995). Understanding the link between joint attention and language. In C. Moore & P. J. Dunham (Eds.), *Joint attention: Its origins and role in development* (pp. 131–158). Hillsdale, NJ: Erlbaum.

Ban, T., Shiwa, T., & Kawamura, K. (1991). Cortico-cortical projections from the prefrontal cortex to the superior temporal sulcal area (STS) in the monkey studied by means of HRP method. *Archives of Italian Biology, 129*, 259–272.

Bard, K., Platzman, K., Lester, B., & Suomi, S. (1992). Orientation to social and nonsocial stimuli in neonatal chimpanzees and humans. *Infant Behavior and Development, 15*, 43–56.

Baron-Cohen, S. (1989). Perceptual role taking and protodeclarative pointing in autism. *British Journal of Developmental Psychology, 7*, 113–127.

Baron-Cohen, S. (1995). *Mindblindness*. Cambridge, MA: MIT Press.

Bates, E. (1976). *Language and context: The acquisition of pragmatics*. New York: Academic Press.

Bates, E., Benigni, L., Bretherton, I., Camaioni, L., & Volterra, V. (1979). *The emergence of symbols: Cognition and communication in infancy*. New York: Academic Press.

Birrell, J., & Brown, V. (2000). Medial-frontal cortex mediates perceptual attention set shifting in the rat. *Journal of Neuroscience, 20*, 4320–4324.

Blair, C. (2002). School readiness: Integrating cognition and emotion in a neurobiological conceptualization of children's functioning at school entry. *American Psychologist, 57*, 111–127.

Block, J., Mundy, P., Pomares, Y., Vaughan, A., Delgado, C., & Gomes, Y. (2003, April). *Different developmental profiles of joint attention skills from 9 to 18 months*. Poster session presented at the biennial meeting of the Society for Research in Child Development, Tampa, FL.

Bono, M., Daley, T., & Sigman, M. (2004). Joint attention moderates the relation between intervention and language development in young children with autism. *Journal of Autism and Related Disorders, 34*, 495–505.

Bretherton, I. (1991). Intentional communication and the development of an understanding of mind. In D. Frye & C. Moore (Eds.), *Children's theories of mind: Mental states and social understanding* (pp. 49–75). Hillsdale, NJ: Erlbaum.

Brooks, R., & Meltzoff, A. (2002). The importance of eyes: How infants interpret adult looking behavior. *Developmental Psychology, 38*, 958–966.

Bruner, J. S. (1975). From communication to language: A psychological perspective. *Cognition, 3*, 255–287.

Bruner, J., & Sherwood, V. (1983). Thought, language, and interaction in infancy. In J. Call, E. Galenson, & R. Tyson (Eds.), *Frontiers of infant psychiatry* (pp. 38–55). New York: Basic Books.

Brunet, E., Sarfati, Y., Hardy-Bayle, M. C., & Decety, J. (2000). A PET investigation of the attribution of intentions with a nonverbal task. *NeuroImage, 11*, 157–166.

Bush, G., Luu, P., & Posner, M. (2000). Cognitive and emotional influences in the anterior cingulate cortex. *Trends in Cognitive Science, 4*, 214–222.

Calder, A., Lawrence, A., Keane, J., Scott, S., Owen, A., Christoffels, I., et al. (2002). Reading the mind from eye gaze. *Neuropsychologia, 40*, 1129–1138.

Calkins, S., & Fox, N. (2002). Self-regulatory processes in early personality development: A multilevel approach to the study of childhood social withdrawal and aggression. *Development and Psychopathology, 14*, 477– 498.

Campbell, R., Heywood, C., Cowey, A., Regard, M., & Landis, T. (1990). Sensitivity to eye gaze in prosopagnosic patients and monkeys with superior temporal sulcus ablation. *Neuropsychologia, 28*, 1123–1142.

Caplan, R., Chugani, H., Messa, C., Guthrie, D., Sigman, M., Traversay, J., et al. (1993). Hemispherectomy for early onset intractable seizures: Presurgical cerebral glucose metabolism and postsurgical nonverbal communication patterns. *Developmental Medicine and Child Neurology, 35*, 582–592.

Carpenter, M., Nagell, K., & Tomasello, M. (1998). Social cognition, joint attention, and communicative competence from 9 to 15 months of age. *Monographs of the Society for Research in Child Development, 63*(4, Serial No. 255).

Carter, A., & Briggs-Gowan, M. (2000). *Infant-toddler social and emotional assessment*. New Haven, CT: Yale University, Connecticut Early Development Project.

Case, R. (1987). The structure and process of intellectual development. *International Journal of Psychology, 22*, 571–607.

Castelli, F., Happe, F., Frith, U., & Frith, C. (2000). Movement and mind: A functional imaging study of perception and interpretation of complex intentional movement patterns. *NeuroImage, 12*, 314–325.

Charman, T., Baron-Cohen, S., Swettenham, J., Baird, G., Cox, A., & Drew, A. (2000). Testing joint attention, imitation, and play: Infancy precursors to language and theory of mind. *Cognitive Development, 15*, 481–498.

Charwarska, K., Klin, A., & Volkmar, F. (2003). Automatic attention cuing through eye movement in 2-year-old children with autism. *Child Development, 74*, 1108–1123.

Claussen, A. H., Mundy, P. C., Mallik, S. A., & Willoughby, J. C. (2002). Joint attention and disorganized attachment status in infants at risk. *Development and Psychopathology, 14*, 279–291.

Corkum, V., & Moore, C. (1998). The origins of joint visual attention in infants. *Developmental Psychology, 34*, 28–38.

Craik, F., Moroz, T., Moscovich, M., Stuss, D., Winocur, G., Tulving, E., et al. (1999). In search of the self: A positron emission tomography study. *Psychological Science, 10*, 26–34.

Crowson, M. M. (2001). Attachment quality and infant joint attention skills: Predictors of mother-toddler interactions. *Dissertation Abstracts International: Science and Engineering, 62*, 2515.

Curcio, F. (1978). Sensorimotor functioning and communication in mute autistic children. *Journal of Autism and Childhood Schizophrenia, 8*, 281–292.

Dawson, G., Meltzoff, A., Osterling, J., Rinaldi, J., & Brown, E. (1998). Children with autism fail to orient to naturally-occurring social stimuli. *Journal of Autism and Developmental Disorders, 28*, 479–485.

Dawson, G., Munson, J., Estes, A., Osterling, J., McPartland, J., Toth, K., et al. (2002). Neurocognitive function and joint attention ability in young children with autism spectrum disorder versus developmental delay. *Child Development, 73*, 345–358.

Dawson, G., Osterling, J., Rinaldi, J., Carver, L., & McPartland, J. (2001). Brief report: Recognition memory and stimulus-reward associations: Indirect support for the role of the ventromedial prefrontal dysfunction in autism. *Journal of Autism and Developmental Disorders, 31*, 337–341.

D'Entremont, B., Hains, S., & Muir, D. (1997). A demonstration of gaze following in 3- to 6- month-olds. *Infant Behavior and Development, 20*, 569–572.

Eacott, M. J., Heywood, C. A., Gross, C. G., & Cowey, A. (1993). Visual discrimination impairments following lesions of the superior temporal sulcus are not specific to facial stimuli. *Neuropsychologia, 31*, 609–619.

Eisenberg, N., Guthrie, I., Fabes, R., Reiser, M., Murphy, B. C., Holgren, R., et al. (1997). The relations of regulation and emotionality to resiliency and competent social functioning in elementary school children. *Child Development, 68*, 295–311.

Eisenberger, N., Lieberman, M., & Williams, K. (2003). Does rejection hurt? An fMRI study of social exclusion. *Science, 302*, 290–292.

Elliott, C. D. (1990). *Differential Ability Scales*. San Antonio, TX: Harcourt Brace Educational Measurement.

Emery, N. (2000). The eyes have it: The neuroethology, function, and evolution of social gaze. *Neuroscience and Biobehavioral Reviews, 24*, 581–604.

Fantuzzo, J., Sutton-Smith, B., Coolahan, K. C., Manz, P. H., Canning, S., & Debnam, D. (1995). Assessment of preschool play interaction behaviors in young low-income children: Penn Interactive Peer Play Scale. *Early Childhood Research Quarterly, 10,* 105–120.

Faw, B. (2003). Prefrontal executive committee for perception, working memory, attention, long-term memory, motor control and thinking: A tutorial review. *Consciousness and Cognition, 12,* 83–139.

Filipek, P., Accardo, P., Baranek, G., Cook, E., Dawson, G., Gordon, B., et al. (1999). The screening and diagnosis of autism spectrum disorders. *Journal of Autism and Developmental Disorders, 29,* 439–484.

Fletcher, P., Happe, F., Frith, U., Baker, S., Dolan, R., Frackowiak, R., et al. (1995). Other minds in the brain: A functional imaging study of "theory of mind" in story comprehension. *Cognition, 57,* 109–128.

Flom, R., & Pick, A. (2003). Verbal encouragement and joint attention in 18-month-old infants. *Infant Behavior and Development, 26,* 121–134.

Fombonne, E. (2003). The prevalence of autism. *Journal of the American Medical Association, 289,* 87–79.

Fox, N. (1991). It's not left, it's right: Electroencephalograph asymmetry and the development of emotion. *American Psychologist, 46,* 863–872.

Fox, N., Henderson, H., Rubin, S., Calkins, S., & Schmidt, L. (2001). Continuity and discontinuity of behavioral inhibition and exuberance: Physiological and behavioral influences across the first four years of life. *Child Development, 72,* 1–21.

Frith, C., & Frith, U. (1999). Interacting minds: A biological basis. *Science, 286,* 1692–1695.

Frith, U., & Frith, C. (2001). The biological basis of social interaction. *Current Directions in Psychologic Science, 10,* 151–155.

Gallagher, H., Happe, F., Brunswick, P., Fletcher, P., Frith, U., & Frith, C. (2000). Reading the mind in cartoons and stories: An fMRI study of "theory of mind" in verbal and nonverbal tasks. *Neuropsychologia, 38,* 11–21.

Gallese, V., & Goldman, A. (1998). Mirror neurons and the simulation theory of mind-reading. *Trends in Cognitive Science, 2,* 493–501.

George, N., Driver, J., & Dolan, R. (2001). Seen gaze direction modulates fusiform activity and its coupling with other brain areas during face processing. *Neuroimage, 13,* 1102–1112.

Goel, V., Gold, B., Kapur, S., & Houle, S. (1997). The seats of reason? An imaging study of deductive and inductive reasoning. *Neuroreport, 8,* 1305–1310.

Goel, V., Grafman, J., Sadato, N., & Hallett, M. (1995). Modeling other minds. *Neuroreport, 6,* 1741–1746.

Gresham, F. M., & Elliott, S. N. (1990). *Social Skills Rating System.* Circle Pines, MN: American Guidance Service.

Griffith, E., Pennington, B., Wehner, E., & Rogers, S. (1999). Executive functions in young children with autism. *Child Development, 70,* 817–832.

Henderson, L., Yoder, P., Yale, M., & McDuffie, A. (2002). Getting the point: Electrophysiological correlates of protodeclarative pointing. *International Journal of Developmental Neuroscience, 20,* 449–458.

Heywood, C., & Cowey, A. (1992). The role of the "face cell" area in the discrimination and recognition of faces by monkeys. *Philosophical Transactions of the Royal Society of London, 335,* 31–38.

Hobson, P. (2002). *The cradle of thought: Exploring the origins of thinking.* London: Pan McMillan.

Hoffman, E., & Haxby, J. (2000). Distinct representation of eye gaze and identity in the distributed human neural system for face perception. *Nature Neuroscience, 3,* 80–84.

Hogan, A. E., Scott, K. G., & Bauer, C. R. (1992). The Adaptive Social Behavior Inventory (ASBI): A new assessment of social competence in high-risk three-year-olds. *Journal of Psychoeducational Assessment, 10,* 230–239.

Holroyd, C., & Coles, M. (2002). The neural basis of human error processing: Reinforcement learning, dopamine and the error related negativity. *Psychological Review, 109,* 679–709.

Hood, B., Willen, J., & Driver, J. (1998). Adults' eyes trigger shifts of visual attention in human infants. *Psychological Science, 9,* 131–134.

Hooker, C. (2002). The neurocognitive basis of gaze perception: A model of social signal processing. *Dissertation Abstracts International: Science and Engineering, 63,* 2058.

Hornak, J., Braham, E., Rolls, R., Morris, J., O'Doherty, P., Bullock, P., et al. (2003). Changes in emotion after circumscribed surgical lesions of the orbitofrontal and cingulate cortices. *Brain, 126,* 1691–1712.

Jasper, H. (1958). The 10-20 international electrode system. *EEG and Clinical Neurophysiology, 10,* 371–375.

Johnson, S., Baxter, L., Wilder, L., Pipe, J., Heiserman, J., & Prigatano, G. (2002). Neural correlates of self-reflection. *Brain, 125,* 1808–1814.

Kanner, L. (1943). Autistic disturbances of affective contact. *Nervous Child, 2,* 217–250.

Kasari, C., Sigman, M., Mundy, P., & Yirmiya, N. (1990). Affective sharing in the context of joint attention interactions of normal, autistic, and mentally retarded children. *Journal of Autism and Developmental Disorders, 20,* 87–100.

Kingstone, A., Friesen, C-K., & Gazzaniga, M. (2000). Reflexive joint attention depends on lateralized cortical functions. *Psychological Science, 11,* 159–166.

Klin, A. (2000). Attributing meaning to ambiguous visual stimuli in higher functioning autism and Asperger syndrome: The Social Attribution Task. *Journal of Child Psychology and Psychiatry, 41,* 831–846.

Kochanska, G., Murray, K., & Coy, K. C. (2000). Inhibitory control as a contributor to conscience in childhood: From toddler to early school age. *Child Development, 68,* 263–277.

Kroupina, M., Kuefner, D., Iverson, S., & Johnson, D. (2003, April). *Joint attention skills of post-institutionalized children.* Poster session presented at the biennial meeting of the Society for Research in Child Development, Tampa, FL.

Lane, R., Fink, G., Chua, P., & Dolan, R. (1997). Neural activation during selective attention to subjective emotional responses. *Neuroreport, 8,* 3969–3972.

Lau, H., Rogers, R., Haggard, P., & Passingham, R. (2004). Attention to intention. *Science, 303,* 1208–1210.

Leekam, S., & Moore, C. (2001). The development of joint attention in children with autism. In J. Burack, T. Charman, N. Yirmiya, & P. Zelazo (Eds.), *The development of autism: Perspectives from theory and research* (pp. 105–130). Mahwah, NJ: Erlbaum.

Leslie, A. (1987). Pretense and representation: The origins of "theory of mind." *Psychological Review, 94,* 412–426.

Leslie, A., & Thaiss, L. (1992). Domain specificity in conceptual development: Neuropsychological evidence from autism. *Cognition, 43,* 225–251.

Lord, C., Floody, H., Anderson, D., & Pickles, A. (2003, April). *Social engagement in very young children with autism: Differences across contexts.* Poster session presented at the biennial meeting of the Society for Research in Child Development, Tampa, FL.

Loveland, K. A., & Landry, S. H. (1986). Joint attention and language in autism and developmental language delay. *Journal of Autism and Developmental Disorders, 16*, 335–349.

Luu, P., Flaisch, T., & Tucker, D. (2000). Medial-frontal cortex in action monitoring. *Journal of Neuroscience, 20*, 464–469.

Martin, J. (1996). *Neuroanatomy: Text and atlas* (2nd ed.). New York: McGraw-Hill.

Masten, A., & Coatsworth, D. (1998). The development of competence in favorable and unfavorable environments: Lessons from research on successful children. *American Psychologist, 53*, 205–220.

McEvoy, R., Rogers, S., & Pennington, R. (1993). Executive function and social communication deficits in young autistic children. *Journal of Child Psychology and Psychiatry, 34*, 563–578.

Meltzoff, A., & Decety, J. (2003). What imitation tells us about social cognition: A rapprochement between developmental psychology and cognitive neuroscience. *Philosophical Transactions of the Royal Society of London: Series B, 358*, 491–500.

Meltzoff, A., & Moore, M. (1997). Explaining facial imitation: A theoretical model. *Early Development and Parenting, 6*, 179–192.

Moore, C. (1996). Theories of mind in infancy. *British Journal of Developmental Psychology, 14*, 19–40.

Morales, M., Mundy, P., Delgado, C., Yale, M., Neal, R., & Schwartz, H. (2000). Gaze following, temperament and language development in 6 month olds: A replication and extension. *Infant Behavior and Development, 23*, 231–236.

Morales, M., Mundy, P., & Rojas, J. (1998). Following the direction of gaze and language development in 6-month-olds. *Infant Behavior and Development, 21*, 373–377.

Morecraft, R., Guela, C., & Mesulam, M. (1993). Architecture of connectivity within the cingulo-frontal-parietal neurocognitive network for directed attention. *Archives of Neurology, 50*, 279–283.

Mundy, P. (1995). Joint attention and social-emotional approach behavior in children with autism. *Development and Psychopathology, 7*, 63–82.

Mundy, P. (2003). The neural basis of social impairments in autism: The role of the dorsal medial-frontal cortex and anterior cingulate system. *Journal of Child Psychology and Psychiatry, 44*, 793–809.

Mundy, P., Card, J., & Fox, N. (2000). EEG correlates of the development of infant joint attention skills. *Developmental Psychobiology, 36*, 325–338.

Mundy, P., Delgado, C., Block, J., Venezia, M., Hogan, A., & Seibert, J. (2003). *Manual for the Early Social Communication Scales: 2nd Revision.* (Available from the authors, pmundy@miami.edu.)

Mundy, P., & Gomes, A. (1998). Individual differences in joint attention skills in the second year. *Infant Behavior and Development, 21*, 469–482.

Mundy, P., Kasari, C., & Sigman, M. (1992). Joint attention, affective sharing, and intersubjectivity. *Infant Behavior and Development, 15*, 377–381.

Mundy, P., & Neal, R. (2001). Neural plasticity, joint attention and a transactional social-orienting model of autism. *International Review of Mental Retardation, 23*, 139–168.

Mundy, P., & Sigman, M. (1989). Specifying the nature of the social impairment in autism. In G. Dawson (Ed.), *Autism: New perspectives on diagnosis, nature, and treatment* (pp. 3–21). New York: Guilford.

Mundy, P., Sigman, M., & Kasari, C. (1993). The theory of mind and joint attention deficits in autism. In S. Baron-Cohen, H. Tager-Flusberg & D. Cohen (Eds.), *Understanding other minds: Perspectives from autism* (pp. 181–203). Oxford, England: Oxford University Press.

Mundy, P., Sigman, M., & Kasari, C. (1994). Joint attention, developmental level, and symptom presentation in young children with autism. *Development and Psychopathology, 6*, 389–401.

Mundy, P., Sigman, M., Ungerer, J., & Sherman, T. (1986). Defining the social deficits of autism: The contribution of nonverbal communication measures. *Journal of Child Psychology and Psychiatry, 27*, 657–669.

Mundy, P., & Willoughby, J. (1996). Nonverbal communication, joint attention, and early socio-emotional development. In M. Lewis & M. Sullivan (Eds.), *Emotional development in atypical children* (pp. 65–87). New York: Wiley.

Mundy, P., & Willoughby, J. (1998). Nonverbal communication, affect, and social-emotional development. In A. M. Wetherby, S. F. Warren & J. Reichle (Eds.), *Transitions in prelinguistic communication* (Vol. 7, pp. 111–133). Baltimore: Brookes.

Neal, R., Mundy, P., Claussen, A., Mallik, S., Scott, K., & Acra, C. F. (2003). *The relations between infant joint attention skill and cognitive and language outcome in at-risk children*. Manuscript submitted for publication.

Nichols, K. E., Fox, N., & Mundy, P. (2005). Joint attention, self-recognition, and neurocognitive functions. *Infancy, 7*, 35–51.

Norman, D., & Shallice, T. (1986). Attention to action: Willed and automatic control of behavior. In R. Davidson, G. Schwartz, & D. Shapiro (Eds.), *Consciousness and self-regulation* (pp. 1–18). New York: Plenum.

Ochsner, K., Bunge, S., Gross, J., & Gabireli, J. (2002). Rethinking feelings: An fMRI study of the cognitive regulation of emotion. *Journal of Cognitive Neuroscience, 14*, 1215–1229.

Panksepp, J. (1979). A neuro-chemical theory of autism. *Trends in Neurosciences, 2*, 174–177.

Pomares, Y., Mundy, P., Vaughan, A., Block, J., & Delgado, C. (2003, April). *On the relations between infant joint attention, imitation and language*. Poster session presented at the biennial meeting of the Society for Research in Child Development, Tampa, FL.

Posner, M., & Petersen, S. (1990). The attention system of the human brain. *Annual Review of Neuroscience, 13*, 25–42.

Puce, A., Allison, T., Bentin, S., Gore, J., & McCarthy, G. (1998). Temporal cortex activation in humans viewing eye and mouth movements. *Journal of Neuroscience, 18*, 2188–2199.

Raver, C. (2002). Emotions matter: Making the case for the role of young children's emotional development for early school readiness. *Society for Research in Child Development Social Policy Report, 16*, 3.

Reynolds, C., & Kamphaus, R. (1992). *Behavior Assessment System for Children: Manual*. Circle Pines, MN: American Guidance Services.

Rheingold, H. L., Hay, D. F., & West, M. J. (1976). Sharing in the second year of life. *Child Development, 47*, 1148–1158.

Rogers, S., & Pennington, B. (1991). A theoretical approach to the deficits in infantile autism. *Developmental Psychopathology, 6*, 635–652.

Rothbart, M. (1981). Measurement of temperament in infancy. *Child Development, 52*, 569–578.

Rothbart, M., & Bates, J. (1998). Temperament. In W. Damon & N. Eisenberg (Eds.),

The handbook of child psychology: Vol. 3. Social, emotional and personality development (5th ed., pp. 105–176). New York: Wiley.

Rothbart, M., Posner, M., & Rosicky, J. (1994). Orienting in normal and pathological development. *Development and Psychopathology, 6*, 635–652.

Rushworth, M., Hadland, K., Paus, T., & Siplia, P. (2002). Role of the human medial-frontal cortex in task switching: A combined fMRI and TMS study. *Journal of Neurophysiology, 87*, 2577–2592.

Sabbagh, M., & Taylor, M. (2000). Neural correlates of theory of mind: An event related potential study. *Psychological Science, 11*, 46–50.

Scaife, M., & Bruner, J. (1975). The capacity for joint visual attention in the infant. *Nature, 253*, 265–266.

Schölmerich, A., Lamb, M. E., Leyendecker, B., & Fracasso, M. P. (1997). Mother-infant teaching interactions and attachment security in Euro-American and Central-American immigrant families. *Infant Behavior and Development, 20*, 165–174.

Schultz, R., Romanski, L., & Tsatsanis, K. (2000). Neurofunctional models of autistic disorder and Asperger syndrome: Clues from neuroimaging. In A. Klin, F. Volkmar, & S. Sparrow (Eds.), *Asperger syndrome* (pp. 172–209). New York: Guilford.

Seibert, J. M., Hogan, A. E., & Mundy, P. C. (1982). Assessing interactional competencies: The Early Social Communication Scales. *Infant Mental Health Journal, 3*, 244–245.

Sheinkopf, S. J., Mundy, P., Claussen, A. H., & Willoughby, J. (2004). Infant joint attention skill and preschool behavioral outcomes in at-risk children. *Development and Psychopathology, 16*, 273–293.

Sigman, M., & Ruskin, E. (1999). Continuity and change in the social competence of children with autism, Down syndrome, and developmental delay. *Monographs of the Society for Research in Child Development, 64*(11 Serial No. 256), 1–108.

Stern, D. (1985). *The interpersonal world of the infant.* New York: Basic Books.

Stich, S., & Nichols, S. (1992). Folk psychology: Simulation versus tacit theory. *Mind and Language, 7*, 29–65.

Stuphorn, V., Taylor, T., & Schall, J. (2000). Performance monitoring by the supplementary eye field. *Nature, 408*, 857–860.

Stuss, D., Shallice, T., Alexander, M., & Picton, T. (1995). A multidimensional approach to anterior attention functions. In J. Grafman, K. Holyoak, & F. Boller (Eds.), *Structure and function of the human prefrontal cortex.* Annals of the New York Academy of Science (Vol. 769, pp. 191–211). New York: New York Academy of Sciences.

Teasdale, J., Howard, R., Cox, S., Ha, Y., Brammer, M., Williams, S., et al. (1999). Functional MRI of the cognitive generation of affect. *American Journal of Psychiatry, 156*, 209–215.

Tomasello, M. (1995). Joint attention as social cognition. In C. Moore & P. Dunham (Eds.), *Joint attention: Its origins and role in development* (pp. 103–130). Hillsdale, NJ: Erlbaum.

Tomasello, M., & Farrar, M. J. (1986). Joint attention and early language. *Child Development, 57*, 1454–1463.

Travis, L., Sigman, M., & Ruskin, E. (2001). Links between social understanding and social behavior in verbally able children with autism. *Journal of Autism and Developmental Disorders, 31*, 119–130.

Trevarthen, C. (1979). Communication and cooperation in early infancy: A description of primary intersubjectivity. In M. Bullowa (Ed.), *Before speech: The beginning of interpersonal communication* (pp. 49–66). Cambridge, England: Cambridge University Press.

Trevarthen, C., & Aitken, K. (2001). Infant intersubjectivity: Research, theory and clinical applications. *Journal of Child Psychology and Psychiatry, 42*, 3–48.

Ulvund, S., & Smith, L. (1996). The predictive validity of nonverbal communicative skills in infants with perinatal hazards. *Infant Behavior and Development, 19*, 441–449.

Valenza, E., Simion, F., Cassia, V., & Umilta, C. (1996). Face preference at birth. *Journal of Experimental Psychology—Human Perception and Performance, 22*, 892–903.

Vaughan, A., Block, J., Delgado, C., Neal, R., Toledo, Y., & Mundy, P. (2003b). Child, caregiver, and temperament contributions to infant joint attention. *Infancy, 4*, 603–616.

Vaughan, A., & Mundy, P. (in press). Neural systems and the development of gaze following and related joint attention skills. In R. Flom, K. Lee, & D. Muir (Eds.), *The ontogeny of gaze processing in infants and children.* Mahwah, NJ: Erlbaum.

Vaughan, A., Mundy, P., Delgado, C., Block, J., Pomares, Y., & Gomes, Y. (2003a, April). *Joint attention and social emotional outcomes in normal developing children.* Paper presented at the biennial meeting of the Society for Research in Child Development, Tampa, FL.

Venezia, M., Messinger, D., Thorp, D., & Mundy, P. (2004). Timing changes: The development of anticipatory smiling. *Infancy, 6*, 397–406.

Wachs, T., & Chan, A. (1986). Specificity of environmental action, as seen in environmental correlates of infants' communication performance. *Child Development, 57*, 1464–1474.

Werner, H., & Kaplan, B. (1963). *Symbol formation.* Oxford, England: Wiley.

Wetherby, A., Allen, L., Cleary, J., Kublin, K., & Goldstein, H. (2002). Validity and reliability of the Communication and Symbolic Behavior Scales Developmental Profile with very young children. *Journal of Speech, Language and Hearing Research, 45*, 1202–1218.

Wetherby, A. M., & Prutting, C. A. (1984). Profiles of communicative and cognitive-social abilities in autistic children. *Journal of Speech and Hearing Research, 27*, 364–377.

Wicker, B., Michel, F., Henaff, M., & Decety, J. (1998). Brain regions involved in the perception of gaze: A PET study. *NeuroImage, 8*, 221–227.

Woodcock, R. (1991). *Woodcock Language Proficiency Battery-Revised.* Allen, TX: Measurement/Learning/Consultants.

Woodward, A. (2003). Infants' developing understanding of the link between looker and object. *Developmental Science, 6*, 297–311.

5

The Social Dimension in Language Development
A Rich History and a New Frontier

Shannon M. Pruden
Kathy Hirsh-Pasek
Roberta Michnick Golinkoff

> *Learning a word is a social act.*
> (P. Bloom, 2000, p. 55)

> *Language is social.*
> (Clark, 2003, p. 19)

The past 30 years have witnessed an explosion in research on social/emotional and cognitive development in infants and toddlers (Berk, 2003). Within the realm of social/emotional development, research has demonstrated that infants are capable of social referencing, joint attention, emotion regulation, and noting another's social intent (Baldwin, 1991; Bretherton, 1992; Carpenter, Nagell, & Tomasello, 1998; Corkum & Moore, 1995; Eisenberg & Zhou, 2000; Gergely, Nadasdy, Csibra, & Biro, 1995; Meltzoff, 1995; Murray & Trevarthen, 1985). Within the realm of cognitive development, theories have explored the understanding of infant competencies in numeracy, spatial cognition, object and event perception, and early word development (Aguiar & Baillargeon, 2002; Spelke, Katz, Purcell, Ehrlich, & Breinlinger, 1994; Woodward & Markman, 1998; Wynn, Bloom, & Chiang, 2002). Despite the proliferation of scholarship in each domain, this research has largely been conducted on parallel planes, with little attention to how infant and toddler social development impacts upon cognitive growth and how cognitive development might feed social development. Research areas such as social cognition emerged in the 1970s, but with a few exceptions (e.g., theory of mind research), most work in this field had a relatively short shelf life. Recent work on emotion regulation (Eisenberg, 2001; Eisenberg & Zhou, 2000; Fox, 2003; Morris et al., 2002) and on social prerequisites for school readiness (National Institute of Child Health and Human Development Early Child Care Research Network [NICHD], 2003; Raver, 2002) ask anew how our theories of development can move beyond the compartmentalized child to embrace interactions between the cognitive and social self in learning.

One area of research that has struggled with divisions between cognitive and social theories of development is that of language acquisition. Historically, the field of language development was born from two events: Chomsky's views on grammar, and the dominance of Piagetian and information-processing models of cognitive development. Chomsky claimed that children were endowed with a universal grammar that made relatively little or no contact with social skills (Chomsky, 1965, 1975, 1981). The social environment provided but a trigger so that children could link internal representations of grammar with the input they heard (see also Pinker, 2002). Information-processing models use children's cognitive competencies (and sometimes innate grammatical structures) as a foundation, asking how children compute correlations from the available evidence to derive a more complete grammar (Maratsos & Chalkley, 1980; but see Bates & MacWhinney, 1987, and Elman, 2001 for an alternative view; see also Hirsh-Pasek & Golinkoff, 1996, for a review). These theories make little contact with children's developing social competence.

Throughout the 1970s and 1980s, dissenting voices represented the fact that a nativist, modular, and even cognitive information-processing views of language would be insufficient to account for word and grammatical learning. As Slobin (1985) wrote, "The application of particular operating principles depends on a complex of existing linguistic and extralinguistic knowledge, processing constraints, the structure of social interaction, and the structure of the language being acquired" (p. 1245). To truly understand a complex cognitive behavior such as language, we need to pay attention not only to linguistic mechanisms underlying language acquisition but also to the social and emotional characteristics of the child in his or her social environment (Bruner, 1975; Snow & Ferguson, 1977; Snow, 1989).

The area of language development is still largely bifurcated, with researchers emphasizing either the social-interactional (also called social-pragmatic) basis of language or the child's innate contributions. There are, however, serious attempts to unite these camps, attempts that could point to new directions in the study of neurological bases for language acquisition.

This chapter is organized in four sections. The first section reviews theories of language development that endorse a social-pragmatic perspective. The second section proposes a hybrid model of language development, called the emergentist coalition model (ECM), that embeds both the pragmatic and cognitive perspectives in a developmental theory of language acquisition. Language development, in this scenario, occurs as a result of the differential weighting of three cues, perceptual/attentional, social, and linguistic. The third section offers evidence for the differential weighting of cues over time. We present several studies (some old and some new) showing that all three cues are used in tandem as the child progresses through early language acquisition. This model has proved fruitful for the study of grammar and early word learning. Finally, in the fourth section we project how this more complex model can provide a road map for the neurological underpinnings of language development in order to shed some light on both normal and atypical language development.

Social Pragmatics in Language Development: A Long Tradition

The role of social and emotional development has been widely recognized within language development and has a long tradition dating back to the 1970s. Bruner (1975) was among the first to address the role of social development in language learning, suggesting that social interaction could be mapped transparently onto linguistic structure, although he subsequently retracted this claim (Bruner, 1983). Nonetheless, the importance of games like "give and take" that infants and toddlers play with their caregivers cannot be overestimated. In these games, where they alternately become the agents or the recipients of an action, the roles that will be expressed in language become revealed. Social interactions also provide a cultural classroom for language learning by introducing the scripts or routines (Nelson, 1973, 1985; Peters & Boggs, 1986; Snow, 1986; Snow & Godfield, 1983) within which language learning takes place and by introducing the joint attentional episodes that help children find the referent of communication (Adamson, 1995; Tomasello & Farrar, 1986). By way of example, parents participate in common routines with children, such as the diapering routine or the feeding routine. Within these contexts, parents engage in "proto-conversations" with their infants. Consider the following "proto-conversation" between a mother and her 3-month-old daughter, Ann (Snow, 1977, p. 12):

> Ann: (smiles)
> Mother: Oh, what a nice little smile. Yes, isn't that nice? There. There's a nice little smile.
> Ann: (burps)
> Mother: What a nice little wind as well. Yes, that's better, isn't it? Yes. Yes. Yes.
> Ann: (vocalizes)
> Mother: There's a nice noise.

Western parents guide the infant's way in the social interaction by showing the baby how to take turns and how to build a relationship (Golinkoff & Hirsh-Pasek, 1999). These "proto-conversations" may be minimal at first, with the adult supplying all the turns. However, as the child grows, the adult "raises the criterion for what counts as a contribution from their infants" (Clark, 2003, p. 30).

Nelson (1985), for example, articulated the social-interactional position clearly when she wrote:

> Language learning takes place within the framework of social interaction, and the nature of the particular kinds of interaction experienced determines not only the function and context of the language to be acquired but which segments will be learned first and how these segments will subsequently be put together or broken down for reassembly. (p. 109)

L. Bloom's intentionality model of language development (2000; Bloom & Tinker, 2001) takes Nelson's position one step further by proposing that language is learned in a social context by an active language learner who is determined to share the contents of his or her mind. Previous theories emphasizing the role of social and pragmatic cues in language acquisition propose that caregivers structure the learning contexts in relevant culturally specific ways (P. Bloom, 2000).

One of the most prolific champions for social mediation in language learning is Michael Tomasello. He and his colleagues hold that early language learning is bathed in a social context (Akhtar & Tomasello, 2000; Carpenter, Nagell, & Tomasello, 1998; Tomasello, 1992). According to Tomasello's social-pragmatic view, children participate in patterned social interactions or routines that provide a "scaffold" to the prelinguistic child (Akhtar & Tomasello, 2000; Ninio & Bruner, 1978). Evidence for "scaffolding" comes from studies investigating children's games like "peek-a-boo" (Ratner & Bruner, 1978), children's play such as a tea party (Kaye & Charney, 1980), and even studies of picture-book reading (Kaye & Charney, 1980; Ninio & Bruner, 1978; Snow & Godfield, 1983; see Golinkoff & Hirsh-Pasek, 1999, for other examples). A classic example of an adult scaffolding or supporting a child in a language-learning situation comes from Ninio and Bruner's (1978, pp. 6–7) study of book reading:

Mother: Look!
Child: (Touches picture).
Mother: What are those?
Child: (Vocalizes and smiles).
Mother: Yes, they are rabbits.
Child: (Vocalizes, smiles, and looks up at mother).
Mother: (Laughs). Yes, rabbit.
Child: (Vocalizes and smiles).
Mother: (Laughs). Yes.

In this example, the mother structures the situation for the child by formatting and framing the interaction. The mother guides her child in the language-learning process by initiating exchanges and interactions and elaborating on a topic. Notice that the child is really not saying anything comprehensible, yet her contribution to the conversation is honored by the mother as if it were a full-fledged verbal communication.

Tomasello, Akhtar, Baldwin, and P. Bloom claim that language learning is fundamentally social, based on the child's discovery of social intent (Akhtar &

Tomasello, 2000; Baldwin & Tomasello, 1998; P. Bloom, 2000). By noting what people are intending to talk about, children become like Fauconnier's bricklayer (Fauconnier, 1985). As Fauconnier writes, "A brick could theoretically occupy any position in a wall, but at any stage of the actual building process there is only one place for it to go" (pp. 168–169). L. Bloom uses this as a backdrop to posit a "principle of relevance" that guides active young learners to form correct mappings between world and language through social, linguistic, and perceptual cues. Once you can follow eye gaze and interpret another's point of view, you have a window onto language use and meaning. Once you can "read" another's mind, you can determine how the mapping from world to mind works. You can then become an apprentice to a more sophisticated language user.

In a recent review, Clark (2003) explained why social development is an important factor, not to be ignored and underestimated, in language learning:

> Infants are born into a social world, a world of touch, sound, and affect, a world of communication. They develop and grow up as social beings, immersed in a network of relationships from the start. It is in this social setting that they are first exposed to language, to language in use. (p. 25)

From the beginning of life, infants are fundamentally social beings, attending to social information in their environment (Butterworth, 2003; see Golinkoff & Hirsh-Pasek, 1999, and Adamson, 1995, for reviews). Research shows that they attend to social cues, such as eye gaze and pointing in the second 6 months of life (Corkum & Moore, 1995; for a review, see Carpenter, Nagell, & Tomasello, 1998). Thus, the issue at hand is not *whether* infants are social beings, born into a social world, but whether infants can recruit social cues for the purpose of learning both the rules of language (grammar) and words of their language.

The Role of Social Development in Children's Acquisition of Grammar

The earliest work on the intersection of social development and language came from the "social interactionists," who asked how social input promoted grammatical development. Two lines of research characterized this period of study: (a) the study of infant-directed speech and its impact on language development (Snow & Ferguson, 1977), and (b) the role of corrections on the development of grammar (Bohannon & Stanowicz, 1988).

"Motherese" or Infant-Directed Speech

Caregivers around the world talk to their infants very differently than they do with adults and even older children (Fernald et al., 1989; Grieser & Kuhl, 1988). "Motherese," or infant-directed (ID) speech, is characterized as having a slower rate, an extended frequency range, higher overall fundamental frequency, repeated pitch contours, marked intensity shifts, longer pauses between utterances, word lengthening, and simplified vocabulary (Golinkoff & Alioto, 1995; see Morgan & Demuth, 1996, and Snow, 1995, for related definitions). Research indicates that infants do in fact prefer to listen to ID speech rather than adult-directed speech (Fernald, 1985), even as early as at birth (Cooper & Aslin, 1990). According to Clark (2003), ID speech serves three specific functions. First, ID speech is designed to get the baby's attention. This type of speech, whether it is high-pitched or a whisper, differentiates speech addressed to the child from speech addressed to adults. It says to the baby, "Hey, this talk is for you!" Getting an infant's attention is the first step on the road to achieving what has been dubbed "joint attention." Second, ID speech is used to maintain infants' attention. In English, speakers achieve this goal by maintaining a high pitch and exaggerated intonation (Fernald & Mazzie, 1991; Ratner, 1984). Only when infants are able to maintain attention to the speaker can they learn what the speaker is referring to. Finally, to communicate with a listener who has much less knowledge than the speaker, the speaker must tailor his or her utterances and make them stand out in the stream of speech. ID speech is generally tailored to the child's linguistic level, though the modifications that are made are different across cultures (Fernald & Morikawa, 1993; Fernald et al., 1989; Schieffelin & Ochs, 1986).

Research has also established that across various cultures, caregivers use ID speech to talk to infants (Fernald et al., 1989; Grieser & Kuhl, 1988) and even to domestic pets (Burnham & Kitamura, 2002; Hirsh-Pasek & Treiman, 1982), but does this type of speech play a specific role in language acquisition? Some suggest that ID speech may help infants isolate *words* within the speech stream (Golinkoff & Alioto, 1995) and may even provide the foundation for acquiring the grammatical structure of one's language (Gleitman, Gleitman, Landau, & Wanner, 1988; Gleitman & Wanner, 1982; Morgan, 1986). What little research exists showed that ID speech, at the very least, facilitates various phonological awareness (Karzon, 1985; Kuhl et al., 1997) and perceptual processes (Kemler-Nelson, Hirsh-Pasek, Jusczyk, & Cassidy, 1989) that might assist learners in the parsing of speech into language-relevant units. In studies of both infant-directed and adult-directed speech, Hirsh-Pasek and colleagues (1987; Kemler-Nelson et al., 1989) noted that prelinguistic infants preferred to listen to utterances that were parsed at language-relevant boundaries such as before or after a noun phrase rather than at points within the noun or verb phrases (e.g., "the big house PAUSE" vs. "the PAUSE big house"). This finding only emerged, however, when the input was in ID speech. Interestingly, prosodic cues offered hints to language structure at the level of both clauses and phrases (Jusczyk et al., 1992). Taken together, these findings suggest that prosodic qualities of motherese might provide infants with cues to units of speech that corresponded to grammatical units of language. These results also lend support to the prosodic bootstrapping hypothesis, which proposes that infants learn about the syntactic structure of their language through the prosodic characteristics of the speech that they hear

(Gleitman et al., 1988; Gleitman & Wanner, 1982; see Morgan & Demuth, 1996, for a review).

Recasts, Expansions, and Imitation

Once children find a toehold for language through ID speech, one must ask how they arrange words and phrases into grammar. That is, how do they move the units of language around to form the rules for language? Two possibilities were introduced by the social interactionists in the form of imitation and correction (called "negative evidence"). Perhaps children simply imitate much of what they hear, and perhaps when they generate ungrammatical sentences, they are corrected by benevolent social partners who help them move progressively toward grammatical speech. Although these ideas were appealing, there were several challenges that needed to be addressed. First, some researchers argued that children do not generally imitate what they hear (Brown, 1973). In fact, children generate novel sentences like, "I goed to the store" that have never been said before. Further, in his classic book, Brown (1973) held that children could not learn language solely through social interaction because parents did not explicitly correct children's ungrammatical speech. Rather, parents responded to the child's *intended* message rather than to the form it arrived in.

In response to Brown's claims, some social interactionists sought to demonstrate that infant speech was only an approximation of adult speech, and that partial if not complete imitation did have a role to play in later language learning (K. E. Nelson, 1989). Further, while parents do not respond explicitly to ungrammatical speech (e.g., telling the child to say, "I goed" as "I went" instead), they do respond *implicitly* by repeating more ungrammatical utterances or by expanding these utterances in ways that made them grammatically correct. By way of example, Bohannon and others demonstrated that adults directly respond to ungrammatical utterances in their children's speech by using expansions, repeats, recasts, and requests for clarification (Bohannon & Stanowicz, 1988; Chouinard & Clark, 2003; Demetras, Post, & Snow, 1986; Farrar, 1992; Hirsh-Pasek, Treiman, & Schneiderman, 1984). Consider the following anecdote from Clark (2003, p. 427) in which 30-month-old Abe asks his father for milk:

> Abe: Milk, milk.
> Father: You want milk?
> Abe: Uh-huh.
> Father: Ok. Just a second and I'll get you some.

The father reformulates the child's utterance by filling in the missing terms needed to make the utterance more complete and grammatically correct. These contingent replies to ill-formed child utterances are different from the types of responses used to respond to well-formed utterances. The use of different reply types to children's utterances might indicate to children whether their utterance was ill formed or well formed. Chouinard and Clark (2003) argue that when children receive negative evidence, they are presented with two forms: their own ill-formed utterance and the adult's well-formed utterance, both expressing the same underlying meaning. Chouinard and Clark write, "Since these two forms do *not* contrast in meaning (they express the same intention), the one that is conventional has priority" (p. 643). As a result of hearing a well-formed utterance that expresses their intention, children "defer to the adult speakers, the experts on the conventional forms for expressing specific meanings" (p. 643). Taken as a whole, these studies show that adults do correct and reformulate children's errors using various reply types.

Of course, corrections and reformulations are useful to children only if children can detect them and if they are prevalent enough in the input for children to make use of them. Shipley, Smith, and Gleitman (1969) reported just this finding in young children's responses to well-formed versus ill-formed commands. Chouinard and Clark (2003) further investigated children's ability to detect adults' corrections. Longitudinal data, collected from five young children, showed that children do attend to adult reformulations. On average, adult corrections of ill-formed sentences were detected between 10% and 50% of the time. Thus, studies do demonstrate that implicit correction is available. Whether these corrections are frequent enough to assist children in grammatical learning (see Hirsh-Pasek et al., 1984, or Pinker, 1984) is still at issue.

At the grammatical level, then, there is reason to believe that ID speech might capture infant attention (Fernald, 1985) and might carve the perceptual flow into language-relevant units like clauses and phrases (Hirsh-Pasek et al., 1987; Kemler-Nelson et al., 1989; Morgan, 1986). Further, social feedback through expansions and recasts might alert children both to the fact that their own utterances were not "up to snuff" and to ways in which their utterances could be repaired (Chouinard & Clark, 2003). Although this might not solve the grammatical learning problem by itself, it certainly highlights potentially important roles for social input in grammatical learning.

The Role of Social Information in Word Learning

As just described, researchers in the 1970s an 1980s focused on the role that social information might play in grammatical development. In contrast, scientists in the 1990s turned their attention to the role of social input in word learning.

On the surface, word learning seems like a very easy problem to solve. At the simplest level, a child need only attach a word to an object in plain view. Upon closer inspection, however, word learning proves to be a difficult task. To learn a word, infants need to (a) segment the continuous sound stream into units; (b) discover a world of objects, actions, and events, and figure out how those are divided into meaningful units to find the natural "carving joints"; and (c) map the word onto the correct referent in the world.

Quine (1960) highlighted the difficulty of word learning in his well-known vignette on word reference. He wrote about a linguist who sees a rabbit scurrying by while hearing a native exclaim "Gavagai!" Quine argued that the word *gavagai* could refer to an indeterminate number of possible referents, including the whole rabbit, rabbit's ears, or rabbit's hopping. If Quine's example captures the word-learning problem, then we must ask how children ever learn what a word refers to. Three major theories of word learning arose to debate this question: (a) the constraints/principles view, (b) the domain-general view, and (c) the social-pragmatic view. In fact, these theories can largely be distinguished by whether they embrace or reject the Quinean conundrum as a foundational assumption.

Constraints/Principles Views

The constraints/principles view adopts Quine's view of the problem space. Under the constraints/principles view, word-to-world mapping is underdetermined, so human minds must be equipped with constraints or principles that narrow the search space (Golinkoff, Mervis, & Hirsh-Pasek, 1994; Woodward & Markman, 1998). Children approach word learning biased to make certain assumptions over others for what a word might mean. For example, Markman's principle of mutual exclusivity (novel name-novel category principle [N3C]; Markman, 1989; see also Merriman & Bowman, 1989, and Golinkoff et al., 1994) proposes that children hypothesize that an object can have only one label. As a consequence, children assume that an unfamiliar name refers to an unfamiliar object rather than to an object that is labeled. In the last 20 years, numerous constraints and principles have been proposed to address the word-learning problem (see Golinkoff et al., 1994, and Woodward & Markman, 1998, for reviews).

Domain-General Views

The constraints/principles approach spearheaded an early and popular view of word learning, but it has not gone unchallenged. Both the domain-general and the social-pragmatic views reject Quine's assumptions and offer alternatives to the constraints approach. Proponents of the domain-general view, like Smith (1995, 1999, 2000), Samuelson and Smith (1998), and Plunkett (1997), suggest that word learning can be accounted for through "dumb attentional mechanisms" such as perceptual saliency, association, and frequency. Samuelson and Smith (1998) articulated this position when they wrote that "general processes of perceiving, remembering, and attending when placed in the word-learning context may be *sufficient* in and of themselves to create children's smart word interpretations" (p. 95). Abundant evidence is available to support these claims. Smith, Jones, and Landau (1996), for example, showed that young children's extensions of novel names to novel objects were influenced by the relative salience to perceptual features rather than to conceptual knowledge such as functional information. However, when children were asked to judge the similarity of the objects, they used conceptual knowledge to group the objects. Smith et al. suggest young children's initial interpretations of novel words are indeed guided by a "dumb attentional mechanism."

Social-Pragmatic Views

The third dominant view, the social pragmatic alternative also dismissed Quine's conundrum as a basis for word learning. Researchers in this camp argued that children were socially gifted from an early age and that their social precociousness would allow them to learn words as apprentices to the master word users around them. The last 20 years have revealed that infants have remarkable social skills from an early age. Infants have the ability to follow eye gaze (see Butterworth, 1995, for a review; for more recent work, see Brooks & Meltzoff, 2002, and Woodward, 2003) to pointing (Butterworth & Itakura, 1998; see Butterworth, 2003, for a review; for more recent work, see Woodward & Guajardo, 2002); to enter into joint attention with another (see Moore and Dunham, 1995 for a review); to use a significant other's facial expressions for information (see Feinman, 1992, for a review); and even to imitate another's intended, but never completed, actions (Carpenter, Akhtar, & Tomasello, 1998; Meltzoff, 1995; Meltzoff & Brooks, 2001). A voluminous literature appeared linking these social competencies to word learning and later language learning.

Using speaker intent to learn words. Children learn words by reading the social intent of their mentors in this world (P. Bloom, 2000). When an adult says "dog" while looking at a dog, infants follow the gaze of the speaker, interpret speaker intent, and are literally guided to the correct word meaning. Thus, by virtue of being a social animal, language comes for free.

Among the first to demonstrate the link between social engagement and language acquisition were Tomasello and Farrar (1986; also see Tomasello & Todd, 1983), who examined the role of joint attention in early language development. They found that extended periods of joint attention between the adult and child serve as a scaffold for linguistic interactions. Adult references to objects that were already in children's focus were positively correlated with children's later vocabulary (also see Dunham & Dunham, 1992). In addition, words were learned better for objects that were in the child's focus than for those that were not.

More recently, studies investigating the role of social input in word learning have explored children's ability to pick out the adults' intended referent using pragmatic cues, such as eye gaze, head direction, body posture, and voice direction (Baldwin, 1991, 1993; see Baldwin & Moses, 2001, for a review). For example, Baldwin (1991, 1993) showed that 18- to 19-month-olds followed a speaker's eye gaze upon hearing a novel label. Rather than linking the new label to an object occupying their own focus, these children used the speaker's line of regard to guide their inferences about word meaning (also see Dunham, Dunham, & Curwin, 1993). Further, a study by Baldwin and colleagues (Baldwin, Bill, & Ontai, 1996) demonstrated that even infants as young as 12 months actively monitor a speaker's face for information about the referent of a word. By age 2, children demonstrate their sophistication by learning a novel word in an intentional context but not in an accidental context (Diesendruck, Markson, Akhtar, & Reudor, 2004).

These studies demonstrate the utility of social information and social intent in the learning of *object labels*. Research also documents that infants recruit social information to learn *action words or verbs* (Akhtar & Tomasello, 1996; Poulin-Dubois & Forbes, 2002; Tomasello & Akhtar, 1995; Tomasello & Barton, 1994). Poulin-Dubois and Forbes (2002), for example, demonstrated that toddlers use social cues such as a speaker's gesture and eye gaze to learn novel action words. Just as in object word learning, Tomasello and colleagues illustrated that infants were able to learn novel action words even when the referent was absent at the time of naming (Akhtar & Tomasello, 1996; Tomasello & Akhtar, 1995). Moreover, Tomasello and Akhtar (1995) showed infants use pragmatic information to indicate what *kind* (an object or an action) of referent a label is referring to.

Where emotion meets word learning. Finally, children learn words not only by joint attention or by attending to speaker intent but also by being attuned to emotional valence in the word-learning environment. For example, Mumme, Fernald, and Herrera (1996) found that children were very sensitive to the emotional affect of the speaker. When infants heard their mother utter a sentence like "Oh, how frightful," *without* a matching facial expression, 12-month-old infants looked at their mothers longer and showed an increase in negative affect. Facial emotional signals did not elicit the same responses, suggesting that vocal expressions may be more powerful emotional signals than facial expressions (Fernald, 1992).

Akhtar and Tomasello (1996) demonstrated how emotional expression relates to word learning. In their study, 2-year-olds watched as a speaker announced her intention to find a toy in a bucket, saying, "Let's go find the toma!" After retrieving the first toy from the bucket, the speaker displayed disappointment. Upon revealing the second toy, the speaker displayed pleasure and terminated her search. Infants immediately assumed that the object eliciting pleasure was the "toma." In a replication of this study, Tomasello, Strosberg, and Akhtar (1996) noted that even 18-month-olds use speakers' emotional expression and actions to determine an adult's referential intentions.

Finally, L. Bloom investigated how emotional expression by the child affected word production across time (Bloom & Capatides, 1987). Early in language production, children cannot express affect and talk at the same time. Instead, their affect becomes neutral before they speak and is not displayed again until after they produce a word. Those who are less expressive emotionally are more lin-

guistically competent. Further, children tend to say "newer" words using a neutral affect, while those words said with emotional expression are generally familiar (L. Bloom, 1998). The coordination of emotion and language, although
understudied at the current time, is a fruitful area for future research.

The evidence that social and emotional forces are important to language learning is compelling. What is less clear is just how far the social information can
and does take the learner (Golinkoff et al., 2000) in the learning of grammar and
words. Some hold that those endorsing the social-emotional perspective have
overstepped the limits of the theory. In grammatical learning, for example, this
challenge comes from Hoff and Naigles (2002), who find that while children use
social information to inform language learning, by age 2, syntactic frames are
the predominant source of information about word meaning and grammatical
form. Supporting the plausibility of a syntactic bootstrapping hypothesis, Hoff
and Naigles argue that the grammatical input to children provides structural cues
to language learning (also see Naigles & Hoff-Ginsberg, 1995).

In word learning, the challenge comes in two forms. First, some argue that the
social information for the learner might not be social at all. Rather, the percep-
tual/attentional changes that accompany social cues may be the real data for word
learning (Samuelson & Smith, 1998; but see Diesendruck et al., 2004). Samuelson
and Smith (1998), for example, modified a study by Akhtar, Carpenter, and
Tomasello (1996) to show that children could solve the word-learning task by
relying exclusively on attentional cues rather than on social cues. Hoff and Naigles
(2002) support a different but related argument when they stated:

> The usefulness of social-pragmatic bases of information for child word learn-
> ers around 10 to 15 months of age is due to maternal sensitivity, not children's
> social-cognitive abilities…even though children over 18 months of age can
> use speaker intent, it appears not to be a particularly important source of in-
> formation for actual word learning. (p. 428)

Complexity in the sentences that children hear might account for more of variance in word learning than does social input. In these scenarios the social input
to children works through mediating cues like perception and grammar to build
the child's lexicon.

Second, some researchers challenge whether children can really recruit social intent in the service of word learning prior to 18 months of age (Hoff &
Naigles, 2002; Hollich, Hirsh-Pasek, & Golinkoff, 2000). While there are some
data to suggest that infants are sensitive to social intent during the latter half of
the first year (Carpenter, Akhtar, & Tomasello, 1998; Gergely et al., 1995), few
studies have discovered infant ability to use social intent in word learning prior
to 18 months of age. If children are not using social intent to drive word meaning from the outset, then other strategies for word learning must be in play when
children learn their very first words (but see Akhtar & Tomasello, 2000).

At present, each of the camps—be it the researchers emphasizing constraints,
those espousing a domain-general approach, or the social pragmatists—seeks

dominion over the theoretical landscape. Each, however, also pays lip service to the fact that word learning will not be possible without input from the social world, the perceptual world, and perhaps some linguistic principles that guide word learning. Even two of the major proponents of the social-pragmatic view argue that language learning is a complex process that requires a more comprehensive explanation. Baldwin and Tomasello (1998) wrote that language learning "requires an explanation encompassing both its *social* and *cognitive* roots" (p. 19). And L. Bloom (2000) has long argued for considering a whole, active child in explaining the language acquisition process. She noted:

> The acquisition of language is, itself, embedded in other cognitive, social, and emotional developments that occur at the same time. Efforts to explain word learning, therefore, must involve broad principles that account for both developmental process and changes in behavior over time. (p. 19)

Throughout the history of language development, then, be it in the study of grammar or word learning, scientists have made enormous progress determining the role of social input and engagement in language learning. The role of social information weaves a constant thread throughout the fabric of the study of language development, but that thread has not been fully integrated into the tapestry of the science. In the last five years, there has been some movement toward a more integrative theory. Perhaps the question that we need to ask is which components of which theories govern children's grammatical and word learning at different points in developmental time. This would provide us with an integrative and truly developmental theory. It would consider multiple perspectives to solve the complex problem in language development and would afford a role for social, perceptual, and cognitive inputs into the system. This kind of approach is not new (L. Bloom, 1993, 2000). As L. Bloom (1993) argued "*Cognitive* developments bring the infant to the threshold of language only in conjunction with other developments in *expression* and *social* connectedness" (p. 52). More recently, Woodward and Markman (1998) echoed the same sentiment when they wrote that "word learning depends on an ability to recruit and integrate information from a range of sources" (p. 371). The complexity of language learning requires a model that takes into account the findings not only from the social-pragmatic literature but from other literatures as well (e.g. constraints/principles, associationist; Hollich et al., 2000).

The Emergentist Coalition Model

The coalition models of grammatical and word development (Hirsh-Pasek & Golinkoff, 1996; Hollich et al., 2000) offered one attempt to provide an integrative theory that used multiple cues and strategies to break into language learning. For the purposes of this chapter, we consider only one of these models, the emergentist coalition model, which attempts to provide such a theory for word learning. Like its predecessor for grammar, the ECM is an empirically based systems approach that incorporates aspects of the perceptual, social, and linguistic theories of learning. Thus, it embraces the role of social input but sees the role of social input in language learning as interactive with other inputs across time. The ECM rests on three central tenets: (a) that children utilize multiple cues, attentional/perceptual, social, and linguistic, that are always available to them in the language-learning situation; (b) that children's ability to use these cues changes over time, as does the weighting of these cues; and (c) that children develop word-learning principles of language over time through these differential weightings (Hollich et al., 2000).

Children Are Sensitive to Multiple Cues

Figure 5–1 graphically depicts the multiple inputs that are available for during the language-learning process. Among the earliest cues used in the service of word learning are attentional cues, such as perceptual salience, temporal contiguity, and novelty. Studies show that infants, well before the age of language

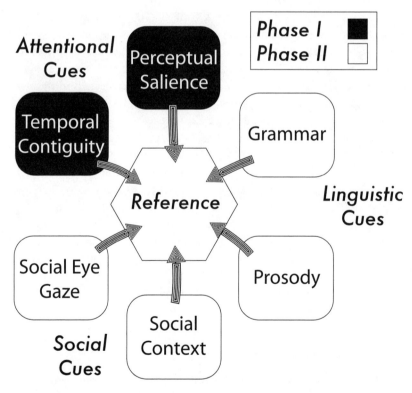

Figure 5–1. Children are sensitive to multiple inputs, including perceptual salience and social and linguistic cues, during the language learning process.

acquisition, detect and link arbitrary relations in intermodal displays (Bahrick, 1983; Gogate & Bahrick, 1998). Literature on word learning also finds the novelty of an object draws children's attention. In the presence of a word, children will map a novel word to a novel object (Golinkoff, Hirsh-Pasek, Bailey, & Wenger, 1992). As noted earlier, research also demonstrates that infants are sensitive to social cues, such as eye gaze, pointing, and speaker intent (Butterworth & Itakura, 1998; Carpenter, Akhtar, & Tomasello, 1998). This vast literature finds that infants can follow another's eye gaze and point. Finally, infants also exploit linguistic input to help them find the words in the speech stream and to identify their part of speech (Hirsh-Pasek et al., 1987; Kemler-Nelson et al., 1989; Morgan, 1986). The question for language researchers, then, becomes not whether children are sensitive to various cues in the word-learning environment, but rather whether and when children exploit these various cues to learn a word.

Children Differentially Weight Cues Over Time

The ECM posits that although these cues are *available* to children at all times, they are not equally *utilized* in the service of word learning. *Not all cues are created equal* (Hirsh-Pasek, Golinkoff, & Hollich, 2000) over the course of development. By way of example, the model posits that infants at the very beginning of word learning will rely more heavily on perceptual salience than on social or linguistic cues. When given a choice between attaching a novel word to a boring object that an adult is looking at and a more perceptually interesting object, children at the very early stages of word learning (10–12 months.) should rely on perceptual salience rather than on social cues (e.g., adults' direction of gaze or pointing). After they can interpret social intent of the speaker, they will realize that a label refers to the object or action that the speaker has in mind. Indeed, as apprentices to master language users, they might even come to overrely on social information about word learning. Finally, as suggested by Hoff and Naigles (2002; Naigles & Hoff-Ginsberg, 1995), children should come to use cues from the sentences they hear in the language to predict word meaning. At around 2 years and later, children comprehend sophisticated language structure and can use this structure to bootstrap word meaning. Indeed, many theories of verb development rely quite heavily on the child's burgeoning ability to detect linguistic structure (e.g., transitive and intransitive) in the input (Fisher, 2002; Lidz, Gleitman, & Gleitman, 2003; Naigles, 1990, 1996).

Principles of Word Learning Are Emergent

The third assumption of the model holds that principles for word learning are emergent. Only through the combination of all sources of information can the process of word learning proceed. Lexical principles are the products, not the engines, of lexical development. They develop from immature principles (e.g., the label goes with the most interesting thing in the environment) to more mature principles (e.g., the label stands for what the speaker has in mind) only as their capabilities develop and they obtain more "practice" in learning words (see also Smith, 2000; Smith, Jones, Landau, Gershkoff-Stowe, & Samuelson, 2002, for arguments that word-learning strategies change with practice). Early versions of the principles are subsequently refined to allow for faster and more precise word learning. For example, children do not start word learning with the N3C. Research shows that this principle is not in place until after the vocabulary spurt (Mervis & Bertrand, 1994).

Research from our laboratories has empirically assessed the assumptions of the ECM within the context of the principles of reference (that words map onto the child's representation of objects, actions, and events) and extendibility (that words map onto more than one exemplar; see Hollich et al., 2000). Three hypotheses are borne from the ECM: (a) children learning their first words (at 10 or 12 months of age) would be informed by multiple cues, of an attentional, social, and linguistic nature; (b) perceptual salience would be more heavily weighted than social cues for the novice than for the expert word learner; and (c) word-learning principles develop along a continuum from immature to mature such that children are first attracted by what is most salient to them, and only later note what is important to the speaker. As they break through the language barrier, children are guided (though not completely) by associationist laws—that is, perceptual salience. As they mature into veteran word learners, they are guided (though not completely) by social-pragmatic strategies—speaker intent.

Evidence for the Emergentist Coalition Model

Investigation of a hybrid model like the ECM demanded experiments that could trace development of the principles of reference and extendibility from their immature to their mature states. To assess the principle of reference, we examined whether infants would attach a label to both interesting and boring objects. We reasoned that a child with an immature principle of reference might attach a novel label to the perceptually interesting object—regardless of which object an adult was labeling. The child with a mature principle, in contrast, should overcome the salience of the object in favor of relying on the speaker's social cues to what is being labeled. To assess the principle of extendibility, we first asked whether infants would extend a label for a given object to one that differed only in color from the original exemplar. We then put infants in a very difficult task and asked whether they would use social information to extend that label to an object that bore no resemblance to the original object. After all, beanbag chairs and dining room chairs bear little resemblance to one another, and yet they are both called "chairs." Children who fail to extend a label or who will only extend the label to close perceptual relatives possess an immature principle of extendibility. Alternatively, children who trust a social mentor extending a label in the face of contrasting perceptual cues are operating with a mature principle of extendibility (Maguire, Hennon, Hirsh-Pasek, & Golinkoff, 2005).

Examination of the emergentist coalition theory required a method that could be used equally effectively with children in the age range of interest (10 to 24 months) and one that would enable researchers to manipulate multiple cues (attentional, social, and linguistic) and their interactions. The Interactive Intermodal Preferential Looking Paradigm (IIPLP) provided this new method (e.g., Hollich et al., 2000). Based on the "Intermodal Preferential Looking Paradigm" (Golinkoff, Hirsh-Pasek, Cauley, & Gordon, 1987; Hirsh-Pasek & Golinkoff, 1996) used to study lexical and syntactic comprehension, Baldwin's (1991) "bucket task," and Fagan's (1971; Fagan, Singer, Montic, & Shepard, 1986) infant intelligence test, the method allows for the study of multiple cues to word learning in the first two years of life. The physical setup is depicted in figure 5–2.

Infants are seated on their blindfolded mother's lap facing the experimenter and our testing apparatus. After preexposure to the toys—familiar toys on some trials and novel toys on others—the toys are fixed with Velcro onto one side of a two-sided black board that can be rotated so that the toys can go in and out of view for a specified period of time. The experimenter hides behind the board while children are inspecting the toys and during test trials. Coding is done off-line from videotaped records, and interrater reliability has consistently been very high.

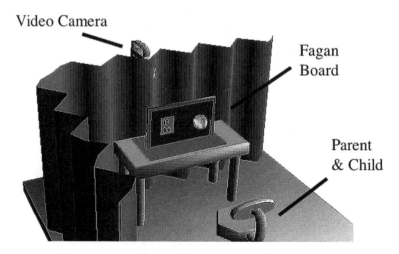

Figure 5–2. Interactive IPLP: The child sits on his or her parent's lap in front of the board. The experimenter stands behind the flip board. A hidden camera behind the curtain records children's looking preferences toward two objects on the display board.

Using this apparatus, it is possible to examine word learning in a controlled setting. Familiar object trials allow us to ask whether the child can "play our game." The use of unfamiliar, novel objects permits exploration of the cues and *combinations* of cues that children use to guide word learning across development. The logic of the design (Golinkoff et al., 1987; Hirsh-Pasek & Golinkoff, 1996) is that children should look more at an object that "matches" the linguistic stimulus than at an object that does not match. Thus, the dependent variable is visual fixation time to the target (named) object versus to the unnamed object.

Validation of the method comes from the familiar trials. Children at three ages were tested: 12- to 13-month-olds just at the beginning of word learning; 19- to 20-month-olds, who may or may not have yet experienced a vocabulary spurt; and 24- to 25-month olds, who typically have sizable production vocabularies. In more than 23 experiments children demonstrated the potency of the method by looking significantly more at the target item than at the nontarget item in the familiar condition when an item was requested (Hollich et al., 2000). Evaluation of the hypotheses comes from children's responses to *novel* stimuli. Using this method, we were able to explore how infants move from immature to mature principles of reference and extendibility and to examine the hypotheses that form the foundation for the emergentist coalition model. We were able to better understand how and when children used social information to buttress word learning.

Evidence From the Studies on the Principle of Reference

Reference, or the assumption that words refer, is the most basic of the word-learning principles. Do infants assume that a word refers to an object, action, or event? How do they decide which object, action, or event should receive a label when one is offered? To investigate these questions, conditions were created in which multiple cues were available to children but were sometimes placed in conflict. In what we called the *coincident* condition, we labeled the novel toy that coincided with children's preferences the "interesting toy." In the *conflict* condition, we labeled the novel toy that did not coincide with the children's preferences the "boring toy." We reasoned that learning the word in the coincident case should be easy for children because all of the "cues"—attentional, social and linguistic—were in alignment. In contrast, learning a novel word in the conflict condition should be more difficult because the coalition of cues is not acting in concert.

The experiment was conducted in four phases. First, children were given the opportunity to explore both the interesting and the boring toys. Second, children participated in a salience trial in which they saw both the interesting and the boring toy mounted side by side on the board. Third, in the labeling phase, the experimenter captured children's attention, displayed both toys and labeled the target five times with a novel word (e.g., "danu"). In the coincident condition, the experimenter looked at and labeled the interesting toy; in the conflict condition, she looked at and labeled the boring toy. Finally, in the test trials, the experimenter, now hiding behind the board, asked for the object that was labeled during training, once again getting the child's attention first. For example, she might say, "Eve, where's the danu?" If children learned the name of the correct toy, they should look more to the target than at the nontarget (see Hollich et al., 2000, for details).

Do children understand that words refer? What cues do they use to determine the referent of a word? The participants in this study were 32 children at each of 12, 19, and 24 months of age. At all three ages, there is evidence that children detected the range of cues available. Importantly, even the 12-month-olds detected the social cue of eye gaze. They could not, however, use the social cues to inform word learning when they were in conflict with perceptual salience. The 12-month-old children learned the name of the object only in the coincident condition, as several further studies indicated (Hollich et al., 2000). The 19-month-olds learned the names of the objects in both conditions but were still influenced heavily by perceptual salience. Even the oldest group who learned the names of the novel objects in both the conflict and the coincident conditions still showed the effects of perceptual salience by looking much longer at the target object in the coincident condition than in the conflict condition. This suggests that children were lured by the perceptual salience of the interesting toy but were able to overcome it when the boring toy was the focus of the experimenter's attention. In short, these data suggest that infants with an immature principle of reference are more dominated by perceptual salience than are their counterparts with a more mature principle of reference. Nineteen- and 24-month old children recruit the speaker's social intent when mapping word to object.

In light of these data, we conducted studies with 10-month-old infants to see whether children who were just beginning to acquire a comprehension vocabulary operated like the 12-month-olds who were starting to produce language. Results from this age-group suggest that 10-month-olds are even more bound to perceptual salience than the 12-month-olds. They demonstrated a clear preference for the interesting toy even in the conflict condition, suggesting these children ignore the presence of conflicting social cues. They apparently assume that labels "go with" interesting rather than boring objects, regardless of what the speaker is labeling (Hirsh-Pasek, Golinkoff, Pruden, & Hennon, 2005)!

What we see in the data is a clear pattern that changes over time, such that infants become increasingly less dependent on perceptual cues and more dependent on social cues to determine reference. Such data speak to both the associationist and the social-pragmatic theorist. The associationist position would predict that children *would* form a mismapping between the *interesting* object and the label in the conflict condition. If the 10-month-old data stand, then these data fit this prediction—but only for the very youngest children. Yet, by as early as 12 months of age, children with only three words in their productive vocabularies are already demonstrating some sensitivity to social information in a word-learning task. These children, at the cusp of word learning, learned the novel labels only in the coincident condition. In the coincident condition, the experimenter labeled the object that the babies were most interested in. For these babies, learning took place when the cues coincided. However, when multiple cues failed to coincide in the conflict condition, infants showed little evidence of word learning. They wanted to look at the interesting object despite the fact that the experimenter persisted in labeling the boring object. Though they looked at the interesting object much more than the boring object in the conflict condition, they did not falsely conclude that the novel label was attached to the interesting object. Even 12-month-olds were sensitive to the fact that the experimenter was looking elsewhere and *not* labeling the interesting object. These children are able to use multiple cues for word learning, but for learning to occur, the cues had to *overlap*. Although the 12-month-olds are not yet social pragmatists, they also defy the predictions made by the associationistic camp. Only a hybrid theory that addresses attention to multiple cues and differential attention to these cues over time can account for the data.

The ECM can and has been readily applied to verb learning. Using a similar design, but using the standard video version of the preferential looking paradigm, Pence et al. (2003) tested 21- to 24-month-old children's ability to attach a novel verb to a natural action and noted a similar pattern of results using the live demonstration of an interesting action and a boring action (see Pence et al., 2003, for condition demonstrating unequal salience of actions).

Evidence From Studies on Extension

Our research examines not only the use of social information in determining word reference but also word extension. That is, what cues do children use to extend a label for an object to another perceptually similar and dissimilar object (Maguire et al., 2005)? As in the study of reference, we reasoned that very young children might accept the same label for objects that are perceptually similar, only later relying on speaker knowledge—social cues—to extend the label to objects that are perceptually distinct. Indeed, this is exactly what Maguire et al. found. Thirty-six children at each of ages 12, 19, and 24 months participated in this research. The experimenter offered a novel label for objects that differed only in color (three lemon juicers), that shared perceptual features for one dominant part (see table 5–1 in the color insert) or that had no features in common.

The results suggested that infants had no trouble extending a novel label to objects that shared shape but not color, or even shape in a dominant part. In stark contrast, we witnessed a developmental progression in children's willingness to accept the same label for objects that did not have any properties in common. Only 24-month-olds were willing to learn a common label for two objects that appeared to be very distinct. Only 24-month-olds were willing to "trust" the social mentor.

Taken together, this research on reference and extendability of words suggests that children are aware of the multiple cues for word learning, but that the potency of these cues changes over time. For word learning, social cues are important for young children because they allow them to tap into the vast resources of adult competencies. While some challenge the universality of the naming explosion (Goldfield & Reznick, 1990, 1996), it is at least interesting that the ability to use social cues in word learning seems to come online at around the time that children begin to amass a large number of words in their vocabulary.

Implications of the Emergentist Coalition Model

Our research suggests that children use multiple cues, at different points along their journey, to learn words. These data further suggest that the myopic views of word learning offer only incomplete snapshots of behavior. If it is the case that we can find testable hypotheses in an integrated view, then it should be possible to apply the theory broadly and gain new insights into how social cues feed into language development as broadly conceived. Two areas that might prove particularly fruitful for study would be the study of language disabilities and the study of the neurological correlates of early language development. What would happen, for example, if one of these critical forms of input (perceptual, social, and linguistic) was unavailable? How might these children and adults coordinate the cues differently, in ways that optimize learning and processing? Further, if language development is about the development of, use of, and coordination of multiple cues across time, then any disruption in the processing of those cues should differentially impair the acquisition and processing of language in both comprehension and production at different points in time.

Neurological studies could also provide insight into how social information and language interact. First, if areas of the brain that control social and emotional development are compromised, one should see concomitant deficiencies in the development of early language ability, especially at around 18 months to 2 years of age, when social information in language acquisition becomes more prominent. It would also be interesting to perform longitudinal studies in typically developing populations looking at both behavioral and neurobiological correlates. There should be not only biological evidence that underlies normal growth but also some biological underpinnings for the coordination of social, perceptual, and linguistic cues across time. Although these are but speculative ideas, the twinning of behavioral and neurobiological measures could offer rich hypotheses about understanding the mechanisms behind language development.

Atypical Language Development

As a comprehensive theory of language development, the ECM allows us to explain the problems observed in both normal and atypical populations. For example, we can ask if language impairments seen in atypical populations come from a dampening of one of the input cues (e.g., social cues) or from a delay in the accessibility of that cue. Language impairments that relate to the use of social information in autism may be best explained using our model.

The work of Baron-Cohen, Baldwin, and Crowson (1997), for example, suggests that some of the key social cues used in language are severely compromised in autistic children. These researchers found that only 29% of autistic children were able to use a speaker's direction of gaze to infer the referent of a novel word, whereas more than 79% of normal children and 70% of mentally handicapped children were able to use a speaker's eye gaze in a word-learning situation. Further, many describe autism's primary impairment as an inability to understand and interpret another's social intent (Baron-Cohen, 1995; Baron-Cohen et al., 1997; Tager-Flusberg, 1999b, 2001). If autistic children do not orient to naturally occurring social stimuli, such as hearing their name called (Dawson, Meltzoff, Osterling, Rinaldi, & Brown, 1998), and they show diminished evidence of joint attention (Baron-Cohen, Tager-Flusberg, & Cohen, 2000), they should show a different and deficient trajectory of language development (see Lord & Paul, 1997, and Tager-Flusberg, 1999a, 2001, for reviews). Indeed, they do. Research in this area shows that lower-functioning autistics either have echolalic speech or never acquire any expressive language at all (mutism; Bailey, Phillips, & Rutter, 1996). Those who exhibit echolalic speech often repeat parts or all of what a speaker said (Fay, 1993). Higher-functioning autistic children acquire language, but they also have both delayed and deviant language development. While these children show vocabulary growth and understand word meanings similar to mental-aged matched children (Tager-Flusberg, 1985; Tager-Flusberg et al., 1990), they show delays in prosody, syntactic development, and pragmatics. Mundy and colleagues (Mundy, Sigman, & Kasari, 1990; Mundy, Sigman, Ungerer, & Sherman, 1987) show that less impaired autistic children who engage in joint attention develop language skills far superior to those who do not engage in joint attention. Research also shows that some autistic children exhibit a regression that entails loss of previously acquired language and social skills, including loss of word use, following directed eye gaze and orienting to one's name (Goldberg et al., 2003). More than half of the autistic children who showed evidence of word loss in their sample also showed a loss of social skills. These losses were evident in the second year of life—an age associated with developments in social intention.

Using a model like the ECM offers a slightly different way to frame the problem. If autistic children have trouble using social information in word learning or grammatical learning, do they compensate by using information from either the perceptual or the grammatical input at their disposal? Given our model of how social information contributes to the process of word learning we might expect (a) that word learning might be slower during the second half of the second year, when social information comes online for word learning, and (b) the word learning that is achieved might be accomplished through different strategies than those used by typically developing children. As our model predicts, these other means might be perceptual, attentional, and/or grammatical elements.

There is evidence to suggest a decrease in the rate of word learning for autistic children in the second year (Goldberg et al., 2003; Lord & Paul, 1997). Recent research in our laboratory directly addressed the second prediction that autistic children come to rely on perceptual strategies as a means to lexical learning (Hennon, Hirsh-Pasek, & Golinkoff, 2003). This research examined the language development of 3- to 7-year-old autistic children and showed that these children do *not* have the ability to use social cues in word learning. Rather, they learned words through increased attention to perceptual salience, responding more like typical 1-year-olds in their language processing (Hollich et al., 2000).

Thus, by looking at atypical populations, one not only can begin to test the ECM of language learning but also can better specify the role and timing of social information in language acquisition. To fully take advantage of this strategy, it would be important to mount longitudinal studies of atypical children who are reported to have particular deficits and to not only chart their language development but also pinpoint the ways in which particular processes come online and interact in the course of language development.

Neurobiological Correlates of Language Acquisition

There is a rich literature on neurological correlates of language (see Bates, Thal, Finlay, & Clancy, 2002, for a recent review). For example, research on the neurological correlates of lexical learning demonstrates that by 20 months of age, processing of linguistic stimuli (both familiar and unfamiliar words) is limited to the temporal and parietal areas of the left hemisphere (Mills, Coffey-Corina, & Neville, 1993; although see Bates et al., 1997, and Neville & Mills, 1997). Some researchers have proposed two postnatal correlates of language development that may underlie the major language milestones. The first of these proposals explores the changes in frontal activity in the brain in 8- to 10-month-olds—a period during which we see a growth in word comprehension and communication, and social development such as imitation, intention, and joint referencing. Chugani, Phelps, and Mazziotta (1987) demonstrated an increase in frontal lobe metabolism in 9- to 12-month-olds that is thought to be caused by a burst in synaptogenesis. Such findings led to the proposal that the frontal lobes "come online" in the first year of life and coincide with language milestones such as word comprehension. More recently, Clancy and Finlay (2001) have argued that the behavioral developments seen between 8 and 10 months of age are a result of the social and cognitive systems reaching "a certain critical level of organization" rather than a sudden maturation of the frontal lobes (p. 324). The second of these proposals explores the changes in the brain correlated with a burst in vocabulary and grammar between 16 and 30 months of age. There appear to be parallels between synaptogenesis and the bursts in both vocabulary and grammar, but little research has explored these parallels. However, some argue that these bursts in language development do not depend entirely on synaptogenesis. Rather, "the compelling parallel between the language burst and the synapse burst may represent a mutually beneficial relationship, but not a crucial and direct relationship of cause and effect" (Clancy & Finlay, 2001, p. 324). Research on the neurological correlates of language acquisition that takes a developmental perspective is just beginning to emerge. Even less of that research is relevant to the ways in which social information might support or interact with language development. In this sense, studies that examine correlations between neurological and behavioral developments might offer insight into the ways in which social information is utilized in word learning and grammatical development.

Not only is there beginning research on neurological development and language, but there is also nascent research on areas of the developing brain related to social development. Studies on joint attention by Mundy, Card, and Fox (2000) found that 14- and 18-month-old infants who had greater left-frontal and left- and right-central cortical activity were more likely to initiate joint attention episodes. Frith and Frith (2001) investigated the biological basis of social interaction and demonstrated that a network of areas in the brain, including the medial prefrontal and temporal cortex, are involved with representing one's own and others' mental states. These areas of the brain may be involved with aspects of social interaction such as representing intention and the goals of actions. Such studies provide evidence for neural processes associated with language development and social development (see also Mundy & Acra, this volume). They do not, however, directly address the underlying neural processes that may be important to the *linkage* between language and social development.

Is there any relation between the brain areas involved in social development and those involved in language acquisition? This is a central question that could help us better understand the mechanisms behind language learning. Mundy, Fox, and Card (2003) are among the first to ask this question by studying whether neurological underpinnings for *joint attention* are *related* to early aspects of *language development*. According to Mundy and colleagues, "Some element of the commonly observed linkage between initiating joint attention and language may involve basic infant brain-related maturation processes" (p. 52). Their research indicates that there is in fact a relationship between brain maturation and joint attention skills on developing lexical abilities. Specifically, later language ability was predicted by both electroencephalographic coherence measures and joint attention.

To date, these studies of language development and social cognition are exploratory. They are already, however, beginning to chart neurological foundations for the social cognition that might mediate language development. From the rich data on typically developing children, several areas of study should prove even more profitable as researchers begin to chart this domain. First, given the behavioral data described in the second section of this chapter, continued exploration of the neurological bases for social constructs like joint attention and social intent would be the best starting points for an understanding of how social cues mediate early lexical learning. There are clear behavioral operational definitions of these constructs that can be used to isolate incidents of these behaviors and to look for neurological underpinnings of these behaviors. There is also a wealth of data relating the use of social intent and joint attention to concurrent and later language skills (e.g., Carpenter, Nagell, & Tomasello, 1998; Tomasello & Farrar, 1986; Tomasello & Todd, 1983).

Looking ahead, it would probably be worthwhile to design not only cross-sectional studies of neurological and behavioral development in social cognition and language but also longitudinal studies. Perhaps social and cognitive developments in the brain jointly pave the way for later language skills (Clancy & Finlay, 2001). Another possibility is that there may be timing shifts such that neurological changes that feed the development of social intent enable concomitant changes in language that allow for behaviors like the so-called naming explosion (Mills, Coffey-Corina, & Neville, 1997), where children move from learning around two new words a day at roughly 19 months of age, to almost nine new words a day at 23 months of age (L. Bloom, 1973; Carey, 1978; Nelson, 1973; but see Goldfield & Reznick, 1990, 1996, for an alternative view).

It would be interesting to examine not only how social behaviors come online to support language development but also how varied behaviors are integrated toward a complex task like language learning. For example, the ECM suggests that perceptual cues give way to social cues as the dominant roadway for language learning. Is there neurological support for this behavioral evidence? Can we examine the ways in which children come to coordinate various sources of information toward an end? Some have argued that children with particular disabilities like autism might have access to independent sources of information, but that they cannot coordinate the information toward a goal like language learning (Frith, 2003). Similarly, the ECM suggests that principles of language learning emerge in the coordination of perceptual, social, and linguistic cues as children move toward language competence.

In short, behavioral data on developing social and language cues offer a looking glass for neurological researchers. As we better understand the neurological foundations for social behaviors and for language development in their parallel planes, we can begin to examine how areas might jointly support both developments. How might the absence of abilities in one area challenge the other? How might the brain compensate for the lack of social cues in language development? Are there specific areas of the brain that specialize in the coordination of cues toward a complex behavior like language development? Looking at neurobiological data in tandem with behavioral accounts will surely help us move from mere descriptions of what the brain does to explanations of why there appears to be a social dimension that might mediate early lexical and grammatical acquisition.

Conclusions

It is becoming increasingly clear that social and cognitive developments are inextricably intertwined. Nowhere has this story been more forcefully told than in the area of language development, where the "interactionists" have struggled to find equal footing with the nativists to account for the acquisition of words and grammar. Language is learned within a social context, and certain social developments seem pivotal to language growth. In the area of word learning, the abilities to use joint attention and to interpret social intent are perhaps necessary ingredients. In grammar, children may also benefit from attention to infant-directed speech and to the recasts and expansions that might offer informal language lessons for the naive grammarian.

Language is a complex cognitive process that no doubt will be served by multiple processes and behaviors. Recently, a number of researchers have tried to develop interactive models that capture that complexity. These models go beyond evidence that social information plays some role in particular parts of language development to ask how social processing, in tandem with other kinds of processing, yields emergent language behavior. The ECM is one such account.

In this chapter, we have argued that accounts like the ECM can be used to reevaluate our understanding of the relationship between social cognition and language in typical populations. The model might help us to better understand how these behaviors interrelate in atypical populations, and it might chart directions for the new frontier of research in neuropsychology and language.

Approaches like the ECM move beyond searching for a single-factor, "smoking gun" explanation for language development. Instead, they encourage us to take multiple, interacting factors into account as we unpack complex behavior. They force us to ask not only what biological foundations might separately underlie aspects of language but also how these factors mediate the path toward language competence as they separately develop, come online in ontogeny, and coordinate with other abilities (social, linguistic, and perceptual input).

Acknowledgments This work was supported by NSF grants SBR9615391 and SBR9601306 to the second two authors.

References

Adamson, L. B. (1995). *Communication development during infancy.* Madison, WI: Brown and Benchmark.

Aguiar, A., & Baillargeon, R. (2002). Developments in young infants' reasoning about occluded objects. *Cognitive Psychology, 45,* 267–336.

Akhtar, N., Carpenter, M., & Tomasello, M. (1996). The role of discourse novelty in early word learning. *Child Development, 67,* 635–645.

Akhtar, N., & Tomasello, M. (1996). Twenty-four-month-old children learn words for absent objects and action. *British Journal of Developmental Psychology, 14,* 79–93.

Akhtar, N., & Tomasello, M. (2000). The social nature of words and word learning. In R. M. Golinkoff, K. Hirsh-Pasek, L. Bloom, L. B. Smith, A. L. Woodward, et al. (Eds.), *Becoming a word learner: A debate on lexical acquisition* (pp. 115–135). New York: Oxford University Press.

Bahrick, L. E. (1983). Infants' perception of substance and temporal synchrony in multimodal events. *Infant Behavior and Development, 6,* 429–451.

Bailey, A., Phillips, W., & Rutter, M. (1996). Autism: Toward an integration of clinical, genetic, neuropsychological and neurobiological perspectives. *Journal of Child Psychology and Psychiatry, 37,* 89–126.

Baldwin, D. A. (1991). Infants' contribution to the achievement of joint reference. *Child Development, 62,* 875–890.

Baldwin, D. A. (1993). Infants' ability to consult the speaker for clues to word reference. *Journal of Child Language, 20,* 395–418.

Baldwin, D. A., Bill, B., & Ontai, L. L. (1996, May). *Infants' tendency to monitor others' gaze: Is it rooted in intentional understanding or a result of simple orienting?* Paper presented at the International Conference on Infant Studies, Providence, RI.

Baldwin, D. A., & Moses, L. J. (2001). Links between social understanding and early word learning: Challenges to current accounts. *Social Development, 10,* 309–329.

Baldwin, D. A., & Tomasello, M. (1998). Word learning: A window on early pragmatic understanding. In E. Clark (Ed.), *Proceedings of the Twenty-ninth Annual Child Language Research Forum* (Vol. 29, pp. 3–23). Cambridge, England: Cambridge University Press.

Baron-Cohen, S. (1995). *Mindblindness: An essay on autism and theory of mind.* Cambridge, MA: MIT Press.

Baron-Cohen, S., Baldwin, D. A., & Crowson, M. (1997). Do children with autism use the speaker's direction of gaze strategy to crack to code of language? *Child Development, 68,* 48–57.

Baron-Cohen, S., Tager-Flusberg, H., & Cohen, D. (2000). *Understanding other minds: Perspectives from developmental cognitive neuroscience.* New York: Oxford University Press.

Bates, E., & MacWhinney, B. (1987). Competition, variation, and language learning. In B. MacWhinney (Ed.), *Mechanisms of language acquisition* (pp. 157–193). Hillsdale, NJ: Erlbaum.

Bates, E., Thal, D., Finlay, B. L., & Clancy, B. (2002). Early language development and its neural correlates. In I. Rapin, & S. Segalowitz (Eds.), *Handbook of neuropsychology: Vol. 7. Child neuropsychology* (pp. 69–110). Amsterdam: Elsevier.

Bates, E., Thal, D., Trauner, D., Fenson, J., Aram, D., Eisele, J., et al. (1997). From first words to grammar in children with focal brain injury. *Developmental Neuropsychology, 13,* 275–343.

Berk, L. E. (2003). *Child development* (6th ed.). Needham Heights, MA: Allyn and Bacon.

Bloom, L. (1973). *One word at a time.* The Hague, Netherlands: Mouton.

Bloom, L. (1993). *The transition from infancy to language: Acquiring the power of expression.* Cambridge, England: Cambridge University Press.

Bloom, L. (1998). Language development and emotional expression. *Pediatrics, 102*, 1272–1277.

Bloom, L. (2000). The intentionality model of word learning: How to learn a word, any word. In R. M. Golinkoff, K. Hirsh-Pasek, L. Bloom, L. Smith, A. Woodward, N. Akhtar, et al. (Eds.), *Becoming a word learner: A debate on lexical acquisition* (pp. 19–50). New York: Oxford University Press.

Bloom, L., & Capatides, J. B. (1987). Expression of affect and the emergence of language. *Child Development, 58*, 1513–1522.

Bloom, L., & Tinker, E. (2001). The intentionality model and language acquisition: Engagement, effort, and the essential tension in development. *Monographs of the Society for Research in Child Development, 66*(4), 1–89.

Bloom, P. (2000). *How children learn the meanings of words*. Cambridge, MA: MIT Press.

Bohannon, J. N., & Stanowicz, L. (1988). The issue of negative evidence: Adult responses to children's language errors. *Developmental Psychology, 24*, 684–689.

Bretherton, I. (1992). Social referencing, intentional communication, and the interfacing of minds in infancy. In S. Feinman (Ed.), *Social referencing and the social construction of reality in infancy* (pp. 57–77). New York: Plenum.

Brooks, R., & Meltzoff, A. N. (2002). The importance of eyes: How infants interpret adult looking behavior. *Developmental Psychology, 38*, 958–966.

Brown, R. (1973). *A first language: The early stages*. Cambridge, MA: Harvard University Press.

Bruner, J. (1975). The ontogenesis of speech acts. *Journal of Child Language, 2*, 1–19.

Bruner, J. (1983). *Child's talk: Learning to use language*. New York: Norton.

Burnham, D., & Kitamura, C. (2002). What's new, pussycat? On talking to babies and animals. *Science, 296*, 1435.

Butterworth, G. (1995). Origins of mind in perception and action. In C. Moore & P. J. Dunham (Eds.), *Joint attention: Its origins and role in development* (pp. 29–40). Hillsdale, NJ: Erlbaum.

Butterworth, G. (2003). Pointing is the royal road to language for babies. In S. Kita (Ed.), *Pointing: Where language, culture, and cognition meet* (pp. 9–33). Mahwah, NJ: Erlbaum.

Butterworth, G. E., & Itakura, S. (1998). How the eyes, head and hand serve definite reference for babies, children and adults. *British Journal of Developmental Psychology, 18*, 25–50.

Carey, S. (1978). The child as a word learner. In M. Halle, J. Bresnan, & G. A. Miller (Eds.), *Linguistic theory and psychological reality* (pp. 264–293). Cambridge, MA: MIT Press.

Carpenter, M., Akhtar, N., & Tomasello, M. (1998). Fourteen- to 18–month-old infants differentially imitate intentional and accidental actions. *Infant Behavior and Development, 21*, 315–330.

Carpenter, M., Nagell, K., & Tomasello, M. (1998). Social cognition, joint attention, and communicative competence from 9 to 15 months of age. *Monographs of the Society for Research in Child Development, 63*(4), 1–176.

Chomsky, N. (1965). *Aspects of the theory of syntax*. Cambridge, MA: MIT Press.

Chomsky, N. (1975). *Reflections on language*. New York: Random House.

Chomsky, N. (1981). *Lectures on government and binding*. Dordrecht, Netherlands: Foris.

Chouinard, M. M., & Clark, E. V. (2003). Adult reformulations of child errors as negative evidence. *Journal of Child Language, 30*, 637–669.

Chugani, H. T., Phelps, M. E., & Mazziotta, J. C. (1987). Positron emission tomography study of human brain functional development. *Annals of Neurology, 22*, 487–497.

Clancy, B., & Finlay, B. (2001). Neural correlates of early language learning. In M. Tomasello & E. Bates (Eds.), *Language development: The essential readings* (pp. 307–330). Malden, MA: Blackwell.

Clark, E. (2003). *First language acquisition*. Cambridge, UK: Cambridge University Press.

Cooper, R. P., & Aslin, R. N. (1990). Preference for infant-directed speech in the first month after birth. *Child Development, 61*, 1584–1595.

Corkum, V., & Moore, C. (1995). Development of joint visual attention in infants. In C. Moore and P. J. Dunham (Eds.), *Joint attention: Its origins and role in development* (pp. 61–83). Hillsdale, NJ: Erlbaum.

Dawson, G., Meltzoff, A. N., Osterling, J., Rinaldi, J., & Brown, E. (1998). Children with autism fail to orient to naturally occurring social stimuli. *Journal of Autism and Developmental Disorders, 28*, 479–485.

Demetras, M. J., Post, K. N., & Snow, C. E. (1986). Feedback to first language learners: The role of repetitions and clarification questions. *Journal of Child Language, 13*, 275–302.

Diesendruck, G., Markson, L., Akhtar, N., & Reudor, A. (2004). Two-year-olds' sensitivity to speakers' intent: An alternative account of Samuelson and Smith. *Developmental Science, 7*, 33–41.

Dunham, P. J., & Dunham, F. (1992). Lexical development during middle infancy: A mutually driven infant-caregiver process. *Developmental Psychology, 28*, 414–420.

Dunham, P. J., Dunham, F., & Curwin, A. (1993). Joint-attentional states and lexical acquisition at 18 months. *Developmental Psychology, 29*, 827–831.

Eisenberg, N. (2001). The core and correlates of affective social competence. *Social Development, 10*, 120–124.

Eisenberg, N., & Zhou, Q. (2000). Regulation from a developmental perspective. *Psychological Inquiry, 11*, 166–171.

Elman, J. (2001). Connectionism and language acquisition. In M. Tomasello & E. Bates (Eds.), *Language development: The essential readings* (pp. 295–306). Malden, MA: Blackwell.

Fagan, J. (1971). Infant recognition memory for a series of visual stimuli. *Journal of Experimental Child Psychology, 11*, 244–250.

Fagan, J., Singer, L., Montic, J., & Shepard, P. (1986). Selective screening device for the early detection of normal or delayed cognitive development in infants at risk for later mental retardation. *Pediatrics, 78*, 1021–1026.

Farrar, M. J. (1992). Negative evidence and grammatical morpheme acquisition. *Developmental Psychology, 28*, 90–98.

Fauconnier, G. (1985). *Mental spaces: Aspects of meaning construction in natural language*. Cambridge, MA: MIT Press.

Fay, W. H. (1993). Infantile autism. In D. Bishop & K. Mogford (Eds.), *Language development in exceptional circumstances* (pp. 190–202). Hillsdale, NJ: Erlbaum.

Feinman, S. (1992). *Social referencing and the social construction of reality in infancy*. New York: Plenum.

Fernald, A. (1985). Four-month-old infants prefer to listen to motherese. *Infant Behavior and Development, 8*, 181–195.

Fernald, A. (1992). Human maternal vocalizations to infants as biologically relevant signals: An evolutionary perspective. In J. Barkow, L. Cosmides, & J. Tooby (Eds.), *The adapted mind: Evolutionary psychology and the generation of culture* (pp. 391–428). Oxford: Oxford University Press.

Fernald, A., & Mazzie, C. (1991). Prosody and focus in speech to infants and adults. *Developmental Psychology, 27*, 209–221.

Fernald, A., & Morikawa, H. (1993). Common themes and cultural variations in Japanese and American mothers' speech to infants. *Child Development, 64*, 637–656.

Fernald, A., Taeschner, T., Dun, J., Papousek, M., De Boysson-Bardies, B., & Fukui, I. (1989). A cross-language study of prosodic modifications in mothers' and fathers' speech to preverbal infants. *Journal of Child Language, 16*, 477–501.

Fisher, C. (2002). Structural limits on verb mapping: The role of abstract structure in 2.5-year- olds' interpretations of novel verbs. *Developmental Science, 5*, 55–64.

Fox, N. (2003). Not quite ready to invest. *Human Development, 46*, 104–108.

Frith, U. (2003). *Autism: Explaining the enigma* (2nd ed.). Malden, MA: Blackwell.

Frith, U., & Frith, C. (2001). The biological basis of social interaction. *Current Directions in Psychological Science, 10*, 151–155.

Gergely, G., Nadasdy, Z., Csibra, G., & Biro, S. (1995). Taking the intentional stance at 12 months of age. *Cognition, 56*, 165–193.

Gleitman, L. R., Gleitman, H., Landau, B., & Wanner, E. (1988). Where learning begins: Initial representations for language learning. In F. J. Newmeyer (Ed.), *Language: Psychological and biological aspects* (pp. 150–193). New York: Cambridge University Press.

Gleitman, L., & Wanner, E. (1982). Language acquisition: The state of the art. In E. Wanner & L. Gleitman (Eds.), *Language acquisition: The state of the art* (pp. 3–48). Cambridge, England: Cambridge University Press.

Gogate, L. J., & Bahrick, L. E. (1998). Intersensory redundancy facilitates learning of arbitrary relations between vowel sounds and objects in seven-month-old infants. *Journal of Experimental Child Psychology, 69*, 133–149.

Goldberg, W. A., Osann, K., Filipek, P. A., Laulhere, T., Jarvis, K., Modahl, C., et al. (2003). Language and other regression: Assessment and timing. *Journal of Autism and Developmental Disorders, 33*, 607–616.

Goldfield, B. A., & Reznick, J. S. (1990). Early lexical acquisition: Rate, content, and the vocabulary spurt. *Journal of Child Language, 17*, 171–183.

Goldfield, B. A., & Reznick, J. S. (1996). Measuring the vocabulary spurt: A reply to Mervis & Bertrand. *Journal of Child Language, 23*, 241–246.

Golinkoff, R. M., & Alioto, A. (1995). Infant directed speech facilitates lexical learning in adults hearing Chinese: Implications for language acquisition. *Journal of Child Language, 22*, 703–726.

Golinkoff, R. M., & Hirsh-Pasek, K. (1999). *How babies talk: The magic and mystery of language in the first three years of life*. New York: Dutton/Penguin.

Golinkoff, R. M., Hirsh-Pasek, K., Bailey, L. M., & Wenger, N. R. (1992). Young children and adults use lexical principles to learn new nouns. *Developmental Psychology, 28*, 99–108.

Golinkoff, R. M., Hirsh-Pasek, K., Bloom, L., Smith, L., Woodward, A., Akhtar, N., et al. (2000). *Becoming a word learner: A debate on lexical acquisition*. New York: Oxford University Press.

Golinkoff, R. M., Hirsh-Pasek, K., Cauley, K. M., & Gordon, L. (1987). The eyes have it: Lexical and syntactic comprehension in a new paradigm. *Journal of Child Language, 14*, 23–45.

Golinkoff, R. M., Mervis, C., & Hirsh-Pasek, K. (1994). Early object labels: The case for a developmental lexical principles framework. *Journal of Child Language, 21*, 125–155.

Grieser, D. L., & Kuhl, P. K. (1988). Maternal speech to infants in a tonal language: Support for the universal prosodic features in motherese. *Developmental Psychology, 24*, 14–20.

Hennon, E., Hirsh-Pasek, K., & Golinkoff, R. M. (2003, April). *Speaker intention? Autistic children may learn words without it.* Poster session presented at the biennial meeting for the Society for Research in Child Development, Tampa, FL.

Hirsh-Pasek, K., & Golinkoff, R. M. (1996). *The origins of grammar: Evidence from early language comprehension.* Cambridge, MA: MIT Press.

Hirsh-Pasek, K., Golinkoff, R. M., & Hollich, G. (2000). An emergentist coalition model for word learning: Mapping words to objects is a product of the interaction of multiple cues. In R. M. Golinkoff, K. Hirsh-Pasek, L. Bloom, L. Smith, A. Woodward, N. Akhtar, et al. (Eds.), *Becoming a word learner: A debate on lexical acquisition* (pp. 136–164). New York: Oxford University Press.

Hirsh-Pasek, K., Golinkoff, R. M., Pruden, S. M., & Hennon, E. (2005). *Birth of words.* Manuscript in preparation.

Hirsh-Pasek, K., Kemler Nelson, D. G., Jusczyk, P. W., Cassidy, K. W., Druss, B., & Kennedy, L. (1987). Clauses are perceptual units for young infants. *Cognition, 26*, 269–286.

Hirsh-Pasek, K., & Treiman, R. (1982). Doggerel: Motherese in a new context. *Journal of Child Language, 9*, 229–237.

Hirsh-Pasek, K., Treiman, R., & Schneiderman, M. (1984). Brown and Hanlon revisited: Mothers' sensitivity to ungrammatical forms. *Journal of Child Language, 11*, 81–88.

Hoff, E., & Naigles, L. (2002). How children use input to acquire a lexicon. *Child Development, 73*, 418–433.

Hollich, G., Hirsh-Pasek, K., & Golinkoff, R. M. (2000). Breaking the language barrier: An emergentist coalition model for the origins of word learning. *Monographs of the Society for Research in Child Development, 65*(3), 1–138.

Jusczyk, P. W., Hirsh-Pasek, K., Kemler Nelson, D. G., Kennedy, L. J., Woodward, A., & Piwoz, J. (1992). Perception of acoustic correlates of major phrasal units by young infants. *Cognitive Psychology, 24*, 252–293.

Karzon, R. G. (1985). Discrimination of polysyllabic sequences by one-to-four-month-old infants. *Journal of Experimental Child Psychology, 39,* 326–342.

Kaye, K., & Charney, R. (1980). How mothers maintain "dialogue" with two-year-olds. In D. Olson (Ed.), *The social foundations of language and thought* (pp. 211–230). New York: Norton.

Kemler-Nelson, D. G., Hirsh-Pasek, K., Jusczyk, P., & Cassidy, K. W. (1989). How the prosodic cues in motherese might assist language learning. *Journal of Child Language, 16*, 55–68.

Kuhl, P. K., Andruski, J. E., Chistovich, I. A., Chistovich, L. A., Kozhevnikova, E. V., Ryskina, V. L., et al. (1997). Cross-language analysis of phonetic units in language addressed to infants. *Science, 277*, 684–686.

Lidz, J., Gleitman, H., & Gleitman, L. (2003). Understanding how input matters: Verb learning and the footprint of universal grammar. *Cognition, 87*, 151–178.

Lord, C., & Paul, R. (1997). Language and communication in autism. In D. Cohen

& F. Volknas (Eds.), *Handbook of autism and pervasive developmental disorder* (2nd ed, pp. 195–225). New York: Wiley.

Maguire, M. J., Hennon, E., Hirsh-Pasek, K., & Golinkoff, R. M. (2005). *When does mother know best? Linguistic cues to lexical category formation in infants.* Manuscript submitted for publication.

Maratsos, M., & Chalkley, M. A. (1980). The internal language of children's syntax: The ontogenesis and representation of syntactic categories. In K. Nelson (Ed.), *Children's language* (Vol. 2, pp. 127–213). New York: Gardner.

Markman, E. M. (1989). *Categorization and naming in children: Problems of induction.* Cambridge, MA: MIT Press.

Meltzoff, A. N. (1995). Understanding the intentions of others: Re-enactment of intended acts by 18–month-old children. *Developmental Psychology, 31,* 838–850.

Meltzoff, A. N., & Brooks, P. (2001). "Like me" as a building block for understanding other minds: Bodily acts, attention, and intention. In B. F. Malle, L. J. Moses, & D. A. Baldwin (Eds.), *Intentions and intentionality: Foundations of social cognition* (pp. 171–191). Cambridge, MA: MIT Press.

Merriman, W. E., & Bowman, L. L. (1989). The mutual exclusivity bias in children's word learning. *Monographs of the Society for Research in Child Development, 54*(3–4), 1–129.

Mervis, C. B., & Bertrand, J. (1994). Acquisition of the novel name-nameless category (N3C) principle. *Child Development, 65,* 1646–1663.

Mills, D. L., Coffey-Corina, S., & Neville, H. J. (1993). Language acquisition and cerebral specialization in 20-month-old infants. *Journal of Cognitive Neuroscience, 5,* 317–334.

Mills, D. L., Coffey-Corina, S., & Neville, H. J. (1997). Language comprehension and cerebral specialization from 13 to 20 months. *Developmental Neuropsychology, 13,* 397–445.

Moore, C., & Dunham, P. J. (1995). *Joint attention: Its origins and role in development.* Hillsdale, NJ: Erlbaum.

Morgan, J. L. (1986). *From simple input to complex grammar.* Cambridge, MA: MIT Press.

Morgan, J. L., & Demuth, K. (1996). *Signal to syntax: Bootstrapping from speech to grammar in early acquisition.* Hillsdale, NJ: Erlbaum.

Morris, A. S., Silk, J. S., Steinberg, L., Sessa, F. M., Avenevoli, S., & Essex, M. J. (2002). Temperamental vulnerability and negative parenting as interacting of child adjustment. *Journal of Marriage and Family, 64,* 461–471.

Mumme, D. L., Fernald, A., & Herrera, C. (1996). Infants' responses to facial and vocal emotional signals in a social referencing paradigm. *Child Development, 67,* 3219–3237.

Mundy, P., Card, J., & Fox, N. (2000). EEG correlates of the development of infant joint attention skills. *Developmental Psychobiology, 36,* 325–338.

Mundy, P., Fox, N., & Card, J. (2003). EEG coherence, joint attention and language development in the second year. *Developmental Science, 6,* 48–54.

Mundy, P., Sigman, M., & Kasari, C. (1990). A longitudinal study of joint attention and language development in autistic children. *Journal of Autism and Developmental Disorders, 20,* 115–128.

Mundy, P., Sigman, M., Ungerer, J., & Sherman, T. (1987). Nonverbal communication and play correlates of language development in autistic children. *Journal of Autism and Developmental Disorders, 17,* 349–364.

Murray, L., & Trevarthen, C. (1985). Emotional regulation of interactions between two-month-olds and their mothers. In T. Field & N. Fox (Eds.), *Social perception in infants* (pp. 101–125). Norwood, NJ: Ablex.

Naigles, L. (1990). Children use syntax to learn verb meanings. *Journal of Child Language, 17*, 357–374.

Naigles, L. (1996). The use of multiple frames in verb learning via syntactic bootstrapping. *Cognition, 58*, 221–251.

Naigles, L. R., & Hoff-Ginsberg, E. (1995). Input to verb learning: Evidence for the plausibility of syntactic bootstrapping. *Developmental Psychology, 31*, 827–837.

National Institute of Child Health and Human Development Early Child Care Research Network. (2003). Do children's attention processes mediate the link between family predictors and school readiness? *Developmental Psychology, 39*, 581–593.

Nelson, K. (1973). Structure and strategy in learning to talk. *Monographs of the Society for Research in Child Development, 38*(1–2), 1–102.

Nelson, K. (1985). *Making sense: The acquisition of shared meaning*. New York: Academic Press.

Nelson, K. E. (1989). Strategies for first language teaching. In M. Rice & R. Schiefelbusch (Eds.), *The teachability of language* (pp. 263–310). Baltimore: Brookes.

Neville, H., & Mills, D. (1997). Epigenesis of language. *Mental Retardation and Developmental Disabilities Reviews, 3*, 282–292.

Nichols, K. E., Fox, N., Mundy, P. (2005). Joint attention, self-recognition, and neurocognitive functions in toddlers. *Infancy, 7*, 35–51.

Ninio, A., & Bruner, J. (1978). The achievement and antecedents of labeling. *Journal of Child Language, 5*, 1–15.

Pence, K. L., Golinkoff, R. M., Pulverman, R., Sootsman, J. L., Addy, D., Salkind, S. J., et al. (2003, June). *The do-it-yourself-guide to verb learning: Infants utilize a coalition of cues*. Poster session presented at the 33rd Annual Meeting of the Jean Piaget Society, Chicago.

Peters, A. M., & Boggs, S. T. (1986). Interactional routines as cultural influences upon language acquisition. In B. Schieffelin & E. Ochs (Eds.), *Language socialization across cultures: Studies in the social and cultural foundations of language* (Vol. 3, pp. 80–96). New York: Cambridge University Press.

Pinker, S. (1984). *Language learnability and language development*. Cambridge, MA: Harvard University Press.

Pinker, S. (2002). *The blank slate: The modern denial of human nature*. New York: Viking.

Plunkett, K. (1997). Theories of early language acquisition. *Trends in Cognitive Sciences, 1*, 146–153.

Poulin-Dubois, D., & Forbes, J. N. (2002). Toddlers' attention to intentions-in-action in learning novel action words. *Developmental Psychology, 38*, 104–114.

Quine, W. V. O. (1960). *Word and object*. Cambridge, England: Cambridge University Press.

Ratner, N. B. (1984). Phonological rule usage in mother-child speech. *Journal of Phonetics, 12*, 245–254.

Ratner, N., & Bruner, J. (1978). Games, social exchange, and the acquisition of language. *Journal of Child Language, 5*, 391–401.

Raver, C. (2002). Emotions matter: Making the case for the role of young children's emotional development for early school readiness. *SRCD Social Policy Report, 16*, 3–24.

Samuelson, L. K., & Smith, L. B. (1998). Memory and attention make smart word learning: An alternative account of Akhtar, Carpenter, and Tomasello. *Child Development, 69,* 94–104.

Schieffelin, B. B., & Ochs, E. (1986). *Language socialization across cultures.* New York: Cambridge University Press.

Shipley, E. F., Smith, C. S., & Gleitman, L. (1969). A study in the acquisition of language: Free response to commands. *Language, 45,* 322–342.

Slobin, D. I. (1985). Crosslinguistic evidence for the language-making capacity. In D. I. Slobin (Ed.), *The crosslinguistic study of language acquisition: Vol. 2. Theoretical issues* (pp. 1157–1256). Hillsdale, NJ: Erlbaum.

Smith, L. B. (1995). Self-organizing processes in learning to learn words: Development is not induction. In C. A. Nelson (Ed.), *Basic and applied perspectives on learning, cognition, and development: The Minnesota Symposia on Child Psychology* (Vol. 28, pp. 1–32). Mahwah, NJ: Erlbaum.

Smith, L. B. (1999). Children's noun learning: How general learning processes make specialized learning mechanisms. In B. MacWhinney (Ed.), *The emergence of language* (pp. 227–305). Mahwah, NJ: Erlbaum.

Smith, L. B. (2000). Learning how to learn words: An associative crane. In R. M. Golinkoff, K. Hirsh-Pasek, L. Bloom, L. Smith, A. Woodward, N. Akhtar, et al. (Eds.), *Becoming a word learner: A debate on lexical acquisition* (pp. 51–80). New York: Oxford University Press.

Smith, L. B., Jones, S. S., & Landau, B. (1996). Naming in young children: A dumb attentional mechanism? *Cognition, 60,* 143–171.

Smith, L. B., Jones, S. S., Landau, B., Gershkoff-Stowe, L., & Samuelson, L. (2002). Object name learning provides on-the-job training for attention. *Psychological Science, 13,* 13–19.

Snow, C. E. (1977). The development of conversation between mothers and babies. *Journal of Child Language, 4,* 1–22.

Snow, C. E. (1986). Conversations with children. In P. Fletcher & M. Garman (Eds.), *Language acquisition* (pp. 69–89). New York: Cambridge University Press.

Snow, C. E. (1989). Understanding social interaction and language acquisition: Sentences are not enough. In M. H. Bornstein & J. S. Bruer (Eds.), *Interaction in human development* (pp. 83–103). Hillsdale, NJ: Erlbaum.

Snow, C. E. (1995). Issues in the study of input: Fine-tuning, universality, individual and developmental differences, and necessary causes. In P. Fletcher & B. MacWhinney (Eds.), *The handbook of child language* (pp. 180–193). New York: Cambridge University Press.

Snow, C. E., & Ferguson, C. A. (1977). *Talking to children: Language input and acquisition.* New York: Cambridge University Press.

Snow, C. E., & Godfield, B. A. (1983). Turn the page please: Situation-specific language acquisition. *Journal of Child Language, 10,* 551–569.

Spelke, E. S., Katz, G., Purcell, S. E., Ehrlich, S. M., & Breinlinger, K. (1994). Early knowledge of object motion: Continuity and inertia. *Cognition, 51,* 131–176.

Tager-Flusberg, H. (1985). The conceptual basis for referential word meaning in children with autism. *Child Development, 56,* 1167–1178.

Tager-Flusberg, H. (1999a). Language development in atypical children. In M. Barrett (Ed.), *The development of language* (pp. 311–348). East Sussex, England: Psychology Press.

Tager-Flusberg, H. (1999b). A psychological approach to understanding the social and language impairments in autism. *International Review of Psychiatry, 11,* 325–334.

Tager-Flusberg, H. (2001). Understanding the language and communicative impairments in autism. In L. M. Glidden (Ed.), *International review of research in mental retardation: Autism* (Vol. 23, pp. 185–205). San Diego, CA: Academic Press.

Tager-Flusberg, H., Calkins, S., Nolin, T., Baumberger, T., Anderson, M., & Chadwick-Dias, A. (1990). A longitudinal study of language acquisition in autistic and Down syndrome children. *Journal of Autism and Developmental Disorders, 20*, 1–21.

Tomasello, M. (1992). The social bases of language acquisition. *Social Development, 1*, 67–87.

Tomasello, M., & Akhtar, N. (1995). Two-year-olds use pragmatic cues to differentiate reference to objects and actions. *Cognitive Development, 10*, 201–224.

Tomasello, M., & Barton, M. (1994). Learning words in non-ostensive context. *Developmental Psychology, 30*, 639–650.

Tomasello, M., & Farrar, M. J. (1986). Joint attention and early language. *Child Development, 57*, 1454–1463.

Tomasello, M., Strosberg, R., & Akhtar, N. (1996). Eighteen-month-old children learn words in non-ostensive contexts. *Journal of Child Language, 23*, 157–176.

Tomasello, M., & Todd, J. (1983). Joint attention and lexical acquisition style. *First Language, 4*, 197–212.

Woodward, A. L. (2003). Infants' developing understanding of the link between looker and object. *Developmental Science, 6*, 297–311.

Woodward, A. L., & Guajardo, J. J. (2002). Infants' understanding of the point gesture as an object-directed action. *Cognitive Development, 17*, 1061–1084.

Woodward, A. L., & Markman, E. M. (1998). Early word learning. In D. Kuhn & R. S. Siegler (Eds.), *Handbook of child psychology: Vol. 2. Cognition, perception, and language* (pp. 371–420). New York: Wiley.

Wynn, K., Bloom, P., & Chiang, W. (2002). Enumeration of collective entities by 5-month-old infants. *Cognition, 83*, B55–B62.

6

Neurocognitive Bases of Preschoolers' Theory-of-Mind Development

Integrating Cognitive Neuroscience and Cognitive Development

Mark A. Sabbagh

Successful engagement and negotiation of the social world rests on many factors. Perhaps one of the most important of these is having a "theory of mind"—a naive theory of how human behavior can be understood in terms of unseen mental states, such as emotions, desires, beliefs, and intentions (Wellman, 1990). The main body of theory-of-mind research lies in the field of preschool cognitive development. In particular, there has been considerable focus on the transition that occurs between children's third and fourth birthdays whereby they come to reason about mental states as distinct representations of the world (Perner, 1991).

More recently, the domain of theory-of-mind research has expanded. Currently, the area serves as an interdisciplinary hub uniting researchers from cross-cultural psychology, infant development, comparative psychology, and neuroscience. In each of these emerging bodies of literature, a very interesting picture is shaping up. For instance, recent cross-cultural research suggests that all languages that have been examined have words that code mental state concepts, thereby suggesting that core aspects of theory-of-mind reasoning may be cross-culturally universal (Lillard, 1997; Wierzbicka, 1999). Recent research with infants suggest that even prelinguistic infants understand that people's actions are motivated by internal mental states (Phillips, Wellman, & Spelke, 2002; Woodward, 2003; Kuhlmeier, Wynn, & Bloom, 2003). Finally, research with nonhuman primates suggests that perhaps only humans are so skilled in this mental domain (Povinelli & Vonk, 2003; though see Tomasello, Call, & Hare, 2003, for a counterpoint).

When taken together, these interdisciplinary findings strongly suggest that the ability to make theory-of-mind-related inferences is a universal, ontogenetically early emerging, and possibly phylogenetically specialized cognitive skill. This general story has prompted a handful of cognitive neuroscience investigations into the basic neural bases of this human specialization (see Gallagher & Frith, 2003, for a recent review). This work has certainly been fruitful, but the bulk of the studies into the neural bases of theory-of-mind reasoning have utilized research paradigms and techniques that are useful only with adult participants. Accordingly, this research has not been directly informative about the possible neurobiological factors that guide theory-of-mind development in the preschool years. The main aim of this chapter is to review some work from our own laboratory that has attempted to better understand and characterize the neurocognitive underpinnings of theory of mind and its development by integrating findings and approaches from studies of cognitive development and cognitive neuroscience.

Decoding and Reasoning About Mental States

Theory-of-mind reasoning has a core component—the ability to impute mental states to others in the service of explaining or predicting their actions. Accordingly, many researchers in the area of cognitive neuroscience have been on the hunt for the circumscribed area of neural tissue that carries out the computations that are critical to this core component of theory of mind (Siegal & Varley, 2002; Frith & Frith, 1999). In our studies, we have approached the problem somewhat differently. In particular, we have taken a more functional perspective that focuses on understanding the cognitive computations required to carry out effective theory-of-mind reasoning. From the outset, this perspective militates for a theoretical distinction between two separate components of theory of mind (Sabbagh, 2004). The first is mental state *decoding*—the use of immediately available information (i.e., facial expression, body posture, tone of voice) in order to make judgments about others' mental states. Importantly, mental state decoding can be done without knowing any background information about a given person. The second kind of theory-of-mind computation is mental state *reasoning*—using established mental state representations to explicitly explain or predict another's behavior. For mental state reasoning, background knowledge about a given person and his or her experiences is central in making appropriate judgments about the person's mental state.

Typically, mental state decoding and mental state reasoning work hand in hand to generate reliable theory-of-mind judgments. However, the distinction is important because they each rely on different kinds of information, and thus may rely on nonoverlapping neurocognitive mechanisms (Sabbagh, 2004). In recent studies, we have focused on understanding the neurocognitive bases of both of these kinds of theory-of-mind computations (e.g., Sabbagh, Moulson, & Harkness, 2004). For the present purposes, however, I am going to focus on our work regarding the neurocognitive bases of mental state *reasoning*. This aspect of theory of mind is the one most well researched with respect to preschoolers' development, and thus provides excellent background for our studies.

Neural Bases of Mental State Reasoning: ERP Studies

A large portion of the theory-of-mind literature on preschool cognitive development focuses on children's performance on the "false-belief" task (Wellman, Cross, & Watson, 2001; Wimmer & Perner, 1983). In a typical false belief task, a protagonist hides some candy in one location and then leaves the room. In his absence, another character enters, takes the candy from its original hiding place, and moves it to an alternative hiding place. The protagonist then returns, and children are asked where he will look for his candy. When the task is designed carefully, with minimal narrative complexity, most older 4-year-olds will correctly reason that the protagonist will look in the original location. By contrast, 3-year-olds consistently and wrongly state that he will look in the new location.

The false-belief task has held prominence in the field of theory-of-mind development because it is an excellent "marker" task. Through correct performance on the task, children convincingly demonstrate that they are reasoning about mental states, and not about a true state of affairs. Moreover, the findings are highly replicable. A recent meta-analysis revealed that these age-related developments are robust and do not interact with various kinds of task manipulations (Wellman et al., 2001). Most important for the present discussion, the false-belief task has the potential to provide a window on whether theory-of-mind reasoning is independent of children's abilities to reason about other kinds of representations. Specifically, by using the general structure of the false-belief task, one can investigate children's abilities to reason about the representational nature of photographs, drawings, or signs.

The first study to introduce a comparison of false beliefs with false photographs was carried out by Zaitchik (1990), who showed that correct performance on both kinds of tasks emerged between the ages of 4 and 5 years, thereby revealing a common developmental trajectory. However, further inspection of these data showed that although they shared a common time line, performance across the tasks was not significantly correlated (Zaitchik, 1990). A second group of studies showed that training that effectively improves performance on the false-belief task does not also improve performance on the false-photograph task, or vice versa (Slaughter, 1998). These findings suggest that in development, there may be a dissociation in the cognitive mechanisms that are used to reason about mental versus nonmental representations.

The most striking evidence for a dissociation in the abilities to reason about mental versus nonmental representations comes from studies done with autistic individuals. Leslie and Thaiss (1992) showed that whereas individuals with autism perform very poorly on the false-belief task, they show no deficit relative to typically developing IQ-matched children on the false-photograph task. This finding has been replicated and extended to show that autistic children show strong performance in reasoning about false drawings as well (Charman & Baron-Cohen, 1995). When taken together with the developmental data, these findings suggest that the ability to reason about mental states may be ontogenetically separated from the ability to reason about other kinds of representations, and mental state reasoning can be selectively disabled by the neuropathic developmental processes at play in autism.

Our first study was an attempt to determine how we might be able to characterize the neural systems that are specially recruited for theory-of-mind reasoning through a comparison of the neural activity that is elicited by false beliefs versus false photographs (Sabbagh & Taylor, 2000). To this end, we used the dense array (128-channel) event-related potential (ERP) technique (Electrical Geodesics, Inc., Eugene, Oregon, USA) to characterize the neural activity that was elicited as 23 typically developing adults made judgments about false beliefs versus false photographs. In this study, participants read a belief version and a photo version of 40 stories (for a total of 80) in which a protagonist carefully placed two elements within a scene and then either took a picture (photo version) or made a mental state comment (belief version) before leaving the room. After the character left the room, a second character moved one of the items. Thus, the main protagonist had a false belief about the location of one object, but a true belief about the location of the other object. Following each story, participants were asked a series of control questions to ensure that they understood the story and the current state of affairs. Participants were also asked a test question in which they were required to judge the contents of the protagonist's representation. The test question was constructed so that participants did not know whether they were being asked about their false or the true representation until the end of the question (i.e., "According to [Marianne/the photo], where is the [moved object/not-moved object]?"). Questions about false versus true representations were equally likely. ERPs were recorded to the onset of the final word in the question, because at this point we were sure they were reasoning about either the belief or the photograph. Two seconds after the final word of the test question, the participants were presented with a candidate answer (i.e., the name of one of the story locations) and participants' task was to determine whether the candidate answer was correct.

Preliminary analyses revealed that there were no effects related to whether participants were asked about their true beliefs or their false beliefs, and so our results were collapsed across test question type. The key result of this study is illustrated in figure 6–1. In short, we found that in this paradigm, the ERP was characterized by a slow-wave effect over frontal regions that was more positive in the belief condition than in the photograph condition. This condition effect

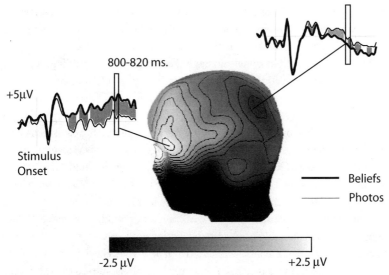

800-820 ms.

+5μV

Stimulus
Onset

-2.5 μV   +2.5 μV

—— Beliefs
—— Photos

Figure 6–1. Grand averaged ERPs and a three-dimensional interpolation of the difference wave (Beliefs-Photos) from Sabbagh & Taylor (2000).

was remarkably focal. Using stringent statistical tests, we found that the slow-wave effect was present only on a cluster of four sites over a lateral prefrontal region of the left hemisphere. Another slow-wave effect was also present at the lateral parietal region of the left hemisphere. Here, however, the direction of the effect was reversed—ERPs elicited in the belief condition were more negative than those elicited in the photograph condition. This pattern of differences began to emerge 300 milliseconds after the onset of the final word in the test question and was maintained throughout the epoch. The differences were most distinct 820 milliseconds through the recording epoch.

These findings provide compelling evidence to suggest that theory-of-mind reasoning might specially require the recruitment of neural systems within the prefrontal and parietal regions of the left hemisphere. However, one thing that was somewhat worrying about this pattern of results is that the spatial distribution of the condition effects bore a surface similarity to those that are classically associated with text processing. Thus, my colleagues and I (Liu, Sabbagh, Gehring, & Wellman, 2004) embarked on a second study designed to replicate this general pattern of results using a methodology that did not rely on text processing, and did not use text as the ERP-eliciting event.

For our second study we also chose a different comparison task. Researchers and theorists have long noted that the false-belief task requires children to "decouple" the content of a mental representation from a true state of affairs (e.g., Perner, 1991). Recent theoretical perspectives in cognitive neuroscience have suggested that "decoupling" may be the computation that sets mental state reasoning apart from reasoning about other kinds of representations (Gallagher &

Frith, 2003). In this second ERP study, we extended our general methodology to see whether the slow-wave effects we observed in our first study would also index differences in reasoning about mental states versus reality.

In this study, a 64–channel montage (Neuroscan Labs, Sterling, Virginia, USA) was used to record ERPs from 17 typically developing adults as they viewed cartoon animations of false-belief vignettes that were narrated by an experimenter. In these animations, a familiar children's character (e.g., Garfield) put one animal into one box and another animal into another box, and then turned his back on the boxes and sang a song. While the character was singing, one of the animals changed locations by jumping from its own box into the other box; the other animal stayed in its own box. Thus, the main character had a false belief about the location of the animal that moved, but a true belief about the animal that did not move. After the vignette was complete, participants were asked test questions about the real (true) or believed location of either of the animals. Specifically, the participants were asked, "Where does Garfield think this is?" Then they were shown a picture of either the animal that moved (false belief) or the animal that did not move (true belief). A question about the real location of either animal was asked in the same way (i.e., "Really, where is this?"). ERPs in both cases were recorded synchronized to the presentation of the pictures.

Again, preliminary analyses revealed no significant differences related to whether participants were asked questions about true versus false beliefs, and so our main analyses were conducted collapsing across question type. The key results for this study are summarized in figure 6–2. What is most striking about these findings is their similarity to the findings from our first study. Specifically, a slow-wave difference between belief and reality was indexed over lateral prefrontal sites on the left hemisphere. This difference started at around 300 milliseconds after the picture was presented and was most pronounced around 800 milliseconds into the recording epoch. In contrast to our first study, we did not also index a slow-wave dissociation over parietal sites in this study. When taken together, these findings suggest that the slow-wave ERP differences that emerged at left lateral prefrontal sites are robust and reliable markers of theory-of-mind reasoning in typically developing adults.

The focal and specific nature of the ERP condition effects in this second study provided the opportunity to use Brain Electrical Source Analysis (BESA) software to gain insight into the neural tissue that might be generating these condition effects (Scherg, 1990). Specifically, we derived a best-fit, single-dipole model that could account for the condition differences sampled between 700 and 900 milliseconds into the recording epoch. The results of this analysis are presented in the lower panel of figure 6–2. The dipole was estimated to be within the left orbitofrontal cortex, and this dipole accounted for just over 87% of the scalp variance associated with the condition effect.

When taken together, the findings from our ERP studies show that the neural systems that are associated with reasoning about mental states can be experi-

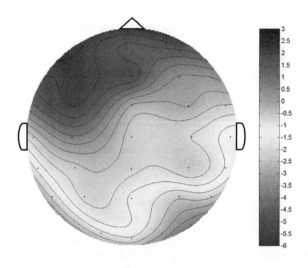

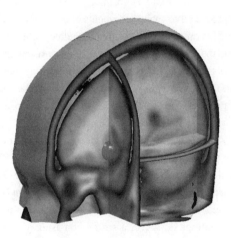

Figure 6–2. Two-dimensional interpolation of the difference wave (Beliefs-Reality) and three-dimensional graphical representation of the BESA solution indicating a dipole within left orbitofrontal cortex, taken from Liu, Sabbagh, Gehring, & Wellman (2004). See also color insert.

mentally dissociated from those that are associated with reasoning about other kinds of representations (i.e., photographs) or reasoning about reality. In particular, left frontal regions seem to be crucial for theory-of-mind reasoning. These findings strengthen the claim that reasoning about mental states rests on special neurocognitive substrates that might be paced by distinct characteristics in development.

We will turn now to a consideration first of how these findings relate to other findings from the cognitive neuroscience literature, and some possible implications that these findings might have for understanding neurodevelopmental factors that may pace the emergence of theory-of-mind reasoning.

Relations Between Our Findings and Others'

Generally speaking, our findings are consistent with a host of other claims regarding the neural regions that are specially recruited when participants engage in theory-of-mind judgments. For instance, recent data from neuropsychiatric patients have shown that individuals with acquired damage to the frontal lobes have difficulty making judgments about others' mental states (Stone, Baron-Cohen, & Knight, 1998; Stuss, Gallup, & Alexander, 2001). Channon and colleagues have reported results suggesting that theory-of-mind impairments might be more profound following acquired left-hemisphere as opposed to right-hemisphere damage (Channon & Crawford, 2000).

These findings regarding the role of the frontal lobes have been underscored by more precise neuroimaging techniques. In a recent review, Gallagher and Frith (2003) reviewed eight functional neuroimaging studies and concluded that when participants are asked to make judgments about others' mental states, the paracingulate region becomes active. The paracingulate cortex is a medial frontal region just anterior to the cingulate. There have been inconsistent findings regarding whether the region of paracingulate cortex that is active during mental state reasoning is lateralized to the left or right hemispheres. Some tasks have revealed left lateralization (i.e., Fletcher et al., 1995; Goel, Grafman, Sadato, & Hallett, 1995); some have shown right lateralization (i.e., Baron-Cohen et al., 1999; Gallagher et al., 2000; Brunet, Sarfati, Hardy-Bayle, & Decety, 2000); and others have found bilateral activation (i.e., Gallagher, Jack, Roepstorff, & Frith, 2002; McCabe, Houser, Ryan, Smith, & Trouard, 2001). Clearly, additional research is required to determine whether laterality differences across studies might be attributable to different kinds of theory-of-mind relevant task demands imposed in each task. Nonetheless, these findings do reveal a strong consistency with respect to the important role of medial frontal regions for engaging theory-of-mind reasoning.

Our own ERP findings are generally consistent with the conclusion of Gallagher and Frith (2003), particularly with respect to the role of medial frontal regions. However, it is worth noting that our source localization techniques suggest that the neural generator that dissociates theory-of-mind reasoning from other closely matched tasks may involve the orbitofrontal cortex, which is more ventral than paracingulate cortex. Gallagher and Frith (2003) note that orbitofrontal cortex has been implicated in several neuroimaging studies of theory-of-mind reasoning (see also Siegel & Varley, 2002), and some researchers have postulated that this region constitutes a core component of the neural bases of theory-of-mind reasoning (Baron-Cohen, 1995; Sabbagh, 2004).

Links With Preschoolers' Brain Development

The finding that circumscribed regions of the medial frontal lobe (including paracingulate and orbitofrontal cortex) have been consistently implicated in theory-of-mind reasoning raises intriguing hypotheses with respect to our understanding of the neurodevelopmental factors that might pace theory-of-mind development. One relatively straightforward hypothesis is that children's emerging abilities to engage in false-belief reasoning might be linked to maturational changes within the frontal lobes. Unfortunately, no research to date has focused specifically on gaining evidence that would support this basic hypothesis. However, there is some circumstantial evidence that militates for further research.

Developmental cognitive neuroscience is an exciting field in its beginning stages (see Nelson & Luciana, 2001). There has long been great interest in the neuromaturational factors that affect different aspects of cognitive development (e.g., Luria, 1973). However, linking specific cognitive processes with specific brain developments has been hard to achieve because of the high cost and logistical difficulties associated with taking direct measures of brain functioning from healthy, typically developing children (see Casey, Thomas, & McCandliss, 2001, for a review).

One especially intriguing methodology that has been used most commonly to study aspects of brain development has been the recording and analysis of electroencephalographic activity (EEG), with a focus on developmental changes in spectral EEG power (Marshall, Bar-Haim, & Fox, 2002) and coherence. Along these lines, groundbreaking research by Thatcher (1992, 1994) has shown that the preschool years may be a particularly important time for the development of the frontal lobes. Specifically, between the ages of 4 and 7 years, EEG coherence measures reflect a major "growth spurt" whereby frontal regions become increasingly connected to posterior sensory areas (Thatcher, 1992, 1994). Thatcher (1994) argues that this particular developmental change is focal to the left hemisphere and stands as the neural correlate of a process of functional integration across neurocognitive subsystems. The fact that these maturational events are occurring around the time when children begin to correctly pass false-belief tasks (which we found is linked to electrophysiological activity in left frontal regions) is suggestive of a functional connection between these two developments.

Demonstrating that two things follow a similar time course is not particularly compelling evidence for a meaningful developmental connection. Fortunately, more suggestive evidence comes from research in which spectral EEG characteristics in preschoolers are directly related to social competence. For example, Nathan Fox and his colleagues have shown that individual differences in left-hemisphere EEG activation correlate with children's social competence. In one study, Fox et al. (1995) showed that 4-year-old children who demonstrated relatively greater left frontal activation were more likely to initiate social interactions and display positive affect in social interactions. In contrast, children with relatively greater right frontal activation were more likely to be withdrawn in social interactions. Fox, Schmidt, Calkins, and Rubin (1996) extended these findings to show that children for whom sociability was coupled with greater relative right frontal activation were likely to have externalizing difficulties. Although these links are speculative at best, it is noteworthy that theory-of-mind functioning is thought to be the foundation of everyday social competence that Fox and his colleagues tapped in their studies. Accordingly, these connections between left frontal EEG asymmetry and children's social competence support the intriguing hypothesis that emerges from our work with adults, suggesting that individual differences in frontal lobe development might pace the emergence of theory-of-mind skills.

Clearly, more research needs to be done linking particular aspects of frontal lobe maturation to children's theory-of-mind development. These intriguing connections, however, instill some confidence that these research efforts are likely to be fruitful.

Theory of Mind and Executive Functioning: A Cognitive Neuropsychological Approach

A second way in which we might gain evidence for a connection between frontal lobe development and preschoolers' emerging theory-of-mind skills is by taking cognitive neuropsychological approach. In this case, we might attempt to determine whether the development of cognitive functions associated with frontal functioning can be associated with preschoolers' performance on relevant theory-of-mind tasks. One specific avenue for this approach is exploring the relations between theory of mind and so-called executive functions—the cognitive processes that serve to monitor and control thought and action (Eslinger, 1996; Zelazo, Muller, Frye, & Marcovitch, 2003). Included among these cognitive processes are self-regulation, planning, response inhibition, and resistance to interference. Some of the earliest research in cognitive neuropsychology has linked executive functions with healthy frontal lobe functioning (e.g., Luria, 1973; Miller, 2000). More direct work has demonstrated that the association also holds for young children (e.g., Dennis, 1991). Most important for the present discussion, the preschool years see important advances in many aspects of executive function. One area that sees particularly striking advances is inhibitory control—the ability to inhibit responses to irrelevant stimuli while pursuing a cognitively represented goal (Kochanska, Murray, Jacques, Koenig, & Vandegeest., 1996; Gerstadt, Hong, & Diamond, 1994).

In addition to the similar time course of development, a number of researchers and theorists have suggested that there may be a more intrinsic relation between inhibitory control and the emergence of preschoolers' theory of mind. In particular, to correctly reason through a typical preschool theory-of-mind task (such as the false-belief task), children must inhibit their own prepotent knowledge of current reality in order to focus their attention on relatively less salient representations of reality. Moreover, to correctly respond, children need to point where the object currently is not—a response that is most likely at odds with a well-practiced tendency to point to where things truly are. Together, these arguments suggest the possibility that the false-belief task, and indeed many tasks that convincingly demonstrate theory-of-mind reasoning (e.g., deception, appearance-reality, etc.), might require fairly well-developed inhibitory control abilities (Leslie & Polizzi, 1998; Bloom & German, 2000).

The findings of several recent studies converge in support of the hypothesis that preschoolers' emerging theory-of-mind skills are related to their developing inhibitory control skills. In one large-scale study of more than 100 preschool children, Carlson and Moses (2001) showed that preschool children's performance on a battery of inhibitory control tasks correlates highly with their performance on a battery of theory-of-mind tasks. These findings were particularly strong for a subset of inhibitory control tasks called "conflict tasks" because they require children to inhibit a response that conflicts with a previously practiced or habitual rule (Kochanska et al., 1996). These findings have been replicated across a number of laboratories (e.g., Hala, Hug, & Henderson, 2003; Perner & Lang, 1999). Indeed, a recent meta-analysis has revealed that over approximately 20 studies, the relation between the emergence of preschoolers' theory-of-mind reasoning and level of inhibitory control functioning is robust. Taken together, these findings clearly strengthen the ties between children's theory-of-mind development and the development of frontal lobe functioning associated with inhibitory control.

Some Evidence for a Specific Relation Between Inhibitory Control and Theory of Mind

An important question concerns how to best characterize the contribution that frontal lobe functioning makes to children's emerging theory of mind. There are two possibilities, each of which maps onto a particular theoretical perspective regarding the emergence of theory of mind (see Moses, 2001; Moses, Carlson, & Sabbagh, 2005). The first is that the frontal lobes provide the computations necessary for negotiating the surface characteristics of theory-of-mind tasks. This perspective has been termed the *expression* account because it suggests that rising inhibitory control functioning enables children to express a nascent understanding of concepts related to theory of mind. The second possibility is that there is something about the conceptual nature of belief itself that requires frontal functioning and inhibitory control. This perspective has been labeled the *emergence* account because it contends that some conceptual aspects of theory of mind might not be acquirable without some level of inhibitory control functioning.

These two broad theoretical perspectives make distinct predictions regarding the *specificity* of the relation between inhibitory control and false belief. On the one hand, the expression account holds that inhibitory control is required to handle the task demands of a standard theory-of-mind task. Accordingly, this account would lead to the prediction that inhibitory control is required for correct performance on any task that has demands similar to the false-belief task. On the other hand, the emergence account posits that inhibitory control is required to acquire aspects of the very concept of belief. On this account, one might predict that inhibitory control is related to children's emerging theory-of-mind skills but not to children's emerging abilities to reason about other kinds of representations.

One line of evidence that would seem to resolve this issue concerns a consideration of relations among children's performance on inhibitory control tasks with their performance on the false-photograph and false-belief tasks. Because of their similarities in task structure (as discussed previously), it would seem that reasoning in both tasks would require similar domain-general skills but distinct domain-specific knowledge. Both tasks have an inhibitory control demand in which they must inhibit a prepotent tendency to refer to a true location in order to refer to a false one. Also, both tasks have the requirement of inhibiting one's own prepotent knowledge regarding what is true in reality in order to focus on a conflicting representation of reality. Thus, any behavioral dissociation between these two tasks could be most readily attributed to differences in domain-specific knowledge.

We explored these issues in two studies (Sabbagh, Moses, & Shiverick, 2005). In our first study, we tested 44 children between the ages of 3 and 5 years on a small battery of false-belief, false-photograph, and inhibitory control tasks. The false-belief tasks included a standard location change and unexpected contents task. The false-photograph tasks were structurally identical to the false-belief tasks, except that they involved photographs instead of beliefs. There were three inhibitory control tasks: (a) "bear-dragon"—a modified "Simon says" game in which children have to (b) "whisper"—children are asked to control their voice and whisper the names of familiar cartoon characters; and (c) "gift delay"—an experimenter noisily wraps a gift while children turn their backs and are instructed not to peek. These tasks were administered to children in a random fixed order over a single session.

Preliminary analyses revealed that performance on all the tasks showed improvement with age. Most important, in our main analysis, we found evidence of a differential association between inhibitory control and false beliefs versus false photographs. Specifically, children's performance on the bear-dragon task correlated highly with children's performance on the false-belief tasks, but not with performance on the false-photograph tasks. This pattern of results held up even when controlling for the effects that were due to age. The finding that false belief was especially related to performance on the bear-dragon task, but not the other two measures of inhibitory control, replicates other findings in the literature (e.g., Carlson & Moses, 2001; Hala et al., 2003). Critically, these findings suggest that false beliefs, but not false photographs, recruit frontal lobe mechanisms associated with inhibitory control.

These findings led us to reason, in line with the emergence account, that there is something special about the conceptual nature of false beliefs that requires recruitment of frontal functioning and inhibitory control. However, this previous study did not clarify why this specific relation exists. One possibility relates to the fact that mental states are more abstract than photographs. In most cases, there is no tangible, lasting physical evidence for the existence of a given mental state. Accordingly, additional inhibitory control might be required for children to disengage from a salient reality in order to focus on these relatively ethereal entities. A second possibility has to do with the conceptual nature of beliefs themselves. Specifically, the job description of a belief is to accurately represent current reality over time. In contrast, photographs are typically inaccurate representations of current reality moments after they are taken. Thus, to consider the possibility that a belief (but not a photo) is false, one must overcome a prepotent tendency to judge the belief as accurate with respect to the current state of affairs. Inhibitory control is likely especially important for overcoming this prepotent tendency. The goal of our second study, then, was to determine whether reasoning about beliefs relies on frontal function and inhibitory control because they are supposed to be up-to-date representations of current reality.

To tease apart these two possibilities, we conducted a second study with 60 preschoolers that replicated the protocol used in the previous study with one key addition—a set of "false-sign" tasks (e.g., Parkin & Perner, 1996). A sign is a nonmental representation that refers (typically truthfully) to something in the world (e.g., a directional arrow in a restaurant that points toward the washrooms). Signs, like beliefs, are supposed to be up-to-date representations of current reality. Thus, the false-sign task provides an elegant way of illuminating the reason for the relation between false belief and inhibitory control. On the one hand, if the relation is best explained by the fact that beliefs are abstract, then we would not expect inhibitory control to be related to reasoning about false signs. After all, signs are like photographs in that they have a clear physical instantiation. On the other hand, if it is because beliefs are supposed to be up-to-date representations of reality, we would expect a robust correlation between inhibitory control measures and false-sign reasoning. Like beliefs, signs are meant to be faithful representations of some real-world situation.

As before, preliminary analyses confirmed that there were age-related improvements in performance on all the measures. In our main analyses, we replicated our previous finding that performance on the bear-dragon task was correlated with children's performance on the false-belief tasks, but not on the false-photograph tasks. Most critically we found that bear-dragon performance as also highly correlated with performance on the false-sign tasks. This pattern of results held up after controlling for effects of age and effects of general language development.

When taken together, these findings confirm that children's emerging theory-of-mind skills are closely related to children's level of frontal functioning, as indexed by measures of inhibitory control. Moreover, these findings suggest that the relation is not a trivial one based on negotiation of task demands. Instead, it seems that there is something about the conceptual characteristics of beliefs that requires recruitment of frontal functioning—in particular the assumptions of representational fidelity. Put in a broader theoretical context, these findings lend support to the "emergence" account of the relation between theory of mind and frontal functioning.

Summary, Implications, and Future Directions

When taken together, our findings help bring to the foreground a couple hypotheses about how theory-of-mind development is paced by the development of frontal lobe functioning. First, we have relatively compelling evidence to suggest that theory of mind specially recruits neurocognitive mechanisms within the frontal lobes, possibly lateralized to the left hemisphere. Second, our research on preschoolers' cognitive development reveals that individual differences in children's performance on some aspects of inhibitory functioning correlate with false beliefs, but not false photographs. Finally, we suggest that the increased inhibitory control demands of beliefs come as a result of the special way in which beliefs are conceptually understood to relate to the world. I turn now to a brief consideration of the implications of these findings and some future directions and challenges that they highlight for understanding the relation between theory of mind and neural development.

Our research has suggested that emerging frontal lobe functioning and inhibitory control are necessary for the emergence of preschoolers' theory-of-mind skills, and in particular their concept of belief. Yet, to date, very little research has focused on understanding the cognitive processes that are important for *acquiring* concepts about belief. In what little work has been done, a common theme that has emerged is that experience in everyday interactions might provide children with the opportunity to talk about and learn about mental state concepts such as belief (Bartsch & Wellman, 1995; Sabbagh & Callanan, 1998). For instance, Ruffman, Slade, and Crowe (2002) have shown that mothers' tendencies to use mental state terms in descriptions of pictures when children were 3 years old correlated with children's theory-of-mind understanding a year later. In addition, children's discussion about mental states in conversations with siblings and peers might also be important for theory-of-mind development (Brown, Donelan-McCall, & Dunn, 1996; Perner, Ruffman, & Leekham, 1994). A crucial direction for future research is characterizing whether and how these important experiences in conversation affect the maturation of the neural systems important for theory-of-mind development.

An equally important area of future research is developing links between direct measures of brain development and children's performance on theory-of-mind tasks. It seems that there are two general directions that this research could take. One way is through assessments of either functional or morphometric characteristics of brain development that could be separately correlated with children's performance on tasks that tap theory-of-mind reasoning. For instance, spectral EEG analyses like those used by Nathan Fox and his colleagues might be a particularly promising avenue for integrating characteristics of preschoolers' brain activity with theory-of-mind development. A second route is through direct *functional* assessments of children's brain activity during tasks that tap theory-of-mind functioning. Such tasks are becoming increasingly common for use with adults (Gallagher & Frith, 2003), as are functional assessments of brain activity in young children (e.g., Casey et al., 2001). Although there are significant difficulties in conducting this later kind of research, there is some reason to believe that these problems will be solvable in the near future.

Finally, it is very important to keep in mind that the developments in the preschool years that set the stage for false-belief understanding should not be mistaken as the onset of theory-of-mind reasoning. As was noted at the outset, some of the core aspects of theory-of-mind reasoning appear to be in place by the end of the first year, if not sooner (e.g., Gergely, Nadasdy, Csibra, & Biro, 1995). Some recent evidence from Henry Wellman and colleagues suggests that children's behavior in some of these early experimental paradigms designed to tap early theory-of-mind understanding correlate with children's scores on a battery of theory-of-mind tasks administered between the ages of 3 and 4 (Wellman, Phillips, Dunphy-Lelii, & Lalonde, 2004). These findings raise the intriguing hypothesis that children's early theory-of-mind skills set the stage for later developments and militate for developing a better understanding of the neurodevelopmental correlates of early theory-of-mind advances, as well as later ones.

Acknowledgments Preparation of this chapter was supported by an NSERC Discovery Grant (200041). Special thanks to Annette Henderson and Beth Seamans for comments on a previous draft of this manuscript. I am indebted to Lou Moses, Stephanie Carlson, and Henry Wellman for ongoing and stimulating discussion of the issues discussed in this chapter.

References

Baron-Cohen, S. (1995). *Mindblindness: An essay on autism and theory of mind.* Cambridge, MA: MIT Press.

Baron-Cohen, S., Ring, H. A., Wheelwright, S., Bullmore, E. T., Brammer, M. J., Simmons, A., et al. (1999). Social intelligence in the normal and autistic brain: An fMRI study. *European Journal of Neuroscience, 11*, 1891–1898.

Bartsch, K., & Wellman, H. M. (1995). *Children talk about the mind.* Oxford, England: Oxford University Press.

Bloom, P., & German, T. P. (2000). Two reasons to abandon the false belief task as a test of theory of mind. *Cognition, 77*, B25–B31.

Brown, J. R., Donelan-McCall, N., & Dunn, J. (1996). Why talk about mental states? The significance of children's conversations with friends, siblings and their mothers. *Child Development, 67*, 836–849.

Brunet, E., Sarfati, Y., Hardy-Bayle, M., & Decety, J. (2000). A PET investigation of the attribution of intentions with a nonverbal task. *NeuroImage, 11*, 157–166.

Carlson, S. M., & Moses, L. J. (2001). Individual differences in inhibitory control and children's theory of mind. *Child Development, 72*, 1032–1053.

Casey, B. J., Thomas, K. M., & McCandliss, B. (2001). Applications of magnetic resonance imaging to the study of development. In C. A. Nelson & M. Luciana (Eds.), *Handbook of developmental cognitive neuroscience* (pp. 137–148). Cambridge, MA: MIT Press.

Channon, S., & Crawford, S. (2000). The effects of anterior lesions on performance on a story comprehension test: Left anterior impairment on a theory of mind-type task. *Neuropsychologia, 38*, 1006–1017.

Charman, T., & Baron-Cohen, S. (1995). Understanding photos, models, and beliefs: A test of the modularity thesis of theory of mind. *Cognitive Development, 10*, 287–298.

Dennis, M. (1991). Frontal lobe function in childhood and adolescence: A heuristic for assessing attention regulation, executive control, and the intentional states important for social discourse. *Developmental Neuropsychology, 7*, 327–358.

Eslinger, P. J. (1996). Conceptualizing, describing and measuring components of executive function: A summary. In G. R. Lyon & N. A. Krasnegor (Eds.), *Attention, memory, and executive function* (pp. 367–395). Baltimore: Brookes.

Fletcher, P. C., Happe, F., Frith, U., Baker, S. C., Dolan, R. J., Frackowiak, R. S. J., et al. (1995). Other minds in the brain: A functional imaging study of "theory of mind" in story comprehension. *Cognition, 57*, 109–128.

Fox, N. A., Rubin, K. H., Calkins, S. D., Marshall, T. R., Coplan, R. J., Porges, S. W., et al. (1995). Frontal activation asymmetry and social competence at four years of age. *Child Development, 66*, 1770–1784.

Fox, N. A., Schmidt, L. A., Calkins, S. D., & Rubin, K. H. (1996). The role of frontal activation in the regulation and dysregulation of social behavior during the preschool years. *Development and Psychopathology, 8*, 89–102.

Frith, C. D., & Frith, U. (1999). Interacting minds: A biological basis. *Science, 286*, 1692–1695.

Gallagher, H. L., & Frith, C. D. (2003). Functional imaging of "theory of mind." *Trends in Cognitive Sciences, 7*, 77–83.

Gallagher, H. L., Happe, F., Brunswick, N., Fletcher, P. C., Frith, U., & Frith, C. D. (2000). Reading the mind in cartoons and stories: An fMRI study of "theory of the mind" in verbal and nonverbal tasks. *Neuropsychologia, 38*, 11–21.

Gallagher, H. L., Jack, A. I., Roepstorff, A., & Frith, C. D. (2002). Imaging the intentional stance in a competitive game. *NeuroImage, 16*, 814–821.

Gergely, G., Nadasdy, Z., Csibra, G., & Biro, S. (1995). Taking the intentional stance at 12 months of age. *Cognition, 56*, 165–193.

Gerstadt, C. L., Hong, Y. J., & Diamond, A. (1994). The relationship between cognition and action: Performance of children 3.5–7 years old on a Stroop-like day-night test. *Cognition, 53*, 129–153.

Goel, V., Grafman, J., Sadato, N., & Hallett, M. (1995). Modeling other minds. *NeuroReport, 6*, 1741–1746.

Hala, S., Hug, S., & Henderson, A. (2003). Executive functioning and false belief understanding in preschool children: Two tasks are harder than one. *Journal of Cognition and Development, 4*, 275–298.

Kochanska, G., Murray, K., Jacques, T. Y., Koenig, A. L., & Vandegeest, K. A. (1996). Inhibitory control in young children and its role in emerging internalization. *Child Development, 67*, 490–507.

Kuhlmeier, V., Wynn, K., & Bloom, P. (2003). Attribution of dispositional states by 12-month-olds. *Psychological Science, 14*, 402–408.

Leslie, A. M., & Polizzi, P. (1998). Inhibitory processing in the false belief task: Two conjectures. *Developmental Science, 1*, 247–253.

Leslie, A. M., & Thaiss, L. (1992). Domain specificity in conceptual development: Neuropsychological evidence from autism. *Cognition, 43*, 225–251.

Lillard, A. (1997). Ethnopsychologies: Cultural variations in theories of mind. *Psychological Bulletin, 123*, 3–32.

Liu, D., Sabbagh, M. A., Gehring, W. J., & Wellman, H. M. (2004). Decoupling beliefs from reality: An ERP study of theory of mind. *NeuroReport, 15*, 991–995.

Luria, A.R. (1973). *The working brain: An introduction to neuropsychology.* New York: Basic Books.

Marshall, P. J., Bar-Haim, Y., & Fox, N. A. (2002). Development of the EEG from 5 months to 4 years of age. *Clinical Neurophysiology, 113*, 1199–1208.

McCabe, K., Houser, D., Ryan, L., Smith, V., & Trouard, T. (2001). A functional imaging study of cooperation in two-person reciprocal exchange. *Proceedings of the National Academy of Sciences, USA, 98*, 11832–11835.

Miller, E. K. (2000). The prefrontal cortex and cognitive control. *Nature Reviews Neuroscience, 1*, 59–65.

Moses, L. J. (2001). Executive accounts of theory of mind development. *Child Development, 72*, 688–690.

Moses, L. J., Carlson, S. M., & Sabbagh, M. A. (2005). On the specificity of the relation between executive function and children's theories of mind. In W. Schneider, R. Schumann-Hengsteler, & B. Sodian (Eds.), *Young children's cognitive development: Interrelationships among executive functioning, working memory, verbal ability, and theory of mind* (pp. 131–145). Mahwah, NJ: Erlbaum.

Nelson, C. A., & Luciana, M. (Eds.). (2001). *Developmental cognitive neuroscience.* Cambridge, MA: MIT Press.

Parkin, L. J., & Perner, J. (1996). *Wrong directions in children's theory of mind: What it means to understand belief as representation.* Unpublished manuscript, University of Sussex.

Perner, J. (1991). *Understanding the representational mind.* Cambridge, MA: MIT Press.

Perner, J., & Lang, B. (1999). Development of theory of mind and executive control. *Trends in Cognitive Sciences, 3*, 337–344.

Perner, J., Ruffman, T., & Leekham, S. R. (1994). Theory of mind is contagious: You catch it from your sibs. *Child Development, 65*, 1228–1238.

Phillips, A. T., Wellman, H. M., & Spelke, E. S. (2002). Infants' ability to connect gaze and emotional expression to intentional action. *Cognition, 85*, 53–78.

Povinelli, D. J., & Vonk, J. (2003). Chimpanzee minds: Suspiciously human? *Trends in Cognitive Sciences, 7*, 157–160.

Ruffman, T., Slade, L., & Crowe, E. (2002). The relation between children's and mothers' mental state language and theory-of-mind understanding. *Child Development, 73*, 734–751.

Sabbagh, M. A. (2004). Understanding orbitofrontal contributions to theory of mind reasoning: Implications for autism. *Brain and Cognition, 55*, 209–219.

Sabbagh, M. A., & Callanan, M. A. (1998). Metarepresentation in action: Children's theories of mind developing and emerging in parent-child conversations. *Developmental Psychology, 34*, 491–502.

Sabbagh, M. A., Moses, L. J., & Shiverick, S. M. (2005). *Executive functioning and preschoolers' understanding of false beliefs, false photographs, and false signs*. Manuscript under review.

Sabbagh, M. A., Moulson, M. C., & Harkness, K. L. (2004). Neural correlates of mental state decoding in human adults: An ERP study. *Journal of Cognitive Neuroscience, 16*, 415–426.

Sabbagh, M. A., & Taylor, M. (2000). Neural correlates of theory-of-mind reasoning: An event-related potential study. *Psychological Science, 11*, 46–50.

Scherg, M. (1990). Fundamentals of dipole source potential analysis. In F. Grandiori, M. Hoke, & G. L. Romani (Eds.), *Advances in audiology: Vol 6. Auditory evoked magnetic and electrical potentials* (pp. 40–69). Basel, Switzerland: Karger.

Siegal, M., & Varley, R. (2002). Neural systems involved in "theory of mind." *Nature Reviews Neuroscience, 3*, 463–471.

Slaughter, V. (1998). Children's understanding of pictorial and mental representations. *Child Development, 69*, 321–332.

Stone, V., Baron-Cohen, S., & Knight, R. T. (1998). Frontal lobe contributions to theory of mind. *Journal of Cognitive Neuroscience, 10*, 640–656.

Stuss, D. T., Gallup, G. G., Jr., & Alexander, M. P. (2001). The frontal lobes are necessary for "theory of mind." *Brain, 124*, 279–286.

Thatcher, R. W. (1992). Cyclic cortical reorganization during early childhood. *Brain and Cognition, 20*, 24–50.

Thatcher, R. W. (1994). Cyclic cortical reorganization: Origins of human cognitive development. In G. Dawson & K. W. Fischer (Eds.), *Human behavior and the developing brain* (pp. 232–266). New York: Guilford.

Tomasello, M., Call, J., & Hare, B. (2003). Chimpanzees understand psychological states—the question is which ones and to what extent. *Trends in Cognitive Sciences, 7*, 153–156.

Wellman, H. M. (1990). *The child's theory of mind*. Cambridge, MA: MIT Press.

Wellman, H. M., Cross, D., & Watson, J. (2001). Meta-analysis of theory of mind development: The truth about false belief. *Child Development, 72*, 655–684.

Wellman, H. M., Phillips, A. T., Dunphy-Lelii, S., & Lalonde, N. (2004). Infant understanding of persons predicts preschool social cognition. *Developmental Science, 7*, 283–288.

Wierzbicka, A. (1999). *Emotions across languages and cultures: Diversity and univerals*. New York: Cambridge University Press.

Wimmer, H., & Perner, J. (1983). Beliefs about beliefs: Representation and constraining function of wrong beliefs in young children's understanding of deception. *Cognition, 13*, 103–128.

Woodward, A. L. (2003). Infants' developing understanding of the link between looker and object. *Developmental Science, 6*, 297–311.

Zaitchik, D. (1990). When representations conflict with reality: The preschooler's problem with false beliefs and "false" photographs. *Cognition, 35*, 41–68.

Zelazo, P. D., Muller, U., Frye, D., & Marcovitch, S. (2003). The development of executive function. *Monographs of the Society for Research in Child Development, 68*.

7

The Neurobiology of Social Bonds and Affiliation

Miranda M. Lim
Larry J. Young

S ocial bonding is one of the most important features of being human. There is little doubt that all human societies rely on social relationships, and that this is a universal human trait that persists across cultures. The formation of selective, long-term social bonds, otherwise known as *attachment*, requires the interaction of many cognitive processes such as sensory and motor function, attention, memory, and, most characteristically, motivation to seek close contact with others. Despite the importance of social relationships in human culture, surprisingly little is known about the neurobiology of social attachment and its underlying cognitive processes. Previous chapters in this book address developmental aspects of social engagement through infancy and childhood; the aim of this chapter is to focus on social bonding between adults, as in romantic attachment between lovers.

The vast majority of what is known about the underlying neurobiology of attachment has been learned through studies of laboratory animals. By understanding mechanisms of social bonding in animal models, we hope to gain insight into the neurobiology of human relationships. Several animal models have great potential for understanding social attachment. These various animal models all have several features in common: the formation of selective, long-lasting social bonds between pairs of animals, a clear onset of bond formation, and the ability to identify and manipulate factors that facilitate or prevent bond formation in the laboratory. Potential mammalian animal models of social attachment range from nonhuman primates, such as the monogamous and biparental marmosets, tamarins, and titi monkeys (Kleiman, 1977; Dewsbury, 1987; Snowdon, 1990; Kostan & Snowdon, 2002); to nonprimate mammals such as the monogamous prairie and pine voles, California mice, Djungarian hamsters, and aardwolves (Gubernick & Alberts, 1987; Richardson, 1987; Carter, DeVries, & Getz,

1995; Jones & Wynne-Edwards, 2000); to nonmammalian species such as birds (Orians, 1969). Current biomedical research relies heavily on rodent models because they are small, breed well in the laboratory, are suitable for many types of experimental manipulations, and are mammalian, and therefore relatively closely related to humans. Microtine rodents (of genus *Microtus*), several species of which are monogamous while the majority are not, fit these criteria and have provided the substrate for much of the ongoing research for understanding the molecular, cellular, and neurobiological bases of pair bonding.

Less than 5% of all mammals display a monogamous social structure where adult mates form selective, enduring pair-bonds (Kleiman, 1977). In contrast, 90% of bird species are considered monogamous over the course of at least one breeding season (Lack, 1968). Here, the culturally charged term *monogamy* does not imply sexual exclusivity with a single individual; rather, biologists use the term to describe a *social* system that includes selective mating, a shared nest, and biparental care of offspring. Until recently, the notion that social systems might have a physiological and neurobiological basis has not been widely considered. In this chapter we will present what is known about the neurobiology underlying social attachment in the monogamous prairie vole animal model.

The Model

Prairie voles (*Microtus ochrogaster*) are small field mice found in the midwestern prairies of the United States. Field studies have shown that adult male and female pairs tend to be trapped together over several months, even when the female is not reproductively active (Getz, Carter, & Gavish, 1981). Pairs form long-lasting, selective social bonds and often produce multiple litters together, and both parents participate equally in the care of their offspring. Pairs split in less than 10% of observed cases in the field, and after the death of one member of the pair, fewer than 20% of the survivors eventually acquire a new mate (Carter et al., 1995).

Pair bonding between adult voles can be observed readily in the laboratory, even with animals bred and raised in a laboratory colony (Getz et al., 1981). The strength of a pair-bond can be assessed using a partner preference test, in which two adult mates that have been paired for some length of time are placed into a testing chamber where the test animal can roam freely between its mate and a novel animal, both tethered at opposite ends of the test chamber (figure 7–1A). The test subject is defined as having developed a partner preference if it spends more than twice as much time in contact with its partner as with the stranger (figure 7–1B). For example, prairie voles typically spend about 1 to 2 hours out of a 3-hour test with their partner and less than 20 minutes with the stranger. Nonmonogamous vole species typically do not show this pattern of preference; in fact, they are much less social and tend to spend most of their time alone in the neutral chamber.

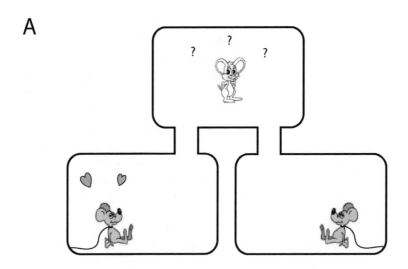

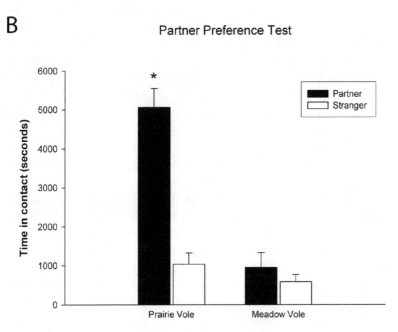

Figure 7–1. A. Partner preference test. Three interconnected chambers house a tethered partner on the left and a tethered stranger on the right. The experimental animal is placed in the neutral cage and allowed to move freely between the partner and the stranger. B. A typical graph showing time spent in contact during the 3-hour test. Monogamous prairie voles tend to spend most of their time huddling with the partner, while nonmonogamous meadow voles spend most of their time alone.

How much social contact time does it take to form a partner preference? It depends on the social and sexual conditions. For example, mating during co-habitation facilitates partner preference formation in voles: 6 hours of cohabitation with mating was sufficient for female prairie voles to form partner preferences, whereas the same length of time without mating was not (Williams, Catania, & Carter, 1992). Similar results were observed with male prairie voles and 14 hours of cohabitation (Insel, Preston, & Winslow, 1995). In the reverse situation, extended periods of cohabitation without mating are sufficient for pair bonding (Williams, Catania, et al., 1992). Using the partner preference paradigm, it is possible to experimentally manipulate, and thus better understand, the social, sexual, and neurochemical factors that affect pair-bond formation.

The Neurochemistry of the Pair-Bond

What neurotransmitter systems might be involved in the mechanisms underlying pair bonding? One might logically hypothesize that similar neural mechanisms may underlie analogous forms of social bonding, such as those detailed in previous chapters in this book. For example, the processes of mother-infant bonding and parturition both involve the same hormones and neurotransmitters (Young & Insel, 2002). In rats, parturition involves the steroid hormones estrogen and progestin and is stimulated by the hormone oxytocin (OT); likewise, maternal behavior is also stimulated by estrogen, progestin, and OT (Pedersen, Ascher, Monroe, & Prange, 1982). OT is a nine amino acid neuropeptide hormone that is produced in the hypothalamus and released both systemically via the posterior pituitary and centrally as a neuromodulator (Gainer & Wray, 1994). Studies in sheep have also suggested that central OT plays a critical role in initiating maternal behavior, as well as maintaining the selective bond between a mother and her infant (Keverne & Kendrick, 1992; Kendrick et al., 1997).

Similarly, studies also show that OT also plays an important role in pair-bond formation in female prairie voles. Infusion of OT into the ventricles of the brain accelerates partner preference even in the absence of mating in female prairie voles (Williams, Carter, & Insel, 1992; Williams, Insel, Harbaugh, & Carter, 1994). Likewise, an injection of OT receptor antagonist just prior to cohabitation inhibits pair bonding in females (Insel & Hulihan, 1995). Pulses of peripheral OT also increase female, but not male, partner preference (Cushing & Carter, 2000).

However, in male prairie voles, a structurally related neuropeptide, arginine vasopressin (AVP), appears to directly modulate social attachment. Central infusion of AVP accelerates pair bonding in males, while the selective antagonist for the V1a subtype of the AVP receptor blocks pair bonding (Winslow, Hastings, Carter, Harbaugh, & Insel, 1993). AVP is also a nine amino acid hormone that is thought to have evolved from the same parent peptide as OT. Like OT, AVP is synthesized in the hypothalamus and released into the periphery and the brain (Gainer & Wray, 1994). AVP fiber density is sexually dimorphic in rodents, appearing higher in males than in females, and AVP synthesis has been shown to be androgen dependent (De Vries, Best, & Sluiter, 1983). In addition, evidence from both mammalian and nonmammalian vertebrates shows that AVP is important for male-specific social behaviors such as paternal care, territoriality, and male courtship (Goodson & Bass, 2001). This supports the notion that OT and AVP systems may function in a gender-specific manner in regulating pair-bond formation in female versus male prairie voles (Insel & Hulihan, 1995).

Although the previously mentioned studies suggest that there may be gender-specific mechanisms for OT and AVP and pair bonding, other studies have shown that both OT and AVP may together regulate bonding in both sexes. A recent study found that both OT and AVP infusions facilitate partner preference formation in both males and females, and blockade of OT and AVP receptors by the administration of selective antagonists blocked pair bonding in both sexes, although AVP was more effective at a lower dose in males (Cho, DeVries, Williams, & Carter, 1999). Another experiment showed that coadministration of AVP and an OT receptor antagonist into a specific brain region blocked pair bonding in male prairie voles (Liu, Curtis, & Wang, 2001). These experiments suggest that the gender differences in response to OT and AVP may not be as clearly demarcated as once believed, and there exists a complex relationship between the OT and AVP systems. However, one should be cautious in interpreting data using exogenously administered AVP and OT because the peptides are very similar in structure and therefore have similar binding affinities to their respective receptors. Thus, it is possible that the behavioral effects of OT could be explained by OT acting on AVP receptors, and vice versa. Pharmacological manipulations using AVP and OT should take into account the dose and physiological relevancy as to the site of injection. Synthetic selective antagonist studies for the specific receptors have contributed more to our understanding of which neurotransmitter systems are involved.

Where are OT and AVP and the selective antagonists acting in the brain to modulate pair bonding? One way to answer this question is to look at where the receptors are expressed, using a technique called *receptor autoradiography*. Two breakthrough studies using receptor autoradiography showed that there are dramatically different species differences in the distribution of OT and V1a receptors between prairie voles and a closely related nonmonogamous species, the montane vole (figures 7–2 and 7–3, respectively; Insel & Shapiro, 1992; Insel, Wang, & Ferris, 1994). Furthermore, central infusion of OT and AVP peptides into nonmonogamous montane voles had no effect on their social behavior (Young, Nilsen, Waymire, MacGregor, & Insel, 1999). This strongly suggests that the specific locations of the OT and V1a receptors within certain brain regions are what modulate pair bonding, and not the presence of

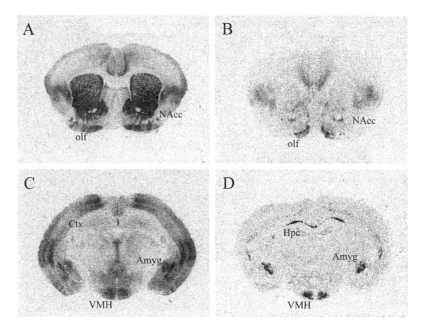

Figure 7–2. Oxytocin receptor distribution in prairie vole brain (A and C) and montane vole brain (B and D). Note the disparity of OT receptor binding in the nucleus accumbens (NAcc) and cortex (Ctx) between the two species. NAcc = nucleus accumbens; olf = olfactory tubercle; Ctx = cortex; VMH = ventromedial hypothalamus; Amyg = amygdala.

the peptides themselves. Thus, the release of OT or AVP in the brain during mating and cohabitation would activate different neural circuits in a monogamous versus a nonmonogamous species.

Besides OT and AVP, a few other neurotransmitter systems have been shown to regulate pair-bond formation in prairie voles. For example, the dopamine system is critical, as dopamine D1 and D2 receptor agonists facilitate, and dopamine D2 receptor antagonists block, partner preference formation in both male and female prairie voles (Wang et al., 1999; Gingrich, Liu, Cascio, Wang, & Insel, 2000; Aragona, Liu, Curtis, Stephan, & Wang, 2003). In addition, a recent study demonstrated that OT and dopamine may interact during pair-bond formation: OT-induced partner preferences were blocked by D2 receptor antagonists; conversely, D2 agonist-induced partner preferences were blocked by OT receptor antagonists (Liu & Wang, 2003). This suggests that both OT and dopamine receptor systems are simultaneously necessary during pair-bond formation.

In addition, the hypothalamic-pituitary-adrenal (HPA) stress axis has been implicated in pair bonding in prairie voles. In general, prairie voles show a much higher basal plasma corticosterone level, ranging from 10- to 20-fold higher than in unstressed rats (Taymans et al., 1997). In both male and female prairie vole

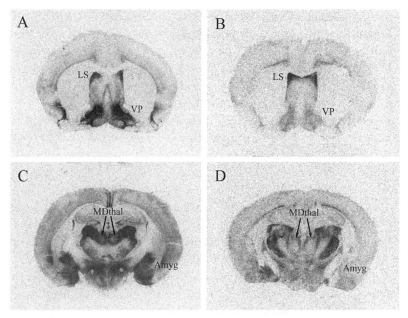

Figure 7–3. Vasopressin V1a receptor distribution in prairie vole brain (A and C) and montane vole brain (B and D). Note the disparity of V1a receptor binding in the ventral pallidum (VP), mediodorsal thalamus (MDthal), and amygdala (Amyg) between the two species. LS = lateral septum; VP = ventral pallidum; MDthal = mediodorsal thalamus; Amyg = amygdala.

pairs, separation was associated with an elevation in serum corticosterone levels, and subsequent reunion with the partner returned serum levels to the baseline state (DeVries, Taymans, & Carter, 1997). Serum corticosterone levels rapidly decline in female prairie voles that are exposed to a novel male, and preventing this decline inhibits the formation of a new pair-bond (DeVries, DeVries, Taymans, & Carter, 1995). Likewise, adrenalectomy, which removes the endogenous source of corticosterone, accelerates partner preference formation in females (DeVries et al., 1995). Interestingly, the effects of stress on social preferences are sexually dimorphic in prairie voles; that is, inflicting stress and injecting corticosterone have opposite behavioral effects in males versus females. Forced swimming or intraperitoneal corticosterone injections have been shown to facilitate partner preference in males, yet both inhibit partner preference in female prairie voles (DeVries, DeVries, Taymans, & Carter, 1996). Central injections of the neuropeptide corticotropin-releasing factor (CRF), which is synthesized in the hypothalamus and co-released with AVP into the pituitary, also facilitate partner preferences in male prairie voles (DeVries, Guptaa, Cardillo, Cho, & Carter, 2002). Preliminary data show that, much like the OT and AVP receptor systems, species differences also exist in CRF receptor distribution between monogamous vole and nonmonogamous vole species (Lim, Nair, & Young, 2005). These studies reveal an additional neuropeptide system that contributes to the neurobiology of social bonding.

Pair-bond formation is a complex social behavior that likely involves many facets of neurobiology, and much of the underlying neurochemistry remains to be dissected. For example, OT and AVP have been implicated in various reproductive and social behaviors and play a major regulatory role in prairie vole monogamy. Neurotransmitters of motivation and reward, such as dopamine, may also modulate the appetitive aspects of pair bonding. Hormones of the HPA axis, such as corticosterone and CRF, which are very sensitive to social stimuli, may relate to the stressful aspects of bond formation and separation. It is possible that corticosterone and CRF directly or indirectly affect AVP and OT systems; in rats, vasopressin is released by stress and is capable of acting as a secretogogue for ACTH, which in turn releases corticosterone. Alternatively, stress or acute corticosterone treatment may release AVP (Wotjak et al., 1996), which in turn could facilitate pair bonding in male prairie voles. Likewise, corticosterone or infliction of stress may inhibit OT release to inhibit pair bonding in female prairie voles. The presence of multiple interacting neurotransmitter systems suggests additional mechanisms through which social experiences can modulate social attachments.

Why Monogamy?

Why do some species form pair-bonds, while others do not? The appearance of monogamous social systems across many different animal species does not follow any obvious taxonomic or phylogenetic pattern, and is thus believed to have evolved in a convergent fashion. What are the ultimate or evolutionary causes for a monogamous versus a polygamous social structure? It has been suggested that monogamous males increase their reproductive fitness by maintaining their association with a single female. For example, harsher environments that would require both parents to successfully rear young might favor pair bonding. In contrast, milder habitats may favor promiscuous males that abandon their mates to seek out additional sexual partners and maximize fitness in that regard.

Prairie voles are believed to have evolved in the tallgrass prairies, which are very low in food resources and population density (Getz, McGuire, Pizzuto, Hofmann, & Frase, 1993; McGuire, Getz, Hofmann, Pizzuto, & Frase, 1993). Under these conditions, males may enhance their reproductive success by nesting with a single female and producing multiple stable litters, rather than risk not finding a fertile mate. The existence of predators such as snakes makes survival and foraging for food even more difficult, but such tasks are easier when both adults in the pair contribute to defending the nest and finding food. In contrast, polygamous species, such as montane voles, occupy densely populated habitats where reproductive success is more dependent on a high number of offspring. Unfortunately, it is difficult to empirically test these potential explanations for the evolution of monogamy in prairie voles.

Interestingly, there exists *intraspecific* variability in monogamous-typical behaviors within prairie voles. A recent discovery within the prairie vole species indicated that animals reared from a stock originally captured in Illinois differ in parental behavior when compared with a subspecies of vole captured in Kansas (Roberts & Carter, 1997). Kansas prairie voles are anatomically more sexually dimorphic in body weight and anogenital distances than are Illinois prairie voles, suggesting that Kansas voles show fewer indices of monogamy than Illinois voles. In addition, Kansas voles were more behaviorally sensitive to peripheral injections of AVP, although there were no observable differences in V1a receptor binding between the two populations (Cushing, Martin, Young, & Carter, 2001). Though the proximate mechanisms for the intraspecies variability are not known, some believe that the differences in ecological habitat, Kansas being more xeric than Illinois, may contribute to the evolution of the differences in social behavior (Cushing et al., 2001). It is possible that these intraspecies differences in social behavior in prairie voles represent genetic drift of two populations, prior to speciation, due to differences in selection pressures within their habitats.

The Genetics of the Pair-Bond

To answer questions about the contribution of genetics to social bonding, one can use the comparative method and contrast the gene sequences of species with different social behaviors. For example, prairie and montane voles are closely related species, physically indistinguishable to the untrained eye, yet their brain neurochemistry and social structure differ dramatically. What causes prairie voles to be affiliative and form pair-bonds, and montane voles to be asocial and promiscuous? OT and V1a receptors are distributed in different brain regions between the two species. This might be explained at the genetic level by examining the regulatory portion of the gene that controls in which brain region the genes are expressed, or the promoter region.

An alignment of the prairie and montane vole vasopressin V1a receptor genes shows, not surprisingly, that the coding sequences are nearly identical between the two species, meaning that the protein itself is virtually identical between the two species. However, analysis of the upstream noncoding regulatory region shows the presence of a 420 base pair stretch of highly repetitive sequence, or microsatellite DNA, in the prairie vole gene that is absent in the montane vole gene (figure 7–4). This microsatellite DNA is genetically unstable and may provide a source of variability for rapid evolution of receptor expression patterns, which in turn could result in the evolution of monogamous behaviors.

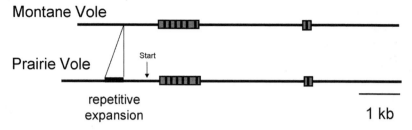

Figure 7–4. A comparison of the prairie vole versus the montane vole vasopressin V1a receptor gene and upstream regulatory sequence. The prairie vole sequence contains a repetitive expansion, or microsatellite polymorphism, in the promoter region of the gene. The striped boxes represent exons in the coding portion of the gene.

For example, within the prairie vole population there is extraordinary individual variability in both microsatellite length and V1a receptor binding pattern in the brain (Hammock & Young, 2002; Phelps & Young, 2003). Recent data have shown that the length of this microsatellite sequence can functionally regulate the amount of V1a receptor expression in cells (Hammock & Young, 2004), and there are meaningful correlations between V1a receptor gene structure, V1a receptor patterns in the brain, and behavioral effects (Hammock, Lim, Nair, & Young, in press). This genetic model provides a convincing evolutionary mechanism for natural selection to produce changes in social behavior within a population by changing the frequency of microsatellite alleles in the V1a receptor.

Is the V1a receptor gene responsible for pair-bonding behavior in this species? Data presented so far suggest that this single gene could have profound effects on the expression of receptors and, subsequently, social behavior. Can this single gene polymorphism determine the entire pattern of receptors in the brain of a monogamous species and subsequently affect behavior? This was addressed by an experiment introducing the prairie vole V1a receptor gene into a nonmonogamous species genome, the mouse. These transgenic mice showed a pattern of V1a receptor binding remarkably similar (though not identical) to prairie voles but very different from wild-type mice. In addition, when injected with AVP, the transgenic mice responded with increased affiliative behavior much like prairie voles, whereas the wild-type mice had no changes in social behavior much like the nonmonogamous montane voles (Young et al., 1999). However, the transgenic mice did not develop partner preferences, suggesting that there are other factors, other genes, and/or environmental cues, besides the V1a receptor gene, that mediate pair bonding. Social engagement is a complex behavioral process that certainly integrates many genes, neural circuits, and environment. Nevertheless, it is intriguing to see that a single gene polymorphism can have such a large impact on V1a receptor expression in the brain and affiliative behavior.

Table 5-1. Perceptual Similar Object Set.

Object	Label
	Similar original category member: purple
	Similar original category member: red
	Similar original category member: green
	Similar possible extension object: same-handle
	Similar possible extension object: juicer

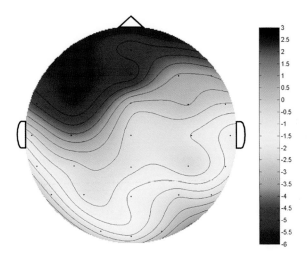

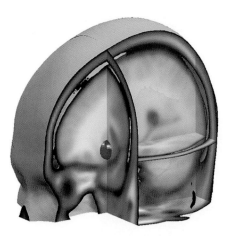

Figure 6-2. Two-dimensional interpolation of the difference wave (Beliefs-Reality) and three-dimensional graphical representation of the BESA solution indicating a dipole within left orbitofrontal cortex, taken from Liu, Sabbagh, Gehring, & Wellman (2004).

Is the V1a receptor gene the "monogamy gene"? The transgenic mouse experiment shows that a single gene polymorphism can dramatically affect social behavior. But the point remains, the transgenic mice did not become monogamous. Although the transgenic mouse approach is a powerful tool for manipulating gene expression, there are limitations. It is difficult to draw conclusions regarding the mechanisms underlying vole social behavior based on comparisons with mice. In addition, since one cannot limit transgene expression to particular candidate brain regions of interest, transgenic mice are of limited use for identifying the contribution of specific brain regions.

To address these issues, one could use viral vectors to deliver transgenes into specific brain regions in any animal species, not just mice. This technique would allow comparative studies in closely related species and would offer better targeting to specific brain regions to potentially study the neural circuits and various neurotransmitter systems involved in pair bonding. For example, one could use a viral vector containing the V1a receptor gene to increase expression in specific brain regions of nonmonogamous voles, where they normally lack V1a receptors, and see if they become monogamous. This experiment was performed recently with astounding results: Nonmonogamous voles with artifically increased V1a receptor gene expression in a specific brain region did, in fact, form partner preferences (Lim, Wang, et al., 2004).

Thus, the plasticity of V1a receptor expression by genetic factors such as gene polymorphisms could represent one possible mechanism for the species differences in behavior between prairie and montane voles. However, as in all biological systems, genetic factors likely act in concert with other aspects, such as environmental factors, to influence OT and V1a receptor expression and ultimately social behavior.

Gene-Environment Interactions

Are individuals destined to follow their genes? Genes provide a basic framework for the biology of an individual that environmental factors can then reshape. With social bonding, for instance, there are likely environmental factors in the lifetime experience of the individual that influence receptor expression in the brain and, subsequently, pair-bond formation. Some possibilities include the quality of nurture received during early development, or sociosexual history within the lifetime of the individual.

Environmental factors have been shown to affect OT and V1a receptor levels in several rodent species. For example, the quality of maternal care that a rat pup receives early in development results in different levels of OT and V1a receptor expression in the brain as an adult (Francis, Champagne, & Meaney, 2000; Champagne, Diorio, Sharma, & Meaney, 2001; Francis, Young, Meaney, & Insel,

2002). Along the same lines, rat pups undergoing neonatal stress have altered levels of OT receptors in the hippocampus (Noonan et al., 1994). V1a receptor expression has also been found to be dependent on corticosterone and glucocorticoids in rats (Patchev & Almeida, 1995; Watters, Wilkinson, & Dorsa, 1996) and testosterone in hamsters (Young, Wang, Cooper, & Albers, 2000). In montane vole species, Insel and Shapiro first found that the onset of maternal behavior induced OT receptor expression density in one brain region to a level similar to that of prairie voles (Insel & Shapiro, 1992). Similarly, in meadow vole species, Parker et al. have found that a variety of sociosexual and environmental factors influence OT and V1a receptor expression. For example, day length and cohabitation experience were found to alter OT receptor expression in female meadow voles, and OT receptor density has been correlated with partner preference formation (Parker, Phillips, Kinney, & Lee, 2001). Likewise, paternal behavior experience has been correlated with both OT and V1a receptor expression in males (Parker, Kinney, Phillips, & Lee, 2001).

In prairie voles, developmental studies have shown that OT and AVP systems are important early in life for social behavior. One such study showed that a single neonatal injection of peripheral AVP increased aggression in male prairie voles when they reached adulthood (Stribley & Carter, 1999). Another study showed that a single injection of testosterone and corticosterone administered to prairie vole pups could affect their social preferences and affiliative behavior as adults (Roberts, Zullo, Gustafson, & Carter, 1996; Roberts, Gustafson, & Carter, 1997). Extensive studies using OT manipulations in neonatal prairie voles have shown that a single neonatal exposure to OT could permanently alter adult measures of social behavior, including alloparenting, aggression, reproductive potential, and partner preference (Bales & Carter, 2003a, 2003b; Bales, Abdelnabi, Cushing, Ottinger, & Carter, 2004; Bales, Pfeifer, & Carter, 2004). Interestingly, species differences in receptor-binding patterns for OT and AVP in the brain are evident early in development and persist through adulthood, suggesting that perinatal manipulations of these systems might explain some of the species differences in social behavior (Wang, Young, Liu, & Insel, 1997).

Clearly, there exist both environmental and genetic components to pair bonding. Regardless of the environmental or genetic origins of monogamy, the interactions of nature and nurture intersect to produce the proximate mechanisms of social bonding in the animal: the underlying neurobiology and neural circuitry that produces social behavior.

The Neural Circuitry of the Pair-Bond

Evidence presented so far suggests that the distribution patterns, that is, the particular brain regions that specifically express V1a and OT receptors, are responsible for affiliative behavior and pair bonding in voles. What specific brain regions are involved in pair bonding in voles? One way to address this question is to compare the brain regions that highly express OT and V1a receptors in the prairie vole versus the montane vole. For example, the nucleus accumbens and prelimbic cortex are rich in OT receptors in prairie voles but are lacking in montane voles (Insel & Shapiro, 1992). Similarly, the ventral pallidum region highly expresses V1a receptors in prairie voles but not in montane voles (see figures 7–2 and 7–3, respectively; Lim, Murphy, & Young, 2004). Even other more distantly related vole species, such as the monogamous pine vole (*Microtus pinetorum*) and the nonmonogamous meadow vole (*Microtus pennsylvanicus*), show a similar species difference in OT and V1a receptor distribution in these brain regions (figure 7–5; Insel & Shapiro, 1992; Insel et al., 1994). Interestingly, V1a receptors in other monogamous species of mammals are also highly expressed in the ventral pallidum. For example, the monogamous California mouse (*Peromyscus californicus*) and the monogamous marmoset monkey both have a high density of V1a receptors in the ventral pallidal region, whereas the closely related nonmonogamous *Peromyscus leucopus* and the nonmonogamous rhesus monkey both lack V1a receptor binding there (see figure 7–5; Young, 1999). This is compelling evidence that V1a receptors in the ventral pallidum are associated with monogamous social structure across taxa, and thus may represent an evolutionary mechanism for social bonding to have convergently evolved.

The nucleus accumbens and ventral pallidum, both located in the ventral forebrain, are two key brain regions in the neural circuitry of reward. For example, the injection of cocaine into these regions in rats results in the development of a "conditioned place preference" to the specific environment where the rat received the drug (Gong, Neill, & Justice, 1996). It is interesting to hypothesize that the activation of OT and V1a receptors in these reward centers might result in the development of a conditioned *partner* preference in prairie voles, where voles would prefer to be near their partners because that is where they associate the reward. Likewise, the scarcity of these receptors in nonmonogamous species might explain their inability to form pair-bonds.

Direct experimental evidence shows that these reward circuits in the ventral forebrain are involved in pair bonding. First, infusion of an OT receptor antagonist into the nucleus accumbens prevents pair bonding in female prairie voles (Young, Lim, Gingrich, & Insel, 2001). Similarly, infusion of a V1a receptor blocker into the ventral pallidum inhibits pair-bond formation in male prairie voles (Lim & Young, 2004). Another experiment used a viral vector approach to deliver the prairie vole V1a receptor gene into the ventral pallidum of male prairie voles, which resulted in a twofold increase in the amount of V1a receptors expressed in that region. These animals with artificially elevated V1a receptors in the ventral pallidum showed increased affiliative behavior, as well as an acceleration of pair-bond formation, even without mating (Pitkow et al., 2001). A third experiment went even further and showed that a viral vector-mediated

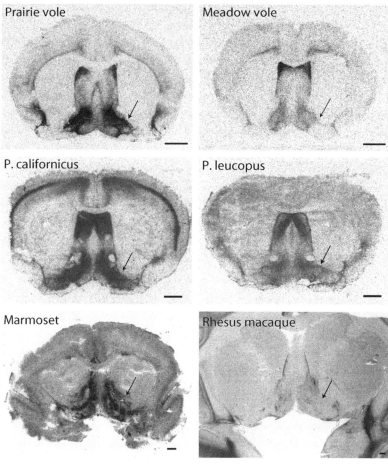

Figure 7–5. Vasopressin V1a receptor distribution across several monogamous species pairs. Monogamous prairie voles, California mice, and marmosets all have dense staining in the ventral forebrain region (arrows). Nonmonogamous sister species montane voles, white-footed mice, and rhesus monkeys all lack V1a receptors in this region (arrows). Scale bar = 1 mm.

V1a receptor increase in the ventral pallidum of nonmonogamous meadow voles could, in fact, induce partner preference formation in these formerly solitary animals (Lim, Wang, et al., 2004). These experiments confirm the necessity of OT and V1a receptors in the reward circuitry for the development of the pair-bond.

In addition to being rich in OT and V1a receptors, these reward regions in the ventral forebrain are also rich in dopamine receptors. In fact, dopamine neurotransmission is also critical in regulating pair-bond formation. Similar to the OT and V1a receptor story, microinjections of a dopamine D2 receptor antagonist, eticlopride, into the nucleus accumbens prevents partner preference, while microinjections of a dopamine D2 receptor agonist, quinpirole, into the same region facilitates partner preference formation in both male and female prairie voles (Gingrich et al., 2000). Both microdialysis and tissue punch experiments have shown that dopamine is also released into this region during mating in both male and female prairie voles (Gingrich et al., 2000; Aragona, Liu, Curtis, Stephan, & Wang, 2002). Interestingly, both dopamine and OT appear to interact to modulate pair bonding in prairie voles: Quinpirole-induced partner preference can be blocked by OT receptor antagonist infusion, and OT-faciliated partner preference can be blocked by the D2 receptor antagonist eticlopride (Liu & Wang, 2002). These data suggest that the activation of either OT or DAergic systems is sufficient to induce partner preferences, but that specific receptor antagonism prevents partner preferences facilitated by the other system, indicating that both systems are necessary for pair bonding (Liu & Wang, 2002).

Recent preliminary data on a third neuropeptide system, CRF and CRF receptors, describe an analogous story to the role of OT and V1a receptors in reward and pair-bond formation. Monogamous prairie and pine voles have much higher levels of CRF receptor subtype 2 (CRFR2) in the nucleus accumbens than nonmonogamous montane and meadow voles (Lim et al., 2005). Furthermore, microinjections of CRF into the nucleus accumbens facilitated partner preference in prairie voles (Lim et al., in press). CRF is involved in stress and learning, and it is possible that CRF may interact with oxytocin and dopamine within the nucleus accumbens to modulate the more subtle aspects of pair-bond formation and maintenance.

Thus, the neural circuits for pair bonding in voles are complex and likely involve interactions between many different neurotransmitter systems. We have hypothesized that it is the convergence of many neurotransmitter systems upon a final common pathway of the activation of reward areas that produces the complex behavior that constitutes a pair-bond (Young & Wang, 2004).

The Cognitive Mechanisms of the Pair-Bond

What are the specific cognitive mechanisms that occur during pair-bond formation? Interestingly, OT and AVP are both involved in learning and memory processes, and both neuropeptides play a critical role in the formation of social memories in rats and mice (Dantzer, Bluthe, Koob, & Le Moal, 1987; Engelmann, Wotjak, Neumann, Ludwig, & Landgraf, 1996; Young, 2002). In fact, mutant mice lacking OT, as well as mutant rats lacking AVP, or Brattleboro rats, both lack the ability to form social memories (Engelmann & Landgraf, 1994; Ferguson et al., 2000). Additionally, mutant mice lacking V1a receptors also show the same phenotype (Bielsky, Hu, Szegda, Westphal, & Young, 2004). A central injection of OT into the medial amygdala of the OT-knockout mice rescues their social memory deficit; similarly, an AVP infusion into the lateral septum of Brattleboro rats restores their social memory (Engelmann & Landgraf, 1994; Ferguson, Aldag, Insel, & Young, 2001). Likewise, OT receptor antagonism blocks social memory in wild-type mice, whereas V1a receptor blockade prevents social recognition in normal rats (Landgraf et al., 1995; Ferguson et al., 2001). One hypothesis to explain the pharmacological effects of OT and AVP on partner preference in the prairie vole is that OT in the medial amygdala may facilitate pair bonding by improving social recognition, while OT receptor antagonist might induce social amnesia. However, this hypothesis does not explain why prairie voles form monogamous relationships but mice and rats do not.

Dopamine release into the nucleus accumbens during mating in rats suggests that this behavior is rewarding (Pfaus et al., 1990); additionally, male rats will bar press for access to a receptive female (Everitt, Fray, Kostarczyk, Taylor, & Stacey, 1987). However, despite both the reinforcing aspects of mating *and* intact social memory faculties, rats still do not develop partner preferences for their mates. Perhaps one of the cognitive mechanisms underlying pair-bond formation in monogamous species involves the formation of a learned association between the memory of the partner and reward. Somehow, the conditioned stimulus, the partner, is paired with the unconditioned stimulus, mating, to result in a conditioned response of the prairie vole seeking to preferentially be with its mate. Overnight cohabitation and mating in prairie voles is inferred to release OT and AVP in the brain, which possibly modulates social memory circuits (Bamshad, Novak, & De Vries, 1994; Wang, Smith, Major, & De Vries, 1994; Cushing et al., 2001). Additionally, dopamine neurotransmission in the ventral forebrain is necessary for partner preference formation (Gingrich et al., 2000). It is possible that the neuronal inputs from reward circuitry and the inputs from social memory both converge onto the ventral forebrain, leading to a "conditioned partner preference," analogous to conditioned place preference. For example, during courtship, olfactory information is processed by the medial amygdala, which is critical for social memory. The medial amygdala has projections to the nucleus accumbens (Coolen & Wood, 1998) and also sends vasopressinergic projections to the ventral pallidum (De Vries & Buijs, 1983). The nucleus accumbens and ventral pallidum are reciprocally connected and project to other limbic regions involved in reward, such as the ventral tegmental area and the mediodorsal thalamus (figure 7–6; Groenewegen, Berendse, & Haber, 1993). The scarcity of OT receptor and V1a receptor in the ventral forebrain of nonmonogamous species may explain their inability to form partner preferences after mating. Conceivably, it is the integration of two preexisting neural circuits, one for reward and the other for social engagement, that has provided the proximate mechanism for pair bonding and driven the evolution of monogamous species.

In reality, a multitude of complex processes underlie the formation of social bonds. The V1a receptor gene does not function alone; it is coupled to a G-protein that activates a cascade of second messengers within the neuron that sub-

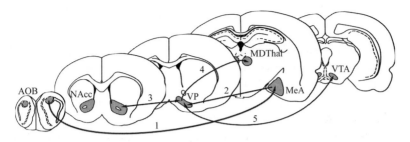

Figure 7–6. A proposed neural circuit for pair bonding. (1) Social olfactory information from the accessory olfactory bulb (AOB) is relayed to the medial amygdala (MeA). (2) The MeA sends vasopressinergic projections to the ventral pallidum (VP). (3) The VP is heavily interconnected with another reward nucleus, the nucleus accumbens (NAcc). (4) and (5) The VP also projects to other regions in the reward pathway, such as the mediodorsal thalamus (MDThal) and the ventral tegmental area (VTA). The convergence of inputs onto the MeA, where social memories are formed, and the VP, which activates reward cicuitry, reinforces the association between the partner and reward. This is the neural substrate for the formation of a pair bond.

sequently modulates the expression of many other genes. Such gene expression is probably different depending on the type of neuron and/or the particular brain region. In addition, brain regions do not function alone; they are heavily interconnected with thousands of synapses to other brain regions that are involved in many different neural circuits with many other neurotransmitter systems, such as OT, dopamine, and stress hormones. Social bonding itself can be dissected into several complex social behaviors, such as pheromone detection, social stimuli processing, social memory formation, learning, and motivation, each of which has its own complicated neural circuit with underlying genes and proteins. On top of all this, sociosexual experience, environmental conditions, and habitat can all interact with genetic factors to modulate social bond formation.

Social Bonding in Humans

The prairie vole model of social bonding has proved useful for understanding the interdisciplinary nature of neurobiology, from the molecular, cellular, and systems levels. These voles have provided us with a detailed understanding of how social attachments form and can lead us to a better understanding of social relationships in humans. They have also provided hypotheses regarding the evolution and diversity in social bonding across many species. Although there is currently no direct evidence that OT or AVP is involved in human bonding, a number of interesting experiments have lent support to this notion. Several studies have shown that OT and AVP are released during sexual intercourse. Plasma

OT levels are increased at the time of ejaculation in males (Carmichael et al., 1987), and plasma AVP levels are elevated during sexual arousal prior to orgasm (Murphy, Seckl, Burton, Checkley, & Lightman, 1987). In addition, OT is released during female sexual arousal and in even greater quantities following orgasm (Blaicher et al., 1999). However, one must be cautious in interpreting these data because the relationship between plasma hormones and brain levels is not always reliable.

Molecular analysis of the V1a receptor gene in voles has shown that mutations in the 5-prime regulatory region could have profound effects on expression patterns in the brain and, subsequently, differences in social behavior. Interestingly, the human V1a receptor gene also contains microsatellite sequences in the same promoter region of the gene (Thibonnier et al., 2000). If V1a receptor expression in the brain is indeed responsible for individual variability in social bonding, then one would predict that some aspects of social attachment in humans might be affected by microsatellite length in the V1a receptor gene. One recent study has found significant transmission disequilibrium between one allele of the human V1a receptor gene and autism, a social bonding disorder (Kim et al., 2002); recently, this result has been independently replicated by another group (Wassink et al., 2004). It would be interesting to perform additional genetic analyses to determine whether social traits in the normal range of behavior might correlate with these variable alleles of the V1a receptor.

It is important to note that although the prairie vole model of social bonding suggests that species differences in social behavior can be largely attributed to a single gene polymorphism, this is likely oversimplified in reference to explaining such a complex behavior. For example, many different genes modulate the release of AVP, as well as the signal transduction cascade that follows the activation of the V1a receptor. Many other genes and proteins are involved in the pathway that links the V1a gene polymorphism to V1a receptors in the brain to pair bonding, and it is likely that several parallel pathways exist that can produce social bonding. Individual as well as species differences in behavior are almost certainly a result of the interaction between numerous genes and environmental factors.

An obvious experiment to do next might be to look at the distribution of OT and V1a receptors in the human brain to see if the pattern resembles the neural circuitry of a monogamous species (see figure 7–5). One might predict that if humans were a species that formed pair-bonds using the same neural mechanisms as other monogamous animals, we would see dense expression of V1a and OT receptors in reward regions of the ventral forebrain. However, the same autoradiographic techniques used for rodent brains do not seem to work well with human brains. It is difficult to obtain freshly frozen human brain samples, and the radiolabeled ligand that selectively binds to the rodent OT receptor does not seem to bind well to the human OT receptor. One study used tritiated [3H]-AVP and [3H]-OT to examine binding sites, but these ligands bound to all subtypes of the vasopressin receptor, including the V1b, as well as the OT receptor (Loup, Tribollet, Dubois-Dauphin, & Dreifuss, 1991). Interestingly, upon using an iodinated [125I]-OT selective antagonist, they did find that OT receptors were concentrated in the some regions of the ventral forebrain, among other regions (Loup et al., 1991).

Another method of examining the neural mechanisms of social bonding in humans is to use functional imaging, with either positron emission tomography (PET) or magnetic resonance imaging (MRI). Recent evidence in humans supports our finding in voles that reward circuits may be involved in the neurobiology of affiliation. A recent study using functional MRI (fMRI) showed brain activation in reward areas with manual stimulation to ejaculation in male human subjects (Holstege et al., 2003), and a PET study in female subjects showed brain activation in the paraventricular nucleus, suggesting release of OT and/or AVP during orgasm (Whipple & Komisaruk, 2002). This suggests that mating in humans, like rodents, not only is subjectively rewarding but also has an observable neurobiological basis. Another fMRI experiment found that even simply viewing beautiful faces has reward value and activates the nucleus accumbens (Aharon et al., 2001), demonstrating that positive salient social stimuli, in this case visual, can activate reward areas. Interestingly, one fMRI study examined brain activation in people while viewing photographs of a person the subject reported being deeply in love with. The authors observed brain activation in regions that were remarkably similar to those seen in other studies after consumption of cocaine (Breiter et al., 1997; Bartels & Zeki, 2000, 2004). Clearly, the subjects who were in love or "pair bonded" with their partners felt hedonic pleasure and reward by just seeing a picture of their partner. This is strikingly analogous to what we think is going on during pair bonding in prairie voles.

In addition to functional imaging studies, structural PET imaging for receptors has shown that D2 receptor densities in the nucleus accumbens and striatum are correlated with "addictive personalities" in the subjective human response to methylphenidate, a cocaine-like compound (Volkow et al., 1999), much like the D2 receptor story and pair-bond formation in prairie voles. This notion of love as an addiction is not new; anecdotally, drug addicts have long maintained the opinion that "the best way to overcome a drug addiction is to fall in love." Even three decades ago, articles and books were written about the similarities between love and addiction: "People can become addicted to other people in the same way they become addicted to drugs" (Peele & Brodsky, 1974, p. 22; 1975).

The neurobiology underlying bonding with a single partner likely involves the same conserved pathways that are required for other forms of motivation, such as those seen in behavioral paradigms of conditioned reinforcement. However, unlike the unnatural cravings of drug addiction that often lead to dysfunction, social bonding enables positive affect in children and socially rewarding approach behaviors in adults. Positive engagement of social behavior is an inherent human feature that provides the foundation for all human societies. The mystery of the neurobiology underlying social bonding has just begun to unravel.

Acknowledgments This research was supported by grants NIH MH65050 to MML, MH56897 and MH 64692 to LJY, and NSF STC IBN-9876754 and the Yerkes Center Grant RR00165.

References

Aharon, I., Etcoff, N., Ariely, D., Chabris, C. F., O'Connor, E., & Breiter, H. C. (2001). Beautiful faces have variable reward value: fMRI and behavioral evidence. *Neuron, 32,* 537–551.

Aragona, B. J., Liu, Y., Curtis, J. T., Stephan, F. K., & Wang, Z. X. (2002). Nucleus accumbens dopamine is important for partner preference formation in male prairie voles. In Society for Neuroscience 2002. Orlando, Florida: 2002 Abstract Viewer/Itinerary Planner CD-ROM; Washington, DC.

Aragona, B. J., Liu, Y., Curtis, J. T., Stephan, F. K., & Wang, Z. (2003). A critical role for nucleus accumbens dopamine in partner-preference formation in male prairie voles. *Journal of Neuroscience, 23,* 3483–3490.

Bales, K. L., & Carter, C. S. (2003a). Developmental exposure to oxytocin facilitates partner preferences in male prairie voles (Microtus ochrogaster). *Behavioral Neuroscience, 117,* 854–859.

Bales, K. L., & Carter, C. S. (2003b). Sex differences and developmental effects of oxytocin on aggression and social behavior in prairie voles (Microtus ochrogaster). *Hormones and Behavior, 44,* 178–184.

Bales, K. L., Abdelnabi, M., Cushing, B. S., Ottinger, M. A., & Carter, C. S. (2004). Effects of neonatal oxytocin manipulations on male reproductive potential in prairie voles. *Physiology and Behavior, 81,* 519–526.

Bales, K. L., Pfeifer, L. A., & Carter, C. S. (2004). Sex differences and developmental effects of manipulations of oxytocin on alloparenting and anxiety in prairie voles. *Developmental Psychobiology, 44,* 123–131.

Bamshad, M., Novak, M. A., & De Vries, G. J. (1994). Cohabitation alters vasopressin innervation and paternal behavior in prairie voles (Microtus ochrogaster). *Physiology and Behavior, 56,* 751–758.

Bartels, A., & Zeki, S. (2000). The neural basis of romantic love. *Neuroreport, 11,* 3829–3834.

Bartels, A., & Zeki, S. (2004). The neural correlates of maternal and romantic love. *NeuroImage, 21,* 1155–1166.

Bielsky, I. F., Hu, S. B., Szegda, K. L., Westphal, H., & Young, L. J. (2004). Profound impairment in social recognition and reduction in anxiety-like behavior in vasopressin V1a receptor knockout mice. *Neuropsychopharmacology, 29,* 483–493.

Blaicher, W., Gruber, D., Bieglmayer, C., Blaicher, A. M., Knogler, W., Huber, J. C. (1999). The role of oxytocin in relation to female sexual arousal. *Gynecologic and Obstetric Investigation, 47,* 125–126.

Breiter, H. C., Gollub, R. L., Weisskoff, R. M., Kennedy, D. N., Makris, N., Berke, J. D., et al. (1997). Acute effects of cocaine on human brain activity and emotion. *Neuron, 19,* 591–611.

Carmichael, M. S., Humbert, R., Dixen, J., Palmisano, G., Greenleaf, W., & Davidson, J.M. (1987). Plasma oxytocin increases in the human sexual response. *Journal of Clinical Endocrinology and Metabolism, 64*, 27–31.

Carter, C. S., DeVries, A. C., & Getz, L. L. (1995). Physiological substrates of mammalian monogamy: The prairie vole model. *Neuroscience and Biobehavioral Reviews, 19*, 303–314.

Champagne, F., Diorio, J., Sharma, S., & Meaney, M. J. (2001). Naturally occurring variations in maternal behavior in the rat are associated with differences in estrogen-inducible central oxytocin receptors. *Proceedings of the National Academy of Sciences of the United States of America, 98*, 12736–12741.

Cho, M. M., DeVries, A. C., Williams, J. R., & Carter, C. S. (1999). The effects of oxytocin and vasopressin on partner preferences in male and female prairie voles (Microtus ochrogaster). *Behavioral Neuroscience, 113*, 1071–1079.

Coolen, L. M., & Wood, R. I. (1998). Bidirectional connections of the medial amygdaloid nucleus in the Syrian hamster brain: Simultaneous anterograde and retrograde tract tracing. *Journal of Comparative Neurology, 399*, 189–209.

Cushing, B. S., & Carter, C. S. (2000). Peripheral pulses of oxytocin increase partner preferences in female, but not male, prairie voles. *Hormones and Behavior, 37*, 49–56.

Cushing, B. S., Martin, J. O., Young, L. J., & Carter, C. S. (2001). The effects of peptides on partner preference formation are predicted by habitat in prairie voles. *Hormones and Behavior, 39*, 48–58.

Dantzer, R., Bluthe, R. M., Koob, G. F., & Le Moal, M. (1987). Modulation of social memory in male rats by neurohypophyseal peptides. *Psychopharmacology (Berl), 91*, 363–368.

De Vries, G. J., & Buijs, R. M. (1983). The origin of the vasopressinergic and oxytocinergic innervation of the rat brain with special reference to the lateral septum. *Brain Research, 273*, 307–317.

De Vries, G. J., Best, W., & Sluiter, A. A. (1983). The influence of androgens on the development of a sex difference in the vasopressinergic innervation of the rat lateral septum. *Brain Research, 284*, 377–380.

DeVries, A. C., Taymans, S. E., & Carter, C. S. (1997). Social modulation of corticosteroid responses in male prairie voles. *Annals of the New York Academy of Sciences, 807*, 494–497.

DeVries, A. C., DeVries, M. B., Taymans, S., & Carter, C. S. (1995). Modulation of pair bonding in female prairie voles (Microtus ochrogaster) by corticosterone. *Proceedings of the National Academy of Sciences of the United States of America, 92*, 7744–7748.

DeVries, A. C., DeVries, M. B., Taymans, S. E., & Carter, C. S. (1996). The effects of stress on social preferences are sexually dimorphic in prairie voles. *Proceedings of the National Academy of Sciences of the United States of America, 93*, 11980–11984.

DeVries, A. C., Guptaa, T., Cardillo, S., Cho, M., & Carter, C. S. (2002). Corticotropin-releasing factor induces social preferences in male prairie voles. *Psychoneuroendocrinology, 27*, 705–714.

Dewsbury, D. A. (1987). The comparative psychology of monogamy. *Nebraska Symposium on Motivation, 35*, 1–50.

Engelmann, M., & Landgraf, R. (1994). Microdialysis administration of vasopressin into the septum improves social recognition in Brattleboro rats. *Physiology and Behavior, 55*, 145–149.

Engelmann, M., Wotjak, C. T., Neumann, I., Ludwig, M., & Landgraf, R. (1996).

Behavioral consequences of intracerebral vasopressin and oxytocin: Focus on learning and memory. *Neuroscience and Biobehavioral Reviews, 20,* 341–358.

Everitt, B. J., Fray, P., Kostarczyk, E., Taylor, S., & Stacey, P. (1987). Studies of instrumental behavior with sexual reinforcement in male rats (Rattus norvegicus): I. Control by brief visual stimuli paired with a receptive female. *Journal of Comparative Psychology, 101,* 395–406.

Ferguson, J. N., Aldag, J. M., Insel, T. R., & Young, L. J. (2001). Oxytocin in the medial amygdala is essential for social recognition in the mouse. *Journal of Neuroscience, 21,* 8278–8285.

Ferguson, J. N., Young, L. J., Hearn, E. F., Matzuk, M. M., Insel, T. R., & Winslow, J. T. (2000). Social amnesia in mice lacking the oxytocin gene. *Nature Genetics, 25,* 284–288.

Francis, D. D., Champagne, F. C., & Meaney, M. J. (2000). Variations in maternal behaviour are associated with differences in oxytocin receptor levels in the rat. *Journal of Neuroendocrinology, 12,* 1145–1148.

Francis, D. D., Young, L. J., Meaney, M. J., & Insel, T. R. (2002). Naturally occurring differences in maternal care are associated with the expression of oxytocin and vasopressin (V1a) receptors: Gender differences. *Journal of Neuroendocrinology, 14,* 349–353.

Gainer, H., & Wray, W. (1994), Cellular and molecular biology of oxytocin and vasopressin. In E. Knobil & J. D. Neill (Eds.), *The physiology of reproduction* (pp. 1099–1129). New York: Raven.

Getz, L. L., Carter, C. S., & Gavish, L. (1981). The mating system of the prairie vole *Microtus ochrogaster*: Field and laboratory evidence for pair-bonding. *Behavioral Ecology and Sociobiology, 8,* 189–194.

Getz, L. L., McGuire, B., Pizzuto, T., Hofmann, J. E., & Frase, B. (1993). Social organization of the prairie vole (*Microtus ochrogaster*). *Journal of Mammalogy, 74,* 44–58.

Gingrich, B., Liu, Y., Cascio, C., Wang, Z., & Insel, T. R. (2000). Dopamine D2 receptors in the nucleus accumbens are important for social attachment in female prairie voles (Microtus ochrogaster). *Behavioral Neuroscience, 114,* 173–183.

Gong, W., Neill, D., Justice, J. B., Jr. (1996). Conditioned place preference and locomotor activation produced by injection of psychostimulants into ventral pallidum. *Brain Research, 707,* 64–74.

Goodson, J. L., & Bass, A. H. (2001). Social behavior functions and related anatomical characteristics of vasotocin/vasopressin systems in vertebrates. *Brain Research. Brain Research Reviews, 35,* 246–265.

Groenewegen, H. J., Berendse, H. W., Haber, S. N. (1993). Organization of the output of the ventral striatopallidal system in the rat: Ventral pallidal efferents. *Neuroscience, 57,* 113–142.

Gubernick, D. J., & Alberts, J. R. (1987). The biparental care system of the California mouse, *Peromyscus californicus. Journal of Comparative Psychology, 101,* 169–177.

Hammock, E. A. D., & Young, L. J. (2004). Functional microsatellite polymorphism associated with divergent social structure in vole species. *Molecular Biology and Evolution, 21,* 1057–1063.

Hammock, E. A. D., & Young, L. J. (2002). Variation in the vasopressin V1a receptor promoter and expression: Implications for inter- and intraspecific variation in social behaviour. *European Journal of Neuroscience, 16,* 399–402.

Hammock, E. A. D., Lim, M. M., Nair, H. P., & Young, L. J. (in press). Vasopressin V1a receptor levels are associated with a regulatory microsatellite and behavior. *Genes, Brain, and Behavior.*

Holstege, G., Georgiadis, J. R., Paans, A. M., Meiners, L. C., van der Graaf, F. H., & Reinders, A. A. (2003) Brain activation during human male ejaculation. *Journal of Neuroscience, 23,* 9185–9193.

Insel, T. R., & Hulihan, T. J. (1995). A gender-specific mechanism for pair bonding: Oxytocin and partner preference formation in monogamous voles. *Behavioral Neuroscience, 109,* 782–789.

Insel, T. R., & Shapiro, L. E. (1992). Oxytocin receptor distribution reflects social organization in monogamous and polygamous voles. *Proceedings of the National Academy of Sciences of the United States of America, 89,* 5981–5985.

Insel, T. R., Preston, S., & Winslow, J. T. (1995). Mating in the monogamous male: Behavioral consequences. *Physiology and Behavior, 57,* 615–627.

Insel, T. R., Wang, Z. X., & Ferris, C. F. (1994). Patterns of brain vasopressin receptor distribution associated with social organization in microtine rodents. *Journal of Neuroscience, 14,* 5381–5392.

Jones, J. S., & Wynne-Edwards, K. E. (2000). Paternal hamsters mechanically assist the delivery, consume amniotic fluid and placenta, remove fetal membranes, and provide parental care during the birth process. *Hormones and Behavior, 37,* 116–125.

Kendrick, K. M., Da Costa, A. P., Broad, K. D., Ohkura, S., Guevara, R., Levy, F., et al. (1997). Neural control of maternal behaviour and olfactory recognition of offspring. *Brain Research Bulletin, 44,* 383–395.

Keverne, E. B., & Kendrick, K. M. (1992). Oxytocin facilitation of maternal behavior in sheep. *Annals of the New York Academy of Sciences, 652,* 83–101.

Kim, S. J., Young, L. J., Gonen, D., Veenstra-VanderWeele, J., Courchesne, R., Courchesne, E., et al. (2002). Transmission disequilibrium testing of arginine vasopressin receptor 1A (AVPR1A) polymorphisms in autism. *Molecuar Psychiatry, 7,* 503–507.

Kleiman, D. G. (1977). Monogamy in mammals. *Quarterly Review of Biology, 52,* 39–69.

Kostan, K. M., & Snowdon, C. T. (2002). Attachment and social preferences in cooperatively-reared cotton-top tamarins. *American Journal of Primatology, 57,* 131–139.

Lack, D. (1968). *Ecological adaptations for breeding in birds.* London: Methuen.

Landgraf, R., Gerstberger, R., Montkowski, A., Probst, J. C., Wotjak, C. T., Holsboer, F., et al. (1995). V1 vasopressin receptor antisense oligodeoxynucleotide into septum reduces vasopressin binding, social discrimination abilities, and anxiety-related behavior in rats. *Journal of Neuroscience, 15,* 4250–4258.

Lim, M. M., Murphy, A. Z., & Young, L. J. (2004). Ventral striatopallidal oxytocin and vasopressin V1a receptors in the monogamous prairie vole (Microtus ochrogaster). *Journal of Comparative Neurology, 468,* 555–570.

Lim, M. M., Nair, H. P., & Young, L. J. (2005). Species and sex differences in brain distribution of CRF receptor subtypes 1 and 2 in monogamous and promiscuous vole species. *Journal of Comparative Neurology,* 487(1): 75–92.

Lim, M. M., & Young, L. J. (2004). Vasopressin-dependent neural circuits underlying pair bond formation in the monogamous prairie vole. *Neuroscience, 125,* 35–45.

Lim, M. M., Liu, Y., Hammock, E. A. D., Nair, H. P., Bai, Y. H., Ryabinin, A. E., Wang, Z. X., Young, L. J. (in press). CRF1 and CRF2 in the nucleus accumbens modulate social attachment. *Nature Neuroscience.*

Lim, M. M., Wang, Z., Olazabal, D. E., Ren, X., Terwilliger, E. F., & Young, L. J. (2004). Enhanced partner preference in a promiscuous species by manipulating the expression of a single gene. *Nature, 429,* 754–757.

Liu, Y., & Wang, Z. X. (2002). Both dopamine and oxytocin receptors are required for partner preference formation in female prairie vole.In Society for Neuroscience. Orlando, Florida: 2002 Abstract Viewer/Itinerary Planner; Washington, DC.

Liu, Y., & Wang, Z. X. (2003). Nucleus accumbens oxytocin and dopamine interact to regulate pair bond formation in female prairie voles. *Neuroscience, 121,* 537–544.

Liu, Y., Curtis, J. T., & Wang, Z. (2001). Vasopressin in the lateral septum regulates pair bond formation in male prairie voles (Microtus ochrogaster). *Behavioral Neuroscience, 115,* 910–919.

Loup, F., Tribollet, E., Dubois-Dauphin, M., & Dreifuss, J. J. (1991). Localization of high-affinity binding sites for oxytocin and vasopressin in the human brain: An autoradiographic study. *Brain Research, 555,* 220–232.

McGuire, B., Getz, L. L., Hofmann, J. E., Pizzuto, T., & Frase, B. (1993). Natal dispersal and philopatry in prairie voles (*Microtus ochragaster*) in relation to population density. *Behavioral Ecology and Sociobiology, 32,* 293–302.

Murphy, M. R., Seckl, J. R., Burton, S., Checkley, S. A., & Lightman, S. L. (1987). Changes in oxytocin and vasopressin secretion during sexual activity in men. *Journal of Clinical Endocrinology and Metabolism, 65,* 738–741.

Noonan, L. R., Caldwell, J. D., Li, L., Walker, C. H., Pedersen, C. A., & Mason, G. A. (1994). Neonatal stress transiently alters the development of hippocampal oxytocin receptors. *Brain Research. Developmental Brain Research, 80,* 115–120.

Orians, G. H. (1969). On the evolution of mating systems in birds and mammals. *American Naturalist, 103,* 589–603.

Parker, K. J., Kinney, L. F., Phillips, K. M., & Lee, T. M. (2001). Paternal behavior is associated with central neurohormone receptor binding patterns in meadow voles (Microtus pennsylvanicus). *Behavioral Neuroscience, 115,* 1341–1348.

Parker, K. J., Phillips, K. M., Kinney, L. F., & Lee, T. M. (2001). Day length and sociosexual cohabitation alter central oxytocin receptor binding in female meadow voles (*Microtus pennsylvanicus*). *Behavioral Neuroscience, 115,* 1349–1356.

Patchev, V. K., & Almeida, O. F. (1995). Corticosteroid regulation of gene expression and binding characteristics of vasopressin receptors in the rat brain. *European Journal of Neuroscience, 7,* 1579–1583.

Pedersen, C. A., Ascher, J. A., Monroe, Y. L., & Prange, A. J., Jr. (1982). Oxytocin induces maternal behavior in virgin female rats. *Science, 216,* 648–650.

Peele, S., & Brodsky, A. (1981). *Love and addiction.* New York: Signet Book.

Pfaus, J. G., Damsma, G., Nomikos, G. G., Wenkstern, D. G., Blaha, C. D., Phillips, A. G., et al. (1990). Sexual behavior enhances central dopamine transmission in the male rat. *Brain Research, 530,* 345–348.

Phelps, S. M., & Young, L. J. (2003). Extraordinary diversity in vasopressin (V1a) receptor distributions among wild prairie voles (Microtus ochrogaster): Patterns of variation and covariation. *Journal of Comparative Neurology, 466,* 564–576.

Pitkow, L. J., Sharer, C. A., Ren, X., Insel, T. R., Terwilliger, E. F., & Young, L. J. (2001). Facilitation of affiliation and pair-bond formation by vasopressin receptor gene transfer into the ventral forebrain of a monogamous vole. *Journal of Neuroscience, 21,* 7392–7396.

Richardson, P. R. K. (1987). Aardwolf mating system: Overt cuckoldry in an apparently monogamous mammal. *Suid-Afrik Tydskrif Wetenskap, 83,* 405–410.

Roberts, R. L., & Carter, C. S. (1997). Intraspecific variation and the presence of a father can influence the expression of monogamous and communal traits in prairie voles. *Annals of the New York Academy of Sciences, 807,* 559–562.

Roberts, R. L., Gustafson, E. A., & Carter, C. S. (1997). Perinatal hormone exposure alters the expression of selective affiliative preferences in prairie voles. *Annals of the New York Academy of Sciences, 807,* 563–566.

Roberts, R. L., Zullo, A., Gustafson, E. A., & Carter, C. S. (1996). Perinatal steroid treatments alter alloparental and affiliative behavior in prairie voles. *Hormones and Behavior, 30,* 576–582.

Snowdon, C. T. (1990). Mechanisms maintaining monogamy in monkeys. In D. A. Dewsbury (Ed.), *Contemporary issues in comparative psychology* (pp. 225–251). Sunderland, MA: Sinauer.

Stribley, J. M., & Carter, C. S. (1999). Developmental exposure to vasopressin increases aggression in adult prairie voles. *Proceedings of the National Academy of Sciences of the United States of America, 96,* 12601–12604.

Taymans, S. E., DeVries. A. C., DeVries, M. B., Nelson, R. J., Friedman, T. C., Castro, M., et al. (1997). The hypothalamic-pituitary-adrenal axis of prairie voles (Microtus ochrogaster): Evidence for target tissue glucocorticoid resistance. *General and Comparative Endocrinology, 106,* 48–61.

Thibonnier, M., Graves, M. K., Wagner, M. S., Chatelain, N., Soubrier, F., Corvol, P., et al. (2000). Study of V(1)-vascular vasopressin receptor gene microsatellite polymorphisms in human essential hypertension. *Journal of Molecular and Cellular Cardiology, 32,* 557–564.

Volkow, N. D., Wang, G. J., Fowler, J. S., Logan, J., Gatley, S. J., Gifford, A., et al. (1999). Prediction of reinforcing responses to psychostimulants in humans by brain dopamine D2 receptor levels. *American Journal of Psychiatry, 156,* 1440–1443.

Wang, Z., Smith, W., Major, D. E., & De Vries, G. J. (1994). Sex and species differences in the effects of cohabitation on vasopressin messenger RNA expression in the bed nucleus of the stria terminalis in prairie voles (Microtus ochrogaster) and meadow voles (Microtus pennsylvanicus). *Brain Research, 650,* 212–218.

Wang, Z., Young, L. J., Liu, Y., & Insel, T. R. (1997). Species differences in vasopressin receptor binding are evident early in development: Comparative anatomic studies in prairie and montane voles. *Journal of Comparative Neurology, 378,* 535–546.

Wang, Z., Yu, G., Cascio, C., Liu, Y., Gingrich, B., & Insel, T. R. (1999). Dopamine D2 receptor-mediated regulation of partner preferences in female prairie voles (Microtus ochrogaster): A mechanism for pair bonding? *Behavioral Neuroscience, 113,* 602–611.

Wassink, T. H., Piven, J., Vieland, V. J., Pietila, J., Goedken, R. J., Folstein, S. E., et al. (2004). Examination of AVPR1a as an autism susceptibility gene. *Molecular Psychiatry, 9,* 968–972.

Watters, J. J., Wilkinson, C. W., & Dorsa, D. M. (1996). Glucocorticoid regulation of vasopressin V1a receptors in rat forebrain. *Brain Research. Molecular Brain Research, 38,* 276–284.

Whipple, B., & Komisaruk, B. R. (2002). Brain (PET) responses to vaginal-cervical self-stimulation in women with complete spinal cord injury: Preliminary findings. *Journal of Sex and Marital Therapy, 28,* 79–86.

Williams, J. R., Carter, C. S., & Insel, T. (1992). Partner preference development in female prairie voles is facilitated by mating or the central infusion of oxytocin. *Annals of the New York Academy of Sciences, 652,* 487–489.

Williams, J. R., Catania, K. C., & Carter, C. S. (1992). Development of partner preferences in female prairie voles (*Microtus ochrogaster*): The role of social and sexual experience. *Hormones and Behavior, 26,* 339–349.

Williams, J. R., Insel, T. R., Harbaugh, C. R., & Carter, C. S. (1994). Oxytocin administered centrally facilitates formation of a partner preference in female prairie voles (Microtus ochrogaster). *Journal of Neuroendocrinology, 6,* 247–250.

Winslow, J. T., Hastings, N., Carter, C. S., Harbaugh, C. R., & Insel, T. R. (1993). A role for central vasopressin in pair bonding in monogamous prairie voles. *Nature, 365,* 545–548.

Wotjak, C. T., Kubota, M., Liebsch, G., Montkowski, A., Holsboer, F., Neumann, I., et al. (1996). Release of vasopressin within the rat paraventricular nucleus in response to emotional stress: A novel mechanism of regulating adrenocorticotropic hormone secretion? *Journal of Neuroscience, 16,* 7725–7732.

Young, L. J. (1999). Frank A. Beach Award. Oxytocin and vasopressin receptors and species-typical social behaviors. *Hormones and Behavior, 36,* 212–221.

Young, L. J. (2002). The neurobiology of social recognition, approach, and avoidance. *Biological Psychiatry, 51,* 18–26.

Young, L. J., & Insel, T. R. (2002). Hormones and parental behavior. In J. Becker, M. Breedlove, & D. Crews (Eds.), *Behavioral endocrinology* (pp. 331–368). Cambridge, MA: MIT Press.

Young, L. J., Lim, M. M., Gingrich, B., & Insel, T. R. (2001). Cellular mechanisms of social attachment. *Hormones and Behavior, 40,* 133–138.

Young, L. J., & Wang, Z. (2004). The neurobiology of pair bonding. *Nature Neuroscience, 7,* 1048–1054.

Young, L. J., Wang, Z., Cooper, T. T., & Albers, H. E. (2000). Vasopressin (V1a) receptor binding, mRNA expression and transcriptional regulation by androgen in the Syrian hamster brain. *Journal of Neuroendocrinology, 12,* 1179–1185.

Young, L. J., Nilsen, R., Waymire, K. G., MacGregor, G. R., & Insel, T. R. (1999). Increased affiliative response to vasopressin in mice expressing the V1a receptor from a monogamous vole. *Nature, 400,* 766–768.

8

The Neurobiology of Maternal Behavior in Mammals

Frédéric Lévy
Alison S. Fleming

B ehaviors associated with the birth and care of young are essential
for the survival of mammals, as the mother provides food, warmth,
shelter, and protection from predators and conspecifics. She also provides the
young with their first social experience and helps them become integrated into
the social group. Through experiences with the mother, the young develop, with
this development depending on the kinds of experiences they have. Mothers are
also affected and changed by their interactions with their young. Sensory and
endocrine changes associated with gestation, parturition, and lactation induce
changes in the mother that have long-term effects on her own neural and behavioral development. In this chapter, we concentrate on factors that influence the
mother's first responses to her offspring, as well as ways she is changed by those
initial responses. We consider the mechanisms that regulate the onset of nurtur-
ing behavior and its maintenance, focusing on both physiological mechanisms
(endocrine, neurochemical, neural) and the variety of behavioral systems that
are also activated by the physiological mechanisms that necessarily underlie the
expression of maternal behavior (affective, perception, learning). Orthogonal to
these themes and in keeping with our particular areas of expertise, we also compare and contrast factors regulating maternal behavior in altricial and precocial
species and, where possible, contrast these with what is known about human
maternal behavior. Maternal behavior displayed directly or indirectly in response
to the young assumes a wide variety of patterns, some of which are common to
most mammals, and others of which depend primarily on the maturity of the
young at birth. The species-characteristic pattern of maternal behavior depends
also on the social structure of the species and the ecology in which they live.

Maternal behavior usually emerges at or close to parturition. Just after birth,
the female shows a very immediate interest in the newborn. Cleaning of the
neonate and the consumption of amniotic fluids and placenta are widespread

behaviors among mammalian orders, except in fully aquatic mammals (Cetacae) and semiaquatic mammals (Pinnipedia). Mothers of many mammals also emit characteristic vocalizations in response to their young and show retrieval, gathering, gathering, herding, or carrying behaviors that protect the young from predation and tend to keep the young in close proximity to the mother. As well, most new mothers protect their young from predators and conspecifics. However, the most important and common pattern of maternal behavior in mammals is nursing, which occurs shortly after the young are born.

In so-called altricial species (most rodents, canids, felids), the main aspects of maternal behavior are (a) nest building, (b) licking, (c) suckling, and (d) retrieving. The mother builds a nest in which she gives birth to a large litter of young that are not fully developed and have limited sensory and locomotor abilities. For instance, in rodents once the mother has retrieved and gathered the pups together into the nest, she spends most of her time in a nursing posture (Stern, 1989, 1990; Stern, Dix, Bellomo, & Thramann, 1992), and she licks the young, a behavior that functions to promote urination and elimination by the offspring and to maintain the mother's fluid balance (Friedman, Bruno, & Alberts, 1981). In most altricial species, the young stay huddled together within the nest for the first 10 or so days of life, and hence there is little need for the mother to recognize individual members of her litter, as long as they remain in or near the nest and the mother can readily locate her own nest site. However, among rodents that live in colonies there may be a need for the mother to recognize the specific characteristics of her litter.

The so-called precocial species (most ungulates) tend to have a small litter of fully developed young that are capable of following the mother shortly after birth. Indeed, these species are constantly on the move in search of food; hence, it is vital that young are able to follow their mothers. The main aspects of maternal behavior in, for instance, sheep, are (a) licking, (b) suckling, and (c) aggression toward alien lambs. Because own and alien young co-occur in the same flock, nursing ungulate females potentially risk having their limited milk supply usurped by young that are not their offspring. Mothers in these species develop discriminative maternal care favoring their own young, allowing them to suck while rejecting any alien young that may approach the udder. In this respect, the establishment of a selective bond within the first few hours after parturition represents one of the essential characteristics of maternal behavior in precocial species. Individual recognition of young has been demonstrated in sheep, goat, cattle, horse (Herscher, Richmond, & Moore, 1963; Hudson & Mullord, 1977; Klopfer, Adams, & Klopfer, 1964; Smith, Van-Toller, & Boyes, 1966; Maletinska, Spinka, Vichova, & Stehulova, 2002). This characteristic is different from maternal responsiveness, which is a nonspecific interest toward any newborn and occurs immediately at birth in both altricial and precocial species.

A continuum of mothering styles can be found between the two extremes of altricial and precocial species. In some types of mammals, neonates have functional sensory systems but limited thermoregulation (e.g., pigs) or locomotion (e.g., primates). Sows build a nest and do not develop selectivity toward their piglets immediately after parturition, although they are able to recognize their young within one day of parturition (Maletinska et al., 2002). Most primates do not build nests; instead, the mother carries the offspring on her body, to which the infants attach, using their strong prehensile hands. Mothers act maternally only toward their own infants, but this selectivity develops later, for example, at about 2 months in crab-eating monkeys (Negayama & Honjo, 1986). Like other primates, humans are able to discriminate their own infants and may show a preference for them, but they do not necessarily reject infants belonging to other mothers.

Considering these behavioral similarities and differences, one would expect that many of the proximal factors (hormonal, neural, and sensory) that control the initial motivation to engage in maternal behavior toward any young (so-called maternal responsiveness) would be shared across mammalian species, while other factors relating to differential treatment of young would differ among species. Hormonal events that are triggered by the onset of parturition and involved in the expression of maternal behavior are likely to have much in common across species, since the neuroendocrine control of pregnancy and parturition is similar across species. Once the initial phase of maternal responsiveness controlled by hormonal factors is established, its maintenance is regulated through the sensory stimuli provided by the young. The first section of this chapter will compare the hormonal and sensory factors and neural mechanisms regulating the onset of maternal behavior in representative altricial and precocial species. In this section, we also discuss the multiple ways that hormones act to promote maternal behavior at the time of parturition, through their effects on the mothers' affective and perceptual systems. The second section will focus on the postpartum period and factors that regulate maternal experience and memory. In this section, we will review the sensory, endocrine, and neural mechanisms that underlie memory for the litter, as described most extensively in an altricial species (rats). The third section explores these same determinants in the regulation of memory for individual offspring as found in a precocial species (sheep). Here, we also briefly describe studies in humans who also show individual recognition of infant odors and cries but independently of selective or exclusive responsiveness. Finally, throughout this chapter we attempt to contrast what is known about the sensory and endocrine correlates of maternal behavior in rats and sheep with primate and human maternal behavior.

Neurobiology of Maternal Responsiveness

Hormonal Determinants

There is now substantial evidence that the hormones associated with late pregnancy and parturition account for the rapid activation of maternal responsiveness

seen at parturition. These include the steroid hormones estradiol and progesterone, which are synthesized by the ovaries and released into the circulatory
system, and the protein hormones prolactin and oxytocin that are released
within the brain and the pituitary gland (Numan, 1994; Rosenblatt & Snowdon,
1996; Rosenblatt, 1990; Bridges, 1990; Insel, 1990). There are also important
changes at parturition in other neurotransmitters such as beta-endorphins,
dopamine, norepinephrine, glutamate, and gamma-aminobutyric acid (Caldwell, Greer, Johnson, Prange, & Pedersen, 1987; Young, Muns, Wang, & Insel,
1997; Keverne & Kendrick, 1990; Rosenberg & Herrenkohl, 1976; Bridges,
1990).

Hormonal Changes During Pregnancy and Parturition

In most mammals, late pregnancy and the periparturitional period are characterized by a decrease in progesterone levels followed by an increase in levels of
estradiol. In sheep, plasma levels of progesterone drop 2 to 4 days before parturition, whereas estradiol levels rise 1 day before parturition, peak at parturition,
and then decrease to a basal level within the first 4 hours postpartum (Challis,
Harrison, & Heap, 1971; Shipka & Ford, 1991). In the rat, a similar pattern is
shown, although the change commences earlier in the pregnancy, peaking at the
time of parturition. However, exceptions to this pattern of steroid change are
found in most female primates and in humans. In the rhesus monkey, there is no
similar shift, with levels of both steroids declining immediately prior to or during parturition (Soares & Talamantes, 1982). In humans, there is also no shift in
the progesterone-to-estrogen ratio at birth, although a 40% decrease of this
ratio in the myometrium has been reported at parturition (Benassayag, Leroy, &
Rigourd, 1999). In addition to estradiol and progesterone, there also occurs a
rise across pregnancy in the activation of the fetal and maternal hypothalamic-
pituitary-adrenal system that peaks at parturition (Fleming, Ruble, Krieger, &
Wong, 1997). The change in the balance of estradiol and progesterone steroids
also induces a rise in levels of the pituitary hormone prolactin. This rise occurs
in most species 24 hours to 48 hours before parturition, and a high level of prolactin is maintained during lactation as a result of suckling stimulation (Chamley
et al., 1973; Bridges & Goldman, 1975).

An extensive literature shows that parturition induces several physiological
changes within the brain itself. In sheep and cattle, oxytocin (OT) concentrations are greatly increased in the cerebrospinal fluid (CSF) within the first minutes after expulsion of the neonate (Kendrick, Keverne, Baldwin, & Sharman,
1986) but not in animals that have had epidural anesthesia (Lévy, Kendrick,
Keverne, Piketty, & Poindron, 1992; Williams, Gazal, Leshin, Stanko, & Anderson, 2001). This increase of oxytocin in the ventricular system appears to be a
common characteristic of mammals, although in humans CSF oxytocin concentrations seem not to change at parturition (Tagaki et al., 1985).

In rats and sheep, oxytocin synthesis at parturition increases in the paraventricular nucleus of the hypothalamus (PVN; Da Costa, Guevara-Guzman, Ohkura, Goode, & Kendrick, 1996) and in the supraoptic nucleus (SON) of the hypothalamus (Neumann, Russell, & Landgraf, 1993), two main sources of oxytocinergic projections in the brain. The increase in oxytocin release from PVN and SON terminals is also associated with an increase of levels of oxytocin receptors in other brain sites that are involved in the expression of maternal behavior. Thus, parturition is characterized by a synchronized synthesis and release of oxytocin in various brain regions, and this tremendous activation is amplified by an increase in the number of OT receptors (Kendrick, 2000).

Other neuropeptides and neurotransmitters that show important variations within the brain at the time of parturition and have both direct and interactive effects on maternal behavior include the beta-endorphins and the catecholamines (Bridges & Ronsheim, 1987; Hammer, Mateo, & Bridges, 1992; Broad, Kendrick, Sirinathsinghji, & Keverne, 1993b; Herbison, 1997; Kendrick, Keverne, Chapman, & Baldwin, 1988; Lévy, Guevara-Guzman, Hinton, Kendrick, & Keverne, 1993). The fact that these simultaneous activations occur in different brain areas that are not directly connected supports the notion that the physiological regulation of maternal motivation is multidetermined (table 8–1).

Hormones and neurochemicals associated with gestation and parturition serve multiple functions. They prepare the prospective mother physiologically, by acting on mammary tissue prior to the initiation of lactation (Tucker, 1988) and by acting on the uteruses, and have analgesic effects during the birth process (Challis & Olsen, 1988; Hodgen & Itskovitz, 1988; Kristal, Thompson, & Abbott, 1986). They also contribute to elevated maternal responsiveness shown by the newly parturient mother by activating various behavioral systems and acting on multiple brain sites (Bridges, 1990; Insel, 1990; Rosenblatt, 1990).

Table 8-1. Plasma and central variations at parturition of the main hormones and neurotransmitters involved in the onset of maternal behavior in mammals

	E2/P	CORT	PRL	OT	ß-End	NA
Rat	Plasma ↗	Plasma ↗	Plasma ↗	Plasma ↗ CNS ↗	Plasma ↗ CNS ↘	Plasma CNS ↗
Sheep	Plasma ↗	Plasma ↗	Plasma ↗ ud CNS	Plasma ↗ CNS ↗	Plasma ↗ CNS ↗	Plasma ↗ CNS ↗
Primate	Nm	Plasma ↗ nc CNS	Plasma ↗ nc CNS	Plasma ↗ nc CNS	Plasma ↗ nc CNS	Plasma ↗ CNS ↗

E2 = estradiol; P = progesterone; CORT = cortisol; PRL = prolactin; OT = oxytocin; ß-End = beta-endorphin; NA = noradrenaline; CNS = central nervous system; ud = undetermined; nc = no change.

Hormonal Regulation of Maternal Behavior

Steroids. In almost all mammals studied, the steroid balance around parturition plays a critical role in the hormonal induction of maternal behavior (table 8–2). In rats whose pregnancies have been terminated through hysterectomy on day 16 of a 21-day gestation, a high percentage of females displayed maternal retrieval, crouching, and licking behavior after 1 day of pup exposure. If pregnancy was not terminated, elevated responsiveness did not occur until close to the time of parturition. This high level of responsiveness appears to result from a decrease in progesterone and increase in estrogen secretion, as would normally occur at the time of parturition (Siegel & Rosenblatt, 1975). Pregnancy-terminated rats injected with estradiol benzoate showed an immediate maternal response on their first exposure to pups. Moreover, a pretreatment with progesterone reduced the necessary effective dose of estrogen (Doerr, Sicgel, & Rosenblatt, 1981). Using a schedule of physiological doses of steroids designed to simulate usual pregnancy changes, it was possible to induce a rapid maternal behavior toward foster pups in virgin rats (Bridges, 1984). Following progesterone and estradiol treatment for 12 days and progesterone withdrawal, females responded maternally after 1 or 2 days of pup exposure. Progesterone withdrawal in the absence of estradiol treatment had no effect, and concomitant progesterone and estradiol treatment was not effective if progesterone was not withdrawn prior to behavioral testing. Overall, these results show that estradiol is essential to stimulate maternal care and that progesterone has two main functions. A prolonged exposure to progesterone primes the female to respond to the rise of estradiol occurring at parturition. Moreover, the fall in progesterone secretion at the end of pregnancy synchronizes the onset of maternal behavior with parturition.

In precocial mammals, as in sheep, a facilitatory effect of estradiol on maternal responsiveness has been reported on several occasions, although results have not always been consistent. Acceptance of a lamb occurs only when estrogen levels are high, at estrus and at the very end of pregnancy (Poindron & Le Neindre, 1980). The period during which parturient ewes are positively responsive to lambs can be extended for 1 day by estradiol injection (Poindron, Martin, & Hooley, 1979). Moreover, a single high dose of estradiol injected into nonpregnant ewes induced maternal responses in 80% of the animals (Poindron & Le Neindre, 1980; Poindron, Lévy, & Krehbiel, 1988). However, this treatment is probably pharmacological, since it produced abnormal sexual behavior: Steroid treatments using more realistic physiological doses and longer period of treatment failed to induce maternal behavior (Kendrick, Da Costa, Hinton, & Keverne, 1992). Contrary to rodents, steroids are not sufficient to induce maternal responsiveness in sheep. Instead, they seem to have priming effects, permitting the action of other physiological factors. In nongestant ewes primed with estradiol, central infusions of cortico-releasing hormone (CRH) potentiate maternal acceptance of lambs after vaginocervical stimulation (VCS). Such acceptance does not occur in the absence

Table 8–2. Neurohormonal substrates involved in maternal behavior in mammals

	Pg/E2	PRL	OT
Rat	++ MPOA	++ MPOA	++ MPOA, OB
Sheep	+	0	++ PVN, MPOA, OB
Primate	++ (marmoset)	ud	ud

Pg = progesterone; E2 = estradiol; OT = oxytocin; ++ = primary action; MPOA = median preoptic area; OB = olfactory bulb; + = moderate action, 0 = no action PVN = paraventricular nucleus of the hypothalamus; ß-End = beta-endorphin; NA = noradrenaline; ud= undetermined.

of VCS, indicating that CRH may exert their effects by modulating VCS induction of oxytocin release (Keverne & Kendrick, 1991).

In nonhuman primates, there is growing evidence that steroids may account for changes in maternal responsiveness during pregnancy and the postpartum period. For instance, red-bellied tamarin females with high prepartum levels of estradiol showed positive behaviors toward their neonates, and those with low prepartum estradiol rejected them (Pryce, Abbott, Hodges, & Martin, 1988). In pigtail macaques, females increase their rate of interactions with other females' infants as pregnancy advances, and this behavioral change is correlated with increases in plasma estradiol and progesterone levels (Maestripieri & Zehr, 1998). More direct evidence for steroid regulation of maternal behavior has been observed in studies using exogenous administration of estradiol and progesterone. Rhesus macaque females whose ovaries had been removed increased their rate of interactions with other females' infants after receiving estradiol in doses similar to those of middle to late pregnancy (Maestripieri & Zehr, 1998). In common marmosets, the rate of bar-press responses for visual presentation of an infant was stimulated by the exogenous administration of late-pregnancy blood levels of estradiol and progesterone (Pryce, 1993, 1996).

In humans, social, economic, demographic, and experiential factors clearly influence how new mothers respond to their infants. However, there is also some evidence that as in other mammals, hormones may also exert important influences on mothers' early interactions with their infants. There is considerable variability among mothers in the pattern of their maternal feelings across pregnancy and the postpartum period. However, for many mothers there is a growth of attachment-related feelings during the second trimester, and once again after the birth of the baby (Fleming, Ruble, et al., 1997). The role of hormones in this elevated responsiveness shown by new mothers has recently received some attention. Consistent with the animal work, Fleming and colleagues have shown that mothers' positive nurturant feelings at birth are related to the shift in the ratio of estradiol to progesterone levels that occurs from pregnancy to the post-partum period (Corter & Fleming, 2002). In contrast, the amount of affectionate behaviors (e.g, stroking, patting, kissing) exhibited toward the infant was related to levels of circulating adrenal hormones in the postnatal period. In a short-term longitudinal study, a significant positive correlation was found between plasma levels of cortisol on days 3 and 4 postpartum and the amount of contact and approach responses shown by mothers toward their nursing infants (Fleming, Steiner, & Anderson, 1987). It is notable that these hormone-behavior relations were considerably stronger in mothers who indicated during the pregnancy that they felt positive toward infants or caretaking activities.

Prolactin. In an elegant series of studies, Bridges and his colleagues showed that prolactin stimulates maternal responsiveness in the female rat. However, prolactin effects are dependent on prior steroidal priming. After removal of the pituitary gland, virgin rats failed to respond maternally to the stimulatory effects of a steroid treatment, while replacement of prolactin reversed this effect (Bridges, DiBiase, Loundes, & Doherty, 1985). In a second set of studies, ovariectomized steroid-treated virgin rats were treated with a prolactin antagonist either with or without concurrent administration of prolactin. Suppression of estradiol-induced rise in prolactin by the antagonist delayed the expression of maternal retrieving and crouching by 4 to 5 days, while the addition of prolactin reversed these effects (Bridges & Ronsheim, 1990). In mice, prolactin also facilitates retrieval and crouching behavior (Voci & Carlson, 1973) and maintains an instrumental response for pup reinforcement (Hauser & Gandelman, 1985). Recent confirmation of prolactin function has come from studies with prolactin-receptor knockout mice where mutant nulliparous females and primiparous females exhibited a dramatic deficit in retrieval and crouching behaviors (Lucas, Ormandy, Binart, Bridges, & Kelly, 1998). The fact that there were no deficits in locomotion, sexual behavior, olfactory function, or learning in these mice indicates that the deficits were indeed specific. Finally, prolactin also plays a role in rabbit maternal behavior. When the prolactin antagonist bromocriptine was injected at the end of pregnancy, the percentage of primiparous rabbits that entered the nest box and crouched over the litter decreased dramatically (Gonzalez-Mariscal & Poindron, 2002; Gonzalez-Mariscal et al., 2000). This same prolactin antagonist also eliminated late-gestation nest building (Anderson, Zarrow, Fuller, & Denenberg, 1971; Gonzalez-Mariscal et al., 2000) and prevented the stimulating effects of estradiol and progesterone on this behavior (Gonzalez-Mariscal & Rosenblatt, 1996). Taken together, these studies on rodents and rabbits suggest that prolactin facilitates some aspects of maternal behavior, but only in the context of steroid priming.

In contrast to findings in altricial species, attempts to show an influence of prolactin on maternal responsiveness in sheep have thus far failed. In parturient ewes, injection of dibromoergocryptine to block prolactin release did not prevent the onset of maternal responsiveness (Poindron & Le Neindre, 1980), and intracerebral infusions of prolactin into steroid-primed, nongestant and multiparous ewes did not induce maternal behavior (Lévy, Kendrick, Keverne, Proter, & Romeyer, 1996). This discrepancy in the role of prolactin could reflect an important difference in the physiological control of maternal responsiveness between rodents and ungulates.

Effects of Vaginocervical Stimulation. As documented earlier in this chapter, steroid hormones have a priming effect, allowing other factors (e.g., the influence of prolactin and oxytocin) to trigger maternal behavior. In addition, steroid hormones appear to prime the effects of somatosensory changes normally associated with parturition. The synchrony between parturition and the various physiological changes described here suggests that the actual process of expulsion of the fetus may be of primary importance to the expression of maternal behavior. Such effects on maternal behavior are most pronounced in sheep and have been extensively studied in this species.

There are several lines of evidence indicating that VCS occurring at parturition is the starting point of a cascade of events that trigger the onset of maternal responsiveness in sheep. In nonpregnant, but multiparous, ewes primed with progesterone and estradiol, the induction of maternal responsiveness in response to a neonate was obtained in 80% of the cases when ewes received 5 minutes of VCS. In contrast, only 20% of females responded maternally without this stimulation (Keverne, Lévy, Poindron, & Lindsay, 1983). These results have been further confirmed in two other breeds of sheep, with low doses of estradiol, and even in ewes at estrus (Kendrick & Keverne, 1991; Kendrick, Da Costa, et al., 1992; Poindron et al., 1988). This stimulation not only increased the number of maternal ewes but also induced the full complement of behaviors associated with maternal responsiveness, including licking, maternal bleats, acceptance at the udder, and reduction in aggressive behavior toward the young. VCS also induced an attraction toward amniotic fluid, which is a characteristic trait of maternal ewes at parturition (see earlier discussion). On the other hand, VCS without a pretreatment of steroids was ineffective, confirming the importance of steroidal priming (Poindron et al., 1988; Kendrick & Keverne, 1991). In contrast, if stimulation of the genital tract was prevented at the time of parturition by peridural anaesthesia, maternal behavior was disrupted (Krehbiel, Poindron, Lévy, & Prud'Homme, 1987).

In rats, there is also evidence that VCS is important to activate maternal care at the time of parturition, although these effects are not as clear or profound as in sheep. Rats whose litters are delivered by cesarean section show a high incidence of pup cannibalism when first presented with foster pups (Orpen & Fleming, 1987). In addition, nonpregnant multiparous females receiving VCS showed immediate maternal behavior. However, as in sheep, this effect is facilitated by steroidal priming: VCS was ineffective in ovariectomized females (Yeo & Keverne, 1986).

In nonhuman primates, cesarean delivery prevents acceptance of the neonate in rhesus monkeys (Meier, 1965; Lundblad & Hodgen, 1980). However, absence of vaginal stimulation is not a prerequisite to maternal care, since swabbing the newborn with amniotic fluid and vaginal secretions allowed its acceptance by the mother (Lundblad & Hodgen, 1980). In humans, the impact of cesarean delivery or peridural anesthesia is poorly documented. However, the research that has been done indicates that neither cesarean delivery nor epidural anaesthesia has effects on new mothers' nurturant feelings, although because of the location of the surgery and influences of pain factors, mothers may cradle and nurse their newborns somewhat differently (Fleming, Ruble, Anderson, & Flett, 1988). The effects of cesarean delivery and epidurals on initial "attachment" behaviors and on affective states in humans have yet to be studied systematically.

Oxytocin. The finding that levels of oxytocin in CSF rise at parturition and following artificial VCS (Kendrick et al., 1986; Lévy et al., 1992) led to the hypothesis of the involvement of this peptide in maternal behavior. This was first demonstrated in nonpregnant ewes in which central injection of oxytocin, after a steroid pretreatment, induced maternal responses within 1 minute (Kendrick, Keverne, & Baldwin, 1987; Keverne & Kendrick, 1991). Central infusion of a receptor antagonist partially blocked the induction of maternal care by oxytocin, and the use of a pharmacological agonist was as efficient as oxytocin itself (Kendrick, 2000). Interestingly, oxytocin, like VCS, was ineffective when given without estradiol priming. In parturient females, inhibiting genital stimulation feedback with peridural anaesthetic prevented both central oxytocin release and maternal behavior (Lévy et al., 1992), and central infusions of oxytocin reversed the behavioral effects.

In rats, the role of oxytocin in the regulation of maternal behavior is not straightforward. In 1979, it was first demonstrated that central infusion of oxytocin induced maternal licking, grouping, nesting, crouching, and retrieving in steroid-primed virgin females (Pedersen & Prange, 1979). Blockade of the positive effects of oxytocin in the induction of maternal care was produced by infusions of antagonists (Van Leengoed, Kerker, & Swanson, 1987; Fahrbach, Morrell, & Pfaff, 1985; Champagne, Diorio, Sharma, & Meaney, 2001) or antisera (Pedersen, Caldwell, Johnson, Fort, & Prange, 1985). However, some research groups have reported difficulty in replicating the induction of maternal behavior by oxytocin (Rubin, Menniti, & Bridges, 1983; Bolwerk & Swanson, 1984; Fahrbach, Morrell, & Pfaff, 1986; Wambolt & Insel, 1987). Discrepancies in the reported effects of oxytocin arise from variations in the procedures used to test maternal behavior, which involve variations in the familiarity of the cage environments used, and/or in the animals' emotional state. Oxytocin clearly has effects in the rat, although these effects are less direct and likely interact with a complicated set of other factors.

In other species of mammals, few studies have focused on the importance of oxytocin in the triggering of maternal behavior. In mice, central infusions of oxytocin prevented infanticide toward pups in nongestant females, but it did not appear to have an effect on maternal care itself (McCarthy, 1990). Furthermore, mice rendered deficient in oxytocin by a targeted mutation of the oxytocin gene had no deficiency in any component of maternal behavior (Nishimori et al., 1996). However, these negative findings do not mean that oxytocin is not important in mice, since some compensatory mechanisms could be responsible for the maternal behaviors seen in these studies.

In humans, effects on maternal behavior of either endogenous oxytocin or following injections of synthetic oxytocin (pitocin) to promote labor have not been reported. However, intercorrelations between levels of plasma oxytocin, anxiety, and the duration of suckling bouts have been reported (Uvnäs-Moberg, 1996).

Hormonal Regulation of Affective Behaviors

Although the parturitional hormones might appear to activate maternal behavior in a unitary fashion, the different hormones and neurochemicals probably exert somewhat different behavioral effects, and any one hormone or neurochemical probably exerts multiple effects. Moreover, their varied effects probably result from their action on a variety of different neural pathways. For instance, progesterone and estradiol might facilitate the expression of maternal behavior in the rat by altering the female's attraction to the odors of pups, her general "fearfulness" in their presence, or the ease with which she learns about their characteristics, possibly by augmenting the pups' reinforcing value. Together, these hormonal effects are seen to indirectly augment maternal responsiveness during the periparturitional period by reducing the competing effects of alternative nonmaternal behaviors, and by ensuring that dams will continue to respond to pups when the period of hormonal priming ends. Thus, as shown in the following discussion, postpartum animals differ from virgins on a number of psychological dimensions because of the action of hormones.

Emotional Changes in the New Mother.   Naturally parturient female rats are less avoidant when presented with pups than are virgin animals: These parturient rats are more willing to approach an unfamiliar intruder and to enter and explore a novel environment (Fleming & Luebke, 1981). Among sheep, it also appears that pregnant ewes display lower fear reactions than do nonpregnant ewes when isolated and when confronted with a novel object (Vierin & Bouissou, 2001). In both these species, these differences in emotionality appear to be hormonally mediated: The regimen of progesterone and estradiol that facilitates maternal behavior in the virgin rat also reduces pup avoidance and measures of timidity in an open-field apparatus (Fleming, Cheung, Myhal, & Kessler, 1989). In sheep, a negative correlation was found between plasma progesterone and level of fear (Vierin & Bouissou, 2001). Moreover, there is now a substantial literature that shows marked hyporesponsiveness of the stress system in lactating animals, and differences between virgin and lactating females in their hypothalamic-pituitary-adrenal responses to stressors, where virgins show enhanced stressor-induced release of corticosterone and ACTH as well as enhanced baseline CRH in the brain (Windle et al., 1997; Neumann et al., 1998). These differences are associated with differences on a variety of tasks, with reduced hyporesponsiveness associated with reduced emotionality (Silva, Bernardi, Nasello, & Felicio, 1997; Neumann et al., 1998). There is also evidence that glucocorticoids enhance arousal, attention, and acuity in a variety of sensory systems (Beckwith, Lerud, Antes, & Reynolds, 1983; Melamed et al., 1999; Wang, 1997; Henry & Wang, 1998). Taken together, this evidence suggests that the combined behavioral effects of glucocorticoids may contribute to maternal responsiveness by reducing fearlike responses and by enhancing the salience of infant stimulation. The assumption that reduced timidity contributes to elevated maternal responsiveness is also supported by findings that manipulations that reduce the animals' timidity or anxiety, like benzodiazepines (Hansen, Ferreira, & Selart, 1985) or early handling (Mayer, 1983), also facilitate maternal responding.

Among humans, evidence relating to changes in emotionality at the time of parturition is widespread. Most notably, 40% to 60% of new mothers become anxious and dysphoric (the so called "baby blues") within the first few days postpartum, and a subset of these (around 10% to 20%) become depressed within the first few postpartum weeks. Among humans, the relation of this depression to prior or ongoing endocrine changes associated with late pregnancy or parturition is assumed, but not as yet proved. However, there is some evidence to implicate the parturitional decline in progesterone in these mood changes (Nott, Franklin, Armitage, & Gelder, 1976; O'Hara, Schlechte, Lewis, & Wright, 1991). Depression that is sustained for 3 months postpartum is quite clearly related to high cortisol levels. In addition, levels of cortisol during the early postpartum period may be related to pueperal lability, anxiety, and well-being (Fleming, Steiner, & Corter, 1997; Handley, Dunn, Waldron, & Baker, 1980). Whatever the endocrine underpinnings of dysphoria in new mothers, it is clear that a mother's mood is related to her interactions with her baby. Although depressed mothers do not report feeling less attached to their infants (Fleming, Flett, Ruble, & Shaul, 1988), and may show considerable warmth and interest (Stein, Gath, Bucher, Bond, Day, & Cooper, 1991), comparisons between depressed and nondepressed mothers indicate that depressed mothers do respond less sensitively and more negatively to their infants than do nondepressed mothers (Fleming, Ruble, Flett, & Shaul, 1988; Cohn,

Campbell, Matias, & Hopkins, 1990; Field, Healy, Goldstein, & Guthertz, 1990; Murray, 1992). Dysphoric mothers were less inclined to respond to their infants' vocalizations by vocalizing themselves, and their overall level of contact, and affectionate behavior was reduced (Fleming, Flett, et al., 1988). At 2 months post-partum their speech tends to contain more negative affect, and in play interactions these mothers exhibit fewer responses to their infant's behaviors (Murray, 1992). During face-to-face encounters, depressed mothers are also more prone to exhibit hostile and intrusive behavior, irritation, or withdrawal and disengagement (Cohn et al., 1990; Field et al., 1998).

Taken together, these studies indicate that among most mammalian species where this has been studied, the parturitional hormones have substantial influence on the new mother's affective state and that this, in turn, influences her responsiveness to her newborn offspring.

Sensory Changes in the New Mother. In addition to their effects on the mother's affective state, parturitional hormones also alter the reinforcing value of young and the mother's responsiveness to infant cues. In the following discussion, we first describe hormonal effects on salience of infant cues for the new mother. Although we know from early studies (Beach & Jaynes, 1956a, 1956b) that maternal motivation is under multisensory control, single denervations of sensory systems in inexperienced animals can also have quite profound effects on the display of maternal care (Fleming & Li, 2002; Lévy et al., 1996). The primary focus will be on the olfactory cues and their involvement in maternal motivation and behavior, since these cues play a key role in most mammals.

Mother rats develop a strong preference for the odors of their own litters. In comparison to virgins, new mothers without direct experience with pups prefer nest material taken from the nest of a new mother and her pups to material taken from a virgin's nest or clean material (Kinsley & Bridges, 1990). Virgins show no such preference (Bauer, 1983; Fleming et al., 1989). Moreover, virgins treated with a regimen of hormones designed to mimic the parturitional changes in progesterone and estradiol also exhibit a preference for pup-related odors (Fleming et al., 1989). The additional observation that injections of morphine can induce an aversion to pup odors (Kinsley, Morse, Zoumas, Corl, & Billack, 1995) suggests that low concentrations of this neuropeptide in relevant parts of the brain at the time of parturition permit heightened attraction to pup-related odors. Experience with these odors can also facilitate maternal responding: Adult virgin rats show more rapid maternal inductions if they have been preexposed to pup odors and vocalizations during their early development (Gray & Chesley, 1984; Moretto, Paclik, & Fleming, 1986). Although difficult to demonstrate, it seems that preexposure to pup cues at a distance (primarily odors and vocalizations) in adulthood also facilitates maternal responding during maternal tests, at least among females whose responsiveness is high to begin with. Thus, a higher proportion of animals exhibit immediate maternal behavior during maternal tests if they have been preexposed to pup odors than if they have not been (Orpen & Fleming, 1987). Finally, if virgins are rendered unable to smell pups, they are not avoidant with pups but instead exhibit a very rapid onset of maternal behavior, as though the pups' odors in the context of other pup cues are aversive (Fleming & Rosenblatt, 1974a, 1974b; Fleming, Vaccarino, Tambosso, & Chee, 1979).

In rats, we have no idea which specific pup or pup-related odors influence the dam's attraction to pups, although recent evidence suggests that anogenital licking of the pup by the mother is facilitated by secretions from the pup preputial glands (Brouette-Lahlou, Vernet-Maury, & Chanel, 1991). Moreover, the relevant component in the secretion seems to be a pheromone-like compound called dodecyl propionate. Because rats do not become attached to individual offspring or even individual litters, it seems likely that the odor of individual pups or litters is less relevant than is the odor that characterizes the developmental age of the pups and/or the mother's postpartum stage. These odors could derive from many sources in addition to preputial glands, including uterine fluids, mother's milk, maternal diet, and maternal excretory products. For instance, mice dams could discriminate pups being nursed by females fed the same diet as themselves from those nursed by mothers fed a different diet (Doane & Porter, 1978).

In sheep, there is considerable evidence that the ewe develops an olfactory attraction to amniotic fluids at parturition, which was not present prior to birth and which begins to fade by 2 hours postpartum (Lévy, Poindron, & Le Neindre, 1983). Attraction to amniotic fluid is a necessary step for the development of maternal responsiveness. Washing the neonate to remove amniotic fluids greatly disrupts the onset of maternal care (Lévy & Poindron, 1987). Amniotic fluid is also sufficient by itself to induce maternal responsiveness in a context where females typically reject young: Parturient-experienced ewes accepted 1-day-old lambs whose coats were treated with amniotic fluid (Lévy & Poindron, 1984; Basiouni & Gonyou, 1988). The origin of amniotic fluid had no reliable effect on maternal acceptance, which suggests that amniotic fluid only contains cues responsible for general attractiveness but not for individual recognition (see earlier discussion). This generalized attraction is apparently induced by the synergistic action of prepartum estrogen, VCS, and oxytocin release associated with parturition (Poindron & Lévy, 1990). Finally, olfactory input clearly constitutes the initial basis of the ewe's selective bond with her lamb. Ewes that are unable to smell their lambs exhibit enhanced maternal behavior to all lambs and do not develop a selective bond with any one lamb (Poindron, 1976; Lévy, Locatelli, Piketty, Tillet, & Poindron, 1995).

Among humans, there is also evidence that the odors of the infant are salient to the mother. Recent findings showed that when mothers interacted with their infants, mothers experienced a decline in their cortisol levels. However, the extent of that decline depended on how attracted mothers were to their infants' body odors: Mothers who gave positive hedonic ratings to their infants' odors on a "pleasantness scale" had higher levels of baseline cortisol (and showed a greater proportional cortisol decline) than did mothers who gave negative ratings (Fleming, Steiner, et al., 1997). Moreover, the strength of these effects depended on the mothers' parity. First-time mothers showed stronger hormone-hedonic correlations than did multiparous mothers. Although we do not know the specific source of the attractive body odor, it is probably associated with secretions from the sebaceous and sweat glands on the back and head regions. Urine, meconium, fecal material, and adult sweat are not attractive to the new mothers (Corter, Fleming, & Steiner, 2005).

Although odors of newborns become attractive to mothers and may facilitate maternal responsiveness and feelings of nurturance, other infant cues are also important. In mother rats, somatosensory cues such as tactile stimulation of the mouth region are essential for the complete expression of maternal behavior during the early postpartum period (Stern, 1989, 1990). In contrast, in mother sheep, stimulation of the perioral region does not appear to be of importance for the onset of maternal behavior. Ewes that are prevented from licking and/or suckling during the first 8 hours postpartum still show maternal responsiveness beyond this period (Poindron & Le Neindre, 1980; Poindron et al., 1988).

Visual and auditory cues are not necessary for the expression of maternal behavior either in rodents or in ungulates, although they may make a contribution. In the absence of both, maternally experienced mother rats or sheep show normal maternal responsiveness toward their young (Poindron et al., 1988; Stern, 1990). However, the combination of odor and cries is a powerful motivator to approach offspring. For instance, ultrasonic calls emitted by pups when they are out of the nest result in the mother's locating them from a distance and retrieving them (Allin & Banks, 1972; Brewster & Leon, 1980). Such directional orientation to pup ultrasounds is facilitated by pup odor cues (Farrell & Alberts, 2002a, 2002b; Smotherman, Bell, Starzec, Elias, & Zachman, 1974). In fact, pup ultrasounds stimulate the initiation of maternal anogenital licking of pups, which is then facilitated or patterned by pup preputial secretions (Brouette-Lahlou, Vernet-Maury, Godinot, & Chanel, 1992; Brouette-Lahlou, Godinot, & Vernet-Maury, 1999). The importance of the combination of sensory cues to approach behavior to offspring is also found in ungulates. The presence of visual cues improves the behavioral response of the mother toward the infant's vocalizations (Shillito-Walser, Hague, & Walters, 1981). In goats, it has recently been shown that the latency to reach a kid at one day postpartum is shorter when visual and auditory cues are available than when only auditory cues are offered (Terrazas, Serafin, Hernandez, Nowak, & Poindron, 2003; Poindron, Gilling, Hernandez, Serafin, & Terrazas, 2003).

Among humans, the importance of multisensory control of maternal responsiveness has not been adequately studied. However, a role for infant crying in motivating mothers to approach and pick up their infants is well established.

Maternal feelings of nurturance are augmented by the cries of infants in the context of the postpartum hormonal environment. A recent study reported that mothers are more sympathetic to infant cries than are nonparent women, and that mothers who are more affectively sympathetic to the cries of newborn infants also have higher levels of circulating cortisol both prior to and after exposure to the infant (Stallings, Fleming, Corter, Worthman, & Steiner, 2001). Cortisol levels were also higher among mothers who were better able to distinguish between pain-related and hunger cries. Interestingly, mothers who were more sympathetic to the recorded cries of unknown infants also reported greater feelings of attachment to their own infants on the second day after birth.

Neural Substrates

As the preceding sections reveal, the regulation of maternal behavior involves multiple hormones and contextual cues, and may take multiple forms depending on the stage postpartum and the species. These endocrine and environmental factors act together to produce a species-characteristic set of behaviors that depend for their expression on activation of a variety of other behavioral systems, which then allow the animal to respond appropriately at the right time. These include systems that regulate affect, perception, and learning. Given this complexity, it is not surprising that the underlying neural circuitry regulating maternal behavior involves structures at all levels of the nervous system, some primary to maternal behavior per se, and others that interface or interconnect with this primary system. The following discussion of the related neuroanatomy will first describe the primary neural circuitry, in terms of where hormones act to stimulate the expression of maternal responsiveness. We will then discuss changes in the maternal neural circuitry that are induced by maternal experience.

The neural bases involved in the regulation of the expression of maternal behavior at the time of parturition are well understood in rodents. Although we have much to learn about the neuroanatomy of maternal behavior in other species such as sheep, what we do know indicates considerable similarity in circuitry across species. Where there are species differences, these map on quite directly to differences in behaviors exhibited by the different species.

In the rat, at least two antagonistic neural systems govern the expression of maternal behavior. One is an excitatory neural system that deals with the activation of maternal responses toward pups, and the other is an inhibitory neural system that regulates avoidance responses to pups or pup-related stimuli. The balance between these two systems determines whether maternal behavior will be expressed at the time of parturition. The sensory cues, parturitional hormones, and experiential factors exert their effects on the excitatory system to bring animals close to pups by increasing the attractive quality of pups or pup-related stimuli, in order to initiate and maintain maternal care. These factors also exert effects on the inhibitory system to reduce animals' natural fearful responses toward novel pups (Schneirla, 1959; Rosenblatt, 1990).

The Excitatory System

The excitatory system is controlled primarily by neurons in the medial preoptic area (MPOA) and ventral part of the bed nucleus of the stria terminalis (vBNST), their efferent projections to the brain stem, and their afferent inputs from the different sensory modalities (Numan, 1988b, 1994). In rats, lesions of MPOA/vBNST cell bodies or knife cuts transecting their lateral projections completely abolish maternal behavior (Numan et al., 1988; Numan & Numan, 1996; Numan, McSparren, & Numan, 1990) in the new mother or maternal virgin, whereas electrical stimulation of this site facilitates maternal responding (Morgan, Watchus, Milgram, & Fleming, 1999).

Hormones that activate maternal behavior act on the MPOA: Implants into MPOA of either estradiol, prolactin, or oxytocin facilitate maternal responding (Numan, Rosenblatt, & Komisaruk, 1977; Insel, 1990; Bridges, Numan, Ronsheim, Mann, & Lupini, 1990), whereas the infusion of oxytocin antagonists, or morphine or beta-endorphin in the MPOA, impairs maternal behavior (Pedersen, Caldwell, Walker, Ayers, & Mason, 1994; Rubin & Bridges, 1984). Implants of antiestrogen in the MPOA also delay the onset of maternal behavior (Ahdieh, Mayer, & Rosenblatt, 1987).

In sheep, a role for MPOA/vBNST in the regulation of maternal responsiveness has not been established. To date there are no studies that explore the effects of lesions or of electrical stimulation of this site on maternal responsiveness and willingness to accept lambs. However, oxytocin infusions into the MPOA reduced aggression toward lambs without affecting acceptance behavior (Kendrick, Da Costa, et al., 1997). In contrast to rats, the primary hypothalamic site for oxytocin induction of acceptance behavior in sheep resides in the PVN. Using retrodialysis, infusions of oxytocin in the PVN induced positive behaviors and reduced negative behaviors toward the lamb in progesterone- and estrogen-primed females (Da Costa et al., 1996).

Another line of evidence supporting the importance of MPOA/vBNST neurons in the control of maternal expression in rat comes from studies using c-fos immunohistochemistry. The proto-oncogene c-fos is one of a class of genes known as *immediate early genes,* which are expressed in response to a variety of stimuli (Sagar, Sharp, & Curran, 1988). Fos expression is often used as a marker for detection of neuronal activation. Several studies have demonstrated that there is a population of neurons in the MPOA/vBNST that appears to regulate maternal responsiveness. For example, postpartum rats exposed to pups had higher numbers of cells showing c-fos expression within the MPOA than did those exposed to adult conspecifics or left alone (Fleming, Suh, Korsmit, &

Rusak, 1994). Heightened MPOA c-fos expression persists in maternally active animals even after animals are rendered anosmic (unable to smell) or anaptic (unable to feel touch sensations around the muzzle) or after temporary anesthetization of the ventral nipple area (Numan & Numan, 1995; Walsh, Fleming, Lee, & Magnusson, 1996).

To understand the function of the MPOA/vBNST in maternal behavior, Numan and his associates have investigated the MPOA/vBNST projections implicated in maternal responding (Numan & Sheehan, 1997). By combining the Fos immunohistochemistry technique with the neural tract-tracing technique, "maternal" neurons (as visualized by Fos-labeling) in the MPOA were found to mainly project to the lateral septum (LS), ventromedial nucleus of the hypothalamus (VMH), and the periaqueductal gray (PAG), whereas the "maternal" neurons in the vBNST project to the retrorubral field, PAG. and ventral tegmental area (VTA Numan & Numan, 1997). The importance of these projections in the control of maternal behavior is consistent with the involvement of these regions in maternal behavior. For instance, the LS has been implicated in the control of the sequential organization of the maternal pattern (Fleischer & Slotnick, 1978), the VTA has been linked to motivational aspects of maternal behavior (Hansen et al., 1991), the VMH is involved in the control of aversive reactions toward pups (Sheehan & Numan, 1997; Bridges, Mann, & Coppeta, 1999), and the PAG is important for the regulation of the upright nursing posture (Lonstein & Stern, 1997; Lonstein et al., 1998). In sheep, the effects on c-fos mRNA expression of VCS given to ewes with hormonal treatment, which would stimulate behavior but which was not actually exposed to lambs, were contrasted with those of parturition and exposure to a lamb (Da Costa, Broad, & Kendrick, 1997). Neural substrates controlling the expression of maternal responsiveness have been found mainly in the hypothalamic regions, (MPOA, PVN, SON, VMH, the periventricular complex) and in the limbic system (BNST, LS, nedial amygdala, hippocampus). In a recent study, Fos immunochemistry expression has been measured in anosmic parturient ewes that are maternal but do not form a memory for their lambs (Keller, Meurisse, & Lévy, 2004). Heightened Fos immunochemistry expression persists in the hypothalamic nuclei (MPOA, PVN, SON) of anosmic ewes, suggesting that these structures represent the core of the maternal circuitry in sheep. Consistent with these studies, c-fos/c-jun antisense infusions into the PVN of parturient ewes impair some aspects of maternal behavior (Da Costa, De La Riva, Guevara-Guzman, & Kendrick, 1999).

The Inhibitory System

The MPOA/vBNST not only projects to the midbrain and motor system involved in the expression of maternal behavior: These nuclear groups also receive input from other parts of the brain, in particular the olfactory and limbic systems (Fleming, 1987; Numan, 1988a), which exert inhibitory influences on the functions of the MPOA/vBNST. For instance, a major input to the MPOA comes from the amygdala, which in turn receives input from the main and accessory olfactory bulbs (Fleming et al., 1987). In contrast to the reduction in maternal behavior with chemosensory denervations in parturient animals, removal of main or accessory olfactory input in nonresponsive virgins facilitates the expression of maternal behaviors, while at the same time reducing certain olfactory-mediated components (like licking) in both maternal virgins and postpartum animals. These data are consistent with the observation that pup odors within the context of other pup cues are aversive to virgin animals but attractive to the postpartum dams (Fleming et al., 1989; Fleming & Rosenblatt, 1974a, 1974b; Fleming et al., 1979). The findings that infusions of oxytocin into the olfactory bulb facilitate the appearance of maternal behavior, whereas infusions of oxytocin antagonist markedly delay all components of maternal behavior, suggest that the olfactory bulb is one site where parturitional hormones act to antagonize the inhibitory control on maternal behavior (Yu, Kaba, Okutani, Takahashi, & Higuchi, 1996). A similar situation occurs in sheep, in which odors associated with amniotic fluids are repellent to nonpregnant animals and to pregnant animals but become attractive within a few hours before parturition (Lévy et al., 1983). This dramatic shift is also observed at the level of the olfactory bulb, where the activity of the main (mitral) cells is inhibited before parturition in response to amniotic fluids but activated on the first days after parturition (Kendrick, Lévy, & Keverne, 1992). Interestingly, infusions of oxytocin into the brain ventricles restore this olfactory attraction in parturient ewes rendered nonmaternal by an epidural anesthesia (Lévy et al., 1992). This suggests an interaction between VCS-induced release of oxytocin and olfactory function to override the aversion to offspring odors.

In rats, behavioral inhibition is also exerted by sites that receive chemosensory projections and that project to the MPOA, such as the medial and cortical nuclei of the amygdala, and the VMH. The amygdala receives inputs from both the olfactory system and the VMH, and projects directly to the MPOA and the VMH. Activation of the olfactory system increases medial amygdala neuronal activity, while electrical stimulation of the medial amygdala predominantly inhibits MPOA neurons, as well as the onset of maternal behavior (Gardner & Phillips, 1977; Morgan et al., 1999). Lesions of the medial amygdala, the stria terminalis (the major efferent pathway from the medial amygdala), the bed nucleus of the stria terminalis, or the VMH all result in the disinhibition of maternal retrieving and crouching in virgin animals exposed to foster pups (Fleming et al., 1979; Fleming, Vaccarino, & Leubke, 1980; Fleming, Gavarth, & Sarker, 1992; Numan, Numan, & English, 1993; Bridges et al., 1999). Importantly, the facilitation of maternal behavior produced by amygdala lesions is abolished by lesions of the medial preoptic area, confirming that the input from amygdala acts through MPOA to exert its inhibitory role in maternal behavior (Fleming, Miceli, & Moretto, 1983; Komisaruk et al., 2000).

Evidence cited previously suggests that the amygdala, especially the medial part, has an inhibitory influence on the onset of maternal behavior. The inhibitory circuit consists of connections between olfactory systems and the MPOA/vBNST via the amygdala and the VMH. Since it has been demonstrated that virgins sustaining amygdala lesions differ from controls in not withdrawing from pups and in maintaining closer proximity to them, and they are less fearful in a series of emotionality tests (Fleming et al., 1980), it is proposed that this circuit inhibits maternal responsiveness by activating a central aversion system (Numan & Sheehan, 1997). These effects of amygdala lesions on the animal's affect are consistent with an extensive literature relating the amygdala to emotional behavior in other contexts (Davis, 1992; Everitt & Robbins, 1992; LeDoux, 1992).

Taken together, maternal behavior is under joint control by two antagonistic neural systems: the excitatory system, which consists mainly of the efferents from MPOA/vBNST to various brain areas, and the inhibitory system, which refers mainly to the projections from the medial amygdala to the MPOA/vBNST and VMH (table 8–3). Finally, in terms of afferents to these systems, the main and accessory chemosensory systems affect both. These systems coordinate in the regulation of neuroendocrine, sensory, and autonomic components necessary for the expression of maternal behavior at the time of parturition.

Effects of Parity on Neural Mechanisms of Behavior

Studies in rodents and sheep suggest that a previous parity alters the underlying neural mechanisms to render mothers more responsive to physiological factors at subsequent births. For instance, the number of estrogen receptors in olfactory cortices is higher in multiparous than in primiparous nonpartum mice (Ehret & Buckenmaier, 1994; Koch, 1990) and postpartum sheep (Meurisse, Gonzalez, Delsol, Caba, Lévy, & Poindron, 2005). In terms of the hypothalamic receptors,

Table 8–3. Neural substrates involved in the onset of maternal behavior in mammals

	OB	AOB	MPOA/vBNST	PVN	Medial AMY/BNST/VMH
Rat	+/–	–	++	0	–
Sheep	+	0	+	+	ud
Primate	ud	ud	ud	ud	ud

OB = olfactory bulb; AOB = accessory olfactory bulb; MPOA = median preoptic area; PVN = paraventricular nucleus of the hypothalamus; medial AMY/ BNST/VMH = medial amygdala/bed nucleus of the stria terminalis/ventromedian hypothalamus; + = moderate activatory action; – = inhibitory action; ++ = primary activatory action; 0 = no action; ud = undetermined.

parity and maternal experience in sheep enhance the level of oxytocin receptors in the PVN (Broad et al., 1999).

At parturition, the brain release of a variety of neurotransmitters and neuropeptides is higher in multiparous than in primiparous ewes. These include oxytocin, noradrenaline, acetylcholine, gamma-amino-butyric acid (GABA), and glutamate (see earlier discussion Keverne, Lévy, Guevara-Guzman, & Kendrick, 1993; Lévy et al., 1993; Lévy, Kendrick, Goode, Guevara-Guzman, & Keverne, 1995). Moreover, experience-based changes have also been reported in glial function in both hippocampus and MPOA (Kinsley et al., 1999). Higher numbers of glial fibrillary acid protein positive cells in the MPOA were observed 4 days after experience with pups in multiparous rats when compared with those of the pup-exposed primiparous rats (Featherstone, Fleming, & Ivy, 2000). Therefore, it appears that maternal experience induces changes in receptors and/or in neural reorganization that mediates the enhanced maternal responsiveness to hormones and pup stimulation.

Neurobiology of Maternal Memory: The Maternal Experience Effect in Rats

Hormonal and Sensory Mechanisms

Processes regulating the long-term maintenance of maternal behavior are quite different from those involved in its onset. As indicated in the following section, the female rat first undergoes a transition period during which hormones interact with environmental and experiential processes in the regulation of behavior. However, once this transition period is over, by the end of the first postpartum week, maternal behavior is maintained primarily by sensory influences and learning and reinforcement processes. Hormonal effects on maternal behavior at this time are minimal. The continued expression of maternal behavior after 4 to 5 days postparturition seems no longer to be based on hormones but is, instead, based both on experiences acquired by the mother when she interacts with pups under the influence of hormones and on experiences acquired during the lactational period (Fleming, Morgan, & Walsh, 1996). Thus, processes of learning and memory sustain the behavior beyond the period of hormonal priming and into the next parity. If pups are removed from newly parturient (or cesarean-delivered) female rats before dams have had the opportunity to interact with the pups, maternal responsiveness declines over the next 3 to 5 days and reaches low (virgin) levels by day 10, by which time animals have usually reinitiated their estrous cycles (Orpen, Furman, Wong, & Fleming, 1987). However, if females give birth (or are cesarean sectioned) and within 24 to 36 hours are permitted to interact with pups for as little as ½ hour before separation, dams continue to be quite maternal in tests undertaken 10 days later (Orpen et al., 1987). Not surprisingly, a longer interactive exposure period results in a longer retention of responsiveness (Bridges, 1975, 1977; Cohen & Bridges, 1981; Fleming & Sarker, 1990).

This long-term change in behavior as a result of experience interacting with pups has come to be known as the *maternal experience effect* and has now been demonstrated in other species such as the rabbit (Gonzalez-Mariscal et al., 1998). However, an increase of exposure period with the young does not result in a longer retention of maternal responsiveness in sheep. Thus, 4 hours of immediate postpartum contact was sufficient to maintain maternal responsiveness for up to 24 hours of mother-young separation in most animals. Longer separations of 36 hours resulted in a substantial reduction in the percentage of maternal animals. Increasing the duration of mother-young contact to 7 days did not reinstate responsiveness under the 36-hour separation conditions (Lévy et al., 1991; Keller, Meurisse, Poindron, et al., 2003).

The parturitional hormones also appear to influence the robustness of maternal learning. Animals that acquire maternal experience under the influence of the parturitional hormones exhibit better retention of maternal behavior 30 days later than do animals that are not being stimulated with hormones at the time of the maternal experience. Moreover, the optimal condition for the expression of maternal behavior occurs when both the initial experience and the test occur during a period of hormonal priming (Fleming & Sarker, 1990). In addition to the ovarian hormones, adrenal hormones are also implicated in the formation of maternal experience and have positive, rather than negative, effects. Adrenalectomy during late pregnancy reduces the retention of maternal behavior 10 days after a maternal experience, whereas glucocorticoid replacement with pellets reverses these effects (Graham, Rees, & Fleming, 2005).

Although most work in this area has focused on mother's learning about her offspring, this enhanced learning ability seems not to be specific to the maternal context. In comparison with virgins or nonmothers, new mothers during the postpartum period also show enhanced learning in other contexts, involving other forms of social learning (Fleming, Kuchera, Lee, & Winocur, 1994) as well as spatial learning (Kinsley et al., 1999).

Taken together, these studies indicate that experiences acquired under hormones are also more easily activated by a combination of hormones and exposure to relevant pup stimuli in the absence of hormones. Hormones could act in a number of ways to promote these robust experience effects. They could increase the salience of associative cues, most likely unconditioned pup cues (e.g., proximal tactile or olfactory) during the learning phase; they could act to facilitate or strengthen the association between the conditioned and unconditioned pup-associated cues; finally, they could produce internal cues that themselves act as conditioned stimuli, a mechanism that could explain the apparent state dependency of the maternal-hormone interactions described earlier. As yet, research has not identified which of these hormone mechanisms is important.

Although it is clear that interactive experience is important for the long-term retention of behavior, which specific aspects of the experience are most important is not known. In this section we consider the different sensory experiences the animal acquires while interacting with pups. As will become apparent, both somatosensory and chemosensory input is important. If the mother is prevented from crouching over her young during the postpartum period, but receives other distal inputs, her responsiveness declines more rapidly with earlier weaning (Jakubowski & Terkel, 1986; Stern, 1983). Moreover, if mothers were separated from their litters by a wire mesh floor during the 1-hour postpartum exposure phase, so that they could see, hear, and distally smell pups, but received no tactile or proximal chemosensory input, 10 days later they showed no long-term benefit of maternal experience but instead responded to pups as virgins do (Orpen & Fleming, 1987). These data indicate that ventral stimulation is probably an essential feature of the maternal experience. The additional findings that dams need to receive somatosensory perioral input from the mouth region to exhibit normal maternal licking and crouching (Stern & Johnson, 1989; Stern & Kolunie, 1989), and that licking during exposure is correlated with responsiveness during test (Morgan, Fleming, & Stern, 1992) point also to the importance of chemosensory and perioral stimulation for the maternal experience effect. As well, somatosensory stimulation is important for the maternal experience effect. Both perioral and ventral trunk stimulation are sufficient to produce a maternal experience, but when both inputs are eliminated by desensitization procedures, the experience effect is eliminated (Morgan et al., 1992).

Olfaction is not essential or necessary for the formation of a maternal experience (Fleming et al., 1992). However, during interactions with pups, dams clearly also learn about specific olfactory and chemosensory features of the pups. If pups are scented with an artificial odorant during the exposure phase, dams respond more rapidly on tests 10 days later to pups labeled with the same scent than to those labeled with a discrepant scent. That this effect depends on the association of the odors with the pups is shown by the additional observation that preexposure to the odor on its own (in the absence of pups) does not result in the same facilitation of responsiveness to similarly scented pups (Malenfant, Barry, & Fleming, 1991).

Neural Substrates of Maternal Memory

Until recently, we had no idea what brain mechanisms underlie maternal memory or the acquisition, consolidation, and retention of a maternal experience, or how these mechanisms or circuits intersect with the "maternal circuit" that mediates the expression of maternal behavior (Li & Fleming, 2003). Immunocytochemical studies assessing densities of cells staining for Fos, glial fibrillary acidic protein (GFAP; astroglial structural proteins), or protein kinase C (PKC; upstream to Fos-signaling protein) showed that the areas of the brain that undergo a long-lasting change with experience were the MPOA, the basolateral amygdala, and the parietal cortex (Fleming & Korsmit, 1996; Featherstone et al., 2000). The MPOA is the region of the brain that is essential for the expression of maternal behavior (see earlier discussion); the basolateral amygdala is the region of the brain that receives input from multiple sensory systems and, in the maternal context, is activated by olfactory and somatosensory input from the pups; and the parietal cortex is involved in processing of tactile and somatosensory input. With experience and a previous parity, hormone receptors in the MPOA are more numerous, rendering this region more sensitive to the hormonal induction of maternal behavior. However, the MPOA region is not involved in the actual acquisition of the experience. Based on an extensive series of lesion studies targeting multiple brain systems known to be involved in memory within other contexts, Lee, Li, Watchus, and Fleming (1999) and Li and Fleming (2003) found that lesions of the nucleus accumbens (NA), a limbic brain site involved in reinforcement, undertaken immediately after a maternal experience, consistently blocked the formation of a maternal experience. Lesions of other sites had no effect, and if NA lesions were conducted 24 hours after pup experience, maternal experience deficits were not seen, suggesting that the NA is critical for the consolidation of a maternal experience but not for its acquisition or storage.

Neurochemical Mechanisms of Maternal Memory

In terms of the underlying neurochemistry of maternal experience in rats, we also know very little: Previous studies have not localized neurochemical effects to a particular brain site. As indicated earlier, with parturition and during the postpartum period before access to pups, the mother undergoes changes in endocrine systems, in autonomic function, and in peptidergic systems (i.e., OT, CRH). These neurochemical changes could affect learning through multiple routes, for example, by altering the rats' arousal, attentional, and/or perceptual function and hence the ability to process information. Other neurochemical systems (e.g., the dopaminergic system) are probably activated later, specifically by pup contact and the expression of maternal behavior (Hansen, Bergvall, & Nyiredi, 1993), and may enhance the "reward" value and salience of stimuli. Together, these systems are likely involved in all phases of maternal experience, and probably interact in various ways at different stages and on different aspects of the learning process. There is some evidence to support these predictions: Manipulations of the noradrenergic, dopaminergic, and opioid systems all affect maternal memory, and some of these are also involved in the initial motivation to be maternal (Hansen et al., 1993; Li & Fleming, 2003; Byrnes & Bridges, 2000). A role for the noradrenergic system is also clear: Injections of a noradrenergic antagonist (propranolol) blocked maternal memory, whereas injections of a noradrenergic agonist (isoproteronol) enhanced maternal memory (Moffat, Suh, & Fleming, 1993). Neuropeptides such as oxytocin are also likely to be involved in the acquisition and consolidation of maternal memory. They are present at parturition, enhance maternal behavior, and are important for the formation of social memories within other functional contexts (Pedersen et al., 1985; Pedersen et al., 1994; Francis, Young, Meaney, & Insel, 2002; Champagne et al., 2001; Dluzen, Muraoka, Engelmann, & Landgraf, 1998; Engelmann, Ebner, Wotjak, & Landgraf, 1998; Popik & Vetulani, 1991; Popik & van Ree, 1998).

Neurobiology of Maternal Selectivity: Individual Recognition of Young in Sheep

During the early phase of maternal responsiveness, ewes progressively learn the characteristics of their offspring, so that they are able to recognize them and accept only them at the udder. Recently, we have systematically investigated the development of selectivity of ewes toward lambs, assessed by ewes' willingness to let their own, but not alien, lambs suckle at the udder. Own and alien lambs were presented consecutively at different postpartum periods ranging from birth to 4 hours postpartum (Keller, Meurisse, Poindron, et al., 2003). A high proportion (65%) of ewes showed selectivity at suckling as early as 30 minutes after parturition, and after 2 hours of contact the majority of ewes (85%) were selective. These data indicate that recognition at suckling is a very rapid learning process that takes place at parturition. The requisite duration of contact between ewe and lamb necessary to produce long-term retention of the recognition learning was also studied. A short exposure to the lamb for 4 hours just after birth, which produces good selectivity, was not adequate to sustain selectivity after a 36-hour mother-young separation (Lévy et al., 1991; Keller, Meurisse, Poindron, et al., 2003). However, if ewes were permitted to interact with their lambs for 7 days, they retained their selectivity over 36-hour separation, but not over a 3-day separation (Keller, Meurisse, Poindron, et al., 2003). Interestingly, unlike the long-term retention of responsiveness found with maternal experience in the rat studies, olfactory recognition memory in sheep is quite short-lived. However, in sheep that are both responsive and selective, the time course of "forgetting" is different (see earlier discussion). Maternal responsiveness declines gradually with time of separation and independently of previous exposure durations, whereas selectivity declines more rapidly but can be reinstated by a longer exposure period (Lévy et al., 1991; Keller, Meurisse, Jouaneau, et al., 2003).

Olfactory Mediation of Lamb Recognition

Numerous observational and experimental studies indicate that the sense of smell plays a primary role in ewes' selective acceptance of lambs for nursing. When ewes are rendered "anosmic" by irrigating the olfactory mucosa with zinc sulfate solution, to destroy the olfactory receptors (Lévy, Locatelli, et al., 1995; Poindron, 1976), they subsequently show no selective preference for their own young but will nurse alien young as well as their own. Sectioning the nerves of the accessory olfactory system is without effect (Lévy, Locatelli, et al., 1995). In related experiments, manipulation of the lambs' sensory cues, rather than the mothers' sensory modality, produced similar effects (Poindron & Le Neindre, 1980). Ewes that were exposed for 12 hours to their lambs that were confined in a double-walled mesh cage (receiving olfactory, but not physical, contact) nonetheless developed a selective bond with that lamb. In contrast, ewes that were exposed to lambs in an airtight, transparent box (thereby eliminating olfactory cues) did not develop a selective bond.

Although ewes depend primarily on olfactory cues to recognize their lambs at suckling, they are also able to recognize their neonate from a distance greater than 1 m without olfactory cues, using auditory and visual cues (Ferreira et al., 2000; Terrazas et al., 1999; Keller, Meurisse, Poindron, et al., 2003). This nonolfactory recognition is already effective as early as 8 hours postpartum. The processes involved in proximal recognition appear independent of those involved in distal recognition, since anosmic ewes that allow suckling any lamb can still discriminate their lambs at a distance (Ferreira et al., 2000). Interestingly, there is some evidence that anosmic ewes that showed no initial suckling selectivity can come to recognize their lambs at suckling at 1 month postpartum, which suggest that ewes can compensate for their loss of olfaction by using the auditory/visual cues from their lambs (Ferreira et al., 2000).

Olfactory Bulb and Lamb Odor Recognition

As described earlier in this chapter, a mother's interest in lambs and her ability to selectively recognize her own offspring depend not only on odor but also on parturition triggering her interest in these sensory cues (Keverne et al., 1983). Neural signals resulting from stimulation of the vagina and cervix feed back to the brain to induce both maternal responsiveness and recognition processes, bringing about changes in the olfactory sensory processing system (Kendrick, Lévy, et al., 1992). The mechanism by which parturition brings about changes in the processing of olfactory signals involves, first and foremost, the olfactory bulb (OB), the first central nervous system projection site for olfactory fibers. Data from a series of experiments in which the electrophysiological and neurochemical activity of the OB were monitored at the time of parturition support this view.

Electrophysiological recordings were undertaken in awake ewes before and after birth from olfactory bulb mitral cells, which receive and transmit olfactory signals (Kendrick, Lévy, et al., 1992). In recordings made during pregnancy, none of these cells responded preferentially to lamb or amniotic fluid odors. Instead, the majority of cells responded preferentially to food odors. After birth, there was a dramatic increase in the number of cells that responded preferentially to lamb odors, supporting the idea that the change in salience of the lamb odor that occurs at the time of parturition is mediated by a shift in olfactory cell responsivity. However, the majority of cells that responded to lamb odors did not differentiate between the odor of the ewe's own lamb and that of an alien lamb. Nevertheless, a proportion of the cells did respond preferentially to the odor of the ewe's own lamb. These results indicate that although the odor of lambs has almost no influence on the activity of olfactory bulb neurons during the period before birth (when there is no attraction to lambs), lamb odors are a very potent olfactory stimulus in the period after birth (when attraction to lambs occurs). As well, a small proportion of cells actually show preferential responsiveness to the odor of own lamb at the time when the recognition of lamb odors is a priority.

These shifts in electrical properties of mitral cells that are associated with maternal responsiveness and with olfactory selectivity are reflected in concurrent parturitional changes in the release of peptides (GABA and glutamate) within the OB (Kendrick, Lévy, et al., 1992), the action of the noradrenergic system projecting into the OB, and the release of OB oxytocin (Lévy et al., 1993; Lévy, Kendrick, et al., 1995). All these neurochemicals are believed to be involved in the olfactory learning associated with the formation of an individual recognition based on odor cues.

VCS, which mimics parturition, induces maternal recognition behavior in non–hormonally-primed multiparous ewes, but it is ineffective in nulliparous ewes. In contrast, the same stimulation, conducted only 6 hours after parturition in primiparous ewes (having given birth for the first time), produces acceptance of an alien lamb, with complete patterns of normal maternal behavior (Kendrick, Lévy, & Keverne, 1991). It would seem, therefore, that the neural substrates associated with maternal recognition are capable of being activated—and reactivated—within the first 6 hours following the first parturition. These neural changes result from the first experience of parturition and interactions with the young. The neurotransmitters released at parturition from intrinsic neurons within the olfactory bulb are higher in ewes that had previously experienced selective bonding with lambs than in those that had not (Keverne et al., 1993). In ewes giving birth for the first time, there is no measurable increase in glutamate or GABA release in the olfactory bulb at parturition. This would suggest that enhanced activity across the cells types within the olfactory bulbs is important for the recognition process.

Of course, changes that occur in the OB induced by parturition and the first interactions with the lamb represent only the first stage in the processing of information that underlies recognition memory. How the rest of the brain handles this information is currently under investigation.

Central Neural Substrates of Lamb Recognition

The main approaches used so far to identify neuranatomical substrates involved in olfactory recognition memory include in situ hybridization to assess presence of mRNA expressed by the immediate early genes, c-fos and zif/268, direct drug infusion into different brain sites, and reversible inactivation of specific neural regions by anesthetic infusion.

Postparturient ewes exposed to their lambs for 30 minutes showed increased c-fos mRNA and/or zif/268 expression compared with animals not exposed to lambs primarily in the main olfactory processing regions (OB, piriform cortex, entorhinal cortex, orbitofrontal cortex; Da Costa et al., 1997). Recently, the number of Fos immunoreactive cells have been compared in intact ewes and in anosmic ewes that do not form an exclusive olfactory memory for their lambs (Keller, Meurisse, Jouaneau, et al., 2003). Consistent with the Da Costa et al. (1997) study, in intact ewes, as compared with anosmic ewes, significant increases of Fos labeling were found in the olfactory structures and projection sites such as the OB and the piriform, orbitofrontal, entorhinal, and medial frontal cortices. In addition, the amygdala also shows enhanced expression in parturient intact animals but not in anosmic animals. Which of these structures is involved in the development of selectivity and the formation of the memory was addressed in a series of implant studies. Reversible inactivation of the medial frontal cortex by infusing tetracaine, a local anesthetic, did not prevent the formation of an olfactory memory for the familiar lamb, but it did inhibit the aggressive rejection directed to strange lambs (Broad, Mimmack, Keverne, & Kendrick, 2002). In contrast, a role for both the medial and the cortical nuclei of the amygdala, which receives olfactory input from the olfactory bulbs, has been recently demonstrated (Keller, Perrin, Meurisse, Ferreira, & Lévy, 2004). Infusion of an anesthetic (lidocaine) for the first 8 hours postpartum in either of these nuclei prevents animals from learning to discriminate their own lamb from an alien lamb, and hence both are permitted to suckle.

The involvement of the basal forebrain cholinergic system, which projects to a variety of olfactory and learning systems, has also been investigated using a specific cholinergic neurotoxin injected into the brain in pregnant ewes (Ferreira, Meurisse, Gervais, Ravel, & Lévy, 2001; Ferreira, Meurisse, Tillet, & Lévy, 2001). Immunotoxic lesions severely impaired olfactory lamb recognition without any evidence for sensorimotor, motivational, or olfactory deficits. Importantly, impairment was observed in animals for which loss of cholinergic neurons in each basal forebrain nucleus and their respective limbic, olfactory, and cortical targets was higher than 75%. However, which of its projection sites is important for the impaired lamb recognition remains to be determined.

Individual Recognition of Young in Humans

Human mothers, like sheep mothers, are also able to recognize their own infants based on both olfactory and auditory cues, although the learning does not seem specialized or infant specific. Mothers can discriminate their own infants' soiled

T-shirts from the T-shirts of same-age infants (Porter, Cernoch, & McLaughlin, 1983; Kaitz, Good, Rokem, & Eidelman, 1987; Schaal et al., 1980). That recognition learning of own infants' odors is based on experience is indicated by the additional observations that mothers who were better at recognizing their own infants' odors had earlier and longer contact with their infants after birth, had spent more time in close proximal contact with their infants during interactions, and had more positive maternal feelings and attitudes (Fleming et al., 1993). In addition, as in both rats and sheep, postpartum learning was related to hormones. In new mothers, heightened attractiveness to their own infants' odors and heightened recognition of those odors were related to elevated levels of salivary cortisol (Fleming et al., 1987).

Recognition of a mother's own infant's cries versus other infants' cries has also been a focus in studies of human mothers. Mothers could identify crying samples belonging to their own infants (Formby, 1967), and patterns of maternal heart rate change differed in response to audiotapes of their own versus another's baby, even though these tapes were presented without identification to the mothers (Wisenfeld, Malatesta, Whitman, Granrose, & Uili, 1985). In the latter study, heart rate acceleration, interpreted as arousal preparatory to active coping, followed cries of other infants. Formby (1967) also reported findings consistent with preparatory arousal to the mother's own infant's cries. The ecological relevance of these studies is suggested by the observations that among mothers who roomed together in the hospital with their infants and with several other infant-mother pairs, 58% reported awakening to their infant's cries on the first few nights, whereas thereafter the percentage rose to 96%.

Conclusion

This chapter has attempted to address and interweave a number of distinct themes. The first is broadly related to the psychobiological and behavioral mechanisms that regulate the expression of maternal behavior, which is clearly one of the most adaptive of the species-characteristic reproductive behaviors. It has been seen that although the actual behavior is often quite stereotyped in its form, the motivation to express maternal behavior requires prior changes in other behavioral systems, especially in the animals' affective, perceptual, and learning systems. Hence, in all animals where this approach has been taken, the new mother is less "neophobic" or fearful than her nonmother counterpart or, as is the case in humans, more emotional. These emotionality changes affect maternal behavior, usually but not always (e.g., in humans) in a positive direction. The new mother also develops an attraction to the initially aversive cues associated with young, and she becomes familiar with those young. In addition, across all species, the mother is changed by her experiences with young. Without these changes, the new mother rat, sheep, or human shows inadequate, abnormal, or no maternal behavior.

Another theme explores similarities and differences in the proximal endocrine, sensory, and neural mechanisms that control the expression of maternal behavior across different species. This theme has mostly been studied in rats and sheep, which constitute clear representatives of altricial and precocial species and about which most is known. Where possible, comparisons have been made between these species and humans, with a view to exploring the extent to which the different nonhuman mammals constitute a meaningful model for our understanding of human maternal behavior. We see that in terms of the comparative endocrinology of maternal behavior, there are striking similarities across species that reflect the similar endocrine mediators of pregnancy, parturition, and lactation, although the particular profile of effective hormones may vary. Where apparent species differences do occur, it is either because the particular hormone has not yet been studied adequately (as in the role of prolactin or oxytocin in humans) or because the hormone in fact does not seem to be very important. For instance, the presence of a clear role for VCS and oxytocin in sheep, but not in rats, could arise from the need in sheep to have a clear, discrete, and strong stimulus timed with parturition and in association with the appearance of the young. This would be necessary in order that mothers recognize and rapidly become attached to their offspring before the offspring move away into the flock. Without this imperative, the onset of the motivation for rats to respond develops more gradually at the end of pregnancy and over the first postpartum hours in response to changing levels of a variety of hormones, especially steroids and prolactin. In humans, like the rat, there is evidence of a relation between nurturant feelings at birth and the change in gestational steroidal hormones across pregnancy.

Whether hormones are necessary for the expression of maternal behavior differs across species. Virgin rats can be induced over time to become maternal through contact with pup stimulation, whereas virgin mice are immediately responsive to pup cues. In both cases, the behavior occurs in the absence of hormones. This "concaveation" effect does not occur in sheep. An analogue in humans is the adoptive mother who, by all accounts, comes to feel nurturant and attached to her infant, although the development of these feelings in adoptive mothers has not been adequately studied. Also not known is whether adoptive mothers in contact with their infants undergo changes in endogenous hormones or in responsiveness to infant cues.

In terms of sensory factors, similar sensory systems are activated in rats, sheep, and humans, but possibly to different extents. For all three, olfaction is important, although its role is most clearly established in sheep. In this species, a primary odor signal (amniotic fluid) is necessary for the initial approach to the young. In addition, the olfactory bulbs undergo extensive change when exposed to this odor. In rats, neither the nature of the motivating chemosensory cue nor the neural bases of their sensory processing mechanisms is well delineated, although at least one study suggests a role for the pup preputial gland mediated by the vomeronasal system. In humans, some infant-related odors are attractive to the mother (e.g., salivary and sebaceous odors), but others clearly are not (e.g., feces and urine). However, we know nothing about the functional specificity of these odors, nor how they are processed. In contrast, in rats, sheep, and humans, infant vocalizations are important to locate the young at a distance from the mother or from the nest site. In rats, these vocalizations are in the ultrasonic range. In sheep, they are bleats, and in humans, the infant cry is a powerful approach stimulus. Finally, whereas rats and humans engage in close-contact behaviors related to thermoregulation, sheep are less affected by somatosensory cues from the young. We have yet to establish in any mammalian species the existence of specific receptors or highly specialized mechanisms for detection or processing of these infant signals.

Neural mechanisms regulating the onset of maternal behavior have been most intensively studied in rats and other rodents, where the MPOA is essential for the expression of the behavior and is part of an excitatory system. Whether the role of the MPOA is in the organization of the consummatory response, or if it is important for maternal motivation is not fully understood. In sheep, oxytocin in the MPOA seems to regulate one aspect of the consummatory response (rejection), but whether the MPOA also regulates acceptance is still not known. There is some evidence that another hypothalamic nucleus, the PVN, may be more important for these positive responses in sheep, whereas in rats its role is more minor. To date, the role of this structure has not been studied in primates or humans.

In all mammals that have been studied, there is a shift in maternal responsiveness at the time of parturition. In the rat, we believe there exists an inhibitory system that is disinhibited by the hormones of parturition. Evidence for this derives from studies in which lesions in olfactory, limbic (amygdala), and hypothalamic (VMH) structures in nulliparous animals disinhibit maternal responsiveness. In other species, as in some mice species, nulliparous animals are already somewhat responsive to young, and hence the inhibitory systems may be less active or absent. Removal of the olfactory bulbs in these species does not result in facilitated maternal behavior, as in rats, but results in cannibalism of young—quite the opposite response. What the effects of lesions to the amygdala or VMH might be in these species has not been investigated. In contrast, in sheep, nulliparous animals are totally unresponsive to young, are repulsed by lamb odors, and are more "fearful" in a novel environment, much like the rat. However, unlike the rat, they are even unresponsive following priming with parturitional hormones. This suggests that in this species the inhibitory system is quite active. However, to date, effects of lesions of the inhibitory olfactory-amygdala-VMH system in nulliparous ewes on any of these end points have not been studied.

The final theme emphasized in this chapter describes the involvement of mechanisms of learning and plasticity in the regulation of maternal behavior. How this plasticity is expressed across species is similar in some respects but not in others. For instance, in both rats and sheep, animals gain from the maternal experience such that after subsequent births, they have altered neurochemical function and are more responsive to maternally relevant physiology and sensory inputs than they were after the first birth. In humans, experience and multiparity also alter the new mothers' responsiveness to infant odor and cry cues. In addition, in the rat, rabbit, and a variety of other species, experiences acquired postpartum are retained throughout lactation. Hence, a brief maternal experience at the time of parturition results in sustained responsiveness beyond the period of hormonal priming. Elevated responsiveness as a function of a brief experience is also reflected in altered brain function and structure. In sheep, this form of experience seems of little importance, since removal of the young after a brief experience with them results in a rapid loss of responsiveness. Sheep are also unique in showing a specialized form of rapid learning, producing recognition learning of individual young. This learning is powerful but again short-lived, functioning only as long as the individuals in question are present. Once they are removed or are lost for too long, they appear to be soon forgotten. The absence of a prolonged memory for either responsiveness or selectivity may be adaptive, but for different reasons. Given that ewes do not go back into estrus for several months after removal of the young, it would not be adaptive to maintain neural and other resources needed to invest in the maintenance of their maternal responsiveness over this period. In contrast, once the mother is separated from her lamb, there is no point in maintaining selectivity toward that lamb, since the next set of progeny are different individuals and must themselves be learned. The relation between the mechanisms underlying a ewe's motivation to respond to any young and her recognition memory is intriguing. Given that the mechanisms are different from one another, these two processes are theoretically separable. While it is clearly possible to be maternal without being selective (in anosmic ewes), it is more difficult to demonstrate selectivity in a nonmaternal animal. However, it would be interesting to develop other tests of selectivity that do not require the ewe to perform acceptance or rejection behaviors to help us dissociate maternal responsiveness and maternal selectivity.

The neural mechanisms involved in recognition memory in sheep are quite different from those involved in maternal memory. This memory involves an olfactory learning mechanism that shares several common features with other forms of olfactory learning found in female mice during mating (Brennan & Keverne, 1997), in social recognition of conspecifics (Insel & Young, 2001; Ferguson, Young, & Insel, 2002), and in olfactory learning of maternal cues in neonatal rats (Wilson & Sullivan, 1994). In each case, odor learning induces structural and functional changes within the main or accessory olfactory bulbs and involves a dependence on noradrenergic transmission. Moreover, oxytocin projections to the olfactory bulb and the medial amygdala are also involved both in lamb recognition and in social recognition. Based on these similarities, it seems that interactions between neuropeptides and classical neurotransmitters acting in these neural systems may constitute a unifying principle of the neural mechanisms of maternal behavior.

Based on the extant data, the neural circuitry that mediates the formation of maternal memory, involving the nucleus accumbens, basolateral amygdala, and the MPOA, has little in common with the olfactory-focused circuitry involved in social recognition. Until more complete analyses are undertaken on the role of the MPOA and striatal structures in recognition memory or on the role of the olfactory structures and oxytocin in maternal memory, the differences in mechanisms controlling these two forms of memory may be more apparent than real (table 8–4).

Up to this point we have concentrated on the mother and the ways in which she responds to her offspring. However, it is also the case that the young also respond to their mothers. Together, mothers and young cooperate in ensuring that the two are together at times that they need to be, to ensure survival of the young. In precocial species, the mother comes to recognize her individual offspring and does so even in a flock context where there are many offspring. In this case, evidence shows not only that it is the mother that regulates the relationship but also that the young of precocial species show selectivity and come

Table 8-4. Comparison between maternal memory in rats and recognition memory in sheep

	Rat	Sheep
Type of recognition	Litter recognition	Individual recognition
Time course	Long-term memory: 30 min of young contact —30 days of retention	Short-term memory: 7 days of young contact —36 hrs of retention
Hormonal systems	Enhanced by hormonal status of parturition	Dependent on hormonal status of parturition
Sensory cues	Somatosensory and olfactory cues	Olfactory cues
Sensory systems	Perioral and ventral tactile and chemosensory systems	Main olfactory system
Neural networks	MPOA + basolateral amygdala + nucleus accumbens	MOB + cortical amygdala + medial amygdala + frontal cortex
Neurotransmitters	Noradrenaline, dopamine, opioids	Noradrenaline, acetylcholine, glutamate, GABA
Plasticity	Medial preoptic area, basolateral amygdala, medial amygdala, parietal cortex	Main olfactory bulb

to recognize their mothers from among other mothers in the flock (Nowak, Porter, Lévy, Orgeur, & Schaal, 2000). In the case of rats, strategies adopted by the mother and her offspring to maintain their relationship are similar. Mothers do not recognize their individual offspring, nor do they need to. Instead, they learn about and become familiar with their litters, which is what is required for a species where the young remain in the nest for a considerable period after birth but the mother leaves the nest to forage and interact with other colony members. Pups in a litter do recognize the cues from the mother, but these primarily provide information about the lactational status of the mother, rather than the individual mother. At birth, young respond to amniotic fluid on the teat, or nipple-search pheromones as demonstrated for rabbits (Schaal et al., 2003), which help them make their first attachment to suckle. As well, when young are somewhat older and more mobile, they come to recognize the mother's caecotrophe and milk composition, which in turn helps them to recognize their own nest sites and to develop appropriate food preferences (Leon, 1978). Together, mechanisms in the young and in their mothers promote a bond between the two that is appropriate to the needs of the young and the social organization in which they reside.

Acknowledgments Supported by funding to F. Lévy from INRA and to A.S. Fleming from NSERC and CIHR. We are grateful to A. C. Rosetti and G. Kraemer for their valuable comments.

Portions of this chapter overlap with material discussed in A. S. Fleming & M. Li, 2002, "Psychobiology of Maternal Behavior and Its Early Determinants in Nonhuman Mammals," in M. H. Bornstein (Ed.), *Handbook of Parenting* (pp. 61–97). Mahwah, NJ: Erlbaum.

References

Ahdieh, H. B., Mayer, A. D., & Rosenblatt, J. S. (1987). Effects of brain antiestrogen implants on maternal behavior and on postpartum estrus in pregnant rats. *Neuroendocrinology, 46*, 522–531.

Allin, J. T., & Banks, E. M. (1972). Functional aspects of ultrasound production by infant albino rats (*Rattus norvegicus*). *Animal Behavior, 20*, 175–185.

Anderson, C. O., Zarrow, M. X., Fuller, G. B., & Denenberg, V. H. (1971). Pituitary involvement in maternal-nest building in the rabbit. *Hormones and Behavior, 2*, 183–189.

Basiouni, G. F., & Gonyou, H. W. (1988). Use of birth fluids and cervical stimulation in lamb fostering. *Journal of Animal Science, 66*, 872–879.

Bauer, J. H. (1983). Effects of maternal state on the responsiveness to nest odors of hooded rats. *Physiology and Behavior, 30*, 229–232.

Beach, F. A., & Jaynes, J. (1956a). Studies of maternal retrieving in rats: II. Effects of practice and previous parturitions. *American Naturalist, 90*, 103–109.

Beach, F. A., & Jaynes, J. (1956b). Studies of maternal retrieving in rats: III. Sensory cues involved in lactating female's response to her young. *Behavior, 10*, 104–125.

Beckwith, B. E., Lerud, K., Antes, J. R., & Reynolds, B. W. (1983). Hydrocortisone reduces auditory sensitivity at high tonal frequencies in adult males. *Pharmacology, Biochemistry and Behavior, 19*, 431–433.

Benassayag, C., Leroy, M. J., & Rigourd, V. (1999). Estrogens receptors (ER/ERß) in normal and pathological growth of the human myometrium: Pregnancy and leiomyoma. *American Journal of Physiology, 276*, E1112–E1118.

Bolwerk, E. L. M., & Swanson, H. H. (1984). Does oxytocin play a role in the onset of maternal behaviour in the rat? *Journal of Endocrinology, 101*, 353–357.

Brennan, P. A., & Keverne, E. B. (1997). Neural mechanisms of mammalian olfactory learning. *Progress in Neurobiology, 51*, 457–481.

Brewster, J., & Leon, M. (1980). Facilitation of maternal transport by Norway rat pups. *Journal of Comparative and Physiological Psychology, 94*, 80–88.

Bridges, R. S. (1975). Long-term effects of pregnancy and parturition upon maternal responsiveness in the rat. *Physiology and Behavior, 14*, 245–249.

Bridges, R. S. (1977). Parturition: Its role in the long term retention of maternal behavior in the rat. *Physiology and Behavior, 18*, 487–490.

Bridges, R. S. (1984). A quantitative analysis of the roles of dosage, sequence, and duration of estradiol and progesterone exposure in the regulation of maternal behavior in the rat. *Endocrinology, 114*, 930–940.

Bridges, R. S. (1990). Endocrine regulation of parental behavior in rodents. In N. A. Krasnegor & R. S. Bridges (Eds.), *Mammalian parenting: Biochemical, neurobiological, and behavioral determinants* (pp. 93–117). New York: Oxford University Press.

Bridges, R. S., DiBiase, R., Loundes, D. D., & Doherty, P. C. (1985). Prolactin stimulation of maternal behavior in female rats. *Science, 227*, 782784.

Bridges, R. S., & Goldman, B. D. (1975). Ovarian control of prolactin secretion during late pregnancy in the rat. *Endocrinology, 97*, 496–498.

Bridges, R. S., Mann, P. E., & Coppeta, J. S. (1999). Hypothalamic involvement in the regulation of maternal behavior in the rat: Inhibitory roles for the ventromedial hypothalamus and the dorsal/anterior hypothalamic areas. *Journal of Neuroendocrinology, 11*, 259–266.

Bridges, R. S., Numan, M., Ronsheim, P. M., Mann, P. E., & Lupini, C. E. (1990). Central prolactin infusions stimulate maternal behavior in steroid-treated, nulliparous female rats. *Proceedings of the National Academy of Sciences of the United States of America, 87*, 8003–8007.

Bridges, R. S., & Ronsheim, P. M. (1987). Immunoreactive beta-endorphin concentrations in brain and plasma during pregnancy in rats: Possible modulation by progesterone and estradiol. *Neuroendocrinology, 45*, 381–388.

Bridges, R. S., & Ronsheim, P. M. (1990). Prolactin (PRL) regulation of maternal behavior in rats: Bromocriptine treatment delays and PRL promotes the rapid onset of behavior. *Endocrinology, 126*, 837–848.

Broad, K. D., Kendrick, K. M., Sirinathsinghji, D. J., & Keverne, E. B. (1993a). Changes in oxytocin immunoreactivity and mRNA expression in the sheep brain during pregnancy, parturition and lactation and in response to oestrogen and progesterone. *Journal of Neuroendocrinology, 5*, 435–444.

Broad, K. D., Kendrick, K. M., Sirinathsinghji, D. J., & Keverne, E. B. (1993b). Changes in pro-opiomelanocortin and pre-proenkephalin mRNA levels in the ovine brain during pregnancy, parturition and lactation and in response to oestrogen and progesterone. *Journal of Neuroendocrinology, 5*, 711–719.

Broad, K. D., Lévy, F., Evans, G., Kimura, T., Keverne, E. B., & Kendrick, K. M. (1999). Previous maternal experience potentiates the effect of parturition on oxytocin receptor mRNA expression in the paraventricular nucleus. *European Journal of Neuroscience, 11*, 3725–3737.

Broad, K. D., Mimmack, M. L., Keverne, E. B., & Kendrick, K. M. (2002). Increased BDNF and trk-B mRNA expression in cortical and limbic regions following formation of a social recognition memory. *European Journal of Neuroscience, 16*, 2166–2174.

Brouette-Lahlou, I., Godinot, F., & Vernet-Maury, E. (1999). The mother rat's vomeronasal organ is involved in detection of dodecyl propionate, the pup's preputial gland pheromone. *Physiology and Behavior, 66*, 427–436.

Brouette-Lahlou, I., Vernet-Maury, E., & Chanel, J. (1991). Is rat-dam licking behavior regulated by pups' preputial gland secretion? *Animal Learning and Behavior, 19*, 177–184.

Brouette-Lahlou, I., Vernet-Maury, E., Godinot, F., & Chanel, J. (1992). Vomeronasal organ sustains pups' anogenital licking in primiparous rats. In R. L. Doty & D. Müoler-Schwarze (Eds.), *Chemical signals in vertebrates* (pp. 551–555). New York: Plenum.

Byrnes, E. M., & Bridges, R. S. (2000). Endogenous opioid facilitation of maternal memory in rats. *Behavioral Neuroscience, 114*, 797–804.

Byrnes, E. M., Rigero, B. A., & Bridges, R. S. (2002). Dopamine antagonists during parturition disrupt maternal care and the retention of maternal behavior in rats. *Pharmacology, Biochemistry and Behavior, 73*, 869–875.

Caldwell, J. D., Greer, E. R., Johnson, M. F., Prange, A. J. J., & Pedersen, C. A. (1987). Oxytocin and vasopressin immunoreactivity in hypothalamic and extrahypothalamic sites in late pregnant and postpartum rats. *Neuroendocrinology, 46*, 39–47.

Challis, J. R., Harrison, F. A., & Heap, R. B. (1971). Uterine production of oestrogens and progesterone at parturition in the sheep. *Journal of Reproduction and Fertility, 25*, 306–307.

Challis, J. R. G., & Olsen, D. M. (1988). Parturition. In E. Knobil, J. D. Neill, L. L. Ewing, C. L. Market, G. S. Greenwald, & D. Pfaff (Eds.), *Physiology of reproduction* (pp. 2177–2216). New York: Raven.

Chamley, W. A., Buckmaster, J., Cereni, M. E., Cumming, I. A., Goding, J. R., Obst, J. M., et al. (1973). Changes in the levels of progesterone, corticosteroids, estrone, oestradiol 17–beta, luteinizing hormone and prolactin in the peripheral plasma of the ewe during late pregnancy and at parturition. *Biology of Reproduction, 9*, 30–35.

Champagne, F., Diorio, J., Sharma, S., & Meaney, M. J. (2001). Naturally occurring variations in maternal behavior in the rat are associated with differences in estrogen-inducible central oxytocin receptors. *Proceedings of the National Academy of Sciences of the United States of America, 98*, 12736–12741.

Cohen, J., & Bridges, R. S. (1981). Retention of maternal behavior in nulliparous and primiparous rats: Effects of duration of previous maternal experience. *Journal of Comparative and Physiological Psychology, 95*, 450–459.

Cohn, J. F., Campbell, S. B., Matias, R., & Hopkins, J. (1990). Face-to-face interactions of postpartum depressed and nondepressed mother-infant pairs at 2 months. *Developmental Psychology, 35*, 119–123.

Corter, C., & Fleming, A. S. (2002). Psychobiology of maternal behavior in human beings. In M. H. Bornstein (Ed.), *Handbook of parenting: Biology and ecology of parenting* (pp. 141–182). Mahwah, NJ: Erlbaum.

Corter, C., Fleming, A. S., & Steiner, M. (2005). *The role of experience in differen-*

tial responsiveness to own and other infants among mothers and fathers of newborns. Manuscript in preparation.

Da Costa, A. P., Broad, K. D., & Kendrick, K. M. (1997). Olfactory memory and maternal behaviour-induced changes in c-fos and zif/268 mRNA expression in the sheep brain. *Brain Research. Molecular Brain Research, 46,* 63–76.

Da Costa, A. P., De La Riva, C., Guevara-Guzman, R., & Kendrick, K. M. (1999). C-fos and c-jun in the paraventricular nucleus play a role in regulating peptide gene expression, oxytocin and glutamate release, and maternal behaviour. *European Journal of Neuroscience, 11,* 2199–2210.

Da Costa, A. P., Guevara-Guzman, R. G., Ohkura, S., Goode, J. A., & Kendrick, K. M. (1996). The role of oxytocin release in the paraventricular nucleus in the control of maternal behaviour in the sheep. *Journal of Neuroendocrinology, 8,* 163–177.

Davis, M. (1992). The role of the amygdala in conditioned fear. In J Aggleton (Ed.), *The amygdala: Neurobiological aspects of emotion, memory, and mental dysfunction* (pp. 255–306). New York: Wiley-Liss.

Dluzen, D. E., Muraoka, S., Engelmann, M., & Landgraf, R. (1998). The effects of infusion of arginine vasopressin, oxytocin, or their antagonists into the olfactory bulb upon social recognition responses in male rats. *Peptides, 19,* 999–1005.

Doane, H., & Porter, R. H. (1978). The role of diet in mother-infant reciprocity in the spiny mouse. *Developmental Psychobiology, 11,* 271–277.

Doerr, H. K., Siegel, H. I., & Rosenblatt, J. S. (1981). Effects of progesterone withdrawal and estrogen on maternal behavior in nulliparous rats. *Behavioral and Neural Biology, 32,* 35–44.

Ehret, G., & Buckenmaier, J. (1994). Estrogen-receptor occurrence in the female mouse brain: Effects of maternal experience, ovariectomy, estrogen and anosmia. *Journal of Physiology (Paris), 88,* 315–329.

Engelmann, M., Ebner, K., Wotjak, C. T., & Landgraf, R. (1998). Endogenous oxytocin is involved in short-term olfactory memory in female rats. *Behavioural Brain Research, 90,* 89–94.

Everitt, B. J., & Robbins, T. W. (1992). Amygdala-ventral striatal interactions and reward-related processes. In J. Aggleton (Ed.), *The amygdala: Neurobiological aspects of emotion, memory, and mental dysfunction* (pp. 401–429). New York: Wiley-Liss.

Fahrbach, S. E., Morrell, J. I., & Pfaff, D. W. (1985). Possible role for endogenous oxytocin in estrogen-facilitated maternal behavior in rats. *Neuroendocrinology, 40,* 526–532.

Fahrbach, S. E., Morrell, J. I., & Pfaff, D. W. (1986). Effect of varying the duration of pre-test cage habituation on oxytocin induction of short-latency maternal behavior. *Physiology and Behavior, 37,* 135–139.

Farrell, W. J., & Alberts, J. R. (2002a). Maternal responsiveness to infant rat ultrasonic vocalizations during the maternal behavior cycle and following steroid and experiential induction regimens. *Journal of Comparative Psychology, 116,* 286–296.

Farrell, W. J., & Alberts, J. R. (2002b). Stimulus control of maternal responsiveness to rat pup ultrasonic vocalizations. *Journal of Comparative Psychology, 116,* 297–307.

Featherstone, R. E., Fleming, A. S., & Ivy, G. O. (2000). Plasticity in the maternal circuit: Effects of experience and partum condition on brain astrocyte number in female rats. *Behavioral Neuroscience, 114,* 158–172.

Ferguson, J. N., Young, L. J., & Insel, T. R. (2002). The neuroendocrine basis of social recognition. *Frontiers in Neuroendocrinology, 23,* 200–224.

Ferreira, G., Meurisse, M., Gervais, R., Ravel, N., & Lévy, F. (2001). Extensive immunolesions of basal forebrain cholinergic system impair offspring recognition in sheep. *Neuroscience, 106,* 103–115.

Ferreira, G., Meurisse, M., Tillet, Y., & Lévy, F. (2001). Distribution and co-localization of choline acetyltransferase and p75 neurotrophin receptors in the sheep basal forebrain: implications for the use of a specific cholinergic immunotoxin. *Neuroscience, 104,* 419–439.

Ferreira, G., Terrazas, A., Poindron, P., Nowak, R., Orgeur, P., & Lévy, F. (2000). Learning of olfactory cues is not necessary for early lamb recognition by the mother. *Physiology and Behavior, 69,* 405–412.

Field, T., Healy, B., Goldstein, S., & Guthertz, M. (1990). Behavior-state matching and synchrony in mother-infant interactions of non-depressed versus depressed dyads. *Developmental Psychology, 26,* 7–14.

Field, T., Healy, B., Goldstein, S., Perry, S., Bendall, D., Schanberg, S., et al. (1998). Infants of depressed mothers show depressed behavior even with non-depressed adults. *Child Development, 59,* 1569–1579.

Fleischer, S., & Slotnick, B. M. (1978). Disruption of maternal behavior in rats with lesions of the septal area. *Physiology and Behavior, 21,* 189–200.

Fleming, A. S. (1987). Psychobiology of rat maternal behavior: How and where hormones act to promote maternal behavior at parturition. In B. R. Komisaruk, H. I. Siegel, M. F. Cheng, and H. H. Feder (Eds.), *Reproduction: A behavioral and neuroendocrine perspective* (pp. 234–251). New York: New York Academy of Sciences.

Fleming, A. S., Cheung, U., Myhal, N., & Kessler, Z. (1989). Effects of maternal hormones on "timidity" and attraction to pup-related odors in female rats. *Physiology and Behavior, 46,* 440–453.

Fleming, A. S., Corter, C., Franks, P., Surbey, M., Schneider, B. A., & Steiner, M. (1993). Postpartum factors related to mother's attraction to newborn infant odors. *Developmental Psychobiology, 26,* 115–132.

Fleming, A. S., Flett, G. L., Ruble, D., & Shaul, D. L. (1988). Postpartum adjustment in first-time mothers: Relation between mood, maternal attitudes, and mother-infant interactions. *Developmental Psychobiology, 24,* 71–81.

Fleming, A. S., Gavarth, K., & Sarker, J. (1992). Effects of transections to the vomeronasal nerves or to the main olfactory bulbs on the initiation and long-term retention of maternal behavior in primiparous rats. *Behavioral and Neural Biology, 57,* 177–188.

Fleming, A. S., & Korsmit, M. (1996). Plasticity in the maternal circuit: Effects of maternal experience on Fos-Lir in hypothalamic, limbic, and cortical structures in the postpartum rat. *Behavioral Neuroscience, 110,* 567–582.

Fleming, A. S., Kuchera, C., Lee, A., & Winocur, G. (1994). Olfactory-based social learning varies as a function of parity in female rats. *Psychobiology, 22,* 37–43.

Fleming, A. S., & Li, M. (2002). Psychobiology of maternal behavior and its early determinants in nonhuman mammals. In M. H. Bornstein (Ed.), *Handbook of parenting* (pp. 61–97). Mahwah, NJ: Erlbaum.

Fleming, A. S., & Luebke, C. (1981). Timidity prevents the nulliparous female from being a good mother. *Physiology and Behavior, 27,* 863–868.

Fleming, A. S., Miceli, M. O., & Moretto, D. (1983). Lesions of the medial preoptic area prevent the facilitation of maternal behavior produced by amygdala lesions. *Physiology and Behavior, 31,* 503–510.

Fleming, A. S., Morgan, H. D., & Walsh, C. (1996). Experiential factors in post-partum regulation of maternal care. *Advances in the Study of Behavior, 25*, 295–332.

Fleming, A. S., & Rosenblatt, J. (1974a). Olfactory regulation of maternal behavior in rats: I. Effects of olfactory bulb removal in experienced and inexperienced lactating and cycling females. *Journal of Comparative and Physiological Psychology, 86*, 221–232.

Fleming, A. S., & Rosenblatt, J. S. (1974b). Olfactory regulation of maternal behavior in rats: II. Effects of peripherally induced anosmia and lesions of the lateral olfactory tract in pup-induced virgins. *Journal of Comparative and Physiological Psychology, 86*, 233–246.

Fleming, A. S., Ruble, D., Anderson, V., & Flett, G. L. (1988). Place of childbirth influences feeling of satisfaction and control in first-time mothers. *Journal of Psychosomatic Obstetrics and Gynecology, 8*, 1–17.

Fleming, A. S., Ruble, D. N., Flett, G. L., & Shaul, D. L. (1988). Postpartum adjustment in first-time mothers: Relations between mood, maternal attitudes and mother-infant interactions. *Developmental Psychology, 24*, 71–81.

Fleming, A. S., Ruble, D., Krieger, H., & Wong, P. Y. (1997). Hormonal and experiential correlates of maternal responsiveness during pregnancy and the puerperium in human mothers. *Hormones and Behavior, 31*, 145–158.

Fleming, A. S., & Sarker, J. (1990). Experience-hormone interactions and maternal behavior in rats. *Physiology and Behavior, 47*, 1165–1173.

Fleming, A. S., Steiner, M., & Anderson, V. (1987). Hormonal and attitudinal correlates of maternal behavior during the early postpartum period in first-time mothers. *Journal of Reproduction and Infant Psychology, 5*, 193–205.

Fleming, A. S., Steiner, M., & Corter, C. (1997). Cortisol, hedonics, and maternal responsiveness in human mothers. *Hormones and Behavior, 32*, 85–98.

Fleming, A. S., Suh, E. J., Korsmit, M., & Rusak, B. (1994). Activation of Fos-like immunoreactivity in the medial preoptic area and limbic structures by maternal and social interactions in rats. *Behavioral Neuroscience, 108*, 724–734.

Fleming, A. S., Vaccarino, F., & Leubke, C. (1980). Amygdaloid inhibition of maternal behavior in the nulliparous female rat. *Physiology and Behavior, 25*, 731–743.

Fleming, A. S., Vaccarino, F., Tambosso, L., & Chee, P. (1979). Vomeronasal and olfactory system modulation of maternal behavior in the rat. *Science, 203*, 372–374.

Formby, D. (1967). Maternal recognition of infant's cry. *Developmental Medicine and Child Neurology, 9*, 292–298.

Francis, D. D., Young, L. J., Meaney, M. J., & Insel, T. R. (2002). Naturally occurring differences in maternal care are associated with the expression of oxytocin and vasopressin (V1a) receptors: Gender differences. *Journal of Neuroendocrinology, 14*, 349–353.

Friedman, M. I., Bruno, J. P., & Alberts, J. R. (1981). Physiological and behavioral consequences in rats of water recycling during lactation. *Journal of Comparative and Physiological Psychology, 95*, 26–35.

Gardner, C. R., & Phillips, S. W. (1977). The influence of the amygdala on the basal septum and preoptic area of the rat. *Experimental Brain Research, 29*, 249–263.

González-Mariscal, G., Díaz-Sánchez, V., Melo, A. I., Beyer, C., & Rosenblatt, J. S. (1994). Maternal behavior in New Zealand white rabbits: Quantification of somatic events, motor patterns, and steroid plasma levels. *Physiology and Behavior, 55*, 1081–1089.

Gonzalez-Mariscal, G., Melo, A. I., Chirino, R., Jimenez, P., Beyer, C., & Rosenblatt, J. S. (1998). Importance of mother/young contact at parturition and across lactation for the expression of maternal behavior in rabbits. *Developmental Psychobiology, 32*, 101–111.

Gonzalez-Mariscal, G., Melo, A. I., Chirino, R., Jimenez, P., Beyer, C., & Rosenblatt, J. S. (2000). Pharmacological evidence that prolactin acts from late gestation to promote maternal behavior in rabbits. *Journal of Neuroendocrinology, 12*, 983–992.

González-Mariscal, G., Melo, A. I., Jiménez, P., Beyer, C., & Rosenblatt, J. S. (1996). Estradiol, progesterone, and prolactin regulate maternal nest-building in rabbits. *Journal of Neuroendocrinology, 8*, 901–907.

Gonzalez-Mariscal, G., & Poindron, P. (2002). Parental care in mammals: Immediate internal and sensory factors of control. In D. W. Pfaff, A. P. Arnold, A. M. Etgen, S. E. Farhbach, and R. T. Rubin (Eds.), *Hormones, brain and behavior* (pp. 215–298). San Diego: Academic Press.

Gonzalez-Mariscal, G., & Rosenblatt, J. S. (1996). Maternal behavior in rabbits: A historical and multidisciplinary perspective. In J. S. Rosenblatt and C. T. Snowdon (Eds.), *Parental care: Evolution, mechanisms and adaptative significance* (333–360). San Diego, CA: Academic Press.

Graham, D., Rees, S., & Fleming, A. S. (2005). Effects of adrenalectomy and corticosterone replacement on maternal memory in the female rat. Manuscript in preparation.

Gray, P., & Chesley, S. (1984). Development of maternal behavior in nulliparous rats (Rattus norvegicus): Effects of sex and early maternal experience. *Journal of Comparative Psychology, 98*, 91–99.

Hammer, R. P. J., Mateo, A. R., & Bridges, R. S. (1992). Hormonal regulation of medial preoptic mu-opiate receptor density before and after parturition. *Neuroendocrinology, 56*, 38–45.

Handley, S. L., Dunn, T. L., Waldron, G., & Baker, J. M. (1980). Tryptophan, cortisol, and puerperal mood. *British Journal of Psychiatry, 136*, 498–508.

Hansen, S., Bergvall, A. H., & Nyiredi, S. (1993). Interaction with pups enhances dopamine release in the ventral striatum of maternal rats: A microdialysis study. *Pharmacology, Biochemistry and Behavior, 45*, 673–676.

Hansen, S., Ferreira, A., & Selart, M. E. (1985). Behavioural similarities between mother rats and benzodiazepine-treated non-maternal animals. *Psychopharmacology, 86*, 344–347.

Hansen, S., Harthon, C., Wallin, E., Lofberg, L., & Svensson, K. (1991). Mesotelencephalic dopamine system and reproductive behavior in the female rat: Effects of ventral tegmental 6–hydroxydopamine lesions on maternal and sexual responsiveness. *Behavioral Neuroscience, 105*, 588–598.

Hauser, H., & Gandelman, R. (1985). Lever pressing for pups: Evidence for hormonal influence upon maternal behavior of mice. *Hormones and Behavior, 19*, 454–468.

Henry, J. P., & Wang, S. (1998). Effects of early stress on adult affiliative behavior. *Psychoneuroendocrinolgy, 23*, 66–83.

Herbison, A. E. (1997). Noradrenergic regulation of cyclic GnRH secretion. *Reviews of Reproduction, 2*, 1–6.

Herscher, L., Richmond, J. B., & Moore, A. U. (1963). Maternal behavior in sheep and goats. In H. L. Rheingold (Ed.), *Maternal behavior in mammals* (pp. 203–232). New York: Wiley.

Hodgen, G. D., & Itskovitz, J. (1988). Recognition and maintenance of pregnancy.

In E. Knobil, J. D. Neill, L. L. Ewing, C. L. Market, G. S. Greenwald, & D. W. Pfaff (Eds.), *Physiology of reproduction* (pp. 1995–2022. New York: Raven.

Hudson, S. J., & Mullord, M. M. (1977). Investigations on maternal bonding in dairy cattle. *Applied Animal Ethology, 3*, 271–276.

Insel, T. R. (1990). Oxytocin and maternal behavior. In N. A. Krasnegor & R. B. Bridges (Eds.), *Mammalian parenting: Biochemical, neurobiological, and behavioral determinant* (pp. 260–280). New York: Oxford University Press.

Insel, T. R., & Young, L. J. (2001). The neurobiology of attachment. *Nature Reviews Neuroscience, 2*, 129–136.

Jakubowski, M., & Terkel, J. (1986). Establishment and maintenance of maternal responsiveness in postpartum Wistar rats. *Animal Behavior, 34*, 256–262.

Kaba, H., & Keverne, E. B. (1988). The effect of microinfusions of drugs into the accessory olfactory bulb on the olfactory block to pregnancy. *Neuroscience, 25*, 1007–1011.

Kaitz, M., Good, A., Rokem, A. M., & Eidelman, A. I. (1987). Mothers' recognition of their newborns by olfactory cues. *Developmental Psychobiology, 20*, 587–591.

Keller, M., Meurisse, M., Jouaneau, N., Vénier, G., Archer, E., & Lévy, F. (2003). Neural networks involved in acquisition and consolidation of the lamb odour by parturient ewes. In *35th Annual General Meeting of the European Brain and Behaviour Society*. Barcelona, Spain: European Brain and Behavior Society.

Keller, M., Meurisse, M., & Lévy, F. (2004). Mapping the neural substrates involved in maternal responsiveness and lamb olfactory offspring memory in parturient ewes using Fos imaging. *Behavioral Neuroscience, 118*, 1274–1284.

Keller, M., Meurisse, M., Poindron, P., Nowak, R., Shayit, M., Ferreira, G., et al. (2003). Maternal experience influences the establishment of visual/auditory, but not of olfactory recognition of the newborn baby lamb by ewes at parturition. *Developmental Psychobiology, 43*, 167–176.

Keller, M., Perrin, G., Meurisse, M., Ferreira, G., & Lévy, F. (2004). Cortical and medial amygdala are both involved in the formation of olfactory offspring memory in sheep. *European Journal of Neuroscience, 20*(12), 3433–3441.

Kendrick, K. M. (1994). Neurobiological correlates of visual and olfactory recognition in sheep. *Behavioural Processes, 33*, 89–112.

Kendrick, K. M. (2000). Oxytocin, motherhood and bonding. *Experimental Physiology, 85*, 111–124.

Kendrick, K. M., Da Costa, A. P., Hinton, M. R., & Keverne, E. B. (1992). A simple method for fostering lambs using anoestrus ewes with artificially induced lactation and maternal behaviour. *Applied Animal Behaviour Science, 34*, 345–357.

Kendrick, K. M., Da Costa, A. P. C., Broad, K. D., Ohkura, S., Guevara, R., Lévy, F., et al. (1997). Neural control of maternal behaviour and olfactory recognition of offspring. *Brain Research Bulletin, 44*, 383–395.

Kendrick, K. M., Guevara-Guzman, R., Zorrilla, J., Hinton, M. R., Broad, K. D., Mimmack, M., et al. (1997). Formation of olfactory memories mediated by nitric oxide. *Nature, 388*, 670–674.

Kendrick, K. M., & Keverne, E. B. (1991). Importance of progesterone and estrogen priming for the induction of maternal behavior by vaginocervical stimulation in sheep: Effects of maternal experience. *Physiology and Behavior, 49*, 745–750.

Kendrick, K. M., Keverne, E. B., & Baldwin, B. A. (1987). Intracerebroventricular oxytocin stimulates maternal behaviour in the sheep. *Neuroendocrinology, 46,* 56–61.

Kendrick, K. M., Keverne, E. B., Baldwin, B. A., & Sharman, D. F. (1986). Cerebrospinal fluid levels of acetylcholinesterase, monoamines and oxytocin during labour, parturition, vaginocerivical stimulation, lamb separation and suckling in sheep. *Neuroendocrinology, 44,* 149–156.

Kendrick, K. M., Keverne, E. B., Chapman, C., & Baldwin, B. A. (1988). Intracranial dialysis measurement of oxytocin, monoamine and uric acid release from the olfactory bulb and substantia nigra of sheep during parturition, suckling, separation from lambs and eating. *Brain Research, 439,* 1–10.

Kendrick, K. M., Lévy, F., & Keverne, E. B. (1991). Importance of vaginocervical stimulation for the formation of maternal bonding in primiparous and multiparous parturient ewes. *Physiology and Behavior, 50,* 595–600.

Kendrick, K. M., Lévy, F., & Keverne, E. B. (1992). Changes in the sensory processing of olfactory signals induced by birth in sheep. *Science, 256,* 833–836.

Keverne, E. B., & Kendrick, K. M. (1990). Neurochemical changes accompanying parturition and their significance for maternal behavior. In N. A. Krasnegor & R. B. Bridges (Eds.), *Mammalian parenting: Biochemical, neurobiological, and behavioral determinant* (pp. 281–304). New York: Oxford University Press.

Keverne, E. B., & Kendrick, K. M. (1991). Morphine and corticotrophin-releasing factor potentiate maternal acceptance in multiparous ewes after vaginocervical stimulation. *Brain Research, 540,* 55–62.

Keverne, E. B., Lévy, F., Guevara-Guzman, R., & Kendrick, K. M. (1993). Influence of birth and maternal experience on olfactory bulb neurotransmitter release. *Neuroscience, 56,* 557–565.

Keverne, E. B., Lévy, F., Poindron, P., & Lindsay, D. R. (1983). Vaginal stimulation: An important determinant of maternal bonding in sheep. *Science, 219,* 81–83.

Kinsley, C. H., & Bridges, R. S. (1990). Morphine treatment and reproductive condition alter olfactory preferences for pup and adult male odors in female rats. *Developmental Psychobiology, 23,* 331–347.

Kinsley, C. H., Madonia, L., Gifford, G. W., Tureski, K., Griffin, G. R., Lowry, C., et al. (1999). Motherhood improves learning and memory: Neural activity in rats is enhanced by pregnancy and the demands of rearing offspring. *Nature, 402,* 137–138.

Kinsley, C. H., Morse, A. C., Zoumas, C., Corl, S., & Billack, B. (1995). Intracerebroventricular infusions of morphine, and blockade with naloxone, modify the olfactory preferences for pup odors in lactating rats. *Brain Research Bulletin, 37,* 103–107.

Klopfer, P. H., Adams, D. K., & Klopfer, M. S. (1964). Maternal imprinting in goats. *Proceedings of the National Academy of Sciences of the United States of America, 52,* 911–914.

Koch, M. (1990). Effects of treatment with estradiol and parental experience on the number and distribution of estrogen-binding neurons in the ovariectomized mouse brain. *Neuroendocrinology, 51,* 505–514.

Komisaruk, B. R., Rosenblatt, J. S., Barona, M. L., Chinapen, S., Nissanov, J., O'Bannon III, R. T., et al. (2000). Combined c-fos and ^{14}C-2-deoxyglucose method to differentiate site-specific excitation from disinhibition: Analysis of maternal behavior in the rat. *Brain Research, 859,* 262–272.

Krehbiel, D., Poindron, D., Lévy, F., & Prud'Homme, M. J. (1987). Peridural anesthesia disturbs maternal behavior in primiparious and multiparous parturient ewes. *Physiology and Behavior, 40,* 463–472.

Kristal, M. B., Thompson, A. C., & Abbott, P. (1986). Ingestion of amniotic fluid enhances opiate analgesia in rats. *Physiology and Behavior, 38,* 809–815.

LeDoux, J. E. (1992). Emotion and the amygdala. In J. Aggleton (Ed.), *The amygdala: Neurobiological aspects of emotion, memory, and mental dysfunction* (pp. 339–351). New York: Wiley-Liss.

Lee, A., Li, M., Watchus, J., & Fleming, A. S. (1999). Neuroanatomical basis of maternal memory in postpartum rats: Selective role for the nucleus accumbens. *Behavioral Neuroscience, 113,* 523–538.

Leon, M. L. (1978). Filial responsiveness to olfactory cues in the laboratory rat. In D. S. Lehrman, R. A. Hinde, & E. Shaw (Eds.), *Advances in the study of behavior* (pp. 117–153). New York: Academic Press.

Lévy, F., Gervais, R., Kindermann, U., Litterio, M., Poindron, P., & Porter, R. (1991). Effects of early post-partum separation on maintenance of maternal responsiveness and selectivity in parturient ewes. *Applied Animal Behaviour Science, 31,* 101–110.

Lévy, F., Gervais, R., Kindermann, U., & Orgeur, P. (1990). Importance of b-noradrenergic receptors in the olfactory bulb of sheep for recognition of lambs. *Behavioral Neuroscience, 104,* 464–469.

Lévy, F., Guevara-Guzman, R., Hinton, M. R., Kendrick, K. M., & Keverne, E. B. (1993). Effects of parturition and maternal experience on noradrenaline and acetylcholine release in the olfactory bulb of sheep. *Behavioral Neuroscience, 107,* 662–668.

Lévy, F., Kendrick, K. M., Goode, J. A., Guevara-Guzman, R., & Keverne, E. B. (1995). Oxytocin and vasopressin release in the olfactory bulb of parturient ewes: Changes with maternal experience and effects on acetylcholine, gamma-aminobutyric acid, glutamate and noradrenaline release. *Brain Research, 669,* 197–206.

Lévy, F., Kendrick, K. M., Keverne, E. B., Piketty, V., & Poindron, P. (1992). Intracerebral oxytocin is important for the onset of maternal behavior in inexperienced ewes delivered under peridural anesthesia. *Behavioural Neuroscience, 106,* 427–432.

Lévy, F., Kendrick, K. M., Keverne, E. B., Proter, R. H., & Romeyer, A. (1996). Physiological, sensory, and experiential factors of prenatal care in sheep. In C. T. Snowdon (Ed.), *Advances in the study of behavior* (pp. 385–416). San Diego, CA: Academic Press.

Lévy, F., Locatelli, A., Piketty, V., Tillet, Y., & Poindron, P. (1995). Involvement of the main but not the accessory olfactory system in maternal behavior of primiparous and multiparous ewes. *Physiology and Behavior, 57,* 97–104.

Lévy, F., & Poindron, P. (1984). Influence du liquide amniotique sur la manifestation du comportement maternel chez la brebis parturiente [The influence of amniotic fluid on maternal behavior in parturient sheep]. *Biology and Behavior, 9,* 65–88.

Lévy, F., & Poindron, P. (1987). The importance of amniotic fluids for the establishment of maternal behavior in experienced and non-experienced ewes. *Animal Behaviour, 35,* 1188–1192.

Lévy, F., Poindron, P., & Le Neindre, P. (1983). Attraction and repulsion by amniotic fluids and their olfactory control in the ewe around parturition. *Physiology and Behavior, 31,* 687–692.

Li, M., & Fleming, A. S. (2003). Differential involvement of nucleus accumbens shell and core subregions in maternal memory in postpartum female rats. *Behavioral Neuroscience, 117*, 426–445.

Lisk, R. D. (1971). Oestrogen and progesterone synergism and elicitation of maternal nest-building in the mouse (Mus musculus). *Animal Behaviour, 17*, 730–738.

Lonstein, J. S., Simmons, D. A., & Stern, J. M. (1998). Functions of the caudal periaqueductal gray in lactating rats: Kyphosis, lordosis, maternal aggression, and fearfulness. *Behavioral Neuroscience, 112*, 1502–1518.

Lonstein, J. S., & Stern, J. M. (1997). Role of the midbrain periaqueductal gray in maternal nurturance and aggression: c-fos and electrolytic lesion studies in lactating rats. *Journal of Neuroscience, 17*, 3364–3378.

Lucas, B. K., Ormandy, C. J., Binart, N., Bridges, R. S., & Kelly, P. A. (1998). Null mutation of the prolactin receptor gene produces a defect in maternal behavior. *Endocrinology, 139*, 4102–4107.

Lundblad, E. G., & Hodgen, G. D. (1980). Induction of maternal-infant bonding in rhesus and cynomolgus monkeys after cesarean delivery. *Laboratory Animal Science, 30*, 913.

Maestripieri, D., & Zehr, J. L. (1998). Maternal responsiveness increases during pregnancy and after estrogen treatment in macaques. *Hormones and Behavior, 34*, 223–230.

Malenfant, S. A., Barry, M., & Fleming, A. S. (1991). Effects of cycloheximide on the retention of olfactory learning and maternal experience effects in postpartum rats. *Physiology and Behavior, 49*, 289–294.

Maletinska, J., Spinka, M., Vichova, J., & Stehulova, I. (2002). Individual recognition of piglets by sows in the early post-partum period. *Behaviour, 139*, 975–991.

Mayer, A. D. (1983). The ontogeny of maternal behavior in rodents. In R. W. Elwood (Ed.), *The ontogeny of maternal behavior in rodents* (pp. 1–21). Chichester, England: Wiley.

McCarthy, M. M. (1990). Oxytocin inhibits infanticide in female house mice (Mus domesticus). *Hormones and Behavior, 24*, 365–375.

Meier, G. W. (1965). Maternal behaviour of feral- and laboratory-reared monkeys following the surgical delivery of their infants. *Nature, 206*, 492–493.

Melamed, S., Ugarten, U., Shirom, A., Kahana, L., Lerman, Y., & Froom, P. (1999). Chronic burnout, somatic arousal and elevated salivary cortisol levels. *Journal of Psychosomatic Research, 46*, 591–598.

Meurisse, M., Gonzalez, A., Delsol, G., Caba, M., Lévy, F., & Poindron, P. (2005). Estradiol receptor-alpha expression in hypothalamic and limbic regions of ewes is influenced by physiological state and maternal experience. *Hormonal Behavior, 48*(1), 34–43.

Moffat, S. D., Suh, E. J., & Fleming, A. S. (1993). Noradrenergic involvement in the consolidation of maternal experience in postpartum rats. *Physiology and Behavior, 53*, 805–811.

Moretto, D., Paclik, L., & Fleming, A. (1986). The effects of early rearing environments on maternal behavior in adult female rats. *Developmental Psychobiology, 19*, 581–591.

Morgan, H. D., Fleming, A. S., & Stern, J. M. (1992). Somatosensory control of the onset and retention of maternal responsiveness in primiparous Sprague-Dawley rats. *Physiology and Behavior, 51*, 549–555.

Morgan, H. D., Watchus, J. A., Milgram, N. W., & Fleming, A. S. (1999). The long lasting effects of electrical simulation of the medial preoptic area and medial amygdala on maternal behavior in female rats. *Behavioural Brain Research, 99*, 61–73.

Murray, L. (1992). The impact of postnatal depression on infant development. *Journal of Child Psychology and Psychiatry, 33*, 543–561.

Negayama, K., & Honjo, S. (1986). An experimental study on developmental changes of maternal discrimination of infants in crab-eating monkeys (Macaca fascicularis). *Developmental Psychobiology, 19*, 49–56.

Neumann, I. D., Johnstone, H. A., Hatzinger, M., Liebsch, G., Shipston, M., Russell, J. A., et al. (1998). Attenuated neuroendocrine responses to emotional and physical stressors in pregnant rats involve adenohypophyseal changes. *Journal of Physiology, 508*, 289–300.

Neumann, I., Russell, J. A., & Landgraf, R. (1993). Oxytocin and vasopressin release within the supraoptic and paraventicular nuclei of pregnant, partutient and lactating rats: A microdialysis study. *Neuroscience, 53*, 65–75.

Nishimori, K., Young, L. J., Guo, Q., Wang, Z., Insel, T. R., & Matzuk, M. M. (1996). Oxytocin is required for nursing but is not essential for parturition or reproductive behavior. *Proceedings of the National Academy of Sciences of the United States of America, 93*, 11699–11704.

Nott, P. N., Franklin, M., Armitage, C., & Gelder, M. (1976). Hormonal changes and mood in the puerperium. *Journal of Psychiatry, 128*, 379–383.

Nowak, R., Porter, R. H., Lévy, F., Orgeur, P., & Schaal, B. (2000). Role of mother-young interactions in the survival of offspring in domestic mammals. *Reviews of Reproduction, 5*, 153–163.

Numan, M. (1988a). Maternal behavior. In E. Knobil and J. Neill (Eds.), *The physiology of reproduction* (pp. 1569–1645). New York: Raven.

Numan, M. (1988b). Neural basis of maternal behavior in the rat. *Psychoneuroendocrinology, 13*, 47–62.

Numan, M. (1994). Maternal behavior. In E. Knobil and J. D. Neill (Eds.), *The physiology of reproduction* (pp. 221–302). New York: Raven.

Numan, M., Corodimas, K. P., Numan, M. J., Factor, E. M., & Piers, W. D. (1988). Axon-sparing lesions of the preoptic region and substantia innominata disrupt maternal behavior in rats. *Behavioral Neuroscience, 102*, 381–396.

Numan, M., McSparren, J., & Numan, M. J. (1990). Dorsolateral connections of the medial preoptic area and maternal behavior in rats. *Behavioral Neuroscience, 104*, 964–979.

Numan, M., & Numan, M. J. (1994). Expression of Fos-like immunoreactivity in the preoptic area of maternally behaving virgin and postpartum rats. *Behavioral Neuroscience, 108*, 379–394.

Numan, M., & Numan, M. J. (1995). Importance of pup-related sensory inputs and maternal performance for the expression of Fos-like immunoreactivity in the preoptic area and ventral bed nucleus of the stria terminalis of postpartum rats. *Behavioral Neuroscience, 109*, 135–149.

Numan, M., & Numan, M. J. (1996). A lesion and neuroanatomical tract-tracing analysis of the role of the bed nucleus of the stria terminalis in retrieval behavior and other aspects of maternal responsiveness in rats. *Developmental Psychobiology, 29*, 23–51.

Numan, M., & Numan, M. J. (1997). Projection sites of medial preoptic area and ventral bed nucleus of the stria terminalis neurons that express Fos during maternal behavior in female rats. *Journal of Neuroendocrinology, 9*, 369–384.

Numan, M., Numan, M. J., & English, J. B. (1993). Excitotoxic amino acid injections into the medial amygdala facilitate maternal behavior in virgin female rats. *Hormones and Behavior, 27*, 56–81.

Numan, M., Rosenblatt, J., & Komisaruk, B. R. (1977). Medial preoptic area and onset of maternal behavior in the rat. *Journal of Comparative and Physiological Psychology, 91*, 146–164.

Numan, M., & Sheehan, T. P. (1997). Neuroanatomical circuitry for mammalian maternal behavior. *Annals of the New York Academy of Sciences, 807*, 101–125.

O'Hara, M. W., Schlechte, J. A., Lewis, D. A., & Wright, E. J. (1991). Prospective study of postpartum blues: Biological and psychsocial factors. *Archives of General Psychiatry, 48*, 801–806.

Orpen, B. G., & Fleming, A. S. (1987). Experience with pups sustains maternal responding in postpartum rats. *Physiology and Behavior, 40*, 47–54.

Orpen, B. G., Furman, N., Wong, P. Y., & Fleming, A. S. (1987). Hormonal influences on the duration of postpartum maternal responsiveness in the rat. *Physiology and Behavior, 40*, 307–315.

Pedersen, C. A., Caldwell, J. D., Johnson, M. F., Fort, S. A., & Prange, A. J., Jr. (1985). Oxytocin antiserum delays onset of ovarian steroid-induced maternal behavior. *Neuropeptides, 6*, 175–82.

Pedersen, C. A., Caldwell, J. D., Walker, C., Ayers, G., & Mason, G. A. (1994). Oxytocin activates the postpartum onset of rat maternal behavior in the ventral tegmental and medial preoptic areas. *Behavioral Neuroscience, 108*, 1163–1171.

Pedersen, C. A., & Prange, A. J. J. (1979). Induction of maternal behavior in virgin rats after intracerebroventricular administration of oxytocin. *Proceedings of the National Academy of Sciences of the United States of America, 76*, 6661–6665.

Pissonnier, D., Theiry, J. C., Fabre-Nys, P., Poindron, P., & Keverne, E. B. (1985). The importance of olfactory bulb noradrenalin for maternal recognition in sheep. *Physiology and Behavior, 35*, 361–363.

Poindron, P. (1976). Mother-young relationships in intact or anosmic ewes at the time of suckling. *Biology of Behaviour, 2*, 161–177.

Poindron, P., Gilling, G., Hernandez, H., Serafin, N., & Terrazas, A. (2003). Early recognition of newborn goat kids by their mother: I. Nonolfactory discrimination. *Developmental Psychobiology, 43*, 82–89.

Poindron, P., & Le Neindre, P. (1980). Endocrine and sensory regulation of maternal behavior in the ewe. In J. S. Rosenblatt, R. A. Hinde, & C. Beer (Eds.), *Advances in the study of behavior* (pp. 75–119). New York: Academic Press.

Poindron, P., & Lévy, F. (1990). Physiological, sensory and experiential determinants of maternal behavior in sheep. In R. S. Bridges (Ed.), *Mammalian parenting: Biochemical, neurobiological and behavioral determinants* (pp. 133–156). New York: Oxford University Press.

Poindron, P., Lévy, F., & Krehbiel, D. (1988). Genital, olfactory and endocrine interactions in the development of maternal behavior in the parturient ewe. *Psychoneuroendocrinology, 13*, 99–125.

Poindron, P., Martin, G. B., & Hooley, R. D. (1979). Effects of lambing induction on the sensitive period for the establishment of maternal behavior in sheep. *Physiology Behavior, 23*, 1081–1087.

Popik, P., & van Ree, J. M. (1998). Neurophyseal peptides and social recognition. *Progress in Brain, 119*, 415–436.

Popik, P., & Vetulani, J. (1991). Opposite action of oxytocin and its peptide antagonists on social memory in rats. *Neuropeptides, 18*, 23–27.

Porter, R. H., Cernoch, J. M., & McLaughlin, F. J. (1983). Maternal recognition of neonates through olfactory cues. *Physiology and Behavior, 30*, 151–154.

Pryce, C. R. (1993). The regulation of maternal behavior in marmosets and tamarins. *Behavioural Processes, 30*, 201–224.

Pryce, C. R. (1996). Socialization, hormones, and the regulation of maternal behavior in nonhuman primates. *Advances in the Study of Behavior, 25*, 423–473.

Pryce, C. R., Abbott, D. H., Hodges, J. K., & Martin, R. D. (1988). Maternal behavior is related to prepartum urinary estradiol levels in red-bellied tamarin monkeys. *Physiology and Behavior, 44*, 717–726.

Rees, S. L., Panesar, S., Fleming, A. S., & Steiner, M. (2004). The effects of adrenalectomy and corticosterone replacement on maternal behavior in the postpartum female rat. *Hormones and Behavior, 46*, 411–419.

Rosenberg, P. A., & Herrenkohl, L. R. (1976). Maternal behavior in male rats: Critical times for the suppressive action of androgens. *Physiology and Behavior, 16*, 293–297.

Rosenblatt, J. S. (1990). Landmarks in the physiological study of maternal behavior with special reference to the rat. In N. A. Krasnegor & R. S. Bridges (Eds.), *Mammalian parenting: Biochemical, neurobiological, and behavioral determinant* (pp. 40–60). New York: Oxford University Press.

Rosenblatt, J. S., & Snowdon, C. T. (1996). *Parental care: Evolution, mechanisms, and adaptive significance*. San Diego, CA: Academic Press.

Rubin, B. S., & Bridges, R. S. (1984). Disruption of ongoing maternal responsiveness in rats by central administration of morphine sulfate. *Brain Research, 307*, 91–97.

Rubin, B. S., Menniti, F. S., & Bridges, R. S. (1983). Intracerebroventricular administration of oxytocin and maternal behavior in rats after prolonged and acute steroid pretreatment. *Hormones and Behavior, 17*, 45–53.

Sagar, S. M., Sharp, F. R., & Curran, T. (1988). Expression of c-fos protein in brain: Metabolic mapping at the cellular level. *Science, 240*, 1328–1330.

Schaal, B., Coureaud, G., Langlois, D., Giniès, C., Sémon, E., & Perrier, G. (2003). Chemical and behavioural characterization of the rabbit mammary pheromone. *Nature, 424*, 68–72.

Schaal, B., Montagner, H., Hertling, E., Bolzoni, D., Moyse, A., & Quinchon, R. (1980). Les stimulations olfactives danes lesrelations entre l'enfants et la mere. *Reproduction, Nutrition, Development, 20*, 843–858.

Schneirla, T. C. (1959). An evolutionary and developmental theory of biphasic process underlying approach and withdrawal. In M. R. Jones (Ed.), *Nebraska symposium on motivation* (pp. 1–42). Lincoln: University of Nebraska Press.

Sheehan, T. P., & Numan, M. (1997). Microinjection of the tachykinin neuropeptide K into the ventromedial hypothalamus disrupts the hormonal onset of maternal behavior in female rats. *Journal of Neuroendocrinology, 9*, 677–687.

Shillito-Walser, E. E., Hague, P., & Walters, E. (1981). Vocal recognition of recorded lambs' voices by ewes of three breeds of sheep. *Behaviour, 78*, 260–272.

Shipka, M. P., & Ford, S. P. (1991). Relationship of circulating estrogen and progesterone concentrations during late pregnancy and the onset phase of maternal behavior in the ewe. *Applied Animal Behaviour Science, 31*, 91–99.

Shipley, M. T., Halloran, F. J., & de la Torre, J. (1985). Surprisingly rich projection from the locus coeruleus to the olfactory bulb in the rat. *Brain Research, 329*, 294–299.

Siegel, H. I., & Rosenblatt, J. S. (1975). Hormonal basis of hysterectomy-induced maternal behavior during pregnancy in the rat. *Hormones and Behavior, 6*, 211–222.

Siegel, H. I., & Rosenblatt, J. S. (1980). Hormonal and behavioral aspects of maternal care in the hamster: A review. *Neuroscience and Biobehavioral Reviews, 4*, 17–26.

Silva, M. R., Bernardi, M. M., Nasello, A. G., & Felicio, L. F. (1997). Influence of lactation on motor activity and elevated plus maze behavior. *Brazilian Journal of Medical and Biological Research, 30*, 241–244.

Smith, F. V., Van-Toller, C., & Boyes, T. (1966). The "critical period" in the attachment of lambs and ewes. *Animal Behaviour, 14*, 120–125.

Smotherman, W. P., Bell, R. W., Starzec, J., Elias, J., & Zachman, T. A. (1974). Maternal responses to infant vocalizations and olfactory cues in rats and mice. *Behavioral Biology, 12*, 55–66.

Soares, M. M., & Talamantes, F. (1982). Gestational effects on placental and serum androgen, progesterone, and prolactin-like activity in the mouse. *Journal of Endocrinology, 95*, 29–36.

Stallings, J., Fleming, A. S., Corter, C., Worthman, C., & Steiner, M. (2001). The effects of infant cries and odors on sympathy, cortisol, and autonomic responses in new mothers and nonpostpartum women. *Parenting: Science & Practice, 1*, 71–100.

Stein, A., Gath, D. H., Bucher, J., Bond, A., Day, A., & Cooper, P. J. (1991). The relationship between postnatal depression and mother-child interaction. *British Journal of Psychiatry, 158*, 46–52.

Stern, J. M. (1983). Maternal behavior priming in virgin and caesarean-delivered Long-Evans rats: Effects of brief contact or continuous exteroceptive pup stimulation. *Physiology and Behavior, 31*, 757–763.

Stern, J. M. (1989). Maternal behavior: Sensory, hormonal, and neural determinants. In F. R. Brush & S. Levine (Eds.), *Psychoendocrinology* (pp. 105–196). New York: Academic Press.

Stern, J. M. (1990). Multisensory regulation of maternal behavior and masculine sexual behavior: A revised view. *Neuroscience and Biobehavioral Reviews, 14*, 183–200.

Stern, J. M., Dix, L., Bellomo, C., & Thramann, C. (1992). Ventral trunk somatosensory determinants of nursing behavior in Norway rats: Role of nipple and surrounding sensations. *Psychobiology, 20*, 71–80.

Stern, J. M., & Johnson, S. K. (1989). Perioral somatosensory determinants of nursing behavior in Norway rats (Rattus norvegicus). *Journal of Comparative Psychology, 103*, 269–280.

Stern, J. M., & Kolunie, J. M. (1989). Perioral anesthesia disrupts maternal behavior during early lactation in Long-Evans rats. *Behavioral and Neural Biology, 52*, 20–38.

Sullivan, R. M., Zysak, D. R., Skierkowski, P., & Wilson, D. A. (1992). The role of olfactory bulb norepinephrine in early olfactory learning. *Developmental Brain Research, 70*, 279–282.

Swanson, L. J., & Campbell, C. S. (1979). Induction of maternal behavior in nulliparous golden hamsters (Mesocricetus auratus). *Behavioral and Neural Biology, 26*, 364–371.

Tagaki, T., Tanizawa, O., Otsuki, Y., Sugita, N., Haruta, M., & Yamaji, K. (1985). Oxytocin in the cerebrospinal fluid and plasma of pregnant and non pregnant subjects. *Hormonal and Metabolism Research, 17*, 308–310.

Terrazas, A., Ferreira, G., Lévy, F., Nowak, R., Serafin, N., Orgeur, P., et al. (1999). Do ewes recognize their lambs within the first day postpartum without the help of olfactory cues? *Behavioral Processes, 47*, 19–29.

Terrazas, A., Serafin, N., Hernandez, H., Nowak, R., & Poindron, P. (2003). Early recognition of newborn goat kids by their mother: II. Auditory recognition and evidence of an individual acoustic signature in the neonate. *Developmental Psychobiology, 43*, 311–320.

Trombley, P. Q., & Shepherd, G. M. (1992). Noradrenergic inhibition of synaptic transmission between mitral and granule cells in mammalian olfactory bulb cultures. *Journal of Neuroscience, 10*, 3985–3991.

Tucker, H. A. (1988). Lactation and its hormonal control. In E. Knobil, J. D. Neill, L. L. Ewing, C. L. Market, G. S. Greenwald, & D. W. Pfaff (Eds.), *Physiology of reproduction* (pp. 2235–2264). New York: Raven.

Uvnäs-Moberg, K. (1996). Neuroendocrinology of the mother-child interaction. *Trends in Endocrinology Metabolic, 7*, 126–130.

Van Leengoed, E., Kerker, E., & Swanson, H. H. (1987). Inhibition of postpartum maternal behavior in the rat by injecting an oxytocin antagonist into the cerebral ventricles. *Journal of Endocrinology, 112*, 275–282.

Vierin, M., & Bouissou, M. (2001). Pregnancy is associated with low fear reactions in ewes. *Physiology and Behavior, 72*, 579–587.

Voci, V. E., & Carlson, N. R. (1973). Enhancement of maternal behavior and nest building following systemic and diencephalic administration of prolactin and progesterone in the mouse. *Journal of Comparative and Physiological Psychology, 83*, 388–393.

Walsh, C. J., Fleming, A. S., Lee, A., & Magnusson, J. E. (1996). The effects of olfactory and somatosensory desensitization on Fos-like immunoreactivity in the brains of pup-exposed postpartum rats. *Behavioral Neuroscience, 110*, 134–153.

Wambolt, M. Z., & Insel, T. R. (1987). The ability of oxytocin to induce short latency maternal behavior is dependent on peripheral anosmia. *Behavioral Neuroscience, 101*, 439–441.

Wang, S. (1997). Traumatic stress and attachment. *Acta Physiologica Scandinavica, 161*, 164–169.

Williams, G. L., Gazal, O. S., Leshin, L. S., Stanko, R. L., & Anderson, L. L. (2001). Physiological regulation of maternal behavior in heifers: Roles of genital stimulation, intracerebral oxytocin release, and ovarian steroids. *Biology of Reproduction, 65*, 295–300.

Wilson, D. A., & Sullivan, R. M. (1994). Neurobiology of associative learning in the neonate: Early olfactory learning. *Behavioral and Neural Biology, 61*, 1–18.

Windle, R. J., Wood, S., Shanks, N., Perks, P., Conde, G. L., da Costa, A. P., et al. (1997). Endocrine and behavioural responses to noise stress: Comparison of virgin and lactating female rats during non-disrupted maternal activity. *Journal of Neuroendocrinology, 9*, 407–414.

Wisenfeld, A., Malatesta, C. Z., Whitman, P. B., Granrose, C., & Uili, R. (1985). Psychophysiological response of breast-and bottle-feeding mothers to their infants' signals. *Psychophysiology, 22*, 79–86.

Yeo, J. A., & Keverne, E. B. (1986). The importance of vaginal-cervical stimulation for maternal behaviour in the rat. *Physiology and Behavior, 37*, 23–26.

Young, L. J., Muns, S., Wang, Z., & Insel, T. R. (1997). Changes in oxytocin receptor mRNA in rat brain during pregnancy and the effects of estrogen and interleukin-6. *Journal of Neuroendocrinology, 9*, 859–865.

Yu, G. Z., Kaba, H., Okutani, F., Takahashi, S., & Higuchi, T. (1996). The olfactory bulb: A critical site of action for oxytocin in the induction of maternal behaviour in the rat. *Neuroscience, 72*, 1083–1088.

Yuan, Q., Harley, C. W., & McLean, J. H. (2003). Mitral cell beta1 and 5-HT2A receptor colocalization and cAMP coregulation: A new model of norepinephrine-induced learning in the olfactory bulb. *Learning and Memory, 10*, 1–14.

9

Play and the Development of Social Engagement: A Comparative Perspective

Sergio M. Pellis
Vivien C. Pellis

In both the human and the nonhuman animal literature, the study of play has had a rocky history in that play has been seen as either minor and irrelevant to the development of normal behavior, or as critical for normal development to occur (Sutton-Smith & Kelly-Byrne, 1984; Smith, 1988a). When seen as important, it has been claimed that play is necessary for the development of many physical, social, and cognitive skills. Unfortunately, empirical evidence in support of these hypothesized benefits is either absent or weak at best (Martin & Caro, 1985; Power, 2000). We believe there are two fundamental reasons for this confusion about play. First, play has tended to be a wastebasket category, often defined by what it is not, such as "any behavior without any apparent immediate purpose" (Bekoff & Byers, 1981). With such a loose definition, many behaviors end up being lumped together but are unlikely to form a coherent behavioral category. This has important implications for comparative research: A hypothesis about the developmental function of play derived from its structure and pattern of development in one species may be refuted when tested on another species. Second, utilitarian and cognitive perspectives have tended to focus on the development of skills. Indeed, the emphasis on skill acquisition via play has driven much of the developmental and comparative research (Power, 2000). However, the central role of emotional regulation in the proper exercise of physical and cognitive skills has only had a relatively recent reawakening (Damasio, 1994), and the link of play to emotional development has just begun to be touched upon (Bekoff, 2002; Fagen & Fagen, 2004). Thus, by having focused on the wrongly presumed benefits of play, researchers have found inconsistent evidence about the role of play in development. Resolution of these two problems leads to the realization that play is instrumental for the ability to engage in appropriate social interactions.

Even though playlike behavior occurs in a variety of species across the animal kingdom, it is most widespread among mammals (Burghardt, 2005). Even among mammals, however, some species do not play at all, and of those that do, the frequency and complexity of play are extremely variable across species (Iwaniuk, Nelson, & Pellis, 2001; Pellis & Pellis, 1998a). This diversity makes it difficult to ensure that the presumed play behaviors being compared are in fact the same phenomenon. The problem is further compounded by the fact that most play occurs in childhood, most markedly in the juvenile phase (i.e., between weaning and sexual maturity), which is a time when all systems are undergoing massive transformations (Gans, 1988; Spear, 2000). During these transitional stages, behavioral systems may be expressed in an incomplete form due to the inadequate maturity of the necessary control mechanisms. Thus, behavior patterns that are expressed in incomplete form are more than likely not associated with the typical, functional consequences present in adults. Such immature or precocial behavioral expression may be mistakenly labeled as play (Coppinger & Smith, 1989; Hogan, 1988; Kortland, 1955). If play were simply a synonym for immature behavior, then the term *play* would be of little added value. Therefore, a set of criteria that can distinguish play from immature behavior is needed (Burghardt, 2001, 2005). Given the emphasis on social engagement in this volume, we will focus our discussion on socially directed play to illustrate both the difference between immature behavior and play, and to develop the thesis that "true" play facilitates the development of an affective system that is capable of dealing with the vicissitudes of social interaction.

The most commonly occurring form of play in nonhuman animals is play fighting or rough-and-tumble play (Pellis & Pellis, 1998a). Even in humans, play fighting accounts for 5% to 10% of all play (Bjorklund & Pellegrini, 2002). Such play involves two or more animals competing for some advantage, which typically is to contact the partner on some specific body target (Aldis, 1975). These body targets are most commonly derived from targets that are contacted during conspecific aggression, sexual behavior, or predation in adulthood (Pellis, 1988; Pellis & Pellis, 1998b). In murid rodents (i.e., rats and their relatives), play fighting involves competition over the body targets contacted during the precopulatory phase of sexual interactions (Pellis, 1993). In play, one animal will attempt to contact the target, while the other attempts to prevent the partner from doing so. Following successful evasion, the defender may then launch an attack on its partner's target. When the pattern of attack and defense in juveniles is compared with the pattern present in adult interactions, marked differences emerge among species. In some species (e.g., voles), the pattern is similar between juvenile play and adult sex (Pellis & Pellis, 1998a). In contrast, for other species (e.g., rats), even though the same targets and behavior patterns are used, the organization of attack and defense during play fighting has little resemblance to that seen in sex. Therefore, in play fighting, the behavior patterns rarely present in sexual encounters are the most common, whereas the behavior patterns that are common during sex are the most uncommon in play (Pellis & Iwaniuk, 2004). These comparisons suggest that the structure of play fighting in voles is fairly close to what would be expected if it were the precocial expression of sexual behavior. This is not true for rats, in which play cannot be equated with immature behavior; this lends support to the argument that for such species, new levels of control have been added to transform immature behavior that appears "playlike" into "true" play (Pellis, 1993; Pellis & Iwaniuk, 2004). For comparisons to test the proposed functions of play, species with a comparable level of control over play need to be used. This necessity is reflected in studies on the developmental consequences of play.

Various studies have shown that depriving juvenile rats of peer contact leads to various social and nonsocial deficits in behavior and cognition after puberty (Moore, 1985). In contrast, mice, gerbils, and guinea pigs do not suffer from comparable deficits following such deprivation (Einon, Humphreys, Chivers, Field, & Naylor, 1981). Our comparative analyses suggest that mice, gerbils, and guinea pigs do not have true play, as do rats; rather, their juvenile, playlike behavior is closer to an immature expression of the adult pattern of sexual encounters (Pellis & Iwaniuk, 2004; Pellis & Pellis, 1998a). These studies suggest that grouping species together as "playful" when in fact only some have true play and others have some form of rudimentary play is likely to lead to confusion and, most important, to inappropriate critical tests of particular hypotheses about the developmental functions of play. Therefore, to be able to evaluate the functional consequences of experience in social play, all the species studied need to exhibit true play. Among rodents, rats have been shown to have true play, and although they do not have all the control mechanisms present in groups such as the higher primates (Iwaniuk et al., 2001; Pellis & Pellis, 1998a), they do share with these groups a pattern of juvenile play that cannot be classified as an immature expression of adult behavior. For this reason, when evaluating the experimental evidence for the functions of such play, special attention will be given to the literature on rats and primates, especially anthropoid primates (including humans).

The Functions of Juvenile Play

As indicated earlier, many functions for play have been proposed that are related to physical, social, and cognitive skill development (Fagen, 1981; Smith, 1978), but these have had little or no empirical support (Martin & Caro, 1985; Power, 2000). When only species with true play are considered, the evidence begins to look better. Indeed, rats and monkeys deprived of peer interactions during the juvenile phase exhibit consistent deficiencies in all these domains.

As mentioned previously, deficiencies in skills are likely to be the overtly measured manifestations of a deeper deficiency: Without play experience, emotional regulation is disrupted. In turn, this degrades the animal's capacity to use physical, social, and cognitive skills in their appropriate contexts. However, before this argument can be fleshed out, another problem needs to be resolved.

The classical experimental design for studying the effects of the lack of social play is to house the test animals in isolation for some period of time. In the absence of all social contact, it cannot be concluded that the resulting deficits, whatever they may be, are due to the lack of play (Bekoff, 1976). Two sets of experiments pinpoint social play as the key ingredient missing during this period of deprivation. The classic experiments by Harlow and his colleagues, in which they reared infant rhesus monkeys with only a terry cloth mother until adolescence, led to socially incompetent animals. As infants, these monkeys attracted hostile reactions from the mother-reared monkeys, and as adults they failed to engage in sexual behavior with a receptive member of the opposite sex (Harlow, Dodsworth, & Harlow, 1965; Sackett, 1968). However, if monkeys being reared by surrogate mothers are given half an hour a day of peer contact, and then are group housed, they integrate normally into the group and do not have sexual inadequacies as adults (Harlow & Suomi, 1971). These researchers called these daily peer contact episodes "playtime," and with good reason. In a variation of this procedure at the Washington Regional Primate Research Center in Seattle, young monkeys that have been weaned from their mothers are given daily periods of peer contact for approximately 30 minutes (Ruppenthal, Walker, & Sackett, 1991). From personal experience, we can attest to the fact that when these infants are together, virtually all their time is occupied with play. However, it could still be argued that it is the social contact itself that is crucial, rather than how the monkeys occupy that contact time.

A series of studies on rats done by Einon and her colleagues provides a clearer illustration that play is a crucial component of the juvenile social experience. First, observations of family groups showed that in a 24-hour period, juveniles played together for a total of 60 minutes. Second, it was found that social isolation during the juvenile phase led to a variety of social and cognitive deficits. Third, when the isolated juveniles were given access to a peer for 1 hour a day, these deficits were alleviated. However, providing the juveniles with access to a nonplayful, adult female did not alleviate the deficits (Einon, Morgan, & Kibbler, 1978). That is, the juveniles did not just need a warm body to huddle up against; they also needed the rigorous playful exchanges that are possible with peers (see also van den Berg et al., 1999; Holloway & Suter, 2004). Indeed, active, but nonplayful, drugged peers are not found rewarding by young rats and so are not sought out for interaction (Humphreys & Einon, 1981); if forced to interact with such unresponsive peers, undrugged rats find the experience aversive (Pellis & McKenna, 1995). Similarly, isolation housing where pairs of rats are separated by a wire mesh, and so have the opportunity to huddle, smell, and even groom one another, is not sufficient to offset later social deficiencies (Pellis, Field, & Whishaw, 1999). It should also be noted that many of these deficits that arise from social deprivation are the result of the rats being isolated during the juvenile phase, but not before or after this phase (Arakawa, 2003; Einon & Morgan, 1977).

Test paradigms in which rats that have been subjected to extended periods of social isolation are group housed for several weeks before testing (so as to subtract the effects of the acute stress of encountering another rat) still show the rats to have deficits (Einon & Potegal, 1991; Pellis et al., 1999; Potegal & Einon, 1989; Wright, Upton, & Marden, 1991). That is, the rats' deficiencies are chronic and arise from the isolation imposed upon them during the juvenile phase. Unlike the long-term effects of prolonged isolation, short-term isolation (between 1 and 24 hours) leads to an elevation of social behavior on reintroduction, which appears to be structurally and functionally the same as the social behavior that occurs in the home cage when the pups are living together (Pellis & Pellis, 1983, 1987, 1990). For the sake of the present argument, it is important to note that the social behavior of these short-term isolates mostly involves play fighting, and not other social behaviors, such as social investigation. Also, whether rats are deprived of only social play, or both social play and other social contact, when given the opportunity, they increase their engagement in play, not other forms of social behavior (Holloway & Suter, 2004). These data suggest that it is the lack of social play, and not general social contact, that is deficient during the period of isolation (Panksepp, 1981; Panksepp, Siviy, & Normansell, 1984; Pellis & Pellis, 1990).

The effects of social isolation in the juvenile phase have been shown to produce changes in the brain (Hall, 1998), such as a decrease in the density of striatal dopamine receptors. These effects are not reversed by subsequent resocialization after the juvenile phase (Bean & Lee, 1991). Furthermore, if juvenile rats are housed with a peer treated with haloperidol (a dopamine antagonist), which fails to interact as a result of the drug, the striatal dopamine receptor levels of the untreated rat are as low as those of juveniles that have been isolated (Bean & Lee, 1991). Thus, having a partner, even an age-matched one that is physically present, is not enough to offset the effects of isolation: The peers need to actively interact. Taken together, these studies strongly suggest that the deficiencies arising from social isolation during the juvenile phase result from the lack of interaction with peers, and, more specifically, that the crucial peer interactions are those that involve play. Of course, it is possible that the presence of cage mates may indirectly influence the subject's activity and interaction with the environment. For example, when rats are housed in enriched environments, more exploration and general activity occur if the rats are housed in groups (Rosenzweig & Bennett, 1972). However, some of the evidence presented strongly suggests that actual peer-peer interaction is a necessary factor for normal development.

Given that deprivation of social play during the juvenile phase leads to a wide range of deficiencies in the later stages of development, a question is raised as to what it is that is disturbed by the lack of play experience. A favorite explanation for the function of play, in both the professional (Caro, 1988) and lay (Angier, 1995) literature, is that play provides practice for physical, social, and cognitive skills. Closer examination of the scientific literature indicates that social play, in all its forms, is instrumental for the development of emotional regulation.

Mother cats bring live prey to their kittens (Baerends-van Roon & Baerends, 1979). The youngsters "play" with the prey, repeatedly attacking it until it is successfully killed or the mother intervenes with a killing bite. It has been argued that because such predatory play allows for practice, it enhances the physical skills needed for predation. However, attempts to show that play with prey or prey substitutes (such as inanimate objects) or with conspecifics improves predatory skills have failed (Hill & Bekoff, 1977; Caro, 1980). In the Hill and Bekoff (1977) study, some members of a coyote litter naturally engaged in more play than others, but this did not translate into superior predatory skill. In the Caro (1980) study, a different approach was used. It is known that different predatory techniques are used to dispatch different types of prey (e.g., Ben-David, Pellis, & Pellis, 1991). Therefore, different groups of kittens were given early practice with either mice or canaries, with the expectation that early play exposure to one type of prey should improve the skills needed to kill that prey type, but not the other. Irrespective of exposure, all the cats had equal facility with all types of prey as adults. It may be that playing with live prey when young is but one avenue by which predatory skills can be honed (Martin & Caro, 1985), and thus it is difficult to isolate the specific effects of play. However, there is another possibility.

It is well known that in a random selection of adult cats, some are better hunters than others (Leyhausen, 1979). In a study conducted on 10 cats born and raised in the laboratory, we found that on their very first exposure to live mice, three were excellent mouse killers, four engaged in long, playful interactions with the mice before finally killing them, and three did all they could to avoid the mice. Following an injection of the anxiolytic diazepam, all 10 cats interacted more forcefully with the mice: The three good killers became a little faster in their attacks, the "playful" killers became as quick and efficient as the good killers had been originally, and those that had previously avoided the mice became playful killers (Pellis et al., 1988). It is unlikely that an injection of diazepam improved the cats' physical skills. Rather, the most likely explanation is that the diazepam reduced the cats' fearfulness of the mice and so enabled them to shift their predatory behavior toward killing, but in an individual-specific manner. As has been noted, not all cats were the same at the beginning of the experiment: While some had little fear of mice, others appeared to have an extreme fear of them. The shift in behavior with the diazepam revealed a graded escalation toward killing, having little effect on the good killers and a strong effect on the more fearful ones. The suggestion that it is fear that was being modulated rather than physical skills is further indicated by the fact that when the good killers were confronted with larger prey (i.e., rats), they shifted their attacks to the playful mode seen in the moderate attackers when confronted with mice (see also Biben, 1979). Playful exposure to live prey as kittens may simply reduce the capacity for live prey to induce fear in the predator—playing with mice as a kitten may teach the animal that these little fur balls with tails are not so scary. That is, it is only once kittens do not react to prey with fear that they can gain potential skill enhancement from further interactions.

Consistent with the view that play may enhance or modulate emotional reactions is a growing literature showing that stress interferes with various neurobehavioral functions. It is well known that when an individual is stressed, cognition is impaired (McEwen & Sapolsky, 1995). For example, stressed rats perform poorly on cognitive tasks and exhibit heightened emotionality when placed in an open field (i.e., they freeze for longer periods of time, defecate more; Roozendaal, 2002). Similarly, stressed rats walk in a more stilted fashion (Metz, Schwab, & Welzl, 2001) and perform poorly on such skilled tasks as reaching (Gerlinde Metz, personal communication, August 2003). Heightened emotionality in stressed animals thus appears to erode both cognitive and motor function. In this light, playful experiences during the juvenile period that help dampen the intensity or duration of emotional responses arising from stressful situations would greatly enhance the ability of animals to function effectively in a wider range of contexts. Our reading of the literature on juvenile play and its long-term effects suggests that such a function for play is indeed plausible.

Juvenile Play Experience and the Development of Emotional Regulation

Evidence from both rats and monkeys suggest a similar role for social play with conspecifics in the development of social behavior and more general cognitive capabilities. For example, rats that are reared in social isolation during the juvenile phase (and are thus denied the chance to play) are more prone to get into fights with unfamiliar rats (Byrd & Briner, 1999; Lore & Flannelly, 1977; van den Berg et al., 1999). In part, this seems to be due to their hyperdefensiveness, in that they respond with inappropriate ferocity to a benign contact by another rat, but they do not seek out conspecifics to attack offensively (Arakawa, 2002; Einon & Potegal, 1991). That is, the isolates do not match their emotional response to another rat in an appropriately scaled manner but instead tend to overreact. The emotional inadequacy of rats reared in isolation has been clearly demonstrated in a recent set of studies (van den Berg et al., 1999; von Frijtag, Schot, van den Bos, & Spruijt, 2002). In standardized dyadic pairings with a large, unfamiliar male, isolates seemed to behave in a way that attracted attacks by the other animal (van den Berg et al., 1999). Similarly, when groups of young adults, composed of individuals that had been reared in groups or reared in isolation, were placed in large enclosures containing a large, unfamiliar, resident male, the isolates were more likely to be attacked. The rats that had been reared in groups decreased their level of activity and moved into a huddle or on top of a platform available in one corner of each enclosure (von Frijtag et al., 2002). In contrast, the rats that had been reared as isolates continued to move around and so attracted the attention of the resident male. Following removal of the resident male, the group-reared rats, but not the isolation-reared rats, increased their level of social play and allogrooming—two rewarding behaviors that likely serve to reduce the effects of stress (von Frijtag et al., 2002). The endocrinological profiles of group- and isolation-reared rats support the behavioral differences. In the group-reared rats, corticosterone levels spiked quickly, but also dissipated quickly, whereas in the isolation-reared rats, corticosterone persisted at high levels for longer (van den Berg et al., 1999). The authors suggested that play experiences fine-tune the coping skills needed for dealing with different social situations (van den Berg et al., 1999; von Frijtag et al., 2002). Play may thus have a more general effect on the development of emotional regulation, in that emotions can be scaled appropriately for the occasion, be it social or nonsocial.

In rats, relatively short-term social isolation of only 1 or 2 weeks during the juvenile phase can lead to impairments in adult social behavior, while nonsocial behaviors remain fairly intact (Hol, van den Berg, van Ree, & Spruijt, 1999; van den Berg et al., 1999). If the isolation is extended to include the whole juvenile phase, then the impairments extend to nonsocial as well as to social skills and behaviors (da Silva, Ferreira, de Padua Gorabrez, & Morato, 1996; Einon et al., 1978; although see Arakawa, 2003, for time sensitivity for nonsocial behaviors). When tested on an elevated plus-maze, rats that had been reared in social isolation from weaning (21 days) until puberty (60 days) failed to solve the problem. It could be concluded that this deficit reflects diminished cognitive abilities in isolates. In opposition to this conclusion, da Silva et al. (1996) showed that if these rats are given an injection of an anxiolytic, they are able to solve the problem as well as the control rats. Furthermore, if the controls are given an injection of an anxiogenic substance, their performance is degraded to the level of the isolates. That is, manipulating the fear state of the subjects changes their cognitive performance. The isolates are not cognitively impaired; they simply overreact emotionally to a situation, and it is this exaggerated emotional response that interferes with their ability to effectively bring their physical, cognitive, and social skills to bear on the problem at hand. Thus, by affecting emotional development, play can indirectly affect all manner of skilled actions.

Studies with monkeys tell a similar story. Male rhesus monkeys that have been reared in social isolation will fail to mount a sexually receptive female correctly. Such a monkey may mount from the front or side, but even if he does mount correctly from the rear, he may not use the normal foot clasp, in which the female's ankles are gripped by the male's feet. Similarly, a female that has been reared in social isolation will fail to present her rump appropriately to the male or will move inappropriately just as the male begins to mount; this will likely then lead to a failed copulatory attempt (Goy & Goldfoot, 1974). These deficits in sexual performance have also been interpreted as being due to impaired physical, social, or cognitive skills (Moore, 1985). However, when such isolates are presented with a carved wooden model of a monkey standing on all fours, these males have been shown to be quite capable of mounting the model from the rear and will even employ the normal foot clasp. Similarly, isolation-reared females can position themselves in front of this wooden model, present their rumps, and remain stationary in the appropriate manner (Deutsch & Larsson, 1974). These isolates are not impaired in their motor, social, or cognitive skills; rather, the live partner is frightening to them, and so they overreact to its slightest movement, thus failing to coordinate their movements effectively with those of their partner. The wooden model, however, because it is immobile and does not emit visual or vocal signals, is nonthreatening; thus, the animals are not fearful and so can perform the behavioral sequence appropriately. Once again, it is the inappropriate emotional response that interferes with the correct behavioral performance.

Another reasonably well-studied form of social play in primates is "play mothering," where a juvenile playfully handles an infant. Play mothering has been proposed to function as a means by which mothering skills are learned or perfected (Lancaster, 1971). A review of the literature on both New World and Old World monkeys suggests that although preadult experience is not essential for the later expression of maternal behavior, it can enhance its performance to some degree. However, the primary effect of play mothering appears to be a reduction of the fear evoked by an unfamiliar infant (Pryce, 1996). For example, female rhesus monkeys without play mothering experience spend more time out of arm's reach of the infant and lip-smack more (a species-typical fear response) at the infant (Holman & Goy, 1981). Again, the social play experience affects the animal's ability to regulate its emotional response, and this, in turn, affects its ability to perform appropriate actions in the correct context.

During the juvenile phase in rats, social isolation leads to decreases in brain levels of noradrenaline and dopamine and increases in serotonin levels; isolated rats are also more sensitive to the effects of amphetamine (Robbins, Jones, & Wilkinson, 1996; Siviy, 1998). That is, there are changes to the basic neurochemistry regulating the emotional-motivational systems. Not surprisingly, some of the core circuitry involved in play has been mapped to the limbic system (Panksepp, 1998). Indeed, brain imaging has shown that in children, activities such as play therapy stimulate the limbic system (work by Bruce Perry discussed by Blum, 2002, p. 287). Of course, play involves many brain systems (Pellis & Iwaniuk, 2004), but its performance seems to have a feedback effect on the limbic system (Gordon, Burke, Akil, Watson, & Panksepp, 2003) and, presumably, on its appropriate development. This suggestion is consistent with the data reviewed previously concerning the effects of the lack of play experience during the juvenile phase on the ability to respond appropriately to social and nonsocial contexts.

How Does Play Allow for the Fine-Tuning of Emotional States?

Data for children show that popular boys engage in more play fighting and are also better at solving social problems (Pellegrini & Boyd, 1993; Pellegrini & Smith, 1998). Indeed, it has been argued that some of the features of play fighting, such as restraint and role reversals between attacker and defender, are similar to the kinds of problems posed in social competency skills (see also Bekoff, 2002). This connection between play fighting and social problem solving may arise because play experience is so highly variable that it enhances the acquisition of flexibility in combining and recombining motor acts (Fagen, 1984). That is, the subjects may learn the connectivity of behavior patterns through play (Poirier & Smith, 1974). Some of the experimental and observational studies can be interpreted as animals with little or no play experience being less flexible in their responses (Einon et al., 1978; Enomoto, 1990). But exactly how is play experience translated into later flexibility? For at least two reasons, the connection between the two may be illusory, or the nature of the connection may need to be reconsidered.

Firstly, even though play in young animals does appear to be less stereotyped than behavioral sequences in adults (Poole & Fish, 1975; Yamada-Haga, 2002), the lack of predictability in behavior may be a function of childhood, and not of play. For example, a multidimensional scaling analysis of presumed communicatory body postures at three ages in wolves shows that the postural components become more structured with age (McLeod, 1996; for a nonmammalian example, see Lovern & Jenssen, 2003). Similarly, an information theory analysis of solitary and social behavior (not involving play) in dyads of rhesus monkeys at two ages (3 and 25 years) shows that the relative frequencies of behaviors predicted the behavior of the younger monkeys better than they did for the older ones, and that the preceding behavior predicted the behavior of the older monkeys better than it did for the younger ones. In essence, this suggests that younger subjects are more stereotyped in *what* behaviors they exhibit, whereas older subjects are more stereotyped in the *order* in which the behaviors are performed (Fitts, 1982). Thus, reduced serial order may be a function of age, not play, as the behaviors examined in these cases were not playful ones. Furthermore, the latter study reveals that at a different level of analysis, the behavior of younger animals *is* stereotyped. These studies not only belie the fact that a lack of stereotypy based on serial order is a function of age rather than a property of play but also have implications for the quality of playful experiences.

In Fitts's study, frequency and preceding behavior are more predictive in age-matched pairs than in age-disparate pairs, and both younger and older animals engaged in more affiliative behavior in age-matched pairs than they did with younger or older partners. Juveniles across a wide range of species prefer to play with other juveniles (Fagen, 1981). This preference may arise because age-matched peers have a similar pattern of organization in their behavior: Interactions with peers are therefore likely to be more pleasurable, partly because less adjustment is needed to accommodate a peer. Indeed, juvenile rats engage in play fighting just as readily with an unfamiliar juvenile as with a pairmate (Panksepp, 1981; Smith, Forgie, & Pellis, 1998). Although such play fights among unfamiliar juveniles may require some behavioral adjustments (Kahana, Rozin, & Weller, 1997), and may even result in escalation to serious aggression (Pellis & Pellis, 1991; Takahashi & Lore, 1983), neither the adjustment nor the escalation to aggression is as marked or as frequent as in postpubertal rats (Smith et al., 1998; Smith, Fantella, & Pellis, 1999; Takahashi, 1986). Unlike adults, juvenile rats do not show a difference in the stress response to familiar and unfamiliar play partners (Cirulli, Terranova, & Laviola, 1996). The role of the frequency of performance of motor actions in organizing the sequences of play fighting performed by juveniles may be undetected by observers, and so may give the mistaken impression that the behavior during play lacks structure. This impression may be enhanced by the fact that when playing together, one animal will facilitate the play of the other; by such contagion, the frequency of behavioral acts becomes even more exaggerated (Pellis & McKenna, 1992, 1995).

Second, even though the range of actions performed by juveniles during play may seem large, the organization of playful encounters is highly constrained so as to follow a particular script. During play fighting, many animals attack and defend particular body targets (Aldis, 1975). Once such a target is identified for a particular species, then any behavior pattern performed during a play fight can be evaluated with regard to whether it is associated with gaining access to the target or preventing a partner from gaining access to that target (Pellis & Pellis, 1998b). For example, in rats, play fights are organized around attack and defense of the nape area, which, if successfully contacted, is gently nuzzled with the snout (Pellis & Pellis, 1987; Siviy & Panksepp, 1987). Although rats may perform many actions during play fighting, such as pouncing, leaping, chasing, boxing, and wrestling (Meaney & Stewart, 1981; Takahashi & Lore, 1983; Taylor, 1980), most are in the service of gaining or avoiding nape contact (Pellis, 1988; Pellis & Pellis, 1987). When viewed from this perspective, the play fights of rats are very repetitive, with the animals basically repeating the same sequence of attack and defense again and again. A source of variation that can be misleading is when one sequence differs from another because the attacker or defender performs a different action for attack or defense, which in turn influences the actions of the partner. That is, a small deviation by one animal leads to a compensatory deviation by the other; this leads to a seeming lack of similarity between play bouts. But such a deviation away from a stereotyped routine can be seen to be superficial, once the target of attack and defense is identified.

It may be a mistake, then, to view play, especially by juveniles, as involving a near-random mixing of behavior patterns from various functional systems

(Heymer, 1977; Millar, 1981). The lack of stereotypy is only apparent, as is the intermixing of behavior patterns (Pasztor, Smith, MacDonald, Michener, & Pellis, 2001; Pellis, Pasztor, Pellis, & Dewsbury, 2000). Over broader spans of time, there may well be flexibility in the content of play fighting, but at any given instant, an animal's action is highly constrained by the target of attack and by the actions of its partner (Pellis & Pellis, 1998b). It is in this highly structured pattern of interaction that the possibility of using flexible responses must be understood. This leads to a modified view of flexibility in play. To reiterate, play fighting follows a strict routine, but within that routine the participants may enact small deviations away from the expected. The deviations that do not aid in attack and defense of the target or, indeed, those that may hamper such a functional outcome, are those most relevant to understanding the role of play in promoting the development of flexibility and its emotional underpinnings.

The core routine of play provides a safe, known set of actions that are familiar and hence nonaversive. The small deviations to this routine enable the subject to experience moderate novelty; this can enhance the experience and yet provide new knowledge about the situation without provoking an aversive response. From such a base, the subject can test the partner by adding novelty (as with flirting; Moore, 1995). If things get out of hand, the subject can always revert to a more stereotyped version of play, which is more calming and so reduces stress. Variability in play fighting thus occurs in small increments, from the vantage point of a well-established routine, and so provides partners with valuable information about the state of their relationships (see Wolf, 1984). This model can be thought of as one of "structured flexibility"—not unlike that which was proposed by Bowlby (1988) with regard to a toddler's use of its mother as a safe haven from which to make exploratory forays, or for rats establishing a home base when exploring a new test arena (Eilam & Golani, 1989). Two questions arise from this schema: Do animals really insert such incremental uncertainty into their play? And what is it about the experiences from these transgressions in their play that lead to emotional fine-tuning?

As has already been mentioned, play fighting in rats involves attack and defense of the nape of the neck, which, if contacted, is gently rubbed with the snout (Pellis, 1988). To achieve such contact, the attacker chases and pounces on its partner. To avoid this contact, the recipient can flee, jump, or dodge away, or it can actively defend itself by turning to face its partner and thereby blocking access to its own nape (Pellis & Pellis, 1987). What changes with age is the propensity to launch playful attacks and the types of defensive actions most likely to be used (Pellis, 2002b). In rats, the incidence of playful attack is most common in the central phase of the juvenile period (30–40 days postnatally; Thor & Holloway, 1984). In this phase, the most prevalent form of defense is to roll over onto one's back, thus blocking the partner's attempts to contact the nape (Pellis & Pellis, 1990, 1997a). For both males and females, in the week following weaning and preceding this peak pubertal period, rats are more likely to adopt defensive maneuvers that involve maintaining postural support on the ground with their hind paws. Similarly, with the onset of puberty, male rats switch from predominantly using the on-the-back defense to the standing defenses (Pellis, 2002b). Thus, in the juvenile phase, rats switch to using a pattern of defense that not only promotes body-to-body contact but also curtails the defender's capacity to counterattack successfully or to terminate the encounter. Because the defender is lying on its back, its mobility is limited, and so it is unable to maneuver into an advantageous position as readily as when it adopts a standing defense (Pellis & Pellis, 1987). That this preference for the on-the-back defense is not some accidental by-product of juvenility is suggested by the behavior of the partner standing on top of the supine defender.

When lying on its back, the defender squirms so as to block its partner's ongoing attempts to contact its nape. To gain control over the supine partner, and so limit its movements, the attacker places its forepaws on the defender's ventrum and keeps its hind paws planted on the ground. In this way, the movements of the forelimbs used to restrain the supine animal are buttressed against a firm base of support. Surprisingly, the attacker sometimes stands on the supine animal with all four paws, which reduces its stability, making it more likely to fall over (Foroud & Pellis, 2003) and so more likely for the supine defender to counterattack successfully. This leads to a nape contact by the original defender, which results in a role reversal (Pellis, Pellis, & Foroud, 2005). Thus, the rats will relinquish an anchored, stable posture for an unanchored, unstable posture. Both in early postweaning and with the onset of puberty, rats are most likely to adopt an anchored position when standing over a supine partner, whereas in the juvenile phase, the rats switch to adopting predominantly the unanchored posture (Foroud & Pellis, 2002). Therefore, at the age when the defender is most likely to adopt the supine defense, and so limit its ability to gain control over its attacker's movements, the attacker is most likely to adopt a posture that relinquishes its own advantage.

These findings for the correlated changes in the patterns of attack and defense support the idea that in their peak play period, rats adopt behaviors that are most likely to lead to a deviation from successfully contacting the partner's nape. That is, within the well-established routine of nape attack and nape defense, the rats interject movements that limit their success and that cause some uncertainty to arise as to which course of action will occur next. The pattern of play fighting in rats, especially in the juvenile phase, is consistent with play being conceptualized as involving "structured flexibility." In using the behaviors that they do, there is a moment-to-moment uncertainty in the bodily and spatial configuration of the rats. It has been suggested that play offers animals the opportunity to learn how to deal with the unexpected (Spinka, Newberry, & Bekoff, 2001). This example in rats provides a model for how the organization of play can be structured to provide the opportunity for experiences relevant for this function. It remains to be empirically determined if these experiences are indeed the ones needed for rats or other animals to fine-tune their emotional response to the sudden onset of an unexpected, and potentially aversive, social stimulus. Nonetheless, as has already been noted, rats with play experience can more quickly recover from an aversive social stimulus, and so are more able to engage rapidly in a course of action to lessen the potential danger from that stimulus (von Frijtag et al., 2002).

Data from rhesus macaques suggest the direct role of experiencing moderate levels of uncertainty in developing such coping skills. Mason and Berkson (1975), working with laboratory-raised rhesus monkeys that had been separated from their mothers at birth, gave the animals exposure to one of two types of artificial, cloth, surrogate mothers. While one group of artificial, cloth mothers remained stationary, the others, although otherwise identical, were mobile and moved up, down, and around the cage on an irregular schedule throughout the day. Later in life, those macaques reared by mobile surrogate mothers were more outgoing, were more likely to approach other animals, and made fewer threats and attacks than those that were reared by the stationary surrogate mothers (Mason & Berkson, 1975); they also were more attentive to novel social stimuli (Eastman & Mason, 1975). Furthermore, when they were 4 to 5 years old, these macaques were also more likely to engage in the proper sequencing of behaviors necessary to achieve copulation (Anderson, Kenney, & Mason, 1977). They thus behaved much more like animals that had been wild born and raised by natural mothers (Mason, 1978). A closer examination of the experiences of the monkeys reared by the mobile surrogate mothers shows a clear link to the experiences described earlier for play fighting. As noted by Mason, the movements of the mobile surrogate mothers were not predictable; they withdrew from the infant at one moment and bumped into its rear at another. Thus, the mobile surrogate mothers stimulated and sustained interactions with their infants, in that these infants were able to withdrew from them or chase, pounce on, and then wrestle with them. Infants reared with mobile surrogate mothers initiated such play fighting with their mothers three times more often than did infants reared by the stationary surrogate mothers (Mason, 1978). That is, the "mother"-infant experiences that most resembled those typical of play fighting—especially in providing an element of uncertainty in social interactions—had a subsequent bearing on the development of their coping skills. These data support the idea that play fighting has a role in developing coping skills and, most important, in developing the emotional substrates that underpin such skills.

A Model for the Developmental Role of Play Fighting

Rat pups that are given daily exposure to being handled by humans in the first 2 or 3 weeks postnatally show very different physiological and behavioral profiles as adults to those that have not been handled (Pryce & Feldon, 2003). Adult rats, if exposed to a stressor, such as being briefly restrained, respond with a release of adrenocorticotropic hormone (ACTH) by the pituitary gland. In turn, this causes a release of corticosteroid hormones from the adrenal glands, which prepare the body to cope with stressful environmental challenges. Whereas rats that have been handled in early development exhibit a sharp rise in these hormones followed by a rapid decrease in them, rats that have not been handled exhibit a slower onset of these hormones, and these levels remain higher for a longer period (van Oers, de Kloet, Li, & Levine, 1998). Concomitantly, other researchers have shown that rats that have been handled from infancy show a less inhibited behavioral response to novel situations, in that they are more likely to explore a novel enclosure and learn novel tasks (see review in Gandelman, 1992). Furthermore, since it has also been shown that aged rats that have been handled in infancy are still able to acquire new tasks more rapidly, it appears that these advantages persist well into adulthood (Anisman, Zaharia, Meaney, & Merali, 1998). These early handling effects appear to tap into the naturally occurring effects of maternal care on the young. During day-to-day mother-infant interactions, the mother will lick, step on, and carry her infants. She will also leave the infants periodically to feed or explore the surrounding area. Therefore, it is a normal part of an infant rat's experience to be unexpectedly handled—sometimes roughly—and to be deprived of its mother's presence for brief periods.

It is important to note that the consequences of the experimentally induced effects of handling appear to depend on the levels of stress experienced as infants. Brief handling, accompanied by short periods of separation from the mother, seem to have a positive effect on the development of the physiological and behavioral responses to stressors later in life. In contrast, a more prolonged separation from the mother can lead to a longer-lasting hormonal response and a greater expression of behaviors that indicate heightened anxiety levels (Boccia & Pedersen, 2001; Ogawa et al., 1994; Plotsky & Meaney, 1999; Pryce, Bettschen, Barhr, & Feldon, 2001; Pryce, Bettschen, & Feldon, 2001; Suchecki, Nelson, van Oers, & Levine, 1995). That is, it seems that the effects of early stress on the development of the stress-response system are most beneficial when the stress is of moderate intensity. Under normal conditions of rearing, mother rats of laboratory strains provide too little stimulation; the short bouts of handling and separation stimulate additional maternal attention, and so benefit the development of the stress-response system (Bateson & Martin, 2000). But as noted earlier, too much maternal deprivation or stimulation may be detrimental (e.g., Allen, 1995; Zahr & Balian, 1995). Indeed, several studies suggest that positive benefits, for the optimal development of several morphological, physiological, and behavioral systems, may accrue from experiencing mild stress during early infancy (Gandelman, 1992).

Thus, the literature on early handling suggests that exposure to some of the normal trials and tribulations of life is good for the development of a variety of neurobehavioral systems, including an affective system that has a good range of responses to the events in the world impinging on an individual. These effects, however, are very general, as the infant does not have the sensory, motor, and cognitive capacities to link these mild stressors to particular features of its environment. We suggest that the experience of play in the juvenile phase, an age after which animals typically benefit from these general effects of mild stress, provides animals with the opportunity to fine-tune the affective response system and, more specifically, to learn to associate particular stimuli and actions with particular emotional states. In this model, we envision that play fighting between peers provides fine-tuning that is additive to those effects on the affective system derived from maternal interactions. Of course, while all mammals should experience the early maternal effects, not all mammals demonstrate play, and so only some species will have the added benefits that experiencing play fighting provides.

Several predictions arise from this hypothesis: (a) Species that play should have a greater range of responses to social situations than animals with only the early handling effects; (b) the effects of early handling should not affect the effects of juvenile play, or, if they do, should do so only indirectly; (c) the experience of play should be linked to better coping skills; (d) the behavior performed during play should provide experiences with moderate degrees of uncertainty; and (e) individuals with more play experience should be better at making subtle distinctions between similarly appearing social contexts. We will now examine each of these predictions in turn.

Adult male rats that encounter each other for the first time in a neutral arena will investigate one another and will then proceed to interact by engaging in play fighting. This play fighting will be a rougher version than that seen in juveniles. These playful interactions will lead either to the formation of a dominance-subordinance relationship or to a serious fight, which will then, in turn, lead to the formation of a dominance-subordinance relationship (Smith et al., 1999). In contrast, adult male mice in a similar situation have only one option following the initial social investigation. If, based on this information, one male does not assume a subordinate role, a serious fight to determine dominance will follow (Pellis, 2002a). That is, mice have fewer options than rats. As juveniles, rats, but not mice, engage in play fighting (Pellis & Pasztor, 1999; Poole & Fish, 1975). Like mice, but unlike rats, many other species of murid rodents that do engage in play fighting as juveniles do not have the capacity to use play fighting in adulthood (Pellis & Pellis, 1998a). It appears that by having added novel levels of control over the expression of play, the rat lineage is able to use play in various contexts in adulthood (Pellis & Iwaniuk, 2004). Yet not only rats but also mice and other laboratory animals have been shown to exhibit early handling effects (Denenberg, 1958; Wyly, Denenberg, de Santis, Burns, & Zarrow, 1975). Therefore, the effects of juvenile play fighting on coping styles are additive to, if not independent of, those arising from early handling experiences.

Many primates and carnivores, like rats, also make use of playful modes of interaction to manipulate social situations in adulthood (Pellis & Iwaniuk, 2000). Furthermore, these uses are particularly evident in the adolescent and early adult stages of development (Pellis, 2002a) and have been identified in postpubescent children for the purposes of reinforcing relationships and testing the limits of those relationships (Pellegrini, 1994, 1995b). In humans, both in the teenage years (Lockard & Adams, 1980; Moore, 1995) and in early adulthood (Ballard, Green, & Granger, 2003), "play-fighting-like" forms of contact are employed during flirtation. Indeed, in humans, the use of play-fighting styles of interaction in dominance relationships, during affiliative encounters, and during courtship suggests that, as in rats, experiences accrued during juvenile play fighting may be instrumental in fine-tuning coping skills and associated strategies.

Another piece of evidence indicating that the effects of neonatal handling on the stress-response system are independent from those arising from play fighting is that handling does not seem to affect the performance or structure of play fighting. Rats subjected to neonatal handling and maternal separation do not play in a manner different than that of controls, although there is one indirect effect: It appears that these early experiences can have a feminizing effect on the structure of the play fighting in males (Arnold & Siviy, 2002). That is, it seems that the hormonal changes induced during these early experiences can damage the normal processes of masculinization. Nonetheless, even though the early handled rats showed less anxiety-related behaviors during playful encounters, the frequency of the play was unaffected. The positively rewarding features of play fighting in the juvenile phase (Panksepp, 1998; Siviy, 1998) do not seem to be adversely affected by the presence or absence of neonatal handling. And, as has already been noted, play experience, especially of the social form seen in rats, has an effect on the subsequent development of coping strategies (van den Berg et al., 1999; von Frijtag et al., 2002). Therefore, the effects of play are independent or additive to those of early handling, and the presence of play experience in the juvenile phase influences the expression of coping skills later in life.

As with Mason's mobile surrogate mothers, we have seen that the juvenile phase of play fighting by rats involves the orchestration of situations that increase the uncertainty of the events to follow, as rats appear to relinquish the control they have over their partner's and their own actions (Pellis et al., 2005). Comparative evidence suggests that actions that promote such uncertainty are also present in the play of other species, especially in many species of primates (Pellis & Pellis, 1998b). Indeed, many species of carnivores and primates use signals to defuse playful situations if they escalate to more aversive levels (Bekoff, 1995; Pellis & Pellis, 1996). For example, an unexpected, overly firm bite to the partner's rump may lead them to turn and threaten the perpetrator. The perpetrator may then maintain a facing orientation and perform a signal that informs the recipient that the bite was a playful one (e.g., Pellis & Pellis, 1997b). It thus appears that for many animals, there are behavioral mechanisms by which playful interactions can be maintained so as to provide a moderate degree of uncertainty.

Starting with the seminal work of Bandura (Bandura, Ross, & Ross, 1961) and continuing to the present (e.g., Potts, Huston, & Wright, 1986; Sanson &

DiMuccio, 1993), a major difficulty with the studies related to the effects of observational learning on the development of aggression has been in the confounding of playful and serious aggression (Smith, 1994; Sutton-Smith, Gerstmyer, & Meckley, 1988). For example, the films of children's attacks on the bobo dolls that are available from Bandura's classic studies often show the children with facial expressions typical of play, not aggression (Smith, 1988b). Although episodes of punching and kicking may be codified as aggression by the adult researchers, this does not mean that the children who are involved view their actions as aggressive. Playful and aggressive fighting can be distinguished by a variety of behavioral criteria (Blurton Jones, 1967; Boulton, 1991; Costabile et al., 1991; Fry, 1987). Moreover, when children are involved, the judgments of the observers can be confirmed by asking the children themselves (Smith, Smees, & Pellegrini, 2004). It appears, then, that when children are engaged in play fighting, they are cognizant that this is "make-believe," and that what is operating within this framework is not to be counted as aggression (Goldstein, 1995). Indeed, very aggressive boys, who do not play within the agreed-upon framework, are excluded more often from opportunities to engage in play fighting (Willmer, 1991). Clearly, although the two forms of fighting can be distinguished, making the distinction is not necessarily easy.

The judgment of whether children are playing or are engaged in aggression is also influenced by the age, sex, and experience of the observers (Goldstein, 1992, 1995). For example, child observers are generally better able to make the distinction between play fighting and aggression than are adult observers (Smith & Boulton, 1990). Furthermore, of adult observers, women are more likely to interpret play fighting as aggression than are men, although if the women have engaged in play fighting as children, they are more apt to interpret such interactions as play (Conner, 1989). Nonetheless, given that play fighting can shift back and forth from gentle to rough depending on age, sex, and social context (Pellis, 2002a, 2002b; Pellis et al., 2005), the distinctions to be made may become quite subtle. For example, an episode of play fighting can be either prosocial and affiliative or antisocial and aggressive, depending on the socioeconomic standing of the children and their relationships (Pellegrini, 1989, 1994). The little evidence available for humans suggests that individuals who have more personal experience with play fighting are the ones more likely to make accurate distinctions between observed episodes of playful and serious fighting.

In nonhuman animals, those with play experience in the juvenile phase are seemingly better skilled at distinguishing between the aggressive and nonaggressive actions of conspecifics (e.g., Byrd & Briner, 1999; Einon & Potegal, 1991; Potegal & Einon, 1989) and in not provoking aggressive responses from others (van den Berg et al., 1999; von Frijtag et al., 2002). These animals may have these enhanced capabilities because they are better at making distinctions about the meaning of the actions of the other animal as well as their own, or because they are more competent in solving a social problem.

Indeed, the finding that it is socially experienced rats, not socially inexperienced rats, that seek the relative safety of a small platform to avoid a large, male, resident intruder (von Frijtag et al., 2002) indicates some enhanced skill in solving social problems. Similarly, in the human literature, when researchers focus on features of social problem solving that are comparable to the problems of reciprocity encountered in play fighting, there does seem to be an effect of play experience on subsequent social competence (Pellegrini, 1995a).

In summary, all five predictions arising from the hypothesis that juvenile play fighting experience fine-tunes the development of the stress-response system in a way that enhances the individual's ability to respond appropriately when faced with novel social challenges have been shown to receive support from the existing literature. These findings provide a good degree of confidence in the use of juvenile play fighting as a research tool for examining the linkage between emotional, motor, and cognitive systems.

Conclusion

The model developed and presented in this chapter shows that social play experience provides the opportunity to fine-tune the stress-response system and emotional regulation in general, in a way that builds on the effects of early maternally derived enhancement of these systems. During play fighting, juveniles learn the emotive value of particular events, which can be generated by themselves or a conspecific. Through play, juveniles learn that social interactions may involve some pain and uncertainty, and so dampen their emotional weighting in order for that discomfort to be regarded as "background noise." In this way, animals with play experience are better able to prevent an overreaction to a particular situation, and instead produce more subtle and graded responses to novel, social contexts (Biben, 1998; Pellis & Pellis, 1998b). After all, overreacting to a situation by being too scared or too angry can interfere with one's decision-making processes. Overreacting or underreacting may lead to maladaptive responses, such as fleeing when it is better to remain still, or remaining still when it is better to flee (von Frijtag et al., 2002). Such impulse control can be impaired by experimentally damaging the amygdala and related limbic structures (Bachevalier, Malkova, & Mishkin, 2001; Emery et al., 2001). The negative effects of early lesions in these brain areas (Daenen, Wolterink, Gerrits, & van Ree, 2002) can be attenuated by social rearing, whereby the youngsters gain experiences from interacting playfully with intact peers (Diergaarde, Gerrits, Stuy, Spruijt, & van Ree, 2004). Social experiences with peers in the juvenile phase therefore are important not only for fine-tuning the ability to regulate emotional responses to particular situations but also can even reduce limitations in behavioral regulation arising from brain damage to emotional centers. Understanding the exact content of the juvenile play experiences that serve these therapeutic benefits may greatly enhance our ability to develop rehabilitation regimes for various neurodevelopmental disorders (e.g., as in autism; Goldstein, 2002; Parsons & Mitchell, 2002).

References

Aldis, O. (1975). *Play fighting*. New York: Academic Press.

Allen, A.-M. (1995). Stressors to neonates in the neonatal unit. *Midwives, 108*, 139–140.

Anderson, C. O., Kenney, A. M., & Mason, W. A. (1977). Effects of maternal mobility, partner, and endocrine state on social responsiveness of adolescent rhesus monkeys. *Developmental Psychobiology, 10*, 421–434.

Angier, N. (1995). *The beauty of the beastly*. Boston: Houghton Mifflin.

Anisman, H., Zaharia, M. D., Meaney, M. J., & Merali, Z. (1998). Do early life events permanently alter behavioral and hormonal responses to stressors? *International Journal of Developmental Neuroscience, 16*, 149–164.

Arakawa, H. (2002). The effects of age and isolation period on two phases of behavioral response to foot shock in isolation-reared rats. *Developmental Psychobiology, 41*, 15–24.

Arakawa, H. (2003). The effects of isolation rearing on open-field behavior in male rats depends on developmental stages. *Developmental Psychobiology, 43*, 11–19.

Arnold, J. L., & Siviy, S. M. (2002). Effects of neonatal handling and maternal separation on rough-and-tumble play in the rat. *Developmental Psychobiology, 41*, 205–215.

Bachevalier, J., Malkova, L., & Mishkin, M. (2001). Effects of selective temporal lobe lesions on socioemotional behavior in infant rhesus monkeys (*Macaca mulatta*). *Behavioral Neuroscience, 115*, 545–559.

Baerends-van Roon, J. M., & Baerends, G. P. (1979). *The morphogenesis of the behavior of the domestic cat, with a special emphasis on the development of prey catching*. Amsterdam: North Holland.

Ballard, M. E., Green, S., & Granger, C. (2003). Affiliation, flirting, and fun: Mock aggressive behavior in college students. *Psychological Record, 53*, 33–49.

Bandura, A., Ross, D., & Ross, S. A. (1961). Transmission of aggression through imitation of aggressive models. *Journal of Abnormal and Social Psychology, 63*, 575–582.

Bateson, P., & Martin, P. (2000). *Design for life*. New York: Simon and Schuster.

Bean, G., & Lee, T. (1991). Social isolation and cohabitation with haloperidol-treated partners: Effect on density of striatal dopamine D2 receptors in the developing rat brain. *Psychiatry Research, 36*, 307–317.

Bekoff, M. (1976). The social deprivation paradigm: Who's being deprived of what? *Developmental Psychobiology, 9*, 499–500.

Bekoff, M. (1995). Play signals as punctuation: The structure of social play in canids. *Behavior, 132*, 419–429.

Bekoff, M. (2002). *Minding animals*. New York: Oxford University Press.

Bekoff, M., & Byers, J. A. (1981). A critical reanalysis of the ontogeny and phylogeny of mammalian social and locomotor play: An ethological hornet's nest. In K. Immelmann, G. W. Barlow, L. Petrinovich, & M. Main (Eds.), *Behavioral development: The Bielefield interdisciplinary project* (pp. 155–168). Cambridge, England: Cambridge University Press.

Ben-David, M., Pellis, S. M., & Pellis, V. C. (1991). Feeding habits and predatory behavior of marbled polecats (*Vormella peregusna syriaca*): I. Killing methods in relation to prey size and prey behavior. *Behavior, 118*, 127–143.

Biben, M. (1979). Predation and play behavior of domestic cats. *Animal Behavior, 27*, 81–94.

Biben, M. (1998). Squirrel monkey play fighting: Making the case for a cognitive training function for play. In M. Bekoff & J. A. Byers (Eds.), *Animal play: Evolutionary, comparative, and ecological perspectives* (pp. 161–182). Cambridge, England: Cambridge University Press.

Bjorklund, D. F., & Pellegrini, A. D. (2002). *The origins of human nature*. Washington, DC: American Psychological Association.

Blum, D. (2002). *Love at Goon Park: Harry Harlow and the science of affection*. Cambridge, MA: Perseus.

Blurton Jones, N. (1967). An ethological study of some aspects of social behavior of children in nursery school. In D. Morris (Ed.), *Primate ethology* (pp. 347–368). London: Weidenfeld and Nicolson.

Boccia, M. L., & Pedersen, C. (2001). Animal models of critical and sensitive periods in social and emotional development. In D. B. Bailey & F. J. Symons (Eds.), *Critical thinking about critical periods* (pp. 107–127). Baltimore: Brookes.

Boulton, M. J. (1991). A comparison of structural and contextual features of middle school children's playful and aggressive fighting. *Ethology and Sociobiology, 12*, 119–145.

Bowlby, J. (1988). *A secure base: Parent-child attachment and healthy human development*. New York: HarperCollins.

Burghardt, G. M. (2001). Play: Attributes and neural substrates. In E. M. Blass (Ed.), *Handbook of behavioral neurobiology: Vol. 15. Developmental psychobiology, developmental neurobiology and behavioral ecology: Mechanisms and early principles* (pp. 317–356). New York: Kluwer Academic/Plenum.

Burghardt, G. M. (2005). *The genesis of play*. Cambridge, MA: MIT Press.

Byrd, K. R., & Briner, W. E. (1999). Fighting, nonagonistic social behavior, and exploration in isolation-reared rats. *Aggressive Behavior, 25*, 211–223.

Caro, T. M. (1980). The effects of experience on the predatory patterns of cats. *Behavioral and Neural Biology, 29*, 1–28.

Caro, T. M. (1988). Adaptive significance of play: Are we getting closer? *Trends in Ecology and Evolution, 3*, 50–54.

Cirulli, F., Terranova, M. L., & Laviola, G. (1996). Affiliation in periadolescent rats: Behavioral and corticosterone response to social reunion with familiar or unfamiliar partners. *Pharmacology, Biochemistry and Behavior, 54*, 99–105.

Conner, K. (1989). Aggression: In the eye of the beholder? *Play and Culture, 2*, 213–217.

Coppinger, R. P., & Smith, C. K. (1989). A model for understanding the evolution of mammalian behavior. In H. Genoways (Ed.), *Current mammalogy* (Vol. 2, pp. 53–73). New York: Plenum.

Costabile, A., Smith, P. K., Matheson, L., Aston, J., Hunter, T., & Boulton, M. (1991). A cross-national comparison of how children distinguish serious and playful fighting. *Developmental Psychology, 27*, 881–887.

Daenen, E. W., Wolterink, G., Gerrits, M. A., & van Ree, J. M. (2002). The effects of neonatal lesions in the amygdala or ventral hippocampus on social behavior later in life. *Behavioral Brain Research, 136*, 571–582.

Damasio, A. R. (1994). *Descartes' error*. New York: Avon.

da Silva, N. L., Ferreira, V. N. M., de Padua Gorabrez, A., & Morato, G. S. (1996). Individual housing from weaning modifies the performance of young rats on elevated plus-maze apparatus. *Physiology and Behavior, 60*, 1391–1396.

Denenberg, V. H. (1958). The effects of age and early experience upon conditioning in the C57BL/10 mouse. *Journal of Psychology, 46*, 211–226.

Deutsch, J., & Larsson, K. (1974). Model oriented sexual behavior in surrogate-reared rhesus monkeys. *Brain, Behavior and Evolution, 9*, 157–164.

Diergaarde, L., Gerrits, M. A. F. M., Stuy, A., Spruijt, B. M., & van Ree, J. M. (2004). Neonatal basolateral lesions and play deprivation in the rat: Differential effects on locomotor and social behavior later in life. *Behavioral Neuroscience, 118*, 298–305.

Eastman, R. F., & Mason, W. A. (1975). Looking behavior in monkeys raised with mobile and stationary artificial mothers. *Developmental Psychobiology, 8*, 213–222.

Eilam, D., & Golani, I. (1989). Home base behavior of rats (*Rattus norvegicus*) exploring a novel environment. *Behavioral Brain Research, 34*, 199–211.

Einon, D. F., Humphreys, A. P., Chivers, S. M., Field, S., & Naylor, V. (1981). Isolation has permanent effects upon the behavior of the rat, but not the mouse, gerbil, or guinea pig. *Developmental Psychobiology, 14*, 343–355.

Einon, D. F., & Morgan, M. J. (1977). A critical period for social isolation in the rat. *Developmental Psychobiology, 10*, 123–132.

Einon, D. F., Morgan, M. J., & Kibbler, C. C. (1978). Brief periods of socialization and later behavior in the rat. *Developmental Psychobiology, 11*, 213–225.

Einon, D. F., & Potegal, M. (1991). Enhanced defence in adult rats deprived of playfighting experience as juveniles. *Aggressive Behavior, 17*, 27–40.

Emery, N. J., Capitanio, J. P., Mason, W. A., Machado, C. J., Mendoza, S. P., & Amaral, D. G. (2001). The effects of bilateral lesions of the amygdala on dyadic social interactions in rhesus monkeys (*Macaca mulatta*). *Behavioral Neuroscience, 115*, 515–544.

Enomoto, T. (1990). Social play and sexual behavior of the bonobo (*Pan paniscus*) with special reference to flexibility. *Primates, 31*, 469–480.

Fagen, R. (1981). *Animal play behavior*. New York: Oxford University Press.

Fagen, R. (1984). Play and behavioral flexibility. In P. K. Smith (Ed.), *Play in animals and humans* (pp. 159–173). Oxford, England: Blackwell.

Fagen, R., & Fagen, J. (2004). Juvenile survival and benefits of play behaviour in brown bears, *Ursus arctos*. *Evolutionary Ecology Research, 6*, 89–102.

Fitts, S. S. (1982). Behavioral stereotypy in old and young rhesus monkeys. *Primates, 23*, 406–415.

Foroud, A., & Pellis, S. M. (2002). The development of "anchoring" in the play fighting of rats: Evidence for an adaptive age-reversal in the juvenile phase. *International Journal of Comparative Psychology, 15*, 11–20.

Foroud, A., & Pellis, S. M. (2003). The development of "roughness" in the play fighting of rats: A Laban Movement Analysis perspective. *Developmental Psychobiology, 42*, 35–43.

Fry, D. P. (1987). Differences between playfighting and serious fighting among Zapotec children. *Ethology and Sociobiology, 8*, 285–306.

Gandelman, R. (1992). *The psychobiology of behavioral development*. Oxford, England: Oxford University Press.

Gans, C. (1988). Adaptation and the form-function relation. *American Zoologist, 28*, 681–697.

Goldstein, H. (2002). Communication intervention for children with autism: A review of treatment efficacy. *Journal of Autism and Developmental Disorders, 32*, 373–396.

Goldstein, J. H. (1992). Sex differences in aggressive play and toy preference. In K. Bjorkquist & P. Niemela (Eds.), *Of mice and women: Aspects of female aggression* (pp. 65–76). San Diego, CA: Academic Press.

Goldstein, J. H. (1995). Aggressive toy play. In A. D. Pellegrini (Ed.), *The future of play theory* (pp. 127–147). Albany: State University of New York, Press.

Gordon, N. S., Burke, S., Akil, H., Watson, S. J., & Panksepp, J. (2003). Socially-induced brain "fertilization": Play promotes brain derived neurotrophic factor transcription in the amygdala and dorsolateral frontal cortex in juvenile rats. *Neuroscience Letters, 341*, 17–20.

Goy, R. W., & Goldfoot, D. A. (1974). Experiential and hormonal factors influencing development of sexual behavior in the male rhesus monkey. In F. O. Schmitt & F. G. Worden (Eds.), *The neurosciences: Third study program* (pp. 571–581). Cambridge, MA: MIT Press.

Hall, F. S. (1998). Social deprivation of neonatal, adolescent, and adult rats has distinct neurochemical and behavioral consequences. *Critical Reviews in Neurobiology, 12*, 129–162.

Harlow, H. F., Dodsworth, R. O., & Harlow, M. K. (1965). Total social isolation in monkeys. *Proceedings of the National Academy of Sciences, 54*, 90–97.

Harlow, H. F., & Suomi, S. J. (1971). Social recovery by isolation-reared monkeys. *Proceedings of the National Academy of Sciences, 68*, 1534–1538.

Heymer, A. (1977). *Ethological dictionary*. Berlin, Germany: Paul Parey.

Hill, H. L., & Bekoff, M. (1977). The variability of some motor components of social play and agonistic behavior in infant eastern coyotes *Canis latrens*, var. *Animal Behavior, 25*, 907–909.

Hogan, J. A. (1988). Cause and function in the development of behavior systems. In E. M. Blass (Ed.), *Handbook of behavioral neurobiology: Developmental and behavioral ecology* (pp. 63–106). New York: Academic Press.

Hol, T., van den Berg, C. L., van Ree, J. M., & Spruijt, B. M. (1999). Isolation during the play period in infancy decreases adult social interactions in rats. *Behavioral Brain Research, 100*, 91–97.

Holloway, K. S., & Suter, R. B. (2004). Play deprivation without social isolation: Housing controls. *Developmental Psychobiology, 44*, 58–67.

Holman, S. D., & Goy, R. W. (1981). Effects of prior experience with infants on behavior shown to unfamiliar infants in nulliparous rhesus monkeys. In A. B. Chiarelli & R. S. Corruccini (Eds.), *Primate behavior and sociobiology* (pp. 72–74). Berlin, Germany: Springer.

Humphreys, A. P., & Einon, D. F. (1981). Play as a reinforcer for maze-learning in juvenile rats. *Animal Behavior, 29*, 259–270.

Iwaniuk, A. N., Nelson, J. E., & Pellis, S. M. (2001). Do big-brained animals play more? Comparative analyses of play and relative brain size in mammals. *Journal of Comparative Psychology, 115*, 29–41.

Kahana, A., Rozin, A., & Weller, A. (1997). Social play with an unfamiliar group in weanling rats (*Rattus norvegicus*). *Developmental Psychobiology, 30*, 165–176.

Kortland, A. (1955). Aspects and prospects of the concept of instinct (vicissitudes of the hierarchy theory). *Archives Néerlandaises Zoologie, 11*, 155–284.

Lancaster, J. B. (1971). Play-mothering: The relations between juvenile females and young infants among free-ranging vervet monkeys (*Cercopithecus aethiops*). *Folia Primatologica, 15*, 161–182.

Leyhausen, P. (1979). *Cat behavior*. New York: Garland STPM Press.

Lockard, J. S., & Adams, R. M. (1980). Courtship behaviors in public: Different age/sex roles. *Ethology and Sociobiology, 1*, 245–253.

Lore, R. K., & Flannelly, W. (1977). Rat societies. *Scientific American, 236*, 106–118.

Lovern, M. B., & Jenssen, T. A. (2003). Form emergence and fixation of head bobbing displays in the green anole lizard (*Anolis carolinensis*): A reptilian model of signal ontogeny. *Journal of Comparative Psychology, 117*, 133–141.

Martin, P., & Caro, T. M. (1985). On the functions of play and its role in behavioral development. *Advances in the Study of Behavior, 15*, 59–103.

Mason, W. A. (1978). Social experience and primate cognitive development. In M. Bekoff & G. M. Burghardt (Eds.), *The development of behavior: Comparative and evolutionary aspects* (pp. 233–251). New York: Garland STPM Press.

Mason, W. A., & Berkson, G. (1975). Effects of maternal mobility on the development of rocking and other behaviors in rhesus monkeys: A study with artificial mothers. *Developmental Psychobiology, 8*, 197–211.

McEwen, B. S., & Sapolsky, R. M. (1995). Stress and cognitive function. *Current Opinions in Neurobiology, 5*, 205–216.

McLeod, P. J. (1996). Developmental changes in associations among timber wolf (*Canis lupus*) postures. *Behavioral Processes, 38*, 105–118.

Meaney, M. J., & Stewart, J. (1981). A descriptive study of social development in the rat (*Rattus norvegicus*). *Animal Behavior, 29*, 34–45.

Metz, G. A., Schwab, M. E., & Welzl, H. (2001). The effects of acute and chronic stress on motor and sensory performance in male Lewis rats. *Physiology and Behavior, 72*, 29–35.

Millar, S. (1981). Play. In D. McFarland (Ed.), *The Oxford companion to animal behavior* (pp. 457–460). Oxford, England: Oxford University Press.

Moore, C. L. (1985). Development of mammalian sexual behavior. In E. S. Gollin (Ed.), *The comparative development of adaptive skills* (pp. 19–56). Hillsdale, NJ: Erlbaum.

Moore, M. M. (1995). Courtship signaling and adolescents: "Girls just wanna have fun"? *Journal of Sex Research, 32*, 319–328.

Ogawa, T., Mikuni, M., Kuroda, Y., Muneoka, K., Mori, K. J., & Takahashi, K. (1994). Periodic maternal deprivation alters stress response in adult offspring, potentiates the negative feedback regulation of restraint-induced adrenocortical response, and reduces the frequencies of open field-induced behaviors. *Pharmacology, Biochemistry and Behavior, 49*, 961–967.

Panksepp, J. (1981). The ontogeny of play in rats. *Developmental Psychobiology, 14*, 327–332.

Panksepp, J. (1998). *Affective neuroscience*. New York: Oxford University Press.

Panksepp, J., Siviy, S. M., & Normansell, L. (1984). The psychobiology of play: Theoretical and methodological perspectives. *Neuroscience and Biobehavioral Reviews, 8*, 465–492.

Parsons, S., & Mitchell, P. (2002). The potential of virtual reality in social skills training for people with autistic spectrum disorders. *Journal of Intellectual Disability Research, 46*, 430–443.

Pasztor, T. J., Smith, L. K., MacDonald, N. K., Michener, G. R., & Pellis, S. M. (2001). Sexual and aggressive play fighting of sibling Richardson's ground squirrels. *Aggressive Behavior, 27*, 323–337.

Pellegrini, A. D. (1989). Elementary school children's rough-and-tumble play. *Early Childhood Research Quarterly, 4*, 245–260.

Pellegrini, A. D. (1994). The rough-and-tumble play of adolescent boys of differing sociometric status. *International Journal of Behavioral Development, 17,* 525–540.

Pellegrini, A. D. (1995a). Boys' rough-and-tumble play and social competence: Contemporaneous and longitudinal relations. In A. D. Pellegrini (Ed.), *The future of play theory* (pp. 107–126). Albany: State University of New York Press.

Pellegrini, A. D. (1995b). A longitudinal study of boys' rough-and-tumble play during early adolescence. *Journal of Applied Developmental Psychology, 16,* 77–93.

Pellegrini, A. D., & Boyd, B. (1993). The role of play in early childhood development and education: Issues in definition and function. In B. Spudek (Ed.), *Handbook of research on the education of young children* (pp. 105–121). New York: Macmillan.

Pellegrini, A. D., & Smith, P. K. (1998). Physical activity play: The nature and function of a neglected aspect of play. *Child Development, 69,* 577–598.

Pellis, S. M. (1988). Agonistic versus amicable targets of attack and defense: Consequences for the origin, function and descriptive classification of play-fighting. *Aggressive Behavior, 14,* 85–104.

Pellis, S. M. (1993). Sex and the evolution of play fighting: A review and a model based on the behavior of muroid rodents. *Journal of Play Theory and Research, 1,* 56–77.

Pellis, S. M. (2002a). Keeping in touch: Play fighting and social knowledge. In M. Bekoff, C. Allen, & G. M. Burghardt (Eds.), *The cognitive animal: Empirical and theoretical perspectives on animal cognition* (pp. 421–427). Cambridge, MA: MIT Press.

Pellis, S. M. (2002b). Sex-differences in play fighting revisited: Traditional and non-traditional mechanisms for sexual differentiation in rats. *Archives of Sexual Behavior, 31,* 11–20.

Pellis, S. M., Field, E. F., & Whishaw, I. Q. (1999). The development of a sex-differentiated defensive motor-pattern in rats: A possible role for juvenile experience. *Developmental Psychobiology, 35,* 156–164.

Pellis, S. M., & Iwaniuk, A. N. (2000). Adult-adult play in primates: Comparative analyses of its origin, distribution and evolution. *Ethology, 106,* 1083–1104.

Pellis, S. M., & Iwaniuk, A. N. (2004). Evolving a playful brain. *International Journal of Comparative Psychology, 17,* 92–118.

Pellis, S. M., & McKenna, M. M. (1992). Intrinsic and extrinsic influences on play fighting in rats: Effects of dominance, partner's playfulness, temperament and neonatal exposure to testosterone propionate. *Behavioral Brain Research, 50,* 135–145.

Pellis, S. M., & McKenna, M. M. (1995). What do rats find rewarding in play fighting? An analysis using drug-induced non-playful partners. *Behavioral Brain Research, 68,* 65–73.

Pellis, S. M., O'Brien, D. P., Pellis, V. C., Teitelbaum, P., Wolgin, D. L., & Kennedy, S. (1988). Escalation of feline predation along a gradient from avoidance through "play" to killing. *Behavioral Neuroscience, 102,* 760–777.

Pellis, S. M., & Pasztor, T. J. (1999). The developmental onset of a rudimentary form of play fighting in mice, *Mus musculus. Developmental Psychobiology, 34,* 175–182.

Pellis, S. M., Pasztor, T. J., Pellis, V. C., & Dewsbury, D. A. (2000). The organization of play fighting in the grasshopper mouse (*Onychomys leucogaster*):

Mixing predatory and sociosexual targets and tactics. *Aggressive Behavior, 26,* 319–334.

Pellis, S. M., & Pellis, V. C. (1983). Locomotor-rotational movements in the ontogeny and play of the laboratory rat *Rattus norvegicus. Developmental Psychobiology, 16,* 269–286.

Pellis, S. M., & Pellis, V. C. (1987). Play-fighting differs from serious fighting in both target of attack and tactics of fighting in the laboratory rat *Rattus norvegicus. Aggressive Behavior, 13,* 227–242.

Pellis, S. M., & Pellis, V. C. (1990). Differential rates of attack, defense and counterattack during the developmental decrease in play fighting by male and female rats. *Developmental Psychobiology, 23,* 215–231.

Pellis, S. M., & Pellis, V. C. (1991). Role reversal changes during the ontogeny of play fighting in male rats: Attack versus defense. *Aggressive Behavior, 17,* 179–189.

Pellis, S. M., & Pellis, V. C. (1996). On knowing it's only play: The role of play signals in play fighting. *Aggression and Violent Behavior, 1,* 249–268.

Pellis, S. M., & Pellis, V. C. (1997a). The pre-juvenile onset of play fighting in rats (*Rattus norvegicus). Developmental Psychobiology, 31,* 193–205.

Pellis, S. M., & Pellis, V. C. (1997b). Targets, tactics and the open mouth face during play fighting in three species of primates. *Aggressive Behavior, 23,* 41–57.

Pellis, S. M., & Pellis, V. C. (1998a). The play fighting of rats in comparative perspective: A schema for neurobehavioral analyses. *Neuroscience and Biobehavioral Reviews, 23,* 87–101.

Pellis, S. M., & Pellis, V. C. (1998b). The structure-function interface in the analysis of play fighting. In M. Bekoff & J. A. Byers (Eds.), *Play behavior: Comparative, evolutionary, and ecological aspects* (pp. 115–140). Cambridge, England: Cambridge University Press.

Pellis, S. M., Pellis, V. C., & Foroud, A. (2005). Play fighting: Aggression, affiliation and the development of nuanced social skills (pp. 47–62). In R. Tremblay (Ed.), *Developmental origins of aggression.* New York: Guilford.

Plotsky, P. M., & Meaney, M. J. (1999). Early, postnatal experience alters hypothalamic corticotropin-releasing factor (CRF) mRNA, median eminence CRF content and stress-induced release in adult rats. *Molecular Brain Research, 19,* 195–200.

Poirier, F. E., & Smith, E. O. (1974). Socializing functions of primate play. *American Zoologist, 14,* 275–287.

Poole, T. B., & Fish, J. (1975). An investigation of playful behavior in *Rattus norvegicus* and *Mus musculus* (Mammalia). *Journal of Zoology, 175,* 61–71.

Potegal, M., & Einon, D. (1989). Aggressive behaviors in adult rats deprived of play fighting experience as juveniles. *Developmental Psychobiology, 22,* 159–172.

Potts, R., Huston, A. C., & Wright, J. C. (1986). The effects of television form and violent content in boys' attention and social behavior. *Journal of Experimental Child Psychology, 41,* 1–17.

Power, T. G. (2000). *Play and exploration in children and animals.* Mahwah, NJ: Erlbaum.

Pryce, C. R. (1996). Socialization, hormones, and the regulation of maternal behavior in nonhuman simian primates. *Advances in the Study of Behavior, 25,* 423–473.

Pryce, C. R., Bettschen, D., Barhr, N. I., & Feldon, J. (2001). Comparison of infant handling, isolation, and nonhandling on acoustic startle, prepulse inhibition, locomotion, and HPA activity in the adult rat. *Behavioral Neuroscience, 115,* 71–83.

Pryce, C. R., Bettschen, D., & Feldon, J. (2001). Comparison of the effects of early handling and early deprivation on maternal care in the rat. *Developmental Psychobiology, 38,* 239–251.

Pryce, C. R., & Feldon, J. (2003). Long-term neurobehavioral impact of the postnatal environment in rats: Manipulations, effects and mediating mechanisms. *Neuroscience and Biobehavioral Reviews, 27,* 57–71.

Robbins, T. W., Jones, G. H., & Wilkinson, L. S. (1996). Behavioral and neurochemical effects of early social deprivation in the rat. *Journal of Psychopharmacology, 10,* 39–47.

Roozendaal, B. (2002). Stress and memory: Opposing effects of glucocorticoids on memory consolidation and memory retrieval. *Neurobiology of Learning and Memory, 78,* 578–595.

Rosenzweig, M. R., & Bennett, E. L. (1972). Cerebral changes in rats exposed individually to an enriched environment. *Journal of Comparative and Physiological Psychology, 80,* 304–313.

Ruppenthal, G. C., Walker, C. G., & Sackett, G. P. (1991). Rearing infant monkeys (*Macaca nemestrina*) in pairs produces deficient social development compared with rearing in single cages. *American Journal of Primatology, 25,* 103–113.

Sackett, G. P. (1968). Abnormal behavior in laboratory-reared rhesus monkeys. In M. W. Fox (Ed.), *Abnormal behavior in animals* (pp. 293–331). Philadelphia: Saunders.

Sanson, A., & DiMuccio, C. (1993). The influence of aggressive and neutral cartoons and toys on the behavior of preschool children. *Australian Psychologist, 28,* 93–99.

Siviy, S. M. (1998). Neurobiological substrates of play behavior: Glimpses into the structure and function of mammalian playfulness. In M. Bekoff & J. A. Byers (Eds.), *Animal play: Evolutionary, comparative, and ecological perspectives* (pp. 221–242). Cambridge, England: Cambridge University Press.

Siviy, S. M., & Panksepp, J. (1987). Sensory modulation of juvenile play in rats. *Developmental Psychobiology, 20,* 39–55.

Smith, E. O. (1978). A historical view of the study of play: Statement of the problem. In E. O. Smith (Ed.), *Social play in primates* (pp. 1–32). New York: Academic Press.

Smith, L. K., Fantella, S.-L., & Pellis, S. M. (1999). Playful defensive responses in adult male rats depend upon the status of the unfamiliar opponent. *Aggressive Behavior, 25,* 141–152.

Smith, L. K., Forgie, M. L., & Pellis, S. M. (1998). Mechanisms underlying the absence of the pubertal shift in the playful defense of female rats. *Developmental Psychobiology, 33,* 147–156.

Smith, P. K. (1988a). Children's play and its role in early development: A re-evaluation of the "play ethos." In A. D. Pellegrini (Ed.), *Psychological bases for early education* (pp. 207–226). New York: Wiley.

Smith, P. K. (1988b). Ethological approaches to the study of aggression in children. In J. Archer & K. Browne (Eds.), *Human aggression: Naturalistic approaches* (pp. 65–93). New York: Routledge.

Smith, P. K. (1994). The war play debate. In J. H. Goldstein (Ed.), *Toys, play and child development* (pp. 67–84). New York: Cambridge University Press.

Smith, P. K., & Boulton, M. (1990). Rough and tumble play, aggression and dominance: Perception and behavior in children's encounters. *Human Development, 33,* 271–282.

Smith, P. K., Smees, R., & Pellegrini, A. D. (2004). Play fighting and real fighting: Using video playback methodology with young children. *Aggressive Behavior, 30,* 164–173.

Spear, L. P. (2000). The adolescent brain and age-related behavioral manifestations. *Neuroscience and Biobehavioral Reviews, 24,* 417–463.

Spinka, M., Newberry, R. C., & Bekoff, M. (2001). Mammalian play: Can training for the unexpected be fun? *Quarterly Review of Biology, 76,* 141–176.

Suchecki, D., Nelson, D. Y., van Oers, H., & Levine, S. (1995). Activation and inhibition of the hypothalamic-pituitary-adrenal axis of the neonatal rat: Effects of maternal deprivation. *Psychoneuroendocrinology, 20,* 169–182.

Sutton-Smith, B., Gerstmyer, J., & Meckley, A. (1988). Play-fighting as folkplay amongst preschool children. *Western Folklore, 47,* 161–176.

Sutton-Smith, B., & Kelly-Byrne, D. (1984). The idealization of play. In P. K. Smith (Ed.), *Play in animals and humans* (pp. 305–321). Oxford, England: Basil Blackwell.

Takahashi, L. K. (1986). Postweaning environmental and social factors influence the onset of agonistic behavior in Norway rats. *Behavioral Processes, 12,* 237–260.

Takahashi, L. K., & Lore, R. K. (1983). Play fighting and the development of agonistic behavior in male and female rats. *Aggressive Behavior, 9,* 217–227.

Taylor, G. T. (1980). Fighting in juvenile rats and the ontogeny of agonistic behavior. *Journal of Comparative and Physiological Psychology, 94,* 953–961.

Thor, D. H., & Holloway, W. R., Jr. (1984). Developmental analysis of social play in juvenile rats. *Bulletin of the Psychonomic Society, 22,* 587–590.

van den Berg, C. L., Hol, T., van Ree, J. M., Spruijt, B. M., Everts, H., & Koolhaas, J. M. (1999). Play is indispensable for an adequate development of coping with social challenges in the rat. *Developmental Psychobiology, 34,* 129–138.

van Oers, H. J. J., de Kloet, E. R., Li, C., & Levine, S. (1998). The ontogeny of glucocorticoid negative feedback: Influence of maternal deprivation. *Endocrinology, 139,* 2838–2846.

von Frijtag, J. C., Schot, M., van den Bos, R., & Spruijt, B. M. (2002). Individual housing during the play period results in changed responses to and consequences of a psychosocial stress situation in rats. *Developmental Psychobiology, 41,* 58–69.

Willmer, A. H. (1991). Behavioral deficiencies of aggressive 8–9 year old boys: An observational study. *Aggressive Behavior, 17,* 135–154.

Wolf, D. P. (1984). Repertoire, style and format: Notions worth borrowing from children's play. In P. K. Smith (Ed.), *Play in animals and humans* (pp. 175–193). Oxford, England: Blackwell.

Wright, I. K., Upton, N. & Marden, C. A. (1991). Resocialization of isolation-reared rats does not alter their anxiogenic profile on the elevated X-maze model of anxiety. *Physiology and Behavior, 50,* 1129–1132.

Wyly, M. V., Denenberg, V. H., de Santis, D., Burns, J. K., & Zarrow, M. X. (1975). Handling rabbits in infancy: In search of a critical period. *Developmental Psychobiology, 8,* 179–186.

Yamada-Haga, Y. (2002). Characteristics of social interaction between unfamiliar male rats (*Rattus norvegicus*): Comparison of juvenile and adult stages. *Journal of Ethology, 20,* 55–62.

Zahr, L. K., & Balian, S. (1995). Responses of premature infants to routine nursing interventions and noise in the NICU. *Nursing Research, 41,* 179–185.

10

Evolutionary Perspectives on Social Engagement

Heidi Keller
Athanasios Chasiotis

Evolutionary Perspectives on Social Engagement

In this chapter, we first introduce the main conceptions of modern evolutionary theory and present conceptions derived from game theory of the evolution of cooperation, especially reciprocal altruism and punishment. We then discuss life history theory and the extended developmental phase of human childhood. The evolved characteristics of human development, especially language acquisition, contingency detection, joint attention, and theory of mind, which are fundamental aspects of the development of social engagement, are then presented. Finally, we discuss social structure and dominance with respect to social engagement.

The Evolution of Social Behavior

Despite an initial and intensive rejection (e.g., Valsiner, 1989), evolutionary theorizing has successfully pervaded the social and behavioral sciences (e.g., Bjorklund & Pellegrini, 2002; Heckhausen & Boyer, 2000). The basic and most provocative assumption of evolutionary theory is constituted by the Darwinian credo that humans do not play a special role in the array of species. Human phylogeny has been shaped by adaptations to selective pressures that arose through contextual demands our ancestors had to face. The contribution that sociobiology (E. O. Wilson, 1975) added to this assumption was that not only somatic and biological systems in a narrower sense follow the reproductive logic, but also social behavior and the complex psychology of human beings.

The second landmark of evolutionary theorizing consists of the transformation of the Darwinian formulation of preservation of the species through reproduction of individuals (Darwin, 1859) to the conception of inclusive fitness of the individual resulting from its own procreation (Darwinian fitness) and the procreation of relatives with whom the individual shares genes (indirect fitness; Hamilton, 1964). The focus on inclusive fitness implies that the evolutionary perspective centers on the gene as the unit of analysis. However, "It is not the naked gene that is exposed to selective forces directly" (Mayr, 1994, p. 206) but the "realized animal" that lives or dies, breeds, or helps relatives (Daly & Wilson, 1983, p. 32). Although individuals are considered as "vehicles," they are also "active replicators" (Dawkins, 1976), since changes in the genes lead to changes in the phenotype as well.

The shift from the species to the individual level has substantial implications for the conception of human nature (Keller, 1996; Keller & Chasiotis, in press-a, in press-b). It implies that altruism, that is, a prosocial orientation and behavior, is not an unconditional human trait but results from—mostly implicit and unconscious—cost-benefit calculations. As a consequence, it is assumed that relationships are constituted out of individual self-interest and are therefore genuinely conflictual. Two main concepts describe the evolution of cooperative social behavior in self-interested organisms: kin selection (Hamilton, 1964) and reciprocal altruism (Trivers, 1971).

Kin Selection

Kin selection as part of inclusive fitness theory is the proposal to understand the dynamics of social preferences and social denials (Hamilton, 1964; Trivers, 1971). According to this conception, individuals' social behaviors will vary according to the degree of genetic relatedness among group members. Individuals will be more cooperative with closely related others as compared with more distantly related or nonrelated others. The underlying assumption is that genetic closeness fosters cooperation and the reciprocation of investments, and thus reciprocity of social exchanges. Cooperation and altruism based on the perception of reciprocity is known as Hamilton's rule (Hamilton, 1964) and expressed in the following equation: $Br - C > 0$ (r = coefficient of relatedness between actor and recipient; B = benefit to the recipient; C = cost to the actor). Considerable empirical evidence has been presented in supporting this assumption. In Great Britain, Dunbar and Spoors (1995) found that adults nominate a high proportion of kin relative to non-kin for help and support (see also Burnstein, Crandall, & Kitayama, 1994), and Fijneman et al. (1996) reported from the Netherlands that the family has been identified as the most salient in-group in the lives of individuals. Based on a large-scale cross-cultural research program, Georgas and colleagues (in press) also conclude that relationships among family members are the most significant relationships in literally all parts of the world (cf., e.g., Georgas, Berry, van de Vijver, Kağitçibaşi, & Poortinga, in press; Kağitçibaşi, 1990; Lay et al., 1998; Rhee, Uleman, & Lee, 1996).

In the environment of evolutionary adaptedness (EEA), social groups presumably consisted of a relatively high proportion of kin (Hinde, 1980). However, the members of these groups not only shared genes to differing degrees but also shared past experiences and plans related to the future (Bjorklund & Pellegrini, 2002). They were familiar and thus predictable to each other. Familiarity can therefore be regarded as the primary mechanism that enables individuals to recognize kin (Cheney & Seyfarth, 1999), generalizing to trustworthy individuals in general. Consequently, establishing familiarity is the first step in the development of infants' attachment to their caregivers, while unfamiliarity is a major cause of distress. Familiarity is the basis of predictability and thus exerts control over the environment as a major mechanism of psychological homeostasis. The extension of cooperative interactions with kin to interactions with non-kin can be illuminated by making inferences about the environments in which these strategies evolved.

Reciprocal Altruism

The conception of reciprocal altruism was proposed by Trivers (1971) in order to capture the social relations among individuals who are not genetically related. It predicts that individuals will cooperate with those with whom there is a perspective of future social exchange and the expectation, implicit or explicit, that the costs of cooperative and altruistic behaviors that an individual invests are to be reciprocated in the future. It is assumed that these expectations are based on prior experiences of cooperative interactions. Accordingly, it has been demonstrated empirically that even relatively small-scale acts of care can precipitate much greater returns from the individual to whom the original altruistic act was directed (Cialdini, 2001; Dickinson, 2000).

Game theorists have analyzed reciprocal altruism mainly within the empirical paradigm of the "prisoner's dilemma." The prisoner's dilemma constitutes an imaginary situation in which two separately imprisoned individuals are accused of having cooperated to perform some criminal act. Meanwhile, an experimenter attempts to induce each one to implicate the other. Each prisoner has the option to cooperate (not implicating the other) or to defect (implicating the other), with the temptation to defect to have the biggest payoff (cf. Trivers, 1985). The pioneering work of Axelrod and Hamilton (1981) on repeated variants of the prisoner's dilemma successfully demonstrated that a strategy called tit-for-tat was superior to all others. This strategy had only two rules. On the first move, cooperate; on the next move, do what your partner did in the previous move. More generally, the result implies that the most successful features of tit-for-tat are "never be the first to defect," "retaliate after the partner has defected," and "be forgiving after retaliation." For Axelrod (1984), the analogy to the evolutionary process of reciprocal altruism was obvious.

Recently, computer simulations based on the prisoner's dilemma paradigm have also confirmed that cooperation between unrelated individuals increased when there had been a previous, sustained history of caring (Roberts & Sherratt, 1998). Similarly, those who have been perceived as neglectful in relationships were less likely to receive future cooperation. Thus it has been demonstrated in laboratory studies (Kruger, 2001) as well as field studies (Kaniasty & Norris, 1995) that a caring nonrelative would be more likely to benefit from another's altruism than would be a neglectful nonrelative.

Beyond Reciprocal Altruism: Altruistic Punishment and Altruism as Costly Signal

Despite the theoretical appeal of the concept of reciprocal altruism, the impressive quantity and quality of cooperation between genetically unrelated individuals in human societies remain mostly unexplained. The main reason is that reciprocal altruism in the form of tit-for-tat or similar strategies of the repeated prisoner's dilemma (Axelrod & Hamilton, 1981) is restricted to two-person interactions and is thus at most applicable to small and stable groups that were characteristic for hunter-gatherer societies (Kaplan, Hill, Lancaster, & Hurtado, 2000). Modern large-scale societies, however, are characterized by multiple and often anonymous interactions where familiarity and predictability are not existent. Future discounting therefore becomes a challenge (Chisholm, 1999): If future economic benefits or reciprocations are uncertain, why should one behave altruistically in the first place? During the last decade, two new game theoretical concepts were introduced, enhancing the understanding of human cooperation: altruistic punishment and altruism as a costly signal (Fehr & Fischbacher, 2003). After introducing these concepts, their application to the development of social engagement will be discussed.

Strong Reciprocity: Reciprocal Altruism as Altruistic Punishment and Altruistic Rewarding

Strong reciprocity is conceived of as a predisposition to combine cooperative behavior ("altruistic rewarding") with a propensity to impose sanctions on defectors ("altruistic punishment"). Altruistic rewarding is the pan-culturally observed trustful exchange that has been widely documented in games like the prisoner's dilemma (Buchan, Croson, & Dawes, 2002). Humans experience subjective rewards in behaving altruistically (Rilling, 2002). Another cross-culturally robust result is altruistic punishment as the costly rejection of social imbalance, for example, unfair sharing (e.g., Henrich, 2001). However, this combination of altruistic rewarding and punishment is often not sufficient to explain social engagement in public or common-good situations involving larger groups with potentially anonymous interactions. Human conditional cooperation is based on implicit assumptions whether or not all or most group members will cooperate. This assumption in turn is mainly determined by the possibility of punishment by third parties (Fischbacher, Gächter, & Fehr, 2001). Thus, even more important than altruistic punishment in dyadic interactions is the altruistic propensity to punish norm violators by third parties who are not economically affected (Fehr & Fischbacher, in press). This seems to be a key element of the enforcement of social norms in human societies (Hill, 2002; see later discussion).

Cooperation as Reputation Formation: Altruism as Costly Signal for Non-Kin

Another important reason that humans maintain cooperation with non-kin can be attributed to the mechanism of reputation formation. Reputation formation through indirect reciprocity (e.g., "image scoring"; Nowak & Sigmund, 1998) or social reputation (e.g., Milinski, Semmann, & Krambeck, 2002; Milinski, Semmann, Bakker, & Krameck, 2001) constitutes another powerful mechanism for the enforcement of cooperation. Reputation-forming behavior can consist of, for example, tough bargaining with an insistence on a fair exchange combined with the readiness to pay a costly price to punish deceivers (Fehr & Fischbacher, 2003). From an evolutionary perspective, this kind of cooperation can be subsumed under the "costly signal" or "handicap theory" (Zahavi, 1995). This mechanism explains why we show costly signals, that is, behave altruistically, although we might not gain anything, not even indirectly. The underlying assumption is that individuals can afford to show off because they have as a consequence a higher reputation and thus a higher genetic fitness, which lowers again the costs of showing the particular behavior or trait ("good genes"; Zahavi, 1975).

Human Altruism and the Evolution of Culture

The interpretation of altruistic acts as costly signaling can explain why we contribute to the public good, but it cannot explain why we should show off in social contexts through being altruistic and not trying to appear particularly brave, powerful, or healthy (Voland & Grammer, 2003). A supplementary explanatory mechanism for human altruism might be cultural group selection (Gintis, Smith, & Bowles, 2001; Smith, Bliege Bird, & Bird, 2003). Despite the skepticism against group selection in the early times of modern evolutionary biology (Williams, 1966; E. O. Wilson, 1975), purely genetic group selection and its phenotypic outcome of a gene-based reciprocal altruism is very unlikely, but not impossible in principle (D. S. Wilson, 2002). Subjective evaluations of fairness and inequity aversion, that is, the disapproval of unequal transactions, differ from economic payoffs, since economic rationality would imply self-interested freeloading without any considerations of fairness (Fehr & Fischbacher, 2003). But cooperative behavior is likely to be imitated when everybody cooperates, because then punishers do not have any punishment costs at all. Thus, in special contextual circumstances, as in the human case of cultural transmission through accumulative cultural evolution, norms and institutions are maintained through altruistic punishment by third parties. Human cultural transmission, in turn, is probably based on the unique theory-of-mind abilities of humans (the "ratchet effect"; Tomasello, 1999; see also Bowles, Choi, & Hopfensitz, 2003; Boyd, Gintis, Bowles, & Richerson, 2003). We will now turn to a life history perspective to discuss how these evolutionary concepts are manifested during human ontogenesis.

Life History Theory

Genetic Programs and Life History Theory

Adaptations are environmental information that has become represented in phenotypes. This is old information about an organism's ancestors' environments that is acquired via copies of their DNA. The information can also be more recent and acquired through "inborn environmental" experiences shaping the phenotype (Bischof, 1996). Thus, phenotypic plasticity provides an adaptive advantage if an organism's fitness depends more on recent information than on old information (Chisholm, 1999). Genes exert their effects on behavior within two kinds of programs that can be differentiated with respect to the directness of the gene-behavior relationship. *Fixed genetic programs* are invariably coded in the DNA of the genotype and expressed in phenotypical characteristics without further transmission mechanisms. However, there is no one-to-one relationship between individual genes and behavioral characteristics, since most behaviors are coded in multiple loci of different genes (pleiotropy). The expression of the genetic information into behavior can occur during different stages of the human life span, which is also part of fixed programs. In fact, the influence of fixed genetic programs may become stronger with development (Keller, 2000a).

Besides the action of fixed behavioral programs, behavior and behavioral development of higher animals and especially humans is organized to a great extent by *open genetic programs* (Mayr, 1997) that are susceptible to recent information. It is difficult to describe open genetic programs with an encompassing definition, since their modes of influencing and directing behavior are manifold (Mayr, 1997). They are products of evolutionary fixed programs but constitute "facultative" or "open" developmental processes (Laland, Odling-Smee, & Feldman, 2000). These processes are based on specialized information-acquisition subsystems in individual organisms, covering single associations as well as domain-specific functioning (MacDonald, 1988). For example, for language acquisition a different interplay between genetic preparedness and learning might be operating than for motor development or social competencies. Learning based on open genetic programs therefore has to be understood as a highly specified mechanism: "The more we have studied learning abilities, the more impressed we have become with their specificity" (Trivers, 1985, p. 102).

Open genetic programs prepare individuals with "epigenetic rules" (E. O. Wilson, 1975), "central tendencies" (MacDonald, 1988), or "informed hypotheses" (Chisholm, 1996) for the acquisition of specific environmental information at specific phases of development. The open or closed nature of these predispositions varies according to the required specificity of the environmental information. The ethological conception of a sensitive period for imprinting builds on one of the most restricted cases (Lorenz, 1965), although even there environmental modifications are possible.

One of the most obvious manifestations of the interplay between open and fixed genetic programs can be demonstrated in ontogenesis, which is the evolution of life spans. This implies that the adult individual is not the end product of evolution but that the whole life span and its patterning are a result of selective forces and thus shaped by evolution (Alexander, 1987; Keller, 2001). Life history theory is thus the evolutionary study of life cycles and life history traits in an ecological context. It is also based on the assumption that the developmental mechanisms that produce life cycles are exposed to selection and evolve (Chisholm, 1999). The individual life course constitutes a trade-off, also mostly implicit and nonintentional, between investment into growth and development (somatic effort) and investment into reproduction, which comprises the functional systems of mating and parental investment (reproductive effort; cf. Chisholm, 1996, 1999). Reproductive decisions are contingent upon environmental conditions, comprising material and ecological resources, as well as social complexity (cf. Dunbar, 1996) and niches that prior generations have created (Laland et al., 2000), forming a continuous scenario of change at the same time. Evolutionary theorizing thus integrates biological and cultural forces in a common framework. Evolutionary psychologists have proposed that hominid psychology evolved to solve adaptive problems in the environment of evolutionary adaptedness (Bowlby, 1969). This time period is conceived as covering the Pleistocene age from about 1.8 million years ago until about 10,000 years before the present time. It can be assumed that our ancestors lived as hunters and gatherers in savanna environments in groups of between around 30 and 60 individuals. Cooperative, altruistic—as well as antisocial—behaviors are assumed to have evolved to regulate life in these groups.

One of the most controversial issues even among scholars of evolutionary theory concerns the applicability of epigenetic rules for human functioning in complex, industrialized, knowledge-based societies. Different scholars accordingly question the usefulness of evolutionary reasoning about ultimate causes beyond subsistence level societies (Tooby & Cosmides, 1992). However, there is also empirical support for the existence of central tendencies in modern environments. The dynamics of allomothering (Hrdy, in press), mating preferences and strategies (Buss, 1994), differential parental investment (Keller & Zach, 2002; Chasiotis, Keller, & Scheffer, 2003), and the relations between variables describing childhood context and reproductive marker variables (Belsky, Steinberg, & Draper, 1991; Chasiotis et al., 2003; Chasiotis, Scheffer, Restemeier, & Keller, 1998) seem to be rooted in evolutionary logic.

The Role of Interindividual Differences

Research in evolutionary psychology has focused mainly on species-typical psychological mechanisms while neglecting individual differences. Evolutionary biologists generally view individual differences as merely proving the raw material on which natural selection operates. Heritable individual differences are often just explained primarily through nonselective forces like random-mutation and accordingly viewed as "noise" or "genetic junk" (Tooby & Cosmides, 1990; D. S. Wilson, 1994). But the consistency of heritable individual differences makes this reasoning not very convincing: Why should natural selection tolerate such a vast interindividual variance, and why are the varying personality traits so closely linked to adaptive activities like sexuality and survival? Evidence from behavioral genetics suggests that heritable and nonheritable characteristics are important for interindividual differences. There are at least three plausible models for exploring the adaptiveness of interindividual differences (cf. Buss, 2004):

1. Niche picking (Sulloway, 1996). In niche picking, an individual seeks niches to avoid or lessen the competition with conspeciWcs. An impressive example is birth order eVects, showing considerable and probably adaptive personality diVerences mainly between Wrstborns (conscientious and conservative) and laterborns (openness to new experiences, more liberal; cf. Sulloway, 1996). This would be an example of noninherited interindividual variance.
2. Reactive heritability (Tooby & Cosmides, 1990). In reactive heritability, individuals take inherited traits into account when they have to make strategic decisions. These assessed traits can be their own (e.g., "Am I strong enough to attack someone physically?") or traits of a social partner ("Is this male attractive for me?").
3. Frequency dependency. Frequency-dependent interindividual diVerences are supposed to result from multidirectional selection processes where more than one adaptive "solution" shows heritable variation (D. S. Wilson, 1994). An example is Mealey's (1995) discussion of the adaptive signiWcance of sociopathy. There seems to be a constant percentage of at least 4% in each population of antisocial personalities who in a way parasitize the majority of cooperative and prosocial subjects in a population: The more cooperative the majority is, the more successful is a small percentage of cheaters.

Thus, nonheritable sources of individual differences are variance in early environmental experiences and alternative niche picking, while heritable sources are reactive heritability and frequency-dependent interindividual variance.

The Evolutionary Significance of an Extended Childhood

Central to the application of evolutionary thinking to human development is the recognition that members of *Homo sapiens* have a life history in which they spend a disproportionate amount of time in a pre-reproductive phase (Bjorklund & Pellegrini, 2002).

Bjorklund (1997) has argued that developmental immaturity had an adaptive role in human phylogeny in that it continues to have an adaptive role for human social—as well as cognitive—ontogeny. He argues that some immature forms and behaviors have been selected in evolution for their immediate or facultative adaptive value. The concept of ontogenetic adaptations implies that neurobehavioral characteristics of young animals serve specific adaptive functions for the developing animal. These are not simply incomplete versions of adult characteristics but have specific roles in survival during infancy or youth, and disappear when they are no longer necessary (Bjorklund, 1997; Bogin, 1997). Some aspects of infants' cognitions may also serve short-term functions rather than preparing for the future. For example, it has been documented that imitation of facial expressions during the first 2 months of life is qualitatively different and unrelated to that observed later in life. The most convincing interpretation of this phenomenon is proposed by Bjorklund (1987), who suggested that imitation during the first 2 months facilitates mother-infant interaction at a time when infants cannot intentionally direct their gaze and control their head movements to social stimulation, whereas at later stages of development it mainly serves the function of acquiring new information. Another example concerns young children's abilities to estimate their competencies in a wide range of tasks. Preschool and school-age children overestimate their abilities in that they think they are smarter, stronger, and generally more skilled than they really are (Bjorklund, Gaultney, & Green, 1993). Children who think they are skilled are more likely to attempt more challenging tasks, which will influence how much they learn.

Nevertheless, there are also costs related to the long phase of immaturity, especially a high level of infant mortality (which still continues in many parts of the world). However, the benefits of extended immaturity must have outweighed the costs, so that it has been proposed that the single most potent pressure on human intellectual evolution was the need to cooperate and compete with conspecifics (Humphrey, 1976). In order to more effectively defend against predators and exploit resources, hominid groups increased in size and thus became socially more complex. Individuals who could better understand their social world gained more of the benefits in terms of available resources, including mating partners, and passed those characteristics on to their offspring. In turn, greater social complexity required greater self-awareness, as well as greater awareness concerning the needs and motives of others. The long childhood and extensive parental investment allow human apprentices to learn from the social environment that represents the pool of local (cultural) expertise. This is particularly important in the development of language and the development of a theory of mind (see later), which have been attributed to the complexities of life in extending social groups.

Parental Investment, Parent-Offspring Conflict, and Cooperative Breeding

For most mammals, investment in offspring is far greater in the female than in the male sex (Trivers, 1972, 1985). In humans, although the amount of time many fathers in contemporary societies spend with their children is higher than in traditional societies (for an exception, see Hewlett, Lamb, Leyendecker, & Schoelmerich, 2000), the overall pattern is still that women devote more of their time to the care and upbringing of children than men (Bjorklund & Pellegrini, 2002). This asymmetry in parental investment in mammals is responsible for three of the most salient sex differences: (a) mating preferences (Buss, 1994), (b) intrasexual competition, and (c) parental certainty (Daly & Wilson, 1988).

However, despite the fact that mothers are the dominant caregivers, the mother-child relationship is not without conflict, since the reproductive interests of mother and offspring differ with respect to when and how much parental investment should be provided, and with respect to the amount of cooperation or altruism a child should demonstrate to siblings and other relatives (Trivers, 1974). Accordingly, children have evolved psychological (e.g., attachment behaviors) and physiological mechanisms to get as much investment from their caregivers as these individuals are willing to give. The fitness considerations for the mother in forming attachments to offspring are more complicated, since her resources to invest in reproduction are finite. Maternal resources must be divided between the demands of multiple offspring, and the mother's health and physical condition, including future reproduction (Thompson et al., in press). Generally, humans can be classified as qualitative strategists, in that they invest quality care in fewer offspring rather than investing less in more offspring (which would be typical of a quantitative strategy; Belsky et al., 1991; Chisholm, 1999). Although in much of the attachment literature (Bowlby, 1969; Cassidy & Shaver, 1999), the primacy of exclusive maternal care is taken as the evolved pattern of care, cultural anthropologists and evolutionary psychologists have challenged this assumption with new scenarios of family life in the Pleistocene environment of evolutionary adaptedness (Hrdy, 1999; Hrdy, in press).

Along the way toward the evolution of hominid social behavior, something has happened that still puzzles anthropologists about human family dynamics: A significantly prolonged life span has placed the helping grandmother on the stage of life (Voland, Chasiotis, & Schiefenhövel, in press). One can assume that our hominid ancestors—comparable to present-day big apes—could reach a maximum age of 40 to 50 years, provided their living conditions were favorable (Hill et al., 2001; Nichida et al., 2003). However, the evolutionary design of the human life span comprises roughly twice as many years. This doubling of the life span would not pose any insurmountable problem for anthropological theory if it were not tied to the obligatory sterility of postmenopausal women, a pattern rarely found in the animal kingdom. Could it be envisaged that the respect one pays to seniors can be regarded as a function of their realized evolutionary utility in terms of increasing the reproductive fitness of offspring? Hrdy (in press) discusses three conditions necessary for the evolution of grandmotherhood. First, the primate heritage provides a motivational tendency for kin support. Second, elderly women must have had a chance to benefit their family, and third, the survival of older individuals must not have caused costs that would have neutralized or even exceeded the support they were able to give. If resources are shared within the family, as, for example, Helle, Käär, and Jokela (2002) report from the Sami in northern Finland, intrafamilial allocation conflicts arise. Postponing childbearing to a later age minimizes the lifetime grandparents and their grandchildren live together, and hence leads to a reduction of intrafamilial competition and thus reduces the costs of the elderly. If getting old affords more resources than the elderly can produce themselves, that is, if the resource flow of kin support would have to go from the young to the old, having support from a grandmother would not have paid off in evolutionary terms. In light of this cost-benefit matrix, it seems possible that a particular emotionality toward grandmothers evolved that adds affect toward the elderly to the balance between the costs old women cause to their kin with the contributions they make (Amoss & Harrell, 1981). Interestingly enough, even in modern times, the helping grandmother can be found in a variety of cultural settings (Nosaka & Chasiotis, in press). Analyses of intergenerational wealth flow indicate that in traditional (Kaplan, 1994) and modern (Kohli, 1999; Lee, 1997) societies, the net flow within the families occurs from the older to the younger generation. The findings from the Hadza and !Kung, where older women take over important subsistence work and are well respected, and those from the Inuit and the Aché, both of whom rely on hunting, seem also to support this (Hill & Hurtado, 1996).

Not only the role of grandmothers but also the roles of siblings and other caretakers have been analyzed with respect to their influence on child survival. Based on these analyses, it has been proposed that allomothers are not just helpful, but that children in the EEA would not have survived without them (Voland et al., in press). Thus, one evolved characteristic of human social evolution is cooperative breeding.

Evolution, Social Learning, and Social Engagement

After having presented the evolution of social cooperation and life history in humans, we now turn to the evolution of the ontogenesis of human social engagement. First, we will discuss the phylogenetic and ontogenetic roots of language acquisition as a uniquely human characteristic and a basic prerequisite for the development of social engagement.

The Evolution of Language

Pinker and Bloom (1990) argue that the facility for human language is a complex biological adaptation that evolved by natural selection for communication in a social environment that is based on the use of knowledge. The most significant aspect of the language faculty is communication, that is, transfer of information (Pinker, 1994, 1999). Pinker regards language as an adaptation to the cognitive niche of humans. The language system seems to have evolved to "encode propositional information—who did what to whom, what is true of what, when, where and why—into a signal that can be conveyed from one person to another" (Pinker, 1994, p. 12). Humans have evolved an ability to encode information about the causal structure of the world and to share it among themselves. The structures of grammar are prepared to convey information about technology (e.g., to combine two artifacts so that a new function emerges), about the spatial environment in order to locate places, and about the social environment (e.g., the structure and intention of social interactions that define social exchange and hierarchy). Gathering and exchanging information is integral to the "cognitive niche" (Tooby & DeVore, 1987) that humans have created and inhabit. Pinker (1994) suggests that language may have evolved gradually after the chimpanzee-human split, in the 200,000 to 300,000 generations that make up the lineage leading to modern humans. Language could be a trait that evolved in one lineage but not its sister lineages.

Although the communication and exchange of information as the evolved function of language is obviously of adaptive advantage, it may not be sufficient to explain its evolution. Robin Dunbar (1996) has proposed an evolutionary account of the evolution of language that is based on the social complexities of group life. He argued that it is likely that language evolved to solve a variety of social problems (see also Miller, 2000). In order to make groups the arenas for individuals' success in terms of protection of predators and better exploitation and acquisition of resources, social bonds were the promise for future behavior. Most primate societies established social bonds through grooming between individuals. In order to establish functional coalitions in larger groups, it became necessary to perceive and process multiple pieces of information in the social context, that is, to become socially intelligent. Selection pressure therefore not only acted on a generally larger brain but acted especially on an increase in the size of the neocortex. The size of the neocortex has been demonstrated to be independent of ecological factors that also require complex information processing, like the proportion of fruits in the amenable food, the size or complexity of food resources, and the difficulties of food provisioning. Rather, the size of the neocortex relates to the group size (Dunbar, 1993). With increasing group size, grooming as a social tool became a highly time-consuming activity. There likely reached a point where more investment in grooming would occur at the expense of food acquisition and defense. It is this changing point that Dunbar (1996) identified as the origin of language, which he understands as acoustical grooming that serves the function of maintaining relations among group members and forming coalitions in larger social units (Keller, 2000a).

The Development of Human Capacities for Social Engagement: Contingency, Joint Attention, and Intersubjectivity

Pinker's (1994) neonativist perspective posits that children are born (a) with a universal grammar, that is, some predisposed knowledge about syntax, and (b) with a language acquisition device, a mental organ prepared to learn from language input. Evidence from second-language learning, proficiency in sign language among deaf people, recovery of damage in language areas of the brain, and differences in brain organization between early and late bilinguals show that the first decade in life can be regarded as a sensitive period for language acquisition. Thus, children are clearly specially prepared to learn language (Bjorklund & Pellegrini, 2002; Keller, 2000b).

Despite this domain-specific evidence, domain-general mechanisms also play a crucial role in language acquisition. The social-pragmatist perspective stresses the importance of a language acquisition support system, which is a natural outgrowth of the emerging understanding of other persons as intentional agents in infancy (Bruner, 1981; Tomasello, 1999, 2001). In this view, language is acquired through more basic social processes like contingency experience, joint attention, and intersubjectivity (see also Pruden, Hirsh-Pasek, & Golinkoff, this volume).

Contingency Experience

From birth onward, infants are endowed with a behavioral repertoire to interact with their social environment. Recent studies have provided evidence that there is some degree of basic differentiation between self and other present from birth on. Newborns respond differently to external and self-administered stimulation (Rochat & Hespos, 1997), 2-month-olds react differently to social and nonsocial stimuli (Legerstee, Corter, & Kienapple, 1990), and infants engage in finely attuned emotional exchanges with others (Stern, 1985; Trevarthen & Aitken, 2001). Self-other differentiation is elaborated with an analytic mechanism that detects contingencies (Watson, 1994). *Contingency* refers to the temporal pattern between two events that potentially reflect a causal dependency. Watson (1994) conceives of contingency as an inborn module that applies two independent mechanisms: a responsiveness index, which looks forward in time and registers an upcoming stimulus event as a function of an emitted response, and a dependency index, which tests backward in time and monitors the relative likelihood that a given stimulus event was preceded by a given response. The provision of contingent responses to infants' signals is part of the intuitive parenting repertoire (Keller, Lohaus, Voelker, Cappenberg, & Chasiotis, 1999; Keller, Schoelmerich, & Eibl-Eibesfeldt, 1988; M. Papoušek & Papoušek, 1991). Caregivers respond within a time range of about 1 second to infants' facial and vocal cues (Keller, Chasiotis, & Runde, 1992; Keller et al., 1999; M. Papoušek & Papoušek, 1991), which may correspond to the short duration of infants' working memory.

In the development of contingent, reciprocal mother-infant interactions and human attachment, right hemispheric processes and areas are involved (Schore, 1994, 1998). Schore (1998, 2001) has offered evidence that face-to-face interactions, which generate high levels of positive arousal between the psychobiologically attuned mother and her infant, represent an essential mechanism in the development of affect regulation. The interpersonal contexts created in mutual gaze transactions allow for the establishment of "affect synchrony" (Feldman, Greenbaum, & Yirmiya, 1999) and "contingent responsivity" (Schore, 2001).

Joint Attention

At about 9 months of age, behavioral changes hasten a new level of infants' social understanding. For example, infants begin to follow the pointing gesture of another person (Carpenter, Nagell, & Tomasello, 1998), and infants understand that another person's attentional directedness is independent of their own (Müller & Carpendale, 2004). Gaze following also involves the understanding of spatial relations (Morisset, Barnard, & Booth, 1995). The ability to coordinate attention with others is essential for the emergence of communicative behaviors. Joint attention mediates a resonance of positive affect and occurs when two individuals simultaneously attend to each other and a third object in social referencing interactions (see Mundy & Acra, this volume). This dyadic mechanism allows the infant to appreciate that "the other person is a locus of psychological attitudes toward the world, that the other is "attending" in such a way that shared experiences are possible" (Hobson, 1993, p. 267), a critical advance in the child's adaptive capacities.

Intersubjectivity and Imitation

Viewing imitation from a developmental perspective allows for consideration of the social influences on developing abilities. Primary intersubjectivity may be the foundation for imitation in humans, but also in chimpanzees (Bard, 2004), providing a mechanism to explain flexibility in response to the social environment (Bard, 2004; Keller, 2003; Miklosi, 1999; H. Papoušek & Papoušek, 1987; Trevarthen & Aitken, 2001). The development of intersubjectivity allows infants to experience that they are the same as other people. Gopnik and Meltzoff (1994) argue that these "like-me" experiences are rooted in the perception of bodily movement patterns. Infants become aware of their own body movements through an internal sense of proprioception so that they can detect cross-modal equivalences between the movement as felt and the movement they see being performed by others. In their seminal contribution, Meltzoff and Moore (1977) outlined that imitation is based on infants' capacity to register equivalences between the body transformations they see in others and the body transformations they feel themselves make. Early imitation therefore implies cross-modal matching. Imitation from memory, that is, deferred imitation in an early capacity, also supports interpersonal development. At about 9 months of age, infants can imitate actions on objects after a 24–hour delay (Meltzoff, 1988). Gopnik and Meltzoff (1997) argue that a body scheme that includes internal proprioceptive sensations serves as a halfway point between purely physical objects and mental states. From this perspective, the capacity to map external visible behaviors onto phenomenologically internal mental states appears to be inborn. Infants have to learn about the nature of the mind from their environment, but they need not learn that something like "mind" exists.

Joint attention as an early understanding of intention can be regarded as an antecedent of false-belief understanding because this sets the stage not only for language (Astington & Baird, 2004) but also for later theory-of-mind achievements (Tomasello, 1999; Wellman, 2004). To understand intentions, one needs to inhibit attention for the self's stream of consciousness (Perner, 2004). In the second year of life, everyday conversations in 2-year-olds might be revealing in this respect, since toddlers' progress in understanding the origin of their own knowledge relates to changes in episodic memory and the end of childhood amnesia, which in turn leads to psychological verbal explanations. In these early conversational exchanges, children learn that different people want and know different things than oneself, thus enhancing their understanding of theory of mind (Astington & Baird, 2004). The connection between conversations and theory of mind might not be straightforward but could be mediated through abilities in conflict inhibition. In this regard, the discussion of Dunn (2004; see also Astington & Baird, 2004) on the importance of semantic versus syntactic and structural components of conversational understanding is interesting. If, as also Nelson (1996) argues, children use mental terms before they fully understand them, thus acquiring "meaning from use" (Astington & Baird, 2004, p. 8) and learning to use language as a tool representing mental states, the pragmatic components of language or the "relationship experiences" themselves (Dunn, 2004, p. 14) of the child become important. In Nelson's (2004) words: "The question is not whether the child can 'read' another's mind, but whether he or she can enter into the cultural discourse that abstracts from ongoing action to talk about what is in the mind of others" (p. 17). One could speculate that to understand these relationship experiences, one needs to control one's own distracting inner impulses of action and to concentrate on the contextual demands of the situation, thus, being skilled in conflict inhibition (cf. Chasiotis, Kießling, Hofer, & Campos, 2005).

The Origins of a Theory of Mind: Sociocultural Influences and Inhibitory Control

In our view, early childhood theory of mind together with language are probably uniquely human and characteristic of persons in all cultural and language communities (Tomasello, 1999, 2001; Wellman, 2004). The other significant ability underlying human social interaction besides language is the understanding that other people have knowledge and desires that may be different from one's one (see Sabbagh, this volume). The core element of our commonsense psychology is the understanding that other humans are mental beings whose behaviors are based on certain states of mind and processes of consciousness (e.g., needs, beliefs, or emotions). How children gain access to such a mental world during their development has become a major research arena in developmental psychology in the past 25 years (Flavell, 1999). Children's understanding of false-belief situations is regarded as a central aspect of their theory of mind because it is generally accepted as a litmus test for the presence of representational abilities (Dennett, 1983). Research has shown that children's understanding of false-belief situations is subject to considerable changes, especially during the age span of 3 to 4.5 years (Wellman, Cross, & Watson, 2001). Findings such as those of Cutting and Dunn (1999) show that, independent of age and family background, verbal competence contributes significantly to the understanding of false-belief situations (cf. also Astington, 2001; Jenkins & Astington, 1996). However, it is not general language competence but particular domains of language development that interact with particular domains of the theory of mind (Astington & Baird, 2004). Although the theory of mind develops at about the same time span in most children (Avis & Harris, 1991), the timing of its development is related to aspects of children's social demographic and cultural environment. For instance, Naito (2004) has demonstrated that Japanese children understood false beliefs and knowledge origins more than 1 year later than European American children. Other research on sociocultural influences demonstrates that contextual variables such as socioeconomic status of the family are significantly related to the development of the child's theory-of-mind understanding, even when age and verbal skill of the child are controlled. One critical factor seems to be the presence of older siblings (Ruffman, Perner, Naito, Parkin, & Clements, 1998). Other contributing contextual factors are greater opportunities to discuss mental states and reasoning about social issues, fantasy play, managing social conflict, and being a silent participant in more ambitious interactions among parents and older siblings. The same factors also tend to increase the speed of language development (Cummins, 1998; Ruffman et al., 1998). Cummins (1998) proposed a further argument with reference to the dominance theory. Younger siblings are always competing for resources with older siblings, with the latter typically having the advantage because of their greater size, force, and mental abilities. Consequently, younger children would be more motivated to develop their talents to improve their competitive abilities. Thus, the number of adults and the number of older peers that a preschool child interacts with on a daily basis are positively related to their understanding of false beliefs (Lewis, Freeman, Kyriakidou, Maridaki-Kassotaki, & Berridge, 1996; see also Cole & Mitchell, 2000; Cutting & Dunn, 1999).

At the same age at which the mental world opens up to the child, his or her executive functioning also undergoes significant development. The term *executive functioning* stands for processes that serve to monitor and control thoughts and actions. Such processes include planning, impulse control, suppression of highly salient but irrelevant reactions, maintenance of strategy, and flexibility in and structured search for appropriate thought and action (Carlson & Moses, 2001; Cole & Mitchell, 2000; Ozonoff, Pennington, & Rogers, 1991; Perner & Lang, 1999). Inhibitory control as an important part of executive functioning designates the ability to suppress reactions to irrelevant (internal as well as external) stimuli when aiming at a certain cognitively represented goal (Bjorklund & Kipp, 2002; Rothbart & Posner, 1985). During childhood, inhibitory abilities lead to an improvement of the immature capability of directing attention selectively to relevant information and being uninfluenced by unimportant information (Bjorklund & Kipp, 2002; Kopp, 1982). Recently, the question of the relation between the development of theory of mind and executive functioning has increasingly attracted attention. Inhibitory control—the ability to suppress contents of thought and ways of behavior—has been investigated as a core component of executive functioning (Carlson & Moses, 2001; Cole & Mitchell, 2000; Hughes, 1998; Perner & Lang, 1999). It is distinguished in delay tasks, in which the child has to demonstrate a certain behavior not immediately but delayed, and conflict tasks, in which the child has to suppress one reaction and activate another depending on the respective stimulus (Carlson & Moses, 2001). Studies investigating the connection between inhibitory control and "theory of mind" (mainly through false-belief tasks) revealed very high, culturally invariant correlations of these two abilities (Cole & Mitchell, 2000), which holds especially for the conflict tasks (Carlson & Moses, 2001; Chasiotis, Kießling, Hofer, & Campos, 2005). However, the directionality of this connection is not clear (see Perner & Lang, 1999, for a review), which suggests that both domains influence each other mutually during their development. For example, a minimum level of inhibitory control seems to be required for a person to direct attention and suppress certain stimuli, and to observe oneself or others in order to discover the mental foundations of one's own or others' thinking and acting. At the same time, an improved understanding of one's own mental processes seems to facilitate the suppression of contents of thought as well as of actions (Perner

& Lang, 1999). According to Moses (2001), there are two groups of opposing theoretical approaches, which he terms "expression" approaches, on the one hand, and "emergence" approaches, on the other. The former approaches stress that young children already possess a belief concept but cannot express it in standard tasks because they are not able to suppress their knowledge of reality. Emergence approaches postulate that a certain degree of executive functioning is necessary for a belief concept to develop at all. To be able to reflect upon thoughts and actions, the person has to dissociate himself or herself from the situation, as well as suppress salient but misleading knowledge (cf. Humphrey, 1993).

An evolutionary theoretical framework trying to clarify the connection between these two abilities has been provided by Bjorklund and Kipp (2002; also see Bjorklund & Pellegrini, 2002). In their opinion, inhibitory control is a necessary condition not only for the development of a theory of mind but for the entire development of social intelligence. Accordingly, the origins of inhibitory control in social mammals are to be found in social selection pressure favoring cooperation. This social pressure required, above all, the inhibition of impulses of aggressive and sexual behaviors. During human phylogeny, as humans have lived in increasingly complex social structures, the ability of inhibition has developed as an increasingly volitionally (i.e., neocortically) controlled domain-general ability that made possible the relatively fast evolution of a theory of mind (see also Humphrey, 1984, 1993). According to Bjorklund and Kipp (2002), inhibitory capabilities and theory of mind coevolved from this point in time. Thus, from a phylogenetic point of view, the postulated sequence could contribute to clarify the controversy currently existing in primatology due to conflicting results obtained by ethological fieldwork and experiments on the theory of mind of higher primates, including humans (see Byrne & Whiten, 1988; Heyes, 1998; Russon, 2002; Tomasello, 1999). According to Bjorklund and Pellegrini (2002; also see Bjorklund & Kipp, 2002), some of the experimental findings of deception in primates could be explained more economically by delay of inhibition abilities. Applied to human ontogenesis, this would imply that at least a small degree of inhibitory functioning is a necessary prerequisite for the development of a theory of mind. This interpretation would support the "emergence" approach (see Moses, 2001; see also Chasiotis & Kießling, 2004).

Although the causal relations between the development of inhibitory and mentalistic abilities is still unclear (see Moses, 2001; Perner & Lang, 1999), the ideas derived from evolutionary developmental psychology on the phylogenesis of inhibitory and theory-of-mind capabilities indicate that at least a slight degree of inhibitory abilities might be a necessary prerequisite for the ontogenetic development of a theory of mind (Bjorklund & Kipp, 2002; Bjorklund & Pellegrini, 2002). The quality of these inhibitory core abilities could be sensorimotor in nature, where higher order cognitive processes like planning are not involved (cf. Chasiotis, Kießling, & Winter, 2005). Thus, the abilities of language, executive control, and theory mind can be regarded as basic prerequisites for the development of social engagement from an evolutionary point of view.

Epilogue: Social Structure, Dominance, and Social Engagement

In the opening section of this chapter, we argued that competition, conflict, and cooperation lie at the core of human social engagement (Trivers, 1985). In particular, the interaction of selfish and cooperative motivation is essential for understanding the nature of human social engagement. The competent application of prosocial and competitive behavior leads to social dominance, which can be regarded as a mechanism to explain social structures in groups. Helpfulness and prosocial interactions are related to popularity and social status at all ages during childhood (Coie, Dodge, & Coppotelli, 1982). Dominant individuals have greater access to resources and will use a variety of techniques to maintain their status through a combination of aggressive and cooperative interactive strategies (Hawley, 1999). The choice of a strategy is influenced by the ecology of the group and the associated costs and benefits. Thus, dominance is in some ways an ideal measure of social development because it explains the ways in which an individual's behavior is related to the more general group structure or group cohesion (Bjorklund & Pellegrini, 2002). Dominance is a variable that reflects the way in which specific individuals interact with each other rather than all members of a group. From this individual selection point of view, individuals must only know their status relative to those with whom they interact frequently (Archer, 1992). Dominance hierarchies are formed based on the history of competitive interactions, with the frequent winners occupying the top of the hierarchy and the frequent losers occupying the bottom. Dominant individuals have preferred access to resources. The presence of dominance hierarchies may have played a critical role in the evolution of social intelligence (Bjorklund & Pellegrini, 2002; Cummins, 1998). Individuals must be aware not only of their rank in the group and that of others, but also of desired and rejected behavioral regulations and their application in the group. Thus social reasoning is a prerequisite as well as a consequence of social structure and dominance in groups.

Ontogenetically, there are some indications that altruistic rewards and altruistic punishment are central to the development of social cooperative behavior within dominance hierarchies. In her evolutionary approach to morality and resource control, Hawley (2003a) recently found evidence for the adaptive interplay of prosocial and coercive control in preschool children: Children who are highly effective resource controllers are simultaneously aggressive and yet well aware of moral norms (see also Charlesworth, 1988, 1996). Interestingly, Sutton, Smith, and Swettenham (1999) could also show that children with socially undesirable behavior do not have deficits in theory of mind and that adolescents who also use dual prosocial/coercive strategies are often the most popular (Hawley, 2003b). Finally, older children are more generous and more willing to punish altruistically in games of social cooperation (Zarbatany, Hartmann, & Gelfand, 1985), a finding that probably is due not to maturational processes but mainly to the presence of an adult or parental socialization influences (Eisenberg et al., 1993).

Thus, although there are strong incentives to obey to within-group prosocial behaviors, even these prosocial or "moral" behaviors are self-serving (MacDonald, 1988, 1992, 1996). Altruistic motives induce humans to cooperate and punish in one-off interactions, and selfish motives induce them to increase rewards and punishment in repeated interactions where reputation formation is possible (Fehr & Fischbacher, 2003). It is intriguing that children's fundamental self-interest guides them to choose the most effective strategy, that is, the bi-strategic cooperative orientation that has also been demonstrated as optimal in modern game theory of human altruism. As a result of a childhood context in which cooperation, conflict, and competition are all simultaneously present, leading to the development of executive control, language, and theory of mind and ultimately fueled by evolutionary-based mechanisms geared to maximize each participant's fitness (Bjorklund & Pellegrini, 2002), children appear to gain reputation by engaging in cooperative and competing interactions in a competent way.

References

Alexander, R. D. (1987). *The biology of moral systems*. Hawthorne, England: Aldine.

Amoss, P. T., & Harrell, S. (Eds.). (1981). *Other ways of growing old*. Stanford, CA: Stanford University Press.

Archer, J. (1992). *Ethology and human development*. Hemel Hempstead, England: Wheatsheaf.

Astington, J. W. (2001). The future of theory-of-mind research: Understanding motivational states, the role of language, and real-world consequences. *Child Development, 72*, 685–687.

Astington, J. W., & Baird, J. (2004). Why language matters for theory of mind. *ISSBD Newsletter, 1*(45), 7–9.

Avis, J., & Harris, P. L. (1991). Belief-desire reasoning among Baka children: Evidence for a universal conception of mind. *Child Development, 62*, 460–467.

Axelrod, R. (1984). *The evolution of cooperation*. New York: Basic Books.

Axelrod, R., & Hamilton, W. D. (1981). The evolution of cooperation. *Science, 211*, 1390–1396.

Bard, K. A. (2004). *Imitation in chimpanzees (Pan troglodytes)*. Manuscript in preparation.

Belsky, J., Steinberg, L., & Draper, P. (1991). Childhood experience, interpersonal development, and reproductive strategy: An evolutionary theory of socialization. *Child Development, 62*, 682–685.

Bischof, N. (1996). *Das Kraftfeld der Mythen. Signale aus der Zeit, in der wir die*

Welt erschaffen haben [The force field of myths. Signals from an area in which we created the world]. Munich: Piper.

Bjorklund, D. F. (1987). A note on neonatal imitation. *Developmental Review, 7,* 86–92.

Bjorklund, D. F. (1997). The role of immaturity in human development. *Psychological Bulletin, 122,* 153–169.

Bjorklund, D. F., Gaultney, J. F., & Green, B. L. (1993). "I watch therefore I can do": The development of meta-imitation over the preschool years and the advantage of optimism in one's imitative skills. In R. Pasnak & M. L. Howe (Eds.), *Emerging themes in cognitive development: Vol. 2. Competencies* (pp. 79–102). New York: Springer-Verlag.

Bjorklund, D. F., & Kipp, K. (2002). Social cognition, inhibition, and theory of mind: The evolution of human intelligence. In R. J. Sternberg & J. C. Kaufman (Eds.), *The evolution of intelligence* (pp. 27–53). Mahwah, NJ: Erlbaum.

Bjorklund, D. F., & Pellegrini, A. (2002). *The origins of human nature: Evolutionary developmental psychology.* Washington, DC: American Psychological Association.

Bogin, B. (1997). Evolutionary hypotheses for human childhood. *Yearbook of Physical Anthropology, 40,* 63–89.

Bowlby, J. (1969). *Attachment and loss: Vol. 1. Attachment.* London: Hogarth.

Bowles, S., Choi, J.-K., & Hopfensitz, A. (2003). The co-evolution of individual behaviors and social institutions. *Journal of Theoretical Biology, 223,* 135–147.

Boyd, R., Gintis, H., Bowles, S., & Richerson, P. J. (2003). The evolution of altruistic punishment. *Proceedings of the National Academy of Sciences of the United States of America, 100,* 3531–3535.

Bruner, J. S. (1981). The social context of language acquisition. *Language and Communication, 1,* 155–178.

Buchan, N. R., Croson, R. T. A., & Dawes, R. M. (2002). Swift neighbors and persistent strangers: A cross-cultural investigation of trust and reciprocity in social exchange. *American Journal of Sociology, 108,* 168–206.

Burnstein, E., Crandall, C., & Kitayama, S. (1994). Some neo-Darwinian decision rules for altruism: Weighing cues for inclusive fitness as a function of the biological importance of the decision. *Journal of Personality and Social Psychology, 67,* 773–789.

Buss, D. (1994). *The evolution of desire: Strategies of human mating.* New York: Basic Books.

Buss, D. (2004). *Evolutionary psychology: The new science of the mind* (2nd ed.). New York: Pearson.

Byrne, R., & Whiten, A. (Eds.). (1988). *Machiavellian intelligence: Social expertise and the evolution of intellect in monkeys, apes and humans.* Oxford, England: Clarendon Press.

Carlson, S. M., & Moses, L. J. (2001). Individual differences in inhibitory control and children's "theory of mind." *Child Development, 72,* 1032–1053.

Carpenter, M., Nagell, K., & Tomasello, M. (1998). Social cognition, joint attention, and communicative competence from 9 to 15 months of age. *Monographs of the Society for Research in Child Development, 63,* 1–143.

Cassidy, J., & Shaver, P. R. (Eds.). (1999), *Handbook of attachment: Theory, research, and clinical applications.* New York: Guilford.

Charlesworth, W. (1988). Resources and resource acquisition behavior during ontogeny. In K. MacDonald (Ed.), *Sociobiological perspectives on human development* (pp. 42–117). New York: Springer.

Charlesworth, W. (1996). Co-operation and competition: Contributions to an evolutionary and developmental model. *International Journal of Behavioral Development, 19*, 25–39.

Chasiotis, A., Keller, H., & Scheffer, D. (2003). Birth order, age at menarche and intergenerational context continuity: A comparison of female somatic development in West and East Germany. *North American Journal of Psychology, 5*, 153–169.

Chasiotis, A., & Kießling, F. (2004). Bleibt die Spezifität der Beziehung zwischen Theory of mind und inhibitorischer Kontrolle über die Lebensspanne bestehen?—Zum Zusammenhang mentalistischer und selbstregulatorischer Kompetenz im Erwachsenenalter [Does the specifity of theory of mind and inhibitory control persist over the life-span?—On the relation of mentalistic and self-regulatory competence in adulthood]. *Zeitschrift für Entwicklungspsychologie und Pädagogische Psychologie* (Journal of Developmental and Pedagogical Psychology), *62*, 210–220.

Chasiotis, A., Kießling, F., Hofer, J., & Campos, D. (2005). *Theory of mind and inhibitory control in three cultures: Conflict inhibition predicts false belief understanding in Germany, Costa Rica, and Cameroon.* Manuscript submitted for publication.

Chasiotis, A., Kießling, F., & Winter, V. (2005). *Sensory motor inhibition as a prerequisite for theory of mind: A comparison of preschoolers with and without sensory integrative deficits.* Manuscript submitted for publication.

Chasiotis, A., Scheffer, D., Restemeier, R., & Keller, H. (1998). Intergenerational context discontinuity affects the onset of puberty: A comparison of parent-child dyads in West and East Germany. *Human Nature, 9*, 321–339.

Cheney, D., & Seyfarth, R. (1999). *How monkeys see the world.* Chicago: University of Chicago Press.

Chisholm, J. S. (1996). The evolutionary ecology of attachment organization. *Human Nature, 7*, 1–38.

Chisholm, J. S. (1999). *Death, hope, and sex: Steps to an evolutionary ecology of mind and morality.* Cambridge, England: Cambridge University Press.

Cialdini, R. B. (2001). *Influence: Science and practice.* Boston: Allyn and Bacon.

Coie, J. D., Dodge, K. A., & Coppotelli, H. (1982). Dimensions and types of social status: A cross-age perspective. *Developmental Psychology, 18*, 557–570.

Cole, K., & Mitchell, P. (2000). Siblings in the development of executive control and a "theory of mind." *British Journal of Developmental Psychology, 18*, 279–295.

Cummins, D. (1998). Social norms and other minds: The evolutionary roots of higher cognition. In D. Cummins & C. Allen (Eds.), *The evolution of mind* (pp. 28–50). New York: Oxford University Press.

Cutting, A. L., & Dunn, J. (1999). "Theory of mind," emotion, language and family background: Individual differences and interrelations. *Child Development, 70*, 853–865.

Daly, M., & Wilson, M. (1983). *Sex, evolution and behavior* (2nd ed.). Boston: PWS Publishers.

Daly, M., & Wilson, M. (1988). *Homicide.* New York: Aldine.

Darwin, C. (1859). *The origin of species.* New York: Modern Library.

Dawkins, R. (1976). *The selfish gene.* New York: Oxford University Press.

Dennett, D. C. (1983). Intentional systems in cognitive ethology: The "Panglossian paradigm" defended. *Behavioral and Brain Sciences, 6*, 343–390.

Dickinson, D. L. (2000). Ultimatum decision-making: A test of reciprocal kindness. *Theory and Decision, 48*, 151–177.

Dunbar, R. (1993). Coevolution of neocortical size, group size and language in humans. *Behavioural and Brain Sciences, 16,* 681–735.

Dunbar, R. (1996). *Grooming, gossip and the evolution of language.* London: Faber and Faber.

Dunbar, R., & Spoors, M. (1995). Social networks, support cliques, and kinship. *Human Nature, 6,* 273–290.

Dunn, J. (2004). Broadening the framework of theory of mind research. *ISSBD Newsletter, 1*(45), 13–14.

Eisenberg, N., Fabes, R. A., Carlo, G., Speer, A. L., Switzer, G., Karbon, M., et al. (1993). The relations of empathy-related emotions and maternal practices to children's comforting behavior. *Journal of Experimental Child Psychology, 55,* 131–150.

Fehr, E., & Fischbacher, U. (2003). The nature of human altruism. *Nature, 425,* 785–791.

Fehr, E., & Fischbacher, U. (in press). Third party punishment and social norms. *Evolution and Human Behavior.*

Feldman, R., Greenbaum, C. W., & Yirmiya, N. (1999). Mother-infant affect synchrony as an antecedent of the emergence of self-control. *Developmental Psychology, 35,* 223–231.

Fijneman, Y. A., Willemsen, M. E., Poortinga, Y. H., Erelcin, F. G., Georgas, J., Hui, C. H., et al. (1996). Individualism-collectivism: An empirical study of conceptual issue. *Journal of Cross-Cultural Psychology, 27,* 381–402.

Fischbacher, U., Gächter, S., & Fehr, E. (2001). Are people conditionally cooperative? Evidence from a public goods experiment. *Economic Letters, 71,* 397–404.

Flavell, J. H. (1999). Cognitive development: Children's knowledge about the mind. *Annual Review of Psychology, 50,* 21–45.

Georgas, J., Berry, J. W., van de Vijver, F., Kağitçibaşi, Ç., & Poortinga, Y. (Eds.). (in press). *Family structure and function across cultures: Psychological variations.* Cambridge, England: Cambridge University Press.

Gintis, H., Smith, E. A., & Bowles, S. (2001). Costly signaling and cooperation. *Journal of Theoretical Biology, 213,* 103–119.

Gopnik, A., & Meltzoff, A. N. (1994). Minds, bodies and persons: Young children's understanding of the self and others as reflected in imitation and "theory of mind" research. In S. Parker & R. Mitchell (Eds.), *Self-awareness in animals and humans* (pp. 168–186). New York: Cambridge University Press.

Gopnik, A., & Meltzoff, A. N. (1997). *Words, thoughts, and theories.* Cambridge, MA: MIT Press.

Hamilton, W. (1964). The genetical evolution of social behaviour (I + II). *Journal of Theoretical Biology, 7,* 1–52.

Hawley, P. H. (1999). The ontogenesis of social dominance: A strategy-based evolutionary perspective. *Developmental Review, 19,* 97–132.

Hawley, P. H. (2003a). Prosocial and coercive configurations of resource control in early adolescence: A case for the well-adapted Machiavellian. *Merrill-Palmer Quarterly, 49,* 279–309.

Hawley, P. H. (2003b). Strategies of control, aggression, and morality in preschoolers: An evolutionary perspective. *Journal of Experimental Child Psychology, 85,* 213–235.

Heckhausen, J., & Boyer, P. (Eds.). (2000). Evolutionary psychology: Potential and limits of a Darwinian framework for the behavioural sciences. *Special Issue of American Behavioral Scientist, 43,* 115–141.

Helle, S., Käär, P., & Jokela, J. (2002). Human longevity and early reproduction in pre-industrial Sami populations. *Journal of Evolutionary Biology, 15*, 803–807.

Henrich, J. (2001). In search of Homo economicus: Behavioral experiments in 15 small-scale societies. *American Economic Review, 91*, 73–78.

Hewlett, B. S., Lamb, M. E., Leyendecker, B., & Schoelmerich, A. (2000). Parental investment strategies among Aka foragers, Ngandu farmers, and Euro-American urban industrialists. In L. Cronk, N. Chagnon & W. Irons (Eds.), *Adaptation and human behavior: An anthropological perspective* (pp. 155–178). New York: Aldine de Gruyter.

Heyes, C. M. (1998). Theory of mind in nonhuman primates. *Behavioral and Brain Sciences, 21*, 101–148.

Hill, K. (2002). Altruistic cooperation during foraging by the Ache, and the evolved human predisposition to cooperate. *Human Nature, 13*, 105–128.

Hill, K., Boesch, C., Goodall, J., Pusey, A., Williams, J., & Wrangman, R. (2001). Mortality rates among wild chimpanzees. *Journal of Human Evolution, 39*, 1–14.

Hill, K., & Hurtado, A. M. (1996). *Ache life history: The ecology and demography of a foraging people*. New York: Walter de Gruyter.

Hinde, R. A. (1980). *Ethology*. London: Fontana.

Hobson, R. P. (1993). *Autism and the development of mind*. Hillsdale, NJ: Erlbaum.

Hrdy, S. B. (1999). *Mother nature: A history of mothers, infants, and natural selection*. New York: Pantheon.

Hrdy, S. B. (in press). Cooperative breeders with an ace in the hole. In E. Voland, A. Chasiotis, & W. Schiefenhövel, W. (Eds.), *Grandmotherhood: The evolutionary significance of the second half of female life*. Piscataway, NJ: Rutgers University Press.

Hughes, C. (1998). Executive function in preschoolers: Links with theory of mind and verbal ability. *British Journal of Developmental Psychology, 16*, 233–253.

Humphrey, N. (1976). The social function of intellect. In P. P. G. Bateson & R. A. Hinde (Eds.), *Growing points in ethology* (pp. 303–317). Cambridge, England: Cambridge University Press.

Humphrey, N. (1984). *Consciousness regained*. Oxford, England: Oxford University Press.

Humphrey, N. (1993). *A history of the mind*. London: Vintage.

Jenkins, J. M., & Astington, J. W. (1996). Cognitive factors and family structure associated with "theory of mind" development in young children. *Developmental Psychology, 32*, 70–78.

Kağitçibaşi, Ç. (1990). Family and socialization in cross-cultural perspective: A model of change. In J. J. Berman (Ed.), *Cross-cultural perspectives: Nebraska symposium on motivation 1989* (pp. 135–200). Lincoln: University of Nebraska Press.

Kaniasty, K., & Norris, F. (1995). Mobilization and deterioration of social support following natural disasters. *Contemporary Directions in Psychological Science, 4*, 94–98.

Kaplan, H. (1994). Evolutionary and wealth flows theories of fertility: Empirical tests and new models. *Population and Development Review, 20*, 753–791.

Kaplan, H., Hill, J., Lancaster, J., & Hurtado, A. M. (2000). A theory of human life history evolution: Diet, intelligence, and longevity. *Evolutionary Anthropology, 9*, 156–185.

Keller, H. (1996). Evolutionary approaches. In J. W. Berry, Y. H. Poortinga & J.

Pandey (Eds.), *Handbook of cross-cultural psychology: Vol. 1. Theory and method* (2nd ed., pp. 215–255). Boston: Allyn and Bacon.

Keller, H. (2000a). Human parent-child relationships from an evolutionary perspective. *American Behavioral Scientist, 43*, 957–969.

Keller, H. (2000b). Sozial-emotionale Grundlagen des Spracherwerbs [The social-emotional foundation of language acquisition]. In H. Grimm (Ed.), *Enzyklopädie der Psychologie: Band 3; Sprachentwicklung* [Encyclopedia of psychology: Vol. 3. Language development] (pp. 379–402). Göttingen, Germany: Hogrefe.

Keller, H. (2001). Evolutionary perspectives on lifespan development. In N. J. Smelser & P. B. Baltes (Eds.), *International encyclopedia of the social and behavioral sciences* (Vol. 13, pp. 8840–8844). Oxford, England: Elsevier Science.

Keller, H. (2003). Socialization for competence: Cultural models of infancy. *Human Development, 46*, 288–311.

Keller, H., & Chasiotis, A. (in press-a). Kultur und Entwicklung [Culture and development]. In M. Hasselhorn & R. Silbereisen (Eds.), *Enzyklopädie der Psychology, Serie V: Entwicklung, Band 4: Psychologie des Säuglings- und Kindesalters* [Encyclopedia of psychology, Series V: Development, Vol. 4: Psychology of babyhood and childhood]. Göttingen, Germany: Hogrefe.

Keller, H., & Chasiotis, A. (in press-b). Zur natürlichen und geschlechtlichen Selektion der menschlichen Individualentwicklung [Natural and sexual selection of the human individual development. Evolutionary and ethological approaches]. In W. Schneider & F. Wilkening (Eds.), *Enzyklopädie der Psychologie: Band 1. Theorien, Modelle und Methoden der Entwicklungspsychologie* [Encyclopedia of psychology: Vol. 1. Theories, models and methods of developmental psychology]. Göttingen, Germany: Hogrefe.

Keller, H., Chasiotis, A., & Runde, B. (1992). Intuitive parenting programs in German, American, and Greek parents of 3–month-old infants. *Journal of Cross-Cultural Psychology, 23*, 510–520.

Keller, H., Lohaus, A., Voelker, S., Cappenberg, M., & Chasiotis, A. (1999), Temporal contingency as an independent component of parenting behavior. *Child Development, 70*, 474–485.

Keller, H., Schoelmerich, A., & Eibl-Eibesfeldt, I. (1988). Communication patterns in adult-infant interactions in Western and non-Western cultures. *Journal of Cross-Cultural Psychology, 19*, 427–445.

Keller, H., & Zach, U. (2002). Gender and birth order as determinants of parental behaviour. *International Journal of Behavioral Psychology, 26*, 177–184.

Kohli, M. (1999). Private and public transfers between generations: Linking the family and the state. *European Societies, 1*, 81–104.

Kopp, C. B. (1982). Antecedents of self regulation: A developmental perspective. *Developmental Psychology, 18*, 199–214.

Kruger, D. J. (2001). Psychological aspects of adaptations for kin directed altruistic helping behaviors. *Social Behavior and Personality, 29*, 323–331.

Laland, K. N., Odling-Smee, F. J., & Feldman, M. W. (2000). Niche construction, biological evolution, and cultural change. *Behavioral and Brain Sciences, 23*, 131–146.

Lay, C., Fairlie, P., Jackson, S., Ricci, T., Eisenberg, J., Sato, T., et al. (1998). Domain-specific allocentrism-idiocentrism. *Journal of Cross-Cultural Psychology, 29*, 434–460.

Lee, R. D. (1997). Intergenerational relations and the elderly. In K. W. Wachter &

C. E. Finch (Eds.), *Between Zeus and the salmon: The biodemography of longevity* (pp. 212–233). Washington, DC: National Academy of Sciences.

Legerstee, M., Corter, C., & Kienapple, K. (1990). Hand, arm, and facial actions of young infants to a social and nonsocial stimulus. *Child Development, 61,* 774–784.

Lewis, C., Freeman, N. H., Kyriakidou, C., Maridaki-Kassotaki, K., & Berridge, D. M. (1996). Social influences on false belief access: Specific sibling influences or general apprenticeship? *Child Development, 67,* 2930–2947.

Lorenz, K. (1965). *Evolution and modification of behavior.* Chicago: University of Chicago Press.

MacDonald, K. B. (1988). *Social and personality development: An evolutionary synthesis.* New York: Plenum.

MacDonald, K. B. (1992). Warmth as a developmental construct: An evolutionary analysis. *Child Development, 63,* 753–773.

MacDonald, K. B. (1996). What do children want? A conceptualisation of evolutionary influences on children's motivation in the peer group. *International Journal of Behavioral Development, 19,* 53–73.

Mayr, E. (1994). Evolution: Grundfragen und Missverständnisse [Evolution: Basic questions and misunderstandings]. *Ethik und Sozialwissenschaften, 5,* 203–209.

Mayr, E. (1997). *This is biology.* Cambridge, MA: Harvard University Press.

Mealey, L. (1995). The sociobiology of sociopathy: An integrated evolutionary model. *Behavioral and Brain Sciences, 18,* 523–599.

Meltzoff, A. (1988). Infant imitation and memory: Nine-month-olds in immediate and deferred tests. *Child Development, 59,* 217–225

Meltzoff, A. N., & Moore, K. (1977). Imitation of facial and manual gestures by newborn infants. *Science, 198,* 75–78.

Miklosi, A. (1999). The ethological analysis of imitation. *Biological Review, 74,* 347–374.

Milinski, M., Semmann, D., Bakker, T., & Krambeck, H. J. (2001). Cooperation through indirect reciprocity: Image scoring or standing strategy? *Proceedings of the Royal Society of London. Series B: Biological Sciences, 268,* 2495–2501.

Milinski, M., Semmann, D., & Krambeck, H. J. (2002). Reputations helps solve the "tragedy of the commons." *Nature, 415,* 424–426.

Miller, G. (2000). *The mating mind: How sexual choice shaped the evolution of human nature.* New York: Random House.

Morisset, C. E., Barnard, K. E., & Booth, C. L. (1995). Toddlers' language development: Sex differences within social risk. *Developmental Psychology, 31,* 851–865.

Moses, L. (2001). Executive accounts of theory-of-mind development. *Child Development, 72,* 688–690.

Müller, U., & Carpendale, J. I. M. (2004). From joint activity to joint attention: A relational approach to social development in infancy. In J. I. M. Carpendale & U. Müller (Eds.), *Social interaction and the development of knowledge* (pp. 215–238). Mahwah, NJ: Erlbaum.

Naito, M. (2004). Is theory of mind a universal and unitary construct? *ISSBD Newsletter, 1*(45), 9–11.

Nelson, K. (1996). *Language in cognitive development: Emergence of the mediated mind.* New York: Cambridge University Press.

Nelson, K. (2004). The future of theory of mind lies in community of minds. *ISSBD Newsletter, 1*(45), 16–17.

Nichida, T., Corp, N., Hamai, M., Hasegawa, T., Hiraiwa-Hasegawa, M., Hosaka, K., et al. (2003). Demography, female life history, and reproductive profiles among the chimpanzees of Mahale. *American Journal of Primatology, 59*, 99–121.

Nosaka, A., & Chasiotis, A. (in press). Exploring the variation in intergenerational relationships among Germans and Turkish immigrants: An evolutionary perspective on behaviour in a modern social setting. In E. Voland, A. Chasiotis, & W. Schiefenhövel (Eds.), *Grandmotherhood: The evolutionary significance of the second half of female life*. Piscataway, NJ: Rutgers University Press.

Nowak, M. A., & Sigmund, K. (1998). Evolution of indirect reciprocity by image scoring. *Nature, 393*, 573–577

Ozonoff, S., Pennington, B. F., & Rogers, S. J. (1991). Executive function deficits in high-functioning autistic individuals: Relationship to "theory of mind." *Journal of Child Psychology and Psychiatry, 32*, 1081–1105.

Papoušek, H., & Papoušek, M. (1987). Intuitive parenting: A dialectic counterpart to the infant's integrative competence. In J. D. Osofsky (Ed.), *Handbook of infant development* (2nd ed., pp. 669–720). New York: Wiley.

Papoušek, M., & Papoušek, H. (1991). Early verbalizations as precursors of language development. In M. E. Lamb & H. Keller (Eds.), *Infant development: Perspectives from German-speaking countries* (pp. 299–328). Hillsdale, NJ: Erlbaum.

Perner, J. (2004). Tracking the essential mind. *ISSBD Newsletter, 1*(45), 4–7.

Perner, J., & Lang, B. (1999). Development of "theory of mind" and executive control. *Trends in Cognitive Sciences, 3*, 337–344.

Pinker, S. (1994). *The language instinct: How the mind creates language*. New York: HarperCollins.

Pinker, S. (1999). *Words and rules: The ingredients of language*. New York: Basic Books.

Pinker, S., & Bloom, P. (1990). Natural language and natural selection. *Behavioral and Brain Sciences, 13*, 707–784.

Rhee, E., Uleman, J. S., & Lee, H. K. (1996). Variations in collectivism and individualism by ingroup and culture: Confirmatory factor analyses. *Journal of Personality and Social Psychology, 71*, 1037–1054.

Rilling, J. (2002). A neural basis for social cooperation. *Neuron, 35*, 395–405.

Roberts, G., & Sherratt, T. N. (1998). Development of cooperative relationships through increasing investment. *Nature, 394*, 175–179.

Rochat, P., & Hespos, S. J. (1997). Differential rooting response by neonates: Evidence for an early sense of self. *Early Development and Parenting, 6*, 105–112.

Rothbart, M. K., & Posner, M. (1985). Temperament and the development of self-regulation. In L. C. Hartlage & C. F. Telzrow (Eds.), *The neuropsychology of individual differences: A developmental perspective* (pp. 93–123). New York: Plenum.

Ruffman, T., Perner, J., Naito, M., Parkin, L., & Clements, W. (1998). Older (but not younger) siblings facilitate false belief understanding. *Developmental Psychology, 34*, 161–174.

Russon, A. E. (2002). Comparative developmental perspectives on cultures: The great apes. In H. Keller, Y. H. Poortinga, & A. Schölmerich (Eds.), *Between culture and biology* (pp. 30–56). London: Cambridge University Press.

Schore, A. (2001). The effects of a secure attachment relationship on right brain development, affect regulation, and infant mental health. *Infant Mental Health Journal, 22*, 7–66.

Schore, A. N. (1994). *Affect regulation and the origin of the self: The neurobiology of emotional development*. Hillsdale, NJ: Erlbaum.

Schore, A. N. (1998). Early shame experiences and infant brain development. In P. Gilbert & B. Andrews (Eds.), *Shame: Interpersonal behavior, psychopathology, and culture* (pp. 57–77). New York: Oxford University Press.

Smith, E. A., Bliege Bird, R., & Bird, D. W. (2003). The benefits of costly signaling: Meriam turtle hunters. *Behavioral Ecology, 14*, 116–126.

Stern, D. N. (1985). *The interpersonal world of the infant: A view from psychoanalysis and developmental psychology*. New York: Basic Books.

Sulloway, F. (1996). *Born to rebel: Birth order, family dynamics, and creative lives*. New York: Pantheon.

Sutton, J., Smith, P. K., & Swettenham, J. (1999). Social cognition and bullying: Social inadequacy or skilled manipulation? *British Journal of Developmental Psychology, 17*, 435–450.

Thompson, R. A., Braun, K., Grossmann, K. E., Gunnar, M. R., Heinrichs, M., Keller, H., et al. (in press). Early social attachment and its consequences: The dynamics of a developing relationship. In L Ahnert, S. Carter, & M. E. Lamb (Eds.), *Attachment and bonding: A new synthesis. Dahlem Workshop Report 92*. Cambridge, MA: MIT Press.

Tomasello, M. (1999). *The cultural origins of human cognition*. Cambridge, MA: Harvard University Press.

Tomasello, M. (2001). Cultural transmission: A view from chimpanzees and human infants. *Journal of Cross-Cultural Psychology, 32*, 135–146.

Tooby, J., & Cosmides, L. (1990). The past explains the present: Emotional adaptations and the structure of ancestral environments. *Ethology and Sociobiology, 11*, 375–424.

Tooby, J., & Cosmides, L. (1992). The psychological foundations of culture. In J. Barkow, L. Cosmides, & J. Tooby (Eds.), *The adapted mind: Evolutionary psychology and the generation of culture* (pp. 19–139). New York: Oxford University Press.

Tooby, J., & DeVore, E. (1987). The reconstruction of hominid behavioral evolution through strategic modeling. In W. G. Kinzey (Ed.), *The evolution of human behavior: Primate models* (pp. 183–237). Albany: State University of New York Press.

Trevarthen, C., & Aitken, K. J. (2001). Infant intersubjectivity: Research, theory, and clinical applications. *Journal of Child Psychology and Psychiatry, 42*, 3–48.

Trivers, R. L. (1971). The evolution of reciprocal altruism. *Quarterly Review of Biology, 46*, 35–57.

Trivers, R. L. (1972). Parental investment and sexual selection. In B. G. Campbell (Ed.), *Sexual selection and the descent of man: 1871–1971* (pp. 136–179). Chicago: Aldine de Gruyter.

Trivers, R. L. (1974). Parent-offspring conflict. *American Zoologist, 14*, 249–264.

Trivers, R. L. (1985). *Social evolution*. Menlo Park, CA: Benjamin/Cummings.

Valsiner, J. (1989). On the glory and misery of sociobiological perspectives on human development: A selfish book review. *Developmental Psychobiology, 22*, 1–5.

Voland, E., Chasiotis, A., & Schiefenhövel, W. (Eds.). (in press). *Grandmotherhood: The evolutionary significance of the second half of female life*. Piscataway, NJ: Rutgers University Press.

Voland, E., & Grammer, K. (Eds.). (2003). *Evolutionary aesthetics*. Heidelberg, Germany: Springer.

Watson, M. W. (1994). The relation between anxiety and pretend play. In A. Slade & D. P. Wolf (Eds.), *Children at play: Clinical and developmental approaches to meaning and representation* (pp. 33–47). New York: Oxford University Press.

Wellman, H. M. (2004). Theory of mind: Developing core human cognitions. *ISSBD Newsletter, 1*(45), 1–4.

Wellman, H. M., Cross, D., & Watson, J. (2001). Meta-analysis of theory-of-mind development: The truth about false belief. *Child Development, 72*, 655–684.

Williams, G. (1966). *Adaptation and natural selection: A critique of some current evolutionary thought*. Princeton, NJ: Princeton University Press.

Wilson, D. S. (1994). Adaptive genetic variation and human evolutionary psychology. *Ethology and Sociobiology, 15*, 219–235.

Wilson, D. S. (2002). *Darwin's cathedral: Evolution, religion, and the nature of society*. Chicago: University of Chicago Press.

Wilson, E. O. (1975). *Sociobiology: The new synthesis*. Cambridge, MA: Harvard University Press.

Zahavi, A. (1975). Mate selection: A selection for a handicap. *Journal of Theoretical Biology, 53*, 205–214.

Zahavi, A. (1995). Altruism as handicap: The limitations of kin selection and reciprocity. *Journal of Avian Biology, 26*, 1–3.

Zarbatany, L., Hartmann, D. P., & Gelfand, D. M. (1985). Why does children's generosity increase with age: Susceptibility to experimenter influence or altruism? *Child Development, 56*, 746–756.

11

Understanding Impairments in Social Engagement in Autism

Raphael Bernier
Sara Jane Webb
Geraldine Dawson

Autism is a developmental disorder characterized by impairments in social interaction and communication, and the presence of a restricted range of activities and interests. It is generally believed that impairments in the social domain, which can include impairments in eye gaze and facial expressions, peer relationships, and social or emotional reciprocity, are the hallmark of this disorder. First described by Leo Kanner in 1943, autism has a neurobiological basis and is quite heterogeneous in its symptom presentation. Thus, the term *autism spectrum disorders* is often used to reflect the fact that autism falls along a spectrum from severe to mildly impaired. Cognitive abilities also are variable, with 70% to 80% of children with autistic disorder scoring in the mentally retarded range on cognitive assessments (Tsai, 1996; Rutter, 1983; Gillberg & Billstedt, 2000). Prevalence estimates for autistic disorder are 1 in 1,000 and increase to 1 in 500 when the broad autism spectrum (e.g., Asperger's syndrome and pervasive developmental disorder–not otherwise specified) is considered. The prevalence rate appears to be unrelated to socioeconomic status and ethnic background. However, boys are affected between three and four times more often than girls (Fombonne, 1999). While twin studies and molecular genetic studies posit heritability estimates over 90% for autism spectrum disorders, the mechanism for genetic transmission is yet unknown (Veenstra-Vanderweele & Cook, 2003; Bespalova & Buxbaum, 2003).

Although the social behavior of individuals with autism has been well characterized, the basic mechanisms underlying impairments in social behavior are unknown. Several early social impairments that are important for social engagement have been studied in young children with autism. Better clarification of the nature of these early social impairments and their neural bases will have implications for understanding the etiology and development course of autism, and hopefully lead to more effective early intervention.

This chapter has two goals: First, we briefly review the core early social impairments affecting social engagement in autism, namely, impairments in social orienting, joint attention, emotion perception, affective sharing, and imitation. Second, we review some current hypotheses regarding the fundamental deficits underlying these impairments, and their neural bases.

Early Social Impairments in Autism

Social Orienting

In the first 6 weeks following birth, typically developing infants demonstrate sensitivity to social stimuli (Rochat, 1999), as reflected in an attentional preference for social stimuli over nonanimate stimuli (Legerstee, Pomerleau, Malcuit, & Feider, 1987), particularly the human face and speech sounds (Maurer & Salapatek, 1976; Morton & Johnson, 1991; Eisenberg, 1970; Butterfield & Siperstein, 1970). These early attentional preferences appear to be obligatory, initially driven by specific perceptual characteristics of social stimuli, but over the course of the first year, infants' attention becomes volitional (Ruff & Rothbart, 1996; Rochat & Striano, 1999). By 5 to 7 months of age, infants will spontaneously orient when someone enters the room or calls their name. These early attentional preferences, especially for social stimuli, provide opportunities for the infant to engage in social exchanges and, in this way, facilitate the acquisition of later social and communication skills (Rochat & Striano, 1999).

A failure to demonstrate this proclivity to orient to social stimuli ("social orienting") is likely one of the earliest and most basic impairments in autism (Dawson, Meltzoff, Osterling, Rinaldi, & Brown, 1998; Dawson, Carver, Meltzoff, Panagiotides, McPartland, & Webb, 2002; Mundy & Neal, 2001; Tantam, 1992). In home videotape studies of first-birthday parties, it was found that, compared with infants later diagnosed with mental retardation or with typical development, infants with autism more often failed to orient to their name and attended less to the people in the environment (figure 11–1; Osterling & Dawson, 1994; Osterling, Dawson, & Munson, 2002). In two other home videotape studies it was found that 8- to 12-month old infants later diagnosed with autism were less likely to orient when their name was called (Baranek, 1999; Werner, Dawson, Osterling, & Dinno, 2000). In an observational study, toddlers with autism have been found to spend less time looking at people than do toddlers with developmental delay and typical development (Swettenham et al., 1998).

An impairment in social orienting in children with autism has also been demonstrated in experimental studies. In a study by Dawson and colleagues (Dawson, Meltzoff, Osterling, Rinaldi, & Brown, 1998), children with autism, Down

Figure 11–1. One-year-old later diagnosed with autism (left) and typically developing 1-year-old (right) at first birthday parties. Based on work from Osterling and Dawson (1994).

syndrome, and typical development were presented with two social stimuli (name calling and hand clapping) and two nonsocial stimuli (rattle and musical jack-in-the-box). It was found that the children with autism more often failed to orient to both social and nonsocial stimuli compared with the other two groups of children. In addition, this failure was much more likely for the social stimuli. When the children with autism did orient to the social stimuli, their response was delayed. More recently, Dawson and colleagues (Dawson, Munson, et al., 2002) replicated these findings using a larger number of stimuli with a larger sample of 3- and 4-year-olds with autism spectrum disorders, mental age–matched children with developmental delay, and those with typical development.

Klin reported that children with autism failed to demonstrate a preference for human speech sounds, while children with typical development and children with mental retardation showed a preference for maternal speech compared with the sounds of a busy restaurant (Klin, 1991). In a sample of 3- to 4-year-old children with autism, Kuhl, Padden, and Dawson (2004) found that listening preferences in children with autism differ dramatically from those demonstrated by typically developing and developmentally delayed children. Given a choice, preschool-aged children with autism preferred listening to mechanical-sounding auditory signals (signals acoustically matched to speech referred to as *sine-wave analog*) rather than speech itself (motherese). The preference for this sine-wave analog was related to level of language ability and characteristics of the event-related potentials (ERPs) to speech sounds. Specifically, preference for motherese was associated with higher language ability and with a more normal pattern of ERP responses to speech syllables. Children with autism who preferred motherese showed mismatch negativity (MMN) waveforms that resembled those of typically developing children, with a larger negative response to the deviant stimuli, indicating the brain's detection of a change in the speech stimulus. When data from the subgroup of children with autism who preferred the sine-wave analogs were examined, there were no differences between the MMN waveforms in response to the two syllables.

In summary, social orienting is an aspect of early social engagement that appears very early in life in typical development and has been shown to be significantly impaired in children with autism. This impairment has been hypothesized to play a fundamental role in the development of later aspects of social engagement. Specifically, it has been proposed that social orienting is a prerequisite and precursor for the development of joint attention (Dawson, Meltzoff, Osterling, Rinaldi, & Brown, 1998; Mundy & Neal, 2001; Tantam, Holmes, & Cordess, 1993). In fact, in the experimental studies of social orienting discussed earlier, it was found that the ability to orient to social stimuli (but not nonsocial stimuli) was highly correlated with joint attention ability in children with autism.

Joint Attention

Joint attention skills begin to develop during the first 6 months of life (Morales, Mundy, & Rojas, 1998; Hood, Willen, & Driver, 1998). By 5 months of age, infants notice changes in others' eye gaze and will attend and smile less when an adult's eyes are looking away (Symons, Hains, & Muir, 1998; Hains & Muir, 1996). By 12 months of age, several joint attention skills are evident in typically developing children (Carpenter, Nagell, & Tomasello, 1998; Slaughter & McConnell, 2003). These skills involve the ability to coordinate attention on an object or event with another person, for example, by alternating eye gaze between an object and another person's eyes and by directing another's attention by pointing to indicate or request an object, or by showing an object (see Mundy & Acra, this volume).

Young children with autism have impairments in joint attention (Mundy & Neal, 2001; Lewy & Dawson, 1992; Mundy, Sigman, Ungerer, & Sherman, 1986; Loveland & Landry, 1986). In fact, joint attention impairment is part of the diagnostic criteria for autism (American Psychiatric Association, 1994) and is considered to be a core symptom of the disorder (Mundy, 2003). Like social orienting, impairments in joint attention can often be observed earlier than other core impairments, such as pretend play and language (Mundy, Sigman, & Kasari, 1994).

Language ability has been found to be correlated with joint attention skills both in children with typical development (Tomasello, 1995) and in those with autism (Sigman & Ruskin, 1999). Sigman and Ruskin (1999), in their longitudinal study of language and social competence of children with autism, developmental delay, and Down syndrome, found that joint attention skills were correlated with concurrent language ability at the initial preschool-age assessment. They also found that joint attention skills were predictive of later expressive language ability at 12 years of age for the autistic group (Sigman & Ruskin, 1999). Dawson and colleagues also found that joint attention ability was related to concurrent language ability in 3- to 4-year-old children with autism, developmental delay, and typical development (Dawson, Webb, Carver, Panagiotides, & McPartland, 2004). Baldwin (1991) proposes that because of the incidental nature of learning language, joint attention skills are necessary to reduce referencing errors. Mundy expands on this by suggesting that joint attention skills increase incidental learning in the social domain (Mundy & Neal, 2001).

Over the course of development in individuals with autism, the ability to respond to a bid for joint attention improves, while the initiation of joint attention tends to remain impaired (Mundy, 2003). Moreover, children with autism are relatively less impaired in using joint attention to make requests, that is, for instrumental purposes, than to show or share experiences with others. The discrepancy in performance for these types of joint attention behaviors is also seen in typically developing children, and Mundy proposes that these behaviors are related to different social-cognitive and social-emotional processes (Mundy, Card, & Fox, 2000). Initiating joint attention for the purpose of showing or commenting requires a motivation for social sharing, an investment in the sharing of an affective experience, and the executive processes to establish the coordination of attention with another person. In contrast, responding to joint attention (e.g., following another's point) involves following another's lead (Mundy, 2003). The motivation for responding to joint attention may be more a function of learning that the object under discussion is of interest and not necessarily a function of sharing an affective experience (Slaughter & McConnell, 2003).

Children with autism can be taught to develop joint attention skills through intervention (Dawson & Zanolli, 2003); however, the acquisition of joint attention in autism appears to be different from that in typical development. In intervention, joint attention skills are taught by reinforcing children's use of pointing for requests, and such requests are typically for an object or activity of interest to the child. The object of interest serves as the reward for the initiation of joint attention. Thus, the motivation for continued joint attention bids centers on the child's interest in the activity or object. In this way, the development of joint attention skills in children with autism differs from that of typical children. For typically developing children, the shared affective experience that accompanies joint attention serves to motivate the child to attend to and engage in further joint attention bids (Mundy et al., 1994; Dawson, Toth, et al., 2004). Positive affective sharing, however, rarely accompanies joint attention bids in children with autism (Kasari, Sigman, Mundy, & Yirmiya, 1990). If the purpose of joint attention bids for children with autism remains instrumental and fails to incorporate the affective sharing, this might subsequently impact social and emotional development for the child. The child would fail to make joint attention bids purely for social reasons, such as showing and sharing, and would miss out on the array of opportunities to learn about the affective expressions and experiences of others (Dawson, Toth, et al., 2004).

Perception of and Memory for Faces and Emotional Expressions

Face perception and recognition abilities develop rapidly during the first 6 months of life. Faces are of significant interest to typically developing infants and provide important information about the actions and intentions of others. Young infants are capable of abstracting direction of gaze, facial gestures, and expressions of emotion within the first year of life. These early developing abilities, particularly attention and response to another's gaze, facilitate successful joint attention and social orienting interactions. Face processing has also been posited as important to the development of social relationships and theory of mind (e.g., Baron-Cohen, 1995; Brothers, Ring, & Kling, 1990).

Given the early development of face-processing abilities, impairment of these skills may serve as an early indicator for abnormalities in brain development in children with autism. To examine this, Dawson and colleagues examined face recognition abilities in 3- to 4-year-old children using ERPs (Dawson, Carver, et al., 2002). In this study, children with autism, developmental delay, or typical development viewed pictures of familiar (mother) and unfamiliar (another female) faces and familiar (favorite toy) and unfamiliar (novel toy) objects. While viewing these images, high-density ERPs were recorded. Results showed that typical children demonstrated increased amplitude to novel faces and objects for two ERP components. The children with autism showed the same differential ERP response to the objects but failed to show a differential response for the faces. Thus, children with autism demonstrate face recognition impairments as early as 3 years of age. In another ERP study with an older sample of adolescents and adults with autism, McPartland and colleagues also found face-processing impairments (McPartland, Dawson, Webb, Panagiotides, & Carver, 2004). In this study, individuals with autism showed a smaller amplitude and slower latency to the face-sensitive ERP component (N170) in response to faces, as compared with a typical comparison group.

Behavioral studies have also shown that individuals with autism have impairments in face processing. Individuals with autism demonstrate poorer performance on face recognition and matching tasks than do typical individuals (Boucher, Lewis, & Collis, 1998), fail to show the typical advantage of viewing faces presented upright rather than inverted (Hobson, Ouston, & Lee, 1988b), and rely more on individual features to identify faces than comparison groups (Weeks & Hobson, 1987). Many researchers have suggested that one of the core deficits in autism is an impairment in the ability to understand facial informa-tion (Baron-Cohen, Baldwin, & Crowson, 1997; Dawson, Carver, et al., 2002; Frith, 1989; Hobson et al., 1988b), and while a review of face-processing im-pairments in autism is beyond the scope of this chapter, ample research suggests that individuals with autism display impairments in face processing (Dawson, Carver, et al., 2002; for review see Dawson, Webb, & McPartland, 2005).

These face-processing impairments extend to the processing of facial expres-sion of emotion. Typically developing infants as young as 6 months of age re-spond differentially to the affective displays of those around them (Trevarthen, 1979). For example, young infants smile more and direct more attention to happy faces than to a neutral or sad expression (Rochat & Striano, 1999; Tronick, Als, Adamson, Wise, & Brazelton, 1978). Between 9 and 12 months of age infants will utilize others' facial expressions to guide their own behavior when presented with an unfamiliar stimulus (Feinman, 1982; Moore & Corkum, 1994). The ability to empathically respond to another's distress also emerges early in de-velopment, within the second year of life, and is demonstrated in such behav-iors as showing concern, sharing, helping, and comforting (Rheingold & Hay, 1976; Zahn-Waxler & Radke-Yarrow, 1990).

The finding that individuals with autism are impaired in the recognition of affective cues was included in Kanner's initial report of autistic disorder. Rely-ing on a variety of experimental designs, many studies have shown that chil-dren with autism fail to respond normally to affective displays of others (Blair, 1999; Hall, Szechtman, & Nahmias, 2003; Sigman, Kasari, Kwon & Yirmiya, 1992; Dawson , Meltzoff, Osterling, & Rinaldi, 1998; Charman et al., 1998; Bacon, Fein, Morris, Waterhouse, & Allen, 1998); have impairments in the rec-ognition of emotional expressions (Braverman, Fein, Lucci, & Waterhouse, 1989; Bormann-Kischkel, Vilsmeier, & Baude, 1995; Hobson, 1986; Macdonald et al., 1989); and have difficulty recognizing correspondence between different modali-ties of affective information (Hobson, Ouston, & Lee, 1988a; Loveland et al., 1997).

Sigman and colleagues observed the behavioral responses of 3- to 4-year-old children with autism, mental retardation, and typical development to an adult displaying different emotions (Sigman et al., 1992). In this study, for example, a familiar examiner pretended to hurt himself or herself by hitting one finger with a plastic hammer. The examiner displayed facial and vocal expressions of distress without using words. Children with autism often failed to notice or ig-nored the affective displays of the adults, whereas the control groups were very attentive to the emotional displays regardless of type of display. When the adult was showing a hurt expression, the individuals with autism were much more likely to remain involved with playing with a toy than to attend to the adult. However, in a similarly designed study, Dawson, Meltzoff, Osterling, and Rinaldi (1998) found that individuals with autism were able to distinguish between nega-tive affective displays and neutral emotions; they were more likely to attend to a distress emotion in comparison to a neutral expression. This failure to attend to an emotional display has also been found in children with autism as young as 2 years of age (Charman et al., 1998).

Dawson and colleagues (Dawson, Webb, et al., 2004) used ERPs to examine brain responses to a fear face and a neutral face in 3- to 4-year-old children with autism compared with typically developing, age-matched peers, and chronological and mental aged matched children with developmental delay. Similar to many ERP studies with infants, this study used passive viewing to eliminate confounds of verbal directions or responses. In contrast to the typically developing children, the toddlers with autism failed to demonstrate increased amplitude to the fear face at both an early component and a late component of the ERP wave. The authors concluded that children with autism demonstrate a disordered pattern of emotion perception by 3 years of age. Moreover, a longer latency to an early ERP component to the fear face was associated with lower level of social attention in experiments conducted on a different day. Specifically, longer ERP latency to a fear face was associated with less attention to an experimenter expressing distress, fewer joint attention episodes, and fewer episodes of social orienting (figure 11–2). Notably, ERP latency to fear was not correlated with performance on tasks involving attention to nonsocial stimuli (e.g., orienting to nonsocial sounds). This study suggests that impairments in basic aspects of emotion perception are impaired at least by 3 years of age in children with autism and that abnormal neural responses to facial expressions, particularly fear, are associated with poor social attention abilities in general.

Imitation

Imitation skills also emerge early in life and are believed to play a role in the development of social engagement. Newborns as young as 42 minutes have the capability to imitate facial expressions (Meltzoff & Moore, 1977, 1979, 1983). These early imitation skills develop rapidly over the first years of life, with the ability to imitate actions on objects and gestures, such as waving, emerging around 1 year of age. Deferred imitation, in which actions are imitated later in new contexts, emerges between the first and second year, although some psychologists suggest it emerges much earlier (Meltzoff & Moore, 1994; Bauer, 1996, for review). Imitation skills progress from simple and familiar behaviors to increasingly complex, novel, and sequenced actions (Piaget, 1962; Meltzoff & Moore, 1994). For example, while 22-month-old infants are able to imitate both meaningful and nonmeaningful actions with the same frequency, infants prior to 16 months imitate meaningful actions more consistently (Killen & Uzgiris, 1981; McCabe & Uzgiris, 1983). Infants younger than 20 months old tend to imitate actions on objects more than actions without objects (Masur & Ritz, 1984).

Researchers have proposed many functions of imitation. It has been suggested that imitation initially serves as a basis for social reciprocity and connectedness

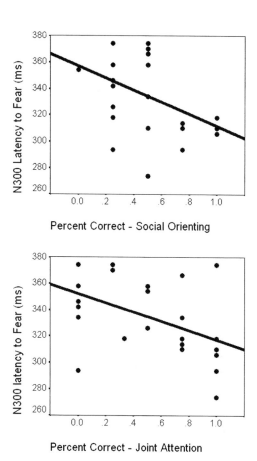

Figure 11–2. Percent responses to a social orienting and joint attention task (horizontal axis) and the relation to the latency of the N300 ERP component to a fear expression (vertical axis) in 3- to 4-year-old children with autism.

with others, as well as the child's ability to differentiate self from others (Meltzoff & Gopnik, 1993; Eckerman, Davis, & Didow, 1989; Uzgiris, 1981; Nadel, Guerini, Peze, & Rivet, 1999; Trevarthen, Kokkinaki, & Fiamenghi, 1999). Imitation also promotes learning and understanding about others' intentions and goals (Uzgiris, 1999; Kugiumutzakis, 1999). Meltzoff (1995) showed that 18-month-old children could imitate others' intended but not completed actions and proposed that imitation serves as an avenue to understand others' internal states. This understanding of seeing what another person does and knowing that the child can produce the same action sequence likely serves as a precursor for the development of a theory of mind (Meltzoff & Gopnick, 1993; Rogers & Pennington, 1991). In addition to serving as a basis for understanding the internal states of others, imitation has also been suggested to play a role in symbolic play (Piaget, 1962), peer relationships (Trevarthen et al., 1999), language

(Avikainen, Wohlschlager, Liuhanen, Hanninen, & Hari, 2003; Charman et al., 2003), and emotional sharing (Hatfield, Cacioppo, & Rapson, 1994).

Many researchers have suggested that impairments in imitation are another core impairment in autism (Dawson & Adams, 1984; Dawson & Lewy, 1989; Rogers, Bennetto, McEvoy, & Pennington, 1996; Rogers & Pennington, 1991; Williams, Whiten, Suddendorf, & Perrett, 2001). Such impairments discriminate between children with autism versus mental retardation or communication disorder by 2 years of age (Stone, Lemanek, Fishel, Fernandez, & Altemeier, 1990; Stone, Ousley, & Littleford, 1997). In a number of studies, it has been shown that individuals with autism perform worse than control participants in all forms of imitation (Rogers, Hepburn, Stackhouse, & Wehner, 2003), including imitating motor movements (Hertzig, Snow, & Sherman, 1989; Sigman & Ungerer, 1984); facial expressions (Loveland et al., 1994); the style of tasks (Hobson & Lee, 1999); actions involving imaginary objects (Rogers et al., 1996); and vocalizations (Dawson & Adams, 1984). Moreover, the differences in imitation ability between groups are substantial. In a study by Rogers and colleagues (Rogers, Bennetto, McEvoy, & Pennington, 1991), 17 high-functioning adolescents with autism and 15 peers from a clinical comparison group completed imitation tasks, and a difference of between-group means of 1.5 standard deviations was found. More recently, Rogers and colleagues (2003) found that young children just under 3 years of age with autism showed significantly more deficits in overall imitation, oral-facial imitation, and imitation on objects when compared with children with developmental delay, fragile X syndrome, as well as typical development (Rogers et al., 2003). Stone and colleagues (1997) studied motor imitation involving body movements and objects and meaningful and nonmeaningful actions. Using the Motor Imitation Scale, in which half of the items require imitation of body movements and half require the manipulation of objects, they found that the young children with autism, as compared with children with developmental delay and typical development, performed much worse on all types of imitation. Hobson and Lee found no differences between adolescents with autism and adolescents with mild mental retardation in their ability to imitate actions that were goal directed. However, fewer teens with autism than those in the control group imitated the style with which the experimenter performed the action. The researchers concluded that in autism there is an impairment in imitation, but specifically it is a deficit in the "intersubjective experience" and "the coordination of the representation between the self and other" (Hobson & Lee, 1999, p. 658).

In addition to impairments in imitation of body movement and affective style (Stone et al., 1997; Hobson & Lee, 1999), impairments in oral-facial imitation are consistently found in individuals with autism (Rogers et al., 2003), and the impairment is greater when there is no instrumental purpose to the imitated action. Rogers and colleagues propose that these differences between types of imitation impairments suggest that imitation is not a unitary skill in autism.

Rather, they propose, imitation with objects relates to instrumental learning, while oral-facial imitation relates to interpersonal engagement (Rogers et al., 2003).

These early impairments in imitation persist into late childhood and adolescence as well (Rogers et al., 1996). Rogers found that high-functioning adolescents with autism, as compared with matched control teens, performed more poorly on imitating face and hand movements, in addition to single or multiple sequence actions. In a study of children between 6 and 14 years of age, Ohta (1987) found that higher-functioning individuals with autism (IQs over 70) demonstrated only partially correct imitation of hand movements. Adults with autism also fail to capitalize on the mirror image of the experimenter's presentation of an action to improve performance on a task (Avikainen et al., 2003). Hobson and Lee (1999) have also found that adolescents with autism perform as well as peers on goal-directed actions, such as applying an inked stamp to paper and making a spring-operated toy policeman move, but fail to imitate the "style" of presentation during deferred imitation of novel, nonsymbolic actions.

In a review of imitation in autism, Williams et al. (2001) conclude that imitation of meaningless actions (as compared with functional actions on objects), novel actions, and sequences of actions are more difficult for individuals with autism. Reversal errors also are common. These are errors in which children with autism pantomime hand movements in such a way that their own hands appear exactly as the model's hands do to them rather than switching to the perspective of the model. Based on these findings, Williams and colleagues propose that the imitation deficits observed in autism are the result of an impairment in the ability to map others' complex actions onto a reference for the self.

Hypotheses Regarding the Nature and Neural Bases of Early Social Impairments in Autism

As reviewed earlier, autism involves impairments in multiple domains that affect social engagement, including social orienting, joint attention, face and emotional processing, and imitation. We now describe three hypotheses regarding the neural mechanisms that might account for this wide range of social impairments found in autism. These hypotheses are not mutually exclusive.

The first hypothesis posits that autism is fundamentally a disorder of attention, especially the ability to rapidly shift attention to multiple stimuli (Courchesne et al., 1994); we will refer to this as the *attentional hypothesis*. The second hypothesis, which we will refer to as the *"Like Me" hypothesis*, posits that the same mechanisms that underlie a child's understanding that others are "like me" provide the foundation for imitation. These mechanisms provide the foundation for social cognition, such that autism could be conceptualized as an impairment of imitation rather than attention (Meltzoff & Gopnik, 1993; Meltzoff & Decety, 2003; Rogers & Pennington, 1991). The third hypothesis is the *social motivation hypothesis*, proposed by our group (Dawson, Carver et al., 2002; Dawson et al., 2005), as well as others (Mundy & Neal, 2001; Grelotti, Gauthier, & Schultz, 2002). This hypothesis proposes that early fundamental impairments in social motivation deprive the infant of significant social interactions and the learning that accompanies these interactions, and this leads to further disruptions in the development of the brain (Dawson, Carver et al., 2002; Dawson et al., 2005; Mundy & Neal, 2001). We next review each of these hypotheses.

Attentional Hypothesis

In the *attentional hypothesis*, Courchesne and colleagues (1994) propose that the ability to rapidly shift attention between different stimuli and different modalities is compromised in autism. Given that early social exchanges require appropriately timed, rapid shifting of attention, young children with autism may be unable to participate in these early social exchanges. The deficits in these early social and affective exchanges result in later deficits in more complex social abilities. For example, to share attention with someone, the child needs to be able to rapidly shift his or her attention between another's gaze toward a stimulus, and the stimulus itself (Courchesne, Akshoomoff, Townsend, & Saitoh, 1995). This ability to disengage from one stimulus and shift to another has been linked to the cerebellum (Harris, Courchesne, Townsend, Carper, & Lord, 1999). A study using spatial cuing tasks and structural imaging conducted with adults with autism, adults with cerebellar damage, and typical individuals found a correlation between slowed orienting behaviors and cerebellar abnormalities (Townsend et al., 1999). In this study, participants with autism or with cerebellar damage showed slowed orienting to visual-spatial cues and greater orienting deficits, which were associated with smaller vermal lobes in the cerebellum. These findings were extended to children with autism in a subsequent study that examined the correlation between orienting speed and cerebellar abnormalities (Harris et al., 1999). A number of other neuroimaging and autopsy studies have found that the cerebellum is abnormal in individuals with autism. Purkinje neurons in the cerebellum have been found to be reduced by 35% to 50% in brains of individuals with autism as compared with brains of typical individuals (Courchesne, 1997). Using magnetic resonance imaging (MRI) technology, two groups of males with autism (aged 2 to 4 years and 5 to 16 years) were found to have cerebellar white matter volume alterations. In the younger group, children with autism had cerebellar white matter volumes 39% larger than the control group (Courchesne et al., 2001). In the autism group, the older children showed a 7% increase in white matter compared with the younger group. In contrast, the older typical group demonstrated a 50% increase in size compared with the younger group. In addition, the cerebellar vermis lobules VI through VII were significantly larger in the typical group than in the group with autism. The authors hypothesized that these results may have been due to excessive premature myelination or an excess of axons or glial cells in the autism group.

Ahskoomoff, Pierce, & Courchesne (2002) have proposed a growth dysregulation hypothesis to explain the etiology of the cerebellar abnormalities that subsequently result in the social engagement impairment in autism. They propose a genetically based dysregulation of brain growth results in overgrowth in some areas of the brain (e.g., enlarged total cerebral volume) and excessive cell loss in the cerebellum in autism. Further research exploring the growth dysregulation hypothesis and its role in the cerebellar abnormalities and the attentional theory is needed.

Like-Me Hypothesis

The *"Like Me" hypothesis* proposed by Meltzoff suggests that the social impairments in autism arise because of an impairment in imitation rather than attention (Meltzoff & Gopnik, 1993; Meltzoff & Decety, 2003). Meltzoff and Decety (2003) have argued that typical infants distinguish themselves from others early on but intrinsically represent others as "like me." Imitation then builds upon this representational capacity. That is, to recognize the connection between one's own emotional and mental experiences and those of others, the ability to match one's own physical behavior with another's behavior must be in place. Through imitation, children develop the continued understanding that others are "like me" in ways that extend beyond physical behaviors and into mental states. It is proposed that the developmental sequence begins with an innate imitation mechanism, which allows for the association between acts that are perceived and acts that are performed by the self. Through experience, infants develop associations between their own behaviors and their own emotional and mental states. From this follows the ability to understand that others have internal mental states like one's own because the others act "like me" behaviorally. If the innate "like-me" mechanism, which is necessary for imitation, is disrupted in autism, then it would follow that the development of the association between the self and others would be impaired.

Several brain regions have been identified as playing a role in imitation. Patients with lesions to the left frontal lobe demonstrate an inability to imitate actions performed by others, even after showing adequate motor control (Goldenberg, 1995; Goldenberg & Hagman, 1997; Merians et al., 1997). The left hemisphere has also been implicated in imitation using electroencephalogram (EEG). Dawson and colleagues found increased EEG activity over the left hemisphere during imitation of hand and facial movements in typical individuals, whereas individuals with autism showed right hemisphere activation when asked to imitate another person (Dawson, Warrenburg, & Fuller, 1985).

Specialized neurons in the superior temporal sulcus of monkeys have been shown to respond expressly to visual information regarding others' postures or movements of the face, limbs, and body (Oram & Perrett, 1994; Perrett et al., 1984; Perrett, Smith, Mistlin, et al., 1985; Perrett, Smith, Potter, et al., 1985; Perrett et al., 1989). Other neurons of this region in macaque brains selectively respond to the sight of reaching behaviors, but only if the reacher is intending to reach for the specified target (Jellema, Baker, Wicker, & Perret, 2000). In a functional neuroimaging study, Decety and colleagues reported activation in the left inferior parietal cortex when participants imitated others and right inferior parietal cortex when participants observed others imitating them (Decety, Chaminade, Grezes, & Meltzoff, 2002).

Finally, specialized neurons that respond to specific actions have also been identified in the prefrontal cortex (area F5) in monkeys (Gallese, Fadiga, Fogassi, & Rizzolatti, 1996; Rizzolatti et al., 1996). These mirror neurons activate when a monkey is performing a certain task or when the monkey watches another monkey performing an equivalent action. Other neurons respond not only to visual stimuli but also if the monkey hears another monkey performing the equivalent action (Kohler et al., 2002; Keysers et al., 2003). In humans, functional imaging studies have demonstrated that viewing and imitating hand motions results in activation of the parietal and prefrontal regions, specifically the premotor cortex and Broca's area (Iacoboni et al., 1999; Grafton, Arbib, Fadiga, & Rizzolatti, 1996; Rizzolatti et al., 1996). Several subsequent neuroimaging studies have found that action recognition and speech production share common neurological structures (Hamzei et al., 2003; Heiser, Iacoboni, Maeda, Marcus, & Mazziotta, 2003; Nishitani & Hari, 2000; Rizzolatti & Arbib, 1998).

Despite the emerging knowledge of the neurobiology of imitation, it is still unclear which brain regions are important in the imitation impairment in autism. Williams and colleagues (2001) propose that a disruption of mirror neurons may be a candidate for a neural basis for the imitation impairments in autism. However Avikainen and colleagues (Avikainen, Kuolomaki, & Hari, 1999) used magnetoencephalography (MEG) to examine differential mirror neuron activity in the primary motor cortex area. In this preliminary study, one individual with autism and four adults with Asperger syndrome manipulated an object in their right hand while also observing a model manipulate the object similarly. No differences between the autistic spectrum and control groups were found. It is important to note that only a portion of the mirror neuron system was examined in this paradigm, and the sample included individuals with milder impairments. The authors suggest future work should include Broca's area to capture the mirror neuron system activity more comprehensively. In addition, research is needed to explore the neurobiological basis of imitation in typically developing children, as well as in children with autism.

Social Motivation Hypothesis

The third hypothesis, the *social motivation hypothesis*, posits that the social impairments result from, or at least are compounded by, a fundamental deficit in social motivation (Dawson, Carver, et al., 2002; Grelotti et al., 2002; Mundy & Neal, 2001). An impairment in social motivation would be expected to result in reduced attention to faces, voices, and hand gestures, which in turn results in a failure to develop efficient, expertise ability to process such stimuli (see Dawson et al., 2005).

Decreased social motivation might be based on abnormalities in (a) the dopaminergic reward system (Schultz, 1998); (b) the amygdala (Baron-Cohen et al., 2000; Howard, 2000); and/or (c) the neuropeptides vasopressin and oxytocin (e.g., Insel, O'Brien, & Leckman, 1999). Research has shown that in the striatum and frontal cortex, particularly the orbitofrontal cortex, dopaminergic projections play a role in approach behavior by acting as a mediator for the effects of reward (Schultz, 1998). Recent studies have further demonstrated that social rewards, including eye contact, activate the dopaminergic reward system (Kampe, Frith, Dolan, & Frith, 2001). In children with autism, we found that performance on neurocognitive tasks that tap into the medial temporal lobe–orbitorfrontal circuit is correlated with severity of social impairments in autism (Dawson, Munson, et al., 2002). Importantly, it appears that reward value as represented in the orbitofrontal cortex depends on input from the basolateral amygdala (Schoenbaum, Setlow, Saddoris, & Gallagher, 2003).

Studies of lesioned animals and brain-damaged individuals suggest that the amygdala is critical for social perception (Baron-Cohen et al., 1999; Baron-Cohen et al., 2000; Bachevalier, 2000); the interpretation of emotional and social signals (Leonard, Rolls, Wilson, & Baylis, 1985; Nakamura, Mikami, & Kubota, 1992; Perrett, Hietanen, Oram, & Benson, 1992; Scott et al., 1997); recognition of faces and facial expressions (Aggleton, 1992; Jacobson, 1986); the ability to make accurate judgments about emotion expression (Breiter et al., 1996; Adolphs, Tranel, Damasio, & Damasio, 1994; Adolphs et al. 1999; Young, Hellawell, Van De Wal, & Johnson, 1996); recognition of the affective significance of stimuli (Lane et al., 1997; LeDoux, 1987); perception of gaze direction (Brothers et al., 1990); and the use of facial gestures (Brothers & Ring, 1993; Kling & Steklis, 1976; Perrett & Mistlin, 1990). In a study conducted in our laboratory collaboratively with Dager (Sparks et al., 2002), it was found that 3- to 4-year-old children with autism have significantly increased amygdala volume, in excess of increased cerebral volume, compared with typical and developmentally delayed children. Furthermore, larger amygdala volume was found to be associated with slower development of social skills during the preschool period (Dager et al., 2002). In autopsy studies, Bauman and Kemper (1985, 1994) found an increase in density and decrease in neuron size in the amygdala of individuals with autism. Functional imaging studies also implicate the amygdala in autism. Baron-Cohen and colleagues found that individuals with high-functioning autism failed to activate the amygdala in response to a task in which participants made decisions about others' emotional states using cues from the eyes (Baron-Cohen et al, 2000). Critchley and colleagues found similar results in a functional magnetic resonance imaging (fMRI) study in which participants identified a person's gender based on a photograph (Critchley et al., 2000).

Finally, oxytocin and vasopressin are neuropeptides that influence social affiliation and have receptors in multiple brain systems, including the limbic system and the brain stem (Barberis & Tribollet, 1996). Oxytocin is known to be involved in nursing, mating, social attachment, bonding, parental behaviors, stereotypic behaviors, and learning and memory in mammals (see Insel et al., 1999, for review). Although there are few reports, there is gathering evidence that oxytocin and vasopressin may have a role in autism. Compared with typical children, children with autism have been found to have lower plasma oxytocin levels and fail to show the same developmental trajectory in oxytocin levels; these may be salient findings, since oxytocin levels have been found to be related to social mastery (Green et al., 2001; Modahl et al., 1998). Adults with autism show reduced incidence and number of repetitive behaviors following oxytocin induction (Hollander et al., 2003). Elevated oxytocin levels have been found in individuals with obsessive-compulsive disorder and in those with Prader-Willi syndrome (Leckman et al, 1994; Martin et al., 1998). In addition, individuals with autism have been found to have chromosomal abnormalities proximal to the oxytocin genes (Cook, 1998).

We have speculated that the social motivation impairment in autism is related to difficulty in forming representations of the reward value of social stimuli (Carver & Dawson, 2002; Dawson, Ashman, & Carver, 2000; Dawson et al., 2005). The ability to form representations of the reward value for a given stimulus begins to develop during the later months of the first year of life (Ruff & Rothbart, 1996). These anticipated representations then motivate and guide the developing child's attention. If the child fails to attend to the naturally occurring social stimuli in the surroundings, the social system would then be deprived of the necessary and expected input. Without the attention to the social stimuli, the child would fail to become an expert in processing social information. This hypothesis reflects others' proposals regarding experience-driven development. For example, Grelotti and colleagues (2002) propose that one example of expert processing is face processing, Nelson (2001) theorizes that face-specific cortical specialization is driven by experience, and Kuhl hypothesizes that phonetic discrimination narrows with native language experience (e.g., Kuhl, 1991). Decreased cortical specialization and efficiency of information processing would result from this failure to develop specialization of these neural regions that mediate social engagement.

Conclusion

In conclusion, the impairments in social engagement that are observed in autism provide an avenue for understanding aspects of social engagement in individuals with typical development. Insights into the neural basis of the disorder allow for further understanding of the nature of the impairment in social engagement in autism. Despite the volume of research into social impairments in autism and the development of various theories to explain this disorder, more research is necessary. In particular, very little research has directly explored the social motivation hypothesis. New imaging technologies and existing research paradigms, including psychophysiological techniques, provide avenues for understanding the neural bases of social impairment in autism. Furthermore, exploring the similarities and differences between populations that have impairments related to social interactions, such as children with conduct disorder, those who fail to respond to rewards, or children with Williams syndrome, who show increased social engagement (see Tager-Flusberg & Plesa-Skwerer, this volume), can provide insight into the neurobiological bases of aspects of social engagement. The theories that have been presented to explain the social impairments in autism can help guide research for future study of both autism and typical development.

Acknowledgments The writing of this chapter was funded by a program project grant from the National Institute of Child Health and Human Development and the National Institute on Deafness and Communication Disability (PO1HD34565), which is part of the NICHD/NIDCD Collaborative Program of Excellence in Autism, and by a center grant from the National Institute of Mental Health (U54MH066399), which is part of the NIH STAART (Studies to Advance Autism Research and Treatment) Centers Program.

References

Adolphs, R., Tranel, D., Damasio, H., & Damasio, A. (1994). Impaired recognition of emotion in facial expressions following bilateral damage to the human amygdala. *Nature, 372*, 669–672.

Adolphs, R., Tranel, D., Hamann, S., Young, A., Calder, A., Phelps, E., et al. (1999). Recognition of facial emotion in nine individuals with bilateral amygdala damage. *Neuropsychologia, 37*, 1111–1117.

Aggleton, J. (1992). *The amygdala: Neurobiological aspects of emotion, memory, and mental dysfunction.* New York: Wiley-Liss.

Ahskoomoff, N., Pierce, K., & Courchesne, E. (2002). The neurobiological basis of autism from a developmental perspective. *Development and Psychopathology, 14*, 613–634.

American Psychiatric Association. (1994). *Diagnostic and statistical manual of mental disorders* (4th ed.). Washington, DC: Author.

Avikainen, S., Kuolomaki, T., & Hari, R. (1999). Normal movement reading in Asperger subjects. *NeuroReport, 10*, 3467–3470.

Avikainen, S., Wohlschlager, A., Liuhanen, S., Hanninen, R., & Hari, R. (2003). Impaired mirror-image imitation in Asperger and high-functioning autistic subjects. *Current Biology, 13*, 339–341.

Bachevalier, J. (2000). The amygdala, social cognition, and autism. In J. Aggleton (Ed.), *The amygdala: A functional analysis* (pp. 509–543). New York: Oxford University Press.

Bacon, A., Fein, D., Morris, R., Waterhouse, L., & Allen, D. (1998). The responses of autistic children to the distress of others. *Journal of Autism and Developmental Disorders, 28*, 129–142.

Baldwin, D. (1991). Infants' contribution to the achievement of joint reference. *Child Development, 62*, 875–890.

Baranek, G. (1999). Autism during infancy: A retrospective video analysis of sensory-motor and social behaviors at 9–12 months of age. *Journal of Autism and Developmental Disorders, 29*, 213–224.

Barberis, C., & Tribollet, E. (1996). Vasopressin and oxytocin receptors in the central nervous system. *Critical Reviews in Neurobiology, 10*, 119–154.

Baron-Cohen, S. (1995). *Mindblindness: An essay on autism and theory of mind.* Cambridge, MA: Bradford/MIT Press.

Baron-Cohen, S., Baldwin, D., & Crowson, M. (1997). Do children with autism use the speaker's direction of gaze strategy to crack the code of language? *Child Development, 68*, 48–57.

Baron-Cohen, S., Ring, H., Bullmore, E., Wheelwright, S., Ashwin, C., & Williams, S. (2000). The amygdala theory of autism. *Neuroscience and Biobehavioral Reviews, 24*, 355–364.

Baron-Cohen, S., Ring, H., Wheelwright, S., Bullmore, E., Brammer, M., Simmons, A., et al. (1999). Social intelligence in the normal and autistic brain: An fMRI study. *European Journal of Neuroscience, 11*, 1891–1898.

Bauer, P. (1996). What do infants recall of their lives? Memory for specific events by one- to two-year-olds. *American Psychologist, 51*, 29–41.

Bauman, M., & Kemper, T. (1985). Histoanatomic observations of the brain in early infantile autism. *Neurology, 35*, 866–874.

Bauman, M., & Kemper, T. (1994). Neuroanatomic observations of the brain in autism. In M. Bauman & T. Kemper (Eds.), *The neurobiology of autism* (pp. 119–145). Baltimore: Johns Hopkins University Press.

Bespalova, I., & Buxbaum, J. (2003). Disease susceptibility genes for autism. *Annals of Medicine, 35*, 274–281.

Blair, R. (1999). Psychophysiological responsiveness to the distress of others in children with autism. *Personality and Individual Differences, 26*, 477–485.

Bormann-Kischkel, C., Vilsmeier, M., & Baude, B. (1995). The development of emotional concepts in autism. *Journal of Child Psychology and Psychiatry, 36*, 1243–1259.

Boucher, J., Lewis, V., & Collis, G. (1998). Familiar face and voice matching and recognition in children with autism. *Journal of Child Psychology and Psychiatry, 39*, 171–181.

Braverman, M., Fein, D., Lucci, D., & Waterhouse, L. (1989). Affect comprehension in children with pervasive developmental disorders. *Journal of Autism and Developmental Disorders, 19*, 301–316.

Breiter, H., Etcoff, N., Whalen, P., Kennedy, W., Rauch, S., Buckner, R., et al. (1996). Response and habituation of the human amygdala during visual processing of facial expression. *Neuron, 17*, 875–887.

Brothers, L., & Ring, B. (1993). Mesial temporal neurons in the macaque monkey with responses selective for aspects of social stimuli. *Behavioral Brain Research, 57*, 53–61.

Brothers, L., Ring, B., & Kling, A. (1990). Responses of neurons in the macaque amygdala to complex social stimuli. *Behavioral Brain Research, 41*, 199–213.

Butterfield, E., & Siperstein, G. (1970). Influence of contingent auditory stimulation upon non-nutritional suckle. In J. Bosma (Ed.), *Symposium on oral sensation and perception: The mouth of the infant* (pp. 313–334). Springfield, IL: Thomas.

Carpenter, M., Nagell, K., & Tomasello, M. (1998). Social cognition, joint attention, and communicative competence from 9–15 months of age. *Monographs of the Society for Research in Child Development, 63*, 1–143.

Carver, L., & Dawson, G. (2002). Development and neural bases of face recognition in autism. *Molecular Psychiatry, 7*(Suppl. 2), S18–S20.

Charman, T., Baron-Cohen, S., Swettenham, J., Baird, G., Drew, A., & Cox, A. (2003). Predicting language outcome in infants with autism and pervasive developmental disorder. *International Journal of Language and Communication Disorders, 38*, 265–285.

Charman, T., Swettenham, J., Baron-Cohen, S., Cox, A., Baird, G., & Drew, A. (1998). An experimental investigation of social-cognitive abilities in infants with autism: Clinical implications. *Infant Mental Health Journal, 19*, 260–275.

Cook, E. (1998). Genetics of autism. *Mental Retardation Developmental Disabilities Review, 4*, 113–120.

Courchesne, E. (1997). Brainstem, cerebellar and limbic neuroanatomical abnormalities in autism. *Current Opinion in Neurobiology, 7*, 269–278.

Courchesne, E., Akshoomoff, N., Townsend, J., & Saitoh, O. (1995). A model system for the study of attention and the cerebellum: Infantile autism. *Electroencephalography and Clinical Neurophysiology, 44*(Suppl.), 315–325).

Courchesne, E., Karns, C., Davis, H., Ziccardi, R., Carper, R., Tigue, Z., et al. (2001). Unusual brain growth patterns in early life in patients with autistic disorder: An MRI study. *Neurology, 57*, 245–254.

Courchesne, E., Townsend, J., Akshoomoff, N., Saitoh, O., Yeung-Courchesne, R., Lincoln, A.,et al. (1994). Impairment in shifting attention in autistic and cerebellar patients. *Behavioral Neuroscience, 108*, 848–865.

Critchley, H., Daly, E., Bullmore, E., Williams, S., Van Amelsvoort, T., Robertson, D., et al. (2000). The functional neuroanatomy of social behavior: Changes in cerebral blood flow when people with autistic disorder process facial expressions. *Brain, 123*, 2203–2212.

Dager, S., Munson, J., Friedman, S., Webb, S., Shaw, D., Sparks, B., et al. (2002, November). *Neuroimaging relationship to behavioral performance and clinical course in young children with ASD*. Presented at the annual meeting of the International Society for Autism Research, Orlando, FL.

Dawson, G., & Adams, A. (1984). Imitation and social responsiveness in autistic children. *Journal of Abnormal Child Psychology, 12*, 209–226.

Dawson, G., Ashman, S., & Carver, L. (2000). The role of early experience in shaping behavioral and brain development and its implications for social policy. *Development and Psychopathology, 12*, 695–712.

Dawson, G., Carver, L., Meltzoff, A., Panagiotides, H., McPartland, J., & Webb, S. (2002). Neural correlates of face and object recognition in young children with autism spectrum disorder, developmental delay, and typical development. *Child Development, 73*, 700–717.

Dawson, G., & Lewy, A. (1989). Arousal, attention, and socioemotional impairments of individuals with autism. In G. Dawson (Ed.), *Autism: Nature, diagnosis and treatment* (pp. 49–74). New York: Guilford.

Dawson, G., Meltzoff, A., Osterling, J., & Rinaldi, J. (1998). Neuropsychological correlates of early symptoms of autism. *Child Development, 69*, 1276–1285.

Dawson, G., Meltzoff, A., Osterling, J., Rinaldi, J., & Brown, E. (1998). Children with autism fail to orient to naturally occurring social stimuli. *Journal of Autism and Developmental Disorders, 28*, 479–485.

Dawson, G., Munson, J., Estes, A., Osterling, J., McPartland, J., Toth, K., et al. (2002). Neurocognitive function and joint attention ability in young children with autism spectrum disorder versus developmental delay. *Child Development, 73*, 345–358.

Dawson, G., Toth, K., Abbott, R., Osterling, J., Munson, J., Estes, A., et al. (2004). Early social attention impairments in autism: Social orienting, joint attention, and attention to distress. *Developmental Psychology, 40*, 271–283.

Dawson, G., Warrenburg, S., & Fuller, P. (1985). Left hemisphere specialization for facial and manual imitation in children and adults. *Psychophysiology, 22*, 237–243.

Dawson, G., Webb, S., Carver, L., Panagiotides, H., & McPartland, J. (2004). Young children with autism show atypical brain responses to fearful versus neutral facial expressions. *Developmental Science, 7*, 340–359.

Dawson, G., Webb, S., & McPartland, J. (2005). Electrophysiological studies of face processing: Implications for understanding the nature of social impairments in autism. *Developmental Neuropsychology, 27*, 403–424.

Dawson, G., Webb, S., Schellenberg, G., Dager, S., Friedman, S., Aylward, E., et al. (2002). Defining the broader phenotype of autism: Genetic, brain, and behavioral perspectives. *Development and Psychopathology, 14*, 581–611.

Dawson, G., & Zanolli, K. (2003). Early intervention and brain plasticity in autism. *Novartis Foundation Symposium, 251*, 266–274.

Decety, J., Chaminade, T., Grezes, J., & Meltzoff, A. (2002). A PET exploration of the neural mechanisms involved in reciprocal imitation. *NeuroImage, 15*, 265–272.

Eckerman, C., Davis, C., & Didow, S. (1989). Toddlers' emerging ways of achieving social coordination with a peer. *Child Development, 60*, 440–453.

Eisenberg, R. (1970). The organization of auditory behavior. *Journal of Speech and Hearing Research, 13*, 453–471.

Feinman, S. (1982). Social referencing in infancy. *Merrill-Palmer Quarterly, 28*, 445–470.

Fombonne, E. (1999). The epidemiology of autism: A review. *Psychological Medicine, 29*, 769–786.

Frith, U. (1989). *Autism: Understanding the enigma.* Malden, MA: Blackwell.

Gallese, V., Fadiga, L., Fogassi, L., & Rizzolatti, G. (1996). Action recognition in the premotor cortex. *Brain, 119*, 593–609.

Gillberg, C., & Billstedt, E. (2000). Autism and Asperger syndrome: Coexistence with other clinical disorders. *Acta Psychiatrica Scandinavica, 012*, 321–330.

Goldenberg, G. (1995). Imitating gestures and manipulating a manikin: The representation of the human body in ideomotor apraxia. *Neuropsychologia, 33*, 63–72.

Goldenberg, G., & Hagman, S. (1997). The meaning of meaningless gestures: A study of visuo-imitative apraxia. *Neuropsychologia, 5*, 333–341.

Grafton, S., Arbib, M., Fadiga, L., & Rizzolatti, G. (1996). Localization of grasp representations in humans by PET. *Experimental Brain Research, 112,* 103–111.

Green, L., Fein, D., Modahl, C., Feinstein, C., Watherhouse, L., & Morris, M. (2001). Oxytocin and autistic disorder: Alterations in peptide forms. *Biological Psychiatry, 50,* 609–613.

Grelotti, D., Gauthier, I., & Schultz, R. (2002). Social interest and the development of cortical face specialization: What autism teaches us about face processing. *Development and Psychopathology, 40,* 213–225.

Hains, S., & Muir, D. (1996). Infant sensitivity to adult eye direction information. *Child Development, 67,* 1940–1951.

Hall, G., Szechtman, H., & Nahmias, C. (2003). Enhanced salience and emotion recognition in autism: A PET study. *American Journal of Psychiatry, 160,* 1439–1441.

Hamzei, F., Rijntjes, M., Dettmers, C., Glauche, V., Weiller, C., & Buchel, C. (2003). The human action recognition system and its relationship to Broca's area: An fMRI study. *NeuroImage, 19,* 637–644.

Harris, N., Courchesne, E., Townsend, J., Carper, R., & Lord, C. (1999). Neuroanatomic contributions to slowed orienting of attention in children with autism. *Cognitive Brain Research, 8,* 61–71.

Hatfield, E., Cacioppo, J., & Rapson, R. (1994). *Emotional contagion.* New York: Cambridge University Press.

Heiser, M., Iacoboni, M., Maeda, F., Marcus, J., & Mazziotta, J. (2003). The essential role of Broca's area in imitation. *European Journal of Neuroscience, 17,* 1123–1128.

Hertzig, M., Snow, M., & Sherman, M. (1989). Affect and cognition in autism. *Journal of the American Academy of Child and Adolescent Psychiatry, 28,* 195–199.

Hobson, R. (1986). The autistic child's appraisal of expressions of emotion. *Journal of Child Psychology and Psychiatry, 27,* 321–342.

Hobson, R., & Lee, A. (1999). Imitation and identification in autism. *Journal of Child Psychology and Psychiatry, 40,* 649–659.

Hobson, R., Ouston, J., & Lee, A. (1988a). Emotion recognition in autism: Coordinating faces and voices. *Psychological Medicine, 18,* 911–923.

Hobson, R., Ouston, J., & Lee, A. (1988b). What's in a face? The case of autism. *British Journal of Psychology, 79,* 441–453.

Hollander, E., Novotny, S., Hanratty, M., Yaffe, R., DeCaria, C., Aronowitz, B., et al. (2003). Oxytocin infusion reduces repetitive behaviors in adults with autistic and Asperger's disorders. *Neuropsychopharmacology, 28,* 193–198.

Hood, B., Willen, J., & Driver, J. (1998). Adult's eyes trigger shifts of visual attention in human infants. *Psychological Science, 9,* 131–134.

Howard, M. (2000). Convergent neuroanatomical and behavioral evidence of an amygdala hypothesis of autism. *NeuroReport, 11,* 2931–2935.

Iacoboni, M., Woods, R., Brass, M., Bekkering, H., Mazziotta, J., & Rizzolatti, G. (1999). Cortical mechanisms of human imitation. *Science, 286,* 2526–2528.

Insel, T., O'Brien, D., & Leckman, J. (1999). Oxytocin, vasopressin and autism: Is there a connection? *Biological Psychiatry, 45,* 145–157.

Jacobson, R. (1986). Disorders of facial recognition, social behavior and affect after combined bilateral amygdalectomy and subcaudate tractotomy: A clinical and experimental study. *Psychological Medicine, 16,* 439–450.

Jellema, T., Baker, C., Wicker, B., & Perrett, D. (2000). Neural representation for the perception of the intentionality of actions. *Brain and Cognition, 44,* 280–302.

Kampe, K., Frith, C., Dolan, R., & Frith, U. (2001). Reward value of attractiveness and gaze. *Nature, 413*, 589.

Kanner, L. (1943). Autistic disturbances of affective contact. *Nervous Child, 2*, 217–250.

Kasari, C., Sigman, M., Mundy, P., & Yirmiya, N. (1990). Affective sharing in the context of joint attention interactions of normal, autistic, and mentally retarded children. *Journal of Autism and Developmental Disorders, 20*, 87–100.

Keysers, C., Kohler, E., Umilta, M., Nanetti, L., Fogassi, L., & Gallese, V. (2003). Audiovisual mirror neurons and action recognition. *Experimental Brain Research, 153*, 628–636.

Killen, M., & Uzgiris, I. (1981). Imitation of actions with objects: The role of social meaning. *Journal of Genetic Psychology, 138*, 219–229.

Klin, A. (1991). Young autistic children's listening preferences in regard to speech: A possible characterization of the symptom of social withdrawal. *Journal of Autism and Developmental Disorders, 21*, 29–42.

Kling, A., & Steklis, H. (1976). A neural substrate for affiliative behavior in non-human primates. *Brain, Behavior and Evolution, 13*, 216–238.

Kohler, E., Keysers, C., Umilta, M., Fogassi, L., Gallese, V., & Rizzolatti, G. (2002). Hearing sounds, understanding actions: Action representation in mirror neurons. *Science, 297*, 846–848.

Kugiumutzakis, G. (1999). Genesis and development of early infant mimesis to facial and vocal models. In J. Nadel & G. Butterworth (Eds.), *Imitation in infancy* (pp. 36–59). Cambridge, England: Cambridge University Press.

Kuhl, P. (1991). Human adults and human infants show a "perceptual magnet effect" for the prototypes of speech categories, monkeys do not. *Perception and Psychophysiology, 50*, 93–107.

Kuhl, P., Padden, D., & Dawson, G. (2004). Auditory preference for speech versus acoustically matched sine-wave speech analogs in young children with autism, developmental delay, and typical development. Manuscript in preparation.

Lane, R., Reiman, E., Bradley, M., Lang, P., Ahern, G., Davidson, R., et al. (1997). Neuroanatomical correlates of pleasant and unpleasant emotion. *Neuropsychologia, 35*, 1437–1444.

Leckman, J., Goodman, W., North, W., Chappell, P., Price, L., Pauls, D., et al.. (1994). Elevated cerebrospinal fluid levels of oxytocin in obsessive-compulsive disorder comparison with Tourette's syndrome and healthy controls. *Archives of General Psychiatry, 51*, 782–792.

LeDoux, J. (1987). Emotion. In F. Plum (Ed.), *Handbook of physiology: Section 1. The Nervous System. Vol. 5. Higher Functions of the Brain* (pp. 419–460). Bethesda, MD: American Physiological Society.

Legerstee, M., Pomerleau, A., Malcuit, G., & Feider, H. (1987). The development of infants' responses to people and a doll: Implications for research in communication. *Infant Behavior and Development, 10*, 81–95.

Leonard, C., Rolls, E., Wilson, F., & Baylis, G. (1985). Neurons in the amygdala of the monkey with responses selective for faces. *Behavioral Brain Research, 15*, 159–176.

Lewy, A., & Dawson, G. (1992). Social stimulation and joint attention in young autistic children. *Journal of Abnormal Child Psychology, 20*, 555–565.

Loveland, K., & Landry, S. (1986). Joint attention and language in autism and developmental language delay. *Journal of Autism and Developmental Disorders, 16*, 335–349.

Loveland, K., Tunali Kotoski, B., Chen, R., Ortegon, J., Pearson, D., Brelsford, K., et al. (1997). Emotion recognition in autism: Verbal and nonverbal information. *Development and Psychopathology, 19*, 579–593.

Loveland, K., Tunali Kotoski, B., Pearson, D., Brelsford, K., Ortegon, J., & Chen, R. (1994). Imitation and expression of facial affect in autism. *Development and Psychopathology, 6*, 433–444.

Macdonald, H., Rutter, M., Howlin, P., Rios, P., LeCouteur, A., Evered, C., et al. (1989). Recognition and expression of emotional cues by autistic and normal adults. *Journal of Child Psychology and Psychiatry, 30*, 865–877.

Martin, A., State, M., Anderson, G., Kaye, W., Hanchett, J., McConaha, C., et al. (1998). Cerebrospinal fluid levels of oxytocin in Prader-Willi syndrome: A preliminary report. *Biological Psychiatry, 44*, 1349–1352.

Masur, E., & Ritz, E. (1984). Patterns of gestural, vocal, and verbal imitation performance in infancy. *Merrill-Palmer Quarterly, 30*, 369–392.

Maurer, D., & Salapatek, P. (1976). Developmental changes in the scanning of faces by young children. *Child Development, 47*, 523–527.

McCabe, M., & Uzgiris, I. (1983). Effects of model and action on imitation in infancy. *Merrill-Palmer Quarterly, 26*, 69–82.

McPartland, J., Dawson, G., Webb, S., Panagiotides, H., & Carver, L. (2004). Event-related brain potentials reveal anomalies in temporal processing of faces in autism spectrum disorder. *Journal of Child Psychology and Psychiatry, 45*, 1235–1245.

Meltzoff, A. (1995). Understanding the intentions of others: Re-enactment of intended acts by 18–month-old children. *Developmental Psychology, 31*, 838–850.

Meltzoff, A., & Decety, J. (2003). What imitation tells us about social cognition: A rapprochement between developmental psychology and cognitive neuroscience. *Philosophical Transactions of the Royal Society of London. Series B: Biological Sciences, 358*, 491–500.

Meltzoff, A., & Gopnik, A. (1993). The role of imitation in understanding persons and developing a theory of mind. In S. Baron-Cohen, H. Tager-Flusberg, & D. Cohen (Eds.), *Understanding other minds* (pp. 335–366). Oxford, England: Oxford University Press.

Meltzoff, A., & Moore, M. (1977). Imitation of facial and manual gestures by human neonates. *Science, 198*, 74–78.

Meltzoff, A., & Moore, M. (1979). Interpreting "imitative" responses in early infancy. *Science, 205*, 217–219.

Meltzoff, A., & Moore, M. (1983). Newborn infants imitate adult facial gestures. *Child Development, 54*, 702–709.

Meltzoff, A., & Moore, M. (1994). Imitation, memory, and the representation of persons. *Infant Behavior and Development, 17*, 83–99.

Merians, A., Clark, M., Poisner, H., Macauley, B., Gonzalez-Rothi, L., & Heilman, K. (1997). Visual-imitative dissociation apraxia. *Neuropsychologia, 35*, 1483–1490.

Modahl, C., Green, D., Fein, D., Morris, M., Watherhouse, L., Feinstein, C., et al. (1998). Plasma oxytocin levels in autistic children. *Biological Psychiatry, 43*, 270–277.

Moore, C., & Corkum, V. (1994). Social understanding at the end of the first year of life. *Developmental Review, 14*, 349–372.

Morales, M., Mundy, P., & Rojas, J. (1998). Following the direction of gaze and language development in 6-month-olds. *Infant Behavior and Development, 21*, 373–377.

Morton, J., & Johnson, M. (1991). CONSPEC and CONLERN: A two-process theory of infant face recognition. *Psychological Review, 2,* 164–181.

Mundy, P. (2003). Annotation: The neural basis of social impairments in autism: The role of the dorsolateral medial-frontal cortex and anterior cingulate system. *Journal of Child Psychology and Psychiatry, 44,* 793–809.

Mundy, P., Card, J., & Fox, N. (2000). EEG correlates of the development of infant joint attention skills. *Developmental Psychobiology, 36,* 325–338.

Mundy, P., & Neal, R. (2001). Neural plasticity, joint attention, and autistic developmental pathology. In L. Glidden (Ed.), *International review of research in mental retardation* (Vol. 23, pp. 139–168). New York: Academic Press.

Mundy, P., Sigman, M., & Kasari, C. (1994). Joint attention, developmental level, and symptom presentation in autism. *Development and Psychopathology, 6,* 389–401.

Mundy, P., Sigman, M., Ungerer, J., & Sherman, T. (1986). Defining the social deficits of autism: The contribution of non-verbal communication measures. *Journal of Child Psychology and Psychiatry, 27,* 657–669.

Nadel, J., Guerini, C., Peze, A., & Rivet, C. (1999). The evolving nature of imitation as a format for communication. In J. Nadel & G. Butterworth (Eds.), *Imitation in infancy* (pp. 209–234). Cambridge, England: Cambridge University Press.

Nakamura, K., Mikami, A., & Kubota, K. (1992). Activity of single neurons in the monkey amygdala during performance of a visual discrimination task. *Journal of Neurophysiology, 67,* 1447–1463.

Nelson, C. (2001). The development and neural bases of face recognition. *Infant and Child Development, 10,* 3–18.

Nishitani, N., & Hari, R. (2000). Temporal dynamics of cortical representation for action. *Proceedings of the National Academy of Science of the United States of America, 97,* 913–918.

Ohta, M. (1987). Cognitive disorders of infantile autism: A study employing the WISC, spatial relationships, conceptualization, and gestural imitation. *Journal of Autism and Developmental Disorders, 17,* 45–62.

Oram, M., & Perrett, D. (1994). Responses of anterior superior temporal polysensory (STP) neurons to "biological motion" stimuli. *Journal of Cognitive Neuroscience, 6,* 99–116.

Osterling, J., & Dawson, G. (1994). Early recognition of children with autism: A study of first birthday home videotapes. *Journal of Autism and Developmental Disorders, 24,* 247–257.

Osterling, J., Dawson, G., & Munson, J. (2002). Early recognition of 1 year old infants with autism spectrum disorder versus mental retardation. *Development and Psychopathology, 14,* 239–251.

Perrett, D., Harries, M., Bevan, R., Thomas, S., Benson, P., Mistlin, A., et al. (1989). Frameworks of analysis for the neural representation of animate objects and actions. *Journal of Experimental Biology, 146,* 683–694.

Perrett, D., Hietanen, J., Oram, M., & Benson, P. (1992). Organization and functions of cells responsive to faces in the temporal cortex. *Philosophical Transactions of the Royal Society of London. Series B: Biological Sciences, 335,* 23–30.

Perrett, D., & Mistlin, A. (1990). Perception of facial characteristics by monkeys. In W. Stebbins & M. Berkley (Eds.), *Comparative perception II* (pp. 187–215). New York: Wiley.

Perrett, D., Smith, P., Mistlin, A., Chitty, A., Head, A., Potter, D., et al. (1985).

Visual analysis of body movements by neurons in the temporal cortex of the macaque monkey: A preliminary report. *Behavioral Brain Research, 16*, 153–170.

Perrett, D., Smith, P., Potter, D., Mistlin, A., Head, A., Milner, A., et al. (1984). Neurons responsive to faces in the temporal cortex: Studies of functional organization, sensitivity to identity and relation to perception. *Human Neurobiology, 3*, 197–208.

Perrett, D., Smith, P., Potter, D., Mistlin, A., Head, A., Milner, A., et al. (1985). Visual cells in the temporal cortex sensitive to face view and gaze direction. *Proceedings of the Royal Society of London. Series B: Biological Sciences, 223*, 293–317.

Piaget, J. (1962). *Play, dreams and imitation in childhood*. New York: Norton.

Rheingold, H., & Hay, D. (1976). Sharing in the second year of life. *Child Development, 47*, 1148–1158.

Rizzolatti, G., & Arbib, M. (1998). Language within our grasp. *Trends in Neuroscience, 21*, 188–194.

Rizzolatti, G., Fadiga, L., Matelli, M., Bettinardi, V., Paulesu, E., Perani, D., et al. (1996). Localization of grasp representation in human by PET. *Experimental Brain Research, 112*, 246–252.

Rochat, P. (Ed.). (1999). *Early social cognition: Understanding others in the first months of life*. Hillsdale, NJ: Erlbaum.

Rochat, P., & Striano, T. (1999). Social-cognitive development in the first year. In P. Rochat (Ed.), *Early social cognition: Understanding others in the first months of life* (pp. 3–34). Hillsdale, NJ: Erlbaum.

Rogers, S., Bennetto, L., McEvoy, R., & Pennington, B. (1991). Imitation and pantomime in high-functioning adolescents with autism spectrum disorders. *Child Development, 67*, 2060–2073.

Rogers, S., Bennetto, L., McEvoy, R., & Pennington, B. (1996). Imitation and pantomime in high-functioning adolescents with autism spectrum disorders. *Child Development, 67*, 2060–2073.

Rogers, S., Hepburn, S., Stackhouse, T., & Wehner, E. (2003). Imitation performance in toddlers with autism and those with other developmental disorders. *Journal of Child Psychology and Psychiatry, 44*, 763–781.

Rogers, S., & Pennington, B. (1991). A theoretical approach to the deficits in infantile autism. *Development and Psychopathology, 3*, 137–162.

Ruff, H., & Rothbart, M. (1996). *Attention in early development: Themes and variations*. New York: Oxford University Press.

Rutter, M. (1983). Cognitive deficits in the pathogenesis of autism. *Journal of Child Psychology and Psychiatry, 24*, 513–531.

Schoenbaum, G., Setlow, B., Saddoris, M., & Gallagher, M. (2003). Encoding predicted outcome and acquired value in orbitofrontal cortex during cue sampling depends upon input from basolateral amygdala. *Neuron, 39*, 855–867.

Schultz, W. (1998). Predictive reward signal of dopamine neurons. *Journal of Neurophysiology, 80*, 1–27.

Scott, S., Young, A., Calder, A., Hellawell, D., Aggleton, J., & Johnson, M. (1997). Impaired auditory recognition of fear and anger following bilateral amygdala lesions. *Nature, 385*, 254–257.

Sigman, M., Kasari, C., Kwon, J., & Yirmiya, N. (1992). Responses to the negative emotions of others by autistic, mentally retarded, and normal children. *Child Development, 63*, 796–807.

Sigman, M., & Ruskin, E. (1999). Continuity and change in the social competence of children with autism, Down syndrome, and developmental delays. *Monographs of the Society for Research in Child Development, 64*(Serial No. 256), 1–108.

Sigman, M., & Ungerer, J. (1984). Cognitive and language skills in autistic, mentally retarded and normal children. *Developmental Psychology, 20,* 293–302.

Slaughter, V., & McConnell, D. (2003). Emergence of joint attention: Relationships between gaze following, social referencing, imitation, and naming in infancy. *Journal of Genetic Psychology, 164,* 54–72.

Sparks, B., Friedman, S., Shaw, D., Aylward, E., Echelard, D., Artru, A., et al. (2002). Brain structural abnormalities in young children with autism spectrum disorders. *Neurology, 59,* 184–192.

Stone, W., Lemanek, K., Fishel, P., Fernandez, M., & Altemeier, W. (1990). Play and imitation skills in the diagnosis of autism in young children. *Pediatrics, 64,* 1688–1705.

Stone, W., Ousley, O., & Littleford, C. (1997). Motor imitation in young children with autism: What's the object? *Journal of Abnormal Child Psychology, 25,* 475–485.

Swettenham, J., Baron-Cohen, S., Charman, T., Cox, A., Baird, G., Drew, A., et al. (1998). The frequency and distribution of spontaneous attention shifts between social and nonsocial stimuli in autistic, typically developing, and non-autistics developmentally delayed infants. *Journal of Child Psychology and Psychiatry, 39,* 747–753.

Symons, L., Hains, S., & Muir, D. (1998). Look at me: Five-month-old infants' sensitivity to very small deviations in eye-gaze during social interactions. *Infant Behavior and Development, 21,* 531–536.

Tantam, D. (1992). Characterizing the fundamental social handicap in autism. *Acta Paedopsychiatrica, 55,* 83–91.

Tantam, D., Holmes, D., & Cordess, C. (1993). Nonverbal expression in autism of Asperger type. *Journal of Autism and Developmental Disorders, 23,* 111–133.

Tomasello, M. (1995). Joint attention as social cognition. In C. Moore & P. Dunham (Eds.), *Joint attention: Its origins and role in development* (pp. 103–130). Hillsdale, NJ: Erlbaum.

Townsend, J., Courchesne, E., Covington, J., Westerfield, M., Harris, N., Lyden, P., et al. (1999). Spatial attention deficits in patients with acquired or developmental cerebellar abnormality. *Journal of Neuroscience, 19,* 5632–5643.

Trevarthen, C. (1979). Communication and cooperation in early infancy: A description of primary intersubjectivity. In M. Bullowa (Ed.), *Before speech: The beginnings of interpersonal communication* (pp. 321–347). Cambridge, England: Cambridge University Press.

Trevarthen, C., Kokkinaki, T., & Fiamenghi, C. (1999). What infants' imitations communicate: With mothers, with fathers and with peers. In J. Nadel & G. Butterworth (Eds.), *Imitation in infancy* (pp. 127–185). Cambridge, England: Cambridge University Press.

Tronick, E., Als, H., Adamson, L., Wise, S., & Brazelton, T. (1978). The infant's response to entrapment between contradictory messages in face-to-face interaction. *Journal of the American Academy of Child Psychiatry, 17,* 1–13.

Tsai, L. (1996). Brief report: Comorbid psychiatric disorders of autistic disorder. *Journal of Autism and Developmental Disorders, 26,* 159–163.

Uzgiris, I. (1981). Two functions of imitation during infancy. *International Journal of Behavioral Development, 4,* 1–12.

Uzgiris, I. (1999). Imitation as activity: Its developmental aspects. In J. Nadel & G. Butterworth (Eds.), *Imitation in infancy* (pp. 186–206). Cambridge, England: Cambridge University Press.

Veenstra-Vanderweele, J., & Cook, E. (2003). Genetics of childhood disorders: XLVI. Autism, Part 5: Genetics of autism. *Journal of Academy of Child and Adolescent Psychiatry, 42,* 116–118.

Weeks, S., & Hobson, R. (1987). The salience of facial expression for autistic children. *Journal of Child Psychology and Psychiatry, 28,* 137–151.

Werner, E., Dawson, G., Osterling, J., & Dinno, N. (2000). Recognition of autism spectrum disorder before one year of age: A retrospective study based on home videotapes. *Journal of Autism and Developmental Disorders, 30,* 157–162.

Williams, J., Whiten, A., Suddendorf, T., & Perrett, D. (2001). Imitation, mirror neurons and autism. *Neuroscience and Biobehavioral Reviews, 25,* 287–295.

Young, A., Hellawell, D., Van De Wal, C., & Johnson, M. (1996). Facial expression processing after amygdalectomy. *Neuropsychologia, 34,* 31–39.

Zahn-Waxler, C., & Radke-Yarrow, M. (1990). The origins of empathic concern. *Motivation and Emotion, 14,* 107–130.

12

Social Engagement
in Williams Syndrome

Helen Tager-Flusberg
Daniela Plesa-Skwerer

W illiams syndrome (WS) was first "discovered" by researchers in Australia (Williams, Barratt-Boyes, & Lowe, 1961) and Germany (Beuren, 1972). Early descriptions of this disorder focused on the physical, medical, and craniofacial characteristics that distinguish it from other mental retardation syndromes. Psychologists became interested in WS two decades ago, when Ursula Bellugi first learned about the striking and precocious linguistic skills of individuals with WS (Bellugi & St. George, 2000). Since that time, WS has been studied intensively by geneticists, cognitive scientists, and neuroscientists primarily because people with WS have a striking and unusual profile of cognitive and behavioral strengths and weaknesses (particularly visual-spatial cognition) that has the potential of revealing links between specific genes, neuropathology, and behavior (Bellugi, Mills, Jernigan, Hickok, & Galaburda, 1999; Karmiloff-Smith et al., 2003).

We now know that WS is a rare syndrome caused by a hemizygous microdeletion spanning approximately 1.6 Mb on the long arm of chromosome 7 (Ewart et al., 1993). This region encompasses about 20 to 25 genes, many of which have been identified and some of which have even been linked to aspects of the physical or behavioral phenotype (e.g., Danoff, Taylor, Blackshaw, & Desiderio, 2004; Frangiskakis et al., 1996; Osborne et al., 1997; Stock et al., 2003). This kind of research depends on developing clear and objective definitions of the phenotype, which has been achieved in investigations of the cognitive profile (Mervis & Klein-Tasman, 2000). In addition to their relative strengths in language and related memory skills (Bellugi, Bihrle, Neville, Jernigan, & Doherty, 1992; Mervis, Morris, Bertrand, & Robinson, 1999), individuals with WS are especially interested in people: They are outgoing and extremely warm, friendly, and empathic toward others. This aspect of the WS phenotype, which has been documented in numerous behavioral studies, suggests that WS may provide a model syndrome for investigating social engagement (e.g., Gosch & Pankau, 1997; Udwin & Yule, 1991). In this chapter, we review the research that has been conducted on the social characteristics and social cognition in WS with a view to understanding the behavioral, cognitive, and neurobiological underpinnings of the social phenotype in WS.

Behavioral and Cognitive Studies of Social Engagement in WS

Overview of the Social Phenotype of WS

Although the behavioral phenotype of people with WS has been the focus of many studies in the last decade (e.g., Davies, Udwin, & Howlin, 1998; Dykens & Rosner, 1999; Einfeld, Tonge, & Florio, 1997; Gosch & Pankau, 1994, 1997; Jones et al. 2000; Klein-Tasman & Mervis, 2003; Morris & Mervis, 1999; Sarimski, 1997; Tomc, Williamson, & Pauli, 1990; Udwin, & Yule, 1991; Udwin, Yule, & Martin, 1987), researchers have only recently started to investigate systematically specific aspects of social engagement in this population, including in infants and young children with WS (Laing et al., 2002; Mervis et al., 2003). As noted, a distinctive behavioral characteristic of people with WS of all ages is their strong propensity for social interaction with both familiar and unfamiliar people. Even very young children with WS have been described as intensely engaging socially, to the extent that parents worry about their indiscriminate friendliness toward strangers (Gosch & Pankau, 1994; Jones et al., 2000; Sarimski, 1997).

When considering these characteristics in conjunction with relatively spared language abilities, high expressiveness in verbal communication (Reilly, Klima, & Bellugi, 1990), and an outgoing, affectionate, friendly personality (Gosch & Pankau, 1994), it would seem that people with WS should be at ease navigating the social world. However, by the time they reach adulthood, many people with WS have experienced a history of difficulties in social interactions and in establishing and maintaining successful relationships over time, and a significant proportion have developed high levels of anxiety and social isolation (Davies et al., 1998; Dykens & Rosner, 1999; Udwin & Yule, 1991). Difficulties in making friends and in sustaining positive peer relations become apparent by middle childhood, despite an unrelenting strong interest and affection for people manifested by individuals with WS in their social behavior from an early age.

Thus, research investigating the behavioral and personality profile of people with WS has produced a complex picture, suggesting a paradoxical combination of high sociability and empathy, but poor social relationships and difficulties in social functioning. Given the unique cognitive and behavioral profile characteristic of WS, an important research objective is to investigate how this early selective deployment of attention to social stimuli may impact the development of cognitive and affective competencies relevant for the maturation of social engagement skills—such as joint attention, language development, especially pragmatic aspects of linguistic communication, face processing, decoding of emotional expressions and emotion regulation, and, more generally, social cognition or theory of mind.

Attention Patterns and Sociocommunicative Behaviors

The importance of joint attention skills for developing social competence and for language learning processes has been demonstrated in numerous studies with typically developing children (Bakeman & Adamson, 1984; Carpenter, Nagell, & Tomasello, 1998; Mundy & Gomes, 1998; Tomasello, 1988; Tomasello & Farrar, 1986). Impairments in joint attention skills, investigated so far in children with autism or Down syndrome, have been related to deficits in social cognition and delays in language development (see Dawson, this volume). Children with WS are usually delayed in language onset, and they exhibit unusual patterns of sociointeractive behaviors in infancy, although by school age, their language and social skills have been described as relative strengths compared with other aspects of their cognitive profile (Bellugi, Marks, Bihrle, & Sabo, 1988; Bellugi et al., 1992; Bellugi, Wang, & Jernigan, 1994; Bellugi & St. George, 2000; Karmiloff-Smith et al., 1997; Mervis et al., 1999; Singer-Harris, Bellugi, Bates, Jones, & Rosen, 1997). Recently, researchers have started to explore the relationships between early sociointeractive behaviors, patterns of social attention and the development of language, communication skills, and social understanding in children with WS, to clarify whether and how the interdependencies and developmental pathways of these domains may be atypical in this population (Laing et al., 2002; Bertrand, Mervis, Rice, & Adamson, 1993; Mervis et al., 1999; Mervis et al., 2003).

Mervis et al. (2003) report on two studies examining the attention behavior of infants and toddlers with WS in naturalistic situations, following up on an early case report (Bertrand et al., 1993; Rice, 1992). The first study compared the looking behavior of one toddler with WS, with the given name of Jenny, to two comparison groups of normal children, one matched on chronological age, and the second on developmental age. The main findings confirmed earlier reports of distinctive patterns of attention distribution during mother-infant and stranger-infant play sessions. Jenny's attention patterns differed both in the amount of time spent looking at the play partner's face and in the unusual intensity of her gaze toward faces, radically different from the intensity ratings of either control group. This difference was most dramatic during the stranger session, when Jenny was engaged 99.5% of the time, of which 78% of her gazing at the stranger's face and 30% of her looking at objects were coded as intense. However,

Jenny's gazes at her mother during free play were of normal intensity, but significantly longer, compared with the control groups. Both quantitatively and qualitatively, Jenny's looking behavior differed significantly from that of the two control groups: She spent far more time looking at her partner, mother or stranger, and the quality of her gaze directed at the stranger during play sessions was unusually intense. The second study compared a group of children with WS between 8 and 43 months, observed during a medical evaluation by a clinical geneticist, to a large sample of age-matched children assessed in a similar setting. Their looking behavior was noted by the geneticist and by a second researcher present in the room during the physical exam. The children with WS in all age-groups looked primarily at the geneticist throughout the session, and the majority of them, especially those younger than 30 months, evidenced intense looking behavior, whereas none of the control participants ever looked intensely at the geneticist.

Mervis et al. (2003) explain these findings in terms of highly increased arousal during social interaction in the infants and toddlers with WS, coupled with "an extreme form of focused attention" (p. 262), possibly leading to attentional inertia (Anderson, Choi, & Lorch, 1987), which precludes normal disengagement from the target, even when a salient change in the environment occurs. Although these episodes of intense looking may be instances of "sticky fixation" leading to difficulty in disengaging attention, the authors point out that in older children attention to faces is voluntary, reflecting the highly motivating role of people and the appetitive nature of social interaction for individuals with WS.

Similar evidence for an atypical pattern of social attention resulted from experimental studies investigating early sociointeractive precursors to language in toddlers with WS. Laing and her colleagues (2002) administered the Early Social Communication Scales (ESCS; Mundy & Hogan, 1996) to a group of toddlers with WS and a group of normal toddlers matched on developmental age. Consistent with findings from observational studies, the toddlers with WS showed fewer object-related behaviors (pointing, reaching, requesting toys) and more social interactive behaviors (requests for tickling, turn-taking behaviors, eye contact not related to objects) than the control group. The WS children produced significantly fewer pointing gestures either in an instrumental or declarative function compared with controls and made fewer requests for toys. They used eye contact mostly in dyadic interactions and less often for social referencing or combined with requesting or reaching behaviors than the controls. The different patterns of correlations between categories of behaviors in the two groups indicated that for the WS toddlers the social interaction behaviors were less integrated with aspects of joint attention than for the controls. Overall, the WS group scored higher on dyadic social interaction behaviors, while the control group scored higher on all joint attention–related behaviors, especially object requesting and producing more triadic eye contact. Interestingly, the findings from this study confirmed earlier research by Mervis and Bertrand (1997) showing that in contrast to normally developing children, in WS, there is no relationship between sociocommunicative behaviors, such as joint attention, and measures of language acquisition.

Another study that found a lack of relationship between nonverbal communicative behaviors and language in WS was reported by Bertrand, Mervis, and Neustat (1998), who conducted a longitudinal investigation on the use of different communicative gestures by toddlers and preschoolers with WS and Down syndrome. After age 18 months, the WS children produced more give gestures than the children with Down syndrome. However, they produced significantly fewer *pointing* gestures, which emerged later in this group than among the children with Down syndrome. Moreover, in contrast to the Down syndrome children, and normally developing children, the use of pointing gestures was not related to receptive vocabulary among the children with WS. Taken together, the findings related to attention patterns and early sociocommunicative behaviors suggest that, for young children with WS, the use of gaze and gestures may not serve primarily referential and communicative goals, as in typical development, but serve primarily as a means for engaging people and maintaining social interaction.

Temperament and Personality

There are likely to be consequences of this attentional focus on people for the ability of individuals with WS to monitor the rest of their environment, to respond with appropriate cognitive solutions to different situations, and to learn about their world (Mervis et al., 2003). For example, Jones et al. (2000) reported that, during cognitive assessments, many young children with WS showed such concentrated interest in the examiner's face that they failed items on tasks requiring object manipulations. In contrast to controls, WS children did not respond to the frustration elicited by task difficulties with distress or anger; instead, they often attempted to engage the experimenter or other people in the room by smiling, looking, babbling, or waving. Such socially engaging behaviors, coupled with positive emotional expressions whenever a social partner is available for interaction, suggest an unusually people-oriented pattern of temperament and personality, already manifest in infancy.

Most studies exploring temperament and personality profiles in WS have used various parent/caregiver or teacher questionnaires and rating scales as informational sources. Studies of temperament in toddlers and young children with WS found that many fall into the category of "difficult" children, although unlike other difficult children, they show more approach, rather than withdrawn behavior (Tomc et al., 1990), confirming earlier reports of behavioral and emotional difficulties (Udwin et al., 1987).

Studies focusing on syndrome-specific behavioral and personality profiles that included matched controls (e.g., Einfield et al., 1997; Udwin & Yule, 1991) revealed higher rates of anxiety, overfriendliness, social disinhibition, attention-seeking behaviors, hyperactivity, and concentration problems for children and young adolescents with WS. Similarly, Sarimski (1997) noted that children with WS are more likely to be rated as worrying, talking too much, being overfriendly to strangers, and less likely to be rated as self-conscious compared with children with other developmental disabilities (see also Dilts, Morris, & Leonard, 1990; Gosch & Pankau, 1997; Greer, Brown, Pai, Choudry, & Klein, 1997).

Many of the behavioral and emotional difficulties identified in these studies of children with WS persist into adulthood and become more apparent and pervasive with age, as shown by Davies et al. (1998) in a study based on interviews with parents and other caregivers. Among the most prevalent social difficulties reported by parents and caregivers were problems in establishing and maintaining friendships, social disinhibition, excessive chatter, and a tendency to exaggerate and to be physically overdemonstrative, inappropriate in conversations, and too trusting of others. Almost three-quarters of the individuals with WS were described as socially isolated, despite their persistent efforts toward social contact. Gosch and Pankau (1997) compared the personality profiles of children, adolescents, and adults with WS. Overall, the characteristic personality profile of individuals with WS appeared to be stable over time, but the study also revealed certain age-related changes reflected in parental ratings of personality adjectives and problem behaviors in adults compared with children with WS: Adults with WS were rated by their parents as calmer, more inhibited, more withdrawn, and less lively, active, restless, tearful, quarrelsome, and overfriendly than the children.

Studies that have attempted to delineate the specific and unique personality profile of WS have found that people with WS differ from those with other genetic syndromes in being more agreeable (van Lieshout, De Meyer, Curfs, & Fryns, 1998) and showing more attention-seeking behavior and empathy toward others (Dykens & Rosner, 1999). Klein-Tasman and Mervis (2003) confirmed this distinct personality profile that focuses on other people: Children with WS were rated as more sociable and empathic, a profile that clearly differentiated WS from other matched children with disabilities. In light of the evidence for a distinctive, syndrome-specific personality profile, it appears that WS may provide a fertile testing ground for psychobiological models of temperament and personality, models that would take into account the complex interactions between genetic background, brain neurobiology, development, and environmental transactions in defining behavioral patterns of reactivity and affective expression (Fox, Henderson, & Marshall, 2001).

To date, few experimental studies directly examined patterns of emotionality and empathy in individuals with WS, but the existing evidence broadly supports the results based on parental report data. Jones, Anderson, Reilly, and Bellugi (1998) used a subset of the Laboratory Temperament Assessment Battery (LabTab; Goldsmith & Rothbart, 1992) to code emotional responses during a parental separation task in infants and toddlers with WS and normally developing controls. The children with WS showed less negative facial and vocal affect than controls and a lower intensity of distress, while control children showed clear signs of frustration or distress in the parent's absence. The children with WS also recovered more quickly and needed less consoling than the controls. It is difficult to conclude from this study whether young children with WS experience negative emotions during parental separation but manage to regulate their expression in anticipation of resuming social interaction upon the parent's return, or whether they show an abnormal pattern of attachment, possibly related to their indiscriminate approach behavior toward strangers.

One of the highly distinctive personality characteristics of people with WS is their empathic stance toward others. The capacity of children with WS to empathize with a person in distress has been tested experimentally in two investigations, using a simulated distress procedure adapted from Sigman, Kasari, Kwon, and Yirmiya (1992). In this procedure, children's responses to an experimenter who feigned hurting her knee and displayed distress are coded. Tager-Flusberg and Sullivan (1999) used this procedure with a group of children with WS, who were compared with a matched group of children with a different genetic syndrome, Prader-Willi syndrome. Although both groups spent most of the time during the distress scene looking at the experimenter, clearly observing her distress, the children with WS showed significantly greater empathy as evidenced by their comforting behavior, expressions of sympathy and help, validating comments, and overall concern. Similar findings were reported by Thomas, Beccera, and Mervis (2002), who used the same procedure with WS preschoolers in comparison with matched groups of normal children and children with developmental delays. The young children with WS showed higher levels of empathic behavior relative to both comparison groups, suggesting that this distinctive personality characteristic is evident by age 4 and is manifest to a greater degree than in the typically developing children of similar age.

Social-Affective Information Processing

Studies of social attention, temperament, and personality have provided important clues about the development of positively valenced approach behaviors in people with WS, a syndrome unique in its pervasive hypersociability. How do these behavioral characteristics relate to their ability to process social and affective information, and to their style of affective expression? Current research on social perception in people with WS has uncovered a mixture of relatively preserved abilities in face recognition coupled with difficulties in reading and interpreting social cues from facial, vocal, and body expressions.

Given the strong interest of people with WS in looking at faces, it is not surprising that on standardized tests of face recognition and face memories children and adults with WS generally perform within the normal range, and better than mental age–matched controls (Bellugi et al., 1988, 1994; Karmiloff-Smith, 1997; Udwin & Yule, 1991). These preserved face-processing skills are all the more remarkable given that WS is characterized by significantly impaired visual-spatial abilities (Mervis et al., 2000). Some researchers have argued that despite their good performance on standardized measures, people with WS process faces using atypical piecemeal strategies instead of encoding them holistically, which is how normal children and adults process faces (Deruelle, Mancini, Livet, Cassé-Perrot, & de Schonen, 1999; Elgar & Campbell, 2001; Gagliardi et al., 2003; Karmiloff-Smith, 1997; Karmiloff-Smith, Scerif, & Thomas, 2002). In a recent study (Tager-Flusberg, Plesa-Skwerer, Faja, & Joseph, 2003), we used the whole-part method introduced by Tanaka and his colleagues (Tanaka & Farah, 1993; Tanaka, Kay, Grinnell, Stansfield, & Szechter, 1998), which compares recognition of face features presented in the context of whole faces or in isolation for upright and inverted faces. A large group of adolescents and adults with WS were compared with age-matched controls, and we found that although overall performance was lower in the participants with WS, both groups showed similar patterns of performance across the different conditions, performing significantly better in the whole-face condition for upright faces, but not for inverted faces. The whole-face advantage only in the upright condition provides strong evidence that people with WS encode and recognize faces holistically in the same way as normal controls and confirms the relative preservation of face-processing skills in this population.

In contrast, several experimental studies examining emotion recognition by children, adolescents, and adults with WS found no sparing in the ability to discriminate, match, or label facial expressions of basic emotions. Tager-Flusberg and Sullivan (2000a) administered an emotion-matching task developed by Hobson, Ouston, and Lee (1988) to children with WS, children with Prader-Willi syndrome, and children with nonspecific mental retardation, matched on age, IQ, and language. The children with WS were as proficient as but no better than the control groups in discriminating and matching facial expressions of emotion. Similar results were reported by Gagliardi et al. (2003), who used an animated facial expression comprehension test based on Ekman and Friesen's (1976) standardized set of expressive faces to compare emotion recognition accuracy in children with WS and two control groups, one matched on chronological age and the other matched on mental age.

Using a standardized measure of emotion recognition—the Diagnostic Analysis of Nonverbal Accuracy test (DANVA-2; Nowicki & Duke, 1994)—we compared adolescents and adults with WS to two control groups: One group of age-matched nonretarded controls and a second group of learning or intellectually disabled (LD) participants, matched on both age and IQ (Plesa-Skwerer, Kaminski, & Tager-Flusberg, 2002). The DANVA-2 includes sets of child and adult faces and voices, which express four basic emotions: happy, sad, angry, and fearful. The task, which is administered by computer, involves selecting the appropriate emotion label for each face or voice presented. Overall, the participants with WS were less accurate than age-matched normal control participants, but no different from the LD comparison group on either the faces or the voices subtests of the DANVA-2. At the same time, despite their poorer overall scores, all groups showed the same pattern of performance, across both modalities and all emotions. Thus the three groups all had greater difficulty reading emotions from adult faces and voices and distinguishing between the negative emotions.

The findings across all these studies conflict with an earlier study we conducted with adults with WS using the original "Reading the Mind in the Eyes task," developed by Baron-Cohen and his colleagues (Baron-Cohen, Jolliffe, Mortimore, & Robertson, 1997). The stimuli for this task included a set of photographs showing just the eye region of the face that portrayed a range of subtle and fairly complex mental states. For each photograph the participant was asked to select which of two semantically opposite mental state labels (e.g., concerned-unconcerned; friendly-hostile) best matched the expression depicted. In this small-scale study we found that the adults with WS performed significantly better than the adults with Prader-Willi syndrome, matched on age, IQ, and language (Tager-Flusberg, Boshart, & Baron-Cohen, 1998). However, given the way the original task was constructed, the participants with WS may have relied simply on choosing between positive or negative valenced terms. More recently, Baron-Cohen, Wheelwright, Hill, Raste, & Plumb (2001) revised the Reading the Mind in the Eyes task: Now all the choices of terms have the same valence, making it considerably harder to select a correct label for each eye expression. We administered an adapted version of this task to a larger sample of adolescents and adults with WS, compared with age-matched normal control participants, and to a group of age- and IQ-matched participants with LD (Plesa-Skwerer et al., 2002). Our findings using this revised task showed that the performance of the WS participants was significantly worse than that of the normal controls and no different from that of the LD group, no longer suggesting relative sparing in WS on this task of social perceptual or "mentalizing" ability.

Another social-perceptual task that has been used with adults with WS taps the ability to infer trustworthiness of strangers from external facial cues. Bellugi, Adolphs, Cassady, and Chiles (1999) administered the approachability/trustworthiness task (Adolphs, Tranel, & Damasio, 1998) to quantify the tendency of individuals with WS to approach and engage strangers. Participants were shown a set of faces, one at a time, and asked to rate how much they would like to go up to each person and begin a conversation with them. The adults with WS gave abnormally positive ratings overall, judging the persons as more approachable and more trustworthy than did matched controls. This tendency is consonant with anecdotal reports about the indiscriminant trust and friendliness of people with WS toward strangers and suggests possible deficits or positive biases in processing the social and psychological significance of facial displays from external cues.

People with WS "never go unnoticed in a group" (Dykens & Rosner, 1999) and usually make a distinct impression on others, partly due to the high expressiveness of their language and communicative behavior. Thus, during everyday social interactions, impairments in their ability to interpret appropriately social cues may be masked by an overabundance of linguistic and dramatic expressive devices used to engage and involve the social partners or audience and maintain social contact. Several studies have documented how the verbal expressiveness of people with WS functions as a means for social engagement across of variety of discourse domains and emerges as early as children are able to use language for conversational and narrative purposes (Jones et al., 2000; Losh, Bellugi, Reilly, & Anderson, 2000; Harrison, Reilly, & Klima, 1995; Reilly et al., 1990; Reilly, Losh, Bellugi, & Wulfeck, 2004).

One of the commonly used narrative tasks requires participants to tell a story based on a picture book. The narratives produced provide a rich context for assessing the linguistic, cognitive, and social engagement abilities of the storyteller. Bellugi and her colleagues have shown in several studies that children and adolescents with WS used significantly more lexical evaluative devices, such as character speech, sound effects, affect, emphatic markers, and vocal prosody, than age-matched participants with Down syndrome and normal control participants of the same mental age. The participants with WS also used phrases and exclamations meant to capture the listener's attention ("audience hooks") to a greater extent than the control groups. However, an analysis of the thematic and structural aspects of the narratives produced by children with WS revealed significant difficulties with the referential content and coherence of their stories, compared with both typically developing children and children with language impairment (Reilly et al., 2004). Similarly, Pearlman-Avnion and Eviatar (2002) showed that 7- to 11-year-old children with WS did not differ from a comparison group of matched children with high-functioning autism on measures of informational elements in a narrative task (e.g., an index of the use of language to transfer information), although they performed at the level of the normal control group on measures of the emotional elements of the storytelling task. Finally, Harrison et al. (1995) report that adolescents and adults with WS used significantly more evaluative devices and affectively enriched language in spontaneous conversation collected in the course of a semistructured biographical interview. Moreover, their participants sometimes took over the lead from the interviewer by asking questions and taking responsibility for keeping the conversation going. In our experience, individuals with WS not only show a desire for continued social interaction, even when asked to participate in tiresome experiments, but also often express exaggerated positive emotional feelings about having met and interacted with our research team. As one adolescent research participant repeatedly told us: "This is the best day of my life!" As Jones et al. (2000) conclude, these results demonstrate the "pervasiveness of linguistically conveyed hypersociability" in WS.

In spite of the apparent language fluency and high expressiveness in the use of communicative devices, more stringent assessments of the pragmatic aspects of language in people with WS have revealed significant levels of impairment (e.g., Laws & Bishop, 2004; Stojanovik, Perkins, & Howard, 2001). Based on parental ratings on the Children's Communication Checklist (CCC; Bishop, 1998), a standardized instrument developed to identify abnormalities in pragmatic aspects of the language of children with language disorders, Laws and Bishop (2004) found that more than 75% of the children and young adults with WS scored below the cutoff considered indicative of pragmatic impairment, compared with 50% of the participants with Down syndrome and 41% of children with specific language impairment. There was considerable variability in ratings on the different subscales of the CCC, yielding an uneven profile of pragmatic language abilities. The WS group differed from typically developing controls in all five areas covered by the subscales: inappropriate initiation of conversation, coherence, stereotyped conversation, use of context, and rapport. Moreover, the WS group scored significantly worse than the comparison groups in two areas of pragmatic competence: the use of stereotyped conversation and inappropriate initiation of conversation.

These results suggest that children with WS tend to rely on the use of superficial social engagement devices in their conversational strategies, lacking fine attunement to the conversational partner, including inappropriate statements and questions, and often reflecting a lack of normal social inhibition in interacting with strangers. Parents also describe excessive chatter and a propensity for socially inappropriate statements and questions and for talking to themselves (Davies et al., 1998). Despite their usually high verbal expressiveness, it appears that individuals with WS are deficient in the pragmatic use of language, and this contributes to difficulties in forming and maintaining social relationships that extend beyond momentary social engagements or interactions.

Theory of Mind

Over the past decade, there has been considerable interest in exploring how people with WS make sense of the social world, and in particular whether they are able to understand mental states in other people. Karmiloff-Smith and her colleagues (Karmiloff-Smith, Klima, Bellugi, Grant, & Baron-Cohen, 1995) gave a number of different theory-of-mind tasks to older children, adolescents, and young adults with WS, including standard first- and second-order false-belief tasks and a higher-order task that involved interpreting nonliteral utterances. The majority of the participants in their study passed these tasks, leading Karmiloff-Smith et al. to conclude that theory of mind may be an "islet of preserved ability" in WS (p. 202).

However, later studies have demonstrated that theory of mind may not be as spared in WS as originally believed. Karmiloff-Smith et al. (1995) studied relatively older individuals with WS and did not include their own well-matched control groups. In a series of follow-up studies, we systematically investigated performance on false-belief and other theory-of-mind tasks in younger children with WS. The children with WS were matched to two comparison groups on age (4 to 10 years), IQ, and standardized language measures. The comparison groups included children with Prader-Willi syndrome and children with nonspecific mental retardation. In each experiment, between 15 and 25 children were included in each group. On three different first-order theory-of-mind tasks, false belief, explanation of action (Tager-Flusberg & Sullivan, 1994), and understanding of intended action (Joseph & Tager-Flusberg, 1999), we found that the children with WS performed no better than the matched comparison groups (Plesa-Skwerer & Tager-Flusberg, in press; Tager-Flusberg & Sullivan, 2000b).

We also investigated higher-order theory-of-mind tasks in adolescents with WS and matched groups of adolescents with Prader-Willi syndrome and mental retardation. Again, no differences were found among these groups in second-order belief reasoning (Sullivan & Tager-Flusberg, 1999), in distinguishing lies and jokes (Sullivan, Winner, & Tager-Flusberg, 2003), or in using trait information to attribute intentionality (Plesa-Skwerer & Tager-Flusberg, in press). Across these higher-order tasks, most of the participants with WS, as well as those in the comparison groups, had difficulty passing test questions, and especially in justifying their answers by correctly referring to mental states.

Our studies on theory of mind in WS thus provide no evidence of relative sparing in this domain for either children or adolescents with WS compared with age-, IQ-, and language-matched controls. On the contrary, we found that children and adolescents with WS had problems in social cognitive abilities that involve inferences and also in attending to many pieces of information in narratives that entail characters whose mental states are relevant for interpreting knowledge, false belief, intention, or intended meaning in communication. The poor performance of the children and adolescents with WS on theory-of-mind tasks may be partly related to attention problems, which have been well documented in this population (Dilts et al., 1990; Udwin, 1990) and which may have hindered their ability to integrate the task information and formulate an inference about the contents of others' mental states.

Summary of Behavioral Studies

Research on social attention, social engagement, and social cognition in WS provides a complex picture of the strengths and weaknesses that define the phenotype of this highly unusual genetic syndrome. Across all ages, people with WS are hypersociable, defined in terms of their strong interest in approaching and engaging with other people, even strangers (Doyle, Bellugi, Korenberg, & Graham, 2004). At a cognitive level, this behavioral/temperamental characteristic is perhaps manifest in their spared face-processing skills, in their empathy toward people in distress, and in their verbal expressive ability. But, as we have seen, hypersociability does not translate into relatively spared processing of affective information or theory of mind. The consequences of this unusual and uneven social profile may be difficulties with peer relations and a relatively high rate of emotional and behavioral problems (Dykens & Rosner, 1999; Einfeld et al., 1997). Higher levels of anxiety compared with the general population are common in people with WS, many of whom develop depression as adults. These mood disorders may in part be related to the accumulation of unsuccessful social experiences (Einfeld et al., 1997; Gosch & Pankau, 1997; Morris & Mervis, 1999).

Neurobiological Basis of Social Engagement in WS

Investigating the Brain in WS

Few research teams have studied the brain structure or function in people with WS. One exception is the research group at the Salk Institute, headed by Ursula Bellugi, which has undertaken a systematic program investigating the neurobiology and neuropathology of individuals with WS, using a range of methodologies. The most consistent finding across numerous studies is that people with WS of all ages have small brains (Galaburda, Wang, Bellugi, & Rossen, 1994; Galaburda & Bellugi, 2000; Jernigan, Bellugi, Sowell, Doherty, & Hesselink, 1993; Reiss et al., 2000). This is also true for people with some (but not all) other neurodevelopmental disorders, including Down syndrome (Jernigan & Bellugi, 1990). Beyond the size of the overall brain, research has explored whether specific regions of the brain show particular atypical patterns of growth or functional organization. In the final section of this chapter, we summarize the studies that focus on aspects of brain structure and function that may be related to the social phenotype of WS described in the previous sections.

Research on the relationship between social behavior in WS and brain pathology has focused on two key aspects of the WS phenotype: hypersociability and face perception. At this stage, most of the studies have been exploratory and have generally involved relatively small numbers of participants. Detailed studies of autopsied brains are very limited by the number of specimens available. Nevertheless, work by Galaburda and his colleagues has yielded interesting findings, drawn from a small number of case studies. As methods for functional brain imaging improve, especially the introduction of high-resolution scanners and protocols that limit the amount of time needed to collect whole-brain images, studies are now able to include larger groups of participants. However, there remain significant challenges to collecting such data from people with WS for either structural or functional studies because the scanning environment is often experienced as highly claustrophobic, with frightening, loud sounds.

Neurobiological Basis of Hypersociability in WS

One of most interesting findings from studies of both autopsied brains and structural magnetic resonance imaging (MRI) is that despite the overall reduction in size of the brain in WS, certain regions are relatively preserved in size. Two regions of particular interest to the link to hypersociability are the cerebellar vermis and the superior temporal gyrus (STG). In one systematic study, Schmitt, Eliez, Warsofksy, Bellugi, and Reiss (2001) compared the neuroanatomical structure of the cerebellar vermis and related neocerebellar structures in 20 adults with WS and 20 age- and gender-matched controls using high-resolution MRI. They found that relative to total brain size, the neocerebellum in the WS group was relatively enlarged, which they suggest reflects relative preservation both structurally and functionally. They speculate, based on comparisons with other neurodevelopmental disorders, that the neocerebellum sparing may relate to the relative sparing of language and especially social-emotional behavior in WS. Jones and colleagues (2002) followed up this study by asking radiologists to rate MRI scans collected from 9 infants and toddlers with WS and 9 matched controls. They found that the main difference noted by radiologists, who were blind to diagnosis and the key hypotheses, was the enlarged cerebellum among the young children with WS. This suggests that the atypical cerebellar enlargement is present from a very early age, consistent with the behavioral findings of early sociability in infants with WS. Both these studies confirm earlier findings reported in several publications from the Salk group (e.g., Jernigan & Bellugi, 1990, 1994; Reiss et al., 2000).

In addition to relative or even enlarged size of the neocerebellum, another area that has been identified as relatively preserved is the STG (Reiss et al., 2000). Reiss and his colleagues compared 14 adults with WS to 14 age- and gender-matched controls. They found that when they controlled for overall cerebral gray matter, the gray matter volumes for STG were proportionally larger in the group with WS. Again, this study replicated earlier studies that included smaller groups of participants (Hickok et al., 1995). This brain region is related to auditory, language, and music processing, and Reiss and his colleagues suggest that the preservation of STG may relate to the strong language abilities and emotional responsiveness to music that characterize people with WS. These aspects of the WS phenotype are closely linked to their social-affective responsiveness toward other people.

Another area of the brain that has been discussed in relation to the unusual social behavior of people with WS is the amygdala. Bellugi and her colleagues (1999) highlight the similarity of the atypical performance of adults with WS on the approachability/trustworthiness task (see earlier discussion) to patients with bilateral amygdala damage (Adolphs et al., 1998), who also gave more positive ratings to the untrustworthy faces. These individuals share the same behavior patterns as people with WS, approaching strangers and acting overly friendly in everyday life. Interestingly, patients with bilateral amygdala damage have preserved face recognition skills, as has been found in WS (see earlier discussion).

Structural MRI studies have yielded inconsistent findings on the relative size of the amygdala in WS. Earlier studies, which compared WS with Down syndrome, found that the size of the amygdala was preserved, relative to total brain size (e.g., Jernigan & Bellugi, 1994). This was replicated in a recent unpublished study conducted in Australia in which 22 children and adults with WS were compared with 22 controls matched on age, gender, and handedness (Martens et al., unpublished data). This study found no differences between the groups in the absolute volumes of either the left or right amygdala. Furthermore, they found a significant correlation between the volume of the right (but not left) amygdala to the participants' approachability ratings on a modified version of Adolph's task.

In contrast to these structural MRI studies, Galaburda and his colleagues (Galaburda & Bellugi, 2000) found that in one of their autopsy specimens, the overall volume of the amygdala was smaller, about half the size compared with matched controls; the dorsal portion of the lateral nucleus was especially small and abnormal in shape compared with the control amygdalae. Galaburda and Bellugi (2000) speculate that since this nucleus of the amygdala receives connections from visual cortex, perhaps in WS a reduction in connectivity between these brain regions means that sensory experiences fail to acquire the appropriate emotional valence, including the danger associated with unfamiliar people. This neuroanatomical difference in WS could account for the unusual approach and overfriendliness toward strangers.

At this point, there are clearly still controversies regarding which brain areas in WS putatively linked to social behavior might be either too small or too large relative to those of controls. Moreover, there have been almost no systematic investigations that specifically relate brain structure to social behavior in WS. For now, we can only speculate on the possible relationships between the social-emotional characteristics of WS to differences in the neocerebellum, STG, and amygdala.

Neurobiological Basis of Face Processing in WS

Perhaps the most preserved cognitive skill in WS is face recognition (see earlier discussion). The most striking feature of the cognitive profile in individuals with WS is the enormous discrepancy between their good face-processing skills and their impaired visual-spatial skills (Bellugi et al., 1992). One consistent hypothesis in the literature on WS is that this dissociation between face and visual-spatial perceptual abilities reflects the anatomical distinction between dorsal visual stream, which processes visuospatial information (the "where" system), and the ventral stream, which processes face and object information (the "what" system). In WS, it is hypothesized that the dorsal stream is impaired both structurally and functionally (Atkinson et al., 1997). Consistent with this hypothesis, Galaburda and Bellugi (2000) report that in autopsied brains from four WS children and adults, there is a curtailment in the posterior-parietal and occipital regions. Furthermore, across all the brains, they found a short central sulcus, which they argue may indicate a developmental anomaly affecting the dorsal half of the hemispheres. These findings were confirmed in an MRI study comparing 21 adults with WS to 21 matched controls (Galaburda et al., 2001). In this study, the researchers found that the dorsal central sulcus was less likely to reach the interhemispheric fissure in the WS adults, but there were group differences in the ventral extent of the central sulcus. These structural findings are consistent with the hypothesis that ventral pathway functions, including face perception, may be relatively spared in WS.

More direct investigations of the neurobiological substrate for face processing in WS comes from electrophysiological and functional MRI (fMRI) studies. The most comprehensive ERP studies were reported by Mills and colleagues (Mills, Alvarez, St. George, & Appelbaum, 2000). The main study compared 18 adults with WS to 23 age- and gender-matched controls on a task that required the participants to judge whether two faces were the same or different; faces were presented in either upright or inverted orientations. A similar study was run with children, but their data were not presented systematically. Mills and colleagues compared the groups on both early (indexing attention to faces) and late (indexing recognition of faces) ERP components in the two groups. The main findings were that the adults with WS showed an unusually small N100 but large N200 peaks to all the face stimuli. Mills and colleagues suggest that the unusual N200 peak reflects the increased attention that people with WS pay to faces. On the later N320 component, which is considered to be linked to face recognition processes, the ERP patterns found among the adults with WS were similar to those found among younger typically developing adolescents, but were somewhat larger and delayed compared with the matched adults. The authors conclude from these findings that "in WS, the brain systems that mediate face recognition might be normally organized but developmentally delayed" (Mills et al., 2000, p. 59).

The use of fMRI methodologies allows researchers to locate more precisely which brain regions are functionally involved in particular cognitive tasks. Face perception has been extensively studied using fMRI by a large number of research groups, and these investigations, in addition to studies of patients with prosopagnosia, support the view that there are specialized brain regions or networks, primarily involving the so-called face fusiform area (FFA) located on the underside of the temporal lobes along the fusiform gyrus, that support face processing (Damasio, Tranel, & Damasio, 1990; Haxby et al., 1994; Kanwisher, Tong, & Nakayama, 1998). Schultz and his colleagues (Schultz, Grelotti, & Pober, 2001) report on a preliminary study investigating FFA activation to faces in adults with WS. They found that the adults with WS had normal activation patterns in both right and left hemisphere FFA (in both size and intensity of activation) that were selective to faces.

A more recent study by Mobbs et al. (2004) compared 11 adults with WS to 11 age- and gender-matched controls in a paradigm that required participants to monitor eye gaze direction in faces presented at different orientations (head-on or averted). Although Mobbs et al. (2004) report on numerous significant differences in brain activation patterns between the WS and control groups, these are not easy to interpret given the complex nature of the task and stimuli used in their study. Nevertheless, the study highlighted three main a priori regions of interest selected on the basis of their known connection to face and gaze processing: fusiform gyrus, superior temporal sulcus, and the amygdala. In these regions of interest, there were no significant differences between the groups in activation patterns for either the left or right hemisphere. Thus these findings replicate those reported by Schultz et al. (2001) and confirm that in WS, the same areas of the brain are used to process faces as in controls. These functional imaging studies confirm the conclusions drawn earlier from behavioral studies; namely, that in WS, the same cognitive and neurobiological mechanisms are involved in processing and recognizing faces as in normally developing individuals.

Conclusions

Genetically based neurodevelopmental disorders can offer unique insights into understanding gene-brain-behavior relationships. WS is especially useful for exploring the genetic and neurocognitive systems that underlie social-emotional behavior because the phenotype associated with this disorder is so striking. Although there is still much to be learned about the precise cognitive-affective mechanisms that underlie the hypersociability, empathy, unusual attention to people, and emotional responsiveness that define the WS social phenotype, significant progress has been made over the past two decades. Less is known about the neurobiological systems that are specifically related to the behavioral patterns that distinguish WS from other groups. Although connections have been made with particular brain areas such as the neocerebellum, STG, and amygdala, the sparse evidence to date is based on a limited number of studies, and no studies have yet demonstrated explicit connections between brain structure or function and socially relevant behaviors in WS. Moreover, even though WS is a developmental disorder, there have been very few developmental studies investigating how the social phenotype of WS changes over time in response to maturational or contextual influences at different developmental stages. Future studies on WS will help to elucidate the foundations and developmental trajectories for the neurocognitive systems that serve basic functions such as social engagement and emotional relatedness, as well as more complex aspects of social cognitive systems that are fundamental to our unique human capacity for forming and maintaining social relationships.

Acknowledgments Preparation of this chapter was supported by a grant from the National Institute of Child Health and Human Development (RO1 HD 33470).

References

Adolphs, R., Tranel, D., & Damasio, A. R. (1998). The human amygdala in social judgment. *Nature, 393,* 470–475.

Anderson, D. R., Choi, H. P., & Lorch, E. P. (1987). Attentional inertia reduces distractibility during young children's TV viewing. *Child Development, 58,* 798–806.

Atkinson, J., King, J., Braddick, O., Nokes, L., Anker, S., & Braddick, F. (1997). A specific deficit of dorsal stream function in Williams syndrome. *NeuroReport, 8,* 1919–1922.

Bakeman, R., & Adamson, L. B. (1984). Coordinating attention to people and objects in mother-infant and peer-infant interaction. *Child Development, 55,* 1278–1289.

Baron-Cohen, S., Jolliffe, T., Mortimore, C., & Robertson, M. (1997). Another advanced test of theory of mind: Evidence from very high-functioning adults with autism or Asperger syndrome. *Journal of Child Psychology and Psychiatry, 38,* 813– 822.

Baron-Cohen, S., Wheelwright, S., Hill, J., Raste, Y., & Plumb, I. (2001). The "Reading the Mind in the Eyes" test revised version: A study with normal adults, and adults with Asperger syndrome or high-functioning autism. *Journal of Child Psychology and Psychiatry, 42,* 241–251.

Bellugi, U., Adolphs, R., Cassady, C., & Chiles M. (1999). Towards the neural basis for hypersociability in a genetic syndrome. *Neuroreport, 10,* 1653–1657.

Bellugi, U., Bihrle, A., Neville, H., Jernigan, T., & Doherty, S. (1992). Language, cognition, and brain organization in a neurodevelopmental disorder. In M. Gunnar & C. Nelson (Eds.), *Developmental behavioral neuroscience: The Minnesota symposium* (pp. 201–232). Hillsdale, NJ: Lawrence Erlbaum Associates.

Bellugi, U., Marks, S., Bihrle, A., & Sabo, H. (1988). Dissociation between language and cognitive functions in Williams syndrome. In D. Bishop & K. Mogford (Eds.), *Language development in exceptional circumstances* (pp. 177–189). London: Churchill Livingstone.

Bellugi, U., Mills, D., Jernigan, T. L., Hickok, G., & Galaburda, A. (1999). Linking cognition, brain structure, and brain function in Williams syndrome. In H. Tager-Flusberg (Ed.), *Neurodevelopmental disorders: Contributions to a new framework from the cognitive neurosciences* (pp. 111–136). Cambridge, MA: MIT Press.

Bellugi, U., & St. George, M. (2000). Linking cognitive neuroscience and molecular genetics: New perspectives from Williams syndrome [Special issue]. *Journal of Cognitive Neurosciences 12*(1).

Bellugi, U., Wang, P. P., & Jernigan, T. L. (1994). Williams syndrome: An unusual neuropsychological profile. In S. H. Broman & J. Grafman (Eds.), *Atypical cognitive deficits in developmental disorders: Implications for brain function* (pp. 23–56). Hillsdale, NJ: Erlbaum.

Bertrand, J., Mervis, C. B., & Neustat, I. (1998). Communicative gesture use by preschoolers with Williams syndrome: A longitudinal study. *Infant Behavior and Development, 21*, 294.

Bertrand, J., Mervis, C., Rice, C. E., & Adamson, L. (1993, March). *Development of joint attention by a toddler with Williams syndrome*. Paper presented at the Gatlinburg Conference on Research and Theory in Mental Retardation and Developmental Disabilities, Gatlinburg, TN.

Beuren, A. J. (1972). Supravalvular aortic stenosis: A complex syndrome with and without mental retardation. *Birth Defects, 8*, 45–46.

Bishop, D. V. M. (1998). Development of the Children's Communication Checklist (CCC): A method for assessing qualitative aspects of communicative impairment in children. *Journal of Child Psychology and Psychiatry, 39*, 879–891.

Carpenter, M., Nagell, K., & Tomasello, M. (1998). Social cognition, joint attention and communicative competence from 9 to 15 months of age. *Monographs of the Society for Research in Child Development, 63* (4 Serial No. 255).

Damasio, A. R., Tranel, D., & Damasio, H. (1990). Face agnosia and the neural substrates of memory. *Annual Review of Neuroscience, 13*, 89–109.

Danoff, S. K., Taylor, H. E., Blackshaw, S., & Desiderio, S. (2004). TFII-I, a candidate gene for Williams syndrome cognitive profile: Parallels between regional expression in mouse brain and human phenotype. *Neuroscience, 123*, 931–938.

Davies, M., Udwin, O., & Howlin, P. (1998). Adults with Williams syndrome. *British Journal of Psychiatry, 172*, 273–274.

Deruelle, C., Mancini, J., Livet, M., Cassé-Perrot, C., & de Schonen, S. (1999). Configural and local processing of faces in children with Williams syndrome. *Brain and Cognition, 41*, 276–298.

Dilts, C., Morris, C. A., & Leonard, C. A. (1990). Hypothesis for development of a behavioral phenotype in WS. *American Journal of Medical Genetics Supplement, 6*, 126–131.

Doyle, T. F., Bellugi, U., Korenberg, J. R., & Graham, J. (2004). "Everybody in the world is my friend": Hypersociability in young children with Williams syndrome. *American Journal of Medical Genetics, 124*, 263–273.

Dykens, E. M., & Rosner, B. (1999). Refining behavioral phenotypes: Personality-motivation in Williams and Prader-Willi syndromes. *American Journal of Mental Retardation, 104*, 158–169.

Einfeld, S., Tonge, B., & Florio, T. (1997). Behavioral and emotional disturbance in individuals with Williams syndrome. *American Journal of Mental Retardation, 102*, 45–53.

Ekman, P., & Friesen, W. V. (1976). *Pictures of facial affect*. Palo Alto, CA: Consulting Psychological Press.

Elgar, K., & Campbell, R. (2001). Annotation: The cognitive neuroscience of face recognition: Implications for developmental disorders. *Journal of Child Psychology and Psychiatry, 42*, 705–717.

Ewart, A. K., Morris, C. A., Atkinson, D., Weishan, J., Sternes, K., Spallone, P., et al. (1993). Hemizygosity at the elastin gene locus in a developmental disorder, Williams syndrome. *Nature Genetics, 5*, 11–16.

Fox, N. A., Henderson, H. A., & Marshall, P. J. (2001). The biology of temperament: An integrative approach. In C. A. Nelson & M. Luciana (Eds.), *The handbook of developmental cognitive neuroscience* (pp. 631–645). Cambridge, MA: MIT Press.

Frangiskakis, J. M., Ewart, A. K., Morris, C. A., Mervis, C. B., Bertrand, J., Robinson, B. F., et al. (1996). LIM-kinase hemizygosity implicated in impaired visuospatial constructive cognition. *Cell, 86*, 59–59.

Gagliardi, C., Frigerio, E., Burt, D. M., Cazzaniga, I., Perrett, D., & Borgatti, R. (2003). Facial expression recognition in Williams syndrome. *Neuropsychologia, 41*, 733–738.

Galaburda, A. M., & Bellugi, U. (2000). Multi-level analysis of cortical neuroanatomy in Williams syndrome. *Journal of Cognitive Neuroscience, 12*(Suppl.), 74–88.

Galaburda, A. M., Schmitt, E., Atlas, S. W., Eliez, S., Bellugi, U., & Reiss, A. L. (2001). Dorsal forebrain anomaly in Williams syndrome. *Archives of Neurology, 58*, 1865–1869.

Galaburda, A. M., Wang, P. P., Bellugi, U., & Rossen, M. (1994). Cytoarchitectonic anomalies in a genetically based disorder: Williams syndrome. *NeuroReport, 5*, 757–758.

Goldsmith, H., & Rothbart, M. (1992). The laboratory temperament assessment battery: Locomotor version. Unpublished test manual. Eugene, OR: Department of Psychology, University of Oregon.

Gosch, A., & Pankau, R. (1994). Social-emotional and behavioral adjustment in children with Williams-Beuren syndrome. *American Journal of Medical Genetics, 52*, 291–296.

Gosch, A., & Pankau, R. (1997). Personality characteristics and behavior problems in individuals of different ages with Williams syndrome. *Developmental Medicine and Child Neurology, 39*, 527–533.

Greer, M. K., Brown, F. R., Pai, S., Choudry, S. H., & Klein, A. J. (1997). Cognitive, adaptive and behavioral characteristics of Williams syndrome. *American Journal of Medical Genetics, 74*, 521–525.

Harrison, D., Reilly, J., & Klima, E. S. (1995). Unusual social behavior in Williams symdrome: Evidence from biographical interviews [abstract, special issue]. *Genetic Counseling, 6*, 181–183.

Haxby, J. V., Horwitz, B., Ungerleider, L. G., Maisog, J. M., Pietrini, P., & Grady, C. L. (1994). The functional organization of human extrastriate cortex: A PET-rCBF study of selective attention to faces and locations. *Journal of Neuroscience, 14*, 6336–6353.

Hickok, G., Neville, H., Mills, D., Jones, W., Rossen, M., & Bellugi, U. (1995). Electrophysiological and quantitative MR analysis of the cortical auditory system in Williams syndrome. *Cognitive Neuroscience Society Abstracts, 2*, 66.

Hobson, R. P., Ouston, J., & Lee, A. (1988). What's in a face? The case of autism. *British Journal of Psychiatry, 79*, 441–453.

Jernigan, T. L., & Bellugi, U. (1990). Anomalous brain morphology on magnetic resonance images in Williams syndrome and Down syndrome. *Archives of Neurology, 47*, 529–533.

Jernigan, T. L., & Bellugi, U. (1994). Neuroanatomical distinctions between Williams and Down syndromes. In S. Broman & J. Grafman (Eds.), *Atypical cognitive deficits in developmental disorders: Implications in brain function* (pp. 57–66). Hillsdale, NJ: Erlbaum.

Jernigan, T. L., Bellugi, U., Sowell, E., Doherty, S., & Hesselink, J. R. (1993).

Cerebral morphologic distinctions between Williams and Down syndromes. *Archives of Neurology, 50*, 186–191.

Jones, W., Anderson, D., Reilly, J., & Bellugi, U. (1998). Emotional expression in infants and children with Williams syndrome: A relationship between temperament and genetics? *Journal of International Neuropsychological Society, 4*, 56.

Jones, W., Bellugi, U., Lai, Z., Chiles, M., Reilly, J., Lincoln, A., et al. (2000). Hypersociability in Williams syndrome. *Journal of Cognitive Neuroscience, 12*(Suppl.), 30–46.

Jones, W., Hesselink, J., Courchesne, E., Duncan, T., Matsuda, K., & Bellugi, U. (2002). Cerebellar abnormalities in infants and toddlers with Williams syndrome. *Developmental Medicine and Child Neurology, 44*, 688–694.

Joseph, R., & Tager-Flusberg, H. (1999). Preschool children's understanding of the desire and knowledge constraints on intended action. *British Journal of Developmental Psychology, 17*, 221–243.

Kanwisher, N., Tong, F., & Nakayama, K. (1998). The effect of face inversion on the human fusiform area. *Cognition, 68*, B1–B11.

Karmiloff-Smith, A. (1997). Crucial differences between developmental cognitive neuroscience and adult neuropsychology. *Developmental Neuropsychology, 13*, 513–524.

Karmiloff-Smith, A., Grant, A., Ewing, S., Carette, M. J., Metcalfe, K., Donnai, D., et al. (2003). Using case study comparisons to explore genotype-phenotype correlations in Williams-Beuren syndrome. *Journal of Medical Genetics, 40*, 136–140.

Karmiloff-Smith, A., Klima, E., Bellugi, U., Grant, J., & Baron-Cohen, S. (1995). Is there a social module? Language, face processing and theory of mind in individuals with Williams syndrome. *Journal of Cognitive Neuroscience, 7*, 196–208.

Karmiloff-Smith, A., Scerif, G., & Thomas, M. (2002). Different approaches to relating genotype to phenotype in developmental disorders. *Developmental Psychobiology, 40*, 311–322.

Klein-Tasman, B. P., & Mervis, C. B. (2003). Distinctive personality characteristics of 8-, 9-, and 10-year-olds with Williams syndrome. *Developmental Neuropsychology, 23*, 269–290.

Laing, E., Butterworth, G., Ansari, D., Gsodl, M., Longhi, E., Panagiotaki, G., et al. (2002). Atypical development of language and social communication in toddlers with Williams syndrome. *Developmental Science, 5*, 233–246.

Laws, G., & Bishop, D. (2004). Pragmatic language impairment and social deficits in Williams syndrome: A comparison with Down's syndrome and specific language impairment. *International Journal of Language and Communication Disorders, 39*(Suppl.), 45–64.

Losh, M., Bellugi, U., Reilly, J., & Anderson, D. (2000). Narrative as a social engagement tool: The excessive use of evaluation in narratives from children with Williams syndrome. *Narrative Inquiry, 10*, 265–290.

Martens, M., Wilson, S., & Reutens, D. (2004). *The amygdala and the development of sociability: Insights from Williams syndrome.* Unpublished manuscript, Monash University, Australia.

Mervis, C. B., & Bertrand, J. (1997). Developmental relations between cognition and language: Evidence from Williams syndrome. In L. Adamson & M. A. Romski (Eds.), *Research on communication and language disorders: Contributions to theories of language development* (pp. 75–106). New York: Brookes.

Mervis, C. B., & Klein-Tasman, B. P. (2000). Williams syndrome: Cognition, personality, and adaptive behavior. *Mental Retardation and Developmental Disabilities Research Reviews, 6,* 148–158.

Mervis, C. B., Morris, C. A., Bertrand, J., & Robinson, B. (1999). Williams syndrome: Findings from an integrated program of research. In H. Tager-Flusberg (Ed.), *Neurodevelopmental disorders* (pp. 65–110). Cambridge, MA: MIT Press.

Mervis, C., Morris, C. A., Klein-Tasman, B. P., Bertrand, J., Kwitny, S., Appelbaum, L. G., et al. (2003). Attentional characteristics of infants and toddlers with Williams syndrome during triadic interactions. *Developmental Neuropsychology, 23,* 243–268.

Mervis, C. B., Robinson, B. F., Bertrand, J., Morris, C. A., Klein-Tasman, B. P., & Armstrong, S. C. (2000). The Williams syndrome cognitive profile. *Brain and Cognition, 44,* 604–628.

Mills, D. L., Alvarez, T. D., St. George, M., & Appelbaum, L. G. (2000). Electrophysiological studies of face processing in Williams syndrome. *Journal of Cognitive Neuroscience, 12*(Suppl.), 47–64.

Mobbs, D., Garrett, A. S., Menon, V., Rose, F. E., Bellugi, U., & Reiss, A. L. (2004). Anomalous brain activation during face and gaze processing in Williams syndrome. *Neurology, 62,* 2070–2076.

Morris, C. A., & Mervis, C. B. (1999). Williams syndrome. In S. Goldstein & C. R. Reynolds (Eds.), *Handbook of neurodevelopmental and genetic disorders in children.* New York: Guilford.

Mundy, P., & Gomes, A. (1998). Individual differences in joint attention skill development in the second year. *Infant Behavior and Development, 21,* 469–482.

Mundy, P., & Hogan, A. (1996). *A preliminary manual for the abridged Early Social Communication Scales (ESCS).* Coral Gables, FL: University of Miami.

Nowicki, S., Jr., & Duke, M. P. (1994). Individual differences in the nonverbal communication of affect: The Diagnostic Analysis of Nonverbal Accuracy Scale. *Journal of Nonverbal Behavior, 18,* 9–35.

Osborne, L. R., Sodar, S., Shi, X.–M., Pober, B., Costa, T., Scherer, S. W., et al. (1997). Hemizygous deletion of the syntaxin 1A gene in individuals with Williams syndrome. *American Journal of Human Genetics, 61,* 449–452.

Pearlman-Avnion, S., & Eviatar, Z. (2002). Narrative analysis in developmental social and linguistic pathologies: Dissociation between emotional and informational language use. *Brain and Cognition, 48,* 494–499.

Plesa-Skwerer, D., Kaminski, S., & Tager-Flusberg, H. (2002, July). *Perception of emotions and mental states by adolescents and adults with Williams syndrome.* Paper presented at the Ninth International Professional Conference on Williams Syndrome, Long Beach, CA.

Plesa-Skwerer, D., & Tager-Flusberg, H. (in press). Social cognition in Williams-Beuren syndrome. In C. A. Morris, H. M. Lenhoff, & P. Wang (Eds.), *Williams-Beuren syndrome: Research and clinical perspectives.* Baltimore: Johns Hopkins University Press.

Reilly, J., Klima, E., & Bellugi, U. (1990). Once more with feeling: Affect and language in atypical populations. *Development and Psychopathology, 2,* 367–391.

Reilly, J., Losh, M., Bellugi, U., & Wulfeck, B. (2004). "Frog, where are you?" Narratives in children with specific language impairment, early focal brain injury and Williams syndrome. *Brain and Language, 88,* 229–247.

Reiss, A., Eliez, S., Schmitt, J. E., Strous, E., Lai, Z., Jones, W., et al. (2000). Neuroanatomy of Williams syndrome: A high-resolution MRI study. *Journal of Cognitive Neuroscience, 12*(Suppl.), 67–73.

Rice, C. E. (1992). *The development of joint attention by a young child with WS.* Unpublished honors thesis. Emory University, Atlanta, GA.

Sarimski, K. (1997). Behavioral phenotypes and family stress in three mental retardation syndromes. *European Child and Adolescent Psychiatry, 63*, 26–31.

Schmitt, J. E., Eliez, S., Warsofksy, I., Bellugi, U., & Reiss, A. L. (2001). Enlarged cerebellar vermis in Williams syndrome. *Journal of Psychiatric Research, 35*, 225–229.

Schultz, R. T., Grelotti, D. J., & Pober, B. (2001). Genetics of childhood disorders: XXVI. Williams syndrome and brain-behavior relationships. *Journal of the American Academy of Child and Adolescent Psychiatry, 40*, 606–609.

Sigman, M. D., Kasari, C., Kwon, K., & Yirmiya, N. (1992). Responses to the negative emotions of others by autistic, mentally retarded, and normal children. *Child Development, 63*, 796–807.

Singer-Harris, N. G., Bellugi, U., Bates, E., Jones, W., & Rosen, M. (1997). Contrasting profiles of language development in children with Williams and Down syndromes. *Developmental Neuropsychology, 13*, 345–370.

Stock, D. A., Spallone, P. A., Dennis, T. R., Netski, D., Morris, C. A., Mervis, C. B., et al. (2003). Heat shock protein 27 gene: Chromosomal and molecular location and relationship to Williams syndrome. *American Journal of Medical Genetics, 120A*, 320–325.

Stojanovik, V., Perkins, M., & Howard, S. (2001). Language and conversational abilities in Williams syndrome: How good is good? *International Journal of Language and Communication Disorders, 36*(Suppl.), 234–239.

Sullivan, K., & Tager-Flusberg, H. (1999). Second-order belief attribution in Williams syndrome: Intact or impaired? *American Journal of Mental Retardation, 104*, 523–532.

Sullivan, K., Winner, E., & Tager-Flusberg, H. (2003). Can adolescents with Williams syndrome tell the difference between lies and jokes? *Developmental Neuropsychology, 23*, 87–105.

Tager-Flusberg, H., Boshart, J., & Baron-Cohen, S. (1998). Reading the windows to the soul: Evidence of domain-specific sparing in Williams syndrome. *Journal of Cognitive Neuroscience, 10*, 631–639.

Tager-Flusberg, H., Plesa-Skwerer, D., Faja, S., & Joseph, R. M. (2003). People with Williams syndrome process faces holistically. *Cognition, 89*, 11–24.

Tager-Flusberg, H., & Sullivan, K. (1994). Predicting and explaining behavior: A comparison of autistic, mentally retarded and normal children. *Journal of Child Psychology and Psychiatry, 35*, 1059–1075.

Tager-Flusberg, H., & Sullivan, K. (1999, April). *Are children with WS spared in theory of mind?* Paper presented at the biennial meeting of the Society for Research in Child Development, Albuquerque, NM.

Tager-Flusberg, H., & Sullivan, K. (2000a, July). *Are theory of mind abilities spared in Williams syndrome?* Paper presented at the International Conference on Williams Syndrome Research, Dearborn, MI.

Tager-Flusberg, H., & Sullivan, K. (2000b). A componential view of theory of mind: Evidence from Williams syndrome. *Cognition, 76*, 59–89.

Tanaka, J. W., & Farah, M. J. (1993). Parts and wholes in face recognition. *Quarterly Journal of Experimental Psychology, 46A*, 225–245.

Tanaka, J. W., Kay, J. B., Grinnell, E., Stansfield, B., & Szechter, L. (1998). Face recognition in young children: When the whole is greater than the sum of its parts. *Visual Cognition, 5*, 479–496.

Thomas, M., Beccera, A., & Mervis, C. B. (2002, July). *The development of empathy in 4-year-old children with Williams syndrome*. Paper presented at the Ninth International Professional Conference on Williams Syndrome, Long Beach, CA.

Tomasello, M. (1988). The role of joint attentional processes in early language development. *Language Sciences, 10*, 69–88.

Tomasello, M., & Farrar, J. (1986). Joint attention and early language. *Child Development, 57*, 1454–1463.

Tomc, S. A., Williamson, N. K., & Pauli, R. M. (1990). Temperament in Williams syndrome. *American Journal of Medical Genetics, 36*, 345–352.

Udwin, O. (1990). A survey of adults with Williams syndrome and idiopathic infantile hypercalcaemia. *Developmental Medicine and Child Neurology, 32*, 129–141.

Udwin, O., & Yule, W. (1991). A cognitive and behavioral phenotype in Williams syndrome. *Journal of Clinical and Experimental Neuropsychology, 13*, 232–244.

Udwin, O., Yule, W., & Martin, N. (1987). Cognitive abilities and behavioral characteristics of children with idiopathic infantile hypercalcaemia. *Journal of Child Psychology and Psychiatry, 28*, 297–309.

van Lieshout, C., De Meyer, R. E., Curfs, L. M. G., & Fryns, J.-P. (1998). Family contexts, parental behavior, and personality profiles of children and adolescents with Prader-Willi, Fragile-X, or Williams syndrome. *Journal of Child Psychology and Psychiatry, 39*, 699–710.

Williams, J. C., Barratt-Boyes, B. G., & Lowe, J. B. (1961). Supravalvular aortic stenosis. *Circulation, 23*, 1311–1318.

13

The Psychological Effects of Early Institutional Rearing

Michael Rutter

For more than half a century, since the writings of pioneers such as Spitz (1946), Goldfarb (1945), and Bowlby (1951), there has been a recognition that rearing in an institutional environment involves substantial risks to the psychological development of children. The general recognition of the many adverse features associated with residential institutions for young children led to important improvements in the care provided for children— particularly in hospitals. Critical reviews of the research findings, both human and animal, led to an acceptance that children's early experiences did have important psychological effects and, moreover, that some of the key elements in those experiences concerned qualities in the relationships between caregivers and children, with continuity in such relationships being a significant feature (Rutter, 1972).

During the 1980s and 1990s, the acceptance that children's early rearing experiences mattered came under threat once again as a result of critiques from behavioral geneticists (Plomin, 1994; Plomin & Bergeman, 1991; Rowe, 1994; Scarr, 1992). The main substance of the critique was that statistical associations between adverse rearing environments and children's psychological development probably reflected, in part, genetic mediation as well as environmental effects. This was likely to be the case because of gene-environment correlations of both a passive and active variety. Parents pass on their genes to their children, as well as creating the rearing environment for them, and on the whole, there is a tendency for genetic risks to be correlated with environmental ones (a passive gene-environment correlation). Thus, for example, when children are admitted into residential institutions because of a breakdown in parenting, it is reasonable to assume that the parents who proved unable to cope with parenting or whose children were removed from them as a result of abuse or neglect are likely to have qualities that involve genetic risks. The problem, then, is how to differentiate the consequences for the children that derive from the genetic risks and the consequences that derive from the adverse experiences to which such genetic risks give rise. In addition, however, genes come into operation because children's experiences, as they grow older, increasingly reflect the role of their own (genetically influenced) behavior in shaping and selecting environments and in eliciting particular behaviors from the people with whom they interact (parents, siblings, teachers, peers, and so forth)—reflecting an active gene-environment correlation.

It was essential for psychosocial researchers to take these challenges seriously and to devise research strategies that could serve to separate genetic mediation from environmental mediation of risk effects. A substantial range of research strategies that can serve that purpose effectively are available (Rutter, Pickles, Murray, & Eaves, 2001). These include not only twin and adoptee designs but also a range of natural experiments. As a consequence of such better-designed studies, it has become clear that there are indeed important environmentally mediated effects of children's early rearing experiences (Rutter, 2000, 2002a; Rutter, 2005b).

Curiously, despite all the progress in the field of psychosocial research, there has been surprisingly little attention to the effects of institutional rearing, despite its importance as the feature that was most prominent in initiating the interest in what came to be called maternal deprivation (Rutter, 2002a; Rutter & O'Connor, 1999). In this chapter, the limited available evidence is reviewed in relation to four key questions. First, it is necessary to address the question of whether or not any adverse psychological sequelae found derive from the basic differences between group rearing in an institutional setting and the more personalized rearing that characterizes growing up in an ordinary family setting. Second, there is the issue of whether or not the patterns of psychopathology associated with institutional rearing are distinctive and different from those seen in children without that experience. Third, there is the rather different question of whether or not the effects are confined to institutional experiences during a particular sensitive period of development and whether or not the sequelae persist after provision of a normal rearing environment. Fourth, attention is paid to the universal finding that there are huge individual differences in outcome even after the most severe forms of institutional deprivation. The questions that arise concern the extent to which these reflect individual differences in genetic liability, prenatal experiences of one kind or another, and adverse early postnatal experiences. The findings are used to discuss the possible mechanisms that might underlie the continuities and discontinuities over time that are found. Throughout, the questions are addressed primarily in terms of the results of an ongoing study comparing the psychological development of children initially reared in very depriving institutions in Romania and later adopted into UK families, and children from noninstitutional backgrounds without serious lasting deprivation and adopted within the United Kingdom before the age of 6 months. However, where relevant, attention is drawn to other findings in the literature.

Design of Study of Romanian Adoptees

When the Ceaucescu regime fell in the late 1980s, it was discovered that a large number of children were being reared in institutions under the most appalling conditions of deprivation. Television programs in the United Kingdom provided graphic pictures of the suffering of the children; as a result, there were multiple humanitarian missions to Romania. In addition, concerned with the plight of the children, many parents sought to adopt them. Between February 1990 and September 1992, 324 children were adopted from Romania into UK families, through applications processed through the Department of Health and/ or the Home Office. The situation provided a particularly striking example of a natural experiment (see Rutter, Pickles, et al., 2001) in which there was a sharp discontinuity between earlier and later rearing environments, and in which the change was extremely sudden (and therefore easy to time exactly) and also involved an unusually radical shift from a profound and pervasive institutional deprivation to somewhat above-average rearing circumstances in a low-risk family setting. A prospective longitudinal study was set up to examine the effects of this "natural experiment." A stratified random sampling design, based on the child's age at the time of coming to the United Kingdom, was used (Rutter & the ERA Study Team, 1998; Rutter, O'Connor, & the ERA Study Team, 2004). A detailed investigation was undertaken of 144 children reared from infancy in very depriving institutions and who were adopted into UK families at various ages up to 42 months (there was also a small sample of children adopted from noninstitutional settings in Romania, but they will not be considered further in this chapter). Detailed assessments were made at age 4 years, 6 years, and 11 years. A comparison sample, comprising 52 UK-born children who were placed into adoptive families before the age of 6 months, was studied in exactly the same way. None of the comparison sample had been removed from parents because of abuse or neglect, and none had experienced an institutional rearing.

To understand the likely mechanisms involved in the adverse effects associated with depriving institutional care, it was considered essential to cover a range of possible outcomes. These included cognitive deficits (O'Connor, Rutter, Beckett, et al., 2000; Rutter & the ERA Study Team, 1998); attachment disturbances (O'Connor, Rutter, & the English and Romanian Adoptees Study Team, 2000; O'Connor et al., 2003); quasi-autistic patterns (Rutter et al., 1999); inattention/overactivity (Kreppner, O'Connor, Rutter, & the English and Romanian Adoptees Study Team, 2001; Rutter, Roy and Kreppner, 2002); common patterns of emotional and behavioral disturbance (Rutter, Kreppner, et al., 2001);

and unusual specific symptoms such as stereotypies (Beckett et al., 2002). Details of the measures used (which included psychometric testing, videotaped observations, parental questionnaires and standardized, investigator-based interviews, teachers' questionnaires, and interviews with the children) are provided in the publications cited.

At the time of leaving the Romanian institutions and coming to the United Kingdom to join their adoptive families, the group of adoptees showed marked developmental retardation, gross malnutrition, and a range of health problems. That observation constitutes the starting point for the questions to be considered in this chapter. So far as this book is concerned, the key issue concerns the neurobiological mechanisms involved in both the immediate effects and the persistent sequelae. Unfortunately, there is an extreme paucity of evidence on this topic. Accordingly, although the chapter ends with some suggestions, which is all that is possible now—suggestions rather than conclusions.

Were the Adverse Psychological Sequelae Caused by the Depriving Circumstances in the Institution?

Two main tests of the causal hypothesis are available. First, if the severe deficits evident at the time of UK entry were a consequence of the children's experiences in depriving institutions, removal from the adverse environment and its replacement by somewhat above-average quality rearing in a normal family environment should be associated with a substantial degree of recovery. That is precisely what was found. The findings for IQ are illustrated in figure 13–1. At the time of UK entry, the average developmental quotient—based on the Denver Pre-Screening and Developmental Questionnaire (Frankenburg, van Doorninck, Liddell, & Dick, 1986) completed retrospectively by the parents at the age 4 assessment—showed that the average developmental level was way down in the retarded range. Even among the older children, very few had any language, and all the contemporaneous assessments indicated that the parental report was likely to be valid. In sharp contrast, the average IQ at age 11 years, as assessed by the Wechsler Intelligence Scale for Children (Wechsler, 1991), showed that the mean IQ score of 91 was only a little below the population mean of 100. Consideration of the measurements at age 4, 6, and 11 showed that the catch-up was mainly evident in the first 2 years after coming to the United Kingdom, with much less change thereafter. This dramatic improvement after the children were placed in good-quality adoptive homes means that it is reasonable to infer that the original deficits were a consequence of the depriving experiences in Romania. Although the findings given in figure 13–1 are confined to cognitive functioning, the overall picture was very much the same on all aspects of the children's development.

However, although the degree of recovery was dramatic, it was not complete in all children. Accordingly, the second test of the causal hypothesis is provided

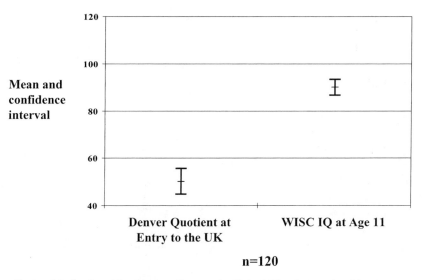

Mean and
confidence
interval

Denver Quotient at
Entry to the UK

WISC IQ at Age 11

n=120

Figure 13–1. Cognitive level at entry to the United Kingdom and at 11 years.

by determination of whether or not the degree of deficit after adoption showed
a strong dose-response relationship with the duration or severity of depriving
experiences, checking that it was not a consequence of individual differences in
the circumstances in the adoptive families. The findings showed that there was
a strong linear relationship between the duration of depriving institutional care
and the degree of deficit as measured at age 4, age 6, and age 11. The relationship is illustrated with respect to IQ at age 11 in figure 13–2 and that for
disinhibited attachment disturbances in figure 13–3; the findings for other outcomes are considered later in the section dealing with the specificity of institutional effects.

However, it was necessary to take account of the fact that, because the children went straight from the institution to the adoptive home (in almost all cases),
there was a total confound between the duration of institutional deprivation and
the duration of time in the adoptive home. The availability of longitudinal data
allowed this confound to be eliminated. Figure 13–4 shows the comparison for
IQ, within a group of children all of whom had spent 2½ to 4 years in their adoptive homes, between those children who had experienced less than 18 months
of depriving institutional care and those who had experienced 24 to 42 months
of such care. The findings were dramatic and surprisingly clear-cut. That is to
say, even after controlling for the duration of the children's time in their adoptive families, the duration of institutional deprivation was associated with an IQ
difference of about a dozen points. Again, it may be inferred that the deficit was,
therefore, a consequence of the duration of institutional deprivation. The same
applied to disinhibited attachment disturbances (figure 13–5).

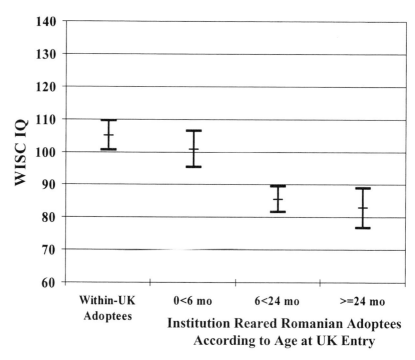

Figure 13–2. Intelligence at 11 years.

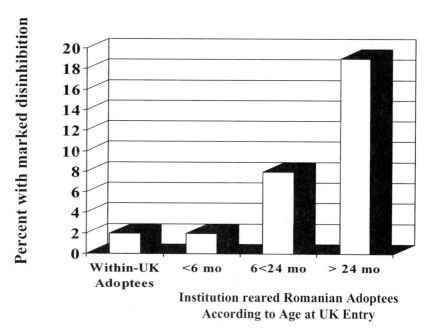

Figure 13–3. Percentage showing marked disinhibited attachment at 11 years.

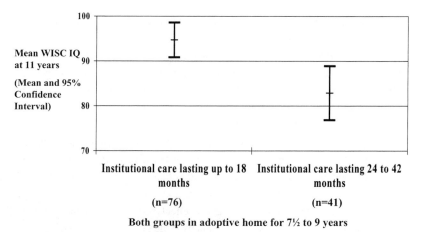

Figure 13–4. Effects of duration of privation, controlling for time in adoptive home.

The second, somewhat related, question is whether or not the adverse psychological sequelae were a consequence of severe deprivation or, rather, a consequence of group rearing in the institution. To answer that question, it is necessary to turn to the findings from other studies dealing with children reared in much better quality residential institutions. Two other British studies (Hodges & Tizard, 1989a; Roy, Rutter, & Pickles, 2000) both found that the children initially brought up in residential nurseries and Group Homes showed no

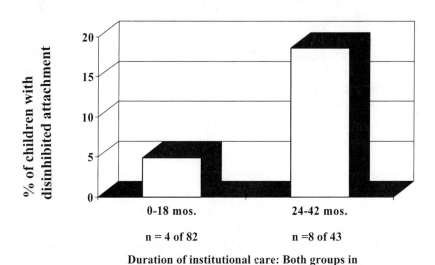

Figure 13–5. Marked attachment disinhibition related to duration of institutional care, controlling for time in adoptive home.

significant intellectual deficit as compared with controls. It may be concluded that the intellectual deficits are a consequence of seriously depriving circumstances in the institutions, and not just institutional rearing as such (see Castle et al., 1999). The findings on attachment disturbances and nonselective peer relationships were, however, quite different. Both of these two British studies found that there were social deficits associated with institutional rearing even when it did not involve overall deprivation of life experiences (Hodges & Tizard, 1989b; Roy, Rutter, & Pickles, 2004). Accordingly, it may be inferred that, unlike the situation with respect to intelligence, deficits in selective social relationships are a consequence of an institutional rearing rather than deprivation of a broad kind. The findings in the literature do not provide a clear-cut answer as to what it is about an institutional rearing that has this effect, but it is likely that the main risk factor derives from the arrangements by which child care is provided by a roster of a large number of different caregivers who, although they provide good-quality care at the time, do not have the opportunity to develop continuous close relationships with the children that extend over long periods of time. The Bucharest Early Intervention Project (Zeanah et al., 2003), in which there is a randomized controlled trial of foster placement and institutional care for abandoned infants and toddlers, should be especially informative on this issue once results are available.

The third query is whether, as is usually assumed, the ill effects are a consequence of the patterns of rearing in institutions or, rather, whether they are a consequence of other risk factors that just happen to be associated with institutional care. Three main possibilities have to be considered. First, the sequelae could be due to prenatal risk factors (Rutter, 2005a). Thus, for example, there is reason to suppose that some of the biological mothers were drinking heavily during the pregnancy, and this may have resulted in damage to the fetus. The records in Romania were quite inadequate for any systematic assessment of the extent to which this was the case, and they do not allow any assessment of possible fetal alcohol effects as experienced by individual children. Although the effects of alcohol (or other substances) might play a role in the deficits found, there is no reason to suppose that they could account for the dose-response relationship with the duration of institutional care. That is to say, there is no reason to believe that prenatal experiences had any effect on the time the children spent in institutions. Virtually no children were either adopted or returned to their biological parents before the fall of the Ceaucescu regime. Accordingly, the duration of institutional care was largely a consequence of the coincidence in timing between the child's age and the fall of the regime.

The same applies to obstetric and perinatal complications. As available from the records, the average birth weight of the Romanian children was below population norms in the United Kingdom, and several children were born after markedly short periods of gestation. However, although possibly important in a few individual children, prematurity, prenatal exposure to alcohol, and other major obstetric complications were not associated with the psychological outcomes studied at age 6, other than inattention/overactivity (Beckett et al., 2003). The third factor that could be important was the nutritional level of the children. At the time of UK entry, most of the children were severely malnourished, and over half had a weight below the third percentile. The findings showed that the degree of malnutrition, as indexed by weight, showed a significant, but only modest, relationship with the IQ level at the various follow-ups (O'Connor, Rutter, Beckett, et al., 2000; Rutter et al., 2004). It did not account for the effects of duration of deprivation; also, the risk effect of length of time in the depriving institutions was much greater than that of degree of malnutrition. It may well be that the poor nutrition of these children made them much more vulnerable than would otherwise be the case to the psychological deprivation experienced in the institutions. On the other hand, the degree of malnutrition accounted for little of the variance in cognitive outcome, and it was unassociated with other outcomes (apart from a weak but statistically significant association with inattention/ overactivity).

Specificity of Psychological Responses to Profound Institutional Privation

The specificity of children's responses to institutional deprivation was examined by Rutter, Kreppner, and colleagues (2001) in relation to the findings at age 6. On the whole, the psychological consequences of psychosocial stress and adversity are diagnostically nonspecific (McMahon, Grant, Compas, Thurm, & Ey, 2003; Rutter, 2000). However, this was not found to be the case in relation to the sequelae at age 6 in the Romanian adoptees. For specificity to be inferred it was necessary that there be both a significant difference in the frequency with which the psychological feature was shown in the Romanian adoptees and in the comparison group of within-UK nondeprived adoptees, and that, within the Romanian sample, there was a significant dose-response relationship with duration of institutional deprivation. Only four features met these dual criteria at age 6: quasi-autistic patterns, disinhibited attachment, inattention/overactivity, and cognitive impairment. Strikingly, neither emotional disturbances nor conduct disturbances showed specificity, and neither did peer relations to a significant degree.

The quasi-autistic pattern was associated with social and communicative deficits of a kind ordinarily associated with autism, and especially with marked circumscribed interests. At 4 years of age, the pattern of behavior, as measured by standardized research measures, was closely comparable with that found in "ordinary" autism unassociated with deprivation experiences (Rutter et al., 1999). However, by age 6 many of the children showed improvement in these autistic-like features. The improvement was even more marked by the age of 11 years (in some, but not all, children), and at that age some of the social deficits appeared to have more in common with attachment disinhibition than with autism. The analysis of findings at age 11 is still under way, and this behavioral pattern will not be considered further in this chapter. Rather, attention will be focused on disinhibited attachment disorder, using comparison with cognitive impairment as a means of considering possible mediating mechanisms.

Disinhibited attachment at age 6 was characterized by a relatively undiscriminating social approach, a seeming lack of awareness of social boundaries, and a difficulty in picking up social cues on what is socially appropriate or acceptable to other people (O'Connor, Rutter, & the English and Romanian Adoptees Study Team, 2000; O'Connor et al., 2003). It was indexed in parental reports by a definite lack of differentiation among adults, a clear indication that the child would readily go off with a stranger, and a definite lack of checking back with the parent in anxiety-provoking situations. A modified separation reunion procedure showed that disinhibited attachment was associated with an unusual nonnormative response. This was more evident in relation to the response to the stranger than to the mother. An unusually friendly initial approach to the stranger was common, but this was sometimes followed by later wariness. In addition coy, silly, overexuberant or overexcited behavior was common.

One or the other of two additional criteria were relevant to specificity. First, if the feature was specific to institutional deprivation, it should be found only rarely in noninstitutionalized children. That did apply to quasi-autistic features, which were found in none of the within-UK adoptees, and disinhibited attachment, which was found in only 3.8% (i.e., 2 children) at age 6. Cognitive impairment was also rare in the comparison group (2.0%; i.e., 1 child), but inattention/overactivity occurred in some 6%. The second criterion was that the overall pattern across the different features should differentiate the groups. Clearly, it did.

What was most distinctive about the Romanian sample was that the pattern usually involved some admixture of attachment problems, inattention/ overactivity, and quasi-autistic problems. This was not found in any of the children in the comparison group. It was also noteworthy that of the children with cognitive impairment in the Romanian sample, half also showed quasi-autistic patterns, and a third showed attachment disturbances. The overlap between inattention/overactivity and attachment disturbances was also found by Roy and colleagues (2004) in a study of children in residential care within the United Kingdom of a kind that did not involve any of the marked deprivation associated with the Romanian institutions. The implication is that although inattention/overactivity may represent a specific response to deprivation (Kreppner et al., 2001), it probably does not follow the same pattern normally associated with attention deficit disorders with hyperactivity found in children who have been reared in family settings.

The findings at age 11 were much the same. Again, the same four features showed specificity (although the association with duration of institutional deprivation fell just short of statistical significance in the case of quasi-autistic features), and, again, the overall pattern (representing overlap among features) was quite different in the two groups.

The one important difference between the age 6 and age 11 findings concerned emotional disturbance. At 6 years of age, this was not more common in the Romanian sample and showed no association with duration of institutional deprivation. By contrast, at age 11 it was more common in the Romanian sample, although there was not a significant association with duration of institutional deprivation. The new emergence of emotional disturbance was particularly common in the children who had shown one of the four deprivation-specific patterns, but the rate was increased even in those who had not shown those at age 6.

None of the psychological features examined was significantly more frequent in the Romanian adoptees who had experienced less than 6 months institutional deprivation. Because the institutional deprivation virtually always began shortly after birth, it is not possible from this finding to determine whether the lack of sequelae was a function of children's young age at the time of institutional deprivation or, rather, from the brevity of the period of institutional deprivation.

Canadian Study

Ames and colleagues (Ames, 1997; Chisholm, Carter, Ames, & Morison, 1995; Chisholm, 1998; Fisher, Ames, Chisholm, & Savoie, 1997; MacLean, 2003; Morison, Ames, & Chisholm, 1995) undertook a somewhat comparable systematic study of children adopted in Canada from Romania. Forty-six children who had spent at least 8 months in institutional care were compared with 29 noninstitutionalized children adopted from Romania before the age of 4 months, together with 46 nonadopted Canadian-born children. As in the British study, institutional rearing was associated with significant cognitive deficit, and indiscriminate friendly behavior, as shown by a tendency to wander without distress and willingness to go home with a stranger, was particularly common. Unlike the British study, however, the indiscriminate friendliness was not significantly associated with the duration of institutional care (although the sample size was rather small to test for this). As in the British study, there was considerable heterogeneity in outcome.

Dutch Study

Hoksbergen and colleagues (Hoksbergen, van Dijkum, & Jesdijk, 2002; Hoksbergen, ter Laak, van Dijkum, Rijk, Rijk, et al., 2003; Hoksbergen, ter Laak, van Dijkum, Rijk, & Stoutjesdijk, 2003b) similarly studied 83 children from Romania adopted by Dutch families. According to parental report, only 13% did not show psychosocial problems 4 years after adoption; indiscriminate friendliness, inattention/overactivity, autistic-like behavior, and post–traumatic stress features were especially noted. The sample was a volunteer one, and there was no comparison group. Accordingly, there must be some caution with respect to the conclusions. Nevertheless, the findings are similar to those in the British and Canadian studies.

Are the Effects of Institutional Care Age-Specific?

Several rather different notions have come to be included within the broad concept of age specificity of effects. First, many people with a special interest in the early years of life have used supposed neuroscience findings to argue that, if experiences are to have lasting effects, they need to occur during the first 3 years of life, when brain development is both particularly great and associated with important elements of organization and reorganization (Schore, 1994). It certainly is true that these early years are associated with radical changes in brain structure and function. Initially, there is a period of neuronal growth, the development of connections among neurons, and neuronal migration; this is followed by a period of neuronal pruning to sort out the "errors" that have taken place during the initial phase of growth. On the face of it, it would seem reasonable to suppose that if experiences during this phase of radical development could influence brain structure, then the effects (either beneficial or adverse, according to the nature of experiences) could be both particularly great and particularly enduring.

However, there are all sorts of problems with this expectation (Bruer, 1999). To begin with, brain development is far from over by the end of the infancy period. Indeed, important changes are still taking place during late adolescence and early adult life (Curtis & Nelson, 2003; Giedd et al., 1999; Huttenlocher, 2002; Keshavan, Kennedy, & Murray, 2004; Paus et al., 1999; Sowell, Thompson, Tessner, & Toga, 2001; Sowell et al., 2003). Second, it has been well demonstrated by both animal experiments and human studies that experiences in adult life can and do have effects on the structure of the brain. For example, this was shown in Greenough's studies of environmental deprivation and enrichment in rats (Greenough & Black, 1992; Greenough, Black, & Wallace, 1987) and Gage's studies of mice (Kempermann, Brandon, & Gage, 1998). It is also evident in the brain-imaging evidence that London taxi drivers' intense training in routes across the city is associated with structural changes in the hippocampus (Maguire, Frackowiak, & Frith, 1997). Much further evidence all points in the same direction. It is clear that it is necessary to reject the blanket expectation that experiences during the early years of life are the only ones that can affect the brain (Rutter, 2002b).

With respect to the specific experience of institutional care, there is remarkably little evidence in the literature of whether or not there is any age-specificity in effects. One of the major problems in examining this question is that the prior experiences of children admitted to institutions when older will usually be quite different from the prior experiences of those entering institutions in early infancy. Accordingly, any human evidence is likely to be quite ambiguous in its implications. However, Wolkind (1974), in a study of 92 children aged 5 to 13 years in residential care (most of whom had been admitted because of a breakdown in parenting or because of parental neglect or cruelty), found that most forms of psychopathology (as assessed using standardized interviews with the children and their house parents) were unrelated to the children's age at the time of admission. The one exception was the pattern of indiscriminate friendliness and lack of social inhibition that was especially a feature of children admitted before the age of 2 years.

Quinton and Rutter (1988) undertook a long-term prospective study of 103 girls placed in residential children's homes run on group cottage lines. The sample, together with a comparison group of girls from the same socially disadvantaged area in London, was followed up in their mid-20s. Social disinhibition was not specifically examined (because the women were adult), but the quality of social relationships and overall social functioning was assessed in detail. It was found that the rate of poor social functioning was quite low in children admitted to the institutions over the age of 2 after having experienced nondisruptive parenting in the early years. By contrast, some two fifths of the women admitted under the age of 2 years, or admitted over the age of 2 after having experienced disruptive parenting, showed poor social functioning.

The implication from both these studies is that the first 2 years may be particularly important with respect to the development of later social relationships. The risks, however, appear to derive from either residential care that involves multiple changing caregivers or severely disrupted parenting outside of an institution. In the Quinton and Rutter (1988) study, however, it should be noted that disrupted parenting often involved short-term admissions to residential care lasting at least 1 month.

Vorria and colleagues' (1998a, 1998b) study of 41 nine-year-old children in long-term residential group care in Greece, together with a similar-sized sample of children being cared for in their own families in the ordinary way, is also informative. Again, social disinhibition was not assessed as such. However, it was found that a lack of close confiding peer relationships was much more common in the group care children than in the family care children. The group care children were much more likely to be reported as indiscriminate in their friendships, to show a limited attachment to their friends, and to exhibit limited confiding in friends; teachers also reported that more of them were inappropriately affection seeking. There were few children admitted as infants, but children admitted before the age of 3 years 6 months were compared with those admitted at an older age. No differences in behavior were found according to age at first admission. In particular, there was no indication that an institutional rearing in the first 3 years was especially likely to be associated with a lack of confiding peer relationships.

The findings for children suffering extreme deprivation in early childhood are also potentially relevant (Skuse, 1984a, 1984b). These reports concern children brought up outside of institutions but whose upbringing involves severe exclusion, physical restraint, cruelty, and lack of human interaction other than of a sporadic kind. At the time that the children were discovered and removed from these extremely depriving conditions, most showed marked motor retardation, malnutrition, little or no language development, and emotional/behavioral disturbance. In the series described by Skuse (1984a, 1984b), the age at which the children were removed from the severely depriving circumstances ranged from 3 years 9 months to 13 years 7 months. Most of the children, apart from the child rescued at the age of 13 years (Curtiss, 1977; Rymer, 1993), gained good language skills and attained an IQ within the normal range (although usually below 100). Unfortunately, the published reports are relatively uninformative about the degree of normality of social functioning at follow-up.

A further study of two children experiencing extreme early environmental deprivation (being kept shut up in a small outdoor shack) for 5 to 6 years gives rise to similar conclusions (Fujinaga, Kasuga, Uchida, & Saiga, 1990). That is, removal from the depriving environment was followed by very substantial cognitive and social gains, but some deficits were evident.

So-called feral children, meaning those supposedly brought up by animals, might also be relevant. Unfortunately, although these children give rise to some fascinating stories (see Candland, 1993; Douthwaite, 2002; Newton, 2002), there are doubts about the true nature of their experiences, and there is a lack of systematic data on their development.

It may be concluded that, although the claims on age specificity of effects have sometimes been overstated, it does appear that the early years may be particularly important for the establishment of basic psychological capacities—perhaps particularly in the domain of relationships. With that in mind, it is necessary to turn to the concept of sensitive periods.

Sensitive Periods

Sensitive periods have been conceptualized in several rather different ways. At one extreme, they have been viewed as no more than the presence of a phase of heightened responsiveness to certain kinds of stimuli (Oyama, 1979). Such phases clearly exist, but they reflect a wide diversity of mechanisms. For example, the sensitivity may reflect children's ability to process (both cognitively and affectively) their experiences. For example, it seems that very young infants (say, under the age of 6 months) are much less vulnerable to the effects of stressful separations from their parents than are toddlers. It is usually supposed that this is because infants have yet to develop a selective attachment with a parent and because of their limited ability to conceptualize the separation experience and its meaning. Conversely, older children (those of school age and older) also appear less vulnerable to the stresses of separation from family, but in this case, probably because they do have the cognitive capacity to understand why the separation happened (e.g., for hospital admission) and that the separation will be temporary and that, hence, they will be able to maintain a relationship even during a period of noncontact.

The point of this digression into sensitive periods is to underline that there are many different sorts of sensitive period and that they do not imply a single underlying causal process. Accordingly, in all cases, it is necessary to determine, first, whether there appear to be effects that are largely restricted to a particular developmental phase and, second, to consider other evidence that might point to the causal mechanisms involved. The increased (or decreased) sensitivity may reflect social context, or the vulnerability left behind by prior experience, or the person's physiological state. In other words, the mere existence of a phase of heightened sensitivity carries no implications for any particular causal mechanism.

On the other hand, sensitive periods have been viewed as being restricted to a very narrow period of development during which specific experiences are supposed to have relatively permanent and irreversible effects. The original notion of imprinting constitutes a well-studied example of this kind. However, the sensitive period associated with imprinting is not as innately fixed and absolute as first supposed (Bateson, 1966, 1990). In any case, it is somewhat dubious whether there are exact parallels of imprinting with human development.

There is, then, the rather different notion that the effects of experiences on a well-established developmental function are likely to be quite different from the effects at a time when that skill is only just beginning to be developed, and has yet to be established. Thus, once a person has gained spoken language, it is not lost as a result of later depriving experiences (unless there is associated brain disease or damage). Even the effects of brain damage are likely to be different. The best-known example concerns the effects of unilateral brain damage on language development (Bates & Roe, 2001; Feldman, 1994; Varga-Khadem & Mishkin, 1997). Unilateral lesions of the left cerebral cortex, however extensive, do not usually result in aphasic symptoms if the injury was sustained before the age of about 5 years. That stands in sharp contrast to the situation in later childhood or adult life, when lasting aphasic deficits are usual. However, see also the quite different effects of amygdala lesions according to the age of monkeys at the time the lesion was made (Amaral & Corbett, 2003) and the different effects on brain size and neuronal spine density of environmental complexity in rodents according to the age of the animal at the time of intervention (Kolb, Forgie, Gibb, Gorny, & Rowntree, 1998; Kolb, Gibb, & Gorny, 2003).

An extension of this concept of sensitive period involves the further notion that somatic development is lastingly affected by the experiences encountered during the phase of development when somatic structures are being laid down and when particular functions are being acquired. These have usually been described under the designation of biological programming.

Biological Programming

A particular form of sensitive period concept is implied by the notion of experience-expectant developmental programming. The notion is that normal somatic development requires particular experiences during the relevant sensitive phase of development if the appropriate somatic structure is to be laid down (Greenough et al., 1987). The best-established model here is that provided by the role of visual input in the development of the visual cortex (Blakemore, 1991; Hubel & Wiesel, 1965; Hubel, Wiesel, and Le Vay, 1977; Le Grand, Mondloch, Maurer, & Brent, 2001, 2003). Not only is patterned binocular visual input necessary for the normal development of the visual cortex in the brain, but the resulting cortical structures are necessary for later normal visual functioning. In humans it is evident, for example, that the finding that unless strabismus (a visual squint) is corrected in the first few years of life, normal binocular vision later is unlikely. Studies have shown that, to a limited extent, there may be later modifications to these effects (see, e.g., Chow & Stewart, 1972), but on the whole the recovery tends to be partial rather than complete. A key feature of this concept is that the required experiences that must be available cover a very broad range of expectable environments, and not variations within the normal range. The effects are developmental phase specific, being operative only within the sensitive period of development in which the somatic structure is being developed. If such experiences are lacking, the usual assumption is that the ill effects are universal, without much in the way of marked individual differences.

A further example is provided by the evidence that male zebra finches must hear song from approximately 20 to 40 days of age to be able to produce that song later in development (Bottjer, 1991; Bottjer & Arnold, 1997). It has also been found that auditory experience in the juvenile period shapes neuronal response properties in the thalamus in owls, with implications for sound localization (Miller & Knudsen, 2003). Visual experience (manipulated by prismatic spectacles) was also important, but the effects were on the forebrain rather than the thalamus. Experience in adult life has more effects than used to be supposed, but plasticity in early life is greater (Linkenhoker & Knudsen, 2002).

A related, but quite different, process is implied with the concept of experience-adaptive development (Rutter, 2002b; Rutter et al., 2004). This notes that particular forms of somatic development, both structural and functional, are shaped by the specifics of experiences during a relatively sensitive period of development in such a way that there is optimal adaptation to the specifics of that environment (see Bateson and Martin, 1999; Caldji, Diorio, & Meaney, 2000; Sackett, 1965). The concept has been written about most extensively in relation to the role of early subnutrition in bringing about a much increased risk for later coronary artery disease, hypertension, and diabetes because, it is argued, the biological programming has been for low nutrition and not the richer diets encountered in adulthood (Barker, 1997; O'Brien, Wheeler, & Barker, 1999). The physiological basis of these well-established connections remains poorly understood, but the general notion that the organism adapts to deal with the environments that it encounters would be generally accepted. Animal experiments have supported the hypothesis that fetal exposure to undernutrition has a biological programming effect that influences later risk for cardiovascular disease (Kwong, Wild, Roberts, Willis, & Flemig, 2000; Langley-Evans, Welham, & Jackson, 1999). In addition to the subnutrition effects, similar findings have been found in relation to immunity and infection (Bock & Whelan, 1991).

The most obvious parallel within the field of psychological development is provided by phonology. Infants in all countries show broadly comparable skills in phonological discrimination, but from the second half of the first year onward, phonological discrimination skills are increasingly shaped by the language of the rearing environment (Kuhl, 1994; Kuhl et al., 1997; Maye, Werker, & Gerken, 2002; Werker, 2003). Thus it has often been observed that Japanese people find great difficulty in discriminating r from l, a discrimination that is taken for granted by those who have been English speakers from infancy onward. As with experience-expectant programming, the effects are found only during the sensitive period of development when the somatic structure is being established, but there are two key differences: namely, that the relevant experiences and outcomes include variations within (as well as outside) the normal range, and, second, that the nature of such experiences will foster somatic development that is well adapted for the environment experienced during the sensitive phase. Whether such development will be well adapted for later environments will depend on whether or not they are similar to those provided by earlier experiences.

A further concept of sensitive periods concerns developmental phase-specific differences in vulnerability to toxins and trauma. One of the best-known examples concerns the so-called fetal alcohol syndrome (Institute of Medicine, 1996). The physical sequelae of fetal alcohol exposure (e.g., the facial features) are mainly evident with heavy exposure in the first trimester, at a time when the structures that come together to form the face are developing. The neurobehavioral effects are probably also found in connection with heavy maternal drinking during the later phases of the pregnancy, but the worst effects still apply to the first trimester. In this alcohol example, the sensitive period concerns unusual vulnerability to damage.

Three particular issues arise in the application of programming concepts to psychological development. To begin with, it is necessary to consider what is meant by "development" (Rutter, 1984; Rutter & Rutter, 1993). On the one hand, it would seem obvious that development must mean a progressive increase in the level of structure and function up to the level when maturity, and therefore stabilization, is reached. Thus, that is how one would consider the development of height. There is, probably, a fairly close parallel with the development of language and, to some extent, intelligence. On the other hand, it is not quite so obvious how to apply it to socioemotional development. It makes no sense to view development as simply change, or even lasting change. The concept is inevitably a somewhat fuzzy one. However, Rutter and Rutter (1993) suggested that development might be viewed as "systematic, organized, intra-individual change that is clearly associated with generally expectable age-related progressions and which is carried forward in some way that has implications for a person's patterns or level of functioning at some later time" (p. 64).

The second issue concerns difficulty in deciding which types of social functioning are more "mature" than others. The dilemma is well illustrated by the difficulties provided by attachment relationships. The term *attachment* is usually taken to mean the development of a selective attachment to a particular individual, with the relationship serving as a basis for security. What develops is the capacity to form such a protective relationship, and not just the particular dyadic relationship that is involved. Thus, if toddlers lose the caregiver with whom they have an attachment relationship, they will ordinarily form a selective attachment with a new caregiver. Insofar as that is what develops, it could be considered that "maturity" is ordinarily reached by at least the age of 2 years, despite the fact that such attachment relationships go on being important throughout life (Shaver & Cassidy, 1999). However, that ignores the fact that the existence of early parent-child attachments is likely to play some role in the qualities needed for the development of peer relationships, confiding friendships, love relationships, and parenting (Rutter, 1995). Insofar as that is the case, although it would probably be misleading to call these relationships "attachment-relationships," they nevertheless may well be involved in the same developmental pathway. Such animal evidence as is available is in keeping with that general notion. Thus, the social isolation of older chimpanzees has not been found to have the devastating effect on social functioning that it has on infants (Davenport, Menzel, & Rogers, 1966). More recently, the issue has been examined systematically by Suomi and collegues with rhesus monkeys (Suomi, 2003; Barr et al., in press). Monkeys reared only with peers (a situation that has no parallel in the wild) for 7 months were compared with monkeys reared with their mother for the same period of time. Both groups were then brought together in a peer group rearing setting. In effect, then, the experimental design compared the effects of early and late peer rearing. Because the effects were shown to be stable over time, it was possible to introduce controls for the duration of peer rearing. The findings showed that the major effects were associated with early, rather than late, peer rearing—the cutoff being roughly equivalent to 28 months of age for humans. It is reasonable to infer that there was some kind of sensitive period effect.

The third issue is whether biological programming effects on development can occur even when there is not a sensitive period as such. Thus, so far as is known, there is not a sensitive period for intellectual development in the sense described earlier. That is, intellectual development proceeds right up through adolescence, and it is open to the effects of experiences throughout the whole of that period. On the other hand, brain growth is particularly great during the early years, and it could be that a lack of the necessary experiences during that early period of development could have lasting effects on brain structure and function.

In summary, it may be concluded that there is a growing body of empirical evidence that sensitive periods do exist for some aspects of psychological development and that the notion of biological programming is valid. The questions have turned from uncertainties about the reality of the phenomena (these are no longer in doubt) to queries on possible mediating mechanisms and on the psychological constructs to which they apply. With that rather lengthy digression on concepts, we need to turn now to the findings from the study of Romanian adoptees.

Possible Programming Effects of Institutional Deprivation

Three key tests may be suggested. If there has been some form of biological programming, it would be expected that (a) the sequelae should be relatively persistent over time even after a normal rearing environment has been provided; (b) the dose-response relationship between the duration of institutional deprivation and the psychological outcome should continue well after the period of institutional deprivation came to an end; and (c) the sequelae should be relatively unresponsive to variations in the rearing environment after the end of institutional deprivation.

The findings have been examined most closely in relation to cognitive functioning and disinhibited attachment patterns in the British study of Romanian adoptees (Rutter et al., 2004). Cognitive impairment showed marked stability across the age span from 6 years to 11 years. Thus, 14 of the 23 children showing cognitive impairment at age 6 still showed cognitive impairment at age 11, and almost all the remaining children were still below average in IQ. This resulted in a phi of .50 for the category between ages 6 and 11. The stability for attachment disinhibition was less strong. Of the 32 children showing this feature to a marked degree at age 6, only 7 showed it to the same extent at age 11. Eighteen showed it to a lesser degree, but 7 of the 32 showed no evidence of disinhibited attachment at age 11. This general fading of disinhibited attachment is reflected in the fact that whereas 32 children showed this to a marked degree at 6, only 13 did so at 11. This resulted in a phi of .23. Inattention/overactivity persisted between 6 and 11 years in half the children showing it at 6—giving a phi of .40.

Similarly, the Pearson correlation between the WISC full-scale IQ at age 11 and the duration of institutional deprivation ($r = -.39$) was nearly as strong as that previously found ($r = -.50$) between the general cognitive index on the McCarthy Scale and the duration of institutional deprivation at age 6 (figure 13–6). In addition, the association between length of institutional deprivation and attachment disinhibition was about as strong at age 11 ($r = .35$) as it had been at age 6 ($r = .27$; see figure 13–7).

With respect to the third criterion, there was a zero association between the educational level of the adoptive parents and either the general cognitive index at 6 years or the WISC IQ at 11 years. Little is known about the family qualities that predispose children to disinhibited attachment, other than the risks associated with institutional care; accordingly, it is difficult to know which aspects of the adoptive home environment might be expected to influence this behavior. However, none of the family measures taken were related either to disinhibited attachment or to changes over time in disinhibited attachment.

Very little is known about the neural correlates of these psychological sequelae. Chugani and colleagues (2001) reported a positron emission tomography (PET) scan study of 10 children, with a mean age of 8.8 years, adopted from Romanian orphanages after a mean period of 38 months in Romanian institutions. The findings were compared with a group of 17 normal adults and 7 children with medically refractory focal epilepsy (in which the comparison was with the contralateral hemisphere). The Romanian children showed a reduced head circumference, and their mean full scale IQ was just 81. It was found that there was decreased glucose metabolism in the Romanian orphans bilaterally in the orbital frontal gyrus, infralimbic prefrontal cortex, the medial temporal structures (amygdala and head of hippocampus), the lateral temporal cortex, and the

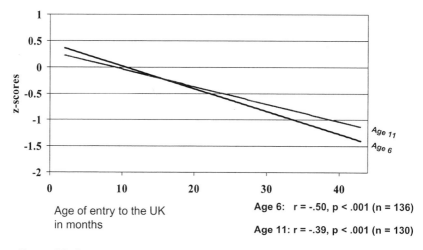

Figure 13–6. Age of entry and cognitive outcomes, age 11 and 6 (Romanian institution–reared adoptees only).

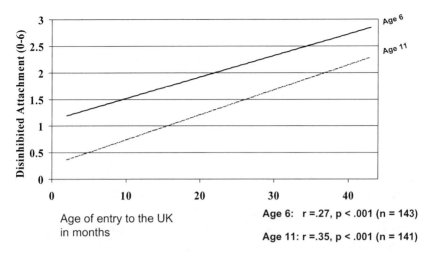

Figure 13–7. Age of entry and disinhibited attachment, age 11 and 6 (Romanian institution–reared adoptees only).

brain stem. The authors argued that the decreased metabolism implied a dysfunction of these brain regions and then inferred that it was likely to derive from the stress of early global deprivation (drawing parallels with stress studies). However, it cannot be assumed that the pattern represents dysfunction, and there was no indication of whether the PET scan findings were associated in any way with any of the psychological features (the sample size was too small for this to be meaningful).

One further relevant finding with respect to cognitive impairment in our own study was that it was quite strongly, and significantly, associated with head circumference, both at the time of leaving the institution and at the various follow-up points. Thus, children with cognitive impairment at age 6 had a head circumference that was approximately one standard deviation lower than that of those without cognitive impairment. Moreover, the head circumference at age 6, for those both with and without cognitive impairment, remained well below general population norms for the United Kingdom. Thus, for the children who had at least 24 months of institutional deprivation, but who did not show severe subnutrition, the mean head circumference at age 6 years was – 1.32 standard deviations. The deficit in those with severe subnutrition was even greater (– 2.52 standard deviations). The findings at age 11 were closely comparable.

The association with head circumference, however, did not apply to the same extent in the case of disinhibited attachment. There was no association between the head circumference at the time of UK entry, or at age 6, and disinhibited attachment at age 6. However, there was some association with respect to head circumference and disinhibited attachment at age 11 (meaning the subgroup for which this feature persisted). The pattern of findings with respect to these two outcomes also differed with respect to severe subnutrition. This was significantly associated with cognitive impairment, but it had no association with disinhibited attachment. The interpretation to be placed on these findings is considered further later, after considering heterogeneity in outcome.

Heterogeneity of Response

However assessed, at both age 6 and age 11 years there was striking heterogeneity within the Romanian sample. Moreover, this heterogeneity was as marked in those experiencing the most prolonged deprivation as in those experiencing only a quite short period. This is shown, using a scattergram and regression line, in the association between WISC full-scale IQ at 11 years and duration of institutional deprivation (figure 13–8). The findings on disinhibited attachment showed equal heterogeneity. Even among those with the most prolonged institutional deprivation, only a minority showed marked disinhibited attachments, and many showed no evidence of this feature. Some of those who showed no disinhibited attachment at age 11 had shown this pattern at age 6, but many had not shown it at either age. In other words, some of the most deprived children showed apparently normal attachment behavior throughout, and some showed disinhibited attachment only when younger. Altogether, at age 11, two fifths of the children who entered the United Kingdom between 24 and 42 months of age showed no evidence of impairment, but just over a quarter showed impairment on at least three out of seven domains (as compared with about 4% in those who

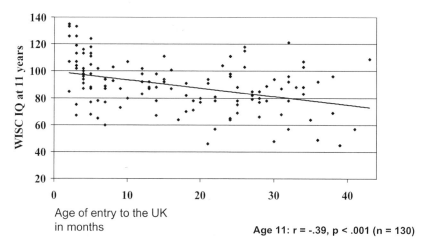

Figure 13–8. Age of entry and cognitive outcomes, age 11 (Romanian institution–reared adoptees only).

entered the United Kingdom at or below 6 months of age and in a similar proportion in the group of nondeprived within-UK adoptees).

Possible Mediating Mechanisms

In considering possible mediating mechanisms, it is important to differentiate between cognitive impairment and disinhibited attachment. Comparisons across studies make it clear that cognitive impairment is not ordinarily a consequence of an institutional upbringing per se. Rather, it is the result of severely deprived circumstances. The case examples of children in family environments who have suffered equally severe deprivation make it evident, too, that the deprivation does not necessarily have to be in an institutional setting. One of the risk factors is severe subnutrition, but the findings on Romanian adoptees indicate that cognitive impairment is associated with deprived institutional care even when there is not marked subnutrition, although the risks are greatest when the two are combined. It is also striking that cognitive impairment was associated with a small head circumference both at the time of leaving the institutions and at follow-up. The fact that this was so even in the children who are not subnourished makes it clear that the effects on head growth are not dependent on general subnutrition and are not simply a consequence of reduced body size. That is, the children largely, or completely, caught up in their body weight, but the catch-up was much more limited in the case of head circumference.

The correlation between head circumference and brain size is quite substantial (van Valen, 1974). Ordinarily, it is the size of the brain that determines the growth of the head; hence, a reduced head circumference can be inferred to represent reduced brain size. The conclusion is that profound institutional deprivation, with or without subnutrition but especially when subnutrition is involved, is associated with effects on neural structure that involve impaired brain growth. These effects have been shown to persist to at least the age of 11 years, with only a small diminution over time in the strength of the effect of the duration of institutional deprivation. Also, these effects were found to be uninfluenced by the educational level of the adoptive parents (or by other measured aspects of parent-child interaction). On the other hand, there was marked heterogeneity in response such that, even with the most prolonged institutional deprivation, some children nevertheless showed superior intellectual functioning at 11 years.

The findings on disinhibited attachment are very similar in some respects but completely different in others. The main similarities lie in the strength of the effects of duration of institutional deprivation, the persistence of such effects up to age 11 years with no apparent effects of the adoptive home environment, and the moderate stability of the psychological feature of disinhibited attachment. It is evident, therefore, that there has been a strong carryover of the effects of early institutional experiences despite the radical change of environment and the provision of good-quality rearing in the adoptive family for at least 7½ years. The differences between cognitive impairment and disinhibited attachment are that the latter outcome was not associated with severe subnutrition and was less consistently associated with reduced head circumference.

Most crucially, too, other studies have shown that disinhibited attachment is associated with an institutional upbringing even when there is no general deprivation in the institution, other than with respect to multiple changing caregivers. The number of studies with relevant data is quite small, but they are consistent in suggesting that the risk lies in some aspect of the institutional rearing, rather than in general deprivation as such.

The findings on persistence up to age 11 years point to the likelihood of some form of intraorganismic change (brought about by the early institutional experiences) that is relatively resistant to the ameliorative effects of a later good environment. Rutter and colleagues (2004) have suggested, therefore, that some form of biological programming constitutes the most likely mediating mechanism. From both a theoretical and a practical point of view, it does matter, however, whether such programming is of the experience-expectant or experience-adaptive type. The latter variety implies that it is not normal development of the brain that has been prevented, but rather that the particular form of brain development has been of a kind that was adaptive to the institutional environment during the key phase of development, even though this proved nonadaptive in relation to the environment experienced later in the adoptive family. If that were to be the case, it might be expected that a more gradual adaptation could foster recovery and that immediate provision of a supernormal social environment to counteract the earlier deprivation would pose problems in adaptation (see Ozanne & Hales, 2004, for an example in relation to nutrition). Unfortunately, there is a distinct lack of evidence on the neural changes involved and even less evidence on what is most likely to bring about functional recovery.

Several questions arise with respect to the possible neural effects of an institutional upbringing that is associated with disinhibited attachment. Much of the literature has focused on the evidence that severe stress in early life has effects on both the neuroendocrine system and the structure of the hippocampus (Caldji et al., 1998; Gunnar & Donzella, 2002). Thus, early maternal deprivation in rats has been shown to affect neuropeptides in the adult brain in such a way that it might be involved in the mediation of risk for affective disorder (Jiménez-Vasquez, Mathé, Thomas, Riley, & Ehlers, 2001; Husum, Termeer, Mathé, Bolwig, & Ellenbroek, 2002; Husum & Mathé, 2002). Human data, too, indicate that maternal stress beginning in infancy may sensitize children to later stress exposure (Essex, Klein, Cho, & Kalin, 2002). It seems that environmental conditions in early life affect later glucocorticoid receptor gene expression (Weaver et al., 2001).

The notion that severe stress experiences may damage the brain has largely been shown by changes in the hippocampus (McEwen, 1999; McEwen & Lasley,

2002). However, important though these effects are, it is doubtful whether they are relevant to disinhibited attachment. To begin with, that psychological feature has been found in children reared in institutions that were not generally depriving and not particularly accompanied by an excess of stress experiences. Also, the behavioral pattern of disinhibited attachment does not seem to be at all associated with an increased sensitivity to stress. It is doubtful, therefore, whether this constitutes a relevant parallel. It is likely that the main risks derive from the *lack* of key attachment experiences in the early years, rather than the presence of severely stressful experiences.

What is potentially more relevant is the evidence on the neurobiology of attachment (Insel & Young, 2001). It has been suggested that the findings from studies across a range of animal species suggest that the neuropeptides oxytocin and vasopressin are implicated, and that for attachment to occur, these neuropeptides must link social stimuli to dopamine pathways associated with reinforcement. It is clear that important leads have been provided, but so far, the findings do not provide answers on the neural basis of disinhibited attachment as brought about by institutional rearing.

Whatever the neural basis, it is necessary to go on to account for the marked heterogeneity in response. Theoretical postulates with respect to biological programming ordinarily imply that the effects are universal even though they may differ in degree (see Rutter et al., 2004). However, that does not seem to be the case here. Three main alternatives need to be considered. First, it could be that the heterogeneity simply reflects measurement error or a failure to assess a sufficiently broad range of aspects of social relationships. Although that cannot be ruled out entirely, it does not seem likely to account for the individual differences because the heterogeneity in response still applies no matter how wide a range of variables are included.

Second, the mechanism could lie in the variation among children in the mix of risk and protective factors encountered in the institution. It is likely that even with an institution run along group lines, some children may have developed more individualized relationships with caregivers than was the case with other children. Similarly, there is likely to have been variation in the extent to which children were drugged, and there will have been variation in prenatal risk factors. Unfortunately, there is no direct evidence of the operation of these risk and protective factors, but it is quite likely that they played some part.

It might be supposed that the marked heterogeneity on outcome at age 11 could reflect the degree of initial deficit or impairment. We examined the possibility with respect to the Denver score at entry to the United Kingdom, the children's use of Romanian language at entry, the degree of subnutrition, and the presence of major health problems. For this purpose, we focused on those children who were at least 2 years of age at the time of UK entry, because this was the group most at risk, and because we wished to take account of the major effect of duration of institutional care. The Denver score at UK entry was unrelated to disinhibited attachment at age 11, but it did have a significant association with the WISC full-scale IQ at age 11. The small group ($n = 12$) of children who had experienced institutional care up to the age of 2 years but who nevertheless acquired a few words of Romanian had a significantly lower rate of cognitive impairment at age 11 (0%) than the remainder of the children (44%). However, they were not less likely to show disinhibited attachment at age 11 (17% vs. 11%). The finding that their minimal language predicted cognitive impairment but not disinhibited attachment suggests that the language was not just an index of their degree of deprivation. Rather, the implication is that the language is more likely to reflect their potential cognitive resources, probably because of a lesser degree of impairment of their neural structure. Whatever the explanation, the implication is that their resilience derived from what happened in the institution rather than in the adoptive home.

As already noted, the degree of subnutrition in the overall sample was related to the WISC IQ at age 11, but it was not associated with disinhibited attachment. Health problems at the time of UK entry were not related to either outcome. No measures of the adoptive family environment were associated with individual differences in outcome in this subgroup. In short, there was some indication that the heterogeneity in outcome was related to the degree of the initial deficit at UK entry, but this accounted for only a minority of the resilience. Postadoptive experiences, at least with respect to those measured, accounted for none of the individual differences in outcome.

The third possibility is that genetic factors may have been influential. Two rather different modes of genetic influence need to be considered. First, it is bound to be the case that the children vary in their genetic background. Thus, the genetic factors that influence individual differences in intelligence may be assumed to operate in these children just as they do in any others. That could be relevant with respect to the individual differences found in IQ. On the other hand, there is some suggestion that genetic factors account for less of the population variance in the case of children from disadvantaged backgrounds (Rowe, Jacobson, & van den Oord, 1999; Turkheimer, Haley, Waldron, D'Onofrio, & Gottesman, 2003). The lack of diminution in spread of scores with an increasing duration of institutional deprivation makes it somewhat unlikely that this adequately accounts for the variation.

Such an explanation is even less plausible in the case of disinhibited attachment. The point is that disinhibited attachment is not ordinarily found in nondeprived populations who have not experienced an institutional rearing. Accordingly, individual differences in these features are likely to be quite minor in the general population. There is no genetic evidence as such, but this mode of genetic operation does not seem very likely. On the other hand, one of the very important modes of genetic influence concerns the effects on sensitivity to the environment (Rutter, 2004; Rutter & Silberg, 2002). Interactions have been found between specific genotypes and measured specific environmental risks in humans such as maltreatment and life stresses (Caspi et al., 2002; Caspi et al., 2003). Animal evidence shows much the same (Bennett et al., 2002; Champoux et al., 2002). Nothing is known about the role of genes in individual differences in children's responsivity to the ill effects of institutional rearing, but it is reasonable to suppose that these will be operative.

The final issue concerns the extent to which the remarkably persistent effects of early experiences may nevertheless be modifiable by later experiences. Such later modification could come about either because compensatory or restorative neural changes occur or because compensatory psychological strategies have been learned and are able to be used in real-life situations. No unequivocal answers are available as yet. It is evident that important brain development is still taking place during adolescence. and, hence, that might provide potential for restorative brain changes. Also, however, it is clear that deprivation and enrichment of various kinds has neural effects even in adult life. Thus, this was shown in Greenough's experiments with rats (Greenough & Black, 1992; Greenough et al., 1987) and by the imaging studies of human taxi drivers (Maguire et al., 1997). It is also apparent that there is a degree of brain plasticity in terms of a capacity for brain areas to take on functions that they would not ordinarily have. For example, this is apparent in the human evidence on the effects of unilateral brain lesions on language (Vargha-Khadem & Mishkin, 1997) and by the evidence from functional imaging that people who have been blind from an early age can have their primary visual cortex activated by Braille reading and other tactile discrimination tasks, even though this does not occur in normally sighted subjects (Cohen et al., 1997). Furthermore, there is evidence that the human hippocampus retains its ability to generate neurons throughout life (Eriksson et al., 1998), although whether or not this applies to other parts of the brain is unclear. A study with mice showed that nonspatial memory deficits caused by the knockout of NMDA receptors in the hippocampal area can be overcome by environmental enrichment (Eichenbaum & Harris, 2000; Rampon et al., 2000). The evidence is far too sparse for firm conclusions, but it appears that it might be possible for later experiences to alleviate at least some of the effects of early deprivation-induced biological programming. Of course, too, compensatory psychological strategies might be possible, but even less is known about them. Although there have been attempts to develop psychological treatments for attachment disorders, they have been inadequately evaluated, and they lack a sound experimental basis (Minde, 2003).

Conclusion

An institutional upbringing has been found to have major effects on children's psychological development. Subsequent rearing in a good-quality family environment does much to alleviate the ill effects, but significant deficits remain in a substantial minority of children. However, it is clear that several rather different risk processes must be involved. An institutional upbringing leads to cognitive impairment only if the institutional care also involves a global deprivation of learning experiences, with the ill effects increased by associated subnutrition. In these circumstances, cognitive impairment is associated with diminished head growth, implying limitations in brain growth. The pattern of findings suggests that normal cognitive development and normal brain growth require adequate experiential input for the biological programming of the neural structure that underpins both.

By contrast, from the limited number of relevant studies, it seems that disinhibited attachment tends to occur with an institutional upbringing even when global deprivation is not involved. The suggestion is that the rotation of multiple caregivers that tends to characterize institutional care impedes the normal development of selective attachment, and that this effect is not wholly removed by a subsequent rearing in a good-quality family setting. Subnutrition does not appear to play a significant mediating role, and there is not the major effect on head growth associated with, and partially mediating, the effects of profound deprivation on cognitive development. It is suggested that some form of biological programming may be involved, but possibly it is of the experience-adaptive rather than experience-expectant variety.

For these effects to be apparent, it seems that at least 6 months of institutional upbringing is required. Very few data are available on the effects of institutional upbringing that does not begin until after the infancy years, but it seems likely that the effects are not the same. To that extent, if that proved to be the case, some sort of sensitive period effect is implied.

Biological programming concepts are usually thought to imply universal effects, even though there may be individual differences in the degree of effects. Our study of UK adoptees from Romanian institutions raises queries about that implication because substantial heterogeneity in outcome was found and because, even after at least 2 years rearing in a profoundly depriving institution, some children showed no detectable sequelae. The processes that underlie such apparent resilience are not known, but the partially protective effect of even minimal language acquisition suggests that the mechanisms need to be sought in the institutional experiences rather that the experiences after leaving the institution. Rearing in a good-quality adoptive home was crucially important in alleviating the sequelae of an institutional upbringing, but variations in the qualities of the adoptive family setting did not appear to account for the heterogeneity in outcome.

The neural underpinning of these institutional effects remain unknown. For the most part, reviewers have sought the biological mechanisms in neuroendocrine and neurochemical processes with consequent brain sequelae. However, it is doubtful if this constitutes the most appropriate paradigm. To begin with, the psychological sequelae of an institutional upbringing do not seem to be common outcomes of noninstitutional stress and adversity (although systematic data on this point are few). But, also, although multiple stressful experiences were a regular part of the life of children in Romanian institutions (e.g., being hosed down with cold water and occasional instances of sexual and physical abuse), this was not the case for most of the children in the British residential nurseries and residential Group Homes studied by Roy et al. (2000), Hodges and Tizard (1989a, 1989b), and Quinton and Rutter (1988). It may be inferred that the risk mechanism probably lay in the relationship experiences that the children lacked, rather than the stress experiences to which they were exposed.

In itself, that does not point to any particular mediating mechanism. It has been argued earlier that the mediation probably does not lie in an increased neuroendocrine response to stress. To begin with, that is not, on the whole, what the findings show in institution-reared children, but, also, an undue sensitivity to stress does not stand out behaviorally as particularly characteristic of the children adopted from Romanian institutions. Nevertheless, that does not mean that there are not important neuroendocrine consequences of an institutional rearing. The evidence suggests a complex mixture of increased and decreased cortisol levels, together with alterations in the diurnal rhythm (Gunnar & Donzella, 2002). It should be noted, too, that numerous studies have shown that the hormonal and behavioral responses to stress do not exactly parallel one another, the meaning of the discrepancy patterns remaining rather obscure. A key question is whether the hormonal effects index, or reflect, altered social functioning or, rather, whether they provide the underlying process causing abnormal social relationship patterns. The former appears more likely, but what is needed at this point is the appropriate data analytic approach to test for mediating and moderating effects (Baron & Kenny, 1986; Kraemer et al., 2001).

An alternative mediating mechanism concerns the effects on brain development and functioning as a social relationship parallel, in effect, to what happens with vision and phonological discrimination. Animal studies, as with the latter two functions, will be crucially important. However, structural and functional imaging studies on humans could be highly informative. Not much is likely to be gained by steady-state functioning imaging. Rather, what are needed are quantitative studies of responses to specific tasks, with respect to disinhibited attachment (and also quasi-autistic patterns). Such tasks might include various aspects of face perception (Schultz, et al., 2003), responses to extreme emotions or suffering (Blair et al., 1996), and theory-of-mind tasks (Frith, 2003). Both functional magnetic resonance imaging (fMRI) and magneto-encephalography (MEG) could be informative.

Initially, many traditional, conservatively inclined behavioral scientists were inclined to dismiss studies of Romanian adoptees as of little theoretical interest because the situation was unique and because the available information on the children's background was so meager. Indeed, at a key point, the (British) Medical Research Council would not fund the research on these grounds. It is now very evident that the situation has more parallels than were at first apparent and that the theoretical interest is very high just because it constitutes such a special "natural experiment" (Rutter, Pickles, et al., 2001). It constitutes a key research opportunity in the broader agenda of understanding experience-based brain and biological development (see Nelson et al., 2002).

Acknowledgments   I am most grateful to Celia Beckett, Jenny Castle, Emma Colvert, Christine Groothues, Jana Kreppner, and Edmund Sonuga-Barke for helpful suggestions and comments on an earlier draft of this chapter. In addition, I am deeply appreciative of the immense input from the families involved in the follow-up study of adoptees from Romania and the United Kingdom, which provided many of the findings that formed the basis of this chapter. I am also grateful for the funding for the research provided by the UK Department of Health and the Helmut Horten Foundation.

References

Amaral, D. G., & Corbett, B. A. (2003). The amygdala, autism and anxiety. In G. Bock & J. Goode (Eds.), *Autism: Neural basis and treatment possibilities* (pp. 177–197). Chichester, England: Wiley.

Ames, E. W. (1997). *The development of Romanian orphanage children adopted to Canada*. Final report to Human Resources Development Canada.

Barker, D. J. (1997). Fetal nutrition and cardiovascular disease in later life. *British Medical Bulletin, 53*, 96–108.

Baron, R. M., & Kenny, D. A. (1986). The moderator-mediator variable distinction in social psychological research: Conceptual, strategic, and statistical considerations. *Journal of Personality and Social Psychology, 51*, 1173–1182.

Barr, C. S., Newman, T. K., Shannon, C., Parker, C., Dvoskin, R. L., Becker, M. L., et al. (in press). Rearing condition and rh5-HTTLPR interact to influence LHPA-axis response to stress in infant macaques. *Biological Psychiatry.*

Bates, E., & Roe, K. (2001). Language development in children with unilateral brain injury. In C. A. Nelson & M. Luciana (Eds.), *Handbook of developmental cognitive neuroscience* (pp. 281–307). Cambridge, MA: MIT Press.

Bateson, P. (1966) The characteristics and context of imprinting. *Biological Review, 41*, 177–211.

Bateson, P. (1990). Is imprinting such a special case? *Philosophical Transactions of the Royal Society of London, 329*, 125–131.

Bateson, P., & Martin, P. (1999). *Design for a life: How behaviour develops*. London: Jonathan Cape.

Beckett, C., Bredenkamp D., Castle J., Groothues C., O'Connor T. G., Rutter M., et al. (2002). Behavior patterns associated with institutional deprivation: A study of children adopted from Romania. *Developmental and Behavioral Pediatrics, 23*, 297–303.

Beckett, C., Castle, J., Groothues, C., O'Connor, T. G., Rutter, M., & the English and Romanian Adoptees (ERA) Study Team. (2003). Health problems in children adopted from Romania: Association with duration of deprivation and behavioural problems. *Adoption and Fostering, 27*, 19–29.

Bennett, A. J., Lesch, K. P., Heils, A., Long, J. D., Lorenz, J. G., Shoaf, S. E., et al. (2002). Early experience and serotonin transporter gene variation interact to influence primate CNS function. *Molecular Psychiatry, 7*, 118–122.

Blair, J., Sellars, C., Strickland, I., Clark, F., Williams, A., Smith, M., et al. (1996). Theory of Mind in the psychopath. *Journal of Forensic Psychiatry, 17*, 15–25.

Blakemore, C. (1991). Sensitive and vulnerable periods in the development of the visual system. In G. R. Bock & J. Whelan (Eds.), *The childhood environment and adult disease* (pp. 129–146). Ciba Foundation Symposium 156. Chichester, England: Wiley.

Bock, G. R., & Whelan, J. (Eds.). (1991). *The childhood environment and adult disease*. Ciba Foundation Symposium 156. Chichester, England: Wiley.

Bottjer, S. W. (1991). Neural and hormonal substrates for song learning in zebra finches. *Seminars in Neuroscience, 3*, 481–488.

Bottjer, S. W., & Arnold, A. P. (1997). Developmental plasticity in neural circuits for a learned behavior. *Annual Review of Neuroscience, 20*, 459–481.

Bowlby, J. (1951). *Maternal care and mental health*. Geneva, Switzerland: World Health Organization.

Bruer, J. T. (1999). *The myth of the first three years*. New York: Free Press.

Caldji, C., Diorio, J., & Meaney, M. J. (2000). Variations in maternal care in infancy regulate the development of stress reactivity. *Biological Psychiatry, 48*, 1164–1174.

Caldji, C., Tannenbaum, B., Sharma, S., Francis, D., Plotsky, P., & Meaney, M. J. (1998). Maternal care during infancy regulates the development of neural systems mediating the expression of fearfulness in the rat. *Proceedings of the National Academy of Science of the United States of America,, 95*, 5335–5340.

Candland, D. K. (1993). *Feral children and clever animals: Reflections on human nature*. New York: Oxford University Press.

Caspi, A., McClay, J., Moffitt, T. E., Mill, J., Martin, J., Craig, I. W., et al. (2002). Role of genotype in the cycle of violence in maltreated children. *Science, 297*, 851–854.

Caspi, A., Sugden, K., Moffitt, T. E., Taylor, A., Craig, I. W., Harrington, H. L., et al. (2003). Influence of life stress on depression: Moderation by a polymorphism in the 5–HTT gene. *Science, 301*, 386–389.

Castle, J., Groothues, C., Bredenkamp, D., Beckett, C., O'Connor, T., Rutter, M., et al. (1999). Effects of qualities of early institutional care on cognitive attainment. *American Journal of Orthopsychiatry, 69*, 424–437.

Champoux, M., Bennett, A., Shannon, C., Higley, J. D., Lesch, K. P., & Suomi, S. J. (2002). Serotonin transporter gene polymorphism, differential early rearing, and behavior in rhesus monkey neonates. *Molecular Psychiatry, 7*, 1058–1063.

Chisholm, K. (1998). A three-year follow-up of attachment and indiscriminate friendliness in children adopted from Romanian orphanages. *Child Development, 69*, 1092–1106.

Chisholm, K., Carter, M. C., Ames, E. W., & Morison, S. J. (1995). Attachment security and indiscriminately friendly behavior in children adopted from Romanian orphanages. *Developmental Psychopathology, 7*, 283–294.

Chow, K. L., & Stewart, D. L. (1972). Reversal of structural and functional effects of long-term visual deprivation in cats. *Experimental Neurology, 34*, 409–433.

Chugani, H. T., Behen, M. E., Muzik, O., Juhász, C., Nagy, F., & Chugani, D. C. (2001). Local brain functional activity following early deprivation: A study of postinstitutionalized Romanian orphans. *NeuroImage, 14*, 1290–1301.

Cohen, L. G., Celnik, P., Pascual-Leone, A., Corwell, B., Faiz, L., Dambrosia, J., et al. (1997). Functional relevance of cross-modal plasticity in blind humans. *Nature, 389*, 180–183.

Curtis, W. J., & Nelson, C. A. (2003). Toward building a better brain: Neurobehavioral outcomes, mechanisms, and processes of environmental enrichment. In S. S. Luthar (Ed.), *Resilience and vulnerability: Adaptation in the context of childhood adversities* (pp. 463–488). Cambridge, England: Cambridge University Press.

Curtiss, S. (1977) *Genie: A psycholinguistic study of a modern-day "wild child."* London: Academic Press.

Davenport, R. K., Menzel, E. W., & Rogers, C. M. (1966). Effects of severe isolation on "normal" juvenile chimpanzees: Health, weight gain and stereotyped behaviors. *Archives of General Psychiatry, 14*, 134–138.

Douthwaite, J. V. (2002). *The wild girl, natural man and the monster: Dangerous experiments in the Age of Enlightenment.* Chicago: University of Chicago Press.

Eichenbaum, H., & Harris, K. (2000). Toying with memory in the hippocampus. *Nature Neuroscience, 3*, 205–206.

Eriksson, P. S., Perfilieva, E., Björk-Eriksson, T., Alborn, A-M., Nordborg, C., Peterson, D. A., et al. (1998). Neurogenesis in the adult human hippocampus. *Nature Medicine, 4*, 1313–1317.

Essex, M. J., Klein, M. H., Cho, E., & Kalin, N. H. (2002). Maternal stress beginning in infancy may sensitize children to later stress exposure: Effects on cortisol and bahavior. *Biological Psychiatry, 52*, 776–784.

Feldman, H. M. (1994). Language development after early unilateral brain injury: A replication study. In H. Tager-Flusberg (Ed.), *Constraints on language acquisition: Studies of atypical children* (pp. 75–90). Hillsdale, NJ: Erlbaum.

Fisher, L., Ames, E. W., Chisholm, K., & Savoie, L. (1997). Problems reported by parents of Romanian orphans adopted to British Columbia. *International Journal of Behavioral Development, 20*, 67–82.

Frankenburg, W. K., van Doorninck, W. J., Liddell, T. N., & Dick, N. P. (1986). *Revised Denver Prescreening Developmental Questionnaire (R-PDQ).* High Wycombe, England: DDM Incorporated/The Test Agency Ltd.

Frith, C. (2003). What do imaging studies tell us about the neural basis of autism? In G. Bock & J. Goode (Eds.), *Autism: Neural basis and treatment possibilities* (pp. 149–176). Chichester, England: Wiley.

Fujinaga, T., Kasuga, T., Uchida, N., & Saiga, H. (1990). Long-term follow-up study of children developmentally retarded by early environmental deprivation. *Genetic, Social and General Psychology Monographs, 116*, 37–104.

Giedd, J. N., Blumenthal, J., Jeffries, N., Catellanos, F., Liu, H., Zijdenbos, A., et al. (1999). Brain development during childhood and adolescence: A longitudinal MRI study. *Nature Neuroscience, 2*, 861–863.

Goldfarb, W. (1945). Effects of psychological deprivation in infancy and subsequent stimulation. *American Journal of Psychiatry, 102*, 18–33.

Greenough, W. T., & Black, J. E. (1992). Induction of brain structure by experience: Substrates for cognitive development. In M. R. Gunnar & C. A. Nelson (Eds.), *Developmental behavior neuroscience* (pp. 155–200). Hillsdale, NJ: Erlbaum.

Greenough, W. T., Black, J. E., & Wallace, C. S. (1987). Experience and brain development. *Child Development, 58*, 539–559.

Gunnar, M. R., & Donzella, B. (2002). Social regulation of the cortisol levels in early human development. *Psychoneuroendocrinology, 27*, 199–220.

Hodges, J., & Tizard, B. (1989a). IQ and behavioural adjustment of ex-institutional adolescents. *Journal of Child Psychology and Psychiatry, 30*, 53–75.

Hodges, J., & Tizard, B. (1989b). Social and family relationships of ex-institutional adolescents. *Journal of Child Psychology and Psychiatry, 30*, 77–97.

Hoksbergen, R. A. C., ter Laak, J., van Dijkum, C., Rijk, S., Rijk, K., & Stoutjesdijk, F. (2003a). Posttraumatic stress disorder in adopted children from Romania. *American Journal of Orthopsychiatry, 73*, 255–265.

Hoksbergen, R. A. C., ter Laak, J., van Dijkum, C., Rijk, K., & Stoutjesdijk, F. (2003b). Attention deficit, hyperactivity disorder in adopted Romanian children living in the Netherlands. *Adoption Quarterly, 6*, 59–72.

Hoksbergen, R., van Dijkum, C., & Jesdijk, F. S. (2002). Experiences of Dutch families who parent an adopted Romanian child. *Developmental and Behavioral Pediatrics, 23*, 403–409.

Hubel, D. H., & Wiesel, T. N. (1965). Binocular interaction in striate cortex of kittens reared with artificial squint. *Journal of Neurophysiology, 28*, 1041–1049.

Hubel, D. H., Wiesel, T. N., & Le Vay, S. (1977). Plasticity of ocular dominance columns in monkey striate cortex. *Philosophical Transaction of the Royal Society of London. Series B: Biological Sciences, 278*, 377–409.

Husum, H., & Mathé, A. A. (2002). Early life stress changes concentrations of neuropeptide Y and corticotrophin-releasing hormone in adult rat brain. Lithium treatment modifies these changes. *Neuropsychopharmacology, 27*, 756–764.

Husum, H., Termeer, E., Mathé, A. A., Bolwig, T. G., & Ellenbroek, B. A. (2002). Early maternal deprivation alters hippocampal levels of neuropeptide Y and calcitonin-gene related peptide in adult rats. *Neuropharmacology, 42*, 798–806.

Huttenlocher, P. R. (2002). *Neural plasticity: The effects of environment on the development of the cerebral cortex.* Cambridge, MA: Harvard University Press.

Insel, T. R., & Young, L. J. (2001). The neurobiology of attachment. *Nature Reviews—Neuroscience, 2*, 1–8.

Institute of Medicine/Stratton, K., Howe, C., & Battaglia, F. (1996). *Fetal alcohol syndrome: Diagnosis, epidemiology, prevention, and treatment.* Washington, DC: National Academy Press.

Jiménez-Vasquez, P. A., Mathé, A. A., Thomas, J. D., Riley, E. P., & Ehlers, C. L. (2001). Early maternal separation alters neuropeptide Y concentrations in selected brain regions in adult rats. *Developmental Brain Research, 131*, 149–152.

Kempermann, G., Brandon, E. P., & Gage, F. H. (1998). Environmental stimulation of 129/SvJ mice causes increased cell proliferation and neurogenesis in the adult dentate gyrus. *Current Biology, 8*, 939–942.

Keshavan, M. S., Kennedy, J. L., & Murray, R. M. (2004). *Neurodevelopment and schizophrenia.* London: Cambridge University Press.

Kolb, B., Forgie, M., Gibb, R., Gorny, G., & Rowntree, S. (1998). Age, experience and the changing brain. *Neuroscience and Biobehavioral Reviews, 22*, 143–159.

Kolb, B., Gibb, R., & Gorny, G. (2003). Experience-dependent changes in dendritic arbor and spine density in neocortex vary qualitatively with age and sex. *Neurobiology of Learning and Memory, 79*, 1–10.

Kraemer, H. C., Stice, E., Kazdin, A., Offord, D., & Kupfer, D. (2001). How do risk factors work together? Mediators, moderators, and independent, overlapping, and proxy risk factors. *American Journal of Psychiatry, 158*, 848–856.

Kreppner, J., O'Connor, T. G., Rutter, M., & the English and Romanian Adoptees Study Team (2001). Can inattention/overactivity be an institutional deprivation syndrome? *Journal of Abnormal Child Psychology, 29*, 513–528.

Kuhl, P. K. (1994). Learning and representation in speech and language. *Current Opinion in Neurobiology, 4*, 812–822.

Kuhl, P. K., Andruski, J. E., Chistovich, I. A., Chistovich, L. A., Kozhevnikova, E. V., Ryskina, V. L., et al. (1997). Cross-language analysis of phonetic units in language addressed to infants. *Science, 277*, 684–686.

Kwong, W. Y., Wild, A. E., Roberts, P., Willis, A. C., & Flemig, T. P. (2000). Maternal undernutrition during the preimplantation period of rat development causes blastocyst abnormalities and programming of postnatal hypertension. *Development, 127*, 4195–4202.

Langley-Evans, S. C., Welham, S. J. M., & Jackson, A. A. (1999). Fetal exposure to a maternal low protein diet impairs nephrogenesis and promotes hypertension in the rat. *Life Sciences, 64*, 965–974.

Le Grand, R., Mondloch, C. J., Maurer, D., & Brent, H. P. (2003). Expert face processing requires visual input to the right hemisphere during infancy. *Nature Neuroscience, 6*, 1108–1112.

Le Grand, R., Mondloch, C., Maurer, D., & Brent, H. P. (2001). Neuroperception: Early visual experience and face processing. *Nature, 410*, 890.

Linkenhoker, B. A., & Knudsen, E. I. (2002). Incremental training increases the plasticity of the auditory space map in adult barn owls. *Nature, 419*, 293–296.

MacLean, K. (2003). The impact of institutionalization on child development. *Development and Psychopathology, 15*, 853–884.

Maguire, E. A., Frackowiak, R. S. J., & Frith, C. D. (1997). Recalling routes around London: Activation of the right hippocampus in taxi drivers. *Journal of Neuroscience, 17*, 7103–7110.

Maye, J., Werker, J. F., & Gerken, L. (2002). Infant sensitivity to distributional information can affect phonetic discrimination. *Cognition, 82*, B101–B111.

McEwen, B. S. (1999). The effects of stress on structural and functional plasticity in the hippocampus. In D. S. Charney, E. J. Nestler, & B. S. Bunney (Eds.), *Neurobiology of mental illness* (pp. 475–493). New York: Oxford University Press.

McEwen, B., & Lasley. E. N. (2002). *The end of stress.* Washington, DC: Joseph Henry Press.

McMahon, S. D., Grant, K. E., Compas, B., Thurm, A. E., & Ey, S. (2003). Stress and psychopathology in children and adolescents: Is there evidence of specificity? *Journal of Child Psychology and Psychiatry, 44*, 107–133.

Miller, G. L., & Knudsen, E. I. (2003). Adaptive plasticity in the auditory thalamus of juvenile barn owls. *Journal of Neuroscience, 23*, 1059–1065.

Minde, K. (2003). Assessment and treatment of attachment disorders. *Current Opinion in Psychiatry, 16*, 377–381.

Morison, S. J., Ames, E. W., & Chisholm, K. (1995). The development of children adopted from Romanian orphanages. *Merrill-Palmer Quarterly, 41*, 411–430.

Nelson, C. A., Bloom, F. E., Cameron, J. L., Amaral, D., Dahl, R. E., & Pine, D. (2002). An integrative, multidisciplinary approach to the study of brain-behavior relations in the context of typical and atypical development. *Development and Psychopathology, 14*, 499–520.

Newton, M. (2002). *Savage girls and wild boys: A history of feral children.* London: Faber and Faber.

O'Brien, P. M. S., Wheeler, T., & Barker, D. J. P. (Eds.). (1999) *Fetal programming: Influences on developmental and disease in later life.* London: RCOG Press.

O'Connor, T. G., Marvin, R. S., Rutter, M., Olrick, J., Britner, P. A., & the E.R.A. Study Team (2003). Child-parent attachment following severe early institutional deprivation. *Development and Psychopathology, 15*, 19–38.

O'Connor, T. G., Rutter, M., & the English and Romanian Adoptees Study Team. (2000). Attachment disorder behavior following early severe deprivation: Extension and longitudinal follow-up. *Journal of the American Academy of Child and Adolescent Psychiatry, 39*, 703–712.

O'Connor, T. G., Rutter, M., Beckett, C., Keaveney, L., Kreppner, J. M., & the English and Romanian Adoptees (ERA) Study Team. (2000). The effects of global severe privation on cognitive competence: Extension and longitudinal follow-up. *Child Development, 71*, 376–390.

Oyama, S. (1979). The concept of the sensitive period in developmental studies. *Merrill-Palmer Quarterly, 25*, 83–103.

Ozanne, S. E., & Hales, C. N. (2004). Lifespan: Catch-up growth and obesity in male mice. *Nature, 427*, 411–412.

Paus, T., Zijdenbos, A., Worsley, K., Collins, D. L., Blumenthal, J., Giedd, J. N., et al. (1999). Structural maturation of neural pathways in children and adolescents: In vivo study. *Science, 283*, 1908–1911.

Plomin, R. (1994). *Genetics and experience: The interplay between nature and nurture*. Thousand Oaks, CA: Sage.

Plomin, R., & Bergeman, C. S. (1991). The nature of nurture: Genetic influences on "environmental" measures. *Behavioral and Brain Sciences, 10*, 1–15.

Quinton, D., & Rutter, M. (1988). *Parenting breakdown: The making and breaking of intergenerational links*. Aldershot, England: Avebury.

Rampon, C., Tang, Y-P., Goodhouse, J., Shimizu, E., Kyin, M., & Tsien, J. Z. (2000). Enrichment induces structural changes and recovery from nonspatial memory deficits in CA1 NMDAR1-knockout mice. *Nature Neuroscience, 3*, 238–244.

Rowe, D. C. (1994). *The limits of family influence: Genes, experience and behavior*. New York: Guilford.

Rowe, D. C., Jacobson, K. C., & van den Oord, E. J. C. G. (1999). Genetic and environmental influences on vocabulary IQ: Parental education level as moderator. *Child Development, 70*, 1151–1162.

Roy, P., Rutter, M., & Pickles, A. (2000). Institutional care: Risk from family background or pattern of rearing? *Journal of Child Psychology and Psychiatry, 41*, 139–149.

Roy, P., Rutter, M., & Pickles, A. (2004). Institutional care: Associations between overactivity and a lack of selectivity in attachment relationships. *Journal of Child Psychology and Psychiatry, 45*, 866–873.

Rutter, M. (1972). *Maternal deprivation reassessed*. Harmondsworth, England: Penguin.

Rutter, M. (1984). Psychopathology and development: II. Childhood experiences and personality development. *Australian and New Zealand Journal of Psychiatry, 18*, 314–327.

Rutter, M. (1995). Clinical implications of attachment concepts: Retrospect and prospect. *Journal of Child Psychology and Psychiatry, 36*, 549–571.

Rutter, M. (2000). Psychosocial influences: Critiques, findings, and research needs. *Development and Psychopathology, 12*, 375–405.

Rutter, M. (2002a). Maternal deprivation. In M. H. Bornstein (Ed.), *Handbook of parenting: Vol. 4. Social conditions and applied parenting* (2nd ed., pp. 181–202). Mahwah, NJ: Erlbaum.

Rutter, M. (2002b). Nature, nurture, and development: From evangelism through science toward policy and practice. *Child Development, 73*, 1–21.

Rutter, M. (2004). Pathways of genetic influences on psychopathology. *European Review, 12*, 19–33.

Rutter, M. (2005a) Adverse pre-adoption experiences and psychological outcomes. In J. Palacios & D. Brodzhinsky (Eds.), *Psychological issues in adoption: Theory, research, and application* (pp. 67–92). Westport, CT: Greenwood.

Rutter, M. (2005b) Environmentally mediated risks for psychopathology: Strategies and findings. *Journal of the American Academy of Child and Adolescent Psychiatry, 44,* 3–18.

Rutter, M., Andersen-Wood, L., Beckett, C., Bredenkamp, D., Castle, J., Groothues, C., et al. (1999). Quasi-autistic patterns following severe early global privation. *Journal of Child Psychology and Psychiatry, 40,* 537–549.

Rutter, M., & the ERA Research Team. (1998). Developmental catch-up and deficit following adoption after severe global early privation. *Journal of Child Psychology and Psychiatry, 39,* 465–476.

Rutter, M., Kreppner, J., O'Connor, T. G., & the English and Romanian Adoptees Study Team. (2001). Specificity and heterogeneity in children's responses to profound privation. *British Journal of Psychiatry, 179,* 97–103.

Rutter, M., & O'Connor, T. (1999) Implications of attachment theory for child care policies. In P. Shaver & J. Cassidy (Eds.), *Handbook of attachment* (pp. 823–844). New York: Guilford.

Rutter, M., O'Connor, T. G., & the ERA Study Team. (2004). Are there biological programming effects for psychological development? Findings from a study of Romanian adoptees. *Developmental Psychology, 40,* 81–94.

Rutter, M., Pickles, A., Murray, R., & Eaves, L. (2001). Testing hypotheses on specific environmental causal effects on behavior. *Psychological Bulletin, 127,* 291–324.

Rutter, M., Roy, P., & Kreppner, J. (2002). Institutional care as a risk factor for inattention/overactivity. In S. Sandberg (Ed.), *Hyperactivity and attention disorders of childhood* (pp. 417–434). Cambridge, England: Cambridge University Press.

Rutter, M., & Rutter, M. (1993). *Developing minds: Challenge and continuity across the lifespan.* New York: Basic Books.

Rutter, M., & Silberg, J. (2002). Gene-environment interplay in relation to emotional and behavioral disturbance. *Annual Review of Psychology, 53,* 463–490.

Rymer, R. (1993). *Genie: An abused child's flight from silence.* New York: HarperCollins.

Sackett, G. P. (1965). Effects of rearing conditions upon the behavior of rhesus monkeys (Macaca mulatta). *Child Development, 36,* 855–868.

Scarr, S. (1992). Developmental theories for the 1990s: Development and individual differences. *Child Development, 63,* 1–19.

Schore, A. (1994). *Affect regulation and the origin of the self: The neurobiology of emotional development.* Hillsdale NJ: Erlbaum.

Schultz, R. T., Grelotti, D. J., Klin, A., Kleinman, J., Van der Gaag, C., Marois, R., et al. (2003). The role of the fusiform face area in social cognition: Implications for the pathobiology of autism. *Philosophical Transactions of the Royal Society of London, 358,* 415–427.

Shaver, P., & Cassidy, J. (eds). (1999). *Handbook of attachment.* New York: Guilford.

Skuse, D. (1984a). Extreme deprivation in early childhood: I. Diverse outcomes for three siblings from an extraordinary family. *Journal of Child Psychology and Psychiatry, 25,* 523–541.

Skuse, D. (1984b). Extreme deprivation in early childhood: II. Theoretical issues and a comparative review. *Journal of Child Psychology and Psychiatry, 25,* 543–572.

Sowell, E. R., Peterson, B., Thompson, P. M., Welcome, S. E., Henkenius, A. L., & Toga, A. W. (2003). Mapping cortical change across the human life span. *Nature Neuroscience, 6,* 309–315.

Sowell, E. R., Thompson, P. M., Tessner, K. D., & Toga, A. W. (2001). Mapping continued brain growth and gray matter density reduction in dorsal front cortex: Inverse relationships during postadolescent brain maturation. *Journal of Neuroscience, 21,* 8819–8829.

Spitz, R. A. (1946). Anaclitic depression. *Psychoanalytic Study of the Child, 2,* 312–342.

Suomi, S. J. (2003). How gene-environment interactions influence emotional development in rhesus monkeys. In C. Garcia-Coll, E. L. Bearer, & R. M. Lerner (Eds.), *Nature and nurture: The complex interplay of genetic and environmental influences on human development* (pp. 35–51). Mahway, NJ: Erlbaum.

Turkheimer, E., Haley, A., Waldron, M., D'Onofrio, B., & Gottesman, I. I. (2003). Socioeconomic status modifies heritability of IQ in young children. *Psychological Science, 14,* 623–628.

van Valen, L. (1974). Brain size and intelligence in man. *American Journal of Physical Anthropology, 40,* 417–424.

Vargha-Khadem, F., & Mishkin, M. (1997). Speech and language outcome after hemispherectomy in childhood. In I. Tuxhorn, H. Holthausen, & H. E. Boenigk (Eds.), *Paediatric epilepsy syndromes and their surgical treatment* (pp. 774–784). Sydney, Australia: Libbey.

Vorria, P., Rutter, M., Pickles, A., Wolkind, S., & Hobsbaum, A. (1998a). A comparative study of Greek children in long-term residential group care and in two-parent families: I. Social, emotional, and behavioural differences. *Journal of Child Psychology and Psychiatry, 39,* 225–236.

Vorria, P., Rutter, M., Pickles, A., Wolkind, S., & Hobsbaum, A. (1998b). A comparative study of Greek children in long-term residential group care and in two-parent families: II. Possible mediating mechanisms. *Journal of Child Psychology and Psychiatry, 39,* 237–245.

Weaver, I. C. G., La Plante, P., Weaver, S., Parent, A., Sharma, S., Diorio, J., et al. (2001). Early environmental regulation of hippocampal glucocorticoid receptor gene expression: Characterization of intracellular mediators and potential genomic target sites. *Molecular and Cellular Endocrinology, 185,* 205–218.

Wechsler, D. (1991). *Wechsler Intelligence Scale for Children—Third Edition (WISC-III),* San Antonio, TX: Psychological Corporation.

Werker, J. F. (2003). Baby steps to learning language. *Journal of Pediatrics, 143,* S62–S69.

Wolkind, S. N. (1974). The components of "affectionless psychopathology" in institutionalized children. *Journal of Child Psychology and Psychiatry, 15,* 215–220.

Zeanah, C. H., Nelson, C. A., Fox, N. A., Smyke, A. T., Marshall, P., Parker, S. W., et al. (2003). Designing research to study the effects of institutionalization on brain and behavioral development: The Bucharest Early Intervention Project. *Development and Psychopathology, 15,* 885–907.

Name Index

Arbib, M., 317
Archer, J., 293
Armitage, C., 208
Arnold, A. P., 370
Arnold, J. L., 263
Ascher, J. A., 174
Ashman, S., 319
Aslin, R. N., 54, 123
Astington, J. W., 289, 290
Atkinson, J., 346
Avikainen, S., 313, 314, 317
Avis, J., 290
Axelrod, R., 277, 278
Ayers, G., 213

Bachevalier, J., 62, 63, 265, 318
Bacon, A., 310
Baerends, G. P., 252
Baerends-van Roon, J. M., 252
Bahrick, L. E., 132
Bailey, A., 139
Bailey, L. M., 132
Baillargeon, R., 118
Baird, J., 289, 290
Bakeman, R., 85, 86, 91, 333
Baker, C., 317
Baker, J. M., 208
Bakker, T., 279
Balaban, M. T., 9, 10, 63
Baldwin, B. A., 200, 201, 206
Baldwin, D. A., 84, 85, 118, 121, 122,
    127, 128, 130, 134, 139, 308, 310
Bales, K. L., 182
Balian, S., 261
Ballard, M. E., 263
Bamshad, M., 186
Ban, T., 102
Bandura, A., 263
Banks, E. M., 211
Baranek, G., 305
Barba, B. D., 59
Barberis, C., 319
Bard, K., 90, 288
Bar-Haim, Y., 10, 161
Barhr, N. I., 261
Barker, D. J., 371
Barker, D. J. P., 371
Barnard, K. E., 288
Baron, R. M., 383
Baron-Cohen, S., 64, 87, 95, 139, 156,
    160, 309, 310, 318, 319, 339, 341

Barr, C. S., 372
Barratt-Boyes, B. G., 331
Barrera, M. E., 47, 50, 51
Barrett, K. C., 21
Barry, M., 219
Bartels, A., 189
Bartholow, J., 54
Barton, M., 128
Bartsch, K., 166
Basiouni, G. F., 210
Bass, A. H., 175
Bates, E., 82, 85, 119, 140, 333, 369
Bates, J. E., 20, 32, 81
Bateson, P., 261, 369, 370
Baude, B., 310
Bauer, C. R., 105
Bauer, J. H., 209
Bauer, P., 311
Bauman, M., 318
Baxter, A., 58
Baylis, G., 59, 318
Beach, F. A., 209
Bean, G., 251
Beccera, A., 337
Beckett, C., 357, 358, 363
Beckwith, B. E., 208
Bednar, J. A., 47
Bekoff, M., 247, 250, 252, 256, 259,
    263
Bell, R. W., 211
Bellomo, C., 198
Bellugi, U., 331, 332, 333, 336, 338,
    339, 340, 341, 342, 343, 344,
    345, 346
Belsky, J., 282, 284
Benassayag, C., 200
Ben-David, M., 252
Benigni, L., 85
Bennett, A. J., 381
Bennett, E. L., 251
Bennetto, L., 313
Benson, P., 53, 318
Bentin, S., 60, 61, 97
Bar-Haim, Y., 10, 161
Berendse, H. W., 186
Bergeman, C. S., 355
Bergvall, A. H., 220
Berk, L. E., 118
Berkson, G., 260
Bernard, C., 61
Bernardi, M. M., 208
Bernzwieg, J., 35

Bruno, J. P., 198
Buchan, N. R., 278
Bucher, J., 208
Buchtal, J., 37
Buckenmaier, J., 216
Bugental, D. B., 6
Buijs, R. M., 186
Bullier, J., 60
Bullmore, E. T., 63
Bunge, S., 102
Burghardt, G. M., 248
Burke, S., 255
Burnham, D., 123
Burns, J. K., 262
Burnstein, E., 276
Burton, S., 188
Bush, G., 34, 101, 102
Bushnell, I. W., 46
Buss, D., 281, 282, 284
Butterfield, E., 305
Butterfield, P., 8
Butterworth, G., 122, 127, 132
Buxbaum, J., 304
Byers, J. A., 247
Byrd, K. R., 253, 264
Byrne, R., 292
Byrnes, E. M., 220

Caan, W., 58
Caba, M., 216
Cacioppo, J. T., 3, 4, 15, 313
Calder, A., 98
Calder, A. J., 62
Caldji, C., 370, 378
Caldwell, J. D., 200, 206, 213
Calkins, S. D., 14, 20, 31, 35, 81, 162
Call, J., 153
Callanan, M. A., 166
Camaioni, L., 85
Camp, C. A., 48
Campbell, R., 59, 64, 98, 338
Campbell, S. B., 35, 209
Campos, D., 290, 291
Campos, J. J., 8, 21
Candland, D. K., 368
Cann, W., 25
Capatides, J. B., 128
Caplan, R., 95
Cappenberg, M., 288
Card, J., 83, 141, 308
Cardillo, S., 177

Carey, S., 61, 142
Carlson, N. R., 204
Carlson, S. M., 163, 164, 167, 291
Carmichael, M. S., 188
Carmichael, T., 61
Caro, T. M., 247, 249, 252
Caron, A. J., 50, 51, 52
Caron, R. F., 50, 52
Carpendale, J. I. M., 288
Carpenter, M., 82, 86, 118, 121, 122,
    127, 129, 132, 142, 288, 307, 333
Carper, R., 315
Carter, A., 107
Carter, C. S., 3, 34, 171, 172, 174,
    175, 177, 179, 182
Carter, M. C., 365
Carver, L., 94, 308, 309, 310, 315,
    318, 319
Cascio, C., 176
Case, R., 88
Casey, B. J., 3, 34, 58, 161, 167
Caspi, A., 381
Cassady, C., 339
Cassé-Perrot, C., 338
Cassia, V., 46, 90
Cassidy, J., 284, 372
Cassidy, K. W., 123
Castelli, F., 104
Castiello, U., 11
Castle, J., 362
Catania, K. C., 174
Cauley, K. M., 134
Cernoch, J. M., 225
Chalkley, M. A., 119
Challis, J. R., 200, 201
Chaminade, T., 317
Chamley, W. A., 200
Champagne, F., 181, 206, 221
Champoux, M., 381
Chan, A., 92
Chanel, J., 210, 211
Channon, S., 160
Chapman, C., 201
Charlesworth, W., 293
Charman, T., 88, 156, 310, 311, 313
Charney, R., 121
Charwarska, K., 95
Chasiotis, A., 276, 281, 282, 284, 285,
    288, 290, 291, 292
Chauvel, P., 65
Checkley, S. A., 188

Chee, P., 210
Cheney, D., 277
Chesley, S., 209
Chess, S., 20
Cheung, U., 208
Chiang, W., 118
Chiles M., 339
Chisholm, J. S., 278, 280, 281, 284
Chisholm, K., 365
Chivers, S. M., 249
Cho, E., 378
Cho, M., 177
Cho, M. M., 175
Choi, H. P., 334
Choi, J.-K., 280
Chomsky, N., 119
Choudry, S. H., 336
Chouinard, M. M., 124, 125
Chow, K. L., 370
Chua, P., 102
Chugani, H. T., 140, 374
Chun, M. M., 58
Cialdini, R. B., 277
Cicchetti, D., 68
Cirulli, F., 257
Clancy, B., 140, 141, 142
Clark, E., 118, 120, 122, 123, 124, 125
Clarke, C., 13
Claussen, A. H., 85, 86, 92, 93, 94, 108
Cleary, J., 83
Clements, W., 290
Coan, J. A., 15, 29
Coatsworth, D., 81
Coffey-Corina, S., 140, 142
Cohen, C., 46
Cohen, D., 7, 46, 50, 63, 139
Cohen, J., 218
Cohen, J. D., 34
Cohen, L. G., 381
Cohn, J. F., 208, 209
Coie, J. D., 293
Cole, K., 291
Cole, P. M., 35
Coleman, M., 64
Coles, M., 102
Collins, P. F., 25, 28, 34
Collins, R., 46
Collis, G., 309
Compas, B., 363
Conner, K., 264

Cook, E., 304, 319
Coolen, L. M., 186
Cooper, G., 66
Cooper, P. J., 208
Cooper, R. P., 123
Cooper, T. T., 182
Coplan, R. J., 31
Coppeta, J. S., 214
Coppinger, R. P., 248
Coppotelli, H., 293
Corbett, B. A., 369
Cordess, C., 307
Corkum, V., 88, 90, 118, 122, 310
Corl, S., 209
Corter, C., 203, 208, 211, 212, 287
Cosmides, L., 281, 282
Costabile, A., 264
Couchoud, E. A., 19
Courchesne, E., 314, 315, 316
Courtois, G., 10
Cowey, A., 98
Coy, K., 35, 81
Craighero, L., 10
Craik, F., 101, 102
Crandall, C., 276
Crawford, S., 160
Critchley, H. D., 62, 63, 319
Croson, R. T. A., 278
Cross, D., 155, 290
Crowe, E., 166
Crowson, M. M., 86, 92, 108, 139, 310
Csibra, G., 50, 118, 167
Culver, C., 67
Cummins, D., 290, 293
Curcio, F., 85, 91
Curfs, L. M. G., 336
Curran, T., 213
Curtis, J. T., 175, 176, 185
Curtis, W. J., 366
Curtiss, S., 368
Curwin, A., 128
Cushing, B. S., 174, 179, 182, 186
Cuthbert, B. N., 63
Cutting, A. L., 290, 291

Da Costa, A. P., 201, 202, 205, 213, 214, 224
da Silva, N. L., 254
Daenen, E. W., 62, 265
Dager, S., 318

Eacott, M. J., 98
Eastman, R. F., 260
Eaves, L., 356
Ebner, K., 221
Eckerman, C., 312
Ehlers, C. L., 378
Ehret, G., 216
Ehrlich, S. M., 118
Eibl-Eibesfeldt, I., 288
Eichenbaum, H., 381
Eidelman, A. I., 225
Eilam, D., 258
Eimer, M., 60
Einfeld, S., 332, 335, 343
Einon, D. F., 249, 250, 251, 253, 254, 256, 264
Eisenberg, N., 19, 32, 35, 81, 118, 294
Eisenberg, R., 305
Eisenberger, N., 90
Ekman, P., 49, 338
Elgar, K., 59, 338
Elias, J., 211
Eliez, S., 344
Ellenbroek, B. A., 378
Elliott, C. D., 106
Elliott, S. N., 106
Ellis, H. D., 46
Ellis, L. K., 35
Ellsworth, C. P., 57
Elman, J., 119
Emde, R. N., 8
Emery, N., 97, 265
Engelmann, M., 185, 186, 221
English, J. B., 215
Enomoto, T., 256
Eriksen, B. A., 34
Eriksen, C. W., 34
Eriksson, P. S., 381
Eslinger, P. J., 162
Essex, M. J., 378
Etcoff, N. L., 53
Evans, D. E., 24
Everitt, B. J., 186, 216
Eviatar, Z., 340
Ewart, A. K., 331
Ey, S., 363
Eysenck, H. J., 28, 29

Fabes, R. A., 35
Fabre-Grenet, M., 46
Fadiga, L., 10, 317

Fagan, J., 134
Fagen, J., 247
Fagen, R., 247, 249, 256, 257
Fahrbach, S. E., 206
Faja, S., 338
Fallshore, M., 54
Fantella, S.-L., 257
Fantuzzo, J., 105
Farah, M. J., 58, 67, 338
Farrar, J., 333
Farrar, M. J., 86, 87, 120, 124, 127, 142
Farrell, W. J., 211
Farrington, D. P., 19
Farroni, T., 50
Fauconnier, G., 122
Faw, B., 102
Fay, W. H., 139
Featherstone, R. E., 217, 220
Fehr, E., 278, 279, 294
Feider, H., 57, 305
Fein, D., 63, 310
Feinman, S., 127, 310
Feinstein, C., 63
Feldman, H. M., 369
Feldman, M. W., 280
Feldman, R., 288
Feldon, J., 260, 261
Felicio, L. F., 208
Ferguson, C. A., 119, 122
Ferguson, J. N., 185, 186, 228
Fernald, A., 58, 122, 123, 125, 128
Fernandez, M., 313
Ferreira, A., 208
Ferreira, G., 222, 224
Ferreira, V. N. M., 254
Ferris, C. F., 175
Fiamenghi, C., 312
Field, E. F., 251
Field, S., 249
Field, T. M., 7, 46, 50, 51, 55, 68, 209
Fijneman, Y. A., 276
Filipek, P., 95
Fink, G., 102
Finlay, B., 140, 141, 142
Fischbacher, U., 278, 279, 294
Fischer, K. W., 3
Fiser, J., 54
Fish, J., 256, 262
Fishel, P., 313
Fisher, C., 132
Fisher, L., 365

Hague, P., 211
Hains, S., 48, 57, 82, 307
Hala, S., 163, 164
Hales, C. N., 378
Haley, A., 380
Halgren, E., 65
Halit, H., 8, 60, 61
Hall, F. S., 251
Hall, G., 310
Hallett, M., 103, 160
Hamilton, W. D., 276, 277, 278
Hammer, R. P. J., 201
Hammock, E. A. D., 180
Hamzei, F., 317
Handley, S. L., 208
Hanninen, R., 313
Hansen, S., 208, 214, 220
Happe, F., 104
Happeney, K., 5
Harbaugh, C. R., 174
Hardy-Bayle, M., 103, 160
Hare, B., 153
Hari, R., 11, 313, 317
Hariri, A. R., 62
Harkness, K. L., 154
Harlow, H. F., 250
Harlow, M. K., 250
Harmon-Jones, E., 31
Harnad, S., 53
Harrell, S., 285
Harris, J. D., 19
Harris, K., 381
Harris, N., 315
Harris, P. L., 290
Harrison, D., 340
Harrison, F. A., 200
Hart, J., 37
Hartmann, D. P., 294
Hasselmo, M., 59
Hastings, N., 174
Hatfield, E., 313
Hauck, M., 63
Hauser, H., 204
Haviland, J. M., 67
Hawley, P. H., 293, 294
Haxby, J. V., 59, 97, 346
Hay, D., 82, 310
Healy, B., 209
Heap, R. B., 200
Hebb, D. O., 28
Heckhausen, J., 275

Heiser, M., 317
Hellawell, D., 318
Helle, S., 285
Hellhammer, D. H., 37
Henaff, M., 97
Henderson, A., 163
Henderson, H. A., 14, 20, 21, 22, 24,
    25, 30, 35, 81, 336
Henderson, L., 83, 99, 100, 101
Henker, B., 37
Hennon, E., 134, 136, 140
Henrich, J., 278
Henriques, J. B., 30
Henry, J. P., 208
Henson, R. N., 60
Hepburn, S., 313
Herbison, A. E., 201
Hernandez, H., 211
Herrenkohl, L. R., 200
Herrera, C., 58, 128
Herscher, L., 198
Hershey, K. L., 19, 23, 24, 33
Hertzig, M., 313
Hertz-Pannier, L., 5
Hespos, S. J., 287
Hess, U., 55
Hesselink, J. R., 343
Hewlett, B. S., 284
Heyes, C. M., 292
Heymer, A., 258
Heywood, C. A., 98
Hickok, G., 331, 344
Hietanen, J., 318
Higuchi, T., 215
Hill, H. L., 252
Hill, J., 278, 339
Hill, K., 279, 284, 285
Hinde, R. A., 277
Hinton, M. R., 201, 202
Hinton, V. J., 5
Hirshfeld, D. R., 19, 32
Hirsh-Pasek, K., 119, 120, 121, 122,
    123, 124, 125, 126, 129, 130,
    132, 134, 135, 136, 140, 287
Hobson, P., 90
Hobson, R., 288, 309, 310, 313, 314,
    338
Hodgen, G. D., 201, 205
Hodges, J., 361, 362, 383
Hodges, J. K., 203
Hofer, J., 290, 291

Hoff, E., 129, 132
Hoff-Ginsberg, E., 129, 132
Hoffman, E., 59, 97
Hofmann, J. E., 178
Hogan, A. E., 82, 83, 105, 334
Hogan, J. A., 248
Hoksbergen, R. A. C., 365
Hol, T., 254
Hollander, E., 319
Hollich, G., 129, 130, 131, 132, 133, 134, 135, 136, 140
Holloway, K. S., 250, 251
Holloway, W. R., Jr., 258
Holman, S. D., 255
Holmes, D., 307
Holroyd, C., 102
Holstege, G., 63, 189
Holt, R., 19
Hong, Y. J., 162
Honjo, S., 199
Hood, B., 88, 307
Hooker, C., 97
Hooley, R. D., 202
Hopfensitz, A., 280
Hopkins, J., 209
Hornak, J., 65, 102
Hornung, K., 68
Horowitz, F. D., 50, 51, 53
Houle, S., 103
Houser, D., 160
Howard, M., 318
Howard, S., 341
Howland, E. W., 34
Howlin, P., 332
Hrdy, S. B., 281, 284, 285
Hu, S. B., 185
Hubel, D. H., 370
Hudson, S. J., 198
Hug, S., 163
Hughes, C., 291
Hulihan, T. J., 174, 175
Humphrey, N., 283, 292
Humphreys, A. P., 249, 250
Humphreys, K., 47
Hurtado, A. M., 278, 285
Huston, A. C., 263
Husum, H., 378
Huttenlocher, P. R., 366

Iacoboni, M., 317
Iglesias, J., 52

Insel, T. R., 174, 175, 176, 181, 182, 183, 186, 200, 201, 206, 213, 221, 228, 318, 319, 379
Ishai, A., 59
Itakura, S., 127, 132
Itier, R. J., 60
Itskovitz, J., 201
Iverson, S., 93
Ivy, G. O., 217
Iwaniuk, A. N., 248, 249, 255, 262
Izard, C. E., 7, 50, 51

Jack, A. I., 160
Jackson, A. A., 371
Jackson, D. C., 29
Jackson, P. L., 12
Jacob, P., 12
Jacobson, K. C., 380
Jacobson, R., 318
Jacques, T. Y., 162
Jaencke, L., 55
Jakubowski, M., 219
Jarvelainen, J., 11
Jasper, H., 96
Jaynes, J., 209
Jeannerod, M., 12
Jellema, T., 317
Jenkins, J. M., 290
Jenssen, T. A., 256
Jernigan, T. L., 331, 333, 343, 344, 345
Jesdijk, F. S., 365
Jiménez-Vasquez, P. A., 378
Joels, M., 37
Johnson, B. W., 11
Johnson, D., 93
Johnson, M., 318
Johnson, M. F., 200, 206
Johnson, M. H., 3, 4, 7, 8, 46, 47, 48, 50, 51, 59, 60, 61, 67, 305
Johnson, M. O., 13
Johnson, S. C., 101, 102
Johnson, S. K., 219
Jokela, J., 285
Jolliffe, T., 339
Jones, G. H., 255
Jones, J. S., 172
Jones, N. A., 30
Jones, S. S., 56, 126, 133
Jones, W., 63, 332, 333, 335, 336, 340, 344

Muir, D., 48, 57, 82, 307
Müller, U., 162, 288
Mullin, J. T., 46
Mullord, M. M., 198
Mumme, D. L., 58, 128
Munakata, Y., 3
Mundy, P., 5, 13, 82, 83, 84, 85, 86,
    88, 89, 90, 91, 92, 94, 95, 96, 97,
    99, 100, 101, 102, 108, 109, 139,
    141, 288, 305, 307, 308, 315,
    318, 333, 334
Muns, S., 200
Munson, J., 305, 306, 318
Muraoka, S., 221
Murphy, A. Z., 183
Murphy, M. R., 188
Murray, K., 35, 81, 162
Murray, L., 118, 209
Murray, R., 356, 366
Muthukumaraswamy, S. D., 11
Myers, I., 57
Myers, R. S., 52
Myhal, N., 208

Nadasdy, Z., 118, 167
Nadel, J., 312
Nagell, K., 82, 118, 288, 307, 333
Nahmias, C., 310
Naigles, L., 129, 132
Nair, H. P., 178, 180
Naito, M., 290
Nakamura, K., 65, 318
Nakayama, K., 346
Narumoto, J., 65
Nasello, A. G., 208
Nawrocki, T., 68
Naylor, V., 249
Neal, R., 84, 85, 86, 89, 90, 94, 96,
    108, 109, 305, 307, 308, 315, 318
Negayama, K., 199
Neill, D., 183
Nelson, C. A., 8, 10, 50, 51, 52, 53, 54,
    56, 64, 68, 70, 161, 319, 366, 384
Nelson, D. Y., 261
Nelson, J. E., 248
Nelson, K., 120, 121, 142, 289
Nelson, K. E., 124
Neumann, I., 185, 201, 208
Neustat, I., 335
Neville, H., 140, 142, 331
Newberry, R. C., 259

Newman, J. P., 27, 34, 35
Newton, M., 368
Nichida, T., 284
Nichols, K. E., 14, 101
Nichols, S., 89, 101, 103
Nichols, S. L., 34, 35
Nicholson, H., 63
Nigg, J. T., 32
Nilsen, R., 175
Ninio, A., 121
Nishimori, K., 206
Nishitani, N., 317
Noonan, L. R., 182
Norman, D., 102
Normansell, L., 251
Norris, F., 278
Nosaka, A., 285
Nott, P. N., 208
Novak, M. A., 186
Nowak, M. A., 279
Nowak, R., 211, 230
Nowicki, S., 338
Numan, M., 200, 213, 214, 215, 216
Numan, M. J., 213, 214, 215
Nuyman, M., 35
Nyiredi, S., 220

Oberklaid, F., 25
Oberman, L. M., 12
O'Brien, D., 318
O'Brien, P. M. S., 371
Ochs, E., 123
Ochsner, K., 102
O'Connor, T. G., 356, 357, 363, 364
Odling-Smee, F. J., 280
Ogan, T. A., 58
Ogawa, T., 261
O'Hara, M. W., 208
Ohkura, S., 201
Ohta, M., 314
Oitzl, M. S., 37
Okutani, F., 215
Olsen, D. M., 201
Ontai, L. L., 128
Oram, M., 317, 318
Orekhova, E., 11
Orgeur, P., 230
Orians, G. H., 172
Ormandy, C. J., 204
Orpen, B. G., 205, 210, 217, 218, 219
Osborne, L. R., 331

Oster, H., 50, 54
Osterling, J., 90, 94, 139, 305, 306, 307, 310
Ottinger, M. A., 182
Ousley, O., 313
Ouston, J., 309, 310, 338
Oyama, S., 368
Ozanne, S. E., 378
Ozonoff, S., 291

Paclik, L., 209
Padden, D., 306
Pai, S., 336
Panagiotides, H., 308, 309
Pankau, R., 332, 336, 343
Panksepp, J., 27, 28, 90, 96, 251, 255, 257, 263
Papoušek, H., 288
Papoušek, M., 288
Parent, A., 27
Parisi, S. A., 50
Parker, K. J., 182
Parkin, L., 290
Parkin, L. J., 165
Parsons, S., 266
Pascalis, O., 8, 46, 50, 60
Pasztor, T. J., 258, 262
Patchev, V. K., 182
Patterson, C. M., 27, 34
Paul, R., 139, 140
Pauli, R. M., 332
Paus, T., 101, 366
Pearlman-Avnion, S., 340
Pedersen, C. A., 174, 200, 206, 213, 221, 261
Pedlow, R., 25
Peele, S., 189
Pellegrini, A., 4, 248, 256, 263, 264, 265, 275, 277, 283, 284, 287, 292, 293, 294
Pellis, S. M., 248, 249, 250, 251, 252, 255, 257, 258, 259, 262, 263, 264, 265
Pellis, V. C., 248, 249, 251, 252, 257, 258, 259, 262, 263, 265
Pelphrey, K., 13
Pence, K. L., 137
Pennington, B., 99, 291, 312, 313, 315
Pennington, R., 100
Perez, E., 60
Perkins, M., 341

Perner, J., 153, 155, 157, 163, 165, 166, 289, 290, 291, 292
Perrett, D., 12, 48, 58, 313, 317, 318
Perrin, G., 224
Perry, B, 255
Persson, J., 11
Peters, A. M., 120
Petersen, I., 11
Petersen, S., 96
Peterson, S. E., 33
Peze, A., 312
Pfaff, D. W., 206
Pfaus, J. G., 186
Pfeifer, L. A., 182
Pfeifer, M., 21, 22, 24
Phelps, E. A., 27
Phelps, M. E., 140
Phelps, S. M., 180
Phillips, A. T., 153, 167
Phillips, K. M., 182
Phillips, M., 62
Phillips, M. L., 66
Phillips, R. D., 52
Phillips, S. W., 215
Phillips, W., 139
Piaget, J., 311, 312
Pick, A., 51, 55, 56, 88
Pickens, J., 68
Pickles, A., 85, 356, 357, 361, 362, 384
Picton, T., 102
Pierce, K., 63, 316
Pierce, S., 37
Piketty, V., 200, 210
Pinker, S., 119, 125, 286, 287
Pinuelas, A., 35
Pitkanen, A., 61
Pitkow, L. J., 183
Pizzagelli, D. A., 62
Pizzuto, T., 178
Platzman, K., 90
Plesa-Skwerer, D., 320, 338, 339, 342
Plomin, R., 355
Plotsky, P. M., 261
Plumb, I., 339
Plunkett, K., 126
Pober, B., 346
Poindron, D., 205
Poindron, P., 200, 202, 204, 205, 210, 211, 216, 218, 221, 222
Poirier, F. E., 256
Poiroux, S., 61

Polak-Toste, C., 13, 14
Polizzi, P., 163
Pollak, S. D., 68
Pomares, Y., 88, 98
Pomerleau, A., 57, 305
Poole, T. B., 256, 262
Poortinga, Y., 276
Popik, P., 221
Porges, S. W., 4
Porter, R. H., 210, 225, 230
Posey, D. J., 63
Posikera, I., 11
Posner, M., 24, 33, 34, 35, 81, 96, 101, 291
Post, K. N., 124
Potegal, M., 251, 253, 264
Potter, D., 317
Potts, R., 263
Poulin-Dubois, D., 128
Povinelli, D. J., 153
Power, T. G., 247, 249
Prange, A. J., Jr., 174, 200, 206
Prescott, A., 21
Preston, S., 174
Price, J. L., 61
Price, T. R., 29
Prinz, W., 12
Prior, M., 25
Proter, R. H., 204
Pruden, S. M., 136, 287
Prud'Homme, M. J., 205
Prutting, C. A., 91
Pryce, C. R., 203, 255, 260, 261
Puce, A., 58, 60, 97
Purcell, S. E., 118

Quine, W. V. O., 126
Quinn, G. E., 67
Quinton, D., 367, 383

Rabionitz, C., 67
Rach-Longman, K., 57
Radke-Yarrow, M., 310
Raichle, M. E., 33, 34
Raine, A., 19, 25, 32
Rakoczy, H., 8
Rampon, C., 381
Rapson, R., 313
Raste, Y., 339
Ratner, N., 121, 123
Ravel, N., 224

Raver, C., 81, 119
Rawling, P., 57
Rebai, M., 61
Reed, A., 68
Reed, M. A., 19, 32
Rees, S., 218
Regard, M., 98
Reilly, J., 21, 332, 336, 340
Reiss, A., 343, 344
Reo, K., 29
Restemeier, R., 282
Reudor, A., 128
Reynolds, B. W., 208
Reynolds, C., 19, 106
Reznick, J. S., 13, 20, 138, 142
Rhee, E., 276
Rheingold, H., 82, 310
Rice, C. E., 333
Richardson, P. R. K., 171
Richerson, P. J., 280
Richmond, J. B., 198
Rickman, M., 21
Rigourd, V., 200
Rijk, K., 365
Rijk, S., 365
Riley, E. P., 378
Rilling, J., 278
Rinaldi, J., 90, 94, 139, 305, 307, 310
Ring, B., 309, 318
Ritz, E., 311
Rivet, C., 312
Rizzolatti, G., 10, 317
Robbins, T. W., 216, 255
Roberts, G., 278
Roberts, P., 371
Roberts, R. L., 179, 182
Robertson, M., 339
Robinson, B., 331
Robinson, R. G., 29
Rochat, P., 287, 305, 310
Roe, K., 369
Roepstorff, A., 160
Rogers, C. M., 372
Rogers, S., 99, 100, 291, 312, 313, 314, 315
Rojas, J., 82, 307
Rokem, A. M., 225
Rolls, E. T., 58, 59, 65, 318
Romanski, L., 104
Romeyer, A., 204
Ronsheim, P. M., 201, 204, 213

Schwartz, G., 51, 56
Schweinberger, S. R., 60
Scott, K., 85
Scott, K. G., 105
Scott, S., 318
Sebanc, A. M., 38
Seckl, J. R., 188
Segerstrale, U., 3
Seibert, J. M., 82, 83, 86
Selart, M. E., 208
Semmann, D., 279
Serafin, N., 211
Serrano, J. M., 52, 53
Setlow, B., 318
Seyfarth, R., 277
Shallice, T., 102
Shapiro, L. E., 175, 182, 183
Sharma, S., 181, 206
Sharman, D. F., 200
Sharp, F. R., 213
Shaul, D. L., 208
Shaver, P., 284, 372
Sheehan, T. P., 214, 216
Sheinkopf, S., 85, 88, 93, 105, 106, 107
Shekhar, A., 63
Shelthon, S. E., 36
Shepard, P., 134
Sherman, M., 313
Sherman, T., 85, 139, 307
Sherratt, T. N., 278
Sherwood, V., 87, 90
Shibata, T., 60
Shillito-Walser, E. E., 211
Shipka, M. P., 200
Shipley, E. F., 125
Shiverick, S. M., 164
Shiwa, T., 102
Siegal, M., 154, 160
Siegel, H. I., 202
Sigman, M., 85, 86, 88, 89, 91, 92, 94, 95, 104, 105, 107, 139, 307, 308, 310, 313, 337
Sigmund, K., 279
Silberg, J., 380
Silva, M. R., 208
Simion, F., 46, 47, 50, 59, 90
Singer, L., 134
Singer-Harris, N. G., 333
Singh, T., 12
Sinha, P., 68
Siperstein, G., 305

Siplia, P., 101
Sirinathsinghji, D. J., 201
Siviy, S. M., 251, 255, 257, 263
Skudlarski, P., 67
Skuse, D., 64, 368
Slade, L., 166
Slater, A., 8, 49
Slaughter, V., 155, 307, 308
Slobin, D. I., 119
Slotnick, B. M., 214
Sluiter, A. A., 175
Smees, R., 264
Smith, C. K., 248
Smith, C. S., 125
Smith, E. A., 279
Smith, E. O., 249, 256
Smith, F. V., 198
Smith, J. R., 11
Smith, L., 85
Smith, L. B., 126, 129, 133
Smith, L. K., 257, 258, 262
Smith, P., 317
Smith, P. K., 247, 256, 264, 293
Smith, V., 160
Smith, W., 186
Smotherman, W. P., 211
Snidman, N., 13, 20
Snow, C. E., 119, 120, 121, 122, 123, 124
Snow, M., 313
Snowdon, C. T., 171, 200
Soares, M. M., 200
Soken, N. H., 51, 55, 56
Sommerville, J. A., 6
Sowell, E., 343, 366
Sparks, B., 318
Spear, L. P., 248
Spelke, E. S., 118, 153
Spinka, M., 198, 259
Spitz, R. A., 32, 57, 355
Spoors, M., 276
Spruijt, B. M., 253, 254, 265
St. George, M., 331, 333, 346
Stacey, P., 186
Stackhouse, T., 313
Stallings, J., 212
Stanko, R. L., 200
Stanowicz, L., 122, 124
Stansbury, K., 37
Stansfield, B., 338
Starr, L. B., 29
Starzec, J., 211

Subject Index

Page references in bold represent illustrations.

autism/autistic spectrum disorders
(*continued*)
Autism Diagnostic Observation
Schedule (ADOS), 105
described, 304
and emergentist coalition model
research, 138–140
and face processing, 63–64, 68
and "false belief" testing, 155–156
imitation deficits, 99, 313–314
Initiating Joint Attention deficits,
91, 96, 108–109
intervention studies and the self-
organizing hypothesis, 86
and joint attention, 94–95, 100–101,
104–109, **312**
language development in, 139–140,
142, 306–308
and mirror neurons, 11–13
neural basis of, 314–319
one-year old at birthday party, **306**
social orienting deficits, 305–307
and Theory of Mind, 88
affective experience, 7–8

BAS. *See* behavioral inhibition
basal ganglia, 66
basolateral amygdala, 28, 220. *See
also* amygdala
behavioral inhibition. *See also*
temperamental exuberance
Behavioral Activation System
(BAS), 26–28, 30–31
Behavioral Inhibition System (BIS),
26–27, 30–31
Behavior Facilitation System (BFS),
28
characteristics of in children, 21
Kagan studies, 13
Behavior Assessment System for
Children (BASC), 106
benzodiazepines, 208
beta-endorphins, 200, 201
BFS. *See* behavioral inhibition
Biological Psychology, 13–14
birds, 370
BIS. *See* behavioral inhibition
Braille, 381
Brain Electrical Source Analysis, 158–
159
Broca's area, 317

bromocriptine, 204
Bucharest Early Intervention Project, 362

cannibalism, rats, 227
catecholamines, 201
cats, 198, 252–253
cattle, 200
caudate motor system, 26
central sulcus, 346
cerebellum, 104, 315–316, 344–345,
347
cerebral cortex, 369, 374–375
cerebrospinal fluid (CSF), 200, 206
c-fos gene, 213–214, 223–224
child abuse, 68
Children's Behavior Checklist
(CBCL), 105–106
Children's Behavior Questionnaire
(CBQ), 24
Children's Communication Checklist
(CCC), 341
chimpanzees, 288, 372
chromosome 7, 331
cingulate, 6
cocaine, 92, 105–106, 183, 189
cognitive neuroscience, 4
color, 53
common coding theory, 12
Conspec/Conlern, 47
constraints/principles views, 126
construct validity, 84–85
content validity, 82
contingency experience, 287–288
cooperative breeding, 284–285
cortex, 29–30
corticosterone, 254
corticotropin-releasing factor (CRF),
177–178, 185, 208
corticotropin-releasing hormone
(CRH), 202–203
costly signal, 278–279
coyotes, 252

Darwinian theory, 275–276, 281
delayed non-match-to-sample testing,
100–101
Denver Pre-Screening and
Developmental questionnaire,
358, 379–380
depression, 208–209, 343
developmental cognitive neuroscience, 4

evolutionary social psychology, 3–4
excitatory system, 213–214, 216
executive functioning, 163, 291–292
expression account, 163–164
extroversion, 28–29
exuberance. *See* temperamental exuberance
eye gaze. *See also* joint attention
  in autism, 139, 304, 307, 315–316
  direction of detected by newborns, 50
  and language learning in infancy, 121–122, 127–128, 131–132
  and the parietal-temporal processes, 97–98
  in Williams syndrome, 333–334, 347

face fusiform area (FFA), 346–347
face processing, adults
  amygdala role in, 62
  categorical perception, 53
  frontal cortex role, 60, 65
  inversion, 54
  occipitotemporal cortex role, 58–59
  simulation theory, 55–56
face processing, monkeys, 97–98
face processing, young. *See also* joint attention; language development
  amygdala role in, 63
  and autism, 311, 319
  and brain development, 8–10
  categorization of emotions, 52–53
  contingency experience, 288
  discrimination of facial emotions, 49–51, 53–55
  facial expression defined, 48–49
  frontal cortex role, 65–66
  imitation, 55–56, 283
  lesions of the cortex and deficits, 102
  preference for, 7, 46–48
  and the social motivation hypothesis, 90, 309–311
  social referencing, 57–58
  still face, 56–57
  visual attention, 56
  visual experience, 67–70
  in Williams syndrome, 337–340, 345–347
"false belief"
  and brain activity, 5
  and expression/emergence account, 164–166

and frontal lobe maturation, 161–162
and joint attention, 289
testing in Williams syndrome, 341–342
and Theory of Mind, 104, 155–160, 290–291
fear. *See also* behavioral inhibition; face processing, young; temperamental exuberance
  and the amygdala, 62
  as basic emotion, 49
  and cognition in animals, 254–255
  in Gray's Motivational Systems Theory, 26–27
  neurochemicals and maternal behavior, 207–208
  orbitofrontal frontal cortex damage and recognition, 65
  and the play effect in mammals, 252–253
fetal alcohol syndrome, 362, 371
fighting, 256
first year, 8, 58
fixed genetic programs, 280–281
flexibility, 256
flight-fight (F-F) system, 26–27
fragile X syndrome, 313
frequency dependency, 282
frontal cortex, 65–66
frontal EEG asymmetry, 13–14
frontal lobes, 160, 316
functional magnetic resonance imaging (fMRI), 3, 5, 189
fusiform gyrus, 6, 13, 59, 347

game theory, 275, 277–279
gamma-amino-butyric acid (GABA), 200, 217, 223
Gavagai, 126
geniculostriate pathway, 59
gerbils, 249
glial fibrillary acidic protein (GFAP), 217, 219–220
glucocorticoids, 208
glutamate, 200
goats, 211
grandmotherhood, 284–285
Gray's Motivational Systems Theory, 26–27

grooming, 254, 286–287
guinea pigs, 249

habituation-dishabituation testing, 51
Hamilton's rule, 277
happiness, 49. *See also* face
    processing, young
hemispherectomy, 95–96
hippocampus, 366, 378, 381
hormones, 199–212. *See also*
    individual hormones; pair
    bonding
humans. *See also* pair bonding
    hormonal changes during
        pregnancy, 200
    olfactory cues and maternal
        responsiveness, 210–211
    oxytocin and maternal
        responsiveness, 206–207
    oxytocin levels after birth, 200
    and parturition, 199, 205–206, 208–
        209
    and play fighting, 263, 264
    sensory cues and maternal responsive-
        ness, 211–212, 224–225
    steroids and maternal
        responsiveness, 203
hypothalamic-pituitary-adrenal (HPA)
    system, 176–178, 200, 208
hypothalamus, 174–175, 201

IBR. *See* Initiating Behavior
    Regulation/Requests (IBR)
IIPLP, **134**–135
IJA. *See* Initiating Behavior
    Regulation/Requests (IBR)
Illinois prairie voles, 179
imitation. *See also* infants
    emergence of, 311
    and face processing in humans, 56
    and intersubjectivity development,
        288–290
    and language development, 312–
        313
    Like Me hypothesis in autism, 316–
        317
    and maternal responsiveness, 283
    and mirror neurons in infants, 10–12
    and the superior temporal sulcus
        (STS), 98–99
    and Theory of Mind, 312–313

impulsivity, 19, 21, 23, 27
inclusive fitness theory, 276–277
Infant Behavior Questionnaire (IBQ),
    23, 93
infants. *See also* face processing,
    young; language development;
    maternal responsiveness
    asymmetry and emotions in, 30
    attachment and familiarity with
        caregivers, 277
    brain development and institutional
        rearing, 366
    imitation skills, 311
    Infant-Toddler Social Emotional
        Assessment (ITSEA), 107
    and sensitive periods of
        development, 368
    social referencing in, 8
    temperament assessment reports,
        23–24
    and Theory of Mind development,
        167
inferior occipital gyrus, 59
inferior parietal cortex, 12
infralimbic prefrontal cortex, 374–
    375
inhibitory system
    and executive functioning, 291–293
    and intention, 289–290
    and maternal responsiveness, 214–
        216
    and Theory of Mind, 162–167, 292–
        293
Initiating Behavior Regulation/
    Requests (IBR), 82, **83**, 93, 107.
    See also joint attention
Initiating Joint Attention (IJA). *See
    also* joint attention
    and age of adoption from
        orphanages, 93
    and the anterior cingulate, 101–102
    and autism, 105
    autism and social approach system,
        96
    deficits and Social Competence, 107
    defined, 82
    frontal processes studies, 99–101
    and imitation, 98–99
institutional rearing. *See also*
    disinhibited attachment; IQ
    Canada study, 365

institutional rearing (*continued*)
  and cognitive impairment, 373–**374**, 377
  duration of and psychological effects, 361–362, 365
  effects of, 355–356, 366–368, 381–384
  inattention/overactivity, 364
  language development, importance of, 379–380, 382
  malnutrition of orphans, 363
  quasi-autistic patterns in orphans, 363–364
  UK studies, 357–358
Interactive Intermodal Preferential Looking Paradigm (IIPLP), **134**–135
interindividual differences, 282
influence, 58
IPLP, 224
IQ
  Canada study, 365
  Dutch study, 365–366
  head circumference in Romanian orphans, 374–375, 377
  and institutional rearing, 359–**361**
  and Romanian orphans, **376**
  Romanian orphans at 11 years, **360**
  Romanian orphans cognitive level, 358–**359**
  and sensitive periods of development, 373
  and subnutrition, 377, 380
isoproteronol, 220

joint attention. *See also* Theory of Mind (ToM)
  after hemispherectomy, 95–96
  and autism studies, 100–101, 104–109, 307–309, **312**
  Disruptive Behavior studies, 106–108
  Early Social Communication Scales studies, 82–84
  and "false belief," 289
  infant directed (ID) speech, 123–124
  Jenny, 333–334
  and language learning, 127–128, 139–142, 288
  neurological studies, 96–97

as predictor of social outcomes in development, 108–109
as secondary intersubjectivity, 91
self-organizing hypothesis, 85–87
social-cognitive hypothesis, 87–89
and social engagement, 81–82, 85
social motivation hypothesis, 90, 94, 318–320
and social orienting, 307
in Williams syndrome, 333–335
joy, 21–22

Kagan, J., 13
Kanner, Leo, 304, 310
Kansas prairie voles, 179

Laboratory Temperament Assessment Battery (LabTab), 336–337
lactation. *See also* pregnancy/parturition
  hormones and maternal behavior, 201, 226
  and maternal responsiveness, 217, 228, 230
  and prolactin levels, 200
language, 85–88. *See also* language development
language development. *See also* emergentist coalition model (ECM); Theory of Mind (ToM)
  in autism, 138–140, 306–308
  contingency experience, 287–288
  and evolutionary theory, 286–287
  and extended childhood, 283–284
  grammar development, 122–125, 287
  infant directed (ID) or motherese, 122–124
  inputs of language learning, **131**
  neurological research on, 140–142
  and open genetic programs, 280
  phonological discrimination, 371
  reference principles, 135–137
  and Romanian orphans studies, 358, 379–380
  and sensitive periods, 369, 382
  social-pragmatic theory, 119–122
  theories on, 118–120, 143
  in Williams syndrome, 333, 340–341
  word learning, 125–130, 137–138

lateral hypothalamus, 28
lateral septum (LS), 214
lateral temporal cortex, 374–375
life history theory, 280–285
Like Me hypothesis (autism), 316–317
limbic system. *See also* amygdala
  and the MPOA/vBNST, 214–215
  pair bonding, 186
  and the paracingulate area, 103
  play in juveniles, 255
  and social affiliation, 319
Linda Ray Intervention Center, 105–106

macaque monkeys, 10, 11
magnetoencephalography (MEG), 3, 317
maternal behavior. *See also* humans;
    individual mammals; maternal
    responsiveness
  altricial species, 198–199
  contingency experience, 288
  emergence of, 197–198
  motivation and mechanisms, 225–230
  precocial species, 198–199
  rats and stress reduction, 261
maternal deprivation. *See also*
    institutional rearing
  and attachment relationships, 372
  and cognitive impairment, 377
  effects of adoption on IQ levels, 359–360
  effects of on relationships, 368
  and stress in infants, 378
maternal experience effect, 217–218
maternal memory, 217–221, **229**
maternal responsiveness. *See also*
    individual mammals
  auditory cues for, 211–212
  defined, 198, 199
  depression in humans, 208–209
  hormonal activation of, 199–209
  and infant imitation, 283
  and maternal memory, 217–221
  neural substrates of, 212–217, **216**
  olfactory cues for, 209–212
  steroids balance, 202–203
meadow voles, 182
medial-frontal cortex, 96, 99, 100, 104, 224

medial prefrontal cortex (MPFC), 5
medial preoptic area (MPOA)
  and the inhibitory system, 214–216
  maternal behavior at parturition, 217
  and maternal memory, 220
  and maternal responsiveness, 213–214, 227
Medical Research Council of Britain, 383
mental retardation, 304, 310, 338–339, 342. *See also* IQ
mental state decoding, 154
mental state reasoning, 154–155, 157–160, 166
mice. *See also* rats
  aggression and play fighting, 262
  arginine vasopressin (AVP) and pair bonding, 180–181
  memory deficits and NMDA, 381
  olfactory memory in, 228
  oxytocin and maternal responsiveness, 206
  peer deprivations and social engagement, 249
  prolactin and maternal responsiveness, 204
mirror neurons
  and autism, 12–13, 317
  and imitation, 10–12, 98
  in monkeys, 317
mirror system activation, 11
mismatched negativity (MMN), 307
modiWes, 8
monkeys. *See also* primates
  amygdala lesions in, 369
  face processing, 97–98
  imitation and brain activation, 317
  and maternal deprivation, 372
  peer deprivations and social engagement, 249–250
  sexual ability and peer depravation, 254–255, 260
monogamy, 172, 178–179, 182, 189–190. *See also* pair bonding
montane voles, 175–179
morphine, 209
motherese, 122–124. *See also* language development
Motor Imitation Scale, 313
MPOA. *See* medial preoptic area (MPOA)

mu rhythm, 10–13
myometrium, 200

nasal hemifield, 59
near infrared spectroscopy (NIRS), 3
Negative Affectivity, 24
neocortex, 286–287
niche picking, 282
noradrenaline, 217, 223, 255
norepinephrine, 200
nucleus accumbens (NA), 176, 183,
    189, 220
nutrition
    and institutional rearing, 382
    of Romanian orphans, 358, 363
    and subnutrition in Romanian
        orphans, 370–371, 377, 380

occipitotemporal cortex, 58–61, 69
olfactory bulbs (OB), 215–216, 222–
    223, 227, 228–229
olfactory systems, 209–211
open genetic programs, 280–281
oppositional disorder, 32
orbitofrontal cortex (OFC)
    damage and emotion processing,
        65–66
    damage and Theory of Mind, 160
    development of in young children,
        5–6
    impairment of in autism, 318
    and mirror neurons, 12
    and the seeking system, 28
    stimulus processing, 6
orphanages, 93. See also institutional
    rearing
oxytocin (OT)
    and attachment relationships, 379
    and autism, 318–319
    maternal memory, 220–221
    maternal responsiveness, 200, 228
    and the medial preoptic area, 213
    olfactory bulbs, 215, 223
    and parturition, 174, 200, 205–**207**,
        217
    prairie vole pair bonding, 174–178,
        176
    sexual intercourse in humans, 187–
        188
    sheep recognition of young, 223,
        226, 227

pair bonding
    animal models, 171–172
    environmental factors influence,
        181–182
    genetics of in prairie voles, 179–181
    in humans, 187–190
    neural circuitry for, 182–185, 187
    partner preference test illustrated,
        173
    prairie voles relationships, 172–178,
        189
    and social memories, 185–187
paracingulate area, 103–104, 160
paracingulate cortex (Brodmann's area
    32), 5
paraventricular nucleus (PVN), 201, 227
parental investment, 284–285
parietal cortex, 220
partner preference test, 172–174
parturition. See pregnancy/parturition
Penn Interactive Peer Play Scale
    (PIPPS), 105
perceptual salience, 131–133, 136
Perceptual Sensitivity, 23
periaqueductal gray (PAG), 214
phonology, 371
pigs, 198–199
pituitary gland
    and maternal responsiveness, 200,
        203–204
    and oxytocin, 174
    and pair bonding in prairie voles,
        177
    and stress in rats, 261
play
    behavior and structured flexibility,
        256–260
    as emotional regulator, 253–256
    and fighting, 260–266
    function of in juvenile mammals,
        249–253
    and imitation, 312
    peer deprivation, effects on brain
        development, 251–252
    and sex in rodents, 248–249
    and social engagement theories,
        247–248
Pleistocene, 281, 284
pointing gestures, **83**, 87, 122, 334–
    335. See also eye gaze; joint
    attention

positive affectivity, 19, 90–92
Positive Affectivity/Extroversion, 25
Positive Anticipation/Approach, 24
positron emission tomography (PET),
    5, 189, 374
posterior orienting network, 33
Prader-Willi syndrome, 337–339, 342
prairie voles
    amygdala role in pair bonding, 186–
    187
    evolutionary causes of mating, 178–
    179
    genetics of pair bonding, 179–181
    neurochemistry of pair bonding,
    174–178
    partner preference test, 172–174,
    173
    reward circuits and pair bonding,
    189
prefrontal cortex (PFC), 5–6
pregnancy/parturition. *See also*
    individual mammals
    delivery, effects on mammals, 204–
    207, 227–228
    hormonal changes during, 199–**201**,
    207–209
    and maternal responsiveness, 209–
    212, **216**–217
    and oxytocin, 174
prelimbic cortex, 183
premotor cortex, 10, 317
preputial gland, 210, 211, 226
Preschool Laboratory Assessment
    Battery (PS-LabTAB), 21–22
primary intersubjectivity, 90
primates
    deception and inhibition, 292
    hormonal changes in, 200, **201, 207**
    maternal responsiveness and
    number of births, 216–217
    parturition and maternal recognition
    of young, 199
    steroids and maternal behavior, 203
prisoner's dilemma, 277, 278
progesterone, 200, 202–203
prolactin, 200, 203–204, 213
propranolol, 220
protein kinase C (PKC), 219–220
proto-conversations, 120–121
punishment, 32–33, 278–279, 280
Purkinje neurons, 315

rabbits, 126, 204, 218, 230
rats. *See also* mice
    Brattleboro, 185–186
    hormonal changes in, 200, **201**,
    206–**207**
    and the inhibitory system, 215
    maternal deprivation effects, 378
    maternal experience effect, 217–
    218
    maternal memory comparison with
    sheep, **229**
    maternal responsiveness in, 203–
    204, 213, 216–217, 226–227
    neonatal stress among, 182
    neural systems in, 212–213
    olfactory cues, 209–210, 211
    parturition and emotional changes,
    207–208
    and peer deprivation, 249–251,
    253–255
    play fighting in, 257–260, 263, 265
    sex and play in, 248–249
    steroids and maternal behavior, 202
    and stress reduction, 260–262
    vaginocervical stimulation (VCS)
    and maternal behavior, 205
reactive heritability, 282
reactive inhibition, 32–33
reactivity, 23
Reading the Mind in the Eyes task,
    339
receptor autoradiography, 175–177
reputation formation, 279–280, 294
Responding to Joint Attention (RJA).
    See also joint attention
    age of adoption from orphanages,
    93
    autism studies, 86, 95
    defined, 82
    emergence of, 88–89
    illustrated, **83**
    and language development, 85, 107
    and parietal-temporal processes, 97–
    99
    at risk children studies, 86–87
Reynell Language Development
    Scales, 86
Rhesus monkeys, 12
Risk Room, 22
RJA. *See* Responding to Joint
    Attention (RJA)

rodents. *See also* mice; rats
  amygdala lesions in, 369
  arginine vasopressin (AVP) in, 175
  maternal behavior of, 198
  play in, 248
  as research models for pair bonding,
    172
Romanian orphans. *See* institutional
    rearing

sadness, 49. *See also* face processing,
    young
salivary cortisol, 36–38, 225
secondary intersubjectivity, 90
seeking system, 27–28
seizure disorders, 95–96
selective attention, 33
self-organizing hypothesis, 85–87
self-regulation, 23
sensitive periods, 368–371, 373, 382
serotonin, 255
serum corticosterone factor (CRF),
    177–178
sex, 187–189, 248–249, 254–255, 260
sheep
  hormonal changes in, 200, **201**, **207**
  maternal behavior and recognition
    of young, 221–224
  maternal memory comparison with
    rats, **229**
  maternal responsiveness in, 216–
    217, 227
  olfactory cues in, 210, 211
  and oxytocin, 174, 200–201, 213
  parturition and emotional changes,
    207–208
  prolactin and maternal behavior,
    204
  steroids and maternal behavior,
    202–203
shyness, 24, 36
simulation theory, 55–56, 66
social attribution task (SAT), 104
social behavior. *See also* pair bonding
  bonding in humans, 171
  components of, 6–8
  and dominance, 293–294
  and evolutionary theory, 275–276
  and institutional rearing, 367
  and language development, 286–287
social cognition, 5–6

social cognitive-hypothesis, 87–89
social engagement, 4, 332–333, 340
social executive function (SEF), 102–
    103
social motivation hypothesis, 90, 94,
    318–320
social orienting, 305–307, **312**
social-pragmatic theory, 119, 126–130
social referencing, 8
Social Skills Rating Scales (SSRS), 106
sociobiology, 275
somatosensory cortex, 6, 66
startle reflex, 9–10
steroids, 202–203, 205
still face, 56–57
strabismus, 370
stress
  damage and the hippocampus, 378–
    379
  and institutional rearing, 383
  moderated in rats, 261–262
  play fighting as stress reducer, 265
  and salivary cortisol, 36–38
stria terminalis (vBNST), 213–216
structured flexibility, 258–260
subcortical retinotectal pathways, 59
subcortical septal-hippocampal
    formation, 26
superior temporal gyrus (STG), 344
superior temporal sulcus (STS)
  activity of and "false belief" stories, 5
  autism, impairment in, 13
  dorsal medial frontal cortex
    interaction and self-information,
    102–103
  face processing, adults, 59, 70
  gaze activation studies, 97–98
  and mirror neurons, 12
  monkeys and imitation behavior,
    317
  stimulus processing, 6
  in Williams syndrome, 347
supervisory attention system (SAS),
    102
supraoptic nucleus (SON), 201
Surgency/Extroversion, 24–25, 36–38
surprise, 49. *See also* face processing,
    young

taxi drivers, 366, 381
temperament, 13, 23–27, 335–337

temperamental exuberance
  anger/frustration, 38–39
  and behavior problems, 31–32
  in children, 13, 25
  and dopamine systems, 30–31
  and neurobiology, 25–26
  and stress, 36–38
  studies in, 19–22
temporal hemifield, 59
temporal poles, 5
thalamus, 370
Theory of Mind (ToM). *See also*
  language development
  as basis for social competence, 162
  and cognitive development, 153–154
  and dorsal-medial frontal cortex, 103–104
  face processing in infants, 309
  and "false belief," 155–160, 289
  frontal lobe damage impairment, 160
  gaze measure and prediction for autism, 88
  and inhibitory control, 162–167, 292
  origins of and language development, 290–293
  in Williams syndrome, 341–342
thermoregulation, 198–199, 227
Turner syndrome, 64

vaginocervical stimulation (VCS), 202–206, 226
vasopressin, 318–319, 379

vasopressin V1a receptor gene, **177,**
  180, 181–183, **184.** *See also* pair
  bonding
vBNST. *See* stria terminalis (vBNST)
ventral tegmental area (VTA), 214
ventral temporal cortex, 59
ventromedial nucleus of the
  hypothalamus (VMH), 214, 215
ventromedial PFC, 5–6
vermal lobes, 315–316
vigilance system, 33
visual cortex, 370, 381
voice recognition, 102
voles. *See* individual species

Wechsler Intelligence Scale for
  Children (WISC). *See* IQ
Williams syndrome (WS)
  brain size in, 343–344
  described, 331–333
  and face processing, 337–340, 345–347
  language development in, 333, 340–341
  and the social motivation
    hypothesis, 320
  temperament and personality, 335–337
  Theory of Mind development, 341–342
wolves, 256
Woodcock Language Proficiency
  Battery-Revised (WLPB-R), 106

zif/268 gene, 224